A HISTORY OF
GREEK PHILOSOPHY

VOLUME I

A HISTORY OF
GREEK PHILOSOPHY

BY

W. K. C. GUTHRIE, F.B.A.

*Master of Downing College and
Laurence Professor of Ancient Philosophy in the
University of Cambridge*

VOLUME I

THE EARLIER PRESOCRATICS AND
THE PYTHAGOREANS

CAMBRIDGE
AT THE UNIVERSITY PRESS
1971

PUBLISHED BY

THE SYNDICS OF THE CAMBRIDGE UNIVERSITY PRESS

Bentley House, 200 Euston Road, London NW1 2DB

American Branch: 32 East 57th Street, New York, N.Y. 10022

© CAMBRIDGE UNIVERSITY PRESS 1962

ISBN: 0 521 05159 2

First published 1962
Reprinted 1967 1971

First printed in Great Britain at the University Press, Cambridge
Reprinted in Great Britain, by lithography,
by John Dickens & Co Ltd, Northampton

CONTENTS

Preface   *page* ix

Note on the Sources   xiii

List of Abbreviations   xv

I   INTRODUCTION AND SUMMARY   I

II   THE BEGINNINGS OF PHILOSOPHY IN GREECE   26

III   THE MILESIANS   39

    A.   Introduction   39

    B.   Thales   45

        (1) Date: the eclipse   46

        (2) Family   50

        (3) Traditional character   50

        (4) Mathematics   52

        (5) Water as *arche*: the unity of all things   54

        (6) Mythical precursors   58

        (7) Rational explanations   61

        (8) Self-change and life: hylozoism   62

        (9) The unity of being: science and myth   67

        Additional note: water and 'life'   71

    C.   Anaximander   72

        (1) Date, writings, interests   72

        (2) The Unlimited as *arche*   76

        (3) The opposites   78

        (4) The meaning of *apeiron*   83

        (5) The *apeiron* divine   87

        (6) Cosmogony and cosmology   89

        (7) Origin of animal and human life   101

        (8) Meteorology   105

        Additional note: 'innumerable worlds'   106

Contents

D. Anaximenes   *page* 115
  (1) Date and writings   115
  (2) Air as *arche*   115
  (3) Unconscious presuppositions   116
  (4) Explanation of change: rarefaction and
      condensation   119
  (5) Air, life, and divinity   127
  (6) Cosmogony and cosmology   132
  (7) Meteorology   139
  (8) Conclusion   139

E. The Milesians: conclusion   140

IV PYTHAGORAS AND THE PYTHAGOREANS   146

A. Difficulties   148

B. Methods of approach   157
  (1) Sources of the sixth and fifth centuries   157
  (2) Fourth-century sources excluding Aristotle
      and his pupils   161
  (3) Post-Platonic sources   169
  (4) The *a priori* method   171

C. Life of Pythagoras and external history of the school   173

D. Outline of the Pythagorean philosophy   181
  (1) Man and his place in nature   182
  (2) Numbers and the cosmos   212
      (a) Introductory: the musical intervals.   212
          Additional note: 'speed' and pitch   226
      (b) Numbers and things: Aristotle's evi-
          dence for the general nature of the
          doctrine   229
      (c) Numbers and things: the generation of
          things from numbers   239
      (d) Cosmology   282
      (e) Abstractions as numbers   301
  (3) The nature of the soul   306

Contents

E.	Individual Pythagoreans	*page* 319
	(1) Hippasus	320
	(2) Petron	322
	(3) Ecphantus	323
	(4) Hicetas	327
	(5) Philolaus	329
	(6) Archytas	333
	Appendix: Time and the Unlimited	336

V	ALCMAEON	341
VI	XENOPHANES	360
	(1) Date and life	362
	(2) Social and political outlook	364
	(3) Writings	365
	(4) Tradition	366
	(5) Destructive criticism	370
	(6) Constructive theology	373
	(7) God identified with the world	381
	(8) All creatures born from earth	383
	(9) Alternation of wet and dry ages	387
	(10) Astronomy and meteorology	390
	(11) Theory of knowledge	395
	(12) Conclusion	401
VII	HERACLITUS	403
	(1) Difficulties and policy	403
	(2) Sources	405
	(3) Writings	406
	(4) Date and life	408
	(5) Obscurity and contempt for mankind	410
	(6) Prophetic character	413

Contents

(7) Relation to earlier thinkers   *page* 415

(8) Philosophical methods: self-search   416

(9) The Logos   419

(10) Three basic statements

     (*a*) Harmony is of opposites   435

     (*b*) Everything is in continuous motion and change   449

     (*c*) The world an ever-living fire   454

(11) Final explanation of the theory of change: fire and soul   459

(12) Change and stability: the concept of measure   464

(13) The complete world-picture: theology   469

(14) Religion and the fate of the soul   473

(15) Astronomy and meteorology   482

(16) Conclusion   486

Appendix: The river-statement   488

Bibliography   493

Indexes

     I. *Index of passages quoted or referred to*   505

     II. *General index*   514

The device on the cover is from a fifth-century coin of
Abdera which shows a bearded head and bears the legend
ΓΥΘΑΓΟΡΗΣ (*see C. T. Seltman,* Greek Coins (*1933*),
pp. 143–4 and Plate 28, no. 11).

PREFACE

This volume marks the beginning of an enterprise undertaken on the initiative of the Syndics of the Cambridge University Press. They decided, first, that there was room for a comprehensive history of ancient Greek philosophy in English, on a considerable scale. The only such history available is the four-volume translation of Theodor Gomperz's *Greek Thinkers*, the last volume of which was finished by Gomperz in 1909. This was a valuable work for its time, though somewhat discursive, but a vast amount of detailed research has been carried out during the last half-century which has left no corner of the field untouched, and in some places has radically altered its contours.

Secondly, the Syndics took the view that the plan of a composite history by several hands, of which the Press has produced such notable examples in the past, had certain drawbacks, and that in this subject it would be preferable for the whole to be the product of a single mind.

Their third wish was that the work should not demand from its readers a knowledge of Greek.

I am well aware of the magnitude of the task, and of my temerity in accepting the proposal of the Syndics that I should undertake it. The difficulties are the reverse of those which beset a pioneer. Far from being a pioneer study, this history deals with a subject of which almost every detail has been minutely worked over many times. What is needed (and few would dispute the need) is a comprehensive and systematic account which will so far as possible do justice to the opposing views of reputable scholars, mediate between them, and give the most reasonable conclusions in a clear and readable form. The qualities called for are not originality and brilliance so much as clearheadedness, sober sense, good judgment and perseverance.

Yet to throw light on the Greek mind calls in addition for gifts of imagination, sympathy and insight. It means entering into the thoughts of men moulded by a civilization distant in time and place from our own who wrote and spoke in a different language. For some of them, though we may call them philosophers, not only reason but also

poetry, myth and divine revelation were paths to truth. Their interpreter must be a scholar with an ear for the subtleties and overtones
of the Greek language, capable of comparing a philosopher's use of it
with that of the writers of non-philosophical poetry and prose. Where
modern techniques of philosophical criticism will aid elucidation, he
should ideally be equipped to invoke them also, while remaining
immune from any tendency to anachronism.

Such a paragon does not exist. By setting forth his qualifications
I have no intention of making any claims for myself: I hope only that
a conscious and explicit awareness of the ideal may induce a proper
humility and help one to fall less woefully short of it. One thing that
no one can do is to master the whole flood of writing on the subject
from the Greek commentators to our own day. I can only hope that
my own selection of authorities has not been too arbitrary or inadequate,
and associate myself with one of the most sensitive of modern critics,
who wrote: 'Although a conscientious working over of the whole
enormous specialist literature would have been highly desirable in
itself, it seemed to me more important to finish during my lifetime.'[1]

A reader new to the subject should perhaps be warned that at the
early period covered by the present volume, from the beginning of
the sixth to the middle of the fifth century B.C., no line is yet drawn
between philosophy, theology, cosmogony and cosmology, astronomy,
mathematics, biology and natural science in general. The word philosophy must therefore be interpreted in a very wide sense, though
possibly not much wider than that which it bore in Europe down to
the seventeenth century A.D. By the fifth century B.C. history, geography, and to a large extent medicine did receive separate treatment
by certain writers. These will only enter incidentally, and our main
concern will be with those who took all nature for their province and
tried to determine its origin and present constitution and (whether
or nor from religious motives) the origin and destiny of human life
and its place in the whole. The medical writers, it is true, had to come
to terms with these broad theories, which they criticized as relying too
confidently on general principles instead of on empirical investigation.
There was action and reaction here, and an acquaintance with the

[1] Hermann Fränkel, preface to *Dichtung und Philosophie* (translated).

medical literature is essential for an understanding of the philosophers. On the other hand, much that might now be regarded as philosophical —ethical and political theory, logic and epistemology—is either wholly lacking in this early period or present only at an embryonic stage.

The importance of the writers of mythical cosmogonies and theogonies—Hesiod, 'Orpheus', Pherecydes and others—as precursors of the philosophers, and the existence within them of a development away from mythopoeic towards rational thought, has become more and more clearly recognized in recent times. Readers aware of the new light that has been thrown on the ideas of the early philosophers by the study of these mythographers may be surprised and disappointed that no preliminary chapters appear to be devoted to them and to their influence exclusively. I hope however that a reading of the chapters on the philosophers themselves will show that this aspect has not been neglected. It was a difficult choice, but I decided that this was the best course, namely that the question of how far the thought of, for example, Thales or Anaximenes was moulded by the myths of their own people, as well as those of Egypt and the Orient, should be discussed in direct connexion with them, but not before. (See also pp. 39 f. below.)

It is my intention, *Deo volente*, to continue this history to include the Hellenistic period, stopping short of the Neoplatonists and those of their predecessors who are best understood in conjunction with them. (Cf. p. 24 below. I understand that the Press has plans for a continuation by other hands.) I had thought to confine the Presocratics to one volume, but as it has turned out, the period down to Heraclitus, with a comprehensive account of Pythagoreanism, has proved sufficient for this if the volumes are not to become uncomfortably large. Although it means that there is a large task ahead, I make no apology for the scale of the work. Excellent short outlines exist already, and there could be no justification for adding to their number. Students of a particular philosopher, school or period will I hope find sufficient in the separate sections to orientate them and form a starting-point for their own researches.

For the benefit of classical scholars, Greek has not been excluded, but for the sake of others it has been confined to footnotes unless translated. As to these, I have tried to follow the principle enunciated

Preface

by Dr Edgar Wind, and make them 'indispensable as foundations for the argument, but superfluous for understanding it'.[1]

Books have usually been referred to in the notes by short titles, and articles by periodical, date and page only. Full particulars of books, and titles of articles, will be found in the bibliography. The standard collection of Greek texts relating to Presocratic philosophy is that of Diels, re-edited by Kranz (abbreviated DK: see bibliography, p. 493), to which reference is constantly made in the following pages. Under each philosopher the texts are divided into two sections. The first (A) contains *testimonia*, that is, accounts in later Greek authorities of the philosopher's life and doctrines, or paraphrases of his writings; in the second (B) are collected what in the opinion of the editors are genuine quotations from the philosopher himself. In this book the number of a 'B' passage is normally preceded by 'fr.' (fragment), while for the others the letter 'A' is retained.

My thanks are due to Mr F. H. Sandbach, Professor H. C. Baldry and Mr G. S. Kirk, who between them have read the volume in typescript. I owe much to their friendly and pertinent comments. I should also like to thank Mr J. D. Bowman for help in the preparation of the index.

May I conclude with a request? To continue this work necessitates keeping up with the flow of periodical literature, and it is all too easy to overlook important articles or monographs. If scholars who see this volume think the enterprise worth while, perhaps they will be kind enough to send me offprints of their articles or particulars of newly published works. I cannot promise any adequate *quid pro quo*: I can only say that I shall be sincerely grateful.

W. K. C. G.

DOWNING COLLEGE, CAMBRIDGE

[1] Preface to *Pagan Mysteries in the Renaissance* (Faber, 1958).

NOTE ON THE SOURCES

The meagreness of our inheritance of original works of the Greek philosophers is commented on in Chapter 1 (24f.). For the Presocratics in particular we depend on excerpts, summaries and comments made by later writers. The problems to which this gives rise have always been recognized, and adequate accounts of the nature of the sources are available in several works, of which the best and most accessible is that of G. S. Kirk in KR, 1–7. (Others will be found in Ueberweg–Praechter, 10–26, Zeller, *Outlines*, 4–8, Burnet, *EGP*, 31–8.) In view of this I am making no attempt at a general appraisal at the beginning, but shall rather deal with particular source-problems as they arise over individual thinkers. (For the all-important Aristotle see especially pp. 41–3.) But a certain amount must be briefly repeated here in order to make intelligible such references as will be necessary to 'Aët.', 'the *Placita*', 'Plut. *Strom.*' or 'Stob. *Ecl.*'

Theophrastus the pupil of Aristotle wrote a general history of earlier philosophy and special works on some individual Presocratics. Only extracts survive, though they include the greater part of the book *On Sensation*. These works of Theophrastus formed the main foundation for what is known as the doxographical tradition, which took different forms: 'opinions' arranged according to subjects, biographies, or somewhat artificial 'successions' (διαδοχαί) of philosophers regarded as master and pupil.

The classification of the doxographical material was undertaken in the monumental work of Hermann Diels, *Doxographi Graeci* (Berlin, 1879), to which all subsequent researchers into Presocratic philosophy owe an incalculable debt. The collections of the works of the early thinkers were known as δόξαι ('opinions', hence 'doxography') or τὰ ἀρέσκοντα (Latinized as *Placita*). There are two such collections or summaries extant, the *Epitome* falsely claimed as Plutarch's, and the *Physical Extracts* (φυσικαὶ ἐκλογαί) appearing in the *Anthology* or *Florilegium* of 'Stobaeus' (John of Stobi, probably fifth century A.D.). From a reference in the Christian bishop Theodoret (first half of fifth century) it is known that both of these go back to a certain Aëtius, and the two are printed by Diels in parallel columns as the *Placita* of Aëtius. Aëtius himself, who is otherwise unknown, was probably of the second century A.D.

Between Theophrastus and Aëtius was a Stoic summary, of the first century B.C. at the latest, which can be detected behind doxographical accounts in Varro and Cicero, and was named by Diels the *Vetusta Placita*.

The doxographies in Hippolytus's *Refutation of all Heresies*, and the pseudo-Plutarchean *Stromateis* ('Miscellanies') preserved in Eusebius, appear to be independent of Aëtius.

The *Lives of the Philosophers* by Diogenes Laertius (probably third century A.D.) exists entire, and contains matter from various Hellenistic sources of uneven value.

To sum up, our information about the Presocratic philosophers depends first of all on extracts or quotations from their works which range from one brief sentence in the case of Anaximander (and of Anaximenes perhaps not even that) to practically the whole of the *True Way* of Parmenides. Secondly we have occasional mention and discussion of Presocratic thought in Plato, and a more systematic exposition and criticism in Aristotle. Finally there is the post-Aristotelian information which (with a few exceptions which will be mentioned in discussing the sources for particular philosophers) depends on brief, and sometimes garbled, epitomes of the work of Theophrastus, the distortions frequently taking the form of adaptation to Stoic thought. To see through this veil to the mind of archaic Greece is the primary task of Presocratic scholarship. Whether it is worth while no one had a better right to say than Hermann Diels, who at the end of his life declared, in a posthumously published lecture: 'I count myself fortunate in that it has been vouchsafed to me to dedicate the best part of my powers to the Presocratics.'[1]

For further details readers are referred to the account of Kirk mentioned above. In addition, an appraisal of the historical work of Theophrastus, which does him more justice than earlier accounts, is to be found in C. H. Kahn, *Anaximander*, 17–24.

[1] 'Ich schätze mich glücklich, dass es mir vergönnt war, den besten Teil meiner Kraft den Vorsokratikern widmen zu können' (*Neue Jahrbb. f. d. klass. Altertum*, 1923, 75).

LIST OF ABBREVIATIONS

In general, the titles of works cited in the text have not been so abbreviated as to be difficult of elucidation. Some periodicals, however, and a few books cited repeatedly, are referred to as follows:

PERIODICALS

AJA	*American Journal of Archaeology.*
AJP	*American Journal of Philology.*
CP	*Classical Philology.*
CQ	*Classical Quarterly.*
CR	*Classical Review.*
JHS	*Journal of Hellenic Studies.*
PQ	*Philosophical Quarterly.*
REG	*Revue des Études Grecques.*
TAPA	*Transactions of the American Philological Association.*

OTHER WORKS

ACP	H. Cherniss, *Aristotle's Criticism of Presocratic Philosophy.*
CAH	*Cambridge Ancient History.*
DK	Diels–Kranz, *Fragmente der Vorsokratiker.*
EGP	J. Burnet, *Early Greek Philosophy.*
HCF	G. S. Kirk, *Heraclitus: the Cosmic Fragments.*
KR	G. S. Kirk and J. E. Raven, *The Presocratic Philosophers.*
LSJ	Liddell–Scott–Jones, *A Greek–English Lexicon,* 9th ed.
OCD	*Oxford Classical Dictionary.*
RE	*Realencyclopädie des klassischen Altertums,* ed. Wissowa, Kroll *et al.*
TEGP	W. Jaeger, *Theology of the Early Greek Philosophers.*
ZN	E. Zeller, *Die Philosophie der Griechen,* ed. W. Nestle.

I

INTRODUCTION AND SUMMARY

To write a history of Greek philosophy is to describe the formative period of our own thought, the making of the framework which supported it until at least the latter part of the nineteenth century. The discoveries about the nature of matter (if that term may still be used), the size and character of the Universe, and the human *psyche* which scientists have been making during the last hundred years are indeed so revolutionary that they may result in a radical reshaping of our fundamental outlook. Apart, however, from the fact that they are still in such a state of rapid transition that it is difficult to see what this new framework of thought will be, the conservatism of ordinary human minds ensures that much in the older outlook will continue to colour our general presuppositions for a long time to come. Even the modern natural philosopher who studies the records of the earliest European thinkers may find that he has more in common with them than he expected. It is this fundamental and dateless character of much Greek thought which makes it worth while to attempt a fresh presentation of it for a contemporary reader.

There is another side to the coin. With the Greeks we stand at the beginning of rational thought in Europe. It follows that we shall not only be concerned with reasoned explanation or scientific observation, but shall be watching the emergence of these activities from the mists of a pre-scientific age. This emergence is not sudden, but slow and gradual. I shall try indeed to justify the traditional claim of Thales to be regarded as the first European philosopher; but I shall not intend by that to assert that at one bound the line was crossed between pre-rational, mythical or anthropomorphic conceptions and a purely rational and scientific outlook. No such clearly-marked line existed, or exists today. Besides appreciating what is of permanent value in Greek thought, we may also learn from observing how much latent mythology it continued to shelter within what appear to be a roof and walls of solid reason. This is naturally more obvious in the earliest period, but even Aristotle, to whom in spite of his critics in all ages we owe so much of the indispensable groundwork of abstract concepts on which our thinking is based, has some fixed ideas which we encounter with a sense of shock; for example, a conviction that the heavenly bodies are living creatures, a belief in the special perfection of circularity or sphericity, and some curious notions about the primacy of the number three which clearly antedate the beginnings of philosophical thought.

This is not a condemnation of myth as false in itself. Its stories and images may be, at an early stage of civilization, the only available means (and an effective one) of expressing profound and universal truths. Later, a mature religious thinker like Plato may choose it deliberately, and as the culmination of a reasoned argument, to communicate experiences and beliefs, the reality and cogency of which is a matter of conviction outrunning logical proof. This is genuine myth, and its validity and importance are undoubted. The danger begins when men believe they have left all that behind and are relying on a scientific method based solely on a combination of observation and logical inference. The unconscious retention of inherited and irrational modes of thought, cloaked in the vocabulary of reason, then becomes an obstacle, rather than an aid, to the pursuit of truth.

The reason for making this point at the outset is that the implicit acceptance of mythical concepts is a habit that never completely relaxes its hold. Today it is even more heavily overlaid than in ancient Greece with the terminology of rational disciplines. This makes it more difficult to detect and therefore more dangerous.

Without belittling the magnificent achievements of the Greeks in natural philosophy, metaphysics, psychology, epistemology, ethics and politics, we shall find that because they were pioneers, and therefore much nearer than ourselves to the mythical, magical or proverbial origins of some of the principles which they accepted without question, we can see these origins clearly; and this in turn throws light on the dubious credentials of some of the principles which gain a similarly unquestioned acceptance among many today.

Examples of these axioms in Greek thought are the assumption of the earliest school in Miletus that reality is one, the principle that like is drawn to, or acts upon, like (in support of which Democritus the atomist was not above quoting the proverb 'Birds of a feather' and a line of Homer), and the aforementioned conviction of the primacy and perfection of circular shape and motion which affected astronomy until the time of Kepler. It is not hard to detect the popular, unscientific origin of these general principles, but what of some to which our own scientists subscribe, or subscribed until recently? Professor Dingle quotes the following:[1] 'Nature abhors a vacuum', 'The Universe is homogeneous' (compare the Milesian premiss), 'Nature always works in the simplest way'. It is not only in the ancient world that, as he says, 'the Universe, instead of being a touchstone, becomes a mould, fashioned first of all to the investigator's liking and then used to give a false form to the things of experience'.

The history of Greek philosophy can be conveniently divided into periods which show a real difference of outlook and interest, corresponding in part to changes of outward circumstances and habits of life. They also differ in the locality of the centres from which the main intellectual influences were exerted upon the Greek world. At the same time, if this division is adopted, it is important not to lose sight of the equally real continuity that runs through the whole development of thought from the Milesians to the Neoplatonists. To bring out this continuity, it will be worth while attempting a brief sketch of the development of Greek philosophy before we proceed to consider it in detail. The next few pages may be regarded as a map of the country which we have to traverse, and it is always as well to run the eye over the map before setting out on the journey itself.

Our attention is first directed to the eastern fringe of Greek settlement. Here in Ionia, on the western border of Asia Minor under Lydian and Persian rule, something happened in the sixth century before Christ which we call the beginning of European philosophy. Here opened the first, or Presocratic period of our subject, with the Milesian school. These men, inhabitants of one of the largest and most prosperous of Greek cities, with numerous colonies of her own and widespread foreign contacts, were endowed with an indefatigable curiosity

[1] *The Scientific Adventure* (Pitman, 1952), 168.

about the nature of the external world, the process by which it reached its present state, and its physical composition. In their attempts to satisfy this intellectual craving for knowledge, they by no means excluded the possibility of divine agency, but they reached a conception of it very different from the polytheism current in contemporary Greek society. They believed that the world arose out of a primal unity, and that this one substance was still the permanent base of all its being, though now appearing in different forms and manifestations. The changes were rendered possible by an everlasting motion of the primary stuff due, not to any external agent, but to its own essential animation. The distinction between a material and an efficient principle had not yet been felt, and the primary entity, since it lived for ever and was the author of its own movement and change, and of all the ordered world of earth, sky and sea, was naturally thought to merit the epithet 'divine'.

Before the end of the century, the philosophical impulse was carried from the eastern to the western borders of the Greek world by the migration of Pythagoras of Samos to the cities of Greek settlement in South Italy. Together with physical translation, it underwent a change of spirit. From now on, the Ionian and Italian branches of philosophy develop in different ways, though the division is not so clearly marked as some later Greek scholars and classifiers supposed, and there was some cross-fertilization, as for example when Xenophanes from Asiatic Colophon followed in the track of Pythagoras and settled in Magna Graecia. So far as Pythagoras and his followers were concerned, the change in spirit affected both the motive and the content of philosophy. From satisfaction of the sheer desire to know and understand, its purpose became the provision of intellectual foundations for a religious way of life; and in itself it acquired a less physical, more abstract and mathematical character. Study of matter gave way to study of form. The logical trend was followed up in the West by Parmenides of Elea and his school, and reached its climax in his teaching that true being was not to be found in the physical world because, from the propositions 'It is' and 'It is one' (on which Milesian cosmology might be said to have been based; in any case Parmenides argued that the second followed from the first), the only valid conclusion was an unqualified denial of

4

physical movement and change. Reason and the senses gave contradictory answers to the question: 'What is reality?', and the answer of
reason must be preferred.

About the same time, or a little earlier, the unique and enigmatic
Heraclitus of Ephesus was also advancing towards the fateful division
between reason and the senses. He preached the folly of relying on
sense-perception unchecked by the judgment of its rightful interpreter,
reason, though without going so far as to reject its witness absolutely
as did Parmenides. In contrast to the Eleatic, who denied the very
possibility of movement, he saw the whole natural world in terms of a
continuous cycle of flux and change. Rest, not movement, was the
impossibility. Any apparent stability was only the result of a temporary
deadlock between the opposite tensions which were ceaselessly at work.
Everlasting is only the *logos*, which in its spiritual aspect is the rational
principle governing the movements of the universe, including the law
of cyclic change. The qualification ('in its spiritual aspect') is necessary
because at this early stage of thought nothing is yet conceived as real
without some physical manifestation, and the *logos* is intimately connected with that substance which had a kind of primacy in the world of
Heraclitus, namely fire, or 'the hot and dry'.

The original and paradoxical philosophies of Heraclitus and
Parmenides both had considerable influence on the mind of Plato.
The rest of the Presocratic period was marked by the efforts of natural
philosophers to escape the distasteful conclusion of Parmenides by a
change from monism to pluralism. If the monistic hypothesis led to
denying the reality of the apparent multiplicity of the world around us,
then in the interests of the phenomena that hypothesis must be
rejected. This was the reasoning of Empedocles, Anaxagoras and the
atomists. Empedocles was a Sicilian, and like other philosophers of
Magna Graecia combined his search for the ultimate nature of things
with the demands of a deeply religious outlook, to which the nature
and destiny of the human soul was of fundamental interest. He saw
the answer to Parmenides in the substitution of four ultimate root-
substances or elements (earth, water, air and fire) for the single principle
of the Milesians. Anaxagoras brought the spirit of Ionian physics from
Asia Minor to Athens, where he lived in the time of Socrates and

Euripides, and enjoyed the friendship of Pericles and his circle. His doctrine of matter as consisting of an infinite number of qualitatively different 'seeds' was a kind of half-way house to the culmination of this pluralistic physics in the atomism of Leucippus and Democritus.

An interesting result of the uncompromising logic of Parmenides was to face philosophers with the problem of a moving cause. At its start, rational thought had inherited from mythology the conception of all physical entities as in some degree animate. The separation of matter and spirit was as yet undreamed-of, and to the Milesian monists it was therefore natural to suppose that the single primary substance of the world—water or mist or whatever it might be—was the author of its own transformations. It did not occur to them that this was something that needed explaining, or that anyone might demand a separate cause of motion. The intellectual drawbacks of this naive combination of matter and spirit, moved and mover, in one corporeal entity are already becoming obvious in Heraclitus. By bringing the world to a full stop, as it were, Parmenides drove home the lesson that motion was a phenomenon in need of its own explanation, and in the later Presocratics we see not only the change from a unity to a plurality of physical elements, but also the emergence of a moving cause beside and apart from the moving elements themselves.

Empedocles, impelled by the needs of his moral and religious, as well as of his physical system, posited two such causes, which he named Love and Strife. In the physical world, these are used in a mechanical way to bring about respectively the combination with, and separation from each other of the four elements, whereby the cosmos is brought into being. In the religious sphere they allow for a moral dualism, being the causes of good and evil respectively. Anaxagoras was hailed by Plato and Aristotle as the first man to assert that *Nous*, Intelligence, was the originator of the motions leading to the formation of a cosmos from the tiny *spermata* of matter which, in his view, were its material constituents. Moreover he explicitly insisted on the transcendent character of this *Nous*, which 'existed alone and by itself' and 'was mixed with no thing'.

Leucippus and Democritus did not provide as their cause of motion any separate entity existing, like the opposite forces of Empedocles or the *Nous* of Anaxagoras, in the same positive way as the elements themselves. For this reason Aristotle condemned them as having neglected the whole problem of the moving cause. In fact their answer was more subtle, and more scientific in spirit than those of the others. Part of the difficulty had been that Parmenides had denied the existence of empty space, on the strength of the abstract argument that if Being is, emptiness could only be the place where Being was not. But nothing exists besides Being, and to say of Being 'it is not' is a logical impossibility. Emptiness is not Being, therefore it does not exist. Outfacing Parmenides on his own ground, the common-sense of the atomists declared that 'not-Being exists as much as Being'; that is, since Being was still conceived as tied up with corporeal existence, they asserted that there must be place which was not occupied by body. They supposed the sum of reality to be made up of tiny solid atoms floating in infinite space. Once this picture is made conscious and explicit, as it now was for the first time, matter is, as it were, set free, and, of atoms let loose in infinite space, it might perhaps seem as reasonable to ask 'Why should they stay still?' as 'Why should they move?' Though he gives them no credit for it, Aristotle comes near to the heart of their achievement when he says that the atomists 'made void the cause of motion'.[1] To appreciate this at its true worth, one must understand what a bold step it was to assert the existence of empty space in face of the new logic of Parmenides.

The gradual emergence into consciousness of the problem of the first cause of motion, bound up as it is with that of the relation between matter and life, is one of the main threads to be followed in an exposition of Presocratic thought.

In the time of Anaxagoras and Democritus, there occurred at Athens the change which the ancients universally associated with the name of Socrates. From the middle of the fifth century to the end of the fourth, we are in our second main period, which most people would agree to call the zenith of Greek philosophy. Athens is its centre, and the outstanding intellectual figures are Socrates, Plato and Aristotle. The shift of interest which marked the beginning of this period may be described as being from the universe to man, from interesting intellectual questions

[1] *Phys.* 265 b 24.

7

of cosmology and ontology to the more pressing business of human life and conduct. Nor was the physical side of the microcosm excluded. Contemporary with Socrates were Hippocrates and the earliest of those anonymous followers of his who with him produced the impressive body of medical and physiological writings known as the Hippocratic Corpus. At this time, says Aristotle roundly, 'the investigation of nature came to a stop, and philosophers turned their attention to practical morality and political thought'.[1] Some three centuries later, Cicero was saying much the same thing. Socrates 'called down philosophy from the skies and implanted it in the cities and homes of men'. He 'brought it into communal life, compelling it to attend to questions of virtue and vice, good and evil'. As for what went on in the heavens, that was far removed from our grasp, and even had it not been, it had no relevance to the good life.[2]

It might indeed be claimed that in Socrates the new spirit found its first genuine philosopher. To say that he was actually responsible for the change of outlook goes much too far. The teaching of the contemporary Sophists was very largely ethical and political, and in this they needed no prompting from Socrates. These were the days of Athens's growth to political maturity, to the leadership of Greece through her conduct in the Persian Wars and the subsequent foundation of the Delian League, and to the democratic form of government which gave every free citizen the right not only to elect his rulers but to vote in person on matters of public policy and even take his turn in exercising high and responsible office. To fit himself for success in the busy life of the city-state became a necessity for everyone. As the power and wealth of Athens grew, there followed her increasing arrogance in external relations, the impact of war between Greeks, the disaster of the Sicilian expedition (in contemporary eyes an inevitable retribution for *hybris*), and the downfall of Athens at the hands of her rival Sparta. The years of war were marked internally by the increasing corruption of Periclean democracy, a murderously cruel oligarchic revolution, and the return of a democracy from which the spirit of vengeance was by no means absent. All these events took place in Socrates's own lifetime, and created an atmosphere inimical to the

[1] *Part. An.* 642a28. [2] *Tusc.* v, 4, 10; *Ac.* I, 4, 15.

prosecution of disinterested scientific research. To Aristophanes, a faithful enough mirror of the better opinion of his time, natural philosophers were a useless sort of people and a suitable butt for not always good-tempered ridicule.

The state of physical speculation itself must also have made the time seem ripe for a reaction against it of common sense. In the absence of precise experiment and the scientific instruments which make it possible, the natural philosophers appeared to be not so much explaining the world as explaining it away. Faced with the choice of believing either, with Parmenides, that motion and change were unreal, or else that reality consisted of atoms and void—atoms which were not only invisible but lacking also the other sensible qualities of taste, smell and sound which mean everything to the human being— it is not surprising if most men decided that the world of the philosophers had little to say to them.

At the same time, the contrast between certain things which were only 'conventional' and others which existed 'in nature' (whether it was borrowed from the physicists or merely shared with them as part of the general spirit of the age) was eagerly seized on by some as the basis for an attack on absolute values or divine sanctions in the ethical sphere. Virtue, like colour, was in the eye of the beholder, it did not exist 'by nature'. In the ensuing controversy, Socrates employed all his powers in the defence of absolute standards, through the implications of his paradoxes: 'Virtue is knowledge' and 'No man does wrong willingly'. His point was that if anyone understood the true nature of goodness its appeal would be irresistible, and failure to comply with its standards could only be due to a lack of full understanding. This full understanding he did not claim to have reached himself, but unlike others he was aware of his ignorance. Since this at least was a starting-point, and an unjustified confidence in ethical matters in his view the chief cause of wrongdoing, he conceived it his mission to convince men of their ignorance of the nature of goodness and so persuade them to seek, with him, to remedy it. In carrying out this task, he developed the dialectical and elenctic methods of argument to which later philosophers owed so much.

To account for the extraordinary influence of Socrates over subsequent philosophy is something that must be left until later. Here it may be said that almost all later schools, whether originating with his own disciples or, like Stoicism, founded long after his death, whether dogmatic or sceptical, hedonistic or ascetic in character, acclaimed Socrates as the fountain-head of all wisdom including their own. This at least suggests that we shall err if we regard him as a simple character. Schools founded by his immediate disciples included the logically subtle Megarians, the pleasure-loving Cyrenaics and perhaps the ascetic Cynics, as well as the Academy of Plato, but only of the last have we anything more than fragmentary knowledge.

Socrates had bequeathed to his successors some of the most intractable of intellectual problems. It might seem that in bidding men seek 'the true nature of goodness' as the sole requirement for right living, he had decided by an act of faith rather than of reason (*a*) that goodness has a 'true nature', (*b*) that the human mind can grasp it, (*c*) that the intellectual grasp of it will be an all-sufficient incentive to right action in practice. But this, in modern terms, is to raise fundamental questions of ontology, epistemology, ethics and psychology. To contemporaries it would seem like begging the question involved in the 'nature-versus-convention' controversy rather than settling it.

Determined to defend and expand his master's teaching, Plato with his more universal genius, though he had no names for the branches of more recent philosophy just mentioned, wove something of all of them into the superb tapestry of his dialogues. Goodness had a real nature because it stood at the head of the world of 'forms'. These were ideal entities having a substantial existence beyond space and time, and constituting the perfect patterns after which were modelled the fleeting and imperfect representations of truth in ethical, mathematical and other spheres which are all that we encounter in this world. Knowledge is possible because, as Pythagorean and other religious teachers claimed, the human soul (of which for Plato the intellect was the highest and best part) is immortal and enters again and again into mortal bodies. Between its incarnations it is face to face with the eternal realities. Contamination with the corporeal dulls the memory of these, which may be reawakened by experience of their imperfect and mutable representations on earth, and, thus started on its way, the philosophic soul may, even in this life, recapture much of the truth by a process of rigorous intellectual and moral self-discipline. Philosophy is a canalization of the will and emotions as well as of the intellect. The soul has three parts, a concupiscent, a spirited or impulsive, and a rational. The *eros*, or *libido*, of each is directed towards a different class of object (physical pleasure, honourable ambition, wisdom). In the soul of the true philosopher the lower two are not allowed to exceed the bounds of their proper functions; the amount of *eros* directed towards their objects is diminished, and it flows with a corresponding increase in strength towards the objectives of reason, which are knowledge and goodness. In this way the Socratic paradoxes receive a broader psychological base.

Plato's was not a static mind. What I have said so far probably represents not unfairly his convictions in middle life, as expressed in the great dialogues of that period, especially the *Meno*, *Phaedo*, *Republic* and *Symposium*. From this root sprang his political theory, aristocratic and authoritarian. Later it became apparent to him that the doctrine of eternal, transcendent forms, which he had accepted with a partly religious enthusiasm, entailed serious intellectual difficulties. As a theory of knowledge it demanded further investigation, nor did the relations between forms and particulars, or between one form and another, lend themselves easily to rational explanation. Plato did not hesitate to tackle these problems, and in doing so was led to produce the critical writings which in the view of some twentieth-century philosophers constitute his most important philosophical achievement, notably the *Parmenides*, *Theaetetus* and *Sophist*. The *Parmenides* raises, without solving, a number of difficulties involved in the theory of forms, the *Theaetetus* is an inquiry into the nature of knowledge, and the *Sophist*, in a discussion of methods of classification, of the relations between the most comprehensive forms, and of the different senses of 'not-being', lays the foundations for much future work in logic.

Plato retained to the end a teleological and theistic view of nature. The *Timaeus* contains a cosmogony which sets out to show the primacy of a personal mind in the creation of the world: it was designed by God's intelligence to be the best of all possible worlds. Yet God is not omnipotent. The world must ever fall short of its ideal model since its raw material is not made by God but given, and contains an irreducible minimum of stubbornly irrational 'necessity'. That the world is the product of intelligent design is argued again in his last work, the *Laws*, as the climax of a detailed legislative scheme. His aim is to undermine the sophistic antithesis of nature and law: law is natural, and if the 'life according to nature' is the ideal, then it should be a law-abiding life.

Aristotle was for twenty years the friend and pupil of Plato, and this left an indelible impression on his thought. Since his own philosophical temperament was very different from his master's, it was inevitable that a note of conflict should be discernible at the heart of his philosophy. His more down-to-earth mentality had no use for a world of transcendent entities which it saw as a mere visionary duplication of the real world of experience. He had a great admiration for his fellow-Northerner Democritus, and it is conceivable that, had it not been for Plato, the atomic view of the world as an undesigned accretion of particles might have undergone remarkable developments in his keen and scientific brain. As it was, he retained throughout life from his Academic inheritance both a teleological outlook and a sense of the supreme importance of form which sometimes led to difficulties in the working out of his own interpretation of nature.

Every natural object is a compound of matter and form, 'matter' in its absolute sense meaning not physical body (all of which possesses some degree of form), but a wholly unqualified substratum with no independent existence but logically demanded as that in which the forms inhere. Immanent form takes the place of the transcendent forms of Plato. Everything has an indwelling impulse towards the development of its own specific form, as is seen most clearly in the organic progress of seed to plant or embryo to adult. The process may also be described as that from potentiality to actuality. This dichotomy of existence into potential and actual was Aristotle's reply to Parmenides's denial of change on the ground that nothing can come to be either out of what is or what is not.

At the apex of the *scala naturae* exists purely actual form, which as perfect Being has no part in matter or potentiality; that is, God. His existence is necessary on the principle that no potentiality is called into actuality save by the presence of an already actual being: in physical generation, a seed is first produced by a mature plant, a child must have a father. (It is fundamental to Aristotle's teleology that the hen came before the egg.) On this plane, actual and potential are only relative terms, but to sustain the teleological order of the whole Universe calls for a perfect and absolute Being. To Aristotle as to Plato, teleology implies the actual existence of a *telos*, an ultimate final and efficient cause for the sum-total of things as well as the individual and relative causes which are at work within the separate species.

In his own nature God is pure mind or intellect, for that is the highest type of being and the only one that can be conceived as existing apart from matter. He is not a deliberate creator, since any concern for the world of forms-in-matter could only detract from his perfection and involve him in one way or another in the potential. But his existence is enough to keep in motion (not 'set in motion', for to Aristotle the world is eternal) the whole world-order by activating the universal and natural impulse towards form. In other words, everything is striving to imitate within its own limitations the perfection of God. Physically, his existence leads directly to the circular motions instigated by the intelligences that move the heavenly bodies, which in turn render possible the processes of terrestrial life. From this point of view mankind exists at many removes from God, but his possession of reason gives him a unique position, a kind of direct line of communication. Thus the way of intellectual contemplation, of philosophy, is for man the way to fulfil his proper nature. For him, as for the rest of nature, it is natural to develop the activity of his highest part, to strive to realize his proper form. For him, unlike the rest of terrestrial nature, this is (as Aristotle says in the tenth book of the *Ethics*) to cultivate a divine spark that is within him.

The abandonment of the transcendent forms of Plato had momentous consequences for ethics. The existence of justice, courage, temperance, etc., among the absolutes of this transcendent world meant that the answers to questions of conduct were bound up with metaphysical knowledge. A man might act rightly by doing what he was told, relying on an 'opinion' implanted by another; but he would have no 'knowledge' of why he was behaving thus. Morals must be securely founded on fixed principles, and for this we need the philosopher who by long and arduous training has recovered his knowledge of reality, that is of the absolute forms of the virtues which are but palely reflected in any virtuous acts on earth. For Aristotle all this is changed. Moral virtue and rules of conduct lie entirely within the realm of the contingent. In the first two books of the *Ethics* he reminds us no less than six times of the principle that precision is not to be sought indiscriminately in all subjects and is out of place in the study of morality, the goal of which is not knowledge but practice. The sentence 'We are not trying to find out what virtue is, but to become good men' seems aimed deliberately at Plato and Socrates.

In psychology, Aristotle defined the soul as, in his technical sense of the word, the 'form' of the body; that is, the highest manifestation of the particular compound of form and matter which is a living creature. This does not of course imply an epiphenomenalist view. That would be to turn his philosophy upside down. Form is the prior cause and is in no way dependent on matter. It does, however, exclude the doctrine of transmigration which Plato shared with the Pythagoreans. Aristotle is shy of the subject of immortality, but seems to have believed in the survival, though not necessarily the individual survival, of *nous*, which is our link with the divine, and, as he once puts it, the only part of us which 'comes in from outside'.

A great part of Aristotle's achievement is scientific, especially in the descriptive and classificatory work of natural history, where the extent of his knowledge and the soundness of his method still excite the admiration of workers in the same field. The identification and description of species was of course a task particularly suited to the genius of the philosopher who, like his master, saw reality in form, yet discovered this form in the natural world instead of banishing it beyond space and time. He was the founder of the natural sciences as separate disciplines, though the doubtful advantage of an admitted cleavage between 'science' and philosophy still lay in the future. In logic, which he regarded not as a part of philosophy but as its *organon* or tool, he stood on Plato's shoulders to a greater extent than is sometimes realized. Yet here as elsewhere, his genius for system and order takes him far beyond the mere rearrangement of other men's ideas, and entitles him to his place as the true founder of formal logic and scientific method.

Aristotle was the tutor of Alexander the Great, remained his friend throughout the period of his conquests, and died within a year of Alexander's death in 323. He stood therefore on the threshold of the new historical order which begins the third main period of Greek philosophy. Whether or not Alexander aimed at establishing a world-wide community (and this is a much-disputed question), he at least succeeded in bringing it about that after his time the small, independent and self-contained city-states, which had formed the essential framework of classical Greek life and thought, lost much of their reality as fully independent communities. Dying early with his work unfinished, he left a vast European, Asiatic and African dominion to his successors, who carved it up into unwieldy empires monarchically ruled. The changes in outlook that followed these momentous military and political events were manifold, though doubtless gradual. Certainly the Greek did not easily or quickly give up his belief in the city as the natural unit, the community to which he belonged and owed his loyalty. These local loyalties were fostered by the successor-kings themselves, who respected the power of the city-states and also saw in their preservation the best hope for the survival of Hellenic civilization among the exotic influences of the Eastern lands to which it was now transplanted. The cities therefore still exerted a direct controlling power over local affairs and the lives of their citizens, though supervised by the central government, and the old political spirit of the Greeks was kept alive, though inevitably, as time went on, it became (as Rostovtzeff has said) rather municipal than political in the true sense. On the mainland, especially, the combination of the cities into leagues went with a growing consciousness of Hellenic unity.

In the early part of the new age, signs were not lacking of a spirit of optimism and confidence, of faith in human capacities and the triumph of reason. The enormous expansion of the Hellenic horizon, the facilities for travel to, and commerce with, what had been little-known and barbarian parts of the world, and the opportunities for a fresh start in new lands, increased the sense of activity and hopefulness. As time went on, however, the continual political struggles and wars between the dynasties, and the disconcerting effect of the sudden new contacts between Greek and Oriental modes of life, as well as the effective absorption of the cities in the new kingdoms, began to create a feeling of uncertainty and depression, which, together with the other general features of the age, was reflected in its philosophy. The growing sense of the unimportance and helplessness of the individual, and even of the long-familiar social and political units, in the face of great and intractable powers which seemed to mould events with the impersonal inevitability of fate, had an effect on the minds of men not unlike that of our own age.

On the one hand, those of studious bent were set free for the pursuit of knowledge for its own sake, in which also they could find a refuge from the uncertainties of the present life. This did not manifest itself in bold and original flights of speculation like those of the dawn of philosophy. Scholarship and the special sciences, which had been given such a remarkable start by Aristotle and his collaborators, were industriously pursued first in the Lyceum itself by men like Theophrastus (Aristotle's friend and successor) and Strato, and then at Alexandria, whither Strato himself migrated to become tutor to the son of the reigning monarch of Egypt. Here at the beginning of the third century B.C. the Museum, with its great library and research centre, was founded by the early Ptolemies, possibly instigated by Demetrius of Phaleron. Exiled from Athens, this scholar-statesman, who was a friend of Theophrastus and had almost certainly attended the lectures of Aristotle himself, carried the spirit of the Lyceum to the Egyptian court of Ptolemy I about 295. A novel and characteristic feature of the age was a serious, well-documented study of the past, and in this the lives and works of previous philosophers had their share of attention. The application of science to technology, especially in the military sphere, also made notable advances in the Hellenistic age.

If the gradual loss of a sense of community, the decreasing opportunity to play a decisive part in public life, meant more freedom for the intellectual to indulge in the secluded pursuits of study and research, it also induced a widespread feeling of uneasiness, loss of direction, homelessness. In earlier, more compact polities the individual was first and foremost a citizen, with comprehensible rights and duties and a niche of his own in society. The largest community known to him was one in which he himself was widely known. All other communities were foreign, to be encountered only in the course of diplomacy or war. His world, like Aristotle's universe, was organically disposed. It had a centre and a circumference. As the Hellenistic age advanced, he became more like a Democritean atom, aimlessly adrift in an infinite void. Under this sense of strangeness, the common accidents of poverty, exile, slavery, loneliness and death took on more frightening shapes and were brooded over more anxiously. One result of this, especially in the later Hellenistic period, was an increase in the popularity of mystery-religions, both Greek and foreign, which in one form or another promised 'salvation'. Cults of this sort, from Egypt and the Asiatic countries, not unknown to Greeks before, gained adherents from all ranks of society. Philosophy also was naturally not unaffected. New systems arose to meet the new needs, systems whose declared goal was the attainment of *ataraxia*, undisturbed calm, or *autarkeia*, self-sufficiency.

The philosophies which dominated the scene from the end of the fourth century onwards were Epicureanism and Stoicism. The latter in particular attained such widespread influence that it might almost be called the representative philosophy of the Hellenistic and Graeco-Roman ages. Both harked back for their inspiration to the thinkers of the great creative period which ended with Aristotle. They were not on this account lacking in originality, to which Stoicism in particular has strong claims. Indeed, to say at what point a philosophic system ceases to be a synthesis of earlier thought and becomes an original creation is by no means easy. Few would deny originality to Plato, yet his philosophy could be plausibly represented as arising simply from reflection on the utterances of Socrates, the Pythagoreans, Heraclitus and Parmenides. What distinguishes the Hellenistic systems is rather, as I have indicated, a difference of motive. Philosophy no longer springs, as Plato and Aristotle rightly said that it did in the first place, from a sense of wonder. Its function is to bring an assurance of peace, security and self-sufficiency to the individual soul in an apparently hostile or indifferent world. It was natural therefore that philosophers should be less directly interested in questions of cosmology and physics, and should choose as the physical setting for their moral teaching an adaptation of some existing scheme. In this way the speculations of the earlier physical schools, though to some extent transmuted, live on in the Hellenistic world.

Epicurus, who was in his late teens when Aristotle and Alexander died, singled out religion as the root of spiritual malaise. The greatest single cause of mental distress lay in fear of the gods and of what might happen after death. It was an outrage that men should be tormented by the notion that our race was at the mercy of a set of capricious and man-like deities such as Greece had inherited from Homer, gods whose malice could continue to pursue its victims even beyond the grave. The atomic theory of Democritus, which accounted for the origin of the Universe and for all that happens therein without the postulate of divine agency, seemed to him at the same time to express the truth and to liberate the mind of man from its most haunting fears. Undoubtedly the gods exist, but if, as true piety demands, we believe them to lead a life of calm and untroubled bliss, we cannot suppose them to concern themselves with human or mundane affairs. At death the soul (a combination of especially fine atoms) is dispersed. To fear death is therefore foolish, since so long as we live it is not present, and when it comes we no longer exist and are therefore unconscious that it has come.

Unlike Democritus, who almost certainly posited an initial random motion of the atoms in all directions, Epicurus supposed the un-impeded motion of the atoms to be uniform in direction and speed, caused by their weight. Since he had the remarkable perspicacity to anticipate the finding of modern science that in a vacuum all bodies will fall at an equal speed, irrespective of their relative weights, he had still to account for their collision and entanglement. This he did by assuming a power in the atoms to make a tiny swerve from their course at a time and place undetermined, and this apparently unexplained hypothesis became a key-point of his system. In conjunction with his theory of the material, atomic composition of the mind, he used it to account for free-will, for, while taking over the atomic system, he was resolved at all costs to avoid the determinism of his predecessor. To suppose oneself a slave to destiny, he said, was worse than believing the old myths about the gods.

The highest good in life he named 'pleasure', but it would be more correctly described as absence of pain. The line of conduct which he recommended was the reverse of a voluptuary's, since indulgence in rich food and drink and other sensual pleasures is by no means calculated to produce that 'freedom from pain in the body and trouble in the mind' in which alone lies the pleasure of the wise man. Moreover 'it is not possible to live pleasantly without living prudently and honourably and justly'. (Cicero said with some reason that Epicurus only succeeded in maintaining that pleasure was the *summum bonum* by giving the word a meaning which no one else would recognize.) Though blameless, the Epicurean ethic was somewhat negative, not to say egoistic, since the attainment of the quiet mind, which was its aim, called for abstention from all public duties and responsibilities. The ideal was 'to live unnoticed'.

However, even if in the wrong hands it was capable of being debased to the level of Horace's pig, yet as taught and lived by Epicurus himself his philosophy was not lacking in intellectual courage or moral nobility. Nevertheless, in spite of his arguments to the contrary, a message of hope and comfort which relies for its effect chiefly on the assurance that death means complete extinction does not seem to the majority of men to carry the word of salvation. As a counter-lure to the mystery-religions it had no great force. At the same time its explicit hedonism, and relegation of virtue to the second rank in the hierarchy of goods, earned it the disapproval of other philosophical schools. Stoicism in its pure form was an even more austere creed, yet it proved capable of existing at different levels and making a wider appeal. Stoicism became a potent force, especially when adapted by the Romans to their own ideals of conduct.

The note of the new Hellenism is struck at the outset by the nationality of the founder of this philosophy, Zeno of Citium, not a Greek at all but a Phoenician Semite, as was almost certainly the great systematizer of Stoic doctrine Chrysippus of Soli near Tarsus. Zeno reacted strongly against the idea that the Universe was the product of chance. He found the germ of truth rather in the mind–matter complex of Heraclitus, and put at the centre of his system the *logos* which has its material embodiment in fire. This union of mind and matter, for Heraclitus a naive assumption, was for Zeno a conscious achievement, following on study and explicit rejection of the Platonic and

Aristotelian forms of dualism. Nothing can exist without material embodiment. The cosmos is the work of a providence which orders all things for the best, a product of conscious art, yet its designer is not transcendent. The divine essence impregnates everything, though not everywhere in the same purity. Only in man among sublunary creatures does it take the form of *logos*, materially represented by warm breath (*pneuma*). In the outer heavens it is even purer, sheer fiery mind free from the lower elements which contaminate it in and around the earth. By the possession of *logos*, which the lower animals lack, man, though his body is animal, shares the highest part of his nature with divinity; and since everything strives to live in accordance with its best nature, this—that is, a life in conformity with the *logos*—is the proper goal for man. Hence the Stoic ideal of the Sage, who has learned that nothing matters but the inner self. Externals (health, possessions, reputation), though the animal side of man may justify him in putting some before others, are intrinsically indifferent. To be right within is all that matters. This knowledge of the indifference of outward circumstances makes the Sage unshakably *autarkes*, and that is the sole requisite for a happy life.

Not pleasure, but virtue (equated with wisdom) is the highest good. Unity was restored to the soul by Chrysippus, who reduced impulse and desire to judgments ('This is good for me', etc.), thus building a new foundation for the Socratic dictum that virtue is knowledge. Virtue is an absolute, like straightness or truth. Hence the much-criticized Stoic paradox that there are no degrees between absolute goodness or wisdom and absolute folly or vice. The perfect Sage is extremely rare, yet all others are fools, and 'all sins are equal'. This was illustrated by various analogies, for instance that a man is drowned just the same whether his head is one foot or several fathoms below the surface. Yet as with externals, the Stoics generally conceded that there must be an intermediate class of actions, some preferable to others, though none properly good or bad.

The unity of virtue, and the universal human possession of *logos*, carried for the Stoics the momentous corollary that wisdom was as likely to be found in women or slaves as in free men. Indeed all men were by nature free and equal. Allied to this is the Stoic conception of the human community. To live communally is as much a natural human instinct as self-preservation, and the ideal community is one that embraces the whole human race, the Cosmopolis or world-city, for all men are kinsmen, sons of the one God. The whole idea of the brotherhood of man, even if it originated (as some would claim) in the mind of Alexander himself, owes much of its development and diffusion to Stoic teaching. It should be said, however, that this conception probably did not mature until some time later than Zeno and his followers, and reached its climax with Epictetus in the late first century A.D. Meanwhile a man has a responsibility to the state in which he finds himself, though existing law may differ widely from the natural law of the Cosmopolis. Unlike Epicureanism, Stoicism recommends active participation in the life around one, and tries to restore to the Greek something of the sense of community which had gone with membership of the independent city-state.

Zeno and Chrysippus made notable contributions to the particular disciplines of epistemology, logic and philology. For the first time, theories of the nature and use of language were being discussed by men who used the Greek language and were steeped in the tradition of Greek thought, but who were yet bilingual, with not Greek but another as their mother-tongue. They adopted the contemporary division of philosophy into logic, ethic and physic, but these elements were united, and the system integrated, by the universality of the *logos*. This vital cosmic force, or deity, has a twofold function as the principle both of knowledge and of causation. One is reminded sometimes of Plato's Idea of the Good, which he compared to the sun as that on which depend not only the existence and life of the natural world but also our perception of it through sight. The *logos* has also obvious affinities with the hylozoistic principle of several of the Presocratic cosmologists besides Heraclitus. They were fond of saying that their single principle, at once the material of the cosmos and the efficient cause of its evolution, both 'knew all things' and 'steered all things'. Yet we may say of Zeno, as of Plato, that however much he owed to his predecessors, his synthesis is infused with that new spirit which entitles it to be called in its own right one of the great philosophical systems of the world.

To trace the later developments of Stoicism is not the function of this preliminary survey. It received fresh impetus and a new direction in the second century B.C. at the hands of Panaetius of Rhodes, who was largely responsible for its introduction at Rome and its adaptation to Roman ideals and habits of thought. Regarding Socrates as the founder of all recent philosophy, he looked to Plato and Aristotle no less than to Zeno. Fitted by nature to be a man of the world, the friend of Scipio and of the historian Polybius, he emphasized the necessity of bringing Stoic principles to bear on practical affairs. His aristocratic leanings led him to abandon the earlier theory of the natural equality of all men for one of natural differences between them, and his relations with Roman society were in fact bound up with his conviction that the ideal state, which he saw as a mean between autocracy and democracy giving to each section of the population its due rights and duties but no more, came nearest to practical realization in the Roman constitution.

Meanwhile other schools—Sceptic, Peripatetic, Academic—continued, but may fairly be said to have been overshadowed by the Stoa. Under Carneades in the second century, a notable opponent of Stoicism, the Academy took a turn towards scepticism and disbelief in the possibility of certain knowledge. This was reversed under Antiochus, the teacher and friend of Cicero, who said of him that he was, 'si perpauca mutavisset, germanissimus Stoicus'. He held indeed that the differences between Academic, Peripatetic and Stoic teaching lay in words rather than substance. In general one may say that in spite of sharp mutual criticisms, there was always felt to be much common ground between these schools, and that, especially in the ethical field, Epicureanism stood isolated and apart, disapproved of by all.

Rome was now a world-power, and the Roman ethos making its impact everywhere. The Roman genius did not lend itself to originality in philosophy, yet the mere act of interpreting the Greek philosophical achievement in the Latin language, which was so successfully carried out by Cicero, was bound to bring its own modifications. Cicero's treatise on 'Duties', the Stoic καθήκοντα, though largely dependent on Panaetius, became a treatise '*De Officiis*', and *officium* was a conception which already had a purely Roman history and associations. Again, the Stoic ideal of the human community was not quite the same when seen through the mirror of the Latin *humanitas*, and similar, either more or less subtle, differences exist between other pairs of equivalents such as the Greek πολιτεία and the Latin *res publica*.

The lifetime of Cicero saw also a revival of the Pythagorean philosophy by certain spirits who were impressed by the religious needs of the age and attracted by a mystical conception of the relation between god and man, but wished to give this a more philosophical basis than was offered by the emotional cults of Isis or Cybele. It is, however, by no means free from the superstitious credulity of its time. It is the existence of this Graeco-Roman school that accounts for much of the difficulty of reconstructing the Pythagoreanism of the time of Plato and earlier. Most of our information about Pythagoreanism comes from writers of the later period, and what they say about the earlier phase is contaminated with post-Aristotelian ideas. Whole books were freely written and promulgated in the name of well-known early Pythagorean thinkers.

Perhaps the chief importance of the Neopythagoreans is that they helped to pave the way for Plotinus in the third century A.D. and the whole of the great and influential movement of Neoplatonism. The Neoplatonists Porphyry and Iamblichus both wrote lives of Pythagoras, and there was a close affinity between the two schools, as was only natural and inevitable, considering how deeply the successors of Pythagoras affected the mind of Plato himself.

We have now crossed the line between the pre-Christian and the Christian eras. In its primitive form, the teaching of Jesus and his handful of Hebrew followers may seem to have had little to do with the impressive and continuous unfolding of Greek philosophy. But after the conquests of Alexander, this continuing development was accompanied by ever widening opportunities for impact on other peoples. Greek and Semite had already met in Zeno and later Stoic philosophers. The first men to set down the new Gospel in writing did so not in their own vernacular but in the language of Plato and Aristotle as it had now adapted itself to its function as the *lingua franca* of the greatly enlarged Hellenic world. The task of converting the Gentiles brought the need to meet them on their own ground, as we see Saint Paul already doing in his famous speech to the Athenians, in which he commends the

Christian belief that all men are sons of God by quoting a line of the Stoic poet Aratus. Later on, there is a continuous interaction between Christian and pagan thought. The Christian attitude varies in individual writers between extreme hostility and considerable sympathy, from the 'What has Jerusalem to do with Athens?' of Tertullian to the idea of Greek philosophy as a *praeparatio evangelica*, the idea that, as Clement of Alexandria put it, philosophy had prepared the Greeks for Christ, as the Law prepared the Jews. With the birth of the highly spiritual religious philosophy of Neoplatonism, the interaction became even more marked. Whether for hostile and apologetic purposes or not, understanding and some degree of assimilation of the views of the opposite camp became indispensable. Thus even with the growth of Christianity to be the recognized religion of the civilized world, the continuity is not broken nor the influence of the Greek tradition at an end. Plato, Aristotle and the Stoics continue to exert their power over the scholastics of the Middle Ages. We have our Cambridge Platonists in the seventeenth century, our Catholic Thomists and our Protestant Platonists today.

To trace this whole story is not the work of one book, nor probably of one man. I mention the continuance of the Greek tradition in Christian philosophy because it is something that must not be forgotten, and constitutes one of the reasons for continuing to study ancient Greek thought today. But the present work will be confined to the non-Christian world, and that being so, I think it is best to make the break before the Neoplatonists rather than attempt to include them. With Plotinus and his followers, as well as with their Christian contemporaries, there does seem to enter a new religious spirit which is not fundamentally Greek (Plotinus himself was an Egyptian and his pupil Porphyry a Syrian who originally bore the name of Malchus), and points rather forward as a preparation for medieval philosophy than back to the ancient world.

One other point must be made clear before we start. In the course of this history I shall mention the names of a large number of philosophers and attempt to assess their achievement. Yet only of three or four of these do we possess any whole or connected writings. Plato's dialogues have come down to us entire. Of Aristotle we have a large amount of miscellaneous writings which are partly the notes for lectures and partly collections of material more or less worked up into scientific treatises on the subjects with which they deal. Within this corpus it is not always easy to be sure whether what we possess is from the pen of Aristotle himself or of one of his pupils, nor how far what is basically Aristotle's has been reworked and enlarged by pupils or editors. In addition to these manuscripts, which were intended for use within the school and have little pretension to literary merit, Aristotle left a number of published dialogues which were greatly admired in antiquity for their style as well as their content. These, however, are lost. We have some complete treatises of his successor Theophrastus. Of Epicurus, who was one of the most prolific writers of antiquity, we now possess only three philosophical letters to friends (of which one, though containing genuine sentiments of Epicurus, is probably not from his hand), a collection of forty 'Principal Doctrines'—each a mere sentence or brief paragraph—and some aphorisms.

For all the other major figures in Greek philosophy, including for example all the Presocratics, Socrates (who wrote nothing), and the Stoics not excepting Zeno himself, we are dependent on quotations and excerpts of varying lengths occurring in other authors, or paraphrases and accounts of their thought which often display a more or less obvious bias. This, the outstanding difficulty for a historian of Greek philosophy, must be appreciated at the outset. Except for Plato and Aristotle, the question of the nature and trustworthiness of our sources inevitably obtrudes itself at every turn.

II

THE BEGINNINGS OF
PHILOSOPHY IN GREECE

nec reditum Diomedis ab interitu Meleagri
nec gemino bellum Troianum orditur ab ovo.

Purely practical considerations ordain that we should not pursue our
subject too far into its embryonic stage, or at least not to a time before
its conception. What may we call the conception of Greek philosophy?
It occurred when the conviction began to take shape in men's minds
that the apparent chaos of events must conceal an underlying order,
and that this order is the product of impersonal forces. To the mind of
a pre-philosophical man, there is no special difficulty in accounting for
the apparently haphazard nature of much that goes on in the world.
He knows that he himself is a creature of impulse and emotion, actuated
not only by reason but by desires, love, hatred, high spirits, jealousy,
vindictiveness. What more natural than that the ways of the world
around him should have a similar explanation? He sees himself to be
at the mercy of superior and incomprehensible forces, which sometimes
seem to act with little regard for consistency or justice. Doubtless they
are the expression of beings like-minded with himself, only longer-
lived and more powerful. Our present purpose does not require us to
enter the troubled regions of anthropological controversy by suggesting
that these remarks have any necessary bearing on the ultimate origin,
or origins, of religious belief. All we have to notice is that these are the
assumptions of that type of polytheism or polydaemonism which
dominated the early mind of Greece and can be studied in all its
picturesque detail in the Homeric poems. Everything there has a
personal explanation, not only external and physical phenomena like
rain and tempest, thunder and sunshine, illness and death, but also
those overmastering psychological impulses through which a man feels
no less that he is in the power of something beyond his own control.

A guilty passion is the work of Aphrodite, an act of folly means that 'Zeus took away his wits', outstanding prowess on the field of battle is owed to the god who 'breathed might into' the hero. In this way human frailty provides for one of its most constant needs, the need for an excuse. Responsibility for impulsive action which is bound to be regretted when (in our significant expression) the doer 'comes to himself' can be transferred from the agent to an external compulsion. In our own age the impersonal factors (repression, complex, trauma and the like), which have replaced Aphrodite or Dionysus, are sometimes put to the same use.

The belief that men are the playthings of powerful but morally imperfect deities may seem to put them in a very humble and pitiable position, and expressions of pessimism about the human lot are frequent in Homer. At the same time it contains an assumption almost of arrogance, which the advent of a more philosophical outlook must dispel; for at least it assumes that the ruling powers of the universe concern themselves intimately with human affairs. The gods take thought not only for the fate of humanity as a whole or of cities, but even for the fortunes of individuals (to whom, if the men are chieftains, they may even be related by blood). If *A* prospers, while his neighbour *B* is ruined, this will be because the one has earned the favour, the other the enmity, of a god. Gods quarrel over whether Greeks or Trojans shall win the war; Zeus pities Hector, but Athena insists on the glorification of Achilles. Men may meet gods and express their feelings to them. When Apollo, after deceiving Achilles by taking the human form of Agenor, finally reveals himself, the infuriated hero bursts out in his presence: 'You have wronged me, Apollo, and if I had the power, I should requite you for it.' In spite of the ultimate invincibility of the gods, this familiar intercourse between earth and heaven must have had its satisfying and stimulating side. Under the influence of the earliest philosophical thinking, the 'Father of gods and men' and his divine family were dissolved into an impersonal 'necessity', an affair of natural laws and the interaction of 'airs, ethers, waters and other strange things', as Socrates calls them in the *Phaedo*. To many this must have brought a feeling of loneliness and desertion, and it is no wonder that the old and colourful polytheism retained its hold to a considerable extent after the rise, in the sixth century B.C., of more rationalistic cosmological views.

Moreover, to appreciate the extraordinary achievement of the early philosophical thinkers, we must recognize that in the prevailing state of knowledge the religious explanation would seem by far the most natural and probable. The world as our perceptions show it to us *is* chaotic and inconsistent. The freedom and irresponsibility of personal will, still more the unpredictable consequences of a clash of conflicting wills, account for its vagaries, on a superficial view, far better than the hypothesis of a single underlying order. Indeed in attempting to explain the world on such a hypothesis, the first philosophers, as Henri Frankfort rightly said, 'proceeded with preposterous boldness on an entirely unproved assumption'.

Religious explanations had sufficed to account not only for the day-to-day events of the contemporary world, but also for its far-off origins. In this respect we can see a considerable development, even before the days of philosophy, in the direction of an orderly process. The tendency towards systematization reaches perhaps its highest point in Hesiod's *Theogony*, yet in that poem the origins of sky, earth and ocean and all that they contain are still represented as the outcome of a series of marriages and begettings on the part of personal beings. The names of these beings—Ouranos (Heaven), Gaia (Earth) and so forth—may seem to indicate that they are no more than a transparent disguise for physical phenomena; yet it must be remembered that Gaia was a genuine goddess who had been from remote antiquity the object of popular belief and widespread cult. In the cosmogony of Hesiod the all-powerful cosmic force is still Eros, 'fairest among the immortal gods'. He is Love, the power of sexual generation, and his presence from the beginning is necessary to set on foot the matings and births which are thought of as the sole means of generation for all parts of the universe as well as for the creatures who inhabit it. How far this earlier view of the world remained an influence even on the minds of those who first sought a more natural and impersonal explanation is something which we must try to determine when we come to consider their work in detail. For the present we may say that in their attempt to conceive of the world as an ordered whole, and their search for its *arche* or beginning, they had predecessors in the genealogies of the theologian and his idea of the *dasmos*, or distribution of provinces and functions between the chief gods: but the final stripping away of anthropomorphic imagery, with all its momentous consequences for the free development of speculation, was theirs alone.[1]

The birth of philosophy in Europe, then, consisted in the abandonment, at the level of conscious thought, of mythological solutions to problems concerning the origin and nature of the universe and the processes that go on within it. For religious faith there is substituted the faith that was and remains the basis of scientific thought with all its triumphs and all its limitations: that is, the faith that the visible world conceals a rational and intelligible order, that the causes of the natural world are to be sought within its boundaries, and that autonomous human reason is our sole and sufficient instrument for the search. The next question to be considered is who were the authors of this intellectual revolution, in what conditions they were living, and to what influences they were open.

Its first exponents, Thales, Anaximander and Anaximenes, were citizens of Miletus, an Ionian Greek city on the west coast of Asia Minor, from the beginning of the sixth century B.C. onwards. In their time Miletus, which had already existed for some five hundred years, was a centre radiating a tremendous energy. Ancient tradition hailed it as the mother of no less than ninety colonies, and modern research confirms the reality of about forty-five of them—in itself an astonishing number.[2] One of the oldest of these was the commercial settlement of Naucratis in Egypt, founded in the middle of the seventh century. Miletus possessed great wealth, which it had obtained both by acting as a trading-centre for materials and manufactured goods brought to the coast from inner Anatolia and by the export of a variety of manufactures of its own. Milesian woollen goods were famous throughout Greek lands. Thus shipping, trade and industry combined to give this

[1] On Hesiod as a predecessor of philosophical cosmogonists see O. Gigon, *Der Ursprung*, ch. 1, and F. M. Cornford, *Princ. Sap.* ch. 11. One of the most interesting of these figures on the borderline between myth and philosophy is Pherecydes of Syros in the sixth century, for whom see the excellent account of Kirk in KR, 48–72.

[2] Pliny, *N.H.* v, 112: *Miletus Ioniae caput...super XC urbium per cuncta maria genetrix.* Cf. Hiller v. Gaetringen in *RE*, xv, 1590.

busy harbour-city a leading position and wide connexions, extending to the Black Sea in the north, Mesopotamia in the east, Egypt in the south and the Greek cities of South Italy in the west. Its government was aristocratic, and its leading citizens lived in an atmosphere of luxury and of a culture which may be broadly described as humanistic and materialistic in tendency. Its high standard of living was too obviously the product of human energy, resource and initiative for it to acknowledge any great debt to the gods. The poetry of the Ionian Mimnermus was an appropriate expression of its spirit in the late seventh century. To him it seemed that, if there were gods, they must have more sense than to trouble their heads about human affairs. 'From the gods we know neither good nor evil.' The poet looked inward, at human life itself. He extolled the enjoyment of momentary pleasures and the gathering of roses while they lasted, mourned the swift passing of youth and the misery and feebleness of old age. The philosopher of the same period and society looked outward to the world of nature, and matched his human wits against its secrets. Both are intelligible products of the same material culture, the same secular spirit. Both in their own way relegate the gods to the background, and explanations of the origin and nature of the world as the handiwork of anthropomorphic deities seem no more appropriate than the notion of a divine providence in the affairs of men. Moreover once the moment for this abandonment of mythological and theological modes of thought seemed to have come, its development was facilitated by the fact that neither here nor in any other Greek state was freedom of thought inhibited by the demands of a theocratic form of society such as existed in the neighbouring Oriental countries.

The environment of the Milesian philosophers, then, provided both the leisure and the stimulus for disinterested intellectual inquiry, and the dictum of Aristotle and Plato, that the source and spring of philosophy is wonder or curiosity,[1] finds its justification. Tradition describes these men as practical, both active in political life and interested in technical progress; but it was curiosity, and no thought of mastering the forces of nature in the interests of human welfare or destruction, which led them to those first attempts at a grand simplification of natural

[1] Ar. *Metaph.* A, 982b12; Plato, *Theaet.* 155D.

phenomena which constitute their chief title to fame. In the application of various techniques to the amelioration of human life the Egyptians of a thousand years before could probably have taught these Greeks some useful lessons. Yet the torch of philosophy was not lit in Egypt, for they lacked the necessary spark, that love of truth and knowledge for their own sakes which the Greeks possessed so strongly and embodied in their own word *philosophia*.[1] Philosophy (including pure science) can only be hampered by utilitarian motives, since it demands a greater degree of abstraction from the world of immediate experience, wider generalization and a freer movement of the reason in the sphere of pure concepts than submission to practical ends will allow. That practical purposes may also be served in the long run, if free rein is given to the flights of pure scientific speculation, is true but irrelevant. Philosophy did not arise from a demand for the necessities or amenities of human life. Rather was the satisfaction of those demands a precondition of its existence. We may agree with Aristotle, who, after making his point that philosophy has its origin in wonder, adds: 'History supports this conclusion, for it was after the provision of the chief necessities not only for life but for an easy life that the search for this intellectual satisfaction began'; as also in this matter with Hobbes, who said much the same thing: 'Leisure is the mother of Philosophy; and Common-wealth, the mother of Peace and Leisure: Where first were great and flourishing Cities, there was first the study of Philosophy.'

A glance at the geographical position of Miletus, and its relations with neighbouring powers, will also be relevant to our subject. Situated on the eastern fringe of the Greek-speaking peoples, it had at its back door the very different world of the East; in fact, as a recent historian of ancient Persia has emphasized, its situation and activities placed it 'in the full current of Oriental thought'.[2] This is something which has long been generally recognized, but the conclusions which have been drawn concerning the actual extent of Oriental influence on the earliest

[1] It is true, and historically important, that the word σοφία developed this meaning of philosophical wisdom out of an original connotation of skill in a particular craft or art. A good carpenter, surgeon, driver, poet or musician had his particular σοφία. Yet this was not the meaning in the minds of those who used the word φιλοσοφία.

[2] A. T. Olmstead, *History of the Persian Empire*, 208.

Greek philosophers show wide discrepancies, and have sometimes tended to be mere guesses based on prejudice rather than knowledge. It was difficult for some philhellenes of the nineteenth century to admit any detraction from the pure originality of Greek thought. When the inevitable reaction set in, it became equally difficult for some, who felt that the adulation of everything Greek had gone to extreme lengths, to grant them any originality at all. In any case, it is no long time since the decipherment of many thousands of clay tablets (even now far from complete) provided material for an appreciation of the science and philosophy of the ancient Near East and hence for a balanced estimate of what it could have taught the Greeks.

To take first of all the question of contacts and opportunity for the interchange of ideas, we must remember that most of Ionia was under the rule of Lydia in the time of its king Alyattes, who had conquered Smyrna but met his match in the Milesians and made a treaty with them.[1] Alyattes ruled from about 610 to 560, a period which covers much of the lifetime of Thales. His son Croesus completed the conquest of the Ionian coastal strip, and after his defeat by Cyrus in 546 it became a part of the Persian Empire. Both these monarchs, however, seem to have felt bound to respect the power and reputation of Miletus, which retained within their dominions a position of privilege and independence and continued to live its own life without much interference. Clearly from this, which might be called the passive, aspect, Milesians like all Ionians must have had plenty of opportunity of getting to know the Oriental mind. On the active side, these enterprising Greeks made journeys by land to Mesopotamia and by sea to Egypt; and the evidence all suggests that the first philosophers were no recluses, who shut themselves off from this ferment of their times, but energetic and practical men, of whom Thales at least made the voyage to Egypt.

We are inclined to think of Egypt and the Mesopotamian states as having been, for all the high level of their civilizations, places where freedom of thought was inhibited by the demands of a religion which weighed heavily on every branch of life and was used in the interests of a despotic central government; where the King was the embodiment

[1] Hdt. I, 17ff.

of divinity, of Ra or Marduk, and the priesthood which surrounded him took care that its authority was not diminished by any encroachment of free thought. This is true, and one of the most striking merits of the Greeks is their intolerance of all such systems. Nevertheless these unwieldy theocratic empires were by no means barren of intellectual achievement. As a historian of science puts it:

To deny the title of men of science to those ingenious workers who created the technique of multiplication and division; who made an error of only one inch in the 755¾ feet base lines of the Great Pyramid; who discovered how to mark out the passing of the seasons by taking as a unit the lapse of time between two heliacal risings of the star Sirius—would be to narrow down the meaning of the term beyond what in this industrial age we should be willing to do.[1]

To predict an eclipse, as he is credited with doing, Thales must have made use of Babylonian knowledge.[2] These were in any case the earliest human civilizations, and had to their credit the fundamental techniques of the domestication of animals, agriculture, pottery, brick-making, spinning, weaving and metallurgy. The Egyptians and Sumerians alloyed copper with tin to make the more useful bronze, and in the manufacture of their famous textiles Ionian cities like Miletus copied the Asiatic technique, which was superior to the Greek.

The debt of Greek mathematics to Egypt and Babylon was one which the Greeks themselves acknowledged. Herodotus writes that in his opinion geometry was invented in Egypt and brought from there into Greece, and that the Greeks learned from the Babylonians the division of the day into twelve parts and the use of the *polos* and *gnomon*, which were instruments (or possibly the same instrument under different names) for marking the time of day and the chief turning-points of the year such as solstice and equinox. Aristotle makes the general statement that the mathematical arts were founded in Egypt.[3] The cuneiform documents so far read suggest that if the Egyptians led in geometry, the Babylonians were even further ahead in arithmetic. In astronomy, arithmetical techniques were used by the

---

[1] W. P. D. Wightman, *The Growth of Scientific Ideas*, p. 4.
[2] Pp. 47 f., below.
[3] Hdt. II, 109, Ar. *Metaph.* 981 b 23. For a comparison of these two passages see below, p. 35.

33

Babylonians to bring the prediction of celestial phenomena to a remarkable degree of accuracy, and these techniques were developed by 1500 B.C. Recent research indeed suggests that, contrary to earlier belief, Babylonian astronomy was based on mathematical calculation rather than observation, which brings it even closer to the mind of Greece, at least as represented by Plato. To mention another branch of knowledge, papyrus documents from Egypt as far back as 2000 B.C. show that considerable progress had already been made there in the arts of medicine and surgery.

All this store of knowledge and skill was waiting, as it were, on the doorstep of the Greeks, so that to call them the first scientists would, we may agree, be to impose an impossibly narrow meaning on the term. Yet if they did not create science, it is generally and on good grounds agreed that they lifted it on to an entirely different plane. What without them would simply have stagnated at a certain elementary level underwent at their hands sudden and spectacular developments. These developments were not in the direction of the better fulfilment of practical ends. They did not, unless accidentally, further the Baconian ideal 'to endow the life of man with infinite commodities'. It is indeed probable, and has been too casually denied in the past, that the Ionian philosophers were keenly interested in technical problems; but it is in this sphere that they were most inclined to be the eager pupils of neighbouring peoples. The uniqueness of their own achievement lies elsewhere. We get a glimpse of it if we consider that although philosophy and science are as yet inseparable, yet whereas we speak of Egyptian and Babylonian science, it is more natural to refer to the philosophy of the Greeks. Why is this?

The Egyptian and Mesopotamian peoples, so far as we can discover, felt no interest in knowledge for its own sake, but only in so far as it served a practical purpose. According to Herodotus, taxation in Egypt was based on the size of the rectangular plots of land into which the country was divided under a system of private ownership. If a plot had its area reduced by the encroachment of the river Nile, the owner could put in a claim and royal surveyors were sent to measure the reduction, in order that the tax might be suitably adjusted. In giving the Egyptians credit for being the first geometers, Herodotus states it as his opinion that it was these problems which gave the stimulus to its development. Aristotle, it is true, attributes the Egyptian achievement in mathematics to the fact that the priests enjoyed leisure for intellectual pursuits. He is arguing that theoretical knowledge ('sciences that are directed neither to the provision of pleasure nor of necessities') only arose after the practical needs of life were satisfied. 'Thus this knowledge first arose in those regions where men had leisure. That is why the mathematical arts first took their rise in Egypt, for there the priestly caste was free to enjoy leisure.' Herodotus too writes elsewhere of the perquisites and privileges attached to the priestly life, which arose from the possession of land by the temples. If a priest was a scribe, he was immune from any other kind of labour. Nevertheless Aristotle is too obviously advancing a favourite theory of his own, which he presses on many other occasions, and Herodotus's account of the practical limitations of Egyptian geometry remains the more probable.[1] In holding that disinterested intellectual activity is a product of leisure, Aristotle is clearly right. His mistake lies in transferring to geometry in Egypt the character and purpose that it had in fourth-century Athens, where it was part of a liberal education and also a subject of pure research. In Egypt it was the handmaid of land-measurement or pyramid-building.[2]

In Babylonia the conduct of practical life was governed to a large extent by religious considerations, and the religion was a stellar one. In this way astronomy was a practical study, its virtue lying in the explanation which it gave to educated men of the behaviour of the stellar gods. The observations and calculations which it called forth were extensive and accurate, but were tied to the service of established religion. Greek philosophy on the other hand was in its beginnings, so far as the traditional gods were concerned, agnostic or positively hostile.

These peoples, then, the neighbours and in some things the teachers of the Greeks, were content when by trial and error they had evolved

---

[1] Cf. the interesting discussion of Hdt. II, 109 and Ar. *Metaph.* 981 b 21 ff. between C. Macdonald and J. Gwyn Griffiths in *CR*, 1950, 12 and 1952, 10.

[2] The practical bent of Egyptian mathematics emerges also from the interesting assessment of it in Plato's *Laws* (819), which is the more impressive because Plato is expressing great admiration and urging the Greeks to follow Egypt's example. Much Egyptian arithmetic was the equivalent of the Greek *logistic*. (See Karpinski's essay 'The Sources of Greek Mathematics' in d'Ooge's translation of Nicomachus's *Introductio Arithmeticae*.)

a technique that worked. They proceeded to make use of it, and felt no interest in the further question why it worked, no doubt because the realm of causes was still governed by religious dogma instead of being open to the free debate of reason. Here lies the fundamental difference between them and the Greeks. The Greek asked 'Why?', and this interest in causes leads immediately to a further demand: the demand for generalization. The Egyptian knows that fire is a useful tool. It will make his bricks hard and durable, will warm his house, turn sand into glass, temper steel and extract metals from their ore. He does these things and is content to enjoy the result in each case. But if, like the Greeks, you ask *why* the same thing, fire, does all these different things, then you are no longer thinking separately of the fire that is lit in the brick-kiln, the fire in the hearth and the fire in the blacksmith's work-shop. You begin to ask yourself what is the nature of fire in general: what are its properties as fire? This advance to higher generalizations constitutes the essence of the new step taken by the Greeks. The methods of the Babylonians have an algebraic character and show them to have been aware of certain general algebraic rules, but 'they formulated mathematical problems only with specific numeral values for the co-efficients of the equations'. 'No attempt was made to generalise the results.'[1] The Egyptians had thought of geometry as a matter of indi-vidual rectangular or triangular fields. The Greek lifts it from the plane of the concrete and material and begins to think about rectangles and triangles themselves, which have the same properties whether they are embodied in fields of several acres or in pieces of wood or cloth a few inches long, or simply represented by lines drawn in the sand. In fact their material embodiment ceases to be of any importance, and we have made the discovery which above all others stands to the especial credit of the Greeks: the discovery of form. The Greek sense of form im-presses itself on every manifestation of their activity, on literature and the graphic and plastic arts as much as on their philosophy. It marks the advance from percepts to concepts, from the individual examples per-ceived by sight or touch to the universal notion which we conceive in our minds—in sculpture no longer an individual man but the ideal of

[1] S. F. Mason, *A History of the Sciences* (1953), 7; V. Gordon Childe, cited by Wightman, *op. cit.* 4.

humanity; in geometry, no longer triangles but the nature of tri-angularity and the consequences which logically and necessarily flow from being a triangle.[1]

Elementary generalizations were of course necessary even for practical and empirical science and mathematics like those of the Egyptians. But they did not reflect on them as single concepts, analyse and define those concepts and so make them usable as the material for, or the constituent units of, yet higher generalizations. To do this one must be capable of dealing with the concept in abstraction, as a unity with a nature of its own. Then further consequences will be seen to flow from its nature as now defined, and a whole scientific or philo-sophical system can be built up which was unattainable so long as thought remained at the utilitarian level. In astronomy the Babylonians might amass data extending over centuries, based on careful observation and involving considerable ingenuity of calculation. But it did not occur to them to use this mass of data as the basis for constructing a rational cosmology like that of Anaximander or Plato. This gift for abstraction, with its limitless possibilities and (we must add) its inherent danger, was the peculiar property of the Greeks. The danger lies, of course, in the temptation to run before one can walk. For the human reason to discover for the first time the extent of its powers is an intoxicating experience. It tends to look down on the pedestrian accumulation of facts, and in trying its wings to soar far beyond the available evidence up to a grand synthesis that is very largely its own creation. It did not occur to the earliest natural philosophers to spend their lives in patiently examining, classifying and correlating the various species of animals and plants; or in developing experimental techniques whereby they might analyse the composition of various forms of matter. That is not how science and philosophy began. They began by

---

[1] Mr Arthur Lane makes this point well in his book on *Greek Pottery* (1948), 11: 'Form can be arrived at by empirical methods, as a happy accident supervening on the experimental manipu-lation of a material; or it may be a concept in the mind, that struggles into tangible shape through whatever channels it can. Their literature, philosophy and art show that the conceptual attitude to form was more deeply ingrained in the Greeks than in any other people of whom we know. To judge from the "geometrical" decoration of their early pottery, they might at that time have been totally blind to the surrounding world of natural phenomena. It was impossible for them to perceive an object, and then fluently translate this percept into a representational work of art. After perception came the agonizing mental process of creating the concept; what the early concept of "man" looked like we can see on a "geometric" vase.'

people asking—and claiming to answer—all-embracing questions like 'What is the *genesis* of existing things?', that is, out of what did they come in the first place and what are they made of now? Is the whole world ultimately of one substance or more? I have spoken of the danger of this mode of procedure, which no doubt strikes a modern scientist as in the literal sense preposterous. Yet if no one had begun in the first place by asking these ultimate and universal questions, science and philosophy as we know them could never have been born. The human mind being what it is, they could not have arisen in any other way. Even today, every scientist would admit that his experiments would be fruitless unless carried out in the light of a guiding idea, that is, on the basis of a hypothesis formed in the mind but as yet unproved, the establishment or refutation of which gives direction to the factual inquiry. Too close an attachment to phenomena, such as was dictated by the practical nature of Oriental science, will never lead to scientific understanding. Scientific inquiry, as a French scholar has put it, presupposes 'not only the love of truth for its own sake, but also a certain aptitude for abstraction, for reasoning on the basis of pure concepts—in other words, a certain philosophic spirit, for science in the strict sense is born of the bold speculation of the earliest philosophers'.[1]

The Greeks themselves had a phrase which sums up well the way in which they went beyond their predecessors and contemporaries. It is the phrase λόγον διδόναι. The impulse 'to give a *logos*' was the typically Greek one. *Logos* cannot be satisfactorily rendered by any single English word. Faced with a set of phenomena, they felt that they must go behind them and account for their existence in the particular form and manner in which they did exist. A complete *logos* is a description which at the same time explains. Besides form or structure, and ratio or proportion, *logos* may mean, according to its context, account, definition and explanation—all typically Greek notions, and all in the Greek mind so closely connected that it seemed natural to express them by the same word.[2] As Aristotle said, the only complete definition is one which includes a statement of the cause.

[1] R. Baccou, *Histoire de la science grecque*, 33.
[2] A fuller account of the uses of λόγος is given later in connexion with Heraclitus (pp. 420 ff.).

III

THE MILESIANS

A. INTRODUCTION

We have outgrown the tendency of which Cornford complained in 1907, to write the history of Greek philosophy 'as if Thales had suddenly dropped from the sky, and as he bumped the earth ejaculated: "Everything must be made of water!"' It was a sign of the changed outlook that, in preparing the fifth edition of Diels's *Fragments of the Presocratic Philosophers* in 1934, Walther Kranz put into effect a suggestion made by Diels himself in his preface to the fourth edition, namely to place at the beginning a chapter of extracts from early cosmological, astronomical and gnomic writings, which in the previous editions had been relegated to an appendix. This raises the difficult question whether the present work should follow the same plan. A strong reason against doing so is the endlessly disputed authenticity and date of the records of this 'pre-philosophical' tradition, which are for the most part preserved only as quotations in writers of a much later period. We may be sure that Hesiod's *Theogony* (the only extant work of its type) preceded the Milesian philosophers, but when we come to the fragments of Orphic cosmogony, or of the *Theogony* of Epimenides, it is difficult to be sure whether they may be reckoned as an influence on the Milesians or, on the contrary, as owing something to the Milesians themselves. Thus Kern saw in the fragments of Epimenides the impact of Anaximenes, and Rohde maintained of the 'Rhapsodic Theogony' attributed to Orpheus that 'in the very few passages in which a real coincidence exists between the Rhapsodies and Pherekydes, Herakleitos, Parmenides or Empedokles, the poet of the Rhapsodies is the borrower not the creditor'.[1] Recent opinion is on the whole inclined to assign the main outlines of the world-view

---

[1] Kern, *De Orphei Epimenidis Pherecydis theogoniis*; E. Rohde, *Psyche*, App. 9, 'The Great Orphic Theogony'. For a general discussion of this question see Guthrie, *Orpheus and Greek Religion*, ch. IV.

expressed in Orphic theogonical and cosmogonical fragments to the sixth century B.C., but doubts remain. All things considered, it seems best to proceed at once to an examination of the remains of those who are usually, and not without reason, called the first of the philosophers. The necessary reference to their actual or possible predecessors can be made where this examination demands it.

It is to Aristotle in the first place that we owe the distinction between those who described the world in terms of myth and the supernatural, and those who first attempted to account for it by natural causes. The former he calls *theologi*, the latter *physici* or *physiologi*, and he ascribes the beginning of the new, 'physical' outlook to Thales and his successors at Miletus, hailing Thales himself as 'first founder of this kind of philosophy'.[1] Such extraneous evidence as we have suggests that he was justified, nor is it likely that the man whose bias towards the scientific outlook led him to speak in strong terms of the uselessness of what he called 'mythical sophistry', and who suspected anthropomorphic religion to have been invented 'for the persuasion of the mob and in the interests of law and utility',[2] would have welcomed these men as his own predecessors if they had not in fact accomplished something like a revolution against the earlier, mythical modes of explanation. When he speaks of philosophy having its origin in wonder, he does indeed reach out a hand, in a sudden flash of understanding, to those on the other side of the gulf, saying in a brief parenthesis that there is a sense in which the lover of myth is also a lover of wisdom, or philosopher, since the material of myth also is that which has occasioned wonder in men's minds; but he makes it quite clear that the resemblance extends no further. The philosopher, he says in the same context, aims at a knowledge which shall be both accurate and all-embracing, and above all shall be knowledge of causes. Only universals are true objects of knowledge: only generalization can lead to the discovery of causes, by which Aristotle already, like a modern scientist, means general laws. Myth on the other hand, thinking in personal terms, demands rather particular causes for particular events. As Frankfort wrote: 'We understand phenomena, not by what makes them peculiar,

[1] *Metaph.* A, 983b20.   [2] *Metaph.* B, 1000a18; Λ, 1074b3.

40

but by what makes them manifestations of general laws. But a general law cannot do justice to the individual character of each event. And the individual character of the event is precisely what early man experiences most strongly.'[1]

To understand the mentality of Aristotle is of primary importance for us as students of the Presocratics, owing to the peculiar nature of the sources of our information about them.[2] Not only is he himself our earliest authority for much of what they taught, but the later doxographical tradition goes back to the historical work of his pupil Theophrastus and is stamped with the impress of his school, and to a considerable extent of his own masterful personality.[3] Here at the outset we may note that, in the sense in which Frankfort uses the word 'we', he is already one of us, though separated from us by some 2300 years and from the beginnings of natural philosophy by only 250. This, incidentally, is some indication of the measure of both Plato's and his own achievement. Some of his results, for example the structure which he attributed to the Universe, may seem absurd today; but in the method of his thought he moves easily among abstract concepts, and his whole effort is directed to explanation by reference to general laws, so much so that he founded formal logic and was already faced with the perennial problem of scientific inquiry: how is scientific knowledge of the individual possible at all, since science only explains by subsuming under laws that operate universally? He has travelled far from the first fumbling attempts to cast off mythological explanation, and this obviously introduces the danger of distortion in his account of what he knew, or thought he knew, about the early doctrines. He was a systematic philosopher first and a historian second, and his examination of his predecessors was explicitly directed towards eliciting how far they had travelled along the path that led to his own conception of reality. That this might not have been their aim, and that they might

---

[1] Arist. *Metaph.* A, 982b 18 and ch. 2 in general; Frankfort, *Before Philosophy*, 24.

[2] See the note on the sources, pp. xiii ff.

[3] That the Φυσικῶν Δόξαι of Theophrastus was largely influenced by Aristotle's accounts of the Presocratics has been shown by J. McDiarmid (*Harv. Stud. in Class. Philol.* 1953). This work, however, must be used with caution. It is over-bold to make statements like that on p. 121: 'There is nothing in Parmenides' poem to justify this interpretation' of the Way of Opinion, when we possess only a few brief quotations from the Way of Opinion itself. A juster verdict on Theophrastus is to be found in Kahn, *Anaximander*, 17–24.

have taken tentative steps in other, and possibly even more promising directions, does not (naturally enough) occur to him.

Nevertheless the probable effect of this on the trustworthiness of what he says about them has sometimes been immensely exaggerated. We possess a large corpus of his works, quite sufficient to allow of a just estimate of his mental quality and powers of judgment. Any reader of these can see that he was a thinker of the first rank, brilliant at times, clear-headed and methodical, sane and cautious. To speak in these terms of one of the leading philosophers of all time sounds ridiculous. Yet it is not superfluous, for it is apparently possible to suppose that whereas in logic, ontology, ethical and political thought, biology and zoology he generally displays these qualities in the highest degree, yet as soon as he comes to assess his predecessors in the philosophical tradition he is so blinded by the problems and presuppositions of his own thought that he loses his common-sense and even any idea of the proper way to handle evidence. This is entirely at variance with the knowledge of his mind which we gain from other portions of his work. We may add, also, first that he has a certain advantage over us in the simple fact that he was an Ionian Greek, writing and speaking the same language as his fellow-Ionians of two or three centuries before and sharing far more of their outlook than we can ever hope to do; secondly that he enjoyed a far more extensive first-hand acquaintance with the writings of some of them; and thirdly that the amount of attention which he bestows on his predecessors is in itself some evidence of a genuine historical approach to his subject which, followed out with the powers of an Aristotle, could hardly have such totally misleading results as are sometimes attributed to it. Not only did he think it proper to begin his investigation of a new topic with a full review of previous opinions; he also wrote separate works on earlier schools of thought. His lost book on the Pythagoreans is one which we might give a good deal to possess.

To sum up, the amount of extant writing either from Aristotle's own pen or taken down by pupils from his teaching is sufficient not only to guarantee the soundness of his judgment in general, but also to warn us where it is most likely to fail him and to give us the material wherewith to counteract for ourselves the effect of his personal philosophical outlook, to show us where distortion is likely to arise, and of what kind. Of course when he describes the Milesians as having discovered only the material cause of things to the neglect of the efficient, formal and final, or castigates the atomists for 'lazily shelving' the problem of the motive cause, we understand that whereas his power of analysis has raced far ahead of theirs, his historical sense has not kept pace with it sufficiently to enable him to see them in a proper perspective. The systems of the earlier *physici* were not unsuccessful or partially successful attempts to fit reality into his fourfold scheme of causation, although in the first book of the *Metaphysics* he cannot well help speaking as though they were. But since we are well acquainted with his philosophy in general and in detail, it should not be too difficult to make the necessary allowances. His most serious fault is likely to be, not actual misunderstanding, but a distortion of the balance of their interests by rigorous selection. He was only concerned with one facet of Milesian thought, the 'philosophical', that is primarily the cosmogonical. Such meagre information as we have from non-Peripatetic sources about Anaximander, for instance, suggests that he had the true Ionian spirit of universal *historie*, and that his remarks about the origins of the universe and of life were only introductory to a descriptive account of the earth and its inhabitants as they at present exist, containing elements of what would now be called geography, ethnology and cultural studies.[1]

The change from a 'mythical' or 'theological' to a 'physical' or 'natural' view of the universe came, Aristotle tells us, with Thales of Miletus, who with his fellow-citizens Anaximander and Anaximenes form what is today referred to as the Milesian School. In support of the expression 'school' we can say with confidence that all were citizens of the same city, their lifetimes overlapped, later tradition described their relations as those of master and pupil, associates or successors of one another, and a thread of continuity is discernible in what we know of their doctrines. To go further is to make inferences or conjectures, though these are indeed probable enough.[2]

[1] See below, p. 75. These remarks about Aristotle's merits as a historian are expanded in Guthrie, *JHS*, 1957 (i), 35–41.
[2] In the doxographical tradition Anaximander is διάδοχος καὶ μαθητής of Thales (Theophr. *ap.* Simpl., DK, 12 A 9; πολίτης καὶ ἑταῖρος (*id.*, DK, A 17; cf. Cic. *Ac. Pr.* II, 118 *popularis et sodalis*,

An appraisal of the Milesian philosophical achievement will best come at the end (pp. 140 ff, below). The questions which excited them were of this kind: Can this apparently confused and disordered world be reduced to simpler principles so that our reason can grasp what it is and how it works? What is it made of? How does change take place? Why do things spring up and grow, then decline and die? How can one explain the alternation of day and night, summer and winter? They claim our attention by having been the first to suggest that answers to these questions may be found by taking thought. They abandoned mythological and substituted intellectual solutions. There might or might not be a divine mind at the back of, or permeating, the works of nature (that was a question to which some of them sought an answer), but it was no longer satisfying to say that storms were roused by the wrath of Poseidon, or death caused by the arrows of Apollo or Artemis. A world ruled by anthropomorphic gods of the kind in which their contemporaries believed—gods human in their passions as well as in their outward form—was a world ruled by caprice. Philosophy and science start with the bold confession of faith that not caprice but an inherent *orderliness* underlies the phenomena, and the explanation of nature is to be sought within nature itself. They did not discard in a generation all preconceptions arising from a mythical or anthropomorphic outlook. Mankind has not done that yet. But so far as we can see, they were the first to make investigations in the faith on which all

Burnet, *EGP*, 50, n. 4); γνώριμος καὶ πολίτης (Strabo, DK, A6); ἀκροατής (Hippol., DK, A11). See Kahn, *Anaximander*, 28f. Anaximenes ἤκουσεν ᾿Αναξιμάνδρου (Diog. Laert., DK, 13A1); is his ἑταῖρος (Theophr. *ap.* Simpl., DK, A5); *auditor, discipulus et successor* (Cicero, Augustine, Pliny in DK, A9, 10, 14*a*).

For modern inferences as to the existence of a regular school cf. L. Robin, *Greek Thought*, 33 f., Burnet, *EGP*, introd. § 14, S. Oświecimski, in *Charisteria T. Sinko*, p. 233: 'I call attention to the fact that the expression "school" is to be taken literally, in suitable proportion, of course, to the modern meaning of the term. I do not think it necessary to prove this statement here, as I suppose L. Robin and A. Rey (*La Science dans l'Antiquité* 11, 32) did it convincingly enough. Considering the evident continuity and consonance in principal questions of ideas, methods, and the general direction of researches of the three Milesians whom tradition always joins by such expressions as [those cited above], it would be very strange if in such an active and rich town as Miletus which besides the inherited old Minoan culture absorbed, too, the Egyptian and Babylonian civilisation, there were not something like either a school or brotherhood or as A. Rey (*op. cit.* 56) calls it "la corporation philosophico-scientifique". It could be the more so in that antiquity, above all the East, already knew different kinds of colleges, of priests, magi, astrologers, not to mention the exclusively Greek creation, Pythagoras's monastically scientific school.'

scientific thought is based, that the bewildering confusion of phenomena conceals a framework which is radically simpler and more orderly,
and so capable of being grasped by the human mind.

B. THALES

Diogenes Laertius (I, 13) says that the Ionian philosophy started with
Anaximander, but that Thales, 'a Milesian and therefore an Ionian,
instructed Anaximander'. There is much to be said for the view of this
late compiler that, so far as our knowledge goes, Thales ought to be
regarded as a forerunner, and that the first philosophical system of
which we can say anything is that of Anaximander. The name of Thales
was always held in high honour among the Greeks as that of an ideal
sage and scientist, and from the time of Herodotus onwards a considerable amount is narrated about him; but all that we have to suggest that
he founded the Ionian school of philosophy is the simple affirmation
of Aristotle, who couples it with the bald statement that he regarded
water as the underlying substance out of which all things are made.
This 'material principle' is described in the terms of Aristotle's own
thought, which are far from any that Thales could have used. How far
the thought itself was different is a question for consideration. In any
case, Aristotle makes it clear that he is relying on secondary authorities
(λέγεται, *Metaph.* A, 984a2), and knows nothing further about the
reasoning on which the statement was based, nor any details about his
cosmological notions save that he believed the earth to rest on water.

In view, however, of the authority of Aristotle, and the fact that he
felt justified in calling Thales 'the founder of this type of philosophy'
(i.e. the philosophy of those who according to Aristotle's ideas acknowledged only the 'material cause' and who were in his view the first to
deserve the name of philosophers), it will be worth while examining
the ancient evidence to discover, not necessarily what sort of man he
was (for he was obviously a shadowy figure even to some of those who
speak of him), but at least what picture of him was current in the
ancient world, and what kind of achievements stood to his credit. We
may then go on to consider the probable implications of the statement
about water which, from Aristotle to the present day, has been universally regarded as constituting his claim to be the first philosopher.

(1) *Date: the eclipse*

The earliest extant author to speak of Thales is Herodotus, who lived roughly 150 years after him and gives us the most important indication of his date in the following passage (1, 74, DK, A5), which refers to the war between Lydia under Alyattes and Media under Cyaxares:

When the war between them had dragged on indecisively into its sixth year, an encounter took place at which it happened that the day suddenly became night. This is the loss of daylight which Thales of Miletus predicted to the Ionians, fixing as its term the year in which it actually took place.

Various dates have in the past been assigned to this eclipse, which must from Herodotus's description have approached totality, but astronomical opinion seems now agreed that it is one which took place on 28 May (22 Gregorian) 585 B.C.[1] Pliny (*N.H.* II, 12, 53), whose ultimate source was the second century B.C. chronologist Apollodorus, gives the date, if not exactly, yet to within one year (Ol. 48.4 = 585/4). This forecast of Thales, which according to Diogenes (1, 23) aroused the admiration not only of Herodotus but also of Xenophanes who was practically his contemporary, is as well attested as most facts of antiquity. Herodotus himself expresses no doubts, in contrast to his treatment of another story about Thales, that he assisted the passage of the Lydian king Croesus across the Halys by diverting the course of the river. 'This', says Herodotus, 'is the favourite version of the Greeks, but I maintain that Croesus used the existing bridges' (1, 75). It should be added that the date 585 for the battle between Cyaxares and Alyattes suits the historical circumstances well, now that it has been established that the chronology of Herodotus, 1, 130, which implies that Astyages son of Cyaxares succeeded his father in 594, is slightly erroneous. It rests on the assumption that the fall of Astyages at the hands of Cyrus took place in the first year of the latter's reign (558), but comparison with the extant records of the Babylonian king Nabonidus shows this

---

[1] 584 by astronomical reckoning, in which the number of the year is one less than that used by chronologists. Tannery (*Pour l'hist. de la science hellène*, 57) still accepted the year 610, but is practically alone. There have been many discussions of this question, of which the following may be cited and will provide the references to others: T. L. Heath, *Aristarchus*, 13–18; ZN, 254, n. 1; Boll, art. 'Finsternisse' in *RE*, VI, 2341 and 2353; G. J. Allman, art. 'Thales' in *Ency. Brit.*[11]; Burnet, *EGP*, 41–4; O. Neugebauer, *The Exact Sciences in Antiquity*, 136.

date to be too early, probably by nine years.[1] Diogenes (I, 22) says that Thales was given the title of Sage (*Sophos*; i.e., as Diogenes adds, was accounted one of the Seven Wise Men) in the archonship of Damasias (582/1).

Now Thales certainly had not the astronomical knowledge necessary to predict solar eclipses accurately for a particular region, nor to foresee their character, whether partial or total. In particular he was ignorant of the sphericity of the earth and of the allowance to be made for parallax. Had it been otherwise, his prediction would not have been isolated, nor, as it appears to have been, merely approximate. Herodotus gives the impression of choosing his words carefully to indicate that Thales did no more than indicate the year of the eclipse.[2] Until recently it was believed that he could have done this with a fair chance of success by means of a period of calculation commonly known as the Saros, from the Sumerian character *šár*. This is a cycle of 223 lunar months (18 years 10 days 8 hours) after which eclipses both of the sun and moon do in fact repeat themselves with very little change, and its probable use by Thales was accepted by authorities of the calibre of Boll and Sir Thomas Heath. The character itself, as Heath knew, in addition to even less relevant meanings, had only a numerical value (3600). Its first association with an astronomical meaning is in the Suda,[3] a passage which was only brought into connexion with the cycle of 223 lunations by an erroneous conjecture of Halley's in 1691, whence it has since found its way into all the textbooks.[4] Neugebauer

[1] So already Ed. Meyer in *RE*, II, 1865, who gives Astyages's reign as 584–550. Cf. How and Wells, *Commentary on Herodotus* (1912, repr. 1949), I, 94, 383; Heath, *op. cit.* 15, n. 3.
[2] C. Brugmann (*Idg. Forsch.* xv, 87–93) argued that the original etymological meaning of ἐνιαυτός was not 'year' but 'resting-place' of the sun (from ἐνιαύω; cf. e.g. *Od.* x, 469), i.e. solstice. Fired by this interpretation, Diels suggested (*Neue Jahrbb.* 1914, 2) that Herodotus was using it in this original sense. If so, Thales's prediction was that the eclipse would take place before the summer solstice, i.e. before the end of June 585. This would tally with the conjecture that it was based on the Egyptian eclipse of 603 as being one cycle earlier (see below), for that took place on 18 May (Gregorian). But the suggestion has received little notice—Kranz in his fifth ed. of Diels's own *Vorsokratiker* writes 'Da Herod. ein ganzes Jahr Spielraum lässt...'—and it is no doubt more probable that Herodotus would use the word in its by then far commoner sense of 'year'. Neugebauer (*loc. cit.*) seems to be ignorant of Diels's suggestion.
[3] Byzantine lexicon of *c.* A.D. 1000, commonly known until recently as 'Suidas'.
[4] This has been demonstrated by O. Neugebauer, *The Exact Sciences in Antiquity*, 136; cf. 114. In interpreting Babylonian material Neugebauer is on his own ground, but some misgiving about his handling of authorities is aroused when he relates to Thales the conclusion of R. M. Cook's article on the Ionians in *JHS*, 1946, 98 ('My tentative conclusion is that we do not

calls it a beautiful example of a historical myth. His conclusion is that even after 300 B.C. the Babylonian texts only suffice to say that a solar eclipse is excluded or is possible. Before 300 the chances of successful prediction were still smaller, though there are indications that an eighteen-year cycle was used for the prediction of eclipses of the moon. The conclusions of Schiaparelli are similar.[1] We see, however, from an early Assyrian text, that 'to say that a solar eclipse is excluded or is possible' was precisely what they did, and that it sufficed for the astrological and religious purposes in which alone they were interested. The tablet in question contains the words:

Concerning the eclipse of the moon...the observation was made and the eclipse took place....And when for an eclipse of the sun we made observation, the observation was made and it did not take place. That which I saw with my eyes to the King my Lord I send.[2]

Drastic political consequences are inferred from the eclipse of the moon, and, as Tannery remarks, the important thing for these people was not so much to make exact predictions as simply to see to it that no eclipse occurred unannounced.

Considering his ample opportunities for contact with Orientals, it is very likely that Thales was acquainted with the limited means of prediction at their disposal, and he could very well have said that an eclipse was possible somewhere in the year which ended during 585 B.C. He may, as has been suggested,[3] have witnessed the eclipse which was visible in Egypt in 603, that is, eighteen years earlier. That the eclipse of 585 occurred at the time and place of a battle, was nearly total, and had the dramatic consequence of causing the combatants to cease fighting and negotiate a truce, was a happy chance by which his statement, in retrospect, acquired very naturally an air of precision that

know enough to say definitely whether in the eighth and seventh centuries the Ionians were generally the pioneers of Greek progress, but that on the present evidence it is at least as probable that they were not'), without mentioning that earlier, on p. 92, Mr Cook has expressly excluded the sixth-century philosophers from this judgment.

[1] G. Schiaparelli, *Scr. sulla storia della astron. antica*, I, 74: 'Quanto alle ecclisse di sole, essi non potevano riuscire, data la loro ignoranza della sfericità della terra, e la nessuna idea che avevano dell'effetto della parallasse.'

[2] From the palace of Sennacherib at Nineveh; first published by G. Smith, *Assyrian Discoveries*, 409. Cf. Schiaparelli, *loc. cit.*, Tannery, *Pour l'hist. de la science hell.* 59, Heath, *op. cit.* 16f.

[3] Diels, *Neue Jahrbb.* XXXIII, 2, n. 1, Boll in *RE*, VI, 2341, Burnet, *EGP*, 44, n. 1.

grew with the centuries and ensured its notoriety among his country-men.

The eclipse is important for two reasons: it fixes a date for what may be called the beginning of Greek philosophy, or at least for the activity of the man whom the Greeks themselves called the first of philosophers, and it accounts for the exaggerated reputation as an astronomer which he enjoyed among his countrymen of later centuries. To take the latter point first, Eudemus, the pupil of Aristotle, in his lost work on astronomy, made a statement which is variously reported as:

(*a*) Thales was the first astronomer: he foretold eclipses and solstices [*sic*]. (D.L. I, 23. T. H. Martin may have been right in regarding the words κατά τινας as part of the quotation, in which case Eudemus would not even be taking responsibility for the statement himself. See Heath, *op. cit.* 14. More probably, however, they are due to Diogenes.)

(*b*) Thales was the first to discover the eclipse of the sun (εὗρε πρῶτος ... ἡλίου ἔκλειψιν) and that its period with respect to the solstices is not always constant. (Dercyllides *ap.* Theon of Smyrna, ed. Hiller, 198.14, DK, A 17.)

(*c*) He foretold the eclipse of the sun which took place at the time of the battle between the Medes and the Lydians.... (Clem. Alex. *Strom.* II, 41 St., DK, A 5.)

In all probability the last of these statements represents most closely what Eudemus actually said. Even if he did attribute to Thales suffi-cient astronomical knowledge to discover the cause of eclipses and predict them accurately, he did so no doubt by an unjustified inference from the impressive incident of 585. Later writers expressly credit Thales with the discovery that solar eclipses were due to the inter-vention of the moon (Aët. II, 24, 1, DK, A 17*a*), and that the moon owes its light to the sun (Aët. II, 28, 5, DK, A 17*b*). These achieve-ments were quite impossible for Thales, and his ignorance becomes even clearer when we see the fantastic explanation of eclipses given by his associate Anaximander.

To return to the question of date, the surest indication is provided by the eclipse, which agrees well with the statement in Diogenes already quoted that he was given the title of Sage in 582/1. The date of his birth as given by Apollodorus will have been calculated by that chronologist's usual method of fixing the *floruit* by some outstanding event in a man's life (for Thales doubtless the eclipse), and accounting him forty years old at that date. In that case he dated Thales's birth in Ol. 39.1 (624)—not 35.1 as our text of Diogenes says—which agrees with Diogenes's other statement that he died in Ol. 58 (548–5) aged seventy-eight. There were other late reports that he lived to ninety or a hundred. We may be content to know that he lived at Miletus in the time of Alyattes and Croesus kings of Lydia, Cyaxares and Astyages of Media, and Cyrus the Persian, and was an almost exact contemporary of Solon of Athens.

(2) *Family*

Herodotus (1, 170) says that his earliest forbears were Phoenician, and it would be interesting to find a trace of Semitic blood at the very beginning of Greek philosophy; but Diogenes in quoting this rightly adds that most writers represent him as a genuine Milesian of distinguished family. His father's name, Examyes, is native Carian—no unlikely ancestry for a citizen of Miletus—and his mother bore the Greek name of Cleobulina. Diogenes explains the Phoenician element by the phrase 'descendants of Cadmus and Agenor', and Zeller suggested that the confusion arose through Thales's ancestors being Cadmeians of Boeotia who, as Herodotus elsewhere says, came over with the Ionian colonists (ZN, I, 255, n. 1; cf. Hdt. I, 146). Cadmus was, of course, in Greek mythology son of Agenor, King of Tyre, whence he had come to Boeotia to found the city of Thebes.[1]

(3) *Traditional character*

In the fluctuations of the traditional list of the Seven Sages, which in our extant authorities goes back to Plato (*Prot.* 343 A), the name of Thales was constant, and he was often regarded as the foremost. This gave him a kind of ideal character, and many of the acts and sayings associated in the popular mind with *sophia* were attributed to him as

---

[1] Interesting, even if not strictly relevant, is the suggestion that the story of Cadmus, and many other Greek references to Phoenicians ('redskins'), may really belong to Minoans. (T. J. Dunbabin, *The Greeks and their Eastern Neighbours*, 35.)

a matter of course. Everything of this kind that we are told about him must be classed as anecdote, but is of interest as showing at least the kind of character that he had in the eyes of the Greeks themselves. He had a reputation for practical statesmanship. Herodotus (I, 170) praises him for his wise advice that in face of the Persian threat the Ionian cities should federate, setting up a common centre of government in Teos,[1] and Diogenes (I, 25) relates a story that he dissuaded Miletus from making an alliance with Croesus. Plutarch (*Solon*, 2, DK, A 11) mentions the tradition that he engaged in trade, and the story related (but not believed) by Herodotus (I, 75), that he diverted the course of the Halys for Croesus and his army, shows a reputation for skill in engineering. His observation of the Little Bear as a better standard than the Great Bear for finding the Pole, mentioned by Callimachus (Pfeiffer, 1923, pp. 43 ff.), indicates a practical interest in navigation. The Phoenicians, as Callimachus says, sailed by the Little Bear, whereas the Greeks, according to Aratus (*Phaen.* 37–9) and Ovid (*Trist.* IV, 3, 1–2), used the Great Bear. Similarly he is said to have put his geometrical knowledge to practical use in measuring the pyramids (Hieronymus of Rhodes, third century B.C., *ap.* D.L. I, 27) and calculating the distance of ships at sea (Eudemus *ap.* Procl. *Eucl.* 352.14 Friedl., DK, A 20).

All this builds up an impressive picture of a practical genius and man of affairs in which there is no doubt some truth. The title of *Sophos* was granted in his day, as for example to Solon, on grounds of practical wisdom, and a similar picture is given of Thales's follower Anaximander. Nevertheless, once he had achieved in the popular mind the status of the ideal man of science, there is no doubt that the stories about him were invented or selected according to the picture of the philosophic temperament which a particular writer wished to convey. Immediately after telling how he frustrated the Milesian alliance with Croesus, Diogenes says that Heraclides Ponticus, the pupil of Plato, represented him (i.e. in a dialogue) as saying that he had lived in solitude and kept apart from public affairs. The most amusing example of mutually cancelling propaganda is provided by the stories of the olive-

---

[1] Though in G. Thomson's opinion the suggestion would have had no value from a military point of view in the contemporary situation after the fall of Sardis (*The First Philosophers*, 253).

presses and of the fall into a well. The former is told by Aristotle (*Pol.* A, 1259 a 6), and is to the effect that by means of his skill in meteorology Thales was able to predict while it was still winter that the coming season would be a bumper one for olives. He accordingly paid small deposits for the hire of all the olive-presses in Miletus and Chios, and when the olives ripened was able to charge his own price for re-letting them, since everyone wanted them at once. He thus demonstrated that it is easy for philosophers to make money if they wish, but that that is not their aim, and the story was told, says Aristotle, as Thales's answer to those who reproached him for his poverty, which was supposed to prove that philosophy is of no practical use. The tale is too much for Aristotle's critical mind, and he comments that this is in fact a commercial device in general use, but men fastened it on to Thales on account of his wisdom.[1] Plato, on the other hand, in the *Theaetetus* (174 A), wants to show that philosophy is above mere practical considerations and that its lack of any utilitarian taint is its chief glory. He therefore says nothing about the olive-presses, but tells instead how Thales, when engaged in star-gazing, fell into a well, and was laughed at by a pert servant-girl for trying to find out what was going on in the heavens when he could not even see what was at his own feet. The process of selection persists, and a modern scholar, who wishes to show that the Milesians were 'not recluses engaged in pondering upon abstract questions...but active practical men' (in which he is probably right), mentions the story of the olive-presses as typical of Thales's reputation without a word about the well.[2]

(4) *Mathematics*

In mathematics, Thales was universally believed to have introduced geometry into Greece, having become acquainted with the study during his travels in Egypt and developed it further for himself (Procl. *Eucl.*

---

[1] Yet this is the man of whom Professor Cherniss would have us believe that when he reports that Thales was said to have regarded water as the beginning of all things, all he had really found was the statement that the earth floats on water, from which he made up the rest. (*J. Hist. Ideas*, 1951, 321.)

[2] Farrington, *Greek Science*, I, 31. The star-gazing story was no doubt also fathered on Thales as a typical or ideal philosopher. A more ribald version of the same kind of tale is told of Socrates in Aristoph. *Clouds*, 171–3.

65.3ff. Friedl., DK, A 11). He was specifically credited with the following theorems:

(1) A circle is bisected by its diameter.
(2) The angles at the base of an isosceles triangle are equal.
(3) If two straight lines intersect, the opposite angles are equal.
(4) The angle inscribed in a semi-circle is a right angle.
(5) A triangle is determined if its base and the angles relative to the base are given.

The ascription to Thales of theorems (1)–(3) and (5) comes from Proclus (DK, A 11 and 20), whose authority was Eudemus. Theorem (4) (actually in the form 'He was the first to inscribe a right-angled triangle in a circle') is quoted by Diogenes (1, 24) from Pamphila, a compiler of the first century A.D. It is impossible to estimate the actual extent of Thales's achievement. The temptation to fasten particular discoveries on to individuals with a general reputation for wisdom was strong in antiquity. The story goes that when he had succeeded with no. 4 he sacrificed an ox, exactly as Pythagoras is said to have done on proving the theorem which commonly bears his name. Theorem (5) is associated with the practical feat of measuring the distance of ships at sea. This, however, like the calculation of the height of the pyramids by measuring their shadows with which he was also credited (Hieronymus *ap.* D.L. I, 27, Pliny, *N.H.* XXXVI, 82, Plut. *Conv.* 147 A, DK, A 21), could have been accomplished by an empirical rule without any understanding of the geometrical propositions involved, as Burnet pointed out.[1] It must always be remembered that, even if we had unimpeachable statements in ancient authorities that Thales 'proved' this or that theorem, the word 'proof' has a meaning only in relation to its historical context.[2] Since no extant authorities, or even their sources, possessed a first-hand written record of any of Thales's proofs,

---

[1] *EGP*, 45 f. Cf. also Frank, *Plato u. d. sog. Pyth.* n. 201, pp. 361 f.
[2] Cf. Cohen and Drabkin, *Source Book in Greek Science*, 34, n. 2 and 44: 'Just as early attempts at demonstrations must have differed considerably from the later canonical proofs, so the modern mathematician cannot in every case be satisfied with Euclid's proofs.' 'The requirements for a mathematical construction or proof may vary from age to age, and indeed in early Greek mathematics probably varied from generation to generation.' Of Thales's theorem (3) above, Eudemus actually says that it was discovered by Thales, but that the scientific proof (ἐπιστημονικὴ ἀπόδειξις) was provided by Euclid (Eud. *ap.* Procl. *Eucl.* p. 299 Friedl.).

they would easily attribute to them the content which the word implied in their own day. Nevertheless, without claiming certainty in details, we may reasonably say that there was some truth in the tradition followed by Proclus, that Thales, besides the knowledge that he obtained in Egypt (which we know to have been limited to the solution of practical problems, as in land-measurement), 'made many discoveries for himself, and in many laid the foundations for those who followed him, employing an approach that inclined now to the theoretical (καθολικώτερον), now rather to the empirical (αἰσθητικώτερον)'. The Greek talent for generalization, for the extraction of the universal law from the particular instances, the 'form' from the 'matter', was already beginning to have its effect.

(5) *Water as 'arche': the unity of all things*

This impulse to generalize, to discard the individual and accidental and bring out the universal and permanent, appears in a more extreme form in the statement which is generally agreed to constitute his claim to fame as the founder of philosophy. That is, the statement that the first principle of all things is water. This statement comes to us first of all from Aristotle, and it is doubtful whether any later occurrence of it is independent of his authority. We must therefore consider it carefully in the context in which he places it. First of all, he tells us that this is what 'is said' of Thales. On the question whether Thales left any written works, we have only the statements of later writers than Aristotle, and these conflict.[1] It seems incredible that he should have written down nothing, and of course the word 'publish' had little meaning in his day; but at least the confusion of later writers and the testimony of Aristotle himself make it plain that no writings of his were available in Aristotle's time and probably long before. Aristotle

---

[1] He wrote nothing but a *Nautical Astronomy* (Simpl.); set forth his views in verse (Plut.); wrote a work *On First Principles* in at least two books (Galen, who quotes a passage containing obvious anachronisms as being from the second book); some say he wrote nothing, the *Nautical Astronomy* being by Phocus of Samos, others that he wrote only two treatises, on the solstice and the equinox respectively (D.L.; all the passages in DK A 2, B 1 and 2). Proclus (A 20) says curiously that in his statement of the proposition that the angles at the base of an isosceles triangle are equal, Thales followed the archaic fashion by using the word 'similar' (ὁμοίας) instead of 'equal' (ἴσας); but, in view of the obvious ignorance and confusion of other writers, little significance can be attached to this.

had no means of knowing the reasons which led Thales to make his statement, and when he ascribes a possible line of thought to him makes no secret of the fact that he is guessing. The frankness and caution with which Aristotle introduces any statement about Thales are highly reassuring, and we may feel confident of the distinction between what he has found on record and what is his own inference. Referring to what he has read or heard he says: 'Thales is said to have declared', 'they say he said', 'from what is recorded he seems to have thought'; to his own conjectures he adds 'perhaps'.

With so much of preface, let us look at the passage in which he introduces the 'first principle' of Thales.

(*Metaph.* A, 983b6ff.) Most of the earliest philosophers thought that the principles which were in the nature of matter were the only principles of all things: that of which all things that are consist, and from which they first come to be and into which they are resolved as a final state (the substance remaining but changing in its modifications), this, they said, is the element and principle of all things, and therefore they think that nothing is either generated or destroyed, since this sort of entity is always preserved, as we say that Socrates neither comes to be absolutely when he comes to be beautiful or musical, nor ceases to be when he loses these characteristics, because the substratum, Socrates himself, remains. So it is, they say, with everything else: there is always some permanent substance, or nature (φύσις), either one or more, which is conserved in the generation of the rest from it.

On the number and nature of such principles they do not all agree. Thales, who led the way in this kind of philosophy, says that the principle is water, and for this reason declared that the earth rests on water. His supposition may have arisen from the observation that the nourishment of all creatures is moist, and that warmth itself is generated from moisture and lives by it; and that from which all things come to be is their first principle. Besides this, another reason for his supposition would be that the semina of all things have a moist nature, and water is for moist things the origin of their nature.

Some think that the very early writers, who first, long before the present generation, wrote about the gods, also had this view of nature; for they named Oceanus and Tethys as the parents of generation, and made the gods swear by water in the oath by the river which they called Styx: what is oldest is most revered, and one swears by what one most reveres. Whether this view of nature is in fact ancient and primitive must perhaps remain in doubt, but Thales at least is said to have described the first cause in this way. No one would think Hippo worthy of inclusion in the same class, owing to the triviality of his thought.

In this, our earliest account of Thales's cosmological views, they are already set forth in the abundant philosophical terminology of a later age. No early Ionian could have expressed his ideas in terms of substance and attribute (οὐσία and πάθος), of coming-to-be in an absolute sense (ἀπλῶς) as opposed to relatively, or of a substratum (ὑποκείμενον) or element (στοιχεῖον). These distinctions, now a part of ordinary speech, were only achieved after much strenuous logical analysis on the part of Plato and its elaboration into a technical vocabulary by Aristotle himself. Great caution is needed here, but in spite of the close interrelation between language and thought, it does not necessarily follow that what Aristotle is giving is a complete misrepresentation of the earlier views.[1] We know more of the thought of Anaximander and Anaximenes, and if we are justified in regarding all three Milesians as representing parts of a continuous movement begun by Thales, we may safely call them the first natural philosophers, meaning by this that they were the first to attempt on a rational basis that simplification of reality which has been the quest of the human mind in all ages. As a modern writer on scientific method has expressed it, with no particular reference to the Greeks:

There seems to be a deep-rooted tendency in the human mind to seek... something that persists through change. Consequently the desire for explanation seems to be satisfied only by the discovery that what appears to be new and different was there all the time. Hence the search for an *underlying* identity, a persistent stuff, a substance that is conserved in spite of qualitative changes and in terms of which these changes can be explained.[2]

---

[1] Not only Aristotle, but a historian of philosophy in any age, is compelled to interpret earlier views in the language of his own day. Even the arrogance of Aristotle's assumption that he knew what his predecessors wanted to say better than they did themselves is an arrogance of which none of us is wholly innocent. It was Whitehead who wrote: 'Everything of importance has been said before by someone who did not discover it.' The ideas here attributed to Thales and his successors by no means involve 'the definition of identity and difference as formulated in consequence of Eleatic logic, and the distinction between subject and attribute as developed first by Socrates and Plato' (McDiarmid, *Theoph. on the Presoc. Causes*, 92), and the statement that Aristotle 'can seriously comment on the material theory of Homer in the same context with those of the physicists' is quite unfair. Thales is for him the ἀρχηγὸς τῆς τοιαύτης φιλοσοφίας.

[2] L. S. Stebbing, *A Modern Introduction to Logic*, 404.

That tendency did not begin with Aristotle. It is as evident in religious as in philosophical accounts of the world. As Professor Broad has remarked, to introduce unity and tidiness into the world is something which appeals to man's aesthetic no less than to his rational interests, and, when pushed to its extreme limits, leads to the view that there is one and only one kind of material.[1]

It was natural that the first philosophical simplification should also be the most extreme. The impulse to simplification was there, and thought had not yet advanced sufficiently for a consideration of the difficulties it involved. Hence the condescension with which Aristotle regarded the (as it seemed to him) dim and fumbling efforts of the earliest philosophers.

Although the terms 'substratum' and 'element' were beyond the reach of the Milesians, Aristotle uses another word, *arche*, to describe their primary substance, which, whether they employed it in this way themselves or not, was in common use in their time and well within their comprehension in the senses of (*a*) starting-point or beginning, (*b*) originating cause. So used it is common in Homer, and the usual translation of it in the Aristotelian passages as '(first) principle' is not far from the mark. In all probability (though the point has been disputed) it was already used of the primary substance by Thales's younger contemporary Anaximander (see below, p. 77), and it is a convenient term which we may regard as standing for a twofold conception in the thought of the Milesians. It means, first, the original state out of which the manifold world has developed and, secondly, the permanent ground of its being, or, as Aristotle would call it, the substratum. All things *were once* water (if that is the *arche*), and to the philosopher all things *are still* water, since in spite of the changes which it has undergone it remains the same substance (*arche* or *physis*, principle or permanent constitution) throughout them all, for there is in fact no other.[2] Since it is Aristotle in particular who insists on the distinction between the first philosophers who believed in a single *arche* of all things and those who held that there were more than one,

[1] *The Mind and its Place in Nature*, 76.
[2] For a fuller discussion of the meaning of ἀρχή, see W. A. Heidel in *CP*, 1912, 215 ff. Kirk (KR, 89) conjectures that only the first sense may have been in Thales's mind. See also his cautious remarks on pp. 92 f.

it is worth noting that it appears in effect before his time also, and is therefore not simply the outcome of an arbitrary classification of his own. The author of the Hippocratic treatise on the *Nature of Man*, which was probably written about 400 B.C.,[1] pours scorn on the un-verifiable theories of non-medical philosophers who think that man is composed of 'air, fire, water, earth or anything else which cannot be clearly discerned in him'. 'They say', he continues, 'that whatever exists is one, being at the same time one and all, but they do not agree on its name. One of them says that this universal unity is air, another fire, another water, another earth, and each supports his own view by evidence that amounts in fact to nothing.'[2]

(6) *Mythical precursors*

For Thales's choice of water as the *arche* various reasons have been suggested, from Aristotle down to modern times. They may be divided into the mythical and the rational. Those who think that Thales was, perhaps subconsciously, influenced by the mythical presuppositions of the society in which he was born and bred have again a choice, between Eastern and Greek mythology. Some point to the undoubted fact that he lived in a country familiar with both Babylonian and Egyptian ideas, and, according to an unchallenged tradition, had himself visited Egypt.[3] In both these civilizations water played a preponderant part which was reflected in their mythology. Both were river-cultures, the one based on the two rivers of Mesopotamia and the other entirely dependent for its life on the annual flooding of the Nile. It was the boast of the Egyptian priests that not only Thales but also Homer had learned from Egypt to call water the principle of all things (Plut.

---

[1] F. Heinimann, *Nomos und Physis*, 158 with n. 1. Cf. W. A. Heidel on Arist. *Metaph.* 1069a25, 988b22 and other passages (*Proc. Am. Acad.* 45, 1910–11, 122, n. 166): 'It is evident that Aristotle is here enlarging upon the criticism of the monists contained in Hippocrates, π. φύσ. ἀνθρ. 1.'

[2] *De Nat. Hom.* 1 (VI, 32 Littré). The writer gives the impression that he is speaking of contemporary thinkers. Cf. the opening words ὅστις μὲν εἴωθεν ἀκούειν λεγόντων, and a little later γνοίη δ' ἄν τις...παραγενόμενος αὐτέοισιν ἀντιλέγουσιν. Some monistic theories do seem to have persisted until the end of the fourth century, but if any known thinker called earth the sole ἀρχή it can only have been Xenophanes (pp. 383 f., below), nor is it easy to identify the contemporary champion of fire.

[3] A Babylonian origin for Thales's theory was suggested as long ago as 1885 by Berthelot (*Les Origines de l'alchimie*, 251).

Is. et Os. 34, DK, A 11). Each year the Nile submerged the narrow cultivable strip beside its banks, and receded leaving it covered with mud of an incredible fertility, in which the growth of new life was extraordinarily rapid. For those who crowded along this strip to get their livelihood it was easy to believe that all life arose in the first place from water. The earth itself had arisen out of Nūn, the primordial waters, which are still everywhere beneath it—as Thales said—and also surrounding it like the Homeric Oceanus. At first the waters covered everything, but gradually sank until a small hillock appeared, to become the seat of primeval life. On this hillock the creator-god made his first appearance. Among Egyptian peasants the belief still persists that the fertile slime left behind by the Nile in its annual flooding has the power of actually originating life, and this belief in the spontaneous origin of life out of mud or slime will shortly meet us in Anaximander.

The attribution to Thales of the notion that the earth floats on water, mentioned by Aristotle in the passage already quoted, is put by him rather more fully in the *De Caelo* (294 a 28):

Others say that [the earth] rests on water. This is the most ancient explanation which has come down to us, and is attributed to Thales of Miletus, namely that the earth is at rest because it can float like wood or similar substances, whose nature it is to rest upon water, though none of them could rest on air.

The Babylonian cosmology of the Enuma Elish, dating from perhaps the middle of the second millennium B.C., gives a similar picture of the primacy of water. I quote from the description by T. Jacobsen in the book *Before Philosophy*, which contains excellent accounts for the non-specialist of Egyptian and Mesopotamian ideas. After quoting from the text, he continues:

This description presents the earliest stage of the universe as one of watery chaos. The chaos consisted of three intermingled elements: Apsu, who represents the sweet waters; Ti'amat, who represents the sea; and Mummu, who cannot as yet be identified with certainty but may represent cloud-banks and mist. These three types of water were mingled in a large undefined mass. There was not yet even the idea of a sky above or firm ground beneath; all was water; not even a swampy bog had been formed, still less an island; and there were yet no gods.

From this initial undifferentiated state cosmogony proceeds, as in Hesiod, by a series of genealogies. Apsu and Ti'amat turn out to be male and female principles who can unite, beget and give birth.

Such stories are common in Near Eastern lands, together with those of great floods (a frequent fact of actual experience in Mesopotamia, as the inhabitants of Iraq learned to their cost in 1954) whereby the all-pervading water sought to reclaim what was once its own. We need only remind ourselves of the Hebrew cosmogony, with its description of the spirit of God moving upon the face of the waters, and its talk of waters under the firmament and waters above the firmament. Olmstead, the historian of Persia, went so far as to say that the water of Thales is simply 'the primordial mist familiar to us in the Biblical Garden of Eden story'.[1]

Parallels from Greek mythology suggested themselves, as we have seen, to Aristotle himself. When he mentions Oceanus and Tethys (*Metaph.* 983b30, above, p. 55), he is thinking of two lines of *Iliad*, XIV. Line 201 runs:

> Ὠκεανόν τε θεῶν γένεσιν καὶ μητέρα Τηθύν

And Oceanus, first parent of the gods, and their mother Tethys,

and line 246:

> Ὠκεανοῦ ὅς περ γένεσις πάντεσσι τέτυκται

Oceanus, who is first parent to them all.

Oceanus dwelt at the farthest limits of the earth (*Il.* XIV, 200); his was the great stream which flowing back upon itself (*Il.* XVIII, 399) encircled the whole earth; he was the source of all rivers, sea, springs and wells (*Il.* XXI, 196). That he antedated the earth and heavens and was the origin of all things is not said; but Homer was not interested in cosmogony, and would take from earlier myths such portions as he wished. In Oceanus and Tethys we at least have male and female principles of water who are the parents of the gods, and the parallel with Apsu and Ti'amat is striking enough. The Greek myth itself may reflect the Oriental.[2] Those Greek mythographers who were interested

---

[1] *Hist. Persian Empire*, 211.
[2] This was suggested long ago by E. H. Meyer. See the critical remarks of F. Lukas, *Kosmogonien*, 154, n., and now U. Hölscher, *Hermes*, 1953, 385, n. 3, 387.

in cosmogony, however, though keeping Oceanus in a high position relative to the other gods, do not seem to have placed him at the very beginning. For Hesiod he is, like Pontus the sea, son of Earth and Heaven, nor is there any strong evidence that a watery principle came first in the earliest Orphic theogonies.

Consideration of these suggestions of a possible origin for Thales's idea is justified by the interest of the subject, but it must be emphasized that they are all conjectural. This applies also to the rational explanations which follow.

(7) *Rational explanations*

The first reason likely to occur to a modern mind is that water is the only substance which can actually be observed, without any apparatus of experiment such as was not available to Thales, to change, according to its temperature, into solid, liquid and gaseous form. That therefore is the reason given for Thales's choice by some modern scholars, for example Burnet. But it was not the reason that occurred to Aristotle, and though he, like ourselves, was making a conjecture, it is possible that he came nearer to the mind of his Ionian predecessor. For him, the most likely thoughts to have been in Thales's mind are those which link water with the idea of life. Hence he observes that food and semen always contain moisture, and that the very warmth of life is a damp warmth. The connexion between heat and animal life, obvious to experience, was insisted on as essential and causative by the ancient world more than it is today. Aristotle himself speaks elsewhere of 'vital heat',[1] and it is obvious that this is also a wet, or damp, heat, provided by the blood. At death two things happen at once. The body goes cold, and it dries up. ὑγρός, indeed, owing to these associations in the Greek mind, is a word rich in meaning which cannot be imparted by any single English equivalent. 'Moist', yes, but that will hardly do when Theocritus applies it to a bow as being flexible, when Plato describes Eros, god of love and generation, by the same word, or applies it to the supple limbs of youth in contrast to the 'hardness' of old age. Pindar uses it of the back of an eagle, Bacchylides of the feet

---

[1] θερμότης ψυχική *Gen. Anim.* 762a20; cf. also *De Vita et Morte*, 469b7ff. For the part played by heat in the earliest development of the embryo in the womb see π. φύσιος παιδίου, 12, quoted by Baldry in *CQ*, 1932, 27.

of dancers, Xenophon of the legs of a swift horse (see the lexicon of Liddell–Scott–Jones).

Burnet (followed by Ross) calls the reasoning which Aristotle here attributes to Thales 'physiological', and suggests that Aristotle may have transferred to the earlier thinker what was known to be true of Hippon, the man whom he dismisses in this same passage as too trivial a thinker to be worth consideration.[1] To introduce modern departmental distinctions like physiology and meteorology in speaking of this early period is a serious anachronism.[2] The thought here attributed to Thales does not link him with a later age when physiology is beginning to show itself as a special interest among others; rather it shows him to be still under the influence of the more primitive stage when all nature alike was conceived to be instinct with life. We saw how, in the mythical cosmogonies of the Near East, the belief that everything was water was closely and directly connected with the observation of its properties as the giver of life. Thales would be well acquainted with Egyptian ideas, and nothing is more likely than that these ancient notions were still at the back of his mind and directing his thought along certain lines, even though, at the conscious level, he had made a deliberate break with mythology and was seeking a rational account.

Moreover, the line of thought here attributed to him by Aristotle consorts well with the only other remarks about the general nature of things which tradition ascribed to him.

(8) *Self-change and life: hylozoism*

Before turning to these, we may consider a little further the general reasons which are likely to have impelled him to choose water as the *arche* primarily on the grounds that, as Aristotle says, it seemed to him to be the stuff of life. These reasons are not far to seek.

---

[1] Hippon was a figure of the mid-fifth century, mentioned again by Aristotle in *De Anima* (405 b 2) as teaching that the soul is water.

[2] Moreover, as Professor Baldry has pointed out (*CQ*, 1932, 28), an interest in birth and other phenomena connected with sex is a regular feature of primitive societies long before other aspects of biology are thought of. We notice Aristotle's reference to the wetness of semen as a possible reason for Thales's choice (cf. Baldry, p. 33). McDiarmid (*Theophr. on the Presoc. Causes*) unfortunately repeats the statement that 'at the time of Thales the prevailing interest appears to have been meteorological' with a mere reference to Burnet, *EGP*, 48–9.

Hylozoism

We come here to something characteristic of all three Milesians alike. To the more advanced, and highly analytical, mind of an Aristotle the notion of principle or cause, ἀρχή or αἴτιον, appeared to be (as it does to us) not simple but manifold, and for full understanding of a phenomenon it was necessary to analyse it into its various components. It was not enough to name the material *arche*, the stuff from which the world is made. Why should this material substratum (if, as they claimed, it is one only) appear in so many different forms? What is the cause of its change into the multiplicity of phenomena? Why not a dead, static world? Besides the one material substance, one must also discover the force which is at work producing movement and change within it. 'Presumably', he writes, in explicit criticism of these same Milesians,

it is not the substratum itself that causes itself to change, just as neither wood nor bronze is the cause of the change of either of them, nor does the wood manufacture a bed nor the bronze a statue. There is something else which is the cause of the change. And to seek this is to seek the second cause, as we should call it: the cause whence comes the beginning of motion (*Metaph.* A, 984a21).

When Aristotle produces his own rigid fourfold scheme of causation and tries to fit the theories of his earliest predecessors into it, then indeed one may suspect that his criticism is not above criticism itself. A little reflexion on the pioneer character of the Milesians, and the undeveloped state of thought in their time, leads to a different conclusion. What he dismisses as absurd, that 'the substratum itself causes itself to change', does in fact more or less represent their view. In this introductory book of the *Metaphysics*, he notes that none of the monist philosophers made earth the primary substance, though each of the other 'elements' had its turn (989a5). This meant little to him, but is perhaps significant nevertheless. In his more advanced view, what he called the four corporeal elements, or simple bodies, were all alike mere matter. All would remain inert were there not some motive cause at work on them. But 'if we would understand the sixth-century philosophers, we must disabuse our minds of the atomistic conception of dead matter in mechanical motion and of the Cartesian dualism of matter and mind'.[1] To them there was no such thing as dead, inert

[1] F. M. Cornford, *Princ. Sap.* 179.

63

matter, and it was therefore impossible for them to see any logical necessity to divide their first principle into a material and a motive element. In accepting water or air or fire as the sole fount of being, they had in mind as much as anything its inherent mobility. Water is life-giving, and the sea shows an apparently causeless restlessness, air rushes hither and thither in the form of wind, fire leaps and flickers and feeds on other substances, and became later to Heraclitus literally the life of the world. It is quaint to speak of those who thought like this as interested in physiology. Rather they reveal themselves as being still on the threshold of rational thought, nearer than we or Aristotle to the animism of the pre-scientific and the childish mind. Earth would not serve their purpose as the *arche*, for they needed something which should be not only the material of change, but also its potential author.[1] This the other elements could be because to these early thinkers they were alive. Aristotle had reached a stage of thought when to call water or air a living, divine power was no longer possible, but he had not advanced far enough to see his predecessors in a proper historical perspective and so do justice to their state of mind, the state of mind of an age before any distinction had been thought of between spirit (or life) and matter, animate and inanimate.

For this reason the term hylozoists, commonly applied to the Milesians, has been criticized as misleading, on the ground that it suggests theories which explicitly deny the separate reality of matter and spirit.[2] We need not share this objection to the term itself, which seems rather to suggest the truth, namely the state of mind of men who still had no clear conception of a distinction between the two. The term which it is above all things important to avoid is the term 'materialists', since that is a word currently applied to those who deliberately deny any place to the spiritual among first principles. It denotes all those who, well aware that a distinction has been drawn between material and non-material, are prepared to maintain in argument that nothing in fact exists which has not its origin in material phenomena. To suppose the sixth-century philosophers to have been

[1] Cf. Simpl. *Phys.* 25.11 διὸ τὴν γῆν δυσκίνητον καὶ δυσμετάβλητον οὖσαν οὐ πάνυ τι ἠξίωσαν ἀρχὴν ὑποθέσθαι. For a similar animism in the thought of children see the work of Jean Piaget, as illustrated in *The Child's Conception of the World*, *The Child's Conception of Causality* and later books.   [2] Burnet, *EGP*, 12, n. 3, Ueberweg–Praechter, I, p. 42.

capable of thinking like this is a serious anachronism. H. Gomperz, on the other hand, goes too far when he rejects the term hylozoism on the grounds that the early Greeks simply accepted certain things as 'happening to be the case' and not needing explanation. The Greek scientists, he says, no longer believed that winds were moved by gods, but neither did they believe them to be living beings.[1] As I shall hope to show, there is evidence to the contrary.

To return to Thales, we have seen that there are some general considerations making it probable that his reasons for the choice of water as *arche* may have been similar to those inferred by Aristotle. The supposition also agrees with the few other statements attributed to him. First, Aristotle in the *De Anima* says that he seems to have identified soul or life (*psyche*) with the cause of motion. He writes (*De An.* 1, 405 a 19): 'Thales too seems, from what is recorded about him, to have regarded the soul as a motive force, since he said that the lodestone has a soul because it makes the iron move.' We are the more inclined to believe him because it was in fact a universal Greek idea to think of the primary and essential character of *psyche* as being its motive power. Secondly, Aristotle also said that Thales considered all things to be full of gods, and connected this on his own account (adding the characteristic 'perhaps') with the belief of other thinkers that 'soul is mingled in the whole' (*De An.* 1, 411 a 7). Plato in the *Laws* (899 B) uses the same phrase, 'that all things are full of gods', without ascribing it to any authority by name, and the late compilation of Diogenes Laertius attributes to Heraclitus the statement that 'all things are full of souls and spirits'. Hence some have thought it to be one of those floating apophthegms which tended to become attached to anyone famous for his wisdom.[2] We may say, first, that Plato at any rate does not attribute it to anyone else, and that Aristotle is a better authority than Diogenes, whose statement is doubtless based on the well-known story about Heraclitus, related by Aristotle himself, that some callers, seeing him warming himself at the kitchen stove, hesitated to enter his house, but he told

[1] *J. Hist. Ideas*, 1943, 166, n. 12.
[2] So Ueberweg–Praechter, 1, 44. Burnet's reference to Arist. *Part. Anim.* 645 a 17 in this connexion (*EGP*, 50, n. 3; *not* 645 a 7) seems irrelevant, and his statement that 'Here too there are gods' 'means only that nothing is more divine than anything else' is surely extraordinary.

65

them not to be afraid, 'for there were gods there too'. Even if this anecdote were true, it would be difficult to know what philosophical significance to attach to it. Secondly, there is no question of claiming that if Thales declared all things to be full of gods he was saying something new or unique. It can easily be seen as a relic of the ineradicable animism, or animatism, of the Greeks, which makes it all the more likely that he should have shared the belief himself. Study of the Milesian thinkers reveals a close affinity between some of their beliefs and the general contemporary climate of thought. The difference— a crucial one—lies in their approach to these beliefs, their critical spirit and determination to fit them into a rational and unified scheme. Even the meagre tradition about Thales gives us a glimpse of this.

That he saw no distinction between animate and inanimate is emphasized by Diogenes (I, 24) on the authority of Aristotle and Hippias: 'Aristotle and Hippias say that he attributed even to the inanimate a share in life, basing his conviction on the behaviour of the magnet and of amber.' If this and the other passages imply, as suggested above, an unconscious relic of mythological thinking, they also show how completely the conscious mind of Thales has left such a stage behind. His argument has a scientific quality, and he attempted to base it on observation of the striking and unexplained phenomenon of magnetism. The lodestone and amber, though belonging neither to the animal nor to the vegetable kingdom, show themselves to possess the psychical property (as it was to the Greeks) of initiating motion.[1]

---

[1] An interesting point arises here, though as it is even more speculative than most of the things that can be said about Thales, it is perhaps best confined to a footnote. Burnet (*EGP*, 50) agrees that he probably did say there was soul in the magnet and amber (this statement not having the character of a floating apophthegm), but argues that we should not suppose him to have generalized from this; for 'to say the magnet and amber are alive is to imply, if anything, that other things are not'. (So also Ueberweg–Praechter, I, 45, and Oświecimski, *Thales*, 249.) *Prima facie* this is plausible: the noticeable thing about the behaviour of magnetic substances is its *difference* from that of other bodies. But the observation of it in something which was neither animal nor vegetable may well have had the opposite effect on the earliest scientific mind. Moreover, amber only exhibits its peculiar property when heated, whether by friction or otherwise, and this might naturally suggest to Thales that other kinds of matter would equally betray their psychic character if we could discover the right way to make them reveal it. If so, this is the earliest Greek instance of an appreciation of the value of experiment.

The argument of Burnet would apply equally well to the statement that all things are water. On the surface it is the *contrast* between the wetness of water, shared by other moist substances, and the nature of, say, iron, that naturally strikes a beholder. It is only under heat that the metal reveals its property of liquefying.

Theophrastus, as we may judge from Aëtius I, 3, 1 (*Dox.* 276), after citing the biological arguments suggested also by Aristotle—that the sperm of animals is moist and that plants are nourished by moisture—added a third: 'that the fire of the sun and stars itself, and the whole cosmos, are nourished by exhalations from water'. Moisture, as Heidel notes,[1] was to the Greeks the nutritive element *par excellence*, as fire is the motive element, and fire is 'fed' by it, in the form of vapour; and so Theophrastus refers Aristotle's words 'warmth itself is generated by moisture and lives by it' to the whole process of evaporation by which the cosmic fire is produced and replenished. The phenomenon of the sun 'drawing water to itself' (Hdt. II, 25) made a deep impression on Greek thinkers from an early date, and on this analogy (which to them was more than an analogy) they explained the fundamental processes of both microcosm and macrocosm, as we shall increasingly discover.

The juxtaposition of these three reasons in the doxography, and the natural use of the same word 'nourished' (τρέφεται) for living organisms and the celestial fires, show once again the error of trying to separate 'physiological' and 'meteorological' considerations in this context. They are united (or rather, they have as yet no meaning) in the thought of those to whom the whole universe is a living organism.

(9) *The unity of being: science and myth*

So far, then, as we can recover the mind of Thales from our meagre authorities, he asserted in the first place that the world was of one substance. To be the *arche* of the world, this substance must contain within itself the cause of motion and change (this, admittedly, would not be argued; it would be an assumption), and to a Greek this meant that it must be of the nature of *psyche*, life- or soul-stuff. This condition he thought best satisfied by water, or more generally the element of moisture (τὸ ὑγρόν, including of course such substances as blood and the sap of plants). This then was the *arche*, and as such was both alive and everlasting.

At this point the Greek mind goes a step further. Ask any Greek

---

[1] *Harv. Stud.* 22, 142, *Arch. f. Gesch. d. Philos.* 1906, 340. Cf. Hipp. *De Victu*, I, 3 (VI, 472 Littré) τὸ μὲν γὰρ πῦρ δύναται πάντα διὰ παντὸς κινῆσαι, τὸ δὲ ὕδωρ πάντα διὰ παντὸς θρέψαι.

what, if anything, in his experience is ever-living (in his own word *athanaton*), and he would have only one answer: *theos*, or *to theion*. Everlasting life is the mark of the divine, and of nothing else. Hence Thales, though rejecting the anthropomorphic deities of popular religion, could retain its language to the extent of saying that, in a special sense, the whole world was filled with gods. One may compare the use of 'the divine' attributed to Anaximander (pp. 87 f., below).

It is not the choice of water as the *arche* that gives Thales his main claim on our attention. As a historian of science has vividly put it: 'If he had championed the cause of treacle as the sole element, he would still have been rightly honoured as the father of speculative science.'[1] Thales decided that, if there is any one thing at the basis of all nature, it must be water. It is the hypothesis, the question he asked, that in the scientist's view constitutes his claim to immortality. Others like Hesiod, he admits, had adumbrated the same idea, but by having recourse to gods and spirits endowed with special powers they begged the question, because the existence of such beings can neither be proved nor disproved by the means wherewith we know the natural world. 'In a word, it was Thales who first attempted to explain the variety of nature as the modifications of something *in* nature.'

The mythological precursors of Thales are worth a little more attention, in view of the importance of understanding something of the climate of thought into which Ionian philosophy was born. It would be too much to say that they anticipated his idea, but they had familiarized a conception of cosmogony which must have smoothed the path for it. It was a common feature of early Greek cosmogonical beliefs, which they shared with those of the Near East and elsewhere, that in the beginning all was fused together in an undifferentiated mass.[2] The initial act in the making of the world, whether accomplished by the fiat of a creator or by other means, was a separation or division. As the Hebrew myth has it, 'God *divided* the light from the darkness...and divided the waters which were under the firmament from the waters which were above the firmament', and so on. Diodorus at the beginning of his universal history gives a Greek account of the origin of

[1] W. P. D. Wightman, *Growth of Scientific Ideas*, 10.
[2] Cf. F. M. Cornford, *Princ. Sap.* ch. 12, K. Marót in *Acta Antiqua*, 1951, 35–63.

the world which appears to go back to an early fifth-century original,[1] and which says that in the beginning heaven and earth had a single form because their nature was mingled. Later these bodies separated, and the world assumed the whole arrangement which it now displays. He supports this with a quotation from Euripides, who as he notes was deeply interested in the physical speculation of his own time. This notion, however, Euripides sets in the legendary past, and there are other indications also that it antedated the beginnings of philosophical inquiry. In his play *Melanippe the Wise*, Euripides makes Melanippe say:[2]

The tale is not mine, I had it from my mother, how heaven and earth were one form; and when they were parted from one another, they gave birth to all things, and gave forth to the light trees, flying things, beasts, the nurslings of the salt sea, and the race of mortals.

For an example of the mythology behind this we need look no further than Hesiod. In the *Theogony* he tells the primitive story of how Ouranos and Gaia, conceived as anthropomorphic figures, lay locked in an embrace until Kronos forced them apart. Again, the theogonies in the Orphic tradition—that is, attributed by the Greeks to Orpheus—spoke of the world as having started in the form of an egg. When it broke, Eros, the spirit of generation, emerged, and, of the two halves of the egg, the upper now formed the sky and the lower the earth. There are several versions in this tradition,[3] but they all seem to teach, of course in mythical form, the central doctrine which is attributed by Diogenes Laertius to Musaeus the pupil of Orpheus 'that all things come to be from one and are resolved again into the same'.[4]

The familiarity of this pre-philosophical conception may well have

---

[1] Diod. 1, 7. Diels–Kranz print this among the fragments of Democritus (68 B 5, vol. II, p. 135), but it more probably antedates the atomists. For its date and sources see the reff. in Guthrie, *In the Beginning*, 122, n. 10, and add Pfligersdorffer, *Stud. ʒu Poseidonios*, 100–46.

[2] Fr. 484 Nauck:

> οὐκ ἐμὸς ὁ μῦθος ἀλλ' ἐμῆς μητρὸς πάρα,
> ὡς οὐρανός τε γαῖά τ' ἦν μορφὴ μία·
> ἐπεὶ δ' ἐχωρίσθησαν ἀλλήλων δίχα
> τίκτουσι πάντα κἀνέδωκαν εἰς φάος
> δένδρη πετηνὰ θῆρας οὕς θ' ἅλμη τρέφει
> γένος τε θνητῶν.

[3] For which see Guthrie, *Orpheus and Greek Religion*, ch. IV.

[4] D.L. *proem.* 1, 3 ἐξ ἑνὸς τὰ πάντα γίγνεσθαι καὶ εἰς ταὐτὸν πάλιν ἀναλύεσθαι.

influenced Thales and his successors in the direction of monism—it is almost impossible to believe that it did not—but does not detract greatly from the extent of their achievement. The evolution of the cosmos in these mythical accounts proceeds in sexual terms. It is achieved by the mating and begetting of a series of pairs of powers imagined in human form, and how near these stories are to the primitive is easily seen in Hesiod's description of the mutilation of Ouranos by his son Kronos and of the birth of Aphrodite. Granted that the Milesians had the ground prepared for them by these myths, it is more important to reflect that they abandoned the whole mythical apparatus of personal agents, and, as Wightman says, tried to explain the variety of nature only in terms of something in nature itself, a natural substance.

The achievement of Thales has been represented by historians in two entirely different lights, on the one hand as a marvellous anticipation of modern scientific thinking, and on the other as nothing but a transparent rationalization of myth. In fact the perennial fascination exercised by the Milesians lies just in this, that their ideas form a bridge between the two worlds of myth and reason. The search for a unity in the universe behind the multiplicity of phenomena is perennial and universal. It is a religious and aesthetic, a philosophic and a scientific need; and it appears at all periods of history. We have seen it in the religious poetry of a pre-philosophical age, and shall encounter it in its most extreme form a hundred years or so after Thales in Parmenides. In modern times we have seen a philosopher remark on the aesthetic appeal of unity and a logician describe it as the only thing which will satisfy the desire for explanation. Turning to the physical scientists, we find one of them writing of 'the endeavour of physics to achieve a unified world-view. We do not accept appearances in their many-coloured fullness, but we want to explain them, that is, we want to reduce one fact to another.'[1] If there is any time and place at which we can say that this search for unity emerged from the mythical and entered its scientific phase, it is here in sixth-century Miletus. There is a long way to go. Philosophy is so recently born that it can scarcely stand on its own legs, and only with many a backward glance at its

[1] C. F. von Weizsäcker, *The World-View of Physics*, 30.

parent and even a grip on her hand; but it is born, because someone has sought the desired unity in a natural substance and removed the gods from the cosmogonical scene. Von Weizsäcker continues his paragraph by saying that in this process of unifying the variety of appearances the scientist finds it necessary to explain what is perceptible by what is not perceptible, and whether or not we can credit this further step to Thales, we shall certainly find it taken by his friend and successor Anaximander.

Additional note: water and 'life'

One hesitates to draw attention to parallels between the views of these early thinkers and those of more recent science, since it is so easy to exaggerate resemblances and invite misleading conclusions. It may well be that the Milesians, as one would expect from their methods and results in other fields of *historie*, were keen observers and may even have had an embryonic awareness of the uses of experiment; but when it comes to the constitution of the universe, there is almost an absurdity in putting their inspired guesses beside the conclusions of modern experimental science. (Another obvious field for pitfalls is the comparison of ancient and modern atomic theory.) Nevertheless the fascination which most people feel at the recurrence of similar ideas at very distantly related phases of human history is natural and justified if the human mind is a subject of interest at all; and, in due segregation from the main argument, one may perhaps allow it a little indulgence.

In choosing water as the one basic substance, Thales was followed by van Helmont, who at the turn of the sixteenth and seventeenth centuries exemplified a similarly transitional phase between superstition and rationalism, with on the one hand his faith in alchemy and devotion to Paracelsus, and on the other his solid scientific achievement which has earned him the title of the father of modern chemistry. In the present century, the following passage from the late Sir Charles Sherrington is of especial interest in view of the likelihood that Thales's choice was determined by the supposed connexion of water with life:

Water is the great menstruum of 'life'. It makes life possible. It was part of the plot by which our planet engendered life. Every egg-cell is mostly water, and water is its first habitat. Water it turns to endless purposes; mechanical support and bed for its membranous sheets as they form and shape and fold. The early embryo is largely membranes. Here a particular piece grows fast because its cells do so. There it bulges or dips, to do this or that or simply to find room for itself. At some other centre of special activity the sheet will thicken. Again at some other place it will thin and form a hole. This is how the mouth, which at first leads nowhere, presently opens into the stomach. In the doing of all this, water is a main means.[1]

Wightman sums up the idea of Thales thus:

Thales was dealing with things as they are, and not with things neatly sorted and cleaned up by chemists. His dictum, then, though certainly not wholly true, was, at its face value, very far from being nonsense. The greater part of the earth's surface is water; water pervades every region of our atmosphere; life as we know it is impossible without water; water is the nearest approach to the alchemist's dream of a universal solvent; water disappears when fanned by the wind, and falls again from the clouds as rain; ice turns into water as does the snow that falls from the skies; and a whole country surrounded by a barren desert is fertile, rich, and populous because a huge mass of water sweeps through it annually.[2]

C. ANAXIMANDER

(1) *Date, writings, interests*

Anaximander was a younger friend and fellow-citizen of Thales (p. 43, n. 2, above). Apollodorus says with unusual precision that he was sixty-four in the year 547/6 (D.L. II, 2).[3] Following the tradition that Thales wrote nothing, Themistius described him as 'the first of the Greeks, to our knowledge, who was bold enough to publish a treatise on nature'. Certain it is that he wrote a book, which seems to have come into the hands of Apollodorus the chronologist, and we may feel some confidence that it was in the library of the Lyceum under Aristotle and Theophrastus. Yet it is perhaps worth remarking that neither Anaximander nor Anaximenes is mentioned by any writer before Aristotle. Plato, though he tells a story about Thales, and quotes the dictum elsewhere attributed to him that all things are full of gods, nowhere mentions the other two Milesians, nor makes any certain reference to their doctrines. This remarkable fact has led the Swiss

[1] *Man on his Nature*, 121 (Pelican ed. 113f.).
[2] *Growth of Scientific Ideas*, 10.
[3] On the date of Anaximander cf. Heidel in *Proc. Am. Ac.* 1921, 253f.

scholar Gigon to suppose that Aristotle, with his deep interest in the historical aspect of his subject, must have sought out the works of these two and discovered copies which up to his time had been lost.

The Suda[1] lists as titles of works by Anaximander: *On Nature*, *Description of the Earth*, *The Fixed Stars*, *Sphere*, 'and a few more'. These probably come from the catalogue of the Alexandrian library and represent divisions of a single work which Anaximander himself would almost certainly, in accordance with the custom of his time, have left unnamed, and, on the assumption that the titles are in fact sub-titles, the lists may well have varied. Throughout antiquity the title 'On Nature' (περὶ φύσεως) was given indiscriminately to the writings of the Presocratics, who from the main bent of their interests were known as 'the natural philosophers' or 'physiologers' (φυσικοί, φυσιολόγοι: so in Aristotle). The phrase was already in use as a title in the fifth and fourth centuries B.C., though this fact is not indeed proved by the passages commonly cited to support it, in which a Hippocratic writer or Plato refers to 'those who write on nature': this and similar phrases mark them off as a recognized group, but cannot be said to indicate anything so definite as a title.[2] More certain proof comes from something which does not seem to have impressed scholars in this connexion, namely the statement that Gorgias the fifth-century Sophist wrote a book which he called 'On the Non-existent or On Nature'.[3] One cannot doubt that the deliberately provocative title was chosen by Gorgias himself, nor that it was intended as a parody of titles already extant. He may have had particularly in mind his contemporary Melissus, whose book according to Simplicius (*Phys.* 70.16, *De Caelo*, 557.10; DK, 30A4) was called 'On Nature or the Existent'.

The classification of his writings in the Suda may be fairly taken to represent the scope of Anaximander's interests. Coupled with the

---

[1] See p. 47, n. 3, above.

[2] Hippocr. *De Vet. Med.* 20 (I, 620 Littré), Plato, *Lys.* 214B, *Phaedo*, 96A, Eur. fr. 910 Nauck, Xen. *Mem.* I, I, 11, Ar. *Gen. et Corr.* 333b18, *Phys.* 185a18 (quoted by Verdenius, *loc. cit.* below). On the strength of some of these, Heidel (*Proc. Am. Acad.* XLV (1910), 81) said: 'It is reasonably certain that philosophical works were familiarly quoted as bearing the title π. φύσεως some time before the close of the fifth century', and Verdenius (*Mnemos.* 1947, 272–3): 'In the fifth and fourth centuries π. φύσεως was obviously regarded as the authentic title of early philosophical works.'

[3] Sext. *Adv. Math.* VII, 65 (DK, 82B3) ἐν τῷ ἐπιγραφομένῳ....

well-authenticated fact that he drew a map of the known world, it suggested to Heidel that he was more of a geographer than a philosopher and that the limited interest of the Peripatetics who were responsible for the doxographic tradition has therefore given a somewhat distorted picture of his achievements as a whole. The reports of his map go back to the great Alexandrian geographer and librarian Eratosthenes, e.g. that of Strabo who in claiming that geography is a study worthy to be called philosophical says, after giving pride of place to Homer (I, I, II, DK, 12 A 6):

Those who followed him were clearly notable men and at home in philosophy, of whom Eratosthenes says that the first after Homer were two, Anaximander the acquaintance and fellow-citizen of Thales, and Hecataeus of Miletus. The one was the first to publish a geographical tablet [map of the earth], whereas Hecataeus left a treatise which is authenticated as his from the rest of his writings.[1]

Anaximander was also noted for his astronomical achievements, a natural accompaniment to his interest in the cosmos as a whole. He is said (D.L. II, 2) to have constructed a sphere, that is, some sort of model of the heavens, but unfortunately we have no details of this, and we are still at the cloudy stage of history when the attribution of particular actions or discoveries to an individual is almost impossible of verification. We read in Cicero that the first celestial sphere was fashioned by Thales (*eam a Thalete Milesio primum esse tornatam, De Rep.* I, 14, 22). Heidel mentions that according to Pliny (II, 31, DK, 12 A 5) Anaximander discovered the obliquity of the zodiac, but does not here note that Eudemus in his *Astronomical History* credited this to Oenopides in the fifth century (DK, 41.7). Like Thales, Anaximander was said to have invented, or introduced, the dial with upright rod (gnomon), and to have shown by its aid the 'solstices, times, seasons, and equinoxes' (Eusebius, DK, A 4, cf. D.L. II, 1). Herodotus, as we have seen (p. 33, above), regarded this as an importation from Babylonia, and the different words used by our authorities indicate at least

---

[1] For supporting passages in the Greek geographical tradition (D.L. II, 2, Agathemerus in DK, 12A6, etc.) see Heidel, *op. cit.* 247; and for conjectural details about the nature of Anaximander's map, Kahn, *Anaximander*, 82–4.

some doubt as to the extent of Anaximander's achievement here.[1] This dial, according to Favorinus (*ap.* D.L. II, 1), he set up at Sparta, a city with which he is further connected by a story in Cicero (*De Div.* I, 50, 112) that he was responsible for a considerable saving of life by warning the Spartans of an impending earthquake and persuading them to spend the night in the open.[2] Thus, as one would expect from his geographical interests, he evidently had the Ionian taste for travel, and Aelian (*c.* A.D. 200) says that he led the expedition to found one of the numerous colonies of Miletus, that at Apollonia on the Black Sea coast (*V.H.* III, 7, DK, A 3). No doubt like Thales he took a full part in the public life of his city, even if we may no longer accept the sixth-century statue bearing the name of Anaximander, the lower part of which has been discovered in the *bouleuterion* of Miletus, as having been erected in honour of the philosopher.[3]

Heidel's minute examination of the evidence from non-Peripatetic sources led him to the conclusion that Anaximander's book was, in short and summary form,[4] a universal history and geography, 'purporting to sketch the life-history of the cosmos from the moment of its emergence from infinitude to the author's own time'. Carrying this tendency even further, Cherniss says: 'Anaximander's purpose was to give a description of the inhabited earth, geographical, ethnological and cultural, and the way in which it had come to be what it was.' This would mean that the only part of Anaximander's doctrine on which we have anything but the smallest and most doubtful bits of information, namely his cosmogony, was to him only incidental or preparatory to the main purpose of his work. We may admit the likelihood that Aristotle and his followers were silent about parts of the book that did not interest them, but to go so far in the opposite direction is to outrun the evidence.

[1] εὗρε D.L., κατεσκεύασε Euseb., εἰσήγαγε Suda.

[2] Cicero denies that this was an act of divination, and compares it to the forecasts made by doctors, seamen and farmers by reason of their special skill and experience, calling Anaximander 'physicus'. It would be interesting to know how Anaximander did it: perhaps by observing the behaviour of the storks, like the inhabitants of the Larissa neighbourhood in the earthquakes of 1954. (*The Times*, 3 May 1954: 'We have watched the storks all day; it is the best way to know when it is coming.')

[3] Burnet had no doubts (*EGP*, 52), but see now W. Darsow in *Jb. D.A.I.* 1954, 101–17: the statue, it appears, is female, and the name must be that of the donor or dedicator.

[4] Cf. D.L. II, 2 τῶν δὲ ἀρεσκόντων αὐτῷ πεποίηται κεφαλαιώδη τὴν ἔκθεσιν.

Here our main purpose must be to attempt a reconstruction of Anaximander's cosmogonical views, and in this, as we have seen, we are better situated than we were with Thales. None of our informants, or their sources, had knowledge of a book by Thales. They were dependent on anecdotes or a few apophthegms, the authenticity of which was doubtful or worse. The treatise of Anaximander could be quoted, and its style criticized, by Theophrastus, and we are told that Apollodorus saw a copy in the second century B.C. Whatever we may think of their interpretations, it is safest to assume that Aristotle and Theophrastus both had the work, and to be correspondingly cautious in criticizing what they say from the standpoint of our own comparative ignorance.

(2) The Unlimited as 'arche'

The best starting-point will be the account which Simplicius gives, in large part from Theophrastus (*Phys.* 24.13, DK, A9 and B1):

Anaximander named the *arche* (cf. p. 57, above) and element of existing things 'the boundless', being the first to introduce this name for the *arche*. He says that it is neither water nor any other of the so-called elements, but a different substance which is boundless, from which there come into being all the heavens and the worlds within them. Things perish into those things out of which they have their being, as is due; for they make just recompense to one another for their injustice according to the ordinance [or perhaps 'assessment'] of time—so he puts it in somewhat poetical terms.

Having thus paraphrased and in part quoted Anaximander's words, Simplicius, with Aristotle and Theophrastus before him, proceeds to interpret them:

It is clear that when he observed how the four elements change into each other, he did not think it reasonable to conceive of one of these as underlying the rest, but posited something else. Moreover he does not account for *genesis* by a qualitative alteration of the element, but by a separation of the opposites caused by the eternal motion.

Few passages descriptive of Presocratic doctrine have escaped a thorough mauling from many modern commentators. The above is no exception, and many difficulties have been discovered, if not created, in it. The casual aside, that Anaximander's language here is rather poetical, gives us the valuable information that the previous sentence, though cast in indirect speech in the Greek, preserves some of his actual words. At a minimum,[1] the criticism must refer to the clause: 'for they make just recompense to one another for their injustice according to the ordinance of time', and this is sufficient guarantee that the preceding clause is a true representation of Anaximander's thought.[2] The statement in Simplicius's explanation that Anaximander accounts for the origin of things 'by a separation of the opposites', etc., depends no doubt on Aristotle, who writes (*Phys.* I, 4, 187a20): 'Others teach that the opposites are in the one and are separated out, as Anaximander says.'[3]

It is clear (though a different view has been taken) that the first sentence in the passage from Simplicius means that Anaximander was the first to give the name *apeiron* (boundless, unlimited) to the *arche*. That he was also the first to use *arche* for that which writers from Aristotle onwards, with rather different ideas in their heads, called 'the substratum' appears not from this but from another passage of Simplicius (*Phys.* 150.22): 'Anaximander says that the opposites were in the substratum, which was a boundless body, and were separated out: he was the first to name the substratum *arche*.' We notice also that Theophrastus deemed it necessary to explain the archaic word by adding the Aristotelian term στοιχεῖον (element).[4]

---

[1] Some previous opinions: Whole sentence ἐξ ὧν δὲ . . τοῦ χρόνου τάξιν is printed as a fr. by DK; so also Cornford in *CQ*, 1934, 11, n. 2, who argues that Theophrastus, a very terse writer, would not write ἡ γένεσίς ἐστι τοῖς οὖσι for γίγνεται τὰ ὄντα or φθοράν γίγνεσθαι for φθείρεσθαι. Quotation is begun at κατὰ τὸ χρεών by Burnet (*EGP*, 52) and Vlastos (*PQ*, 1952, 108, n. 51), who thinks that κατὰ τὴν τοῦ χρόνου τάξιν is also not certain. Heidel is somewhat non-committal in *CP*, 1912, 233. Cf. also U. Hölscher in *Hermes*, 1953, 258f. (who, however, is more concerned with separating Theophrastus from Simplicius), McDiarmid, *Theophr. on Presoc. Causes*, 141f. See also now the sensible remarks of Kahn, *Anaximander*, 166ff., and his review of earlier interpretations, 193ff.

[2] In spite of McDiarmid, *Theophr. on Presoc. Causes*, 96ff. McDiarmid is of course right in saying that 'recompense to one another for injustice' can have nothing to do with the relation of generated things to the *apeiron*.

[3] ὥσπερ 'Αναξίμανδρός φησι. Aristotle here groups Anaximander's 'boundless' with the 'mixture' of Empedocles and Anaxagoras, whose conceptions were in fact different, since they represented conscious attempts to escape the dilemma posed by Parmenides. After him, philosophers were conscious of distinctions and difficulties of which Anaximander had no inkling. This does not, however, invalidate the testimony, and it is probable—if not, as Heidel said, 'proved beyond a doubt' (*CP*, 1912, 231) by this passage—that Anaximander himself used the word ἐκκρίνεσθαι, or perhaps ἀποκρίνεσθαι (Kahn, *Anaximander*, 19f.).

[4] Cf. Heidel, *CP*, 1912, 215–16. McDiarmid (*Theophr. on the Presoc. Causes*, 138ff.) has cast legitimate doubt on this final point, but his contention that Simpl. *Phys.* 150 is no evidence that Anaximander used the word ἀρχή is only maintained by an alteration of the received text. See also on this point Jaeger, *TEGP*, 26f., Kahn, *Anaximander*, 30–2.

The Milesians

With Anaximander physical theory takes a momentous step, to a notion from which it has retreated many times before its reappearance in very different form in the modern world: the notion of the non-perceptible. 'The physical view of the world', writes the physicist von Weizsäcker, 'has always had a tendency towards the non-perceptible. This stems immediately from the endeavour of physics to achieve a unified world-view. We do not accept appearances in their many-coloured fulness, but we want to explain them, that is, we want to reduce one fact to another. In this process what is perceptible is often explained by what is not perceptible.'[1]

Anaximander then rejected the idea that water, or any of the popularly (and later philosophically) recognized elemental masses visible in the world of today, could have served as a basis for all the rest. Instead he posited an unnamed substance behind them all, less definite in character, which he described as *apeiron* (from *a* privative, indicating absence, and *peras* = limit or boundary). There was no reason for regarding water, earth, fire or any such familiar, sensibly manifest phenomenon as prior to the rest. The original matrix of the universe must be something more primitive and ultimate than any of them, of which they are all alike secondary manifestations or modifications, obtained by a process of 'separating out'.

The following questions therefore suggest themselves: Why did he thus go behind the phenomena? What did he mean by *apeiron*? What were the 'opposites', and in what sense 'in the one and separated out'?

(3) The opposites

The assumption of an imperceptible reality behind the perceptible was, for one seeking a unity behind the multiplicity of phenomena, on general grounds a reasonable one, as von Weizsäcker has confirmed from the scientist's standpoint. Anaximander had also a more specific reason for adopting it, and this introduces a fundamental feature of Greek thought with a long and influential history, namely the notion of the primary opposites. Later, when substance and attribute had been clearly distinguished by Plato and Aristotle, it was said that the

[1] *The World-View of Physics*, 30.

elements—earth, water, air and fire—were characterized by one or more of a set of contrary qualities, hot, cold, wet and dry, and because of their contrary attributes were always in a state of conflict. European literature attests the vitality of this semi-anthropomorphic notion. From Ovid—

> Frigida pugnabant calidis, umentia siccis—

we pass to Spenser—

> The earth the air the water and the fire
> Then gan to range themselves in huge array,
> And with contrary forces to conspire
> Each against other by all means they may—

and Milton—

> Hot, cold, wet and dry, four champions fierce
> Strive here for maistery.

When Anaximander first tried to give philosophical expression to the idea, no clear distinction was possible between substance and attribute. Just as he spoke of 'the boundless', so also he designated the opposites by article and adjective as the hot, the cold, the wet and the dry.[1] These, as Cornford has said, are for Anaximander not qualities but things. '"The hot" was not warmth, considered as an adjectival property of some substance which is warm. It is a substantive thing, and "the cold", its contrary, is another thing. Hence it was possible to think of the hot and the cold as two opposed things which might be fused together in an indistinct condition, like a mixture of wine and water' (*Princ. Sap.* 162).

The conflict of the opposites is an undeniable fact of nature. Water for instance, whose nature it is to quench fire whenever it meets it, can hardly be the original substance out of which fire, along with all the

---

[1] Simpl. 150.24, DK, A9. We may note that although by Plato's time the abstract nouns 'heat' or 'dryness' are currently distinguished from 'hot' and 'dry', he still has to apologize for the general term 'quality' (ποιότης) as an uncouth neologism (*Theaet.* 182A).

I cannot agree with the reasoning of Hölscher (following Reinhardt; see *Hermes*, 1953, 266) that the opposites enumerated as Anaximander's by Simplicius are not 'anaximandrisch', nor see why 'τὸ ἄπειρον is in a different class'. 'Because', says Hölscher, 'it stands not for a quality (like the hot), but a phenomenon like fire.' But the hot was also for Anaximander a material phenomenon.

other forms of material existence, had its being. Aristotle puts the argument thus, though without mentioning Anaximander by name:

Some thinkers make this [*sc.* a substance other than the elements, out of which they have evolved] the unlimited, not air or water, to prevent their destruction by that one of them which is unlimited; for they are marked by mutual opposition—e.g. air is cold, water wet, fire hot—so that if one of them were unlimited, the others would have perished. As it is, they say, it is something else, out of which the known elements come (*Phys.* III, 204b24).

The conflict is referred to by Anaximander himself in the only well-attested fragment of his writings: 'They make just recompense to one another for their injustice according to the ordinance of time.'

To avoid misunderstanding, a distinction must be observed here which may at first sight seem rather subtle. There is a sense in which water (the cold and wet) can and does give birth to its opposite, fire (the hot and dry). No other meaning can be attached to Anaximander's sentence than that the 'injustice' which they commit consists in an encroachment, say, of fire by swallowing up some of its rival water, and *vice versa*. It was in fact a common Greek belief, which emerges still more clearly in Anaximenes, that the fiery heat at the circumference of the universe (that is, in the present world-order the sun) not only vaporized the moisture of earth and sea, thus turning it into mist or air, but finally ignited it and transformed it into fire. The process was actually spoken of as the 'nourishment' of the sun by water or moisture, as we saw in connexion with Thales (p. 67 above).

In this sense fire *can* be created out of water, but only because of the simultaneous existence of both, and, as Anaximander says, their balance is always being redressed: the encroachment of one opposite is followed by a retribution in which the other regains the lost ground. Fire becomes cooled into cloud, cloud into rain which once more replenishes the moisture on earth. This alternate advance and retreat of the hot and the dry, the cold and the wet, is an obvious expression of the annual variation of the seasons.[1] It in no way contradicts the observation which led to the abandonment of one of the opposites as primal *arche*, for it remains as true as ever that in a universe which was *all* water, like that

[1] So Heidel, 'On Anaximander', *CP*, 1912, 233–4, and *Proc. Am. Acad.* 1913, 684–5; Vlastos, *CP*, 1947, 172; Cornford, *Princ. Sap.* 168.

of the Mesopotamian and Egyptian myths which Thales perhaps rationalized a little too precipitately, no fire could ever have come into being. For water to turn into fire requires the action of fire already existing.

Thus whether the sentence 'things perish into those things out of which they have their being, according to necessity' is also Anaximander's or is a paraphrase by Theophrastus or Simplicius, it cannot refer (as it has frequently been thought to do) to the primal generation of the opposites out of, and final reabsorption into, the ultimate *apeiron*, but only to their mutual transformations in the present order. Otherwise its connexion with the quotation which follows would make no sense.[1]

To sum up, Anaximander had noticed that it is the natural tendency of each of the elements to swallow up its opposite. Fire and water must inevitably be in conflict. When they meet they struggle until one or the other prevails, and either the fire is put out and nothing but the water remains, or else the water is dried up and fire remains in sole possession of the field. Conversely this may be described, in Simplicius's words, as the conversion of water into fire and *vice versa*.[2] There is of course an intermediate stage, clearly visible to observation, of the conversion of water into steam or vapour, which for the Greeks are included in the term *aer*. In the world as a whole, complete and final victory is never granted to one or the other of the opposing forces (or litigants, as Anaximander imagined them): the balance between them is always being restored or maintained. If one gains a local advantage, the other is encroaching elsewhere.

Now if the world is evolved from a single substance, there must be at least enough of this substance to make the whole world, and probably a good deal more besides. But if fire existed in that quantity, it would inevitably enjoy a permanent victory over its potential

---

[1] Vlastos (*CP*, 1947, 170) thinks the plural ἐξ ὧν 'is strange, for the reference is obviously to the Boundless'; but concludes that 'the Boundless is explicitly thought of as a plurality'. This is much less probable than that the reference is not to the Boundless at all. The view of H. Fränkel (*Dichtung u. Philos.* 345–7) is subtle and interesting, but as Woodbury says (*CP*, 1955, 154f.) it credits Anaximander with a more developed sense of the distinction between possible and actual than he is likely to have possessed. The view here taken is now supported by Kahn, *Anaximander*, 167f., 195f.

[2] τὴν εἰς ἄλληλα μεταβολήν (*Phys.* 24.21).

rivals, none of which could be allowed to come into existence; or if the *arche* and *physis* of the world were water, there could never be fire. This remains true whether we take Anaximander's word *apeiron*, which he applied to his primary state of matter, to mean strictly infinite in extent, as Aristotle did, or simply of an indefinite quantity large enough to serve as source or reservoir[1] from which all that exists has been drawn. What exactly he did mean by the word has been matter of considerable controversy, and is now due for consideration.

It was long customary to regard the Milesians as interested only in the question 'What is the world made of?' They assumed it to be made of one material substance, and asked only whether that substance was water, air or something else. This was Aristotle's view, because when he approached them from the standpoint of his own fourfold scheme, seeking only, as he tells us, for anticipations of the material, efficient, formal and final causes as he conceived them, they appeared to be concerned only with 'principles of a material kind' (τὰς ἐν ὕλης εἴδει μόνας, *Metaph.* 983b7). But by thus limiting the scope and purpose of his review, he has undoubtedly misled those who, ignoring his own explicit declaration of intentions, supposed him to be writing a history of philosophy. Not 'matter' (for which they had no word, since they knew of no other form of existence) but rather 'nature' (*physis*) is the correct keyword. It may be that no certain instance of this word occurs in the scanty fragments of the philosophers before Heraclitus, but we have it in a very similar sense in Homer,[2] and this with the universal consensus of antiquity is enough to justify the claim of Pohlenz that 'the concept of *physis* is a creation of Ionian science, in which they summed up their new understanding of the world'.[3] Most commonly it meant the real constitution or character of things, including the way they behave, though it could also mean 'birth' or 'growth' (e.g. in Empedocles, fr. 8). The two are not unconnected, since, as Aristotle said (*Phys.* 193b12), '*Physis* in the sense of coming-to-be is the path to *physis*' (in the sense of state or structure finally reached).

---

[1] Another meaning of *arche*, as Heidel has illustrated in *CP*, 1912, 219ff.

[2] *Od.* x, 303, the 'bodily form' of a plant. See Kahn, *Anaximander*, 4, n. 1 and 201, n. 2.

[3] 'Nomos und Physis', *Hermes*, 1953, 426. For a good discussion of the meaning of the word see Kirk, *HCF*, 42–3, 228–31.

Physis could be both process and constitution or developed form, and the Milesians were interested in both aspects, though the evidence, such as it is, suggests that the latter sense (which it has in the *Odyssey*) is likely to have predominated in the sixth century.

The 'new understanding of the world' consisted in the substitution of natural for mythological causes, that is, of internal development for external compulsion. This, as Pohlenz says, is well expressed by the generalized use of *physis*,[1] which is something essentially internal and intrinsic to the world, the principle of its growth and present organization, identified at this early stage with its material constituent. The primary assumption is not simply that it consists of a single material substance, but that the diversity of its present order is not from eternity, but has evolved from something radically simpler at a particular point in time.

(4) *The meaning of 'apeiron'*

To this initial simple state or *arche* Anaximander gave the name of the Boundless, and the process by which a world-order emerged from it he described as a 'separating-off'. To consider first the initial state itself, how did he conceive it and why did he call it *apeiron*? Aristotle (*Phys.* 203b15; DK, A15), for whom the word had the strict sense of infinite, mentions five considerations as leading to the belief that something is *apeiron*. We may take it that they include all the traditional aspects of the word up to and including his time. In the first of these aspects, the temporal, the *apeiron* of Anaximander certainly deserves to be called infinite. The notion of temporal infinity was familiar to the Greek mind from remote antiquity in the religious conception of immortality, and Anaximander's description was in terms appropriate to this conception, for like many of his successors, says Aristotle (*Phys.* 203b13; DK, B3), he called his *arche* 'deathless and imperishable'. According to Hippolytus he also applied to it the words 'eternal and ageless' (*Ref.* 1, 6, 1; DK, B2). This marks it off as something of a different order from anything recognizable in the present world, and also illustrates the meaning of *arche* as both the original state of things —for it has existed from all time—and the permanent ground of their

---

[1] Very possibly at this stage with a limiting genitive like τοῦ ὅλου or τῶν ὄντων, though Heraclitus (fr. 123 DK) already uses it absolutely.

6-2

being. The *arche* of all things cannot itself have an *arche*—a beginning
—because then not it but that further *arche* would be the ultimate one.
And what has no *arche*, and also no ending, is *apeiron*, for an *arche*
would be a limit. So, in effect, says Aristotle (*Phys.* 203 b 7), using an
argument which seemed to Cornford to have 'an archaic ring'.[1]

Apart from the temporal sense of 'everlasting', *apeiron* has two main
meanings, according as the 'boundaries' (*perata*) which it lacks are
thought of as external or internal. If a body is limited externally, this
can only be because it comes up against something else, or so at least
it seemed to Aristotle and later writers.[2] Beyond its limit there must
be something other than itself. Conversely, then, a body which is unlimited in this sense must continue infinitely, or at least indefinitely, in
space. In the *Placita* of Aëtius (DK, A 14) we are told that Anaximander regarded the *apeiron* as infinite in this quantitative sense 'in
order that becoming might not fail'. The extant 'opposites', as we have
seen, and more complex bodies composed of them, are continually
perishing. Consequently, it seems to be argued, if the supply of them
is to be kept up—as it is and has been for time out of mind—the
reservoir out of which new supplies come—that is, the *apeiron*—must
be inexhaustible and therefore infinite.

It seems doubtful, however, whether Anaximander used this argument himself.[3] It looks rather as if the author had drawn that inference
from a sentence in which Aristotle denies that this is a valid reason for
supposing the existence of an infinite body, but without suggesting
that Anaximander did so. 'Nor is it necessary', writes Aristotle (*Phys.*
208 a 8; DK, A 14), 'for an infinite sensible body to exist in actuality in
order that becoming may not fail; for the destruction of one thing may
be the genesis of another, while the whole sum remains finite.' What
Aristotle says is clearly right. The process of becoming and perishing
is circular. Perishing does not mean vanishing into nothingness, but
changing into a different form of matter. This circularity, symbolized
by Anaximander as the alternation of 'injustice' and 'reparation',

---

[1] For reasons in favour of supposing that the whole argument goes back to Anaximander himself see C. H. Kahn in *Festschr. Kapp*, 1958, 19–29.

[2] *Phys.* 203 b 20 τὸ πεπερασμένον ἀεὶ πρός τι περαίνειν.

[3] What follows goes against the opinion of Burnet (*EGP*, 57), Cornford (*Princ. Sap.* 173), Cherniss (*ACP*, 379) and others.

seems to have been central in his thought. If he did not see that it does away with the necessity for an inexhaustible reservoir of primal matter which is everlastingly being drawn upon to form new creatures and other things in the world, then his mind was less acute than the evidence suggests it to have been.

It is unlikely that Anaximander was capable of grasping the notion of strict spatial or quantitative infinity, which came with further advances in mathematics. It is indeed purely conceptual, and has no meaning in the world of immediate sensible experience. As one of the five reasons for believing in an infinite, Aristotle says that number, mathematical magnitude and the space beyond the sky are thought to be infinite 'because they never give out in our thought'.[1] It is hardly credible that Anaximander reasoned like this. He certainly regarded the *apeiron* as an enormous mass surrounding (περιέχειν, Ar. *Phys.* 203b11) the whole of our world, but it may even have presented itself to his mind, as Cornford suggested, as a vast sphere. The word was in use in Greek to describe both spherical and circular shape, and, in an age without any sciences of grammar, semantics or logic, men were at the mercy of words to an extent which it is not always easy to realize. A word was more like a single whole entity, and its various meanings, which we without difficulty analyse and separate, could only appear as different aspects or facets of a single meaning.

It is right therefore to take into account the fact that *apeiron* was used of spheres and rings, to indicate no doubt that one can go on and on around them without ever coming to a bounding line. This comes out particularly clearly when Aristotle says (*Phys.* 207a2) that finger-rings are called unlimited if they have no gem-socket. Empedocles (fr. 28) speaks of an unlimited sphere, and the word is also applied to a seamless robe and a circular band of worshippers round an altar.[2]

Secondly *apeiron* was used with internal *perata* chiefly in mind, to indicate that no line could be drawn between part and part within the whole. In this way it approximates to the notion of indeterminacy. A body unlimited in this sense may be made up of different sorts of

---

[1] *Phys.* 203b23 διὰ τὸ ἐν τῇ νοήσει μὴ ὑπολείπειν.
[2] Eur. *Or.* 25 (cf. Aesch. *Ag.* 1382), Aesch. fr. 379 Nauck. (These and other examples are cited by Cornford, *Princ. Sap.* 176f.)

matter, but they are fused into an indistinguishable mass. Standing on the shore, we can see clearly where sea and earth and air begin and end. The world is not *apeiron* in the sense we are considering. But we can imagine some cataclysm occurring which would destroy those boundaries, just as we can imagine an initial state of chaos before the main divisions of the world were so cleanly distinguished as they are now. If earth, sea and sky were fused in one heaving, molten mass, the world might be described as a boundless, or unlimited, mixture (in Greek ἄπειρον μῖγμα), meaning that the boundaries between its various components were non-existent and they were inextricably confused. The extent of the world's own boundaries is not in question.

Let me repeat that we are not at a stage of thought when clear distinctions between different uses of the same word are possible. Some inheritance of the magical idea that a word or name has an independent existence and essence of its own, and can only therefore be one thing, persisted until later times than this, and influenced even the thought of the most enlightened, however far it may have receded into the subconscious. Of that the *Cratylus* of Plato is ample evidence. There is no question then of deciding in which of several senses Anaximander intended us to take his word, but only which sense was uppermost in his mind. This is likely to have been the notion of internal indeterminacy rather than of spatial infinity, since the former offered a solution to the problem that he was trying to solve. He was impressed, as we have seen (pp. 79 ff., above), with the difficulty of supposing the single primary element to be water, or 'the wet', as Thales had done, or any of the actual opposites with their determined characteristics. Owing to his belief in the inherent hostility and 'injustice' of these, any single one of them, far from serving as source of being to the rest, would prevent it altogether. A primitive stuff must be, so to speak, a neutral in these hostilities, and must therefore have no definite characteristics of its own. It must hold, inactive in the first place and suspended as it were in solution, the characteristics of all the future opposites which in due course were to be, in the significant word which was probably his own, 'separated off' (or 'out') from it. Here we may find, in all probability, the chief reason why he called his *arche* simply 'the *apeiron*'. There were no *perata* in it between the hot, the cold, the wet and the dry. Before the formation of a cosmos, the opposites as such could be said to be as yet non-existent, because they were indistinguishably mingled. At the same time (to use a resource of language that was not at Anaximander's disposal) they were present in a potential state, so that their subsequent emergence into actual and active being was always a possibility.

The difficulties of this conception, at least as it was expressed in the crude language of his time, were not immediately apparent. To bring them out fully required the uncompromising clarity of a Parmenides. If the opposites could be separated out from the *arche*, we may say, it must have contained them all the time and therefore could not be described as a unity. In applying the ancient formula 'everything came into being out of one thing', Anaximander virtually cheated.[1] But to make this criticism belonged to a more advanced stage of thought, a necessary stage between the naive monism of the Milesians and the Aristotelian distinction between various modes of being.[2]

(5) The 'apeiron' divine

There is a little more to be said about Anaximander's *arche*, based on the words of Aristotle in *Phys.* 203b6 (DK, A15):

Everything either *is* an origin or *has* an origin: the unlimited has no origin, for that would be a limit of it. Moreover, being an origin [or source or principle: *arche*], it is ungenerated and imperishable.... Therefore, as I say, there is no origin for it, but it appears to be the origin of other things and to encompass all things and direct all things, as those philosophers say who do

---

[1] The fact that this *is* an ancient formula, going back beyond the beginning of philosophy, is our best guarantee that in calling the earliest philosophers monistic in intention we are not (as some modern interpreters have argued) foisting on them the misconceptions that we have absorbed from Aristotle. Cf. pp. 68 f., above.

[2] It is no wonder that later writers, both ancient and modern, have been puzzled to know whether Anaximander's *apeiron* is a single substance or a mixture. (Cf. Cherniss, *ACP*, 375 ff., McDiarmid, *Theophr. on Presoc. Causes*, 100.) Probably the explanation given above comes closer to the mind of Anaximander than an outright denial of Aristotle's supposition that the opposites were in the *apeiron*, which was therefore a mixture. He had not faced the question. The distinction which some have emphasized between separating *out* and separating *off* (ἐκκρίνεσθαι and ἀποκρίνεσθαι) seems to me of little significance in this connexion. (For Hölscher's contrary view see KR, 130.)

Perhaps the explanation which shows most insight is that of Kahn (*Anaximander*, 236). In the light of Anaximander's conception of the universe as a living organism (cf. pp. 90 f., below) he writes: 'For a Milesian they [*sc.* the opposites] were no more pre-existent in the ἄπειρον than children pre-exist in the body of their parents before conception.'

not posit besides the unlimited other causes such as Mind or Love; and this they say is the divine, for it is immortal and imperishable, as Anaximander and most of the writers on nature call it.

Aristotle is here distinguishing later thinkers, to whom the belief in an animate self-moving stuff was beginning to seem unsatisfactory so that like Empedocles and Anaxagoras they moved towards the notion of a separate moving force, from those who like the Milesians were still at the hylozoist stage. For these a single *arche* filled the dual role; it included or surrounded all things, and was also the directive force. This verb (κυβερνᾶν), literally 'to steer', was applied in the fifth century by Diogenes of Apollonia (fr. 5) to air, which he adopted as the *arche* from Anaximander's successor Anaximenes. Elsewhere among the Presocratics we find it in Heraclitus (whatever the correct reading and interpretation of fr. 41, for which see below, p. 429) and Parmenides (fr. 12, *v.* 3). In all probability this word and the rest of the language here quoted from 'philosophers of the unlimited' go back to Anaximander as well as the two epithets explicitly vouched for by Aristotle as his.[1]

These words, as Aristotle says a little later (207a18), impart a certain loftiness of tone to the pronouncements of early philosophers on the *apeiron*. Indeed the attribution to the *arche* not only of life but of directive powers immediately suggests divine status. The same verb (to steer, κυβερνᾶν) is of course applied to divinities in non-philosophical contexts.[2] It is therefore no surprise when Aristotle goes on to ascribe divinity explicitly to the *arche* of Anaximander and those who thought like him. For a Greek indeed, as he indicates in the next clause, it follows directly from the fact of immortality. If it includes directive or governing power it also implies at least some form of consciousness. For Anaximander we have no further evidence on this point, but later monist philosophers ascribe consciousness and intelligence explicitly to their single material *arche*. This is the beginning of the road which will lead ultimately to the separation of matter and

---

[1] Cf. Jaeger, *TEGP*, 29 ff.

[2] πάντα γὰρ...σῇ κυβερνῶμαι φρενί, says Odysseus to Athena in Soph. *Aj.* 35, and the doctor Eryximachus in Plato's *Symposium* says that his own art of medicine πᾶσα ὑπὸ τοῦ θεοῦ τούτου κυβερνᾶται (i.e. by Eros: 186E).

moving cause, that is of matter and spirit, as the difficulty of their identification becomes more apparent; but that is still in the future. At present the very word 'matter' is an anachronism.[1]

(6) *Cosmogony and cosmology*

From the primal state, or original source of all things, we turn to the process by which a world-order comes into being. This is described as being, in general terms, one of 'separating-out', caused by an 'eternal motion' in the *apeiron*. In Aristotle's words (*Phys.* 187 a 20), 'the opposites are in the one and are separated out'. This statement of the process follows well on our description of the primary nature of the *apeiron* as an initial indeterminate fusion of all the opposites.[2] But we are not confined to the general term *ekkrisis* (or *apokrisis*) for our knowledge of how Anaximander supposed a world to be formed from the *apeiron*. Part of a description of his cosmogony, taken by Eusebius

---

[1] It must be stated in fairness that Prof. G. Vlastos has written (*PQ*, 1952, 113): 'There is no good conclusive evidence that either Anaximander or Anaxagoras called their cosmogonic principle "god" or even "divine".' I can only say that for me the evidence of Aristotle makes it much more probable than not. Vlastos produces two arguments *ex silentio*: (i) τὸ θεῖον does not occur as a substantive for 'divinity' in any of the Presocratics or any other text prior to Aeschylus and Herodotus, while it is one of Aristotle's favourite terms; (ii) the ancients did not understand this particular text or any other text at their disposal to say that Anaximander himself taught that the *apeiron* was τὸ θεῖον; even the chapter in Aëtius (1, 7) which generously supplies even Democritus with a god (= fire!) does not say that Anaximander's *apeiron* was god, but only that 'Anaximander declared that the infinite *ouranoi* were gods'. (i) is by no means conclusive when we consider the general frequency of article and neuter adj. at an early stage (cf. τὸ ἄπειρον itself). The expression τὸ θεῖον is frequent in Aristotle not because it is a 'favourite' but because divinity is so frequently his subject. If Herodotus, who uses it several times, had written treatises on natural theology it would no doubt have been a 'favourite' expression of his also. As for (ii), the denial goes beyond the evidence, as arguments *ex silentio*, based on fragmentary sources, are almost bound to do.

But whether or not Anaximander called his principle 'divine', it is of course true and important (and this is Vlastos's main point) that it had nothing whatever to do with the gods or cults of popular religion.

[2] Aristotle is in the context drawing a distinction, from his own point of view, between two kinds of early physical theory, those involving an alteration in the nature of the primitive stuff (ἀλλοίωσις), and those—of which Anaximander's was the first—which speak only of a separating-out of what was there all the time. Thales he leaves out of the account, probably on the grounds that too little was known about him. Following him Simplicius says (*Phys.* 150.20): 'Another way is not to adduce a change of matter as the cause, nor to account for the generation of things by the alteration of the substratum, but by separation (ἔκκρισις). Thus Anaximander says that the opposites were in the substratum, which was an indeterminate (ἄπειρον) body, and are separated out.' This ἀλλοίωσις is a notion that belongs properly to Aristotelian physical theory, and its introduction here throws little light on his early forerunners; but that does not concern us now.

from the compilation called *Stromateis* and originating in Theophrastus, reads thus (DK, A 10):

He says that at the birth of this cosmos a[1] germ of hot and cold was separated off from the eternal substance, and out of this a sphere of flame grew about the vapour surrounding the earth like the bark round a tree. When this was torn away and shut off in certain rings, the sun, moon and stars came into existence.

The last sentence can be better understood by comparison with the following (see further below, p. 93).

(*a*) (Aët. II, 13, 7, DK, A 18) Anaximander says that the stars are wheel-shaped concentrations (lit. 'feltings') of mist filled with fire, breathing out flames through openings in a certain quarter.

(*b*) (Hippolytus, *Ref.* I, 6, 4, DK, A 11) The stars come into being as a circle of fire, separated off from the fire that pervades the cosmos and surrounded by mist. There are breathing-places, certain pipe-like passages,[2] through which the stars appear. When these are blocked, eclipses occur.

The word γόνιμον, here translated 'germ', is an adjective meaning generative, fertile, able to bring to birth, and is used of eggs and seed.[3] It is used again by Theophrastus in *De Igne*, 44 in relation to the life of animals and plants only.[4] We can never know whether it is the actual word used by Anaximander, but it is in keeping with the language of organic generation which seems to pervade the passage and, as we saw in discussing Aristotle's conjecture about Thales, is a likely colour for the thought of these early speculators to have taken (pp. 61 f., above). The whole sentence strongly suggests, as Professor Baldry has well brought out,[5] that Anaximander conceived his cosmogony on the analogy of early views concerning the seed of animals and the develop-

---

[1] Or 'the'; but cf. Diels, *Dox.* 579, crit. n.

[2] Perhaps the simile is intended to compare the breathing-holes to the holes in a (musical) pipe. This would be appropriate, but cannot be said to be a certain translation of the Greek.

[3] Examples: σπέρμα γόνιμον (as opposed to ἄγονον), Ar. *H.A.* 523a25; of eggs, Ar. *G.A.* 730a6, Plato, *Theaet.* 151 E (as opposed to ὑπηνέμιον or ἀνεμιαῖον, a 'wind-egg').

[4] γόνιμος καὶ ζῷων καὶ φυτῶν (of the sun).

[5] *CQ*, 1932, 29 f. There is admittedly an element of speculation in this, and for a more cautious view the reader is referred to Kirk in KR, 132 f., but I should certainly not go further in that direction than to agree with Kahn that though the phrasing may be more recent, nevertheless the idea is old (*Anaximander*, 57).

ment of the embryo. The mythical world-egg of Orphic and other cosmogonies shows how primitive such a notion could be, and the 'separation' (ἀπόκρισις) of the seed in the womb, the part played by hot and cold, the word φλοιός, and the 'detachment' (ἀπορραγῆναι) of the new organism from the parent body, are all familiar from Greek medical writers as well as finding their place in the present account. As to φλοιός (the word translated 'bark' above), one may note with Baldry that it means 'any skin that forms round a growing organism, whether plant or animal'. Aristotle (*H.A.* v, 558a28) uses it of the membrane round an egg, and Anaximander himself is said to have applied it to the prickly skin which on his theory surrounded the earliest forms of animal life. It looks as if Anaximander saw the outer 'skin' of the embryo world, separating it from the womb of the 'Boundless' in which it was formed,[1] as a parallel phenomenon to this membrane which developed round eggs, animal embryos and trees alike.[2] Since the world's skin is spherical, the reference to trees (which may have been added by Theophrastus or even later) is obviously not intended to be pressed.[3]

That cosmogony should be described in terms of organic life is appropriate to the mentality of these intellectual pioneers. The *arche* of Anaximander, the doxographers tell us,[4] was in eternal motion. The reason for this is nowhere explained, an omission censured by Aristotle but no doubt due to persistence of the belief that the *arche* is eternally alive. Since for the Greek the very notion of life involves self-caused motion, no external cause was conceivable, let alone demanded. Anaximander has rejected the anthropomorphic imagery of sexual mating which formed the basis of mythical cosmogonies, but for him it is still natural and rational to regard the matrix of the world as animate and its origin as taking place from a kind of seed or egg.

[1] ἐκ τοῦ ἀιδίου must refer to the ἄπειρον, which Anaximander is elsewhere said to have described as ἀθάνατον and ἀγήρω (p. 88, above).

[2] Cf. e.g. De Nat. Pueri, 12 (VII, 488 Littré): ἡ γονὴ ὑμενοῦται φυσωμένη (quoted by Baldry, 27). Leucippus actually spoke of a ὑμήν forming about the nascent cosmos (D.L. IX, 32).

[3] The word meant sometimes the soft inner rind rather than the outer bark. Herodotus (VIII, 115) speaks of people eating φλοιόν and leaves when no other food was available. In Hellenistic times Nicander uses it for the skin of Marsyas (*Al.* 302) and of serpents (*Th.* 355, 392).

[4] A11 (Hippolytus), 12 (Hermeias).

This fertile nucleus, pregnant with the opposites, becomes detached from the Boundless and develops into a sphere of fire enclosing a cold, moist mass. Between the two is dark mist (ἀήρ). At this stage only two primary opposites can be said to be separated, hot including dry and cold including wet. The mist arises from the action of the hot periphery on the cold-wet centre, and, under the same action of heat, wet and dry become in the end more completely separated, producing land and sea. So Aëtius (DK, A27 *fin.*):

Anaximander says that the sea is a relic of the primal moisture, the greater part of which has been dried up by the fire.

Anaximander was among those whose accounts of the origin of the sea are mentioned by Aristotle in the *Meteorologica* (353b5, trans. Lee):

Those who were more versed in secular philosophy [as opposed to the ancient theological poets] suppose it to have had a beginning. They say that at first the whole region about the earth was wet, and that as it dried up the water that evaporated became the cause of winds and the turnings of the sun and moon, while what was left is the sea: consequently they believe that the sea is still drying up and becoming less, and that in the end a time will come when it is all dried up.

He is mentioned by name in the commentary of Alexander of Aphrodisias on the passage (DK, A27):

Some of them say that the sea is a residue of the primal moisture. The region of the earth was moist, and subsequently part of the moisture was vaporized by the sun...but part of it left behind in the hollows of the earth forms the sea. Hence it is continually becoming less as the sun dries it up, and eventually it will be dry. Of this opinion, according to Theophrastus, were Anaximander and Diogenes.

It is characteristic of Milesian thought that once the separation of the mutually hostile opposites has begun, the process of cosmogony is continued by the natural exercise of their respective powers: heat dries up moisture and so on. Interesting also, after Aristotle's and our own conjectures about Thales, is the immediate prominence of moisture and heat as soon as fertilization and generation are to take place. Heat especially has an important part to play as a first agent of *genesis*, and at a later stage it is the action of heat on moisture which produces animal life. These features of Anaximander's system strengthen the case against those who have disparaged Aristotle's conjecture as arising out of the later progress of physiological and medical knowledge in Greece. We find rather, as might be expected, certain points of contact between the two who were fellow-citizens and fellow-workers in their field.

The next stage in the same continuous process explains the formation of the heavenly bodies. In addition to evidence already quoted, we have the following:[1]

(*a*) Hippolytus, after the words quoted (p. 90, above), adds: 'and the moon is seen to wax and wane according as the passages close or open'. There follows a sentence in which some words have probably dropped out of the manuscripts, but which seems to say that the circle of the sun is twenty-seven times the diameter of the earth[2] and that of the moon eighteen times, and adds that the sun is the highest of the heavenly bodies, and the stars are the lowest.

(*b*) Simpl. *De Caelo* 471.4 (DK, A19, speaking of the planets): 'Anaximander was the first to discuss their sizes and distances, according to Eudemus, who attributes the first determination of their order to the Pythagoreans. The sizes and distances of the sun and moon are reckoned to this day by taking eclipses as the starting-point of our knowledge, and we may reasonably suppose that this too was Anaximander's discovery.'

(*c*) Aët. II, 15, 6 (A18): 'Anaximander, Metrodorus of Chios and Crates held that the sun was situated highest of all, next the moon, and beneath them the fixed stars and planets.'

(*d*) *Ibid.* 20, 1 (A21): 'According to Anaximander, the sun is essentially a circle twenty-eight times the size of the earth, shaped like a cartwheel. The rim is hollow and full of fire, and at a certain point allows the fire to be seen through an orifice like the nozzle of a bellows: this is the sun.'

(*e*) *Ibid.* 21, 1 (A21): 'Anaximander says that the sun is the same size as the earth, but the circle in which is its blowhole, and by which it is carried round, is twenty-seven times the size of the earth.'

(*f*) *Ibid.* 24, 2 (A21): 'According to Anaximander the sun is eclipsed when the orifice through which the fire escapes is shut up.'

(*g*) *Ibid.* 25, 1 (A22): 'According to Anaximander, the moon is essentially

---

[1] I omit (*a*) the passage from Achilles (DK, A21), as being obviously an unintelligently garbled version of what is described more clearly by Aëtius, (*b*) Aët. II, 16, 5 (A18), which as Kahn has seen (*Anaximander*, 59) is only an accidental repetition of the preceding reference to Aristotle.

[2] Though Dreyer (*Planetary Systems*, 15, n. 1) would take the text as it stands.

a circle nineteen times the size of the earth, resembling a cartwheel with the rim hollow and full of fire like that of the sun, lying obliquely as does the sun's and having a single blowhole like the nozzle of a bellows. It is eclipsed according to the turnings of the wheel.'[1]

(*h*) *Ibid.* 29, 1 (A22): 'Anaximander says that the moon is eclipsed when the orifice in the wheel becomes blocked.'

(*i*) *Ibid.* 28, 1 (A22 omits last phrase): 'Anaximander, Xenophanes and Berosus say that the moon has its own light, in some way rarer [than the sun's].'[2]

In spite of minor discrepancies, we may accept the following account as probable. The fiery, spherical membrane about the new-born cosmos parted (doubtless under increasing pressure from the mist or steam caused by its own action in evaporating the watery centre) into separate circles, around each of which the dense mist surged and closed. Where there are apertures in this surrounding envelope, we see the heavenly bodies themselves. Thus the sun and moon are really rotating wheels of fire going right round the earth, but encased in tubes of mist except at one point where there is a hole, through which the fire streams like an ignited jet of gas through a leak in its pipe. (The modern simile is closer than the Greek one of air escaping through the nozzle of a pair of bellows.) The circles of the stars are not so easy to visualize from our fragmentary authorities, but one would suppose that each contained many holes.[3] Mention of the Milky Way, as by some modern authorities, hardly gives an adequate explanation, though its appearance may possibly have helped to put the idea of the wheels into Anaximander's head. They were evidently all regarded as lying in the same spherical plane, nor are the planets yet distinguished in this respect from the

[1] The last sentence, which occurs in Stobaeus but not in Plutarch's *Epitome* (*Dox.* 355), is obscure (and perhaps corrupt: Kahn, *Anaximander*, 60), but cannot be held to be a valid contradiction of the next passage quoted.

[2] This must be preferred to the statement of D.L. II, 1 (DK, A1) that it gets its light from the sun. The correct view was in later antiquity attributed even to Thales (p. 49, above), and also to Anaximenes, in whose somewhat fantastic astronomy it can scarcely have found a place. It seems to be first clearly attested in Parmenides (fr. 14), but Heath (*Aristarchus*, 75 f.) is sceptical about this line and would credit the discovery to Anaxagoras. See further p. 286, below.

[3] For Burnet's suggestion that there is only one 'wheel of the stars', and that it is intended to explain the motions of the morning and evening stars alone (not yet recognized as one), see *EGP* 69 and Taylor, *Timaeus*, 160, n. 1. Even though this would explain why the 'wheel of the stars' was smaller than those of sun and moon, it does not seem to be supported by our texts.

fixed stars. (Eudemus, in passage (*b*) above, attributes the determination of the planetary orbits to the Pythagoreans. Simplicius's introduction of Anaximander in the context of the planets is confusing, as is his apparent suggestion that Anaximander himself might have calculated the sizes and distances of the sun and moon from the observation of eclipses.)

To suppose that the stars are nearer the earth than either sun or moon is contrary to later Greek astronomy, according to which the fixed stars are—as seems most natural—in the plane of the outermost circumference of the spherical cosmos, and the sun, moon and planets revolve in different orbits beneath them. Anaximander's order raises the question in a modern mind how the rings of the stars avoid obstructing, at least at times, the light of the sun and moon, but it is very doubtful whether this consciously troubled him.[1]

We may assume that the rings are one earth-diameter thick. The variants in the reported sizes (diameters) of the rings of sun and moon (27 and 18 or 28 and 19 times the size of the earth) were, since Burnet's time (*EGP*, 68), accounted for as measurements to the inner or outer surface of the rings, until Kirk pointed out the simple fact that this requires a difference of two earth-diameters, not one. He suggests that 'the larger figure might represent the diameter from outer edge to outer edge, the smaller one that from points half-way between the inner and outer edges of the actual felloe of air' (KR, 136). In any case the larger figures are likely to have been some commentator's refinement on the simple scheme of Anaximander expressed in multiples of three. No statement of the size of the star-rings is preserved, but since the diameter of the earth is said to be three times its height (p. 98, below), it looks as if these numbers have a conventional or sacred origin which

[1] See on this point Heath, *Aristarchus*, 31, Burnet, *EGP*, 68, Kahn, *Anaximander*, 89 f. Burnet suggests, referring to Homer, that in early Greek thought *aer* could be seen through, although it had the property of rendering invisible anything enclosed in it. Dreyer (*Planetary Systems*, 14) remarks that astronomical observation must have been still so backward that Anaximander had never noticed the frequent occultation of a bright star by the moon. According to the doxography (D.L. IX, 33), Leucippus also placed the path of the sun furthest from the earth, but with the stars between it and the moon. A single statement in the *Placita* (DK, 28 A 40 *a*) seems to credit Parmenides with having placed the fixed stars nearest the earth. His curious doctrine of στεφάναι may well owe something to Anaximander, from whom he might possibly have taken this feature also. It is, however, more likely that the doxographer misunderstood his words. See ZN, 714 with n. 2.

Anaximander has not outgrown; in which case the missing number seems to be nine.[1]

The statement that the visible sun is the same size (of the same diameter) as the earth is, for Anaximander's time, most remarkable. (In the next century Anaxagoras could be prosecuted for saying that it was an incandescent stone larger than the Peloponnese.) It also causes a difficulty if we try to correlate it strictly with the distance of the sun from the earth, i.e. the diameter of its wheel.[2] This need not have presented itself forcibly to his mind, and all the evidence confirms that he was a fearless and original thinker. Perhaps, however, the possibility that the statement is not authentic cannot be altogether excluded.

The well-attested explanation of eclipses, and of the phases of the moon, as due to alternate contracting and opening of the holes in the tubes of mist through which the heavenly bodies are seen, is another indication of the inchoate state of Anaximander's astronomy, and puts out of court the charitable guess of Simplicius that he might already have been capable of using these phenomena to calculate the sizes and distances of the sun and moon.

One can hardly extract further detail on this part of his system with any approach to certainty. Aëtius speaks of the circles of the sun and moon as 'lying obliquely', presumably to the celestial equator, and the phrase is no doubt, as Heath says, an attempt to explain the annual movement of the sun and monthly movement of the moon. Ingenious

---

[1] So, e.g., Tannery, Burnet, Heath, Cornford. In a predominantly sceptical period of scholarship, there is some pleasure in recording the contrary view of R. Baccou (*Hist. de la sc. gr.* 77): 'Quelle impossibilité y a-t-il à imaginer qu'il a mesuré, de manière plus ou moins approximative, l'angle du diamètre apparent du soleil, et que, d'après l'idée qu'il se faisait de la grandeur de la terre—idée naturellement restreinte à l'*oikumene*—il en a déduit les chiffres plus haut cités?' H. Gomperz, in an interesting discussion of the various types of analogy employed by the Presocratics, connects it rather with the sense of fitness and proportion exhibited by a Greek architect or planner in designing a city or a temple (*Journ. Hist. Ideas*, 1943, 166–7). Cf. also W. I. Matson, *Rev. Metaph.* 1954–5, 447: '*Prima facie*, however, we have here an early example of the insistence that Nature must conform to reason, i.e. a sort of embryonic metaphysics of the mathematizing sort. One is presumably supposed to accept the figures because of their inherent reasonableness (*v.* the Pythagorean harmonies)....Moreover, we must not overlook the fact that these figures occur in the context of an astonishingly rational account of the nature of things, which is by no means devoid of references to observation, as Cornford admits.' (The reference is to Cornford, *Princ. Sap.* 165 and 170.) Kahn (*Anaximander*, 94–7) emphasizes the rational element in Anaximander's scheme.

[2] The question is discussed by G. B. Burch in an article on Anaximander (*Rev. Metaph.* 1949–50, 137–60), though not all of his ideas are acceptable.

ways have been suggested in which Anaximander may have intended to explain the solstices,[1] but all are conjectural. It is not even certain whether the word 'turnings' (τροπαί), occurring in passages which are evidently meant to apply to Anaximander among others, refers to the solstices[2] or simply, as it sometimes does, to the revolutions of the heavenly bodies.[3] In the passage of the *Meteorologica* quoted on p. 92, Aristotle states that the action of the heavenly fire in drying up the water caused 'winds and the turnings of the sun and moon'. Commenting on this Alexander says (omitted from the translation above):

From it [that is, that part of the original moisture which was vaporized by the sun] arose winds and turnings of the sun and moon, the notion being that the turnings (revolutions?) of those bodies too are accounted for by these vapours and exhalations, since they turn in those regions where they receive a plentiful supply of the moisture.

Here is a clear reference to the early idea that the cosmic fires, or heavenly bodies, are 'nourished' by moisture (for which see above, p. 67).[4] Further than that this second- or third-hand description will hardly allow us to go. Anaximander may have been supposing the limits of the sun's path in the ecliptic to be fixed by the abundance, in a certain region of the sky, of the moisture on which it depended for its existence; or he may have been trying to produce a theory to account for the whole fact of the cosmic revolutions, suggesting that the motion was started and maintained by these currents of air which the evaporating process somehow set up. We are not offered any other explanation of the revolving motion of the cosmic circles, and the only alternative is to suppose that the movement was somehow implanted

---

[1] For which see Heath, *Aristarchus*, 32 ff. Heidel (*CP*, 1912, 233, n. 4) thought it very probable that the 'ordinance of time' in the one extant fragment of Anaximander refers to the obliquity of the ecliptic, which, he says, Anaximander is said to have discovered. He notes how well this would fit with the designation of the litigants as the opposites—hot and cold, wet and dry.

[2] And to a parallel phenomenon of the moon, of which, however, Zeller considered that it was most unlikely that Anaximander would have been aware. Dreyer (*Planetary Systems*, 17, n. 1) disagrees.

[3] Arist. *Meteor.* 353b8 (quoted above, p. 92), 355a25. In the latter passage Zeller pointed out that according to the most natural meaning of τὰς τροπὰς αὐτοῦ Aristotle is speaking of the 'turnings' of the *heaven*, not of the sun. (ZN, 298, n. 4, Heath, *Aristarchus*, 33, n. 3.) For the contrary view see Cherniss, *ACP*, 135, n. 544.

[4] Cherniss, *op. cit.* 135, n. 544, disagrees, mainly because *Meteorol.* 355a24-5 'shows definitely that it is *air* and not moisture which causes the turnings'. But there is certainly moisture in ἀήρ.

by the 'eternal motion' of the Boundless, the nature of which is not specified. In 'giving birth' to its 'offspring' the cosmos, it produced no still-born child. Language like this has been shown to be appropriate to Anaximander's thoughts in no merely metaphorical sense. Ingenuous as it sounds, this explanation is on the whole the more likely. Enough remains to show that astronomy was still in its infancy among the Greeks. The strength of someone like Anaximander lay in the bold flight of imaginative reason with which he sketched the outlines of a cosmos, and we may agree with Dreyer that 'probably the system never advanced beyond a mere sketch and was not worked out in detail'.

The evidence for the shape and position of the earth is as follows:

(*a*) [Plut.] *Strom.* (A 10, in same context as the passage quoted on p. 90): 'And he says that the earth is cylindrical in shape, with a breadth three times its depth.'

(*b*) Hippolytus, *Ref.* 1, 6, 3 (A 11): 'The earth hangs freely, not by the compulsion of any force but remaining where it is owing to its equal distance from everything. In shape it is rounded [see below for this word], circular, like the drum of a column; of its surfaces one is that on which we stand, and there is another opposite.'[1] Aëtius (A 25) repeats that the earth 'resembles the drum of a column'.

(*c*) The reason why the earth remains at the centre had previously been more fully given by Aristotle (*De Caelo*, 295 b 10, A 26): 'But there are some who name its "indifference"[2] as the cause of its remaining at rest, e.g. among the ancients Anaximander. These argue that that which is situated at the centre and is equably related to the extremes has no impulse to move in one direction—either upwards or downwards or sideways—rather than in another; and since it is impossible for it to accomplish movement in opposite directions at once, it necessarily remains at rest.'

(*d*) Eudemus, *Astronomy*, quoted by Theo (p. 198.18 Hiller, A 26) *via* Dercyllides: 'Anaximander says that the earth is freely suspended and moves around the centre of the universe.'

The exact meaning of the word γυρόν (translated by 'rounded' in passage (*b*); it is a correction for the impossible ὑγρόν of the manu-

---

[1] This translation depends on several corrections of the received text, for which see Diels's apparatus, and cf. Cornford, *Princ. Sap.* 166, n. 2.

[2] So Burnet and Stocks translate ὁμοιότητα; see Stocks's note *ad loc.* in the Oxford translation. The context makes the meaning clear.

scripts)[1] is difficult to determine. The lexica gloss it as both 'round' and 'convex', and it is used of a round-shouldered person in the *Odyssey* (XIX, 246). Anaximander, if he used the word, may have meant that the surfaces of the earth are not flat but convex, as observation might suggest, though this would make the comparison to 'the stone of a column' less appropriate. The corresponding noun (γῦρος) is used of something ring-shaped, as for example a trench dug round a tree, and another possibility is that Anaximander meant to indicate that the earth had a hole at the centre, thus bringing its shape into line with the circles of the heavenly bodies around it. Column-drums often had such a hole.[2]

The statement quoted from Eudemus in passage (*d*), that the earth is in motion, need not be taken too seriously. In the same passage Eudemus is credited with a probably exaggerated account of Thales's astronomical knowledge and with saying that Anaximenes discovered the cause of eclipses of the moon and the fact that its light is derived from the sun. As Zeller suggests, and Alexander seems to have suspected, there has probably been a misunderstanding of the words in which Anaximander expressed his highly original notion that the earth floats freely in space with nothing to keep it stationary.[3]

Anaximander's most striking contribution to cosmological theory was undoubtedly to emancipate himself from the idea that the earth needed a support. The belief that it floated on water was, as we saw, an inheritance from mythology perpetuated by Thales, and intellectually it was a leap forward when the argument from 'indifference' was invoked in favour of the view that it remained unsupported at the centre of a spherical universe, and that the heavenly bodies revolved in complete circles below as well as above it. Nothing shows more clearly

[1] By Roeper and Diels, and generally accepted. Kahn (*Anaximander*, 56) has recently defended ὑγρόν, but I cannot agree that τὸ σχῆμα ὑγρόν is a natural expression for 'its character is moist', especially when followed by στρογγύλον.

[2] It is interesting that the Babylonian map illustrated by Kahn as a probable prototype of Anaximander's (*Anaximander*, pl. 1) not only shows the world as circular but has a round hole in the middle. This is explained as 'probably left by the scribe's compass', but only because 'there is at any rate no other good explanation' (*op. cit.* 83).

[3] ZN, 303, Alex. *ap.* Simpl. *De Caelo*, 532.6ff. Burnet's contrary view (*EGP*, 66) is bound up with certain other preconceptions which are not necessarily correct. We need not avail ourselves of the emendation of Montucla κεῖται for κινεῖται, though κεῖται περὶ τὸ τοῦ κόσμου μέσον would be a very precise description if, as is quite likely, Anaximander thought of the disc of the earth as having a hole in the centre.

7-2

the independent quality of Anaximander's mind, and, as we shall see, the advance was too rapid for some of his successors. Nearly two centuries later, Plato paid him the compliment of making Socrates adopt his view, when he said in the *Phaedo* (108E, trans. A. J. Church):

In the first place then, I believe that the earth is a spherical body placed in the centre of the heavens, and that therefore it has no need of air or any other force to support it: the equiformity[1] of the heavens in all their parts, and the equipoise of the earth itself, are sufficient to hold it up. A thing in equipoise placed at the centre of what is equiform cannot incline in any direction, either more or less: it will remain unmoved and in perfect balance.

Clearly the recognition of the earth's sphericity could not be long delayed, but it did not appear first in the Milesian tradition, and the mention of air is a reminder that later Ionians went back to the more simple-minded notion that the earth needed material support, for they supposed it to be buoyed up by air.

We are told (and might in any case have assumed) that just as the world-order had a beginning out of the *apeiron*, so also it will have an end, fading back, as it were, into the formless state from which it came. Only the *apeiron* itself is 'eternal and ageless', 'immortal and indestructible'. So Aëtius (A 14):

Anaximander of Miletus, son of Praxiades, says that the first principle of existing things is the Boundless; for from this all come into being and into it all perish. Wherefore innumerable worlds are both brought to birth and again dissolved into that out of which they came.

But our sources nowhere explain how this will occur. It looks as if Anaximander were less interested in the end of a world than in its beginning. The one sentence of his which we possess (if indeed this first part of the sentence is his) has been commonly held to refer to it in the words: 'Things perish into that out of which they have their being': but in fact this obviously describes the transformation of the elements into one another, which, far from signifying the destruction of the world, is the process by which it is maintained.[2]

[1] For ὁμοιότης as similarity in the geometrical sense see Kahn, *Anaximander*, 79, n. 3.

[2] P. 81, above. Heidel saw this, *CP*, 1912, 233–4. As to the destruction of the world, Heidel says (234, n. 3): 'No doubt Anaximander believed in the destruction of the world, and so of the opposites also; but he doubtless thought of this as a question of nutrition.' This is very possible, but we are not told.

Destruction of the Cosmos

What seems more relevant is the mention of a time when there will be no more water left, since fire, its opposite, will have prevailed completely and dried it all up.[1] This will clearly upset the balance of the universe which is maintained by the alternate and mutual encroachment of the opposites on each other, followed by their recession as 'penalty' for their 'injustice'. One cannot suppose this cyclic process, taking place as Anaximander says 'according to the ordinance (or assessment) of time', to be anything other than the annual alternation of the seasons. The permanent victory of the hot and dry would obviously disorganize the whole world-order. Cornford connected this possibility with the archaic idea of a 'great summer' and 'great winter', and assumed 'alternate destructions of the world by the Hot and by the Cold moisture'. Our world will be ultimately destroyed by fire, the next by flood.[2] This may have been what Anaximander meant, but if so, it is something different from reabsorption into the *apeiron*, and it is difficult to see how the Hot, having once been allowed to gain the supreme victory—or commit the supreme injustice—could ever be forced to give up its ill-gotten gains. A cosmos starts from a neutral state, not from an extreme. If that is not the thought from which Anaximander started out, which impressed on him the need for an *apeiron* as the *arche* rather than water or anything else, then we have indeed failed in our interpretation of him and there is little chance of success.

(7) Origin of animal and human life

After the formation of a world-order by the separation of the opposites, or elements, into their proper stations, the next stage is the emergence of animal life. This is explained with remarkable consistency (and complete disregard for religious or mythological modes of thought) as due to a continuation of the same process of 'separating-out' through the action of the hot and dry on the cold and moist: for life arose in the moist element through the action on it of the sun's warmth. This theory was probably connected with the persistent belief that even in the present world life is generated 'spontaneously' from the warmth of

[1] Ar. *Meteor.* 353 b 9, quoted above, p. 92.
[2] *Princ. Sap.* 183 f. Certainly, as Cornford says, 'the notion of alternate destruction of at least a great part of mankind by fire and flood was deeply rooted in Greek thought'. Cf. also p. 388, below.

putrescent matter, a belief doubtless based on observation—'an ob-servation', as Dr W. P. D. Wightman has remarked, 'which must have been only too familiar, though misinterpreted, in a warm climate'.[1]

The testimonies are as follows:

(*a*) Hippolytus, *Ref.* I, 6, 6 (A 11): 'He said that living creatures arose from the evaporation of the moist element by the sun; and that man originally resembled another creature, namely a fish.'

(*b*) Aëtius V, 19, 4 (A 30): 'Anaximander said that the first animals were born in moisture and surrounded by prickly integuments,[2] but that as they grew older they emerged on to the drier part, the integument split off, and they lived on[3] for a short time.'

(*c*) [Plut.] *Strom.* (A 10, continuation of the passages quoted on pp. 90 and 98): 'He says moreover that originally man was born from creatures of a different species, on the grounds that whereas other creatures quickly find food for themselves, man alone needs a long period of suckling; hence if he had been originally what he is now he could never have survived.'

The references to the origin of mankind are naturally of particular interest. So far we have nothing inconsistent with the supposition that Anaximander was describing its gradual evolution, on Darwinian lines, from some marine species. Indeed the statement of Hippolytus, that man 'originally *resembled* another creature, namely a fish', would, by itself, hardly allow a different interpretation. Yet this does not seem to have been in fact what he meant. Plutarch in his *Quaestiones Conviviales* (730E, A 30) says that at first ·men were born *in* fish, and makes this meaning clearer by contrasting it with the more plausible view that they are related to them. The guests are discussing the custom of abstaining from fish on religious grounds. One of them mentions examples of people who do this because they worship Poseidon as Fosterer and Ancestor, believing, like the Syrians, that man arose from the wet element. 'For this reason,' he continues, 'they reverence the fish as

---

[1] *Growth of Scientific Ideas*, 14. Spontaneous generation seemed an incontrovertible fact to Aristotle (unfortunately for him, since it made an awkward exception to his general theory of the workings of nature), and the belief lingered on in Europe until the nineteenth century. See Guthrie, *In the Beginning*, 41 f. J. A. Wilson in *Before Philosophy*, 59, says that the modern Egyptian peasant still believes in the life-giving power of the mud left behind by the retreating Nile. (Both these last writers quote further illustrations of the belief.)

[2] φλοιοῖς, the same word which is used for the bark of a tree in the passage from the *Stromateis* quoted on p. 90, above.

[3] Or 'lived a different life' (i.e. on land). See KR, 141, 142.

kindred and foster-brother, displaying a more reasonable philosophy than Anaximander; for he does not class fish and men together, but declares that men were first born in fish, and having been nurtured in the manner of *galei* and become capable of looking after themselves, they emerged and occupied the land. And so just as fire devours the matter in which it was kindled and which is father and mother to it (as the writer said who interpolated the wedding of Ceyx in Hesiod), so Anaximander, having shown the fish to be the common father and mother of men, put us off eating it.'[1]

The Latin writer Censorinus gives an even clearer account to the same effect (IV, 7, A 30):

Anaximander of Miletus said that in his opinion there arose out of water and earth, when warmed, either fish or creatures resembling fish. In these creatures men were formed, and the young were retained within until the time of puberty; then at last the creatures were broken open and men and women emerged already capable of finding their own nourishment.

The theory of Anaximander seems then to have been that human embryos grew inside the bodies of the early fish-like creatures, and later emerged as fully-formed men and women. His account proceeds in the first place by deduction from the hypothesis that all life had its origin in moist slime acted on by the heat of the sun, this being in its turn only a particular stage in the evolution of the cosmos by the inter-action of the opposites. It would acquire seeming confirmation either from observation or from the lore of Egyptians or Orientals. The first living creatures must therefore have been of a kind suited to a moist habitat, perhaps rather like the prickly sea-urchin. A human infant could hardly have survived under these conditions unless some special

---

[1] The last sentence is troublesome. Its logic seems to require, if Anaximander acted 'just like' the fire, that he did eat fish, or approve of eating it. This would also be a satisfactory reason why his philosophy was less ἐπιεικής ('humane') than that of the Syrians and others. Plutarch no doubt knew nothing of Anaximander's actual habits of diet. But again, if this were so, he would be more likely to assume that like most ordinary men he ate fish than that he preached an absten-tion for which there is no other evidence at all. Yet the negative sense of διέβαλε πρός seems un-doubted, however much one would like it to mean 'he mistreated as food': cf. 727 D ἄπωθεν ἡμᾶς πρὸς ἐκεῖνα τὰ πάθη διαβάλλοντες and 809 F πρὸς τὴν κακίαν διαβαλοῦμεν αὐτούς. If the text is sound, it must be intended to convey that Anaximander deprecated the eating of fish because it resembled the action of fire in devouring parents, and the 'unreasonableness' of his philosophy consists simply in the fact that he justified the ban by his queer idea of men coming out of fish rather than being ὁμογενεῖς καὶ σύντροφοι with them. But if so, it is not very well expressed.

protection were devised, and here the example of the *galeus* came to his mind as a possible solution. This name was applied to dogfish or sharks, and Plutarch, commenting on the parental affection of *galei*, says (*De Soll. Anim.* 982c): 'They produce an egg, and then the creature itself, not outside, but within their own bodies, and nurse it there and carry it as if there had been a second birth. Then when they have grown larger they put them forth'; and more clearly in *De Amore Prolis* 494c: 'The *galei* in particular reproduce viviparously, and allow their young to issue forth and feed, then take them back and enfold them in the womb to rest.'

The species that Plutarch has in mind is no doubt the smooth dogfish (*mustelus levis*, Aristotle's γαλεὸς ὁ λεῖος), a viviparous variety which forms 'the subject of one of Aristotle's most celebrated descriptions, and a famous example of his anatomical erudition'.[1] Aristotle (*HA*, 565b1) refers to the remarkable peculiarity that 'the young develop with the navel-string attached to the womb, so that, as the egg-substance gets used up, the embryo is sustained, to all appearances, just as in the case of quadrupeds. The navel-string is long, and adheres to the under part of the womb (each navel-string being attached as it were by a sucker), and also to the middle of the embryo where the liver lies.' He also associates himself with the common belief that '*galei* in general can extrude their young and take them back again' (565b24), a belief which persisted in the middle ages. Burnet (*EGP*, 71, n. 2) thinks that Anaximander's comparison is sufficiently accounted for by the anatomical details of the placenta and umbilical cord, and that there is no need to associate him with the other belief. Much as one would like to discover such faithfulness to observed fact in the first youth of Greek natural philosophy, it seems hardly likely that Anaximander disowned a belief which was still seriously held by Aristotle, and which undoubtedly provides the best illustration for his purpose.[2]

---

[1] D'Arcy Thompson, *Glossary of Greek Fishes*, 41. See Thompson *s.v.* γαλεός for further information.

[2] After all this discussion, it must be pointed out that the appearance of the γαλεοί in Plutarch's reference to Anaximander depends on an emendation of the MS. text, which reads ὥσπερ οἱ παλαιοί. (See DK, crit. n. *ad loc*.) This makes no sense, and the correction may be taken as certain, especially since the difference between the two words, to a Byzantine copyist, might be no more than that between ΓΑΛΕΟΙ and ΓΑΛΕΟΙ. Kirk however believes (KR, 142) that the comparison may

(8) *Meteorology*

Anaximander's reported views on meteorological phenomena provide further illustration of his principle of consistency, that events in the present world must be attributed to the continued operation of the same forces and processes that brought about its formation in the beginning. This is especially obvious in his explanation of wind, which he regarded as a flow of air, or as air in motion.

(*a*) Aëtius (A24): 'Wind is a flow of air, occurring when the finest [and most moist] elements in it are set in motion [or liquefied] by the sun.' (The reason for the brackets will appear below.)

(*b*) Hippolytus, *Ref.* 1, 6, 7 (A11): 'Winds are produced when the finest vapours of the air are separated off, and being gathered together are set in motion; rain out of the evaporation given off from the earth by the sun's action.'[1]

As O. Gilbert remarked (*Meteor. Theorien*, 512), the brief note about Anaximander inserted by Aëtius in his section on winds seems to have conflated Theophrastus's reports of his explanation of winds on the one hand and rain on the other. Comparison with Hippolytus suggests that the cosmogonic process of *apokrisis* is still at work. After water had been separated from earth, the sun drew vapour up from the water to form the atmosphere. This in its turn, as the 'separating-out' continues, divides into two substances, a lighter (finer, drier) and a heavier (wetter). The former is set in motion as wind, the latter precipitated as rain. It is all part of the same operation of peripheral heat on the moist centre which in due course was responsible for the emergence of life.[2]

not be Anaximander's, but put in by Plutarch as throwing light on Anaximander's theory. This is of course possible, but I do not agree with Kirk that the knowledge which it displays is 'unlikely' for Anaximander. Inhabitants of an ancient seaport probably knew more about the facts of life among fishes than do the unscientific among ourselves.

[1] Reading uncertain. Translated here is τῆς ἐκ γῆς ὑπὸ τοῦ ἡλίου ἀναδιδομένης. Cf. Diels, note on *Dox.* 560.10, Gilbert, *op. cit.* 406, n.

[2] The theory bears a superficial resemblance to Aristotle's, and might therefore come under suspicion of having been brought into conformity by our sources under Peripatetic influence. Starting from his assumption of two sorts of exhalation, a dry and a wet, Aristotle continues (*Meteor*, 360a11): 'Of these the exhalation containing the greater quantity of moisture is the origin of rainwater, whereas the dry one is the origin and substance of winds.' But he goes on to emphasize that, since the two exhalations are specifically different, the natural substances of wind and rain are also different, and from that to criticize those who claim that the same substance, air, becomes wind when set in motion (κινούμενον) and rain when condensed (συνιστάμενον). This

Once the air has been separated into wind (the light and dry part) and rain-cloud (the heavy and wet), these, and in particular the wind, are made to account for thunder and lightning. Thus Aëtius (A23), in his section on thunder, lightning, meteorites, waterspouts and whirlwinds:

Anaximander says that all these are caused by wind. When it is imprisoned in thick cloud and forces a way out by reason of its fine texture and lightness, then the tearing makes the noise, and the contrast with the blackness of the cloud produces the flash.[1]

It would appear that, in the process of 'separating-out' of the air into wind and cloud, some of the lighter and finer sort may find itself so completely surrounded by the denser that it cannot easily complete the process of 'gathering together' with its like. The result is a violent explosion of the cloud, perceived by us as thunder and lightning.

Additional note: 'innumerable worlds'

Anaximander's belief in 'innumerable worlds' has been the subject of vexed and difficult controversy. Its natural place is earlier in the exposition, but it seemed best to reserve it for an addendum owing to its complexity and the fact that the problem cannot be stated at all without constant reference to the Greek. Full discussion demands more minute collation and examination of testimonies than is possible in a general work, but it should be worth while to indicate the points at issue and their bearing on the general history of early Greek thought.

Post-Aristotelian sources speak of Anaximander as having believed in the existence of ἄπειροι κόσμοι or ἄπειροι οὐρανοί—innumerable worlds or heavens. (The phrase is ἄπειροι τῷ πλήθει in Simpl. *Cael.* 202.14.) The main question at issue is whether this means a *succession*

was inevitably the view of the monist Anaximander, whose theory of progressive ἀπόκρισις from a single original substance involves as a necessary consequence that the substance forming wind and rain is ultimately one. Cf. 349a20, where the same people are also said to define wind as κίνησιν ἀέρος, and see also Gilbert, *op. cit.* 523, n. 2. Kahn (*Anaximander*, 63) retains the full text of Aët. and offers an explanation.

[1] Briefer statements are found in Hippolytus (A11) and Seneca (A23). Kahn (*Anaximander*, 108) has pointed out how authentically this theory is reproduced by Aristophanes in the *Clouds* (404–7).

of worlds following one another in time, or an innumerable *crowd* of worlds coexisting in the vast body of the *apeiron*. Zeller argued for an endless succession of single worlds. Burnet (*EGP*, 58 ff.) contested this, and maintained strongly that Anaximander must have taught the existence of an infinite number of coexisting worlds. Nestle, re-editing Zeller's history of Greek philosophy after his death, was persuaded by Burnet's arguments (ZN, 312, n.). Then in 1934 Cornford, in an article in the *Classical Quarterly* (1934, 1–16), vigorously defended the original view of Zeller, subjecting the evidence to a thorough re-examination and adducing fresh arguments in favour of the conception of a temporal succession of single worlds.

Unfortunately Aristotle himself provides no definite lead. He nowhere attributes a doctrine of ἄπειροι κόσμοι or ἄπειροι οὐρανοί explicitly to Anaximander. Speaking in *De Caelo* (303 b 10) of philosophers who posit one element alone, 'either water or air or fire or a substance rarer than water but denser than air', he says that according to them 'this element is infinite and embraces πάντας τοὺς οὐρανούς'; but it is at least doubtful whether in this passage he has Anaximander in mind,[1] even if we could say that by οὐρανοί he meant 'worlds'.

All our testimonies therefore are later, and cannot be directly referred back to Aristotle. They attribute to Anaximander either (*a*) ἄπειροι οὐρανοί or (*b*) ἄπειροι κόσμοι or (*c*) both οὐρανοί and κόσμοι. It may be convenient to have the passages collected, though some of course must be seen in context before being made the basis of further investigations.

(*a*) Aët. *ap.* Stob. (A 17): ᾿Α. ἀπεφήνατο τοὺς ἀπείρους οὐρανοὺς θεούς. The *Placita* however have τοὺς ἀστέρας οὐρανίους θεούς. See Cornford, *op. cit.* 10.

(*b*) (i) Simpl. *Cael.* 615.15 (A 17): ἄπειρον δὲ πρῶτος ὑπέθετο, ἵνα ἔχῃ χρῆσθαι πρὸς τὰς γενέσεις ἀφθόνως · καὶ κόσμους δὲ ἀπείρους οὗτος καὶ ἕκαστον τῶν κόσμων ἐξ ἀπείρου τοῦ τοιούτου στοιχείου ὑπέθετο ὡς δοκεῖ.

(ii) Simpl. *Cael.* 202.14 (not in DK): οἱ δὲ καὶ τῷ πλήθει ἀπείρους κόσμους, ὡς ᾿Α. μὲν ἄπειρον τῷ μεγέθει τὴν ἀρχὴν θέμενος ἀπείρους ἐξ αὐτοῦ

---

[1] Burnet (*EGP*, 55 f.) saw in the intermediate element a reference to Anaximander's *apeiron*, and Stocks in his translation followed him, but most scholars have been against the identification, e.g. Zeller and Diels. See especially the arguments against it in Ross's ed. of Arist. *Physics*, p. 482.

The Milesians

τῷ πλήθει κόσμους ποιεῖν δοκεῖ, Λεύκιππος δὲ καὶ Δημόκριτος ἀπείρους τῷ πλήθει τοὺς κόσμους ἐν ἀπείρῳ τῷ κενῷ καὶ ἐξ ἀπείρων τῷ πλήθει τῶν ἀτόμων συνίστασθαί φησι.

In these two passages the use of δοκεῖ seems to indicate a certain suspension of assent on the part of Simplicius. In the first the argument for the *apeiron* being infinite in quantity may well not have been Anaximander's (p. 84, above).

(iii) Simpl. *Phys.* 1121.5 (A 17): οἱ μὲν γὰρ ἀπείρους τῷ πλήθει τοὺς κόσμους ὑποθέμενοι, ὡς οἱ περὶ ᾽Α. καὶ Λεύκιππον καὶ Δημόκριτον καὶ ὕστερον οἱ περὶ ᾽Επίκουρον, γινομένους αὐτοὺς καὶ φθειρομένους ὑπέθεντο ἐπ᾽ ἄπειρον, ἄλλων μὲν ἀεὶ γινομένων ἄλλων δὲ φθειρομένων, καὶ τὴν κίνησιν ἀΐδιον ἔλεγον.

The statement that there were innumerable worlds 'some always coming into being and others passing away' introduces temporal succession as well as spatial plurality. The atomists of course believed in both. The previous phrase, 'assumed them to come into being and pass away everlastingly', would fit Anaximander on the assumption that he believed in only one world at a time. Here he is simply put with the atomists as a believer in innumerable worlds, but in (ii) above Simplicius correctly notes that the atomic world-view was different in that they recognized (*a*) infinite empty space and (*b*) an infinite number of atoms.

(iv) Aëtius (A 14): ᾽Α.... φησὶ τῶν ὄντων ἀρχὴν εἶναι τὸ ἄπειρον· ἐκ γὰρ τούτου πάντα γίγνεσθαι καὶ εἰς τοῦτο πάντα φθείρεσθαι. διὸ καὶ γεννᾶσθαι ἀπείρους κόσμους καὶ πάλιν φθείρεσθαι εἰς τὸ ἐξ οὗ γίγνεσθαι.

This passage in isolation would certainly be taken to refer to successive, not coexistent, worlds.

(v) Aëtius (A 17): ᾽Α., ᾽Αναξιμένης, ᾽Αρχέλαος, Διογένης, Λεύκιππος, Δημόκριτος, ᾽Επίκουρος ἀπείρους κόσμους ἐν τῷ ἀπείρῳ κατὰ πᾶσαν περιαγωγήν. (So Stobaeus. Ps.-Plutarch mentions only Democritus and Epicurus and has περίστασιν for περιαγωγήν.)

It is clear that after Epicurus had popularized the atomic doctrine of innumerable worlds in infinite space there was a tendency to read this view back into all earlier physical theory. On Anaximenes contrast Simpl. *Cael.* 202.13, where he is said to have believed in ἕνα ἄπειρον κόσμον in explicit contrast to Anaximander's belief in τῷ πλήθει ἀπείρους κόσμους. See on this Cornford, *op. cit.* 5. Moreover, as Cornford noted, Ps.-Plutarch not only omits the Milesians from the believers in innumerable worlds, but speaks of Θαλῆς καὶ οἱ ἀπ' αὐτοῦ (which must surely include Anaximander) as having believed that our world exists alone.

The words κατὰ πᾶσαν περιαγωγήν (or περίστασιν) are rather obscure. Burnet, holding that Anaximander did believe in innumerable coexistent worlds, and that these were visible as the stars, rendered: 'in whichever direction we turn'; Zeller, more reasonably, 'in every cycle' (of generation and destruction).

(vi) Aëtius (A 17): τῶν ἀπείρους ἀποφηναμένων τοὺς κόσμους 'Α. τὸ ἴσον αὐτοὺς ἀπέχειν ἀλλήλων, 'Επίκουρος ἄνισον εἶναι τὸ μεταξὺ τῶν κόσμων διάστημα.

The significance of this sentence will be referred to below.

(vii) Cicero, *N.D.* I, 10, 25 (A 17): *Anaximandri autem opinio est nativos esse deos longis intervallis orientes occidentesque, eosque innumerabiles esse mundos.*

(viii) Augustine, *Civ. Dei* VIII, 2 (A 17): *Non enim ex una re sicut Thales ex umore, sed ex suis propriis principiis quasque res nasci putavit. Quae rerum principia singularum esse credidit infinita, et innumerabiles mundos gignere et quaecumque in eis oriuntur; eosque mundos modo dissolvi modo iterum gigni existimavit, quanta quisque aetate sua manere potuerit, nec ipse aliquid divinae menti in his rerum operibus tribuens.*

This passage by itself would not be inconsistent with the idea of a succession of single worlds, but no doubt Augustine's source shared the view that Anaximander believed in innumerable worlds in the same sense as Epicurus.

I have referred already (p. 87, n. 2) to the difficulty experienced by later interpreters in deciding whether Anaximander's *apeiron* ought to be classed as a monistic substratum or a mixture. His thought was too primitive to recognize its own inconsistency.

(c) (i) Simpl. *Phys.* 24.16 (A9): λέγει δ' αὐτὴν μήτε ὕδωρ μήτε ἄλλο τι τῶν καλουμένων εἶναι στοιχείων, ἀλλ' ἑτέραν τινὰ φύσιν ἄπειρον, ἐξ ἧς ἅπαντας γίνεσθαι τοὺς οὐρανοὺς καὶ τοὺς ἐν αὐτοῖς κόσμους.

The Milesians

(ii) Hippol. *Ref.* 1, 6, 1 (A 11): οὗτος ἀρχὴν ἔφη τῶν ὄντων φύσιν τινὰ τοῦ ἀπείρου, ἐξ ἧς γίνεσθαι τοὺς οὐρανοὺς καὶ τὸν ἐν αὐτοῖς κόσμον.

If Hippolytus in writing the singular κόσμον has correctly reproduced the text of Theophrastus, we may take it that the meaning was, as DK say, not 'worlds in them' but 'order inherent in them'. (Diels, *Dox.* 132f., after lauding Hippolytus as 'fidissimum excerptorem', changed the manuscript reading to κόσμους to bring it into line with passages (i) and (iii).)

(iii) Plut. *Strom.* (A 10): τὸ ἄπειρον...ἐξ οὗ δή φησι τούς τε οὐρανοὺς ἀποκεκρίσθαι καὶ καθόλου τοὺς ἅπαντας ἀπείρους ὄντας κόσμους.

This passage, in which the worlds have become 'innumerable', the words ἐν αὐτοῖς are missing, and ἅπαντας has been transferred from οὐρανούς to κόσμους, has come into line with the atomist conception of innumerable worlds. Simplicius and Hippolytus on the other hand, by putting the κόσμοι in the οὐρανοί, appear to deny it (Cornford, *op. cit.* 11).

In general, 'a close examination of the doxographic tradition shows that the further it gets from Aristotle and Theophrastus, the oftener κόσμοι is substituted for οὐρανοί and the more is heard of ἄπειροι κόσμοι' (Cornford, *ibid.*).

No less than the word ἄπειρον, the words κόσμος and οὐρανός, as used by those who were trying to interpret Anaximander, had more than one meaning. It is perhaps more probable than not that Anaximander himself did not use κόσμος in the sense of world or universe. Basically the word meant 'order', though from an early date it combined with this the meaning of 'adornment'. (Order was after all, in Greek eyes, a beautiful thing.) Because, to a Greek thinker, the most notable thing about the universe was the order which it displayed (above all in events on a cosmic scale like the movements of sun, moon and stars), and this was what contrasted it most radically with the chaos which he supposed to have preceded it, the word took on in addition the special meaning of 'world-order' and then simply 'world'. This happened gradually, and there are passages in which it is difficult to be sure how far it has progressed (for example Heraclitus, fr. 30); but it is unlikely that the word, thus baldly used, would be unequivocally understood as 'world' before the fifth century B.C. It is, however, so used by Empedocles in the middle of that century.[1] Whatever Anaximander wrote, our sources are interpreting, not quoting it.

In later philosophical writing, κόσμος can mean (*a*) world-order, universe; (*b*) a separate region within the world-order. Grammarians say that Homer divided the universe (τὸ πᾶν) into five κόσμοι: οὐρανός, water, air, earth, Olympus. (Other instances also in Cornford, *op. cit.* I.)

Οὐρανός was used in three senses, distinguished by Aristotle in *De Caelo* (278b9ff.): (i) the outermost circumference of the universe; (ii) the heavens in general, including the paths of fixed stars, planets, sun and moon, which were believed to lie in different planes, some nearer to, some further from the centrally situated earth; (iii) the universe as a whole. This certainly seems sufficient to justify Cornford's claim that 'doxographers, meeting with statements derived from Theophrastus about a plurality of κόσμοι or οὐρανοί, might well be in doubt as to the meaning of the word'.

Briefly Cornford's view, which is given here as the most reasonable yet produced, was that when Anaximander spoke, as he doubtless did (in whatever Greek terms), of an infinite plurality of worlds, he meant a succession of single worlds in time. When he mentioned ἄπειροι οὐρανοί, saying for instance that they were gods, he did not mean worlds but something different to which we shall come in a moment. Statements which refer unambiguously to innumerable coexistent worlds (for example (*b*) (vi), above), or in which it would be strained to say that the idea is not present, arose from a confusion between οὐρανοί and κόσμοι. This confusion is not due to Theophrastus, but had its origin in assumptions natural enough once the Epicureans had made generally familiar the atomists' doctrine of innumerable worlds arising haphazard at different points in infinite space.

If we agree that Anaximander held the doctrine of an everlasting succession of single worlds, we need not bring into it, as Cornford did, the wording of our single verbal fragment of Anaximander (discussed above, pp. 80f.). His statement that things perish into that out of which

---

[1] Emped. fr. 134, 5. See p. 208, n. 1, below, and for a good general discussion of the word Kahn, *Anaximander* 219–30.

they come, because they must make just recompense to one another, seems rather to describe the cyclic, seasonal rhythm that goes to the maintenance of a single cosmos, not the reabsorption of the separated contents of a cosmos back into the primal *apeiron*. But he held that the world-order, as it had had a beginning, would also perish, and contrasted it with the immortal and indestructible character of the *apeiron* itself. This is doubtless the meaning of the statement about ἄπειροι κόσμοι in Aëtius ((*b*) (iv), above), which certainly seems to refer to successive worlds.

The statement from Aëtius in Stobaeus, that Anaximander called the ἀπείρους οὐρανούς gods,[1] refers on this view to the innumerable rings of fire which are the stars, and which resulted from the splitting apart of the original sphere of fire which surrounded the world at its beginning. These it would be natural to call οὐρανοί, in a sense corresponding to one of those given by Aristotle, that is, any of the many heavens which carry the heavenly bodies. Up to the time of Anaximander, the Greeks had generally supposed that there was one single Ouranos, and this Ouranos was of course a god, well known as such from the theogony of Hesiod and elsewhere. In the strange and original cosmogony of Anaximander it had split up and become many, and it is reasonable enough that he should both have emphasized the fact that there were now ἄπειροι οὐρανοί and have retained the idea of their divinity, especially since another ancient belief, which persisted in the philosophers down to Plato and Aristotle and beyond, was the belief in the divinity of the stars. When he is reported as having spoken of these οὐρανοὺς καὶ τὸν ἐν αὐτοῖς κόσμον (or τοὺς...κόσμους), then, 'the "heavens" being the rings of the heavenly bodies, the κόσμος or κόσμοι in them may be the region or regions of the world-order framed by them' (Cornford, 11).

Whether or not Burnet was right in maintaining with some of the doxographers the opposite view, that Anaximander believed in the simultaneous existence of a plurality of universes like our own, scattered through the infinity of the *apeiron*, he says one thing which is certainly contrary to what evidence we have. That is, that

---

[1] The substitution of ἀστέρας οὐρανίους in Plutarch's version may represent, as Cornford suggested, a gloss on the other. If so, it is a correct interpretation.

these innumerable worlds are the stars themselves. The stars are parts of *this* cosmos, formed from its original outer envelope of fire.

If Anaximander said that there was an endless succession of single worlds, and also spoke of ἄπειροι οὐρανοί meaning a large number of heavenly circles which we see as the stars, it is obvious that he used language open to misconstruction if there was any antecedent temptation on the part of the doxographers to misconstrue him. This temptation was provided by the fact that the atomists of the fifth century did believe in the coexistence of innumerable worlds in infinite space, and in fact we find Anaximander expressly linked with them, and with their successors the Epicureans, when he is described as having held the same belief (cf. (*b*) (iii), (v), above). The curious post-Epicurean statement quoted above as (*b*) (vi), assuming that the writer is thinking of spatial and not temporal distance (and so far as Epicurus is concerned he doubtless had the *intermundia* in mind), may well reflect the confusion already noted between κόσμοι and οὐρανοί. The distances between the οὐρανοί of Anaximander (sun to moon, moon to stars, stars to earth) were in fact equal, being of nine earth-diameters (Cornford, 12). In Cicero's sentence ((*b*) (vii)) it is very difficult to decide whether the *longa intervalla* are spatial or temporal, but in any case his source was probably influenced by the Epicurean theory.

We know, however, that the belief of the atomists in innumerable worlds was closely reasoned from their ideas about the nature of body and of space. Not only is there no evidence for these ideas in Anaximander, but one may say with confidence that a clear philosophic distinction between body and empty space was not made before the fifth century, when it resulted from the criticism brought to bear by Parmenides on earlier systems. The early monists had identified all that exists (τὸ ὄν) with their primary *physis*, which was a material body. Their logic had gone no further, but, said Parmenides, in effect, if material body comprises the whole of that which exists (τὸ ὄν), then what is not body cannot exist, that is, empty space is μὴ ὄν, non-existent. In the face of this unanswerable reasoning (for so it seemed at the time) it required considerable boldness on the part of Leucippus and Democritus to assert the existence of empty space, and they could only do it in paradoxical terms. 'They said that the non-existent exists no less than the existent.'[1]

Having asserted their right to speak of empty space as distinct from any form of body, they went on to show that it must be strictly infinite, using the kind of arguments which seem obvious today but had probably not been thought of before.[2] In this infinite space they supposed there to be an infinite number of atoms of different shapes, drifting with aimless motion. If they formed a world-order in one part of the infinite void, it was unreasonable to suppose that they would not do so elsewhere, though doubtless all the *cosmoi* would not be the same as ours.[3]

The picture of reality presented by Anaximander is very different from this, and represents, as should now be clear, a much more inchoate state of thought. His *apeiron* is not empty space but body, and, more than that, a body which is living and divine. This last fact gives additional support to the supposition that he did not imagine it as strictly infinite in extent. We have already seen that his mind had probably not grasped the notion of strict spatial infinity, and apart from that it is difficult to believe that any Greek thought of a divine being as infinite in extent. The pantheism of Xenophanes saw the divine All as a sphere, and the aura of divinity still clings to spherical shape in Aristotle, who regards the οὐρανός as divine and says that the sphere is the only fitting shape for it on account of its perfection. Just as the earth is at the centre of the spherical universe, so Anaximander may have vaguely imagined that the universe as a whole arose and had its being and perished within a divine and spherical *apeiron*. 'Vaguely imagined', let us say, for, astonishingly rational as his system was in many ways, it looks as if this were something he had taken for granted because the Greek mind was not yet ready to argue out the implications contained in the notions of the infinity or non-infinity of space.

(Kirk deals with the question of innumerable worlds in Anaximander in KR, 121–6. On pp. 122f. he argues briefly that even the notion of

---

[1] Arist. *Metaph.* 985 b 4 ff. They called the solid τὸ ὄν, and the void τὸ μὴ ὄν: διὸ καὶ οὐθὲν μᾶλλον τὸ ὄν τοῦ μὴ ὄντος εἶναί φασιν.

[2] Some of the arguments repeated by Aristotle in the *Physics* (203 b 23) must come from the atomists.

[3] Hippol. *Ref.* I, 13, 2, Democritus, A 40.

successive worlds, as well as coexistent, is implausible for Anaximander. Jaeger in the second edition of *Paideia* (1, 159) declared himself convinced of the coexistence of innumerable worlds in Anaximander, contrary to his previous opinion, by the arguments of Mondolfo's *L'Infinito nel pensiero dei Greci*. See now Kahn, *Anaximander*, 46–53.)

D. ANAXIMENES

(1) *Date and writings*

Anaximenes was also active about the middle of the sixth century, a younger contemporary of Anaximander and probably still a young man when Ionia changed hands after the defeat of the Lydian king Croesus by Cyrus the Persian. He is described as friend, pupil and successor of Anaximander.[1] Diogenes Laertius (II, 3) says that he wrote in 'a simple and economical Ionian style', and although he no doubt took over this verdict from one of his sources it allows us to assume with confidence that the philosopher's works survived into the Hellenistic period. As a criticism it contrasts with Theophrastus's comment on the somewhat poetical language of Anaximander, and the difference in style perhaps reflects a more prosaic and scientific approach on the part of Anaximenes. We hear no more of the opposites conducting a warfare like hostile powers or 'making reparation' for an 'injustice'.

(2) *Air as 'arche'*

Like Anaximander he was still firmly set in the monist tradition. That is to say, the only conceivable explanation of the nature of things was still one which showed how 'all things proceed from one and are resolved into the same'—that dogma which in the eyes of the ancient world went right back to their legendary poets like Musaeus (D.L. 1, 3). The chief interest of his system lies in his abandonment of the almost nameless *apeiron* of Anaximander and the reasons which led him to the choice of a different *arche* for all things. It was no longer to be something known only by its characteristic mark and so described in the

[1] The question of his precise date is complicated. See G. B. Kerferd in *Mus. Helv.* 1954, 117–21. On p. 121 Kerferd seems to treat the word ἑταῖρος rather cavalierly when he suggests that it may imply no more than affinity in doctrine with Anaximander.

baffling way of early Greek thought by an adjective with the article—the hot, the cold, the boundless. These as we have seen were not qualities but qualified things, but Anaximenes chose rather to give his *arche* a directly substantial name. It was air. Perhaps his thought went further than Anaximander's. The Boundless, when it had acquired 'bounds' and become differentiated into the variously qualified components of a cosmos, was no longer the Boundless, but air could be denser or rarer, hotter or colder and still remain the same substance. Though conscious differentiation is still in the future, we are a step nearer to the distinction between substance and quality, that distinction which Aristotle erroneously supposed to have been fully present to the minds of all his predecessors alike.[1] Yet what of the difficulties which Anaximander had presumably felt in making one of the recognizable forms of matter the *arche* of the rest? Perhaps our best starting-point for a consideration of Anaximenes lies in these words of Cyril Bailey (*Greek Atomists and Epicurus*, 17):

It seems at first sight a retrogression that after the singular insight of Anaximander Anaximenes should have gone back to the idea that the primary substance was one of the things known to experience and selected 'air'. But an examination of his theory shows that it was really an advance on Thales and even on Anaximander himself.

It is not difficult to see the apparent retrogression to cruder ways of thought, for it was an intellectual achievement to have understood that all forms of matter known to experience must be regarded as existing on the same level, so that if there is a single primary substance at all it must be a more primitive, a neutral and no longer perceptible state of things, from which all alike had evolved. Why did Anaximenes go back to one of the familiar forms of matter, and how can it be said that in so doing he was making a real advance on Anaximander?

(3) *Unconscious presuppositions*

To introduce the motives which led Anaximenes to his choice of air, it may be useful to make a general observation, which must certainly

---

[1] There is no need to suppose that this step was taken by Thales, even if he did call the *arche* ὕδωρ and not τὸ ὑγρόν. To give this kind of name to it *after* Anaximander was a different thing.

be made some time, about the nature of philosophical thinking as a whole and that of the earliest philosophers in particular. Though not new, it is essential to remind ourselves of it. Philosophy (and science) develop from two different sources. There is what may be called the scientific element proper, the combination of observation and conscious rational thought which is all that the philosopher supposes himself to be using and is often the only factor taken into account by the historian. But in fact no human being makes use of rational thought and observation alone. The second factor is provided by the unconscious presuppositions which are in his mind before he starts philosophizing at all, and which may be an even more powerful influence than the other on the system which he will ultimately produce.

Under this head comes the difference between one individual and another. William James described the history of philosophy as to a great extent that of a clash of human temperaments. Temperament being no conventionally recognized reason, the philosopher urges impersonal reasons only for his conclusions. Yet his temperament gives him a stronger bias than any of his more strictly objective premises. 'He feels men of opposite temper to be out of key with the world's character and in his heart considers them incompetent and "not in it" in the philosophic business, even though they may far excel him in dialectical ability.... There arises thus a certain insincerity in our philosophical discussions; the potentest of all our premises is never mentioned' (*Pragmatism*, 6). Many have made similar observations, as for example Nietzsche, who in *Beyond Good and Evil* says that every great philosophy is 'the confession of its originator, a kind of involuntary and unconscious autobiography. Plato and Aristotle were wrong in naming the desire of knowledge as the parent of philosophy; in fact another impulse has only made use of knowledge as an instrument.' Like most theses, this one can be falsified by being carried to an extreme, but there is much truth in it.

With this form of unconscious presupposition we are less concerned at the moment. It is obvious that the bias of temperament will be potent, for example, in inclining a man to a religious or a materialistic interpretation of the universe, and it may loom more largely when we are ready to discuss the difference between the two main lines of tradition in early Greek philosophy, the Ionian and the Italian or Pythagorean. But in addition to the vagaries of individual temperament, there is another type of presupposition to which men are born, and which finds expression in the very language which they are compelled to use—'that groundwork of current conceptions shared by all men of any given culture and never mentioned because it is taken for granted as obvious'.[1] These traditional conceptions (or it may be a new outlook moulded by the pressure of recent history, as in some of the forms taken by existentialism after the war of 1939) are powerful in every age, but had freer play in the early Greek philosophical systems than in most others. All later systems have had their predecessors. They start by appraising and modifying the systems of others. But the Milesians had no philosophical predecessors. Before they embarked on their conscious reflective activity, the ideas which filled their heads concerning the nature and working of the universe were derived from popular pre-philosophical thought, steeped in myth, and it is perhaps worth noting that the only literature with which they were acquainted was poetical. Moreover the bonds of language, in which all philosophy is to a greater or less degree enmeshed, lay particularly heavy upon them, for they had not the latter-day advantage of reading in a variety of tongues. The degree to which they attained a rational outlook is admittedly astonishing. The mere fact of writing in prose was a great step forward. Indeed the effect of emphasizing the background of popular mythology against which these men must be seen should be rather to increase than to belittle their intellectual stature, by bringing home the difficulties with which they had to contend. At the same time the world-view with which they grew up was not without effect on their maturer thought, and it may sometimes hold the key to an otherwise unintelligible feature of their systems.

This reminder may be useful at various stages of our inquiry. To return to Anaximenes, I would suggest that there were two kinds of

---

[1] F. M. Cornford. See *The Unwritten Philosophy*, viii, and cf. also W. A. Heidel, *Harv. Class. Stud.* 1911, 114: 'Such common points of view would naturally not be the subject of discussion. Just because they constituted the presuppositions of all reflection they would be ignored, although they foreshadowed the inferences to be drawn from them....This fact renders the history of ideas difficult.'

reason which led to his choice of air as the *arche*, one arising out of the train of thought which he was consciously pursuing, the other more entangled in those unconscious presuppositions which were his inheritance from the current and popular views of his time.

(4) *Explanation of change: rarefaction and condensation*

As to the first, the air, we are told, was to be an *arche* in the same sense as the Boundless of Anaximander, as that out of which all things had their being and into which they were all resolved again. (E.g. Aët., B2; Hippol., A7 *init*.) But the problem which especially interested Anaximenes was that of the process by which these changes occurred. If matter did not always remain in its primary state, was it possible to offer any *natural* explanation of why, or at least how, it changed and developed the many manifestations under which it appears in the present world-order? This question of process receives great prominence in all accounts of his system, and we may safely conclude that he thought it one which his predecessors had failed to tackle satisfactorily.

Anaximander's notion of the primitive state of matter had been a fusion of the opposites so complete that their individual characteristics were entirely submerged and *as* opposites they could not yet be said to exist; in his own eyes the *apeiron* was one. Their subsequent emergence was due to a process of separation, a kind of winnowing caused by the eternal motion of the living matrix (the nature of which motion is nowhere specified in our sources). This was a brilliant conjecture, but it was legitimate to suppose that it was entirely arbitrary. Moreover although it doubtless came to Anaximander with the force of a new idea, and he intended the word *ekkrisis* or *apokrisis* to have a purely scientific meaning, we at least may remind ourselves of something else, while recognizing that Anaximenes was in no position to use it as a criticism. We have seen (pp. 68f., above) how this conception of the creation of a cosmos as the separation of what had previously been mingled was at the bottom of many early mythological and poetic cosmogonies, both Greek and other. The examples are sufficient to suggest that there lies behind it some universal tendency of the human mind. It is one of those preconceptions of tradition of which I have spoken, and it is scarcely credible that it did not exert an influence on a pioneer of rational thought like Anaximander in his assertion of 'separation' as the fundamental process behind cosmogony.

Such criticism was not for Anaximenes, but he could at least lay stress on the arbitrary character of the assumption and point out that Anaximander's explanation of the changing forms of things invoked no known and recognizable process of nature. To account for the world-order by natural causes (he seems to have argued), one must show its origin to have been due to some process which can still be verified today as bringing about the transformation of one form of matter into another. Such a verifiable natural process was exactly what Anaximenes had to offer, the process of rarefaction and condensation.

Aristotle in the *Physics* (187a12) divides the natural philosophers before his time into two classes. There are those who regard the underlying substance of things as one, identifying it with water, air, fire or an intermediate body, and generate the rest from it by a process of rarefaction and condensation; and there are those who suppose the contraries to have pre-existed in the single principle, from which they can then be separated out. Their 'one' is therefore in reality a mixture, and among these he puts not only the pluralists Empedocles and Anaxagoras, but also Anaximander, to whose *apeiron* his more analytic mind could not concede true unity.

Among the first class he mentions no names, but the one early philosopher for whom the process of rarefaction and condensation is attested beyond doubt is Anaximenes, whose choice of air as his primary principle Aristotle himself attests (*Metaph.* 984a5). Theophrastus in one part of his history of philosophy went so far as to attribute this explanation of genesis to Anaximenes alone, a statement which Simplicius felt obliged to correct on the authority of Aristotle, who, as he says, in this passage includes a whole class of thinkers alike. There can, however, be little doubt that what Theophrastus says is nearer the truth. Cherniss has shown how Aristotle here, in attempting to accommodate the earlier natural philosophers to his own outlook, has oversimplified his classification.[1] Probably, as Zeller suggested,

[1] Simpl. *Phys.* 149.32, Cherniss, *ACP*, 49 ff., 55. Here is one case at least where Theophrastus has not slavishly followed Aristotle. McDiarmid's note (*Harv. Class. Stud.* 1953, 143,

Rarefaction and Condensation

Theophrastus[1] had only the early Ionians in mind in the passage quoted by Simplicius, since he would certainly have agreed that Diogenes of Apollonia in the next century followed Anaximenes in this respect. But at least there can be no doubt that he did say 'only Anaximenes', and did not merely mean by this (as Diels proposed) that he was the first to introduce this theory. That was obvious, and Simplicius would have felt no need to contradict him.

Elsewhere Simplicius gives the following description of Anaximenes's theory:

(a) *Phys.* 24.26, A5: 'Anaximenes of Miletus, son of Eurystratus, the companion of Anaximander, also posits a single infinite underlying substance of things, not, however, indefinite in character like Anaximander's but determinate, for he calls it air, and says that it differs in rarity and density according to the different substances. Rarefied, it becomes fire; condensed, it becomes first wind, then cloud, and when condensed still further water, then earth and stones. Everything else is made of these. He too postulated eternal motion, which is indeed the cause of the change.'

The account of Hippolytus clearly goes back in the last resort to Theophrastus also, but is differently expressed and adds some further information.

(b) Hippol. *Ref.* I, 7, 1, A 7: 'Anaximenes, another Milesian and the son of Eurystratus, says the *arche* is infinite air, out of which proceeds whatever comes to be or has done so in the past or will exist in the future, gods also and the divine. Everything else is made from its products.[2] Now in form the air is like this: when it is most evenly distributed (or uniform: ὁμαλώτατος) it is invisible, but it is made visible by hot and cold and wet and movement. It is in constant movement, otherwise the things which change could not do so. It assumes different visible forms as it is rarefied or condensed. When dispersed more finely, it becomes fire. Winds on the other hand are air in process of condensation, and from air cloud is produced by concentration (lit. 'felting').[3] The continuation of this process produces water,

---

n. 72; the passage is much too relevant to his thesis to be thus relegated to a note at the end) cannot alter the fact.

[1] *Not* Simplicius, as McDiarmid (*loc. cit.*) misquotes Zeller into saying.

[2] Lit. 'offspring'. The double sense of *genesis* (coming-to-be in general, and birth in particular) is probably still making its influence felt on cosmogonical thought.

[3] Miletus was, after all, a famous centre of the textile industry, which may account for his even more homely comparison of the starry vault to a 'little felt cap' (πιλίον).

and still further condensation earth, while stones are the most condensed form of all. Thus the most important features in genesis are contraries, hot and cold.'

The early part of this passage should no doubt be read in conjunction with the version given by Cicero.

(c) Cicero, *Acad.* II, 37, 118, A9: 'After Anaximander his pupil Anaximenes postulated infinite air, the products of which are however determined. These are earth, water and fire, and from them comes everything else.'

To get rid of a small and troublesome point first, the odd statement in Hippolytus that air first has its own 'offspring', and everything else is generated from them, seems to be explained by the speaker in Cicero. The 'offspring' of air are the other elements, earth, water and fire, and everything else is made up of these. This suggests two stages in the making of the world, the formation of the elements by condensation and rarefaction of the air, and the production of 'the rest', by which must be meant chiefly organic, living nature. It has been thought unlikely that having once hit on the process of rarefaction and condensation as sufficient to explain even the genesis of stones from air, Anaximenes should feel the need for a secondary process as well, and Theophrastus as the fountain-head of the doxography has therefore been blamed for reading into Anaximenes the later theory of the four elements or 'simple bodies' as such, and their combination. This theory, expressly formulated by Empedocles and adapted by Aristotle to his own explanation of change, was not yet consciously articulated. It was called forth by the criticism of Parmenides and resulted from a deliberate abandonment of the monistic position. But it is incredible that it should have been a sudden invention. Anaximander with his primary oppositions between hot and cold, wet and dry, was preparing the way for it. All our evidence about him indicates that although no doubt there were other opposites, these four had a distinct primacy as cosmogonical agents. We have seen with what consistency he employed the action of hot and dry on cold and wet to explain the origin of everything, from the formation of earth and stars to the birth of the first animals. Cherniss goes too far when he says (*ACP*, 55): 'Neither his "contraries" nor those of any of the Presocratics were a single set of opposed agencies but an indefinite number of physical ingredients.' Moreover by speaking of the *arche* as air, instead of simply denoting it by its leading characteristic with article and adjective, Anaximenes as we have seen took a step towards the distinction between substance and affection. When the inconsistencies of the monistic hypothesis became too obvious to be ignored, the fourfold scheme by which Empedocles replaced it lay almost ready to his hand in the systems of his predecessors, requiring only to be clarified and raised to the position of an ultimate. It is more than likely that Anaximenes followed Anaximander's lead in holding that the first products of the modification of air were fire, water and earth, and that though the Aristotelian 'elements' or the Empedoclean 'roots' are still in the future, these three (the fiery, the wet and the cold *par excellence*) had a certain primacy for him as they had had for his mythological predecessors to whom Ouranos, Gaia and Oceanus were primal divinities.[1]

It does not of course follow that once these were formed, a different *process* supervened to produce the contents of the natural world.[2] What Anaximenes said about this we do not know, for our sources are completely silent about his views on the origin of organic nature. Presumably he had nothing to say on this subject comparable to the bold and imaginative account of Anaximander.

'Anaximenes and Diogenes (of Apollonia)', says Aristotle (*Metaph.* 984a5), 'make air prior to water and in the fullest sense the origin of the simple bodies.' The process by which they are derived from it is simple, and little needs to be added to the explanations of the doxographers. He chooses air as primary because he seems to think that in its invisible state, as atmospheric air, it is somehow at its most natural,

---

[1] Cf. Kahn, *Anaximander*, 133 ff., a detailed discussion of the evidence for the origins of the ideas of elements and opposites. On p. 149 he writes: 'Whatever terminology may have been used by the sixth-century Milesians, it is certain that their conception of the natural world contained, in potential form, a view of earth, water, air, and fire as "members" or "portions" of the cosmos.' However, the account in Simplicius does perhaps suggest, as Kahn later notes (156, n. 2), that the tetrad was not yet exclusive, and that Anaximenes included wind, clouds, and stones among the 'primary products' of air. (My own text was written before Kahn's book appeared.)

[2] It would not necessarily follow even if our authorities in the Aristotelian tradition supposed that it did. But in fact they make no mention of any process other than rarefaction and condensation, and indeed Simplicius (*De Caelo*, 615.20) says that Anaximenes made air the principle, ἀρκεῖν νομίζων τὸ τοῦ ἀέρος εὐαλλοίωτον πρὸς μεταβολήν.

and as it would always be if left alone, so to speak, like a piece of rubber which no force is at the moment either stretching or compressing. But it is not left alone, for he agreed with Anaximander in postulating an everlasting motion as a result of which its 'uniform' state (as Hippolytus says he called it) is disturbed and it becomes rarefied or condensed in different places, taking on various visible forms as a result. It was to him an obvious fact of experience that the air on a damp day becomes visible as mist, and that by a continuation of the same process the mist or cloud solidified still further into rain or other forms of water; and we still give the name of condensation to that unpleasant process so familiar in some parts of England whereby the air turns to water and drips down the walls of our houses. When water is heated the reverse process occurs. It turns first into visible steam, and then mingles with the invisible air. By an extension of these familiar processes he supposed it to be on the one hand further solidified into earth and stones, and on the other, as it became rarer still, to become hotter until it ignited as fire.[1]

We observe that the new process was linked with Anaximander's doctrine of opposites. The hot and dry were connected with rarity, the cold and wet with density. This was done explicitly, and with an attempt at experimental proof, as we learn from an interesting passage of Plutarch in which, along with the account in his own post-Aristotelian terminology, he claims to repeat one of Anaximenes's own technical terms:

(d) Plut. *De Prim. Frig.* 7, 947F, B1: 'As Anaximenes held long ago, we must not allow either the hot or the cold in the category of substances; they are common affections of matter supervening on its alterations. What is compacted and condensed he says is cold, but what is rare and "loose"[2] (that I think is the actual word he used) is hot. Hence, he said, there is

---

[1] We can of course detect an inconsistency here, which Plato pointed out in his *Timaeus*. In A. E. Taylor's words (*Timaeus*, 316): 'If you are really in earnest with the doctrine of cyclical transformations, you must hold that whatever it is that is invariant throughout change, it cannot be a sensible body. *All* sensible bodies must be on the same level; if one of them is a "phase", all must be "phases".' If such a thought did not occur to Anaximenes that is no doubt due, in part at least, to the second kind of motive which, as is suggested below (p. 127), led him to the choice of air as the basic principle. At the same time, in spite of what some have said, Anaximenes certainly deserves the credit of having recognized the invisible atmospheric air as a substance; and it is scarcely a sensible one.

[2] χαλαρόν.

something in the saying that a man blows both hot and cold with his mouth, for the breath is cooled when the lips press and condense it, but when it issues from an open mouth it is rarefied and becomes warm.'

Since one of the minor present-day controversies about Greek philosophers concerns the extent to which they made use of experiment, a brief excursus is perhaps permissible here. It is a controversy from which the recently-mentioned unphilosophical preconceptions are not always absent. Professor Farrington is convinced of the scientific character of Ionian thought, and since his definition of science is a Marxist one ('the system of behaviour by which man acquires mastery over his environment'), he naturally tends to derive their theories from practical techniques and exalt the experimental side of their work. Cornford on the other hand, who saw them in a very different light, was perhaps apt to belittle this aspect of it. Without taking sides in the general argument, one may mention a point in which Cornford seems to have done less than justice to Anaximenes, and, though not of central importance, it has a certain interest of its own. In *Principium Sapientiae* (p. 6) he wrote:

Anaximenes affords another instance of a hypothesis which no one tested. He held that differences of heat and cold can be reduced to differences of density; steam is hotter and less dense than water, water hotter and less dense than ice. If that is so, a given quantity of water ought to fill less space when frozen. Had Anaximenes set a jar full of water outside his door on a frosty night and found it split in the morning, he might have found out that ice fills more space than water and revised his theory.

This result would certainly have puzzled him, but the fact remains that his general theory was right, and if he had performed the experiment and based any generalization on the results, it would only have led him into error. In general, bodies do of course expand as their temperature rises, and contract as it falls, a principle which makes the thermometer possible. Water itself expands as it is heated, and contracts as it is cooled, until it reaches a temperature of 39° F (4° C). Then for some reason as it becomes colder and passes freezing-point it ceases to contract and begins to expand. This exception to the otherwise universal truth that bodies expand by increase of temperature is still unexplained, that is, scientists have still failed to relate it to any general law. It is perhaps hardly fair to Anaximenes to blame him if, having correctly divined an almost universal truth, he failed to observe the single exception which has hitherto baffled the efforts of scientists to explain it.[1]

There are two points in particular in which the achievement of Anaximenes contributed to the progress of thought. (1) With him the word *aer* first comes to mean, in its primary significance, the invisible substance around us which we call air today. Although all things are ultimately formed by modifications of it, yet it is to this that the name is properly applied rather than to mist or cloud or any other of the visible forms of matter. Hitherto the word *aer* had generally signified mist, fog or darkness—something at least which obscured the vision and hid any objects which it surrounded. It stood for the darkness with which Zeus had covered the battle-field before Troy when Ajax uttered his famous prayer: 'Save the sons of the Achaeans from the *aer*.... Slay us, if it be but in the light.' Hearing the prayer, Zeus straightway 'scattered the *aer* and thrust aside the mist, and the sun shone out and all the battle was plain to see'. (*Il.* XVII, 647, 649.) To Anaximander also the substance surrounding and concealing the wheels of fire which were the heavenly bodies was *aer*. For the early Greek mind darkness itself was a substance, the 'sacred darkness' (ἱερὸν κνέφας) of Homer. Not until Empedocles do we meet the idea that it is something merely negative, an absence of light. (2) With Anaximenes apparent differences of kind or quality are for the first time reduced to a common origin in differences of quantity. Burnet remarked (*EGP*, 74) that this makes the Milesian cosmology for the first time consistent, 'since a theory which explains everything as a form of a single substance is clearly bound to regard all differences as quantitative. The only way to save the unity of the primary substance is to say that all diversities are due to the presence of more or less of it in a given space.'

Here again he is well ahead of Anaximander in clarity of thought, and the introduction of a quantitative criterion for qualitative differences not only rounded off the Milesian monistic systems but bore remarkable fruit in later Greek and European thought. We are still at the very beginning, the first dawning of rational explanation, and there is no

[1] G. Vlastos criticizes Cornford's remark on other grounds in *Gnomon*, 1955, 66.

question of Anaximenes having made any mathematical applications of his new principle. That advance may justly be credited to the Pythagoreans. But by the statement of the principle the essential first step has been taken along a path which is still being followed. That physical phenomena—colour, sound or whatever it may be—can be expressed in the form of mathematical equations—in other words, that all differences of quality are reducible to differences of quantity, and only when so reduced can be regarded as scientifically described—is an assumption on which all modern physical science is based. By accounting for all qualitative differences of matter by different degrees of condensation and rarefaction of the one basic stuff, Anaximenes is already, we cannot say providing, but demanding a quantitative explanation. He was the originator of the idea, and such was its importance that it was perhaps an excusable exaggeration on the part of Theophrastus to attribute it to him 'alone'. He probably wished to emphasize that the principle of condensation and rarefaction was Anaximenes's own.

(5) *Air, life, and divinity*

The rational motive, then, which led Anaximenes to his choice of air as *arche* lay in the wish to discover a natural explanation of the manifold variety of physical phenomena consistent with a monistic view of reality. This he thought he had detected in the processes of condensation and rarefaction. There would also, I suggested, be motives influencing him less consciously, because they sprang from the general climate of thought in which he and the other Milesian thinkers were living, and which they shared with their unphilosophical fellow-countrymen. He assumed, like Anaximander, that the original source and fount of being (that is, for him, the air) had been in motion from all time, and that this was what made its changes possible. 'He too makes motion everlasting', said Theophrastus, and added that this eternal motion is the means whereby change takes place.[1] One may rightly say 'assumed', for like Anaximander (and doubtless Thales also) he offered no explanation of this. To Aristotle the omission seemed indefensible. Matter was one

---

[1] *Ap.* Simpl. (A5). So also Hippolytus (A7), the *Stromateis* (A6) and Cicero (A10).

thing, and a moving cause another, so that if matter was in motion, the natural philosopher should be able to point to some separate agent—separate conceptually at least, if not physically—to which the motion was due. But this discrimination belongs to a more sophisticated stage of thought than that of the sixth century, which as yet conceived of no opposition between an inert matter on the one hand and a force arousing it to motion on the other. The *arche* of the universe was not matter in that sense. It was eternal being, and because eternal and the *arche* of everything else, it was of necessity uncaused, or else self-caused. It was not only the matter or subject of motion, but itself the cause. What then, one may ask, in the thought of the time, answered to the description 'self-caused' or 'self-moving'? The answer is soul or life (*psyche*). The *arche* was something alive, not only eternal (ἀΐδιον) but immortal (ἀθάνατον) and therefore divine (θεῖον). So Anaximander called his *apeiron*, and Thales too, as we saw good reason to believe, was impressed by the links uniting moisture and life. These links were so strong that it seemed perfectly reasonable, as it had through the preceding centuries of pre-philosophical imagination, to regard moisture as the original fount and cause of life and therefore of everything else.

In making air his selection, an air in perpetual motion, Anaximenes also was respecting an age-old and still flourishing popular belief which associated, and in fact identified, breath and life. That the air which we breathe should be the life itself which animates us is a common idea, and the breath-soul a world-wide conception. Among the Greeks we meet this idea both outside and inside the realm of philosophical thought. I have dealt with it fairly fully elsewhere,[1] but may perhaps repeat here sufficient to show that the equation of air with soul or life was not the invention of any single philosophic or religious individual or school, but must have originated in the mists of early popular belief.

The idea that a female could be impregnated, and thus new life originated, by the wind alone goes back to the *Iliad*, in which the horses of Achilles were born to their mother Podarge by the wind Zephyros. Eggs laid by birds without sexual union were according to

[1] *The Greeks and their Gods*, ch. 5.

Aristotle called wind-eggs or Zephyr-eggs, 'because in springtime the birds were observed to inhale the breezes'. This reminds us of a passage in Virgil which, although belonging to a later age, no doubt contains the explanation of the birth of Achilles's horses in Homer. In spring, he says, the mares stand on high crags with their mouths turned towards the Zephyr to catch its breezes. In this way they are made pregnant by the winds without sexual union.[1]

According to the sacred poetry of the Orphics 'the soul enters into us from the whole as we breathe, borne by the winds'. At the opposite extreme we find the materialist Democritus saying much the same thing in the terms of his own atomistic world-view: 'In the air there are many of those particles which he calls mind and soul. Hence, when we breathe and the air enters, these enter along with it, and by their action cancel the pressure' (i.e. of the surrounding atmosphere), 'thus preventing the expulsion of the soul which resides in the animal. This explains why life and death are bound up with the taking in and letting out of breath; for death occurs when the compression of the surrounding air gains the upper hand, and, the animal being unable to respire, the air from outside can no longer enter and counteract the compression.'[2] Probably for Democritus the soul-atoms were even smaller and finer than those of air, but at least he subscribed to the general notion that it is by breathing in the air that we acquire the life-principle.

Diogenes of Apollonia took up in the fifth century the doctrine of Anaximenes that air was the primary substance, and developed in particular this point that it was not only the origin of all things but also the element of soul in the universe, and therefore had special affinities with the soul in animal and human beings. The following are among the excerpts from his book on nature which are given by Simplicius (Diog. frr. 4 and 5):

Mankind and the other animals live on air, by breathing; and it is to them both soul and mind.

The soul of animals is the same, namely air which is warmer than the air outside, in which we live, though much colder than that near the sun.

---

[1] *Il.* xvi, 150; Ar. *H.A.* 559b20, 560a6; Virg. *G.* iii, 271 ff. Lucian, *De Sacrif.* 6 calls Hephaestus a wind-child because Hera bore him without Zeus.

[2] The authority for both these statements is Aristotle. See *De An.* 410b28, *De Resp.* 472a8.

In my opinion that which has intelligence is what men call air, and by it everyone is directed (κυβερνᾶσθαι— the verb that Anaximander applied to his *apeiron*), and it has power over all; for it is just this substance which I hold to be god.

It is a logical consequence of these statements that there exists a close affinity between the divine or universal mind and our own, and according to Theophrastus this conclusion was duly drawn by Diogenes, who said that 'the air within us' is 'a small portion of the god' (*De Sensu*, 42, Diog. A 19). It is no wonder that such a belief was made to serve the purposes of a mystical religion like that expounded by the Orphics, as well as those of natural philosophy. When Aristophanes laughs at the new divinities, Air and Respiration, and ridicules the notion of the kinship between the air and the human mind (*Clouds*, 627, 230), he no doubt has in mind the fashionable philosophico-religious theories; but it cannot be denied that in so far as these theories had caught the popular imagination, they owed much of their success to the fact that similar beliefs were rooted in folk-consciousness.

These and other examples which could be adduced, as well as the cumulative effect of evidence from other cultures, put it beyond reasonable doubt that ideas of this sort must have been a part of the familiar background of Anaximenes's upbringing. They would help to make the choice of air as *arche* a perfectly natural one, for, on the hylozoist view which he shared with the other members of the Milesian school, the stuff of the world had at the same time to be the stuff of life. It is therefore only what we should expect when we are told that he said the air was god (Cicero and Aëtius, A 10).[1] There are also, it seems, other gods and 'divine things' which are not eternal but have their origin from air. So Hippolytus (quoted above, p. 121) and St Augustine (*Civ. Dei*, VIII, 2, A 10): *Nec deos negavit aut tacuit; non tamen ab ipsis aerem factum, sed ipsos ex aere ortos credidit.* What Anaximenes had in mind when he spoke of these other gods we are not told, and perhaps there is little point in guessing. He may have tried in this way, like Epicurus in a later age, to find room for the gods of popular belief

---

[1] Cicero's words are (*N.D.* I, 10, 26): *aera deum statuit eumque gigni.* It is a curious mistake, but there is no doubt whatever that for Anaximenes the air as *arche* has existed from all time. Perhaps there has been some confusion between the primal air itself and the θεούς καὶ θεῖα which arise from it.

within the framework of a rational philosophy of nature. He may have had the other elements in mind, the 'offspring' of air as he called them. These were already associated or identified with deities in popular thought: Gaia the earth was a goddess, for water there was Oceanus, and for fire Hephaestus. What he says about the heavenly bodies makes it unlikely that he thought of them as divinities.

There is evidence also that he drew the same analogy as his follower Diogenes of Apollonia between the function of the air in the universe at large and that in man, that is, his soul. This appears from a passage in Aëtius which reads as if it were intended as an actual quotation from Anaximenes, though this has been hotly disputed in recent times:

Aët. I, 3, 4, B2: 'Anaximenes of Miletus, son of Eurystratus, declared that the origin of existing things was air, for out of it all things come to be and into it they are resolved again. "Just as our soul," he says, "which is air, holds us together, so breath and air surround the whole cosmos." Air and breath are used synonymously.'

It is perhaps impossible to decide just how far this sentence preserves the actual wording of Anaximenes,[1] but Theophrastus and his epitomizers evidently believed themselves to be keeping to it pretty closely, nor is there any good reason to doubt that the sentence faithfully communicates his doctrine. Burnet, who accepts the fragment, has perhaps contributed unwittingly to its rejection by later critics, for he comments (*EGP*, 75) that it is 'an early instance of the argument from the microcosm to the macrocosm, and so marks the beginning of an interest in physiological matters'. Kirk adduces the same fact as an argument against its genuineness: 'The parallel between man and cosmos is first explicitly drawn by medical speculation in the

---

[1] Reinhardt, Wilamowitz, Gigon and Kirk hold that it is so altered as to distort its meaning. It is accepted as a genuine fragment by Kranz, Nestle (ZN, 319, n. 1) and Praechter (Ueberweg, 51; the other reff. will be found in Kirk, *HCF*, 312). Vlastos (*AJP*, 1955, 363 with n. 55) holds that 'though much of the wording of this fragment is doubtful, there is no good reason to doubt that it paraphrases an analogy drawn by Anaximenes himself'. Exception is taken in particular to the words συγκρατεῖ, κόσμος and πνεῦμα. That κόσμος in the sense of world-order came into use only later is possible, though if anyone wished, like Nestle, to use this passage as evidence to the contrary, it would be difficult to prove him wrong. The same applies to πνεῦμα, which comes under suspicion of having a Stoic flavour. If this is so, the remark of the doxographer that ἀήρ and πνεῦμα are used here synonymously (by Anaximenes?) is curious. On the use of κόσμος see further p. 208, n. 1, below.

fifth century' (*HCF*, 312). Apart from the fact that this argument comes perilously near to a *petitio principii*, the assumption of an affinity between the soul of man and the all-pervading cosmic divinity has no more to do with the rise of physiological and medical science than had the probable assumption of Thales that moisture was the principle of life (p. 62, above). It is primarily a religious assumption, not one which appealed to the inheritors of the Olympian pantheon of Homer, but one which seems to have belonged particularly to the religious ferment that affected a different stratum of the population in the sixth century and gave rise to the sacred poetry known as Orphic. The promulgators of *teletai* in the name of Orpheus were concerned in the religious sphere with the same problem of the relation between the One and the Many which in a different form was the problem of the Milesian philosophers. In both forms it was a living problem in the sixth century.[1] If then we are to trust to *a priori* reasons drawn from the climate of contemporary thought (which is all that the sceptics would have us do), there is no need to deny to Anaximenes the analogy between microcosm and macrocosm which is expressly attributed to him here, and is in any case a probable consequence of the simple fact that he looked upon the air as (*a*) the *arche* and divine, and (*b*) the stuff of the human soul.[2]

(6) *Cosmogony and cosmology*

In the details of cosmogony and cosmology Anaximenes can hardly be said to have rivalled the combination of reasoning power and bold imagination which characterized Anaximander, but was in some ways more naive. As Anaximander's cosmos was surrounded by the *apeiron*, so is Anaximenes's by the air, which, as we have just seen, is also called breath (*pneuma*) in what purports to be a quotation or near-quotation. The suspicion of Stoic influence here is lessened when one sees that according to Aristotle the Pythagoreans described the universe as

---

[1] Cf. Guthrie, *Greeks and their Gods*, 316 and *Harv. Theol. Rev.* 1952, 87–104.

[2] In Hippocr. *De Nat. Hom.* 1 (VI, 32 Littré), Sabinus (a contemporary of Galen) read οὔτε γὰρ πάμπαν ἀέρα λέγω τὸν ἄνθρωπον ὥσπερ ᾿Αναξιμένης. Cf. also Philoponus, *De An.* 9.9 Hayduck (DK, A23): οἱ δὲ ἀερίαν [*sc.* τὴν ψυχήν] ὥσπερ ᾿Α. καί τινες τῶν Στωϊκῶν. Anaximenes is probably included among the ἕτεροί τινες of whom Aristotle speaks in *De An.* 405a21: Διογένης δὲ ὥσπερ καὶ ἕτεροί τινες ἀέρα [*sc.* τὴν ψυχὴν ἐοίκασιν ὑπολαβεῖν].

breathing in from a 'limitless *pneuma*' outside it.[1]   It may be inferred that, as the analogy with the soul suggests, the world for Anaximenes is alive and breathing.

We are told (*Strom.* III, A6)—though no further explanation is vouchsafed—that the earth was the first part of the cosmos to come into existence, engendered of course by compression of the air. Of its shape and situation we have the following reports:

(*a*) *Stromateis* (A6): 'As the air "felted", earth, he says, came into being first, quite flat; wherefore it rides, as is reasonable, upon the air.'

(*b*) Hippolytus (A7): 'The earth is flat, riding upon the air.'

(*c*) Aëtius (A20): 'Anaximenes says it is table-shaped.'

(*d*) Aëtius (A20): 'Anaximenes says that it rides upon the air owing to its flatness.'

(*e*) Aristotle, *De Caelo*, 294b13 (A20): 'Anaximenes, Anaxagoras and Democritus name the flatness of the earth as the cause of its remaining at rest. It does not cleave the air beneath it, but settles on it like a lid, as flat bodies to all appearances do; owing to their resistance they are not easily moved even by the wind. The earth, they say, owing to its flatness behaves in the same way in relation to the air immediately underneath it, which, not having sufficient room to change its place, is compressed and stays still owing to the air beneath, like the water in *klepsydrai*. For this power of the air to bear a great weight when shut up and its motion stopped, they bring forward plenty of evidence.'[2]

The audacity of Anaximander's idea that the earth remained poised without support at the centre of the universe, simply because it *was* at the centre, was too great for his friend and successor to be able to accept it, and he returned to Thales's hypothesis of a material support.

The earth having been formed first, the heavenly bodies originate from it, and though those of them that are visible are now of fiery substance, they are all in origin earthy.

(*a*) *Stromateis* (A6, continuation of (*a*) above): 'And the sun, moon and other heavenly bodies originate from earth. He argues at any rate that the sun is earth but acquires great heat from its swift motion.'[3]

---

[1] See pp. 278f., below. Aristotle also referred to this breathing of the world in his lost book on the Pythagoreans (fr. 201 Rose). On this Pythagorean doctrine see Baldry, *CQ*, 1932, 30f.

[2] For the *klepsydra* see note *ad loc.* in the Loeb edition.

[3] The reading of the last few words is doubtful, but the sense scarcely affected.

(*b*) Hippolytus (A7): 'The stars originated from the earth, because moisture arose from it, which being rarefied gave rise to fire, and of this, as it rose aloft, the stars are composed. There are also earthy bodies in the region of the stars, revolving with them.'

(*c*) Aëtius (A14): 'Anaximenes said that the stars are of the nature of fire, and that they enclose[1] certain earthy bodies also which revolve together with them and are not seen.'

(*d*) Aëtius (A15): 'He said the sun is flat like a leaf.'

This theory of the origin of the heavenly bodies from the earth, so that even 'the sun is earth', shows at least how consciously emancipated was Anaximenes's mind from any religious preconceptions; but it lacks the cogency of Anaximander's account. His theory of 'separation' allowed for both extremes, fire and wet earth, to be produced together. Vaporization and drying, which accounted for all the rest of the cosmos including animal life, were then readily explicable by the action of the enveloping fire on the cold wet centre, whereas in Anaximenes's scheme it seems that fire itself is to be produced from earth by a vaporization which is difficult to explain. Why he should suppose it necessary that the first result of the air's motion was to condense some of it to earth, and that the rarefaction producing fire should only result secondarily out of moisture from the earth (thus obviously passing once more through the stage of invisible atmospheric air), our fragmentary sources do not enable us to say.

It is arguable that Anaximenes, having advanced his single brilliant and fruitful hypothesis of condensation and rarefaction, did not pay so much attention to the detailed working-out of a system. If so, the common background of these thinkers would lead one to expect him to produce something more closely related to the mythical cosmogonies which preceded them. This is perhaps what happened. To derive all the heavenly bodies from the earth sounds strange and original, but in Hesiod's *Theogony* (126–7) 'Earth first bore the starry Heaven, equal to herself, that he might cover her all round'.

---

[1] περιέχει is a little difficult, but, especially in view of the Hippolytus passage, can hardly mean (as Zeller thought) that each star contained an earthy core. Presumably they 'surround' them, as the air περιέχει the world, i.e. the earthy bodies are all somewhat nearer the centre than are the stars. This would be necessary if they were intended to explain eclipses. (Ἄστρα and ἀστέρες are of course here used of the heavenly bodies in general.)

Lacking Anaximander's curious tubes of mist, Anaximenes must have had to seek another explanation of eclipses, and many modern authorities have thought this to be the reason for the invisible earthy bodies in the heavens. If so, this was one helpful step on the part of a thinker to whom, as Boll rightly remarked, astronomy owes in general very little. It is, however, only a guess.[1]

The sun, he said, is flat like a leaf (Aëtius, A 15), and it and the other heavenly bodies 'ride upon' the air owing to their flat shape, just as the earth does (Hippol. A 7). There is, however, a remarkable, isolated passage in Aëtius (A 14), in which Burnet and others have very reasonably seen some corruption:

Anaximenes held that the stars are fixed like nails in the crystalline (or ice-like) substance; some however that they are fiery leaves like paintings.

Whatever the meaning of the last two words (the constellations—Bear or Wagon, Orion and the rest?), the theory that the heavenly bodies are 'fiery leaves' is surely Anaximenes's, and the statement that owing to their flat shape the air supports them in their revolutions is inconsistent with supposing them to be fixed in a solid crystalline sphere. Some scholars (for example Heath, *Aristarchus*, 42 f.) infer that Anaximenes was the first to distinguish between planets and fixed stars, the former being 'flat like leaves' and free to move irregularly, the latter attached to the solid wheeling outer circumference or dome of the universe. On this view the report of Aëtius (A 15) that 'the stars execute their turnings when pushed aside by condensed and resistant air' would refer to the planets only.[2]

There are obvious objections to attributing a crystalline heaven to Anaximenes. He connected solidity with cold, rarity with heat (B 1); and if fire 'rose aloft' and became the stars at the outer edge of the universe, it is difficult to see how the air in the same region became

---

[1] Kirk (KR, 156) thinks that the invisible earthy bodies were falsely transferred to Anaximenes from Diogenes of Apollonia, to whom they are also attributed. He asserts that in any case their function will have been to explain meteorites, not eclipses, on the grounds that this was the purpose of their introduction by Diogenes and that Anaxagoras posited similar bodies although he knew the true cause of eclipses.

[2] Heath takes τροπαί to refer to their revolutions in their respective orbits, not to solstices, and suggests that this meaning could be got from the original text (Aët. II, 14, 3) by reading ἐνίους (*sc.* ἀστέρας) for ἔνιοι (in spite of the neuter ἄστρα immediately before, a difficulty which he does not mention).

frozen solid. But the lamentably large gaps in our knowledge may preclude us from understanding how his mind worked here, and, more generally, a little further reflexion on the word κρυσταλλοειδής is prompted by the thought that there is no particular reason why Theophrastus or a later doxographer should have fathered it on him unjustifiably. The risk of contamination from any of their favourite schools of thought was slight, for the later spheres of the Pythagoreans, of Aristotle and of the Stoics were not of a kind which could be described by this word. From Aristotle onwards, and probably for many before him, the outer heaven was of pure, invisible fire or *aither*. The notion of a hard, crystalline sphere or spheres, so dear to astronomers and poets of medieval and renaissance days,[1] was a rare one in Greek thought, and where it does seem to occur is a little puzzling. The common arrangement of a cosmos continued to be what it was for Anaximander: earth at the centre with water upon it, air or mist around that, and fire, including the heavenly bodies, taking the outermost place.

There are, however, indications that both Parmenides and Empedocles combined this arrangement with the attribution of a solid circumference to the whole. We read that in Parmenides's 'Way of Seeming', 'that which surrounded' his mysterious heavenly rings 'is solid like a wall, and under it comes the fiery ring'. Not only is no further explanation vouchsafed, but a little later Aëtius is saying that '*aither* is uppermost and surrounds everything', and in a summary of descriptions of the heaven he lists Parmenides with others who say that it is fiery. We are equally unfortunate in having no actual fragment of Empedocles's poem dealing with this point, but according to Aëtius again he believed that fire itself had the power of 'freezing' or solidifying. Lactantius (whose source is Varro) describes Empedocles's heaven as *aerem glaciatum*, and the version of the *Stromateis* is that fire occupies the space under the coagulation (πάγος) of air, a parallel to the situation of the fiery ring of Parmenides.[2]

Perhaps then Anaximenes anticipated Empedocles here, though it is

---

[1] Who in all probability took it over from the Arabs: see Dreyer, *Planetary Systems*, 289.

[2] Aët. II, 7, 1 (Parm. A37), II, 11, 4 (A38); II, 11, 2 (Emped. A51), cf. A60 and Ar. *Probl.* 937a14; Lactant. in Emped. A51, *Strom.* A30.

difficult to see how he would accommodate such a view to his general association of heat with 'the rare and loose'. There is, however, another possibility. In later Greek at least, the word 'crystalline' need by no means imply the hardness of ice or glass, and we need not suppose that either Anaximenes himself, if he used the word, or whoever may have first used it to explain what he found in Anaximenes, intended it to bear that sense. To medical writers like Celsus or Galen the crystalline lens of the eye was known as 'the crystalline *moisture*' or in Latin a *gutta humoris*. The word occurs a number of times in Galen's *De Usu Partium*, and at one point he describes this crystalline moisture as being surrounded with 'a clear moisture like that in an egg'. This finds a near parallel in Celsus, who writes that the liquid called by the Greeks κρυσταλλοειδής is itself *ovi albo similis*.[1]

This use of the term in a physiological setting to mean a viscous transparent liquid 'resembling the white of an egg' makes it at least possible that Anaximenes was following his contemporary and associate Anaximander in supposing the world to be surrounded, not by a hard and glass-like substance, but by a transparent membrane. Since we can say even more confidently than we could of Anaximander that he regarded the world as a living and breathing creature, it is highly probable that he also used the physiological analogy in describing its birth and structure. The word ἧλος, commonly a nail, occurs several times in later Greek meaning a wart or other kind of callus.[2]

With characteristic intellectual boldness, Anaximander had seen the heavenly bodies as performing complete revolutions, carried round both above and below the centrally-poised earth in their rings which were segments of a dissected sphere. Anaximenes revived the idea that they only go round, not under the earth. The testimonies are these:

(*a*) Hippolytus (A 7): 'He says that the stars do not go under the earth, as others have supposed, but round it, as the small felt cap turns about our head. The sun disappears not beneath the earth, but concealed by its higher parts and on account of its greater distance from us.'

(*b*) Aëtius (A 14): 'Anaximenes says the stars circle round the earth, not under it.'

[1] Galen, *De Usu Part.* x, 4 (vol. II, 70.9 Helmreich), Celsus VII, 7, 3 (280.2 Daremberg).
[2] For references see Guthrie in *CQ*, 1956, 40–4, where the suggestions here put forward are elaborated with further evidence.

137

In view of the above, one may add the following from Aristotle in which Anaximenes is not mentioned by name.

(*c*) Aristotle, *Meteor.* II, 354a27 (trans. H. D. P. Lee): 'An indication that the northerly parts of the earth are high is the opinion of many of the ancient meteorologists that the sun does not pass under the earth but round its northerly part, and that it disappears and causes night because the earth is high towards the north.'

What with his stars like paintings, and his cap which turns round on the head, Anaximenes's taste for homely human similes cannot be said to be very helpful.[1] However, he clearly retreated from the progressive view of Anaximander to the more primitive belief that the universe was, effectively at least, a hemisphere rather than a sphere. Mythographers had told how the sun, when he set in the west, was carried round the encircling stream of Ocean in a golden boat to rise in the east again.[2] Under the earth was a mass of compressed air, the shape or extent of which is never mentioned, and if it is to do its job of supporting the earth in the manner described by Aristotle, the earth must reach to the circumference of the cosmos, thus making it practically impossible for the heavenly bodies to pass beneath. How exactly this theory of their disappearance behind higher ground in the north was accommodated to observation is something that we can only guess, and has been much disputed. But on one astronomical point Anaximenes improved on Anaximander, for the report in Hippolytus (A7) that according to him 'the stars give no heat owing to their great distance' shows that he abandoned the strange doctrine that the stars are nearer the earth than is the sun.[3]

[1] Those who wish to take the revolving cap more seriously will find something about it in H. Berger, *Gesch. d. wissenschaftlichen Erdkunde d. Griechen*, 79. Teichmüller found significance in the fact that the ancients, like the members of some public schools, wore their caps on the backs of their heads. (See Heath, *Aristarchus*, 41.) He does not say that they habitually wore them too large. It is the idea of *movement* which makes the simile so bizarre. Could the πῖλον have been a turban, and στρέφεται mean 'is wound' round the head? Turbans may have been worn in Miletus in Anaximenes's time as in later ages until Turkey went republican and western.

[2] U. Hölscher in *Hermes*, 1953, 413 says, on the authority of F. Boll, *Zeitschr. f. Assyr.* 1914, 361, n., that the idea that the sun and moon go round instead of under the earth is Babylonian.

[3] It was revived solely by Leucippus (D.L. IX, 33), who also spoke of the inclination of the earth towards the south, which he invoked in explanation of eclipses!

(7) *Meteorology*

In his description of meteorological phenomena, Anaximenes seems to have followed Anaximander as closely as the difference between their primary world-processes would allow. Air in swift motion, i.e. wind, is already slightly condensed, and further condensation produces clouds, rain, snow and hail. Thunder and lightning were for him, just as for Anaximander, the effect of a cloud being split by the force of wind, and he apparently thought that phosphorescence in the sea provided some sort of parallel to the lightning (Hippol. A7, Aët. A17). He also spoke of the rainbow, no longer a radiant goddess Iris but only the effect of the sun's rays on densely compacted air, which appeared in different colours according as the sun's heat or the cloud's moisture prevailed (A18). He had also observed an occasional rainbow at full moon. Of his opinion about earthquakes we have Aristotle's account:

Anaximenes says that when the earth is in process of becoming wet or dry it breaks, and is shaken by the high ground breaking and falling; which is why earthquakes occur in droughts and again in heavy rains: for in droughts the earth is dried and so, as just explained, breaks, and when the rains make it excessively wet it falls apart.[1]

(8) *Conclusion*

In spite of the scantiness of the record, it needs little imagination to see Anaximenes as a well-defined character, and this may perhaps be permitted in a summing-up. The vivid imagery attributed to him suggests a man interested in and observant of his fellows at their daily tasks, observant also of the more striking and picturesque phenomena of nature, though probably not in the patient and painstaking way that makes the typical scientist. The air is felted like wool, the earth reminds him of a table, the circling sun and moon of leaves borne up in an eddying wind, the stars perhaps of nails or rivets or warts. He recalls the phosphorescent glitter that drips from an oar-blade as it rises from the water, and the faint colours that he has seen ('but not often') in the

---

[1] *Meteor.* 365b6, trans. H. D. P. Lee. If the account in Ammianus (XVII, 7, 12, Anaximander, A28) really refers to Anaximander, we have here also a remarkably close similarity between the theories of master and pupil. But more probably the single MS. which gives instead the name of Anaximenes has preserved the true attribution.

light of a full moon. Like a true Ionian, his freedom of thought is so little inhibited by any sense of awe that he can compare the starry vault to a felt cap, and use the diminutive form in doing so. Ranging thus untrammelled, his mind put later ages in its debt by hitting on the inspired notion that if the genesis of the world was from a single substance, its changes could only be due to there being more or less of it in a given space. Condensation and rarefaction provide the universal clue to becoming and change, and if he was too impetuous to submit himself to the detailed thought and investigation which might have produced a fuller and more consistent cosmological scheme, the central idea remains and has borne its fruit.

Religion had little appeal for him. Perhaps there were gods: if so they like everything else must be formed from the air, which was after all alive (what else could its eternal, uncaused motion mean?) and manifested in our own selves as the *psyche* which at once integrates and animates the body. Such a man would accept this like his fellow-Ionians (and like a later secular thinker of Ionian stock, Democritus) as a fact of nature. A similar belief could be the basis of a mystic's hope, but in the face of other evidence about Anaximenes we cannot credit him, as some have done,[1] with mystical tendencies himself.

E. THE MILESIANS: CONCLUSION

Three main points occur if one wishes to summarize briefly the chief characteristics of the Milesian philosophers and their legacy to later Greek thought. Their view of nature was rational, evolutionary, hylozoist.

(*a*) Essential as it is to be aware of the persistent effects of mythological conceptions and modes of thinking, enough has been said about these, and it should not now be misleading if in a summing-up one emphasizes rather the revolution in man's thought about the world and its history which their purely rational approach brought about. Briefly, it meant that the causes operating in the beginning were to be regarded as the same in kind as those which we see operating now. To one reading in Hesiod of the succession of human ages, the heroic, the

---

[1] 'Auch in diesem Physiker spricht noch ein Mystiker mit' (K. Joel, *Gesch. d. ant. Philos.* 270).

silver and the golden, then further back to the reign of Kronos and the older gods, and finally right back to the very birth of the gods from the marriage of Heaven and Earth, it must have seemed that as one went back in time the world became less and less like that of ordinary experience, and governed by forces of a different kind. It is true that up to and beyond Hesiod's day divine interference was supposed by many to account even for contemporary events to which we should assign perfectly natural causes. But take a passage from the *Theogony*, say the battle of Zeus and his allies with the Titans. Great rocks are hurled, the earth and its forests are set on fire, they crash and cry aloud, the surface of the land heaves and boils as does the sea. Heaven rocks and groans and Olympus is shaken to its base. Lightning and thunder, flame and thunderbolt are the weapons of Zeus, and all nature is convulsed before his enemies the Titans can be overcome and consigned to Tartarus deep beneath the earth. Events of those days, or the days when Prometheus stole the fire, were events of a different order, they were different in kind, from what went on in the Boeotia of Hesiod himself or the world of those who came after him.

Yet until the rise of a more scientific outlook in Miletus, there was no alternative explanation of the past. Aristotle, who was no friend to the 'sophisms' of mythology, makes it clear that with Thales a new spirit emerges, a spirit which the man of reason could respect. The haze of myth is dissipated, with extraordinary suddenness, from the origins of the world and of life. Instead we find what is, all things considered, a remarkably successful attempt to push back to the very beginning of things the operation of familiar natural processes like the condensation of moisture. The formation of the world has become a purely natural event from which the clash of supernatural powers is eliminated, even if the ways in which those powers had been formerly imagined to work must be admitted to have influenced the mechanism of the natural causes in terms of which these men were now speculating. We may be inclined to underrate the astonishing completeness of their triumph because, thanks to the Ionians themselves, their premiss quickly became the universally accepted premiss of all science: that is, the hypothesis that, as Henri Frankfort put it, 'a single order underlies the chaos of our perceptions, and furthermore that we are able to comprehend that order'. Yet, as he truly comments, to act on that hypothesis was at the time to proceed with preposterous boldness on an entirely unproved assumption.

(*b*) Cosmogonies are either creative or evolutionary. With the possible exception of Orphic ideas, which never gained wide popular favour, it may be said that an evolutionary conception of the origins of the world was the only one that had so far been mooted among the Greeks. Brought up in the religious tradition of the Hebrews, we are accustomed to associate this term with the scientific outlook of a Darwin, but in Greece the early mythical accounts were themselves of evolutionary type. Unlike Jahwe, the Greek gods had not created the world, and the Milesians, in so far as they thought along evolutionary lines, were retaining an earlier framework though stripping it of its mythological covering. Mythology too had presented an initial state of confusion—in which for example, as we have noted, heaven and earth were mingled together in 'one form'—out of which the present world-order has gradually emerged. The myths described this evolution in terms of the marriages and begettings of the personified elements themselves, the philosophers ascribed it to natural causes; but neither regarded it as a *creation*, the work of an original god standing apart from, and working on, an original matter distinct from himself. Writing from the different standpoint of a Christian and a Platonist, Augustine thinks it necessary to explain, after saying that Anaximenes believed in the existence of gods, that nevertheless the airy substance of the world was not created by them but they actually took their origin from it.

It follows that neither the writers of theogonies nor the Milesian philosophers admitted the notion of *design* (τέχνη) as responsible for the world-order.

This had immensely important consequences for philosophy, which do not, however, become immediately apparent. For the present, thought rests content in the idea that nature herself has generative power, and by nature (φύσις) is meant an actual material substance— that of which the world is made—which is assumed to be alive and so capable of initiating the changes to which it is itself subject, a fact which the Milesians expressed by referring to it not only as water or air or the boundless, but also as god or the divine. This was not an assumption with which thought could rest content. Later philosophers became dissatisfied with it, and tended in varying degrees to separate the ideas of life and matter and see them as residing in different entities. Anaxagoras in the time of Pericles is the first to separate Mind explicitly as that which ordered the universe in the beginning, declaring it to be entirely apart from matter.[1] This would seem to give more than a hint of conscious design, yet it is well known how loud were the complaints of Socrates and his followers Plato and Aristotle that although Anaxagoras posited Mind at the beginning, when it came to working out the subsequent processes by which the world had evolved he made no use of Mind at all, but alleged purely mechanical causes just like the others.

Diogenes of Apollonia, a younger contemporary of Anaxagoras, restored for a while the unity of matter and spirit in a single living substance which for him, as long before for Anaximenes, was air. Possibly under the influence of Anaxagoras, he laid stress on the mental qualities of this divine element, going so far as to say (fr. 3) that without its intelligence the universe could not have been ordered as it is, everything keeping within its due bounds, summer and winter, night and day, foul weather and fine; and if you reflect, he adds, you will find that everything else is disposed in the best possible manner. This seems to go a long way; yet for Diogenes as for the Milesians intelligence is still only an attribute of the primary matter which is itself subject to the evolutionary process. We have not yet arrived at the true idea of creation, to which Plato attached so much importance, and which sets the divine Craftsman and his material over against and independent of each other from the beginning.

The influence of the Ionian tradition was in fact in the other direction. As the notion of a divine generative power inherent in nature itself became more and more difficult to retain, and the idea of art or design proceeding from the mind of an independently existing being had not yet emerged as a serious competitor, there came to be asserted as the ultimate cause the only possible alternative: chance, or a blind, unreasoning necessity. These were the causes invoked by the Atomists, in whom the Ionian succession finds its logical conclusion. Natural

[1] μέμεικται οὐδενὶ χρήματι (fr. 12).

143

forces work blindly, without any conscious aiming at a particular end, and from their interaction there happens to emerge a cosmos. Empedocles too taught that the cosmos, including plant and animal life, came about by the purely random interplay of the four elemental substances.

This philosophy which exalted as first cause a 'nature' operating in a purely mechanical and non-teleological way, and looked upon intelligent design as something secondary both in time and importance and operating only on the human plane, was seized on in the fifth century by opponents of the traditional framework of religion, morality and law, and threatened to exercise an influence over a far wider field than that of natural philosophy. For Plato, inheriting the moral ideas of Socrates at the beginning of the fourth century, it represented a spiritual peril, and he summoned all his mental powers to oppose it. This controversy will concern us later, but meanwhile, since the attitude so hateful to Plato undoubtedly owes its ultimate origin to the early Ionian philosophers, we may glance at his own description of it and keep it in mind as we proceed.

According to them [writes Plato in the *Laws* (x, 889 A)], the greatest and best things are the work of nature and chance. Smaller things are wrought by art, which received from the hands of nature the formation of the great and primary works, and moulds and contrives all the smaller sort, which in fact we call 'artificial'.... Let me put it more clearly. They assert that fire and water and earth and air all exist by nature and by chance. None of them is the product of art, and the bodies next after them—the earth, sun, moon, stars and so forth—were produced by them acting as purely lifeless agents. Then they drifted at random, each according to its particular capacity, fitting together as happened to be practicable, hot with cold, dry with moist, soft with hard, as many as were combined in the mingling of opposites, of necessity and as chance ordained. In this manner and by these processes were generated the whole heaven and everything in it, all animals also and plants. Neither intelligence, nor god, nor art, they say, is the cause, but, as I have told you, nature and chance. Art, as a product of these forces, came later. It is something mortal, from mortal origins, and later produced certain toys which have no great part in reality but are a kind of imitations resembling the arts themselves.

(*c*) In speaking of the evolutionary character of nature as viewed by the Milesians, it has been necessary to say much about their hylozoism also, since these two aspects prove to be inseparable. It only remains to add that this question of whether, and to what extent, life is inherent in matter, the moving cause identified with the body moved, will be found to run as a leading thread through the whole development of Presocratic thought. For the Milesians the union of matter and spirit in a material substance like air is an assumption that raises no doubts and calls for no argument or defence. As Aristotle rightly said, they were not at all dissatisfied with themselves. Gradually, but only gradually, the difficulties of such a conception become apparent, and some of the obscurity of their successors—Heraclitus for instance—may be explicable by the fact that matter and spirit are tugging more and more strongly at the bonds which unite them, but philosophers have not yet become fully aware of where the trouble lies, nor of the necessity to separate the two. The climax comes with the declaration of Parmenides that motion and change are impossible and inadmissible conceptions. Those who followed him were dominated by the necessity to escape from this disconcerting conclusion, and their attempts to do so led not only to the assumption of a plurality of primary substances in place of the single *arche* of the Milesians, but in the end to the hypothesis of a moving cause outside and above the substance of the physical world.

IV

PYTHAGORAS AND THE PYTHAGOREANS

The history of Pythagoreanism is perhaps the most controversial subject in all Greek philosophy,[1] and much about it must remain obscure. For this there are several good reasons, which are themselves not without interest. The subject is not only obscure but highly complex, and its complexity demands above all a clear statement at the outset of what is to be attempted and the outline of a plan of campaign.

First, is it justifiable to put a general account of the Pythagoreans at this early point in the exposition? Pythagoras was a contemporary of Anaximenes, but his school existed, and its doctrines developed and diverged, for the next two hundred years. Little can be attributed with certainty to the founder himself, and much Pythagorean teaching is associated with the names of philosophers of the late fifth or early fourth century. There is, however, no doubt that Pythagoras inaugurated a new tradition in philosophy, sharply divided in purpose and doctrine, as in external organization, from anything that we have met hitherto, and that from his time onwards this new current is something to be reckoned with. The Italian outlook exists in contrast to the Ionian, and an individual philosopher is likely to be influenced by sympathy with, or reaction against, the one or the other. Pythagoras himself is mentioned by the contemporary writer Xenophanes and by Heraclitus not many years after his death, and for an understanding of the development of thought during the fifth century it is important to have some idea of the main features of Pythagorean teaching which were certainly known to the philosophers of the period.

The attempt might be made to treat at this point only the earliest phase of the school, leaving until their proper chronological place the developments and divergences that culminated in a Philolaus and an

---

[1] No one can claim even to have plumbed what a modern scholar has despondently called 'the bottomless pit' of research on the Pythagoreans. In any case the scope of the present work forbids us to enter into all the detail and take part in every dispute.

Archytas and the use which they made of the latest mathematical and astronomical discoveries. This, however, would immediately meet the difficulty that our sources are in many cases too vague to allow of certain decision concerning the chronological sequence of doctrines or their attribution to a particular thinker. Moreover although divergences occurred, and strongly individual philosophers arose within the school, it was characteristic of the Pythagoreans to combine progressive thought with an immense respect for tradition. All revered the founder and claimed to belong to his brotherhood, and underlying any diversity of doctrine was an abiding unity of outlook. For the historian of philosophy the important thing is to understand as far as possible the spirit and doctrinal basis of this outlook as it existed up to the time of Plato. Lack of this understanding is a severe handicap in the study of Plato himself, on whose thought Pythagoreanism was so obviously a major formative influence. This pre-Platonic Pythagoreanism can to a large extent be regarded as a unity. We shall note developments and differences as and when we can, but it would be unwise to hope that these, in the fragmentary state of our knowledge, are sufficiently distinguishable chronologically to allow the separate treatment of earlier and later phases. The best course will be that which Aristotle himself felt forced to adopt before the end of the fourth century B.C. On the whole he regards the ideas of all previous generations of Pythagoreans as sufficiently homogeneous to be spoken of together, but in his general treatment he sometimes refers to or criticizes a tenet which he confines to 'some' of the school or to a named individual within it. At this distance of time we can hardly hope to do more.

The obscurity which surrounds the Pythagoreans is not merely due to the external circumstance that, as with the Milesians, most of the early records have perished. It is intimately bound up with the nature of the school itself. It was of the essence of Pythagoreanism that it should cause these difficulties to later interpreters, as indeed to most interpreters outside its own fellowship, and a summary of the difficulties that face us will be in part a summary of certain characteristics of the brotherhood itself. In this way the problem of the nature of the evidence, always prominent at this early stage of Greek thought, takes on here an altogether new and enhanced importance.

It seems best therefore first to enumerate the chief difficulties which stand in the way of a historian of the school, secondly to indicate briefly the resources and methods at the disposal of scholars to overcome these difficulties, and only after that to attempt, thirdly, an outline of the most interesting and important tenets and characteristics of the school. If at this third stage it should prove impossible, without undue loss of clarity, to complicate the account by a constant citation of authorities for every statement made, the two foregoing sections will at least have indicated the kind of process by which the results have been attained, and hence the degree of credence which they are likely to merit.

A. DIFFICULTIES

With Pythagoras the motive for philosophy ceases to be primarily what it had been for the Ionians, namely curiosity or technical improvement, and becomes the search for a way of life whereby a right relationship might be established between the philosopher and the universe. Plato will serve as witness to this well-known fact. In the *Republic*, deploring the uselessness of poets, he criticizes Homer thus (600B):

Do we hear that Homer himself in his lifetime became for certain people personally a guide to their education? Are there any who admired him as disciples a master, and handed down to later generations a Homeric way of life, like Pythagoras, who himself was especially admired on this account, and his followers down to this day are conspicuous among the rest of men for the Pythagorean manner of life as they call it?

Pythagoras was indeed as much a religious and political teacher as a philosopher, and founded an organized society of men pledged to uphold his teaching in practice. For the present we are only concerned to notice one or two inevitable consequences of this.

(1) In a society which is a religious sect rather than a philosophical school, the name of the founder is held in particular veneration. He tends to be, if not actually deified, at least heroized or canonized, and in consequence his memory gets surrounded by a haze of legend. This happened early to Pythagoras. Herodotus (IV, 95) tells how he was brought into relation with the Thracian figure of Zalmoxis by a story that Zalmoxis had been his slave and pupil. Herodotus himself is

sceptical, and in fact Zalmoxis was undoubtedly a deity of Thrace. The legends were well launched by the time Aristotle wrote his treatise on the Pythagoreans. Quotations from this work speak of their 'highly secret' division of rational creatures into three classes: gods, men, and beings like Pythagoras. Aristotle told also the stories of how Pythagoras had appeared in two places at once, how when he was seen stripped it was observed that he had a golden thigh, how once when he crossed a river the voice of the river-god was heard saying 'Hail Pythagoras!', how he killed by his own bite a snake whose bite was fatal, and so forth. He was credited with prophecies, and the men of Croton identified him with the Hyperborean Apollo.[1] For the events of Pythagoras's life we have no earlier source than Aristotle, and it is obvious that the existence of these legends tends to cast doubt on other parts of the tradition which in themselves seem credible enough.

(2) In a religious school there is a particularly strong temptation, not only to venerate the founder, but to attribute all its doctrine to him personally. It is 'the word of the Master'. This is not simply due to a pious desire to honour his memory, but is bound up with the religious view of truth which the Pythagoreans shared with adherents of the mystery-religions. They were indeed philosophers, and made scientific discoveries; but these they regarded in much the same light as the revelations which were an essential part of initiation into the mysteries. Many of their most important discoveries were mathematical, and there was always in the Greek mind a close connexion between mathematical, astronomical and religious speculation. Anecdotes may not be true, but their existence is revealing. One about an early Pythagorean called Hippasus says that he was heavily punished either for revealing to the world a secret of geometry or alternatively for accepting the credit for its discovery instead of allowing it to Pythagoras. The secret is sometimes said to have been the incommensurability of the diagonal of a square with its sides, but the traditions both of secrecy and of *ipse dixit*[2] are much too strong for us to believe, as has been suggested in modern times, that this was only disapproved of because the discovery of irrationals was an embarrassing skeleton in the

[1] Arist. frr. 191, 192 Rose, DK, 14, 7.
[2] See e.g. Cic. *N.D.* I, 5, 10, D.L. VIII, 46.

Pythagorean cupboard. The fate of Hippasus was either drowning at sea or expulsion and the raising of a tomb to him as if dead.[1] Where scientific facts are regarded thus as parts of a secret lore, there is a natural tendency to suppose them all to have been implicit in the original revelation of the founder.

Another motive is perhaps more difficult for a modern mind to appreciate. In the ancient world it was considered that a doctrine gained greatly in authority if it could be claimed to be, not the latest word on its subject, but of a venerable antiquity. Although this applied especially to religious teaching, it was by no means confined to it,[2] and indeed, as a study of the Pythagoreans makes clear, there was no sharp distinction between 'scientific' and 'religious' knowledge. An obvious parallel on the religious side is provided by the Orphic writers, and since the religion taught by Pythagoras had much in common with these, the parallel is apt. All Orphic writings were produced under the name of Orpheus, although their composition continued beyond the beginning of the Christian era. According to a tradition going back to the fifth century B.C. (Ion of Chios, DK, 36 B 2), Pythagoras himself was one of those who wrote under this name. A feature of the Orphic teaching was its seemingly conscious rivalry with Homer, to whose conception of the relations between god and man it stood in strong contradiction. But to withstand so great an authority its prophet must claim superiority both in age and inspiration. Orpheus was the son of a Muse, and as an Argonaut he belonged to the earlier, heroic age of which Homer told, not the later age of lesser men in which Homer himself had lived.

(3) Besides the miraculous stories of the founder and the promulgation of later doctrine in his name, an obvious difficulty for the historian is constituted by the secrecy already mentioned. Like the mystery-cults which it in some ways resembled, Pythagoreanism too had its secrets (ἄρρητα or ἀπόρρητα). Aristotle speaks of them in the fragment (192) already quoted, and his pupil Aristoxenus, who was a friend of the Pythagoreans of his day, said in his work on rules of

---

[1] Iambl. *V.P.* 88 *et al.*, DK, 18, 4.

[2] E. Frank noted that the tendency to attribute recent discoveries to ancient wisdom was not confined to the religious schools, but was a more general fashion in Plato's time (*Plato u. d. sog. Pyth.* 72f.).

education that according to them 'not everything was to be divulged to all men'.[1] Isocrates in a bantering vein (*Bus.* 29) remarks that those who claim to be disciples of Pythagoras are more admired for their silence than are the most famous orators for their speech. We may also quote Porphyry here, for the Neoplatonic writers are usually so ready to believe anything that their rare expressions of doubt or scepticism are all the more striking. Iamblichus, who was Porphyry's pupil, cheerfully attributes any Pythagorean doctrine to Pythagoras himself, even when 'the Pythagoreans' was all that stood in his source. In his life of Pythagoras, however (ch. 19), Porphyry writes: 'What he said to his intimates, no man can say with certainty, for they maintained a remarkable silence.' This is sufficiently impressive even if the words are not, like the preceding sentences, excerpted from Dicaearchus, which would take us back again from Neoplatonism to the fourth century B.C.[2]

Iamblichus tells us (*V.P.* 72, 94) that applicants for membership of the brotherhood were made by Pythagoras to keep a five-year silence as part of their novitiate. If this is true, the famous Pythagorean silence was of two kinds, for we cannot suppose that the passages just quoted refer to this rule of training and no more.[3] In reply to the argument that these authorities must be wrong, because in fact a great deal of Pythagorean teaching did become widely known, there is not much that needs to be said. It is perfectly possible for certain doctrines to be held in awe, coupled with a feeling that they should not be spoken of, long after the religious rule of silence imposed by the founders of a sect or cult has been broken and is known to have been broken. Some will be stricter than others, and more deeply shocked to hear the *arcana* openly avowed, but the feeling of *religio* still clings. It was well described by Lobeck in *Aglaophamus* (65–7), where he says, with particular reference to the Pythagoreans: 'De iis rebus quae iam notiores neque apud omnes sanctae essent, adeo religiose locuti sunt veteres nihilque in quo vel umbra quaedam arcani resideret, in publico

---

[1] Fr. 43 Wehrli, D.L. VIII, 15. Wehrli also attributes to Aristoxenus the sentence earlier in the chapter of D.L. that up to the time of Philolaus it was impossible to acquire a knowledge of any Pythagorean doctrine.

[2] Delatte assumed that they were (*Études*, 98, n. 1), but Wehrli omits them from the relevant fragment of Dicaearchus.

[3] Some have of course tried, but the necessity for the distinction was convincingly put by Ritter and Preller, *Hist. Phil. Gr.* 55, note *a*, p. 45.

iactarunt.' He has just quoted the story from Plutarch of how, when the guests at a symposium were discussing the reasons for Pythagorean prohibitions, one of them, mindful of the presence among them of the Pythagorean Lucius who had been sitting silent for some time, said politely: 'If this conversation is offensive to Lucius, it is time we stopped it.' The other prohibitions enjoined by Pythagoras, such as abstention from certain kinds of food, were undoubtedly only observed by some Pythagoreans and not by others, and doubtless the same was true of the injunction to secrecy. It is of course more logical to observe a meatless diet, even though other members of your sect are less strict, than it is to keep silent on matters which others have divulged; but, as Lobeck has well brought out, this is not a matter of logic but of *religio*.

The existence of this feeling against open discussion of Pythagorean doctrine, even if the secrets were not inviolably kept, must inevitably have led to omissions and distortions in ancient writings on the subject; for where the truth is not freely communicated, its place is naturally filled by baseless rumour. Its seriousness as an impediment to the historian has been variously estimated, and of course we have not the evidence for an exact appraisal of the extent either of the official prohibition or of its observance. Some have thought that the rule of secrecy only applied to ritual actions, the 'things done' (δρώμενα) as they were called in the mysteries. As a rough generalization, this seems to have been true of the Eleusinian and Orphic mysteries, and if it were so, the loss might be strictly limited. But for one thing it may be difficult to understand a belief fully without knowledge of the act, if there was one, which embodied and illustrated it. Belief and ritual action, where they coexist, are not unconnected. For another, the evidence of stories like that of Hippasus tells against this view.

It has also been suggested that although doubtless certain dogmas were included among the *arcana*, these will only have been matters of religious faith: there can have been no secrecy about their purely philosophical investigations. The objection to this is similar: there is no ground for separating the religious from the philosophical or scientific side in a system like the Pythagorean. In contrast to the Milesian tradition, it undertook philosophical researches with the conscious purpose of making them serve as a basis for religion. Mathematics was a religious occupation and the decad a holy symbol. If anything, there is more evidence for the jealous guarding of mathematical secrets than for that of any teaching about the gods or the soul. It is certainly difficult to believe that the doctrine of transmigration was ever treated as secret. But the truth is that the two sides are inextricably interwoven. We shall never know just how serious a bar to knowledge was the imperfectly kept rule of secrecy; but of its existence the evidence allows no doubt.[1]

(4) These are three results of the particular character of Pythagoreanism which inevitably make difficulties for the historian: the legends which gathered round the figure of its founder, the tendency—from a variety of motives—to trace back to him all their doctrines and discoveries, and the secrecy with which some at least of their teaching was surrounded. There are other difficulties not arising solely from this cause, chief among them being the scantiness of contemporary sources of information. The word 'contemporary' is used here with the same thought in mind that it is the Pythagoreanism of the period from the lifetime of Pythagoras to the early fourth century which it would be especially desirable to understand, since that is the Pythagoreanism which Plato knew, and to be able to assess its meaning for him would perhaps be a greater gain to the history of philosophy than any assessment of the Pythagoreans for their own sake. Yet Plato only mentions Pythagoras once (in the quotation on p. 148, above) and the Pythagoreans once, in another passage in the *Republic* (530 D) where Socrates says that they regard music and astronomy as sister sciences. Aristotle, if the reference to Pythagoras in *Metaph.* A, 986a30, is genuine, mentions him only twice in his extant works; but the authenticity of the passage is doubtful.[2] The other reference is *Rhet.* B, 1398b14.

---

[1] The reasons for this may have been in part political as well as religious, cf. E. L. Minar, *Early Pyth. Politics*, 26. As Minar shows in this chapter, the Pythagorean society had much in common with political ἑταιρεῖαι elsewhere in Greece. He can, however, produce no positive evidence that their secrets had a political content.

[2] See Ross *ad loc.*; yet it seems a little hard that the rarity of the early mentions of Pythagoras should itself become a ground for depriving us of them ('The suspiciousness of the words is increased by the fact that Aristotle only once elsewhere mentions Pythagoras, and nowhere claims any knowledge of his date'), especially when one takes into consideration the fact that Aristotle's works on the Pythagoreans are lost. Even such quotations from them as we have suffice to prove untrue the statement that he only once elsewhere mentions Pythagoras; this needs to be qualified by adding 'in the extant works'.

Neither is very informative, since the first only says that Alcmaeon lived in the old age of Pythagoras, and in the second Aristotle is quoting from Alcidamas, the pupil of Gorgias, an example of an inductive argument in which the sentence 'the Italians honoured Pythagoras' occurs. When we come to the 'fragments' of Aristotle, it is advisable to be cautious, since most of them are not represented as his actual words, and some in late compilers are doubtless at second or third hand. Moreover we have direct evidence that writers of Neopythagorean or Neoplatonic persuasion felt little compunction in substituting the name of Pythagoras himself for that of the Pythagoreans in citing their authorities. If we can trust our sources, we have half a dozen mentions of Pythagoras quoted from Aristotle, which will be used and criticized later as necessary. Their limitations may here be briefly indicated. They tell us that he believed in Pythagoras's Tyrrhenian descent, made passing mention of Cylon's opposition to him, told of his miracles and the Pythagorean division of rational creatures into gods, men and such as Pythagoras, and spoke of his prohibitions, including that of the eating of beans. Damascius credits him with the attribution to Pythagoras of a philosophical doctrine stated unmistakably in his own and Plato's terminology, which may yet be a genuine Aristotelian restatement of early Pythagorean teaching, and in the *Protrepticus* of Iamblichus we have what is probably an authentic extract from the *Protrepticus* of Aristotle in which he quotes Pythagoras as having said that the chief end of man is the observation of the heavens and of nature.[1]

Of Pythagorean philosophy Aristotle in his surviving works gives plenty of explanation and criticism, though it is not always easy to understand. He likes to refer to the school as 'those who are called Pythagoreans', no doubt implying that it would be uncritical to assume that all their doctrines go back to Pythagoras himself, but also calls them 'the Italians' and their philosophy 'the Italian'. In *De Caelo* (293a20) he gives them the full title: 'The philosophers of Italy who are called Pythagoreans'. He also speaks of 'some Pythagoreans' as

[1] Arist. frr. 190 Rose (Clem. Alex.), 75 (D.L.), 191 (Apoll. Tyan. and others), 192 (Iambl.), 195 (D.L.), 207 (Damasc.), Iambl. *Protr.* 9, p. 51 Pist. (Ross, Arist. *Sel. Frr.*, Oxf. trans. 1952, 45).

maintaining a certain view, which suggests divisions within the school (such as are spoken of in later tradition) and perhaps a feeling of vagueness and uncertainty already existing in his own mind.[1]

Aristotle is the earliest author to give any detailed information about the Pythagoreans, and in trying to recover their views up to the time of Plato it will be necessary to pay the closest attention to what he says. Of Pythagoras himself as a writer we have only the contradictory statements of much later men, some of whom say that he wrote nothing while others claim to give the names of some of his books. Knowing the tendency of the school to attribute all its works to the founder, we shall treat these claims with well-merited suspicion. We have no fragments of Pythagorean writings before the time of Philolaus, the leader of the school at Thebes at the end of the fifth century who is mentioned in Plato's *Phaedo*. Indeed Diogenes Laertius states (VIII, 15) that up to the time of Philolaus knowledge of Pythagorean beliefs was impossible.[2] There exist a number of fragments attributed to him, but unfortunately their genuineness is much disputed. Not only have we no Pythagorean writings before this time, but surviving Greek literature from Pythagoras's lifetime to the end of the fifth century provides only some half-dozen mentions of himself or his school. This is the more unfortunate in that their doctrines were certainly influential from the beginning. Democritus is said (D.L. IX, 38) to have written a book on Pythagoras, yet his extant fragments contain no explicit reference to Pythagorean doctrine.

The most abundant, and on the face of it precise, part of our information originates with the revival of Pythagoreanism which began about the time of Cicero and continued until the rise of the Neoplatonic school in the third century A.D. Indeed the Neoplatonists, who are the direct source of much of this information, absorbed many of its beliefs, as it in its turn had absorbed those of the Academy. From the Neoplatonists we have books on the life of Pythagoras and on the Pythagorean life by Porphyry the pupil of Plotinus and Iamblichus the pupil

---

[1] It is important to avoid translating the word καλούμενοι as 'so-called', for it carries none of the implications of spuriousness which the English phrase suggests. On the dangers of this see the sensible remarks of Cherniss, *ACP*, 384f. (Also *Gnomon*, 1959, 37.)

[2] This observation, which also occurs in Iambl. *V.P.* 199, probably goes back to Aristoxenus (p. 151, n. 1, above).

of Porphyry. Both are compilations—that of Iamblichus a particularly careless one—and their immediate sources are Neopythagorean. From the point of view of one who is anxious to extract from it genuine early Pythagorean doctrine and history, this Neopythagorean material suffered from two related faults:

(i) A love of the marvellous. It arose in an age very different from that of the sixth and fifth centuries B.C., an age when men felt themselves adrift in a world so large that they had lost their bearings and looked to philosophy for an anchor on which they could outride the storm. Philosophy tended to become wholly religious in character, and religion was all too often degenerating into superstition. There was a remarkable recrudescence of primitive religious phenomena. A magical formula, for instance, which at first sight gives the impression of being genuinely primitive, is equally likely to be a product of the declining intellectual standards of this age of credulity, which are amply vouched for by the magical papyri of Alexandrian and Roman times. The religious and magical element, though undoubtedly present in Pythagoreanism from the beginning, was thus easily exaggerated.

(ii) As a natural corollary to their religious and superstitious character, these later writers exhibit a singular lack of any critical faculty in compiling their accounts. Their interest in Pythagoras was after all very different from ours, namely to use him as an inspiration for their own age, not to achieve a strictly historical account of him and his school; and when one considers the number of philosophical schools that by this time existed for them to play with, it is not surprising that earlier and later, Pythagorean and non-Pythagorean material are thoroughly mingled in the 'Pythagoreanism' which they present. Plato and Aristotle, Stoic and Epicurean all play their part, and sometimes a doctrine attributed to an early Pythagorean can be easily recognized as an innovation of Aristotle or the Stoics. Whole books are extant, like the treatise on the World-Soul attributed to Timaeus of Locri, which are associated with the names of individual early members of the school but can be recognized from their content as pious forgeries from the time of its revival.

B. METHODS OF APPROACH

What then are the resources at our disposal, and what methods can we employ, to overcome these difficulties and arrive at a modicum of fact concerning the history and nature of Pythagoreanism in the period from Pythagoras to Plato?

(1) *Sources of the sixth and fifth centuries*

The first thing to do is to note every scrap of early evidence. Though lamentably scanty, it is of value both for itself and as a touchstone to apply in a critical investigation of later information. The few testimonies of the sixth and fifth centuries may be dealt with here.

(*a*) Xenophanes of Colophon must have been born within a few years of Pythagoras, though he probably outlived him for a good many. He left his native Ionia as a young man, and spent the rest of his life as an exile, largely in Sicily and Italy. The tone of his poems is highly satirical in their treatment of others, and Diogenes Laertius (VIII, 36, Xenoph. fr. 7 DK) quotes four of his elegiac lines as having been written about Pythagoras. They ridicule his doctrine of the transmigration of souls by telling the story of how he saw a man beating a dog, and exclaimed: 'Stop, do not beat him: it is the soul of a friend, I recognize his voice.'

(*b*) The life of Heraclitus also in all likelihood overlapped that of Pythagoras. In a passage designed to illustrate his proud and contemptuous nature, Diogenes gives the following as a quotation from his book (D.L. IX, 1, Heracl. fr. 40 DK): 'Much learning does not teach insight (νόον); otherwise it would have taught Hesiod and Pythagoras, and again Xenophanes and Hecataeus.' There is also fr. 129, which runs, literally translated: 'Pythagoras son of Mnesarchus practised inquiry most of all men, and having made a selection of these writings contrived a wisdom (σοφίην; perhaps better "learning" or "cleverness") of his own, a polymathy, a worthless artifice.'[1] The rather obscure words 'having made a selection of these writings', if they are a genuine part of the fragment and correctly transmitted, cannot refer to writings of Pythagoras himself as Diogenes

---

[1] Πυθαγόρης Μνησάρχου ἱστορίην ἤσκησεν ἀνθρώπων μάλιστα πάντων καὶ ἐκλεξάμενος ταύτας τὰς συγγραφὰς ἐποιήσατο ἑαυτοῦ σοφίην, πολυμαθίην, κακοτεχνίην. The authenticity of the fragment has been questioned in the past, but recent opinion rightly accepts it: 'certainly genuine' (Kirk, *HCF*, 390); 'Trotzdem dringt die Ansicht mit recht durch, dass das Fragment echt sei' (Kranz, DK, I, p. 181, n.). See also Wilamowitz, *Gl. d. Hell.* II (1932), p. 188, n. 1, Cameron, *Pyth. Background*, p. 23, n. 11, and for earlier views Delatte, *Vie de Pyth.* 161 ff.

supposes (VIII, 6: he is disputing the view that Pythagoras wrote nothing), but seem to constitute a charge of plagiarism.[1]

(c) The many-sided writer Ion of Chios was born about 490, perhaps little later than the death of Pythagoras, and from a line in the *Peace* of Aristophanes (see 832 ff.) it appears that he was dead by 421 when that play was produced. According to Diogenes, he said in his philosophical work *Triagmoi* (in which after the Pythagorean fashion he exalted the cosmic importance of the triad) that Pythagoras had produced some writings under the name of Orpheus (D.L. VIII, 8, Ion, fr. 2 DK). Diogenes also quotes elegiac lines of his on Pherecydes in which he alludes to the teaching of Pythagoras on the soul (I, 120, Ion, fr. 4): 'So he, endowed with manliness and modesty, has for his soul a joyful life even in death, if indeed Pythagoras, wise in all things, truly knew and understood the minds of men.' There is some doubt about the exact translation of the last two lines, but they certainly appeal to Pythagoras for the doctrine that a good man will be rewarded after death.[2]

The opening of Ion's *Triagmoi* (fr. 1) shows that he admired and adopted Pythagorean ideas,[3] and fr. 2 strongly suggests that he made use of Orphic poems which, rightly or wrongly, were in his time ascribed to Pythagoras. No doubt it was in these that he found the doctrine of rewards (and presumably punishments) after death for which in his elegiacs he claims Pythagoras as the authority.[4]

(d) Herodotus was an almost exact contemporary of Ion, for it is fairly certain that he was born in 485/4. In book IV, ch. 93–4, he describes the religion of the Thracian Getae, who are remarkable for their belief in immortality. They think, he says, that they do not really die, but at death are transported to their god Zalmoxis (who is also mentioned as a Thracian god by Plato, *Charmides*, 156D). The Greeks, however, who live in the Black Sea region have a different story about this Zalmoxis. They say that he was a human being, who had been Pythagoras's slave in Samos. Having gained his freedom and made a fortune he returned to his native people, and, finding them

---

[1] In spite of Kranz, *Hermes*, 1934, 115 f. To provide an antecedent for ταύτας, Gercke (see Delatte, *op. cit.* 162) seems to have taken ἀνθρώπων πάντων as a possessive genitive after ἱστορίην, thus: 'P. worked over the researches of other men, and making a selection of these writings....'

[2] In l. 3 Mr F. H. Sandbach has suggested the simple and convincing emendation σοφὸς ὅς for ὁ σοφός: 'If Pythagoras was truly wise, he who knew and understood the opinions of men about all things.' This might have been written with a sidelong glance at Heraclitus, fr. 129 (*Proc. Camb. Philol. Soc.* 1958/9, 36).

[3] Even to say this is, admittedly, to invoke somewhat later evidence than we have hitherto considered, but I think it is fair enough to refer on this point to a passage like Arist. *De Caelo*, 268a11.

[4] Cf. W. Kranz in *Hermes*, 1934, 227 f., where also different translations of the last two lines are discussed.

primitive and stupid, determined to improve them. 'Since, then,' Herodotus continues, 'he was acquainted with the Ionian standard of life and with habits more civilized than those of the Thracians, having lived among Greeks and indeed with one of the most powerful of Greek teachers, Pythagoras, he constructed a hall in which he received the leading citizens, and in the course of a banquet instructed them that neither he nor his guests nor their descendants would die, but they would go to a place where they would live for ever and enjoy all good things.' This Greek story went on to tell of a trick which Zalmoxis played to gain credit for his new teaching. He retired into a secret underground chamber for three years, during which time the Thracians believed him dead. In the fourth year he reappeared, thus seeming to demonstrate his immortality. Herodotus himself is sceptical about the story, maintaining that if Zalmoxis were indeed a man and not a god, then he must have lived a long time before Pythagoras.

Of course the Thracian belief in immortality, which Herodotus represents as having been accompanied by human sacrifice, owed nothing to Greek influence. The interesting thing is that the Greeks noted the resemblance between it and the teaching of Pythagoras, and used it as evidence that in this, as in so much else, they had been the teachers of the barbarians. The instruction in immortality is represented as the direct consequence of association with the great Greek teacher. Probably the resemblance extended to a common belief in transmigration, which we already know to have been taught by Pythagoras, since the reappearance of Zalmoxis in a body more than three years after his death seems to demand something of the sort. Similar beliefs were in any case common among these northern peoples, and entered from them into Greek mythology. Thus Aristeas of Proconnesus (another figure familiar to 'the Greeks who live by the Hellespont and Pontus') reappeared seven years after he was thought to have died, and again 240 years after that, and also took the body of a raven (Hdt. IV, 14). If there was borrowing here, it is far more likely to have been the other way round.[1]

Herodotus, besides what he says about Pythagoras, provides the first extant mention of a Pythagorean sect. Opinions differ on whether

---

[1] Cf. E. R. Dodds, *The Greeks and the Irrational*, 143 f. Admittedly the parallel is not complete, since in Pythagorean belief the soul was commonly reborn in a *different* body. Pythagoras had lived previously as Aethalides and Euphorbus, not himself.

he is speaking of Pythagoreans or Pythagorean rites, since the adjective as he uses it might be masculine or neuter, but this at present is unimportant. The passage (II, 81) has been in its detailed interpretation the subject of prolonged controversy, into which our present purpose does not compel us to enter.[1] Herodotus has been saying that though the Egyptians (who are the subject of this whole second book) wear wool in ordinary life, they do not wear it in temples nor are they buried in it, for this is against their religion. He continues: 'The Egyptians agree in this with the Orphics, as they are called, and with the Pythagoreans; for it is similarly against the rule for anyone who takes part in these rites to be buried in woollen garments. These customs are the subject of a sacred book.'

It was a favourite thesis of Herodotus, in which he certainly goes beyond both truth and probability, that the Greeks had borrowed their most notable religious ideas, and even their deities, from the Egyptians. It would be captious not to mention here the place in which he gives as Egyptian, 'but borrowed by the Greeks both earlier and later', a more detailed version of the doctrine of transmigration which there is good reason for thinking was shared by the Pythagoreans and the Orphics (II, 123). But since Herodotus does not here cite the Pythagoreans by name (only remarking, to the disgust of the modern historian, that he knows the names of the Greeks concerned but is keeping them to himself), this must find no emphasis in the present brief survey of early references. One may simply add that the doctrine was certainly a Greek one, since in fact Egyptian religion knew nothing of transmigration.

(*e*) I have left until the last, slightly out of chronological order, a writer a little older than Herodotus who was himself a notable religious philosopher and shared with the Pythagoreans an enthusiastic belief in transmigration: Empedocles. This is because, although there can be no reasonable doubt that the subject of his eulogy is Pythagoras, he leaves him unnamed, and it is in keeping with our present strict canon to mark the fact. Our

---

[1] For an exhaustive discussion with full bibliography see I. M. Linforth, *The Arts of Orpheus*, pp. 38–50. The translation which he finally gives may be accepted as a perfectly safe one, except that it seems unnatural, despite his arguments, to suppose that Herodotus meant to refer the 'sacred book' to the Egyptians. With the exception of the last sentence, then, I give Linforth's translation.

source for the quotation, Porphyry in his life of Pythagoras, refers the lines
to him, and this attribution goes back to the Sicilian historian Timaeus in the
fourth century B.C.; but since Diogenes Laertius (VIII, 54) also says that some
referred them (quite impossibly) to Parmenides, we must suppose that the
praise was bestowed anonymously.[1] They are as follows (fr. 129): 'There
was among them a man of surpassing knowledge, who possessed vast wealth
of understanding, capable of all kinds of cunning acts; for when he exerted
himself with all his understanding, easily did he see every one of all the
things that are, in ten and even twenty human lives.'

(2) *Fourth-century sources excluding Aristotle and his pupils*

The chronological divisions in this preliminary survey are inevitably
arbitrary. Plato was born in 427 and when he spoke of the Pythagoreanism of the fifth century knew what he was talking about.[2]
Aristotle was Plato's close associate for twenty years. Nevertheless it is
as well to regard Plato and his contemporaries as reflecting a period
of their own, different in spirit and intellectual content from that of the
early and mid fifth century and again from the new era of research into
which philosophy enters with Aristotle and those trained in his school,
and which gives to his evidence a distinctive stamp. Moreover his
surviving treatises are in themselves so rich a source, comparatively
speaking, that at this stage they can only be mentioned. Later they will
be used.

(*a*) We have noted (p. 153) that Plato only once mentions the Pythagoreans by name, but this single reference is of great importance. In the seventh
book of the *Republic*, discussing the course of study which is to be laid down
for the philosophical Guardians, Socrates comes to astronomy, and explains
that it is not to be limited to a study of the stars and their visible motions.

---

[1] For modern opinions of the attribution to Pythagoras the following may be cited: *Against*:
Zeller, *Sitzungsb. Preuss. Akad.* 1889, 989f.; Rathmann, *Quaestt. Pythag.* 42, 138. *For*: Delatte,
Vie de Pyth. 157, n. 1; Rohde, *Psyche*, 406, n. 96, 598; I. Lévy, *Rech. sur les sources de la légende
de P.* 6, n. 2; Nestle, *Philol. Woch.* 1934, 409; Cameron, *Pythag. Background*, 20f.; Verdenius,
Mnemosyne, 1947, 282. Mondolfo (*Fil. d. Greci*, II, 329f.), Diels, Burnet and Cornford also agree
that the reference is to Pythagoras (see Cornford, *Princ. Sap.* 56).
[2] Heidel adduces no evidence for his statement (*AJP*, 1940, p. 7) that although Plato and his
school owed much to the Pythagoreans, and Socrates had among his associates men who were
somehow affiliated with them, 'it was, however, a revived Pythagoreanism in both cases'; and
in itself the statement seems to have no clear meaning. On the other hand it is reasonable to
assume a certain amount of *development* within the various branches of the school, and that is
what the paragraph above is intended to imply.

These must only be used as a means of reaching beyond them to the mathematical principles and laws of motion which they illustrate, but which, as visible and material objects, they cannot embody with perfect exactitude. The philosopher's aim must be to understand 'the true realities; that is, the movements and bodies in movement whose true relative speeds are to be found in terms of pure numbers and perfect figures, and which are perceptible to reason and thought but not visible to the eye'.[1]

From astronomy Socrates then passes, by what he claims is a natural transition, to harmonics (530D): 'I think we may say that, just as our eyes are made for astronomy, so our ears are made for harmony (ἐναρμόνιον φοράν), and that the two are, as the Pythagoreans say, and as we should agree, sister sciences.'[2] Because of the attention they have given to this study, Socrates continues, we must be prepared to learn from them. Nevertheless their work in this sphere shows a failure analogous to that of contemporary workers in astronomy, in that 'they look for numerical relationships in audible concords, and never get as far as formulating problems and asking which numerical relations are concordant and why'.

Although there is no other mention of the Pythagorean school as such, Plato has something to say about Philolaus, who stayed for a time in Thebes after the anti-Pythagorean revolution in Italy and was later believed to have been the first to put Pythagorean doctrine into writing. (I have omitted his fragments from the certain fifth-century evidence owing to the doubts that have been felt about their authenticity.) In the *Phaedo*, Simmias and Cebes are introduced into the conversation with Socrates as Thebans and pupils of Philolaus. When Socrates speaks of people who hold suicide to be unlawful, Cebes asks him to explain, and he expresses surprise that his friends, who have listened to Philolaus, have not heard all about matters of this sort from him. Cebes replies that he has indeed heard Philolaus and others express this view, but that they did not seem to make their reasons clear. Socrates then goes on to expound what he calls 'the account of it given in secret teachings',[3] a phrase strongly reminiscent of the well-known reticence of the Pythagoreans. According to this account we are in this world as men held in custody, from which it is not right to try to free ourselves or run away, because our guardians are the gods, and human beings are their possessions.

---

[1] 529D. The translations here given are Sir Desmond Lee's.

[2] Archytas, Pythagorean and friend of Plato, wrote of astronomy, mathematics, and music, ταῦτα γὰρ τὰ μαθήματα δοκοῦντι ἦμεν ἀδελφεά (fr. 1, DK, 1, 432, l. 7. On the genuineness of the frr. of Archytas see below, p. 335, n. 3).

For the meaning of 'harmony' or 'harmonics' at this period cf. I. Henderson in the *New Oxford Dictionary of Music*, 1, 340: '*Harmonics* meant *tuning*, or acoustic theory. Greek postulates were melodic and heterophonic, and ignored "harmony" in our sense.'

[3] ὁ ἐν ἀπορρήτοις λεγόμενος περὶ αὐτῶν λόγος (62B).

The explanation can hardly be separated from the injunction itself, and its religious message agrees with what we know of Philolaus from later sources, including an actual quotation attributed to him by Clement of Alexandria.[1]

(*b*) Isocrates, the rival of Plato and his elder by a few years, repeats for his own not very philosophical purposes the legend that Pythagoras owed all his wisdom to Egypt.[2] In his rhetorical exercise in praise of Busiris he repeats a number of Greek commonplaces about the Egyptians, including the belief in their religious genius and example.

'One who was not pressed for time', he continues (ch. 28), 'could tell many wonderful tales of their holiness, which I am not the only nor the first óne to observe. Many have done so both of present and past generations, among them Pythagoras of Samos, who went to Egypt, and having become their pupil was the first to introduce philosophy in general to Greece, and showed a more conspicuous zeal than other men for sacrifices and temple rites; for he reckoned that even if this led to no reward from heaven, among men at least it would bring him the highest reputation. And so it turned out. His fame so surpassed that of others that while all the young men wanted to be his disciples, the older would rather see their sons enjoying his company than minding their own affairs. The truth of this cannot be doubted, for even at the present day those who claim to be his disciples win more admiration by being silent than do those most noted for the gift of speech.'

We detect here the ironical note which so often creeps into the ordinary Greek's remarks on Pythagoras and his school, broadening sometimes into a more or less tolerant contempt. They were a favourite butt for the writers of the Middle Comedy in the late fourth century, who ridicule chiefly their abstention from flesh and other ascetic (and unhygienic) practices. (DK, 1, 478–80.)

(*c*) Heraclides of Pontus was a pupil of Plato, who joined the Academy at about the same time as Aristotle, and a notable philosopher and scientist in his own right. In his writings (of which only fragments remain) he dealt at some length with Pythagoras and his school, and there are signs that they exercised considerable influence on him.[3] Although his works are lost, later writers provide several quotations on this subject. They are referred to here in the numbering of F. Wehrli's edition of the fragments of Heraclides.

Fr. 40. Porphyry (*De Abst.* 1, 26) cites Heraclides among other authorities for the statement that the Pythagorean ban on flesh-eating is not absolute.

---

[1] See frr. 14 and 15, DK, 1, 413f., and further on this subject pages 309–12, below.
[2] Naturally Isocrates did not invent this legend, and it cannot be doubted that Pythagoras is one of those whom Herodotus had in mind at II, 123 (p. 160, above).
[3] Cf. Daebritz in *RE*, VIII, 473, Wehrli, p. 60. For divided opinions on Heraclides in antiquity see I. Lévy, *Rech. sur les sources de la légende de Pyth.* 22f.

Pythagoras and the Pythagoreans

Fr. 41 (Lydus, *De Mens.* IV, 42, p. 99 Wünsch). Heraclides explains the Pythagorean ban on beans by the curious superstition that if a bean is laid in a new tomb and covered with dung for forty days, it takes on the appearance of a man.

Fr. 44 (Clem. *Strom.* II, 84 St.). Heraclides attributes to Pythagoras the statement that happiness consists in knowledge of the perfection of the numbers of the soul.

Fr. 89 (D.L. VIII, 4). Heraclides tells, ostensibly on the authority of Pythagoras himself, of his successive incarnations. He was once Aethalides, who, when his father Hermes offered him any gift except immortality, chose to retain both in life and in death the memory of what happened to him. (Cf. Apollonius Rhodius, I, 640ff.) Later he became the Homeric hero Euphorbus, wounded by Menelaus, who was wont to recount the wanderings of his soul in animals and plants as well as human bodies, and tell of the fate of souls in Hades. Next his soul entered Hermotimus, who authenticated the story of his previous life by identifying the rotting shield of Menelaus in the temple of Apollo at Branchidae. It then became a Delian fisherman named Pyrrhus, and finally Pythagoras, carrying with it still the memory of its previous phases of existence.

Fr. 88. Cicero in the *Tusculans* (v, 3, 8) tells from Heraclides the story of Pythagoras's conversation with Leon the ruler of Phlius.[1] Leon, admiring the genius and eloquence of Pythagoras, questioned him about his art. He replied, however, that he was not a master of any art, but a philosopher. This word was strange to Leon, and, to explain to him what it meant, Pythagoras employed a simile which has become famous. Life, he said, is like the gathering at the Olympic festival, to which people flock from three motives: to compete for the glory of a crown, to buy and sell, or simply as spectators. So in life, to which we come *ex alia vita et natura profecti*, some enter the service of fame and others of money, but the best choice is that of those few who spend their time in the contemplation of nature, as lovers of wisdom, that is, philosophers.

The last quotation is a warning that if this section is to be confined to passages of undoubted independence as authorities for Pythagoreanism, then it is time to stop, for we have already entered the region of controversy. Heraclides wrote dialogues (see frr. 22ff.), and no doubt the conversation between Pythagoras and Leon occurred in one

[1] The other ancient references to the story are collected by Delatte, *Vie de Pyth.* 109, notes to lines 5–10. Phlius was known to Plato as a centre of Pythagoreanism, Cameron, *Pyth. Background*, 35, n. 27.

of these compositions which, like those of his teacher Plato, would have a moral rather than a historical purpose and could contain elements of free invention. Moreover the distinction between the three types of life, and corresponding types of humanity, was a favourite theme of Plato's, expressed most concisely in *Republic*, IX, 581C; and it is probably the prevailing view today that in this story 'Heraclides is projecting Academic ideas on to Pythagoras'.[1] A. Cameron, on the other hand,[2] has ably defended the view that Heraclides is relying largely on fifth-century material. The value of learning (σοφία, μάθος, θεωρία) was deeply rooted in Greek consciousness, as is amply illustrated in Herodotus, tragedy and elsewhere, and Pythagoras was early regarded as an outstanding exemplar of it (Heraclitus, Herodotus). Transmigration was a Pythagorean belief long before it was Platonic, and the notable thing about the presentation of Pythagoras's philosophic ideal in Heraclides is that it is firmly linked to that belief. In this it goes naturally with his other story of how the single soul which became Pythagoras amassed a store of remembered knowledge in its pilgrimage through several lives and the periods between them, which in its turn reminds us of the testimony of Empedocles, fr. 129, even more strongly than of Plato. Jaeger's dismissal of the words *nos...in hanc vitam ex alia vita et natura profectos* as 'nothing but Plato's well-known doctrine of the soul' is falsified by the words 'nothing but'. He continues (*Aristotle²*, 432, n. 1): 'We cannot infer from it that the doctrine of the three "lives" was Pythagorean, on the ground that the transmigration of souls was a demonstrably Pythagorean view'; but since the transmigration of souls *was* a demonstrably Pythagorean view, we cannot with any greater certainty infer that the doctrine of the three lives was not Pythagorean, and there are, as Cameron has shown, strong arguments to suggest that it was.[3]

This does not of course amount to saying that the simile goes back to Pythagoras himself, but only that the Greek ideal of *philosophia* and

[1] So Wehrli, 89, Jaeger, *On the Origin and Cycle of the Philosophic Ideal of Life*, A. J. Festugière, *Les Trois Vies*. Both Wehrli and Festugière ignore the strong arguments of Cameron.
[2] *Pythagorean Background*, ch. 3: 'The Theoretic Life in Pythagoreanism of the Fifth Century.' See also the sensible and well-written article of J. L. Stocks, 'Plato and the Tripartite Soul' (*Mind*, 1915).
[3] Cf. also J. S. Morrison, *CQ*, 1958, p. 208: 'Jaeger's rejection of the story as a fabrication of the later Academy is quite unwarranted.'

theoria (for which we may compare Herodotus's attribution of these activities to Solon, 1, 30) was at a fairly early date annexed by the Pythagoreans for their master, and linked with the doctrine of transmigration. At the same time, when one considers that both this doctrine and the outstanding zeal for knowledge were known to be characteristic of Pythagoras in his own lifetime (Xenophanes) and very soon after (Heraclitus), it would be rash to deny outright that the causal linkage was Pythagoras's own work.[1]

From this survey of the explicit references to Pythagoras and the Pythagoreans down to the time of Plato, it will be seen how much must have been lost and how difficult it is to form any comprehensive idea of their history and beliefs in this period from contemporary sources. Nevertheless it is something to know that, even if we were to take no account either of later evidence or of anything in earlier writers which is not attributed by name to the school but may with great probability be referred to it (and to employ neither of these resources would be unnecessarily defeatist), we could still assert the following:

1. Pythagoras himself taught the transmigration of souls (Xenophanes, lending credibility to Heraclides Ponticus), and posthumous rewards for the meritorious (Ion).[2]

2. He was known to his near-contemporaries as a polymath, a man of prodigious learning and an insatiable thirst for inquiry (ἱστορίη, etc. Heraclitus, σοφιστής Herodotus[3]), and in his teaching the acquisition of knowledge was related to transmigration (Empedocles, and in all probability Heraclides).

3. By the fifth century the veneration of his followers had already exalted him to legendary status, regarding him as more than man and crediting him with miracles (Herodotus; and the tales repeated by Aristotle were naturally not his invention but traditional).

---

[1] We may well agree with Burnet here (*EGP*, 98): 'It would be rash to say that Pythagoras expressed himself exactly in this manner; but all these ideas are genuinely Pythagorean, and it is only in some such way that we can bridge the gulf that separates Pythagoras the man of science from Pythagoras the religious teacher.'

[2] Vlastos has dealt adequately with the unreasonable scepticism of Rathmann (*Philos. Quart.* 1952, 110, n., referring to Rathmann, *Quaestt. Pyth. Orph. Emped.* 3–11).

[3] Vlastos (*op. cit.* 111, n. 64) and Rathmann think this word means here no more than a religious sage. They compare Eur. *Rhesus*, 949, where, however, the word means 'poet', as in line 924 and Pindar, *Isth.* v, 28, and can have no bearing on Herodotus's use.

4. From at least the middle of the fifth century the Pythagoreans were known to practise certain superstitious taboos (on burial in wool, Herodotus; compare Heraclides on eating flesh and beans: here at any rate there is no contamination from Academic doctrine, and the prohibitions are of course much older).

5. Silence and secrecy were prominent features of their behaviour (Isocrates, and compare Aristotle's reference to ἀπόρρητα).

6. They formed a society of their own, practising what was to their contemporaries a distinctive and extraordinary way of life (Plato, *Rep.* 600 B).

7. Philolaus, a leading fifth-century Pythagorean, preached the wickedness of suicide, basing it on a secret *logos* of which the purport was that men are not their own masters but belong to the gods (Plato, *Phaedo*).[1]

8. As to the more scientific side of their teaching, we have learned from Plato that they were the acknowledged experts in astronomy, harmonics and the science of number. They regarded all these studies as closely allied, because in their view the key to the understanding both of the movements of the stars and of the notes in the musical scale lay in the establishment of a numerical relation. We may allow ourselves to note that the actual union of astronomy and harmonics in the remarkable theory of the 'harmony of the spheres', adopted by Plato, is described and attested as Pythagorean in the same century by Aristotle.[2] This is the view that physical objects moving as rapidly as the heavenly bodies must necessarily produce a sound; that the intervals between the several planets and the sphere of the fixed stars correspond mathematically to the intervals between the notes of the octave, and that therefore the sound which they produce has a definite musical character.

The importance of even these scanty items of information becomes evident when we remember that for Plato the problem of the possibility of knowledge was central, and that he solved it by the supposition that since the world of experience is strictly unknowable, such awareness of truth as we acquire in this life must consist in the recollection of what we discovered before birth: i.e. it depends on the doctrine of reincarnation. What may well cause surprise, even allowing for the fragmentary state of the evidence, is the narrowness of the field which our summary covers. Except for the very general remarks of Plato in a single

---

[1] I have been asked in what sense this λόγος was secret, if Socrates knew it and knew that Philolaus used it. I can only reply: Ask Socrates. It was he who said it was ἐν ἀπορρήτοις.

[2] *De Caelo*, II, 9. The Pythagoreans are mentioned at 291a8. On this theory see pp. 295 ff., below.

passage, there is no mention of Pythagorean discoveries (let alone discoveries of Pythagoras himself) in mathematics or music. Of the famous doctrine that 'things are numbers' there is not a whisper before Aristotle. So much of what we usually think of as characteristic of Pythagoras and his school is missing in our evidence until the latter half of the fourth century. Rohde[1] went so far as to say that Pythagoras himself was not a philosopher at all, but only a religious reformer. To him it seemed an important argument *ex silentio* that even Aristotle and his pupil Aristoxenus knew nothing of any physical or ethical doctrines of Pythagoras himself. The sole allusion in the period so far considered to his personal interest in mathematical explanation is Heraclides's attribution to him (in fr. 44) of the statement that happiness consists in knowledge of the perfection of the numbers of the soul, and since this does smack strongly of Academic doctrine it seemed more prudent to omit it from our summary. As for Aristotle, the only safe conclusion to draw from his silence is that he hesitated to write of Pythagoras at all,[2] preferring to speak generally of Pythagoreans because Pythagoras had already become a legend and his critical mind could not feel satisfied that any specific doctrine was to be traced with certainty to the Master himself. Once we speak of the Pythagoreans, however, it might equally well be argued that by Aristotle's time at least they had become a purely scientific school, since it is only as such that they appear in his extant treatises.[3] This argument has in fact been used, but is of little weight. The simple answer is that only their mathematics and philosophy were relevant to Aristotle's subject-matter in his extant treatises. The meagre fragments of his lost works are sufficient to show that he knew of another side to their teaching. As for the silence of our early sources on Pythagoras as a philosopher and mathematician, it is enough to say that all the later biographical writers show him as such, and they obviously preserve much early material. It would be absurd to suggest that the authors down to Plato's time constitute our only hope of

[1] *Rh. Mus.* 1871, 554f. But he seems partially to retract on pp. 556–7.

[2] Yet it is not now quite true to say that he shows no awareness of Pythagoras as a physical philosopher. In a fragment of the *Protrepticus* (Iambl. *Protr.* ch. 9, p. 51 Pistelli: see the Oxf. trans. of Aristotle's fragments, p. 45) he tells a traditional story of Pythagoras, that when asked what is the end of human life he replied 'to observe the heavens', and that he used to say that he was an observer of nature (θεωρὸν τῆς φύσεως), and it was for this that he had entered on life.

[3] Except for the reference to transmigration at *De Anima*, 407b22.

learning anything about him. Nevertheless to begin in this way, so that statements of genuine antiquity are clearly marked off both from later testimonies and from our own inferences, is salutary and methodically sound.

(3) Post-Platonic sources

This general heading brings together sources of very disparate date and unequal value. But all alike can be sharply distinguished from earlier material in that they are to a far greater extent the inevitable subject of controversy and doubt. The reasons are briefly these.

Two pupils of Aristotle, Aristoxenus and Dicaearchus, wrote extensively about the Pythagoreans. Aristoxenus (who, as it is not irrelevant to note, was an expert on music) wrote whole books on Pythagoras and his acquaintances, on the Pythagorean life and other Pythagorean matters, and we are told that he personally knew those who were spoken of as the last generation of the Pythagoreans, that is the pupils of Philolaus and Eurytus including Echecrates.[1] Dicaearchus was a scientific researcher of great learning and independence of mind. Here then are two further fourth-century sources of information who would seem to merit a high degree of trust. In the first place, however, their works have not come down to us, and what they said is known only through quotations in the Neoplatonic lives of Pythagoras by Porphyry and Iamblichus and similar compilations of the Christian era. Although these writers frequently cite their fourth-century predecessors by name, there is often dispute about the actual extent or the accuracy of their quotations, especially as these are not thought to have been made at first hand. Rohde, for instance, in his work on the sources of Iamblichus,[2] concluded that he made direct use only of the works of Nicomachus of Gerasa and Apollonius of Tyana, the former a mathematician of about A.D. 100 whose work was imbued with Neopythagorean number-mysticism, the latter a Neopythagorean sage and wonder-worker of perhaps half a century earlier. Secondly, as we have already seen with Heraclides Ponticus, members of the schools of Plato and Aristotle are themselves already under suspicion of confusing

---

[1] Their names are given by D.L. VIII, 46, and cf. the Suda (Aristox. frr. 19 and 1 Wehrli).
[2] Rh. Mus. 1872, 60f.

Pythagoras and the Pythagoreans

Platonic doctrine with that of the Pythagoreans.[1] In general the separation of early Pythagoreanism from the teaching of Plato is one of the historian's most difficult tasks, to which he can scarcely avoid bringing a subjective bias of his own. If later Pythagoreanism was coloured by Platonic influences, it is equally undeniable that Plato himself was deeply affected by earlier Pythagorean beliefs; but in deciding the extent to which each has influenced the other, most people have found it impossible to avoid being guided by the extent of their admiration for Plato and consequent unwillingness to minimize his originality.

Another source from the turn of the fourth and third centuries B.C. is the Sicilian historian Timaeus from Taormina. He had intimate knowledge of affairs in Magna Graecia, where the Pythagorean society had played an important political role, and seems to have been unbiased by any personal attachment to the school. In his case therefore the one serious disadvantage arises from our fragmentary and indirect knowledge of his writings.[2]

Since, then, this later fourth-century literature is known through writers of the Graeco-Roman period, we have from now on to lean heavily on studies in source-criticism. The source-critic starts from passages which are expressly ascribed to an earlier writer, and, by comparison with these and passages of known origin elsewhere, endeavours to detect other derived material and assign it to its original authority. He may also extract a genuine vein of ancient matter from the ore in which it is imbedded by testing it against whatever is known as certain or probable Pythagorean history and doctrine from sources of the earliest (pre-Platonic) period. The atmosphere of post-Aristotelian philosophy—Stoic, neo-Academic or other—so permeates the literature of the Graeco-Roman period that a passage containing no trace of it may suddenly stand out. Its freshness and difference strike a reader and make him at least suspect that he is dealing with something earlier. The delicacy of this work, and the element of personal judgment inseparable from it, are mitigated by the

[1] Cf. Wehrli, *Aristoxenos*, 59: 'Hauptmerkmal der Ἀποφάσεις [i.e. the Πυθαγορικαὶ ἀποφ. of Aristoxenus] ist aber die Beanspruchung akademisch-peripatetischen Gutes für die Pythagoreer.' Exaggeration of this attitude to Aristoxenus is criticized by E. L. Minar, *Early Pyth. Politics*, 96f.

[2] Cf. Minar, *op. cit.* 52 with reff. in n. 6; von Fritz, *Pyth. Politics in S. Italy*, ch. 3.

habits and methods of writers like Iamblichus. These compilers often made no attempt to rewrite and weld their sources into a new and homogeneous whole, but simply copied out extracts side by side, even repeating conflicting accounts in different parts of their work. Thus in his *Protrepticus*, for example, Iamblichus inserts passages from the *Phaedo*, *Gorgias* and other dialogues of Plato practically verbatim without the slightest acknowledgment of their authorship. Ingram Bywater in the last century, encouraged by this, and observing that other parts of the work also seemed to belong to a pre-Hellenistic stratum of thought as well as being marked by an individual style which was certainly not that of Iamblichus himself, was led on to the discovery that they belonged to the lost *Protrepticus* of Aristotle, considerable portions of which have been in this way recovered for us by Bywater himself and others following in his footsteps. It cannot be denied that the methods employed in source-criticism, and the nature of the task itself, leave plenty of room for individual differences of opinion; but a solid foundation of generally acceptable results has gradually been obtained, of which the recovery of the *Protrepticus* fragments, though not relevant to our immediate subject, may serve as an outstandingly successful instance.[1]

(4) The 'a priori' method

Besides the actual information about the early Pythagoreans which we may extract, directly or indirectly, from ancient writers, there is another resource. This has been made use of in the past, and it will be appropriate to make a brief statement of it here, thought it is not so much a fresh source of evidence as a means of testing, and perhaps by inference expanding, the positive testimony.

The method is to leave aside for a time the small number of explicit statements about what the Pythagoreans of a given period actually said, and argue *a priori*, or from circumstantial evidence, what they are likely to have said. It starts from the assumption that we possess a certain general familiarity with other contemporary schools and indi-

---

[1] See now I. Düring, *Aristotle's Protrepticus: an attempt at reconstruction*, Göteborg, 1961. The work of von Fritz, *Pyth. Politics in S. Italy*, is so exceptionally lucid that it may be taken as a model introduction to source-criticism, whether or not his results are accepted individually.

vidual philosophers, and with the climate of thought in which the Pythagoreans worked. This general knowledge of the evolution of Greek philosophy gives one, it is claimed, the right to make judgments of the sort that the Pythagoreans, let us say, before the time of Parmenides are likely to have held doctrine *A*, and that it is impossible for them at that stage of thought to have already evolved doctrine *B*. Examples of the application of this method in recent English scholarship are the two articles by F. M. Cornford on 'Mysticism and Science in the Pythagorean Tradition' together with their sequel in his book *Plato and Parmenides*, and their criticism by J. E. Raven.[1]

In arguments of this type, considerable weight may be attached to the generally acknowledged existence of two main streams of early Greek philosophy, the Ionian and the Italian, and the equally well established fact that the fountain-head of the Italian tradition was Pythagoras. Individual philosophers were open to the influence of one or the other of these streams, and whichever it was, being aware of the existence of both they are either openly or implicitly critical of the other. Empedocles the Sicilian is deeply imbued with the Italian ideas. Parmenides on the other hand is with good reason believed to have started as a philosopher of the Italian school, and to have rebelled against its teachings. Parmenides indeed, the most original and profound of all Presocratic thinkers, abandoned the fundamentals of all earlier systems alike, declaring any form of monistic cosmogony to be irrational and impossible; but if he had been of the Italian persuasion himself, it seems natural that he should have had its tenets particularly in mind in his criticism.

In such ways as these the development of Pythagorean thought may be reflected in the agreement or disagreement of other thinkers, and it may be possible to infer that certain Pythagorean doctrines existed in the time of Parmenides, of Zeno the Eleatic, or of Empedocles. Clearly, however, such a method may only be used with the greatest possible caution.

[1] Raven, *Pythagoreans and Eleatics*. In mentioning these works purely as examples, I am not of course at this stage expressing any opinion on the correctness of their results.

C. LIFE OF PYTHAGORAS AND EXTERNAL HISTORY
OF THE SCHOOL

No one who has read the preceding section will suppose that an account
of the life, character and achievements of Pythagoras can rest on anything stronger than probabilities; but the evidence is interesting, and
certain conclusions may legitimately be drawn.[1]

The dates of his life cannot be fixed exactly, but assuming the approximate correctness of the statement of Aristoxenus (*ap.* Porph. *V.P.* 9,
DK, 14.8) that he left Samos to escape the tyranny of Polycrates at the
age of forty, we may put his birth round about 570 B.C. or a few years
earlier. The length of his life was variously estimated in antiquity, but
it is agreed that he lived to a fairly ripe old age, and most probably he
died at about seventy-five or eighty.[2] His father Mnesarchus of Samos
(the name goes back to Herodotus and Heraclitus[3]) is described as a
gem-engraver, and it would be in accordance with regular Greek
custom for Pythagoras to be trained in his father's craft. We read of
travels in Egypt and Babylonia, the former first mentioned by Isocrates
in his *Busiris*. The nature of this work does not inspire confidence, and
the tradition connecting Pythagoreanism with Egypt may be thought
to have arisen from the general Greek respect for Egyptian wisdom,
especially religious wisdom.[4] But the same cause would naturally drive
a man like Pythagoras to seek enlightenment in that quarter, and that he
did so is very likely. According to Diogenes (VIII, 3), Polycrates (whether
before or after his assumption of power we do not know) gave him a
letter of introduction to Amasis, the Pharaoh who was the tyrant's
friend and ally. The tyranny of Polycrates may be taken to have begun
about 538,[5] and it may well be that Pythagoras's disapproval of it did

---

[1] See also J. S. Morrison, 'Pythagoras of Samos', *CQ*, 1956.
[2] See esp. Rohde's analysis of the tradition about Pythagoras's dates in *Rh. Mus.* 1871,
pp. 568–74, and E. L. Minar, *Early Pyth. Pol.* appendix.
[3] And may be taken as certain, like the Samian origin of Pythagoras for which Herodotus also
speaks. The tradition that he was of Tyrrhenian origin (Aristoxenus *ap.* D.L. VIII, 1, etc.) may
be reconciled with this (ZN, 380), but may, as Delatte, *Vie de P.* 147f., and Wehrli, *Aristo-*
xenos, 1945, 49 conjecture, have been suggested to explain his possession of secret religious lore.
This would be a parallel to his reputed connexion with Zoroaster and the Magi (Hippol. *Ref.* I,
2, 12, Porph. *V.P.* 6, 12; DK 14.9, 11).
[4] Hdt. II, 81, 123.
[5] T. Lenschau in *RE*, XXI, 1728.

not reach a head until some years later. Polycrates undoubtedly succeeded in raising Samos to an unprecedented height not only of prosperity and power but also of technical achievement. To his reign belong the famous tunnel of the engineer Eupalinus (rediscovered in 1882), the great temple built by Rhoecus and the harbour mole whose line may still be traced in the water, as well as the flourishing practice of those arts to which Dr Seltman has given the combined name of celature and in which Pythagoras and his family were directly concerned.[1] All that we know, or can guess, of Pythagoras suggests that he would be intensely interested in both the artistic and the commercial progress of the island, and in all probability, with his mathematical genius and craftsman's skill, an eager contributor to both.

But there was another side to Polycrates. He encouraged the luxury and dissipation which grew naturally with material prosperity, and in attaining his ends he could be brutal and unscrupulous. The atmosphere in which poets like Anacreon and Ibycus felt at home was not one to appeal to a preacher of the ascetic life. Whether or not political considerations played their part—Polycrates was the enemy of the old landed aristocracy of Samos—we know too little of Pythagoras's connexions and outlook to say; but political considerations are unnecessary to explain the discontent of a religious and philosophical genius at the court of a tyrant of this type.[2]

To escape life under the tyranny, he migrated to Croton, the leading Achaean colony in South Italy. What determined his choice we cannot say, but he may have been encouraged in it by Democedes of Croton who was court physician to Polycrates.[3] Croton was still suffering the demoralizing effects of her defeat by the Locrians at the river Sagra, and historians of the Greek West observe a marked improvement after the arrival of Pythagoras.[4] Arriving no doubt with his reputation made,

[1] P. N. Ure in *C.A.H.* IV, 92 f., C. T. Seltman, *Approach to Greek Art* (1948), pp. 13, 37. Celature (or toreutic) was a free man's art, Gisela Richter in *AJA*, 1941, 379, quoting Pliny, *N.H.* xxxv, 77.

[2] The experiences of the present century make one disinclined to agree with Minar when he writes (*E.P.P.* 4): 'This [Pythagoras's departure] of course shows that a specifically political difference existed between Pythagoras and the democratically-disposed tyrant.'

[3] It is interesting to notice this evidence that a school of medicine existed at Croton before the time of Pythagoras (Burnet, *EGP*, 89, n. 2). Democedes had practised in Athens and Aegina, and attained such fame that he was employed by Darius as well as Polycrates (Hdt. III, 131-2). For further details see pp. 346 f., below).

[4] T. J. Dunbabin, *The Western Greeks*, 359, 360.

he appears to have attained without delay a position of authority and influence in the city and founded his school there. From now on the name of Pythagoras is linked indissolubly, not with the Ionian or Eastern, but with the Italian, Western schools of thought of which he is the fountain-head. Stories going back to Dicaearchus[1] tell how when this impressive and much-travelled man arrived he so won over the elder and ruling citizens with his eloquence that they invited him to address also the younger men, the school-children and the women. Dicaearchus, it is said,[2] as a champion of the practical life exaggerated the political activity of Pythagoras and his school, but the evidence that they took a leading part in politics is overwhelming. The Neo-pythagoreans, who embroidered his story in the light of their own more visionary ideas, liked to represent him as absorbed in religious and contemplative thought, but no outstanding thinker in the small society of a sixth-century city-state (as Dunbabin remarks, *op. cit.* 361) could avoid playing some part in public affairs, nor do any of our earlier sources suggest that Pythagoras had any desire to do so. What we may say, from our knowledge of the Pythagorean philosophy, is that his motive in acquiring power (like that of his near contemporary Confucius) was not personal ambition but a zeal for reforming society according to his own moral ideas. There is no reason to doubt the general statement which we find in Diogenes (VIII, 3) that he gave the Italians a constitution and with his followers governed the state so well that it deserved the name of aristocracy ('government of the best') in its literal sense. Dunbabin gives an excellent summary of the position from the point of view of a historian of the Western Greeks (*op. cit.* 61):

His political influence was, however, a secondary consequence of his teaching. The moral regeneration which he wrought was the necessary condition of Krotoniate expansion, political and otherwise. We need not believe that he was invited to address the citizens on his arrival at Kroton. . . . His influence was no doubt more gradually felt. . . . There is no reason to doubt that the Pythagorean ἑταιρεῖαι [political clubs] did for the first half of the fifth century direct the affairs of Kroton and most of the other South Italian cities. (Von Fritz, 94 ff., Minar, 15 ff.) This they will have done through the

---

[1] Porph. *V.P.* 18, DK, 14. 8*a*.
[2] Burnet, *EGP*, 89, n. 4.

Pythagoras and the Pythagoreans

existing forms of government; the part of the ἑταιρεῖαι in determining the policy of the State may be roughly compared with that of a party caucus in parliamentary government. The importance in the account of the Pythagorean society of ἑταιρεία and other terms with a political meaning, and the history of the revolts against the Pythagoreans, indicate sufficiently clearly that real power was in their hands. In what form this applies to the sixth century is uncertain, but it must be noted that ἑταῖροι are spoken of in connexion with the events of 510 (Iambl. *V.P.* 177). Further, one of the followers of Pythagoras was the athlete Milon, general of the victorious army which defeated Sybaris (Strabo, 263).

The tendency, as well as the reality, of Pythagoras's political influence may be illustrated by a narrative of Diodorus (XII, 9, DK, 14.14). Telys, the leader of the popular party (δημαγωγός) at Sybaris, persuaded his city to banish five hundred of its richest citizens and divide their property among the people. When these oligarchic exiles sought refuge at Croton and Telys threatened war if they were not given up, the Crotonian assembly was at first inclined to give way, and it was Pythagoras who intervened and persuaded them to protect the suppliants. The result was the campaign in which the Crotonians were led to victory by the Pythagorean Milo.

A possibility that must not be overlooked is that Pythagoras may have both introduced and designed the unique incuse coinage which was the earliest money of Croton and the neighbouring South Italian cities under her influence.[1] This is a coinage which excites the enthusiasm of numismatists by its combination of a remarkable and difficult technique with outstanding beauty of design, and Seltman claims that its sudden appearance with no evolutionary process behind it postulates a genius of the order of Leonardo da Vinci: 'for the latter half of the sixth century B.C. there is only one name to fit this role: Pythagoras'. As the son of an engraver he would himself have been a practising

---

[1] This theory was put forward by the Duc de Luynes in 1836, and though it has met with much opposition (partly no doubt because as Seltman says it seems 'too good to be true'), it has recently been vigorously revived by C. T. Seltman ('The Problem of the First Italiote Coins', *Num. Chron.* 1949: his arguments must be read in full to be properly appreciated), and Miss M. White accounts it 'the most reasonable explanation yet proposed for these curious coinages' (*JHS*, 1954, 43). The Belgian P. Naster has even identified the technique of the coins with one introduced by contemporaries of Pythagoras on Samos, and therefore attributes them to an émigré who accompanied the philosopher—a view which Seltman likens to that of the examinee who wrote that the *Iliad* was not written by Homer but by another poet of the same name.

artist, and of his genius there can be no doubt. One begins to appreciate the dictum of Empedocles that he was 'skilled in all manner of cunning works'.

It is scarcely possible (to put the theory in its mildest form) that Pythagoras can have had nothing to do with this apparently contemporary coinage;[1] and this throws a light on his social position and practical interests which is not without its bearing on his philosophy. To have been responsible for the adoption of coinage, he must have belonged to the rising mercantile class with experience of the international market.[2] This is the right sort of man to have befriended the wealthy party (τοὺς πλουσιωτάτους) when they were exiled from Sybaris, and finds support in two statements of Aristoxenus which are seldom quoted. He writes that Pythagoras 'extolled and promoted the study of numbers more than anyone, *diverting it from mercantile practice* and comparing everything to numbers', and in another place attributes to him the introduction of weights and measures among the Greeks.[3] Even the earliest accounts of Pythagoras contain legendary accretions, but these prosaic statements hardly have a legendary ring, nor would the Pythagorean friends of Aristoxenus have any motive for introducing them into their idealized picture of the Master. One may suspect that the aristocracy of which Pythagoras was a

[1] It used to be objected that there exist in this same distinctive series coins of Siris, a town which was destroyed about 550 B.C., that is, at least twelve and possibly twenty years before the migration of Pythagoras. But Seltman has shown (*op. cit.* 2, citing a parallel case) that the coins in question do not belong to Siris but to the town of Pyxus, which called itself Sirinian probably because founded by fugitives from the destroyed city. This is a more likely solution to the question of date than to put Pythagoras's arrival considerably earlier, on the grounds that 'the tyranny of Polycrates' does not mean what it says but only 'the tyranny in Samos' (M. White, *JHS*, 1954, 42).

[2] So G. Thomson, *The First Philosophers*, 263. Sutherland noted that the silver used for the coins had to be imported from Corinth. Arguing as a Marxist, Thomson regards Pythagoras's mercantile interests as the key to his interest in mathematics because trade leads to a purely quantitative interest in the variety of material goods, as opposed to the qualitative criterion of the consumer. The words of Aristoxenus, that he diverted the study of number ἀπὸ τῆς τῶν ἐμπόρων χρείας, though not quoted by Thomson, provide an ancient precedent for this view, which is also supported by a Chinese scholar: '[The Greeks] were primarily merchants. And what merchants have to deal with first are the abstract numbers used in their commercial accounts, and only then with concrete things which may be immediately apprehended through these numbers. ...Hence Greek philosophers...developed mathematics and mathematical reasoning' (Fung Yu Lan, *Short History of Chinese Philosophy*, 25). On the whole, however, the evidence is in favour of supposing that Pythagoras's impulse towards mathematics originated rather from his interest in musical theory. See pp. 220ff., below.

[3] Aristox. frr. 23 and 24 Wehrli, also in DK, 58B2 and 14.12.

leader was not simply of the old land-owning type, but had strong connexions with trade.[1]

The ascendancy of Pythagoras and his followers was uninterrupted for some twenty years, during which Croton extended her influence over the neighbouring cities and in many of them the leading positions were occupied by members of the Pythagorean brotherhood. At the end of this period a Crotonian named Cylon stirred the people to revolt.[2] According to Aristoxenus he was a wealthy and loose-living nobleman who acted from personal spite, having been refused admission to the Pythagorean order on moral grounds.[3] Others, however, more plausibly allege political opposition on the grounds of the ultra-conservatism of the Pythagoreans, reinforced by the suspicion and jealousy aroused by the strange and secret nature of their doctrines. The upshot of the somewhat confused account which Iamblichus (*V.P.* 255 ff.) retails from Apollonius[4] seems to be that opposition came from both sides, Cylon representing the upper classes and a certain Ninon the democratic element. Ninon's indictment includes the obstruction by the Pythagoreans of attempts at popular reform. This combination of forces seems to have been due on the one hand to popular discontent with the concentration of power in the hands of a few, coupled with the ordinary man's dislike of what he considers mumbo-jumbo, and on the other to the native aristocracy's suspicion of the Pythagorean coteries (ἑταιρεῖαι), whose assumption of superiority and esoteric knowledge must at times have been hard to bear.

[1] Dicaearchus (fr. 34 Wehrli) tells a story that when in his flight from Croton he came to Locri, a Locrian deputation met him at the border with the polite but firm request that he should go elsewhere. They admired, they said, his cleverness (σοφὸν μὲν ἄνδρα σε καὶ δεινὸν ἀκούομεν), but were satisfied with their present condition and had no desire for any change. Whether this story is true or only *bien trouvé*, it is perhaps just worth recalling that Locri had no coinage until the fourth century: 'this suggests that the Locrian economy was in the archaic period different from that of her neighbours, and that her relations with them were limited' (Dunbabin, *op. cit.* 356). On such a society Pythagoras would indeed be a disturbing influence.

[2] The earliest extant mention of Cylon as the opponent of Pythagoras is in Aristotle, according to D.L. II, 46, who claims to be quoting 'the third book On Poetry'.

[3] Iambl. *V.P.* 248 (DK, 14.16), Porph. *V.P.* 54. Aristoxenus got his information from fourth-century members of the Pythagorean school who had migrated to Greece after persistent persecution in Italy (D.L. VIII, 46). This means that as to facts, chronology, etc. he could hardly have been better informed, but in moral and political judgments his account may be unduly favourable to the Pythagoreans.

[4] What sources were used by Apollonius is a more complex question. Cf. von Fritz, *Pyth. Pol. in S. It.* 56ff.

In the Cylonian conspiracy a number of leading Pythagoreans were rounded up and killed (the details are variously given), and it seems to have been the signal for outbursts of anti-Pythagorean activity in other cities also, which made it difficult for Pythagoras, banished from Croton, to find a resting-place. As usual, fact and legend mingle in the story of his fate. Aristotle preserves the version that he left Croton before the attack, but since the object of this story is to demonstrate his power of prophecy, it seems to belong to the legend. According to the most credible accounts, he finally reached Metapontum, where he died. About his death there are naturally a number of more or less romantic stories, but the most probable seems to be that of Dicaearchus (D.L. VIII, 40, Porph. *V.P.* 57), that he was forced to take refuge in a temple of the Muses, where he starved to death.

The rebellion of Cylon, which must have taken place about the turn of the sixth and fifth centuries, seems to have caused only a very temporary check to Pythagorean activities, and their influence was even extended over the next forty or fifty years. But it was a troublous period of growing unrest, which led to a second, major anti-Pythagorean outbreak in the middle of the fifth century. In this the house at Croton that had belonged to Milo was said to have been burned down, and according to Polybius[1] the revolutionary movement spread through the whole of Magna Graecia. Pythagorean meeting-houses were destroyed, the leading men of each city perished, and the whole region was in turmoil. This catastrophe, which is dated by Minar to 454 B.C. (*op. cit.* 77), brought about the first emigration of Pythagoreans to the mainland of Greece and led to the establishment of Pythagorean centres at Phlius and Thebes. Among the youngest of the refugees Aristoxenus (Iambl. *V.P.* 249, DK, 14.16) mentions Lysis, who much later at Thebes became the teacher of Epaminondas. Another was Philolaus, mentioned in the *Phaedo* as having taught the Thebans Simmias and Cebes (p. 162, above). Even now, the Pythagoreans who stayed behind seem to have regained a certain amount of political influence in Italy, and to have continued their life as a society, chiefly at Rhegium. Later still, however, when in the words of Aristoxenus (Iambl. 251) 'political conditions got worse', all are said to have left

[1] II, 39, 1–4. Text and translation in Minar, *Early Pyth. Pol.* 75 f.

12-2

Italy except Archytas of Tarentum. It is impossible to date this final exodus, but von Fritz would put it as late as 390.

We see, then, that the life of the Pythagorean societies was by no means peaceful or uninterrupted, and that from the second half of the fifth century they existed in small separate bands scattered widely over South Italy and Greece. The effect of this on the continuity of their philosophical tradition was naturally serious. Porphyry (57ff.) and Iamblichus (252f.) preserve a description of what happened which went back through Nicomachus to Neanthes in the third century B.C. It must contain a great deal of truth, and goes far to account for the inadequacy and obscurity of our material on Pythagorean doctrine. According to this tale the prominent Pythagoreans who lost their lives in the troubles carried their knowledge with them to the grave, for it had been kept secret, only those parts being divulged which would have conveyed little meaning to outsiders. Pythagoras had left no writings of his own, and only a few dim sparks of philosophy were kept alight by men like Lysis and Archippus of Tarentum who escaped, and any who were abroad at the time of the troubles. These exiles were so cast down by events that they lived in isolation, shunning the company of their fellow-men. Nevertheless, to avoid incurring divine displeasure by allowing the name of philosophy to perish altogether, they collected in note form whatever had been written down by an older generation, supplemented by their own memories. Each one left these commentaries, when and where he happened to die, in trust to son, daughter or wife, with instructions that they be kept within the household. The trust was faithfully kept, and the notebooks handed down for several generations, but our sources agree that as an active sect (αἵρεσις) the Pythagorean society practically died out during the fourth century B.C. 'They preserved their original ways, and their science, although the sect was dwindling, until, not ignobly, they died out.' Thus was their epitaph written by Aristoxenus (*ap*. Iambl. *V.P.* 251), speaking of those who were his contemporaries and acquaintances.

It emerges from this troubled history, first, that the Pythagorean School continued to exist through the classical period of Greek thought in the sixth to the fourth centuries B.C., and secondly, that from the middle of the fifth century it existed in the form of separate, scattered communities in various parts of the Greek world. It is only natural that these communities should develop on different lines, and that we should hear, as we do from Aristotle, that 'some Pythagoreans' held certain doctrines and some held others, although all acknowledged allegiance to the same founder. This does not lighten our task, but at least it means that inconsistencies are no cause for despair, or for a hasty conclusion that the authorities are confused: they are no less likely to be a faithful reflexion of historical fact.

D. OUTLINE OF THE PYTHAGOREAN PHILOSOPHY

Pythagoras has been regarded by some scholars as no more than the founder of a religious sect, upon whom were foisted in later days mathematical discoveries made long after his time: he may have played in a superstitious way with 'number-mysticism', but no more.[1] Others have emphasized almost exclusively the rational and scientific side of his thought. Both these portrayals are too one-sided and extreme to be plausible. The religious doctrines of immortality and transmigration are assigned to Pythagoras on incontrovertible positive evidence. His character as one of the most original thinkers in history, a founder of mathematical science and philosophical cosmology, although not directly attested by such early and impregnable sources, must be assumed as the only reasonable explanation of the unique impression made by his name on subsequent thought. It was both as religious teacher and as scientific genius that he was from his own lifetime and for many centuries afterwards venerated by his followers, violently attacked by others, but ignored by none. The attempts to minimize one or the other side of his nature arise from the difficulty which a modern mind experiences in reconciling adherence to a comparatively primitive set of religious and superstitious beliefs with the rational pursuit of mathematical science and cosmic speculation; but in the sixth century B.C. such a combination was not only possible but natural. What we may safely say is that for Pythagoras religious and moral motives were dominant, so that his philosophical inquiries were

---

[1] The most outstanding work of this tendency was Erich Frank's *Plato und die sogennanten Pythagoreer*.

destined from the start to support a particular conception of the best life and fulfil certain spiritual aspirations.

Since the keynote of any philosophical system is struck when we understand its aim,[1] we may make this our starting-point. Philosophy for Pythagoras and his followers had to be first and foremost the basis for a way of life: more than that, for a way of eternal salvation. When the study of man and the cosmos is undertaken as a means of help and guidance in right living, the resulting system of nature must be one that will afford such help. To the Pythagoreans the most important part of philosophy was that which taught of man, of the nature of the human soul and its relations with other forms of life and with the whole. This therefore will be dealt with first. After that it will be in place to say something of Pythagoreanism as a philosophy of *form*, under which heading will conveniently fall its mathematical and numerical aspect.

(1) *Man and his place in nature*

Pythagoreanism contains a strong element of the magical, a primitive feature which sometimes seems hard to reconcile with the intellectual depth which is no less certainly attested. It is not on that account to be dismissed as a mere excrescence, detachable from the main system. All who work on the border-line of philosophy and religion among the Greeks are quickly made aware of a typical general characteristic of their thought: that is, a remarkable gift for retaining, as the basis for their speculations, a mass of early, traditional ideas which were often of a primitive crudity, while at the same time transforming their significance so as to build on them some of the most profound and influential reflexions on human life and destiny. This was true of the Orphic writers, whose religious teaching was almost identical with that of Pythagoras,[2] and the same genius for combining conservatism with innovation, introducing new wine without breaking the old bottles, was particularly strong among the Pythagoreans.

[1] In case this sounds a slightly cynical statement, implying that philosophy is no more than a rationalization of beliefs held before the inquiry begins, let me add that although this is in many cases a fair judgment, clear thinking itself may be a philosopher's aim as much as anything else. If so, this does not make an understanding of the aim any less important.

[2] For this characteristic of Orphic thought cf. Guthrie, *Orph. and Gk. Rel.* 129f., and for the relations between Orphic and Pythagorean, *ibid.* 216–21. As early as the fifth century Ion of Chios could attribute Orphic poems to Pythagoras himself (Ion, fr. 2 DK).

Magical Elements

Their retention of primitive material is well illustrated in their collection of sayings called *Acusmata* or *Symbola*. Although adopted by the sect, many of these precepts are obviously older than Pythagoras, and some are found in non-Pythagorean contexts as well, for example in Hesiod, the sayings of the Seven Wise Men, and the Delphic precepts. Some are straightforward moral precepts, but others had to be later explained as having a hidden, oracular meaning in accord with Pythagorean moral or political ideals.[1] In fact the majority are easily recognizable as primitive taboos. The lists of them which we have in Diogenes, Porphyry, Iamblichus, Hippolytus may be said with confidence to go back to a collection made by Aristotle in the work which he wrote on the Pythagoreans, and which is explicitly quoted as the authority for some.[2] Out of many attributed to Pythagoras, the magical origin of which is obvious, the following will serve as examples:

To abstain from beans.

Not to pick up what has fallen from the table.

Not to stir the fire with a knife.

To rub out the mark of a pot in the ashes.

Not to sit on a bushel-measure.

Not to wear a narrow ring (also given as 'Not to wear a ring').

Not to have swallows in the house.

To spit on one's nail-parings and hair-trimmings.

Not to make water or stand on one's nail-parings or hair-trimmings.[3]

To roll up one's bedclothes on rising and smooth out the imprint of the body.

To touch the earth when it thunders.

[1] C. W. Goettling (*Ges. Abh.* vol. I, 278–316) contended that these latter alone were the σύμβολα (for it is of the essence of a σύμβολον that its true significance does not appear on the surface), the others forming a separate class of ἀκούσματα. The hypothesis was somewhat weakened by the number of times that he had to assume a saying to have been wrongly classified by the ancient authorities. His general interpretation ('quam totam ethicam esse debere ostendi', vol. II, 280) was easier to uphold in the middle of the nineteenth than of the twentieth century.

Their real nature was first explained in detail by F. Boehm, *De Symbolis Pythagoreis*, in the light of the anthropological material of his time, and especially of that contained in *The Golden Bough*. Boehm's competent short work scarcely deserves the slighting expressions of Delatte in *Vie de Pyth.* 186–7. A more weighty as well as more recent critic describes his application of the comparative method as 'circumspect' (Nilsson, *Gesch. d. gr. Rel.* I, 666, n. 3). For the ἀκούσματα in general see Nilsson, 665–9.

[2] D.L. VIII, 34. Cf. Delatte, *Études*, 273 (following V. Rose and Rohde), Nilsson, *Gesch.* I, 665 f.

[3] Only this and the previous one defeated the moralizing zeal of Goettling: 'Ich bin nicht im Stande, aus dieser Vorschrift irgend einen vernünftigen Sinn zu entnehmen' (p. 315).

The moral interpretations attached to these picturesque sayings in our sources show plainly enough that they had nothing to do with them in the beginning. To stir the fire with a knife was taken to mean rousing a man's passions with sharp words, to sit on the bushel was to be content with what one has or to rest on one's laurels, to roll up the bedding meant to be always ready for travel, that is, ready to leave this life for the next, swallows stood for chatterers, and so forth.[1]

A famous and widely commented-on Pythagorean injunction was that which prohibited the eating of beans, and many different explanations of it were offered, some of which may at first sight seem obscure. Beans resembled testicles: they resembled the gates of Hades, or the whole universe (all these were recorded by Aristotle, D.L. VIII, 34): their stems were hollow throughout and unjointed (D.L. VIII, 34; Porphyry connected this fact with the return of souls from beneath the earth, *Antr. Nymph.* 19): they are of a windy or breathy nature and hence full of the life-force (D.L. VIII, 24): they contain the souls of the dead (Pliny, *N.H.* XVIII, 118). When in the creative chaos at the beginning of the world life arose out of the primeval slime, beans and human beings had their origin from the same form of primal matter.[2] There were strange superstitions about the metamorphoses which a bean would undergo if buried in earth or dung. Heraclides Ponticus is reported as saying that it would assume human shape. From later writers we learn that it would be assimilated to a child's head or the female pudenda. Porphyry and others adduced the belief that if chewed and left in the sun a bean would give off an odour of semen.[3]

These explanations all have in common a connexion between beans and life, death or the soul. (In saying that they 'resembled the universe' the Pythagoreans doubtless had in mind their belief that it was animate.) Such a connexion may well have been primitive, and at the

---

[1] There were other explanations too. See Plut. *Quaest. Conv.* 727–8. Iamblichus warns that not all the interpretations were Pythagorean (*V.P.* 86). It is of course by no means improbable that in taking over these primitive superstitions Pythagoras himself interpreted them in this symbolic way.

[2] ἐκ τῆς αὐτῆς σηπεδόνος, Porph. *V.P.* 44. Cf. the unintelligibly abbreviated version in Hippol. *Ref.* I, 2, 14 (Diels, *Dox.* 557), where Pythagoras is said to have learned this from Zoroaster; also Diogenes (i.e. Antonius Diogenes, *Dox.* 557, n.) *ap.* Lyd. *De Mens.* IV, 42, pp. 99–100 Wünsch.

[3] For references see Delatte, *Études*, 38, n. 2.

same time reflects genuine Pythagorean interests. The ban was also rationalized in a political sense. It was said to symbolize the oligarchic tendencies of Pythagoras, since beans were used as counters in the democratic process of election by lot. This explanation also goes back to Aristotle (D.L. *ibid.*), and was repeated in later times by Lucian, Iamblichus, Hippolytus, and in the treatise *De Liberis Educandis* attributed to Plutarch. Presumably it was at some time accepted by the Pythagoreans themselves, but its artificial character is obvious, nor had it ever the wide currency nor the central importance in Pythagorean lore that was accorded the connexion with life and the doctrine of transmigration. There was a Pythagorean saying in the form of a hexameter verse (also attributed to Orpheus, which keeps it in the same circle), to the effect that to eat beans is equivalent to eating the heads of one's parents. Both the actual line and various paraphrases of it are quoted repeatedly in late antiquity,[1] and another hexametric version of the prohibition was not only included in the Orphic poems but used by Empedocles in the fifth century B.C. This ran: 'Wretched, thrice wretched, keep your hands from beans.'[2]

Many of the other examples cited betray their origin in sympathetic magic, which assumes a close, quasi-physical relationship between things that to the civilized mind have no such connexion at all. It exists between a man and his picture or image, or even the imprint of his body in a bed, as well as anything that had once been a part of him like nail-parings or hair-trimmings. These must be treated with respect because owing to the intangible bond which unites them the treatment to which such things are subjected will be reflected in the welfare of the man himself. By gaining possession of them, an enemy can do much harm. The taboo on wearing any unbroken rings about the person, which applies also to knots, is based on the possibility that they will transfer their binding or inhibiting power into regions far beyond their immediate

[1] And by Heraclides Ponticus according to Lydus, *De Mens.* p. 99 Wünsch. For other references see Nauck's ed. of Iambl. *V.P.* 231 ff. Callimachus echoes it, with a mention of Pythagoras himself (DK, 14.9, p. 101):

καὶ κυάμων ἄπο χεῖρας ἔχειν, ἀνιῶντος ἐδεστοῦ,
κἀγώ, Πυθαγόρας ὡς ἐκέλευε, λέγω.

[2] Emped. fr. 141 DK (from Gellius). Taboo on beans is found in many parts of the world, and at Rome they were associated with the cult of the dead. See Boehm, *op. cit.* 14–17 and index to *Golden Bough, s.v.* beans.

physical effect. The general belief in the possibility of transference, which underlies all the taboos of sympathetic magic, rests in turn on an extended notion of kinship or relationship which is foreign to civilized thought. It appears again in the beliefs associated with a totemic organization of society, where the tribe is conscious of a kinship, even an identity, between itself and a non-human species of animal.

Beginning the account with the *Acusmata* or *Symbola* has brought into prominence the initial connexion of much in Pythagoreanism with primitive magical ways of thinking. The essentially magical conception of universal kinship or sympathy, in a more or less refined and rationalized form, permeates its central doctrines of the nature of the universe and the relationship of its parts. To be aware of this will assist an understanding of its mathematical conception of the natural world as well as of its religious beliefs concerning the fate of the human soul.

Porphyry writes of Pythagoras as follows (*V.P.* 19, DK, 14.8*a*):

What he said to his disciples no man can tell for certain, since they preserved such an exceptional silence. However, the following facts in particular became universally known: first that he held the soul to be immortal, next that it migrates into other kinds of animal, further that past events repeat themselves in a cyclic process and nothing is new in an absolute sense, and finally that one must regard all living things as kindred (ὁμογενῆ). These are the beliefs which Pythagoras is said to have been the first to introduce into Greece.

Apart from the fact that Porphyry's informant here may have been Dicaearchus,[1] this passage contains several reassuring features. His language shows unusual caution, an effort for once to confine himself to what he believes he may regard as certain. More important, the immortality of the soul, and its transmigration into various animal bodies, are vouched for as beliefs of Pythagoras by his own contemporary Xenophanes (p. 157, above). Moreover the doctrine of the kinship of all animate nature appears in Empedocles, a philosopher of the Italian tradition in the early fifth century B.C.[2] We may assume that this doctrine, no less

---

[1] Dicaearchus is mentioned by name some sixteen lines earlier. Cf. Rohde, *Rh. Mus.* 1872, 26 f., and n. 2, p. 151, above.

[2] The other theory mentioned by Porphyry, that of the exact recurrence of events, does not immediately concern us, but is vouched for as Pythagorean in the fourth century B.C. by Eudemus (*ap.* Simpl. *Phys.* 732 Diels, DK, 58 B 34). See p. 281, below.

than those of immortality and transmigration, formed part of the teaching of Pythagoras. Indeed our cautious approach is scarcely necessary here, since the kinship of nature provides the general world-view within which alone the transmigration of souls is a tenable belief. Only the fact that the souls of men and of animals are of the same family could make it possible for the same soul to enter now a man's body and now that of a beast or a bird.

In the extraordinary Pythagorean attitude to beans we have already seen an example of the way in which these tenets had their outcome in practice. The mysterious embodiment of the universal life-spirit (and evidently a particularly close connexion with *human* life) which the Pythagoreans saw in this vegetable led to its prohibition as food. Still more close must be the connexion between dogma and practice in their abstention from animal flesh, not only the most notorious, but also the most controversial of the commandments of Pythagoras. The chief testimonies are these:

(*a*) Eudoxus *ap*. Porph. *V.P.* 7 (DK, 14.9): 'Eudoxus in the seventh book of his Description of the Earth says that he [*sc.* Pythagoras] exhibited such purity and such abhorrence of killing and killers that he not only abstained from animal food but would have nothing to do with cooks or hunters.'

(*b*) Onesicritus *ap*. Strabo xv, 716 (DK, *ibid.*). Onesicritus was a Cynic philosopher who accompanied Alexander to India, and is recounting his meeting with an Indian gymnosophist who questioned him about Greek doctrine. Onesicritus told him among other things that Pythagoras 'commanded men to abstain from animal food'.

(*c*) The poets of the Middle Comedy of the fourth and early third centuries B.C. indulge in various jibes at the Pythagoreans of their time. Some suggest that these had taken a leaf out of the Cynics' book (or that the comic poets chose to bait them by maliciously making the confusion), caring nothing for appearances but going about unwashed and in filthy rags. They include, however, digs at their vegetarianism, for example the obvious joke: 'The Pythagoreans eat no living thing.' 'But Epicharides the Pythagorean eats dog!' 'Only after he has killed it.' 'They eat vegetables—or bread—and drink nothing but water' is the general verdict, though Aristophon might amuse himself by observing that some of the modern hangers-on of the sect, in spite of their professions, were ready enough to wolf down fish or meat if you set it before them. (The relevant fragments of Antiphanes, Alexis, Aristophon and Mnesimachus are collected in DK, 58E, vol. I, pp. 478 ff.)

According to these heterogeneous sources the eating of animals was entirely against Pythagorean principles, whatever backsliding might occur. Others, among whom is cited Aristotle, suggest that religious abstention was certainly practised, but that it was limited to certain species.

(*d*) Aristotle, Ross frr., p. 138 (*ap.* D.L. VIII, 34, DK, 58C3): 'Aristotle in his work on the Pythagoreans said that Pythagoras counselled abstention from...white cocks because they are sacred to the lunar god or to the month, and are suppliants [presumably because white was the colour worn by suppliants]—sacred to the lunar god because they announce the hours. Moreover white is of the nature of good, black of evil. Also to abstain from any fish that are sacred, since it is not right that the same creatures should be assigned to gods and to men.'

(*e*) Aristotle, Ross *ibid.* (D.L. VIII, 33, DK, 58B1*a*): 'Purity is achieved by cleansing rites and...abstaining from meat and flesh of animals that have died, mullet, blacktail, eggs and oviparous animals, beans....'[1]

(*f*) Iambl. *V.P.* 85 (DK, 58C4) tells us that according to the Pythagorean *acusmata* only animals which it is proper to sacrifice may be eaten, because only into these does the soul of a man not enter. This sounds more like the genuine Pythagorean reason than the incompatible explanation attributed to Aristotle that it was not right for men and gods to share the same creatures. (It does not follow that the actual prohibition of eating sacred fish—which doubtless were not sacrificed—is not rightly attributed to the Pythagoreans.)

(*g*) Porph. *V.P.* 43 (partly in DK, 58C6), in a list of the *Symbola* of Pythagoras: 'Of sacrificed animals he bade them not to eat the loin, testicles and privy parts, marrow, feet or head.' Porphyry adds as the reason Pythagoras's symbolic interpretation of these parts. They signified for the animal respectively the foundation, genesis, growth, beginning and end. Together these are the leading parts (ἡγεμονίαι) of the body. He added that they must abstain from beans 'as they would from human flesh'.

Finally we find in a few passages a determined attempt, which seems to go back to Aristoxenus, to deny altogether the existence of the prohibition.

(*h*) Aulus Gellius in his *Noctes Atticae*, IV, 11 writes (partly quoted in DK, 14.9): 'There is an old and erroneous, but strongly entrenched,

---

[1] This passage is assigned by Ross to Aristotle, but it is not quite clear that it does not belong to Alexander Polyhistor. In his translation Ross renders βρωτῶν 'meat that has been nibbled'.

belief that the philosopher Pythagoras habitually abstained from animal food, and also from beans, which the Greeks call κύαμοι. This belief made Callimachus write: "I too bid you, as did Pythagoras, keep your hands from beans, an injurious food." Of the same opinion was Cicero, who in his first book *On Divination* has these words: "Plato tells us to go to bed in such a condition of body that there be nothing to induce wandering or disturbance of the mind. This is commonly thought to be the reason why the Pythagoreans are forbidden to eat beans, which have a flatulent tendency inimical to the pursuit of mental tranquillity." So much for Cicero. But Aristoxenus the writer on music, an industrious student of ancient literature and a pupil in philosophy of Aristotle, in the work which he has left us on Pythagoras says that beans were Pythagoras's favourite vegetable on account of their purgative and relieving properties. [Here Gellius quotes the original words of Aristoxenus.] The same Aristoxenus reports that he included young pigs and sucking kids in his diet, and he seems to have got his information from the Pythagorean Xenophilus who was his friend, as well as from older men who were nearer to the time of Pythagoras. Alexis the poet also treats of animal food in his comedy *The Lady Pythagorean*.[1]

'The origin of the mistake about the eating of beans appears to be that in the poem of Empedocles, who followed the teaching of Pythagoras, there occurs this line:

Wretched, thrice wretched, keep your hands from beans.

Most people assumed the word to refer to the vegetable, as it commonly does. But those who have studied the poem of Empedocles with the greatest care and insight say that in this context it signifies testicles, which after the enigmatic and symbolic style of Pythagoras are called beans (κύαμοι) because they bring about pregnancy (κυεῖν) and are the source of human generative power. Thus Empedocles in this line is trying to dissuade men not from eating beans but from sexual indulgence.

'Plutarch too, whose authority in the history of philosophy carries great weight, reports in the first of his books on Homer that Aristotle said the same about the Pythagoreans, namely that they did not abstain from eating animals, with the exception of a few kinds of flesh. As this is contrary to the general opinion, I append his actual words: "Aristotle says that the Pythagoreans abstain from the womb and the heart, and from sea-anemones and certain other similar creatures, but eat the rest."...However Plutarch in his *After-dinner Questions* says that the Pythagoreans also abstain from the fish called mullet.'

[1] The fragments of Alexis quoted by Athenaeus (DK, vol. 1, p. 479), one of which is from this play, all represent the Pythagoreans as eating *no* meat.

189

(*i*) D.L. VIII, 20 (DK, 14.9): 'Pythagoras only sacrificed inanimate things, or according to others no living creatures except cocks, sucking kids and sucking pigs, with special avoidance of lambs. Aristoxenus on the other hand said that he allowed the eating of all other living creatures except the ploughing-ox and the ram.'

(*j*) Porph. *V.P.* 15 says of the athlete Eurymenes that whereas other athletes kept to the traditional diet of cheese and figs, 'on the advice of Pythagoras he was the first to strengthen his body by eating a fixed daily portion of meat'.

(*k*) Iambl. *V.P.* 25 claims that the substitution of a meat diet for dried figs on the part of athletes was due to a namesake of Pythagoras, the son of Eratoclees, 'though it is wrongly attributed to Pythagoras son of Mnesarchus'.

(*l*) D.L. VIII, 12: 'He [Pythagoras] is said to have been the first to train athletes on meat, beginning with Eurymenes, as Favorinus says in the third book of his Commentaries. . . . Others say it was a trainer called Pythagoras who used this diet, not our philosopher, who in fact forbade the killing, let alone the eating, of animals on the ground that they share with us the right to a soul.'

It will be seen that none of these testimonies antedates the fourth century B.C., by which time the prohibition of flesh had already become a matter of doubt and controversy. They fall into three classes. First, those that affirm the prohibition of animal food without qualification, like Eudoxus and the less decisive voices of Onesicritus and the comic poets. Secondly, those (among them Aristotle) who describe the prohibition as selective, certain species or parts of animals being forbidden on religious or superstitious grounds. Abstention from some of the creatures mentioned is a common enough superstition outside the Pythagorean brotherhood and indeed outside the Hellenic sphere. Examples are collected by Boehm in the work already referred to. Cocks for instance were forbidden to epileptics, who were supposed to be daemonically possessed, and Caesar notes that the British held it impious to eat them. The religious reasons adduced by the Pythagoreans are expressly linked by some of our authorities with their belief in transmigration. Sacrifice was limited to certain animals, and these might be eaten because of a belief that the soul of a man never enters them. Perhaps the same, or perhaps a different, school of Pythagoreans held that even of sacrificial animals certain parts were to be avoided, including those, like testicles and marrow, which were particularly associated with the vital force.

Finally we have the categorical denial that Pythagoras imposed on his followers any ban at all on the eating of flesh or beans. The statements to this effect have a positive and polemical tone which suggests that, as Gellius in fact says, they were going against the generally received belief. The most vehement in this direction was evidently Aristoxenus. This man, a Western Greek from Tarentum, who became a member of the Lyceum under Aristotle and Theophrastus, was also a friend of the last generation of Pythagoreans.[1] Since his chief claim to fame was his work on the theory of music (he was in fact generally known by the distinguishing epithet of *Musicus*), it was natural that he should have a prime interest in that school which gave music a central place in its philosophy and was universally recognized as having been responsible for the most fundamental discoveries in musical theory. The friends to whom such a man attached himself would of course belong to the most scholarly and intellectual wing of the school, and would have little use for the old superstitions to which its more devoutly religious members clung. By this time the school was split into a number of groups divided both locally and by the character of their thought, and since all alike continued to claim the authority of Pythagoras for their teaching, the more philosophically-minded would reject the idea that he lent himself to superstitious practices which they themselves had outgrown.

In this connexion may be mentioned the distinction drawn by later writers between two types of Pythagorean, the *acusmatici* and the *mathematici*. Accounts of this are given by the Neoplatonists Iamblichus and Porphyry as follows:

(a) Iambl. *V.P.* 81, 87 (also *De Comm. Math. Sc.* p. 76.16ff. Festa). Iamblichus has been explaining that Pythagoras instituted various grades among his disciples according to their natural talents, so that the highest secrets of his wisdom were only imparted to those capable of receiving them. Even the way of life was not the same for all: some he ordered to hold all their possessions in common, but there was an outer circle of those who

---

[1] D.L. VIII, 46. The Suda says that he was a pupil of the Pythagorean Xenophilus before joining Aristotle. See this and other authorities for his life at the beginning of Wehrli's *Aristoxenos*.

retained their private property. The account continues: 'In another way also there were two forms of the Pythagorean philosophy, corresponding to two classes of those who had part in it, the *acusmatici* and the *mathematici*. Of these the *acusmatici* are admitted to be Pythagoreans by the others, whereas they themselves do not accept the *mathematici*, claiming that their activity does not originate from Pythagoras but from Hippasus.[1] . . . The philosophy of the *acusmatici* consists of undemonstrated sayings, without argument, enjoining certain courses of action. These and other dicta of Pythagoras they endeavour to preserve as divine revelations, making no claim to say anything of their own. Indeed they hold it would be wrong to do so: those of their number are accounted the wisest who have learned the greatest number of *acusmata*.'

(*b*) Porph. *V.P.* 37 (DK, 18.2): 'His teaching took two forms, and of his followers some were called *mathematici* and some *acusmatici*. The *mathematici* were those who had mastered the deepest and most fully worked-out parts of his wisdom, and the *acusmatici* those who had only heard summarized precepts from the writings, without full explanation.'

The account reproduced by Iamblichus implies a claim that the division was instituted by Pythagoras himself in order that justice might be done to those of greater and lesser philosophical capacity. Probably Porphyry was relying on the same sources and meant to say the same, although taken by itself his statement might imply no more than what was probably the truth. In view of the universal Pythagorean practice of attributing everything to the founder, we cannot attach much historical value to the claim. What seems to be obviously true is that 'his teaching took two forms', or at least had two sides. The genius of Pythagoras must have possessed both a rational and a religious quality such as are rarely united in the same man. It is not surprising that he and his school attracted two different types, on the one hand enthusiasts for the promotion of mathematical philosophy and on the other religious devotees whose ideal was the 'Pythagorean way of life', the life of a religious sect strongly resembling that of the Orphics and justifying its practices by a similar system of mystical beliefs. The philosophical wing inevitably neglected, or secretly despised, the simple superstitious faith of the devotees, but could not deny that it had played a part in the foundations laid by Pythagoras. These therefore admitted

[1] The translation follows the order of words in *De Comm. Math. Sc.*, not that of *V.P.* (DK, 18.2) in which *acusmatici* and *mathematici* are reversed.

the claim of the *acusmatici* to call themselves Pythagoreans, and fostered the belief that both wings of the school had their origin in the teaching methods of the Master himself. That at least seems the most probable explanation of the tradition, which serves an obvious apologetic purpose for the *mathematici*. The split is unlikely to have occurred before the second half of the fifth century, when it would be fostered by the geographical dispersion of the school. It may provide the explanation why Aristotle speaks in his more cautious moments of 'some Pythagoreans' as holding certain views, and not of the Pythagoreans as a whole. Rohde noted as further evidence for it that the physical doctrines which Aristotle reports as Pythagorean, as well as the ethical precepts of the friends of Aristoxenus, show no connexion with Pythagorean religious beliefs. This point has some substance, though it must not be pressed too far. It was the physical and mathematical philosophy of the Pythagoreans that Aristotle happened to be interested in, and reference to its religious basis would have been out of place in his purely philosophical discussions. The two in fact could never have been completely separated. Consider for example the reference to their numerical philosophy in such a passage as this from the *De Caelo* (268 a 10):

As the Pythagoreans say, the whole world and all things in it are summed up in the number three; for end, middle and beginning give the number of the whole, and their number is the triad. Hence we have taken this number from nature, as it were one of her laws, and make use of it even for the worship of the gods.

Nevertheless the thesis that there were two kinds of Pythagoreans, the one chiefly interested in the pursuit of mathematical philosophy and the other in preserving the religious foundations of the school, is both inherently probable and supported by a certain amount of positive evidence, among which we may certainly reckon the contradictory reports that have just been quoted concerning the views of Pythagoras on religious abstention from certain foods.[1]

Porphyry wrote a work in four books, which has been preserved, on

---

[1] With this paragraph cf. Delatte, *Pol. Pyth.* 22 f., *Études*, 272–4, Rohde, *Rh. Mus.* 1871, 558–62, Minar, *Early Pyth. Pol.* 31–3. Minar is right to deprecate the assumption of a clear-cut division between two hostile and mutually exclusive sects, but goes too far in belittling the scientific achievement of the *mathematici*.

abstinence from animal flesh. This being its main topic, its references to Pythagorean doctrine and practice have perhaps more weight than more casual allusions, and may be considered together before drawing final conclusions on the subject. His information can be confidently assigned to the fourth or early third century B.C.[1] Porphyry, who is of course arguing in favour of abstinence, begins by stating in full the case of his opponents, whom he describes as 'the ordinary, common run of men' (ὁ πολὺς καὶ δημώδης ἄνθρωπος). In their name he produces a string of arguments, ending with the claim (I, 15) that meat-eating does no harm to soul or body, as is proved by medical opinion and by the fact that athletes eat meat to improve their condition. Immediately he continues: 'And as strong evidence that Pythagoras was wrong, we may mention that no wise man believed him...not even Socrates.' In the eyes of the common man, the wrongness of Pythagoras evidently consisted in the prohibition of meat. In ch. 23 the same common man asserts that according to Pythagoras the eating of pork and beef was equivalent to cannibalism, but in ch. 26 he supports his case by reference to the story that Pythagoras allowed, and even introduced, meat in the diet of athletes, and adds: 'Some report that the Pythagoreans themselves taste flesh when they sacrifice to the gods.'[2]

In II, 4, when Porphyry is arguing his own case, he rebukes his opponents for assuming that because it is right for some men, like athletes, soldiers and manual workers, to eat meat, therefore it is proper for philosophers. We may take it that in his view Pythagoras might indeed have approved of meat for someone who would never make a philosopher (cf. passage (*j*) on p. 190, above), but still forbade it to his own school. The friends of Aristoxenus who rejected the ban will then have made their point by an illegitimate generalization. Later in the same book (ch. 28), he says that the Pythagoreans were[3] life-

---

[1] Most of it comes from Theophrastus. See Burnet, *EGP*, 95, n. 2, and compare especially *De Abst.* II, 32: τὰ μὲν δὴ κεφάλαια τοῦ μὴ δεῖν θύειν ζῷα, χωρὶς τῶν ἐμβεβλημένων μύθων ὀλίγων τε τῶν ὑφ' ἡμῶν προσκειμένων καὶ συντετμημένων, ἐστὶν τῶν Θεοφράστου ταῦτα. The Pythagorean arguments adduced by Sotion for the same purpose (*ap.* Seneca, *Ep.* 108 (bk. XVIII, 5), 17 ff.), which may be compared with Porphyry's, also appear to contain much early material. (Cf. Rostagni, *Verbo di P.* 166 ff.)

[2] So also Plut. *Qu. Conv.* 729 c. The common source here is probably not Theophrastus but Heraclides Ponticus (Burnet, *loc. cit.*).

[3] Porphyry uses the imperfect tense in speaking of them.

long abstainers from animal flesh. When they offered a beast to the gods, they did but taste it, and other animals they never touched. In III, 26 he brings the taboo into explicit relation with the kinship of all life: 'Since then all animals are our kin—if it is clear that, as Pythagoras said, they have the same soul—the man who does not keep his hand off his own relatives is rightly condemned as unholy.'

Porphyry then, whether he is speaking in his own person or through the mouth of an imaginary philistine, is consistent in asserting that in general Pythagoras forbade his followers to eat flesh, that his reason was the kinship of all life, and that as a result the Pythagoreans were life-long vegetarians except for a ritual mouthful on occasions of sacrifice. His account gives a clear hint of how, when a rationalist wing arose in the school, it claimed as authority for neglecting the ban a story which, whether true or not, was never originally intended to grant a dispensation to philosophers, that is, to Pythagoreans. Taking all this in conjunction with the evidence previously discussed, and with the primitive character of the demand itself, we may conclude that abstinence from flesh, on the religious ground that to eat it is a form of cannibalism, was a tenet of Pythagoreanism from the beginning. A sacramental tasting, on special occasions, of the flesh of the forbidden animal is not an exception; rather it brings the system into line with universal primitive practice, as Burnet noted (*EGP*, 95). Later, when the rationalists and the devotees tended to take separate roads, it was denied by some who still laid claim to membership of the school. In support of this conclusion we may add that the belief and practice are independently known to have been current in the thought of the early fifth century, especially in the West. Empedocles of Acragas reasoned explicitly that because of the transmigration of souls a man who eats flesh may unwittingly devour his own son or his own father in altered shape; and a similar abstention was enjoined in the Orphic writings.[1]

To those whose minds run on these lines the soul is obviously something of paramount importance. It occupies an entirely different place in the scheme of things from that which it has, for instance, in the

---

[1] Emped. fr. 137 DK. For Orpheus, Ar. *Frogs*, 1032, Eur. *Hipp.* 952f., and a little later Plato, *Laws*, VI, 782C.

Homeric epics, which set the tone for so much in later Greek religion. For Pythagoras it was immortal (ἀθάνατος), and this implied much more than mere survival. In Homer too the *psyche* survived after death, but that thought brought no consolation to his heroes. The *psyche* by itself was the merest simulacrum of the man, lacking strength and wits, both of which it owed to its association with the body. It is compared to a shadow, an image, a dream, to smoke, to a twittering bat. The only thing that could give it a temporary return to something more like real life was to absorb a draught of blood, that is, to be reanimated momentarily by renewed contact with the life-giving elements of the body.

This was a natural creed for the men of a heroic age, who equated the goodness of life with bodily prowess in battle, feasting and love. The real self was the body. Death meant separation from the body, and hence from life in any sense which these robust fighters could appreciate. Indeed to speak of the human soul as immortal was blasphemy. Only the gods were immortal, and they were exceedingly jealous of their immortality. It would go ill with a mortal who claimed it for himself, for that would be to set himself up against Zeus and the Olympians. We need not here consider in detail the powerful influence on later Greek thought of this conception of the relation between men and gods. Herodotus, the tragedians, Pindar and others are full of the necessity to remember one's mortality and 'think mortal thoughts'. 'Seek not to become Zeus.... For mortals mortal things are fittest' (Pindar, *Isth.* v, 14).

Homeric religion is a product of the Ionian spirit, and shares its matter-of-fact and rational outlook on the world. Indeed, while from the religious point of view its shortcomings are obvious to all, they are probably outweighed by the immense service it did to the mind of Greece by ridding it of so much of the dark underworld of magic and superstition which plagued the life of many other ancient peoples. It was by no means out of tune with the rationalism of the Ionian tradition in philosophy. Similarly the Italian philosophical tradition is not something existing in intellectual isolation, but the philosophical expression of a much more general mode of thought. Side by side with the Olympian religion—which may be called orthodox to the extent that it was inculcated by the official cults of the Greek states as well as being accepted by most of the great figures of literature—there existed a type of belief which implied a very different relationship between gods and men and a different conception of the nature and value of the human soul.[1]

The religion of Homer, after all, was particularly suited to the somewhat artificial and short-lived society for which it was intended, and much less so to the ordinary Greek of later centuries. Living a life quite unlike that of the Homeric hero, he was subject to certain longings and stirrings of the heart from which the hero had been free. The idea of capricious, all-too-human deities, whom one must try to please with material gifts offered in a bargaining spirit but without any certainty that they would make the expected return, began to seem less satisfying. Victims of injustice in this world turned their eyes to the possibility of finding redress in another. Moreover, to meet these resurgent needs, the means were at hand in numerous popular and ancient cults of an agrarian character which had only been thrown into temporary eclipse by the dominance of Homeric ideas. The most notable was the mystery-cult of Eleusis, raised from obscurity to Panhellenic repute when its mother-town was incorporated by Athens (probably towards the end of the seventh century) and its worship taken under Athenian patronage. By initiation into the mysteries of Demeter the Earth-mother and her daughter Persephone, their worshippers believed that they could be actually adopted into the family of the gods, and by this adoption secure for themselves not mere survival—which in some sense, as we have seen, was the lot of everyone—but a far better and happier fate in the life to come. 'Blessed among men who dwell on earth is he who has seen these things; but he who is uninitiated and has no part in the rites has never an equal lot when he has died and passed beneath the dank darkness.'[2]

At Eleusis initiation was all that mattered. The participants returned to their homes and lived their ordinary lives, secure in the knowledge imparted by the visual revelation which was the culmination of the

---

[1] The religious background can only be sketched very briefly here. I have dealt with it more fully in *The Greeks and their Gods*, where references to other literature will be found.

[2] *Homeric Hymn to Demeter*, 480 ff. From internal evidence we can say that this hymn was written for the Eleusinian cult before the incorporation by Athens.

mystic rites. The teaching of the Orphic writers and initiators went further. For them the hope of immortality was based on a complex myth concerning the nature of the human soul as a mixture of divine and earthly. It could only be attained by strenuous efforts, lasting through life, to develop and elevate the divine element and subdue the earthly. Initiation was an essential part, but the rites must be periodically renewed and life as a whole lived differently, with observance of ritual prohibitions among which abstention from meat was, as with the Pythagoreans, of the greatest importance. The whole religious side of this movement, which included an elaborate cycle of rebirths, cannot be separated from that adopted by Pythagoras, and to make the attempt would probably be unhistorical. The Pythagoreans not only used the religious books promulgated under the ancient name of Orpheus: prominent members of the school were named in later antiquity as the authors of some of them, and the tradition ascribing some to Pythagoras himself goes back, as we have already noted, to the fifth century B.C.[1]

The purpose of mentioning these things—Eleusis as the outstanding example of a type of belief that accompanied hundreds of more obscure agricultural cults all over Greece, and the elaborate eschatological schemes of the Orphics—is to put the Pythagoreans in their setting. Owing to the religious foundations of their thought, they were even less isolated than other philosophers from the current beliefs of their time. To recognize the existence and interaction of the two great streams of philosophical tradition, the Ionian and the Italian, is of the first importance for an understanding of Presocratic philosophy: but it is equally important to become aware that they stand in their own sphere for something wider, for two contrasting tendencies in the Greek mind whose conflict and interplay form an essential and fascinating aspect of the study of Greek life and literature in general. These two strains in their turn find their explanation partly in the fusion of races that went to make up the Greek people of historical times, and partly in social conditions, but to pursue them there now would take us too far afield.[2] They may be summed up in the words θνητὰ φρονεῖν ('think mortal thoughts') on the one hand and ὁμοίωσις θεῷ ('assimi-

[1] P. 182, n. 2, above, and for the names of other Pythagoreans see Kern, *Orph. Fr.* p. 52.
[2] See *The Greeks and their Gods*, esp. pp. 301–4.

lation to God') on the other.[1] 'Strive not, my soul, for an immortal life', warned Pindar (*Pyth.* III, 61), whereas Empedocles the Sicilian, apparently without the slightest heed to such a warning, shouted to his fellow-citizens of Acragas: 'I tell you I am a god immortal, no longer a mortal' (fr. 112.4).

It is to this second strain, to the idea of assimilation to the divine as the legitimate and essential aim of human life, that Pythagoras gave his allegiance, and he supported it with all the force of a philosophical and mathematical, as well as a religious, genius. In this last clause lies the originality of Pythagoreanism. This is where it transcends the more widespread idea of 'God shalt thou be instead of mortal' which pre-existed and formed the soil out of which it sprang. Eleusis taught that immortality was to be obtained through the single revelation, after suitable preparation, of the mystic objects or symbols; the Orphics added the need for carrying out in daily life an elaborate system of religious, possibly also moral, prohibitions; to Pythagoras the way of salvation lay through philosophy. Aristoxenus[2] said of Pythagoras and his followers: 'Every distinction they lay down as to what should be done or not done aims at conformity with the divine. This is their starting-point; their whole life is ordered with a view to following God, and it is the governing principle of their philosophy.'

This brief excursus into religious history was necessary, for in the idea of the purification of the soul we come near to the link which joins the religious and the philosophical sides of Pythagoreanism and enables us to see them as two sides of a single unitary system. Hence to understand this system the first essential is to appreciate the religious background out of which it arose and against which it must be seen.

---

[1] The first sentiment, in the above or similar words, is frequent. Cf. e.g. Epicharmus, 263 Kaibel (DK, 23 B 20, vol. I, p. 201) θνατὰ χρὴ τὸν θνατόν, οὐκ ἀθάνατα τὸν θνατὸν φρονεῖν and Soph. *Tr.* 473. For the second phrase see Plato, *Theaet.* 176A διὸ καὶ πειρᾶσθαι χρὴ ἐνθένδε ἐκεῖσε φεύγειν ὅτι τάχιστα. φυγὴ δὲ ὁμοίωσις θεῷ κατὰ τὸ δυνατόν, and cf. the true statement of Arius Didymus (?) *ap.* Stob. *Ecl. Eth.* II, 7, p. 49 Wachsm.: Σωκράτης Πλάτων ταὐτὰ τῷ Πυθαγόρᾳ, τέλος ὁμοίωσιν θεῷ.

[2] *Ap.* Iambl. *V.P.* 137, DK, 58 D 2. The translation is Cornford's (*CQ*, 1922, 142), except for the word ὁμολογίας. Cornford prints ὁμιλίας. So Nauck, but this is due to Scaliger: ὁμολογίας is in all MSS. If it is the true reading, it raises a suspicion that the sentence as it stands is not a word-for-word quotation from Aristoxenus, for ὁμολογία in the particular sense required became something of a technical term of the Stoics. Wehrli does not include the passage in his *Aristoxenos*. Nevertheless it gives a true description of the Pythagoreans of all periods.

Basic is the notion of the kinship of all life, which was a necessary pre-supposition to the doctrine of transmigration. This kinship had a very wide extension, embracing more than what we should be inclined to accept as animate nature, so that Porphyry, while using it as the foundation of his argument against the eating of animals, found himself at the same time under the necessity of opposing the extreme view that even vegetables should be avoided, since logically they were included within its scope.[1] For Empedocles everything had a share of consciousness (fr. 110.10), and even the universe as a whole was in the eyes of the Pythagoreans a living and breathing creature.[2] The Pythagorean Ecphantus (if we may trust an amended text) described the world as a form (ἰδέα) of the divine power called Mind or Soul which was the cause of physical motion.[3]

Since Aristotle wrote of this in the first book of his lost work *On the Philosophy of Pythagoras*, he probably attributed it to Pythagoras himself, and since the belief was already abroad in the sixth century we may safely do the same. In this respect he and his followers did not differ

---

[1] The logical difficulty is obvious, once the attempt is made, as Pythagoras made it, to fit the συγγένεια of all nature into the framework of a philosophical system. The distinction between things that have life only (ζωή) and those that have ψυχή (p. 202, below) suggests that the Pythagoreans were conscious of it. The feeling that animal, but not vegetable food must be avoided at all costs no doubt finds its ultimate explanation in the ancient and deeply-rooted horror of the pollution (ἄγος, μίασμα) incurred by bloodshed, which the Pythagoreans inherited from un-philosophical predecessors. Empedocles, like Pythagoras, made a conscious effort to justify this revulsion on philosophical grounds, but an earlier age is evoked by his agonized cry (fr. 139):

οἴμοι, ὅτι οὐ πρόσθεν με διώλεσε νηλεὲς ἦμαρ
πρὶν σχέτλι' ἔργα βορᾶς περὶ χείλεσι μητίσασθαι.

Empedocles does indeed also issue a command to 'keep off bay-leaves' (fr. 140: although the words are quoted in Plutarch simply in a context of picking leaves off the plants, I presume that Empedocles had consumption in mind as in the similarly-worded injunction about beans, fr. 141); but the bay, Apollo's sacred plant, occupied a rather special position. In fr. 127 he pairs it with the lion, king of plants as the lion is king of beasts. Each forms the best lodging in its kind for a human soul.

[2] For the universe as breathing, Ar. *Phys.* 213 b 22 and in a fragment of the *De Philos. Pythagorae* (DK, 58 B 30; see p. 277, below). Cf. Sext. Emp. *Math.* IX, 127 οἱ μὲν οὖν περὶ τὸν Πυθαγόραν καὶ τὸν Ἐμπεδοκλέα καὶ τῶν Ἰταλῶν πλῆθός φασι μὴ μόνον ἡμῖν πρὸς ἀλλήλους καὶ πρὸς τοὺς θεοὺς εἶναί τινα κοινωνίαν, ἀλλὰ καὶ πρὸς τὰ ἄλογα τῶν ζῴων. ἐν γὰρ ὑπάρχειν πνεῦμα τὸ διὰ παντὸς τοῦ κόσμου διῆκον ψυχῆς τρόπον, τὸ καὶ ἑνοῦν ἡμᾶς πρὸς ἐκεῖνα. Similarly Cicero *N.D.* I, 11, 27.

Cornford (*CQ*, 1922, 140, n. 2), in saying that this passage, though employing later terms, is substantially true, follows Delatte, *Vie de Pyth.* 204: 'Il faut bien admettre que c'est là une doctrine de l'ancien Pythagorisme.'

[3] DK, 51.1. See their apparatus and pp. 324f. below. The MS. reading is obviously corrupt. The date of Ecphantus is uncertain, but at the latest he was a contemporary of Archytas (ZN, 1, 604, n. 5).

from the Milesians, who as we saw assumed as a sufficient explanation of the original generative motion that the stuff of the world was instinct with life. Anaximenes even accepted the corollary that the air which constitutes the human soul is the same substance as that of the god which we must suppose the universe to be. But, so far as we can tell, he treated it in the Ionian way, as an interesting scientific fact. He certainly did not regard it as the basis of a religious way of life. We know¹ both how universal was the early belief that the soul was of the nature of breath or air, and also what widely different conclusions could be drawn from the fact, according as one's inclinations were towards a scientific or a religious conception of the world. Democritus combined it with what was for practical purposes a materialistic atheism, but the Orphics— that is, a mystical religious sect—subscribed to it no less. The conclusion drawn both by them and by the Pythagoreans was that if the world was a living, eternal and divine creature, and lived by breathing in air or breath from the infinite around it;² and if man too got his life by breathing (which was evidence that the human soul itself was air); then the natural kinship between man and the universe, microcosm and macrocosm, must be close. The universe was one, eternal and divine. Men were many and divided, and they were mortal. But the essential part of man, his soul, was not mortal, and it owed its immortality to this circumstance, that it was neither more nor less than a small fragment or spark of the divine and universal soul, cut off and imprisoned in a perishable body. Diogenes Laertius quotes an account of Pythagoreanism which Alexander, a contemporary of Sulla surnamed Polyhistor on account of his encyclopaedic activities, claimed to have found in certain 'Pythagorean notebooks'.³ In this account it is said,

---

¹ Pp. 128 ff., above.

² See pp. 277 ff., below. E. Frank held that Aristotle learned of this 'Pythagorean' doctrine from 'Philolaus', both in inverted commas because he believed this pseudo-Philolaus to have been a Platonist, probably Speusippus. For his present point he refers to the citation of Philolaus's views in *Anon. Londinensis* (DK, 44A27), although in fact that passage only speaks of ordinary animal life and to make his point he has to add on his own account: 'Nun ist aber für Philolaos der Mikrokosmos ein treues Abbild der Weltganzen' (*Plato u. d. sogenn. Pyth.* 327–8). It will not be expedient to refer at every turn to the extreme sceptical views expressed in Frank's book, and this may serve as an example.

³ D.L. VIII, 24 ff. The part quoted here is from ch. 28. Alexander seems to have been an industrious and unoriginal collector of facts, free from the fantasy that characterized the later Neopythagoreans and Neoplatonists. (See *RE*, I, 1449–52.) The Πυθαγορικὰ ὑπομνήματα which

first, that plants as well as animals have life (ʒωή), though not all have soul (ψυχή). Soul is a torn-off fragment (ἀπόσπασμα)[1] of *aither* and the hot and the cold: it is not coterminous with life, and it is immortal *because that from which it has been detached is immortal*.

In this way the doctrine that all life was *homogenes* not only united men in the ties of kinship with animals, but, most important of all, it taught them that their best nature was identical with something higher. It gave them an aim in life, namely to cultivate the soul, shake off the taint of the body, and rejoin the universal soul of which their individual souls were in essence parts. So long as the soul was condemned to remain in the wheel of transmigration—so long, that is to say, as it had to enter a new body of man or animal after the death of the one which it had previously tenanted—so long was it still impure. By living the best and highest type of human life it might ultimately shake off the

he claims to be citing recall the ὑπομνήματα κεφαλαιώδη handed down by the last generation of Pythagoreans in the fourth century B.C. (p. 180, above). However, the date or dates of the contents of these chapters have been variously estimated by scholars. Rohde (*Rh. Mus.* 1872, 47) remarked on their relatively modest content, as indicating an early date. Zeller (ZN, 471 and n. 1) treated Alexander's account with some respect, but attributed his source to the second century and considered it an heir to Platonic and Stoic teaching. M. Wellmann (*Hermes*, 1919, 225–48), though not always sufficiently critical in his use of late sources for comparison, argued persuasively for its fourth-century origin, as also did Delatte (*V. de P.* 198 ff., 232 ff.), and they were followed by Cornford (*P. and P.* 3). Diels was converted by Wellmann, whose arguments nevertheless appeared to Wilamowitz (*Platon*, II, 84, n. 1) to be 'ganz verfehlt', though he says no more. I. Lévy (*Sources de la Légende de Pyth.* 75) also thinks the third century the earliest possible date. But see also Raven, *Pyth. and El.* 159–64.

An exhaustive analysis of the extract has been made by A. J. Festugière in *REG*, 1945, 1–65. It may be difficult to deny his conclusion that the immediate source is a Hellenistic compilation incorporating elements of diverse dates, but his further argument, that none of the doctrines so collected can have antedated Speusippus, does not seem so inescapable. One misses also any suggested explanation of the title Πυθαγορικὰ ὑπομνήματα. According to Clement of Alexandria, Alexander also wrote a work περὶ Πυθαγορικῶν συμβόλων (*RE*, I, 1451).

To give an example of the differing conclusions which may be drawn from the same material, Cornford adduced in favour of an early date that 'no later writer could have escaped the influence of Plato himself and in particular of the *Timaeus*'. For Festugière the extract displays an arrangement of material of which 'l'origine est incontestablement le *Timée*'. (Cornford attributes occasional anachronistic phraseology—e.g. 'the indefinite dyad' for the Pythagorean 'unlimited' —to Alexander himself.) K. von Fritz, like Cornford, saw elements in the account which would be 'certainly impossible in any philosophy influenced by Platonic thought', and concluded that even though some of its parts show the influence of later philosophical terminology, it contains elements of genuine early Pythagorean doctrine. (*CP*, 1946, 34.) With this judicious conclusion one may well agree.

[1] The word ἀπόσπασμα occurs in Plato (*Phaedo*, 113 B), but its use to describe the relation of individual souls to the Universe seems to have been Stoic. Cf. Chrysippus *ap.* D.L. VII, 143, Epictetus, II, 8, 10, M. Aurel. V, 27. Nevertheless the doctrine concerned, like many others held by the Stoics, did not originate with them.

body altogether, escape from the wheel of rebirth, and attain the final bliss of losing itself in the universal, eternal and divine soul to which by its own nature it belonged.[1] The conception of god or divinity, as so far adumbrated, may seem decidedly vague, and it must be admitted that, in so far as we rely on any trustworthy sources for the Pythagoreanism of Plato's time or earlier, it must remain so.[2] The Pythagoreans certainly did not reject the contemporary polytheism, and their particular patron was Apollo, to whom Pythagoras was believed to stand in a special relation. Some at least revered him as an actual incarnation of this god (p. 149, above). Such individual manifestations of the divine, however, by no means ruled out at this stage the conception of 'the divine' (τὸ θεῖον) in general, a conception which had its appeal both to the rationalist (as explaining the ultimate constitution of the universe) and to the mystic, whose deeper longings it satisfied.[3] What exactly the Pythagoreans meant by the soul, and how they reconciled its immortality with certain presuppositions about its composition, is also a difficult problem, which is best left until after an account of their philosophy of number, with which it is intimately bound up.[4]

That then is the situation. Each of us is shut up in his separate body and marked with the impurity of the lower forms of matter. How are we to shake this off and bring the moment nearer when our own small part will reunite with the whole and we shall be god ourselves? What is the way of salvation? Eleusis offered it by way of the revelation, *epopteia*, granted to the initiate after suitable preparatory purification. The Orphic sought it through some form of sacramental *orgia* or *teletai* and the observance of taboos. Pythagoras retained much of this, but because he was a philosopher he added a method of his own.

---

[1] As positive evidence that this was a Pythagorean belief we have so far seen only the statement of Alexander Polyhistor that the soul was an ἀπόσπασμα αἰθέρος. He also says that all within the uppermost air is divine (ch. 27) and that pure souls go ἐπὶ τὸν ὕψιστον (ch. 31). Add that Delatte (*Vie de Pyth.* 225 ff.) shows it to have been a belief at least of later Pythagoreanism, that it was already common in the fifth century, and that there is reason to think it was adopted by the Orphics. See Guthrie, *The Greeks and their Gods*, 262 f., 324.

[2] Cf. ZN, 565–6.

[3] Similarly (and doubtless under Pythagorean influence) Empedocles gave the name Apollo to his highest god, to whom he explicitly denies all anthropomorphic features. See fr. 134, with the introductory words of Ammonius.

[4] Pp. 306 ff., below.

Pythagoras and the Pythagoreans

There are good grounds for thinking that Pythagoras introduced and made familiar a new meaning of the words *philosophos* and *philosophia*. The story told by Heraclides Ponticus (referred to on p. 164, above) makes him the actual inventor of the words. As given by Diogenes (I, 12) it runs: 'Pythagoras first used the term philosophy and called himself a philosopher [i.e. lover of wisdom] in conversation at Sicyon with Leon the tyrant of that city or of Phlius, as Heraclides Ponticus relates in his *De Muliere Exanimi*; for, he said, no one is *wise* save God.' This is probably not strictly true, for the actual words are used quite early, in what one might call an Ionian rather than an Italian sense, although one of these references may just possibly support the attribution. Heraclitus (fr. 35) said: 'Philosophers must be inquirers into a great number of things.' This may indicate that the word was in use independently in his time, but it may on the other hand be aimed personally at Pythagoras, 'the man who called himself philosopher'; for polymathy, or inquiry into many things, was in the eyes of Heraclitus folly, and elsewhere (fr. 40, quoted above, p. 157) he censures Pythagoras by name for indulging in it.[1] Zeno the Eleatic is also said to have written a book *Against the Philosophers*, which almost certainly means the Pythagoreans.[2] On the other hand Herodotus already uses the word in what I have called the 'Ionian' sense, without any of its Pythagorean overtones, when he describes Solon as travelling about φιλοσοφέων, θεωρίης ἔνεκεν, that is, to see the world and acquire information of all sorts (I, 30). Burnet remarked truly (*EGP*, 83): 'In Ionia *philosophia* meant something like "curiosity"....On the other hand, wherever we can trace the influence of Pythagoras, the word has a far deeper meaning. Philosophy is itself a "purification" and a way of escape from the "wheel".' We have seen (p. 199) the Pythagorean ideal as stated by Aristoxenus. Philosophy in this sense is the subject-matter of Plato's *Phaedo*, where Pythagorean influence is obviously strong and seems to be acknowledged by the references to Philolaus. 'I want to give you my reasons', says Socrates (63E), 'for

---

[1] Kirk (*HCF*, 395) agrees that this is a possibility. Wilamowitz thought that the word φιλοσόφους was not a part of the actual fragment of Heraclitus, but both Bywater and Diels–Kranz reasonably retain it. See note *ad loc.* in DK, and cf. Cornford, *Princ. Sap.* 115, J. L. Stocks, *Mind*, 1915, 220. On fr. 35 see also p. 417, below.

[2] Stocks, *loc. cit.* Cf., however, for a more sceptical view ZN, 438.

thinking that the man who has truly devoted his life to *philosophia* is of good courage when death approaches, and strong in hope that the greatest of good things will fall to his lot on the other side when he dies.'

For Pythagoras then the purification and salvation of the soul depended not merely, as in the mystery-cults, on initiation and ritual purity, but on *philosophia*; and this word, then as now, meant using the powers of reason and observation in order to gain understanding. In what way, we may ask, was the connexion established? Does the philosophical side of Pythagorean teaching link up with the religious beliefs of which we have seen something already?

Pythagorean religious beliefs were founded on the world-wide and primitive idea of universal kinship or sympathy. The more philosophical side of the system rests on something which belongs particularly to the Hellenic outlook and is typified in the character of the most Hellenic of the gods, Apollo, to whose worship the sect was devoted. That is, the exaltation of the related ideas of limit, moderation, and order. It was not accidental that they chose as their divine patron the god on whose temple were inscribed the words 'Nothing too much', 'Observe limit', and other precepts in the same sense. The Greek genius, in thought and art, represents the triumph of λόγος or *ratio*, which has been defined as meaning on the one hand 'the intelligible, determinate, mensurable, as opposed to the fantastic, vague and shapeless', and on the other 'the proportions of things both in themselves and as related to a whole'.[1] Of this genius for reducing things to their mensurable characteristics, and insisting on the element of proportion both in their internal structure and in their relations with one another, the Pythagorean philosophy provides the outstanding example. Their philosophico-religious synthesis was, however, in one respect audacious. From their insistence on the cosmic significance of limit and order they did not infer the same consequences for human life and aspirations as did the popular thought and the poets of their day. Dominant in the literature of the sixth and fifth centuries is the idea already referred to,

---

[1] E. Fraenkel, *Rome and Greek Culture* (Inaugural lecture, Oxford, 1935). I may be forgiven for quoting such an aptly worded description of the Greek genius, although in the context Professor Fraenkel is in fact attributing these qualities of *ratio* to the Romans, to explain their success as the preservers of Greek thought.

that if excess is to be avoided and limit observed, if everything in the universe has its proper place and must not seek to encroach on that of others, then this for man means that he must recognize his mortality and content himself with a mortal's life. Between mortals and immortals, gods and men, a barrier was fixed, and it was *hybris* to cross it. Nothing too much, observe the limit; and immortality and divinity were unquestionably beyond the limit appointed for man. This prevailing view has already been noted, as also the fact that by the sixth century there existed a mystical movement which denied it. That movement was especially associated with the Western Greeks. To the evidence already mentioned we may add those verses which, scratched on thin plates of gold, were buried with the initiates of a mystic sect in graves of Magna Graecia. Here among other instructions the dead man is told that if he can prove his credentials to the guardians of the nether world, they will welcome him with the cry: 'Happy and blessed one, thou shalt be god instead of mortal.' To attain this goal he had lived a life of sanctity and purity, as had Empedocles of Acragas who made the same claim for himself.[1] Of this persuasion was Pythagoras, with his denial of the propriety of mortal thoughts for mortal men. Assimilation to God was for him, as we have seen, the goal of life. At the same time, unlike the Orphics and their kind, he and his followers united with these aspirations a philosophy rooted in the twin ideas of limit and order, *peras* and *kosmos*. It is in the interpretation of these key-words, if at all, that we shall find the bridge between their religious and their philosophic ideas.

This bridge was constructed by the following train of thought: (*a*) the world is a *kosmos*—that untranslatable world which unites, as perhaps only the Greek spirit could, the notion of order, arrangement or structural perfection with that of beauty. (*b*) All nature is akin, therefore the soul of man is intimately related to the living and divine universe. (*c*) Like is known by like, that is, the better one knows something the more one is assimilated to it. Hence (*d*) to seek through philosophy for a better understanding of the structure of the divine

---

[1] The gold plates have been many times discussed. See Guthrie, *Orpheus and Gk. Rel.* 171 ff. The oldest may be dated to the fourth century, and the poems from which they contain extracts are obviously older.

kosmos is to realize and cultivate the divine element in oneself. This argument must now be amplified and some evidence for it adduced. The state of our knowledge of early Pythagoreanism is such that part of this evidence must be indirect, that is, taken either from contemporary philosophers who were known to be in sympathy with them, or one like Plato on whom they exercised a powerful influence. Yet he would be a hardened sceptic who would deny its total weight.

Limit (*peras*) and the Unlimited (*apeiron*) were, as will appear more fully later (pp. 240 ff., below), set by the Pythagoreans at the very beginning of things as the two contrasting principles by which the world evolved; and of them they saw *peras* as good and *apeiron* as evil. To quote a simple statement of this, Aristotle says in the *Ethics* (1106 b 29): 'Evil belongs to the unlimited, as the Pythagoreans surmised, and good to the limited.' Now the world is living and divine, and so good. It can only be any or all of these because it is *limited*, and displays an *order* in the relations of its component parts. Full and efficient life depends on organization. We see this in individual creatures, which we (like Aristotle) call organic to indicate that they have all their parts arranged and subordinated as instruments (*organa*) towards the end of keeping the whole being alive and enabling it to perform its functions. So with the world. Were it unlimited, it would have no *telos*, would be *ateles*—which means both 'endless' and 'incomplete';[1] but the world is *teleion*, a complete whole. Observation (it was then thought) supports this view. There may be minor irregularities, but the major cosmic events are marked by their regular order. Dawn and sunset, summer, winter and the intermediate seasons follow one another in unvarying succession. For the Greeks the perfect example of this eternal regularity was provided by the wheeling stars, which exhibited (as was believed from before the time of Pythagoras down to, and including, Copernicus) an everlasting and perfectly circular motion. One can see the reason for the paramount position assigned by the Pythagoreans to astronomy among the sciences.

In short the world is in the full sense a *kosmos*, and we may allow ourselves to note a statement about Pythagoras which, whether literally true or not, is a significant pointer to doctrines which were regarded as

[1] What is ἀτελές is ἄπειρον, cf. Plato, *Philebus*, 24 B.

characteristically his: he was traditionally supposed to have been the first to apply the name *kosmos* to the world, in recognition of the order which it displayed.[1]

The idea of the kinship of all nature has been sufficiently shown to be Pythagorean and to underlie the doctrine of transmigration and the prohibition of animal flesh. It recurs in these connexions in Empedocles.[2]

---

[1] Aët. II, 1, 1 (DK, 14.21) Π. πρῶτος ὠνόμασε τὴν τῶν ὅλων περιοχὴν κόσμον ἐκ τῆς ἐν αὐτῷ τάξεως. See also D.L. VIII, 48 (from Favorinus). Other references in Delatte, *Vie de P.* 203. The attribution has been contested by some modern scholars on the ground that κόσμος with the meaning 'world' did not come into use until very much later. Our knowledge of the actual language used by Presocratic philosophers is terribly meagre, but the position may be summarized thus.

Whether or not Anaximander used the word κόσμος (cf. p. 110, above), it was already being used by philosophers to mean the world (of course in its aspect as an ordered structure) in the early fifth century. In Empedocles fr. 26.5 (ἄλλοτε μὲν φιλότητι συνερχόμεν' εἰς ἕνα κόσμον), it clearly, as Mr Kirk says in his discussion of the term (*HCF*, 313), means only 'order' or 'arrangement', but when in fr. 134.5 he speaks of the divine mind as φροντίσι κόσμον ἅπαντα καταΐσσουσα θοῇσιν, he must mean that it darts through the whole world. The choice of word is still significant: it emphasizes that the world is an ordered structure; but even much later, no Greek could have described the world by this term without having somewhere in his mind the consciousness that it exemplified the combination of order, fitness and beauty. These associations κόσμος never lost. Of κόσμον τόνδε in Heracl. fr. 30 Kirk's own conclusion is (*ibid.* 316, 317) that it means 'things plus order', that is, 'the natural world and the order in it'. 'The natural world' is also the plain meaning in Diog. Apoll. fr. 2 τὰ ἐν τῷδε τῷ κόσμῳ ἐόντα νῦν, and (as Vlastos seems to me to have shown, *AJP*, 1955, 345) in Anaxag. fr. 8.

Kirk points out that 'the parallel between man and cosmos is first explicitly drawn in the fifth century', and even if we reject the word itself in Anaximenes, fr. 2 (and I for one should be prepared to maintain that the comparison between man and the world at least is his: pp. 131 f., above), the phrase quoted from Democritus (fr. 34 ἐν τῷ ἀνθρώπῳ μικρῷ κόσμῳ ὄντι κατὰ Δημόκριτον), which seems genuine, shows that κόσμος = 'world-order' was by his time a familiar notion.

The development of the word through the stages (*a*) order or arrangement of anything, (*b*) order in the world, ὁ τοῦ παντὸς κόσμος, as used for example in Emped. 26.5, Eur. fr. 910, (*c*) the world *as* an order (Emped. fr. 134.5), (*d*) the world in general, with no special reference to its ordered structure, must have been a gradual one; the new shades of meaning came into use beside the older without replacing them. Once the step had been taken from (*a*) to (*b*), there is little point in trying to pin down further developments to any particular date or person. The decisive moment came when the world was first seen to exhibit a rationally comprehensible order, and as such Anaximander had already described it before Pythagoras, though the latter greatly developed and enriched the conception. This first step constituted, in Jaeger's words, 'the spiritual discovery of the cosmos', and, as he rightly says, it entailed a radical break with current religious beliefs. (*Paideia*, I, 158 f.) It is hardly too much to say that it marked the dividing line between religion and philosophy. It would certainly not be surprising if the discoverers themselves added emphasis to the new truth by actually giving the name κόσμος to the world. Tradition ascribes this linguistic advance to Pythagoras, and we know that it was made by Empedocles, who followed him in so many things and at no great distance of time.

For discussions of this point, with further examples and references to earlier scholars, see especially W. Kranz, *Philologus*, 1938–9, 430ff.; Kirk, *HCF*, 313ff.; G. Vlastos, *AJP*, 1955, 345f. with n. 19.

[2] The reason for so frequently calling in the witness of Empedocles may not have been made sufficiently clear. It is twofold: (*a*) the religious ideas of Empedocles are demonstrably almost

The words 'since all nature is akin' occur in Plato in the exposition of a religious doctrine for which he is careful to disclaim originality, ascribing it to 'priests and priestesses whose concern it is to give a reasoned account of their undertakings' (*Meno*, 81 c and A). This idea and the conception of the world as a *kosmos* occur together in a most instructive passage, where again they are ascribed to others, and who should these others be but the Pythagoreans? 'The wise men tell us that heaven and earth, gods and men are bound together by kinship and love and orderliness and temperance and justice; and for this reason, my friend, they give to the whole the name of *kosmos*, not a name implying disorder or licentiousness. But you, for all your wisdom, seem to me to pay no attention to this, nor to have any conception of the powerful influence of geometrical equality among gods and men' (*Gorg.* 507 E).[1] The association of man not only with the lower forms of life but also with the soul or mind of the universe is expressed in the Pythagorean documents quoted by Alexander (p. 202, above), which find some support in Aristotle (DK, 58 B 30), and the potential divinity of man is also emphasized by Empedocles.

That like is known by like was held as a serious philosophical (and even physiological) doctrine in the fifth century, exemplified by Empedocles's theory of 'effluences' from sensa fitting into 'pores' in the body of the perceiver, which is described by Plato in the *Meno* (76 A). On the basis of this theory he wrote in an extant fragment (109): 'With earth we see earth, with water water.' It follows that if we have knowledge of the divine, it cannot be in virtue of any sense-organ (fr. 133) composed of the lower material elements that circulate in the sublunary sphere; it must mean that we have in ourselves a tincture of the divine element—by some equated with pure fire or with *aither*—

identical with those of the Pythagoreans, (*b*) his date is a sufficient answer to those who suspect that when we quote, as we so often must, fourth-century sources for Pythagorean beliefs, they may be referring to beliefs which only entered Pythagoreanism at that time (e.g. as a reflexion of Platonism). A tradition going back to Timaeus in the fourth century B.C. and Neanthes in the third (D.L. VIII, 54–5) said that Empedocles was a Pythagorean who was accused by the School of appropriating and making public their doctrines.

[1] Aristotle (if we may take the *Magna Moralia* to represent his views) had little use for this mixture of morals with mathematics (*MM*, 1182a11): 'Pythagoras also attempted to treat of virtue, but misguidedly, for by referring the virtues to numbers he rendered his investigation irrelevant to its subject: justice is not a square number.' This passage confirms, if any further confirmation were needed, that the σοφοί of Plato are in fact the Pythagoreans.

which enters our world from outside. This is the physical aspect of the doctrine of Pythagoras that, since God alone is wise, the *philosophos* or seeker after wisdom is developing the god-like in himself, and gives further content to Aristoxenus's statement about the Pythagoreans (p. 199, above) that their aim is conformity with the divine, and their whole life and philosophy ordered and governed with a view to following God.

It is Plato again who finally pulls the threads together for us by saying explicitly that what unites the philosopher to the divine (that is, to the living and breathing Whole) is the element of *kosmos* in both. In the *Republic* he writes of the philosopher 'who has his mind fixed on true reality' (500C): 'Contemplating things which are in due sequence and immutable, which neither do nor suffer wrong but are all in order (*kosmos*) and governed by reason, he will reflect them, and so far as possible become assimilated to them. Do you not think it inevitable that a man should come to resemble that with which it delights him to associate? Hence the philosopher through association with what is divine and orderly (*kosmios*) becomes divine and orderly (*kosmios*) in so far as a man may.'

For Plato the objects of the philosopher's contemplation are the transcendent 'Forms' at which he had arrived by bringing Pythagorean notions to bear upon the Socratic search for moral certainty, but the framework into which he fitted this new content of knowledge is wholly Pythagorean. In the *Timaeus* he introduces the idea on its more purely Pythagorean level, saying that to study the visible cosmos in its regular and ordered aspects—that is, the movements of the heavenly bodies—will have the same effect of emphasizing our kinship with the divine. By giving us sight, he says, the gods have made philosophy possible, for it was given us 'in order that we might observe the circuits of intelligence in the heaven and profit by them for the revolutions of our own thought, which are akin to them, though ours be troubled and they are unperturbed; and that, by learning to know them and acquiring the power to compute them rightly according to nature, we might reproduce the perfectly unerring revolutions of the god and reduce to settled order the wandering motions in ourselves'.[1]

[1] *Tim.* 47B–C, trans. Cornford.

'Kosmos' and the Philosopher

A. E. Taylor held the view that throughout this dialogue Plato was doing no more than reproduce a fifth-century Pythagorean account of the world. Few would go all the way with him in this, but we have seen enough to give assent to the following sentences from his commentary (p. 133):

The assumption that 'like is known by like', which Aristotle found in Plato's oral teaching, is common enough in the dialogues and seems to have been as characteristic of both Socrates and Plato as it was of the Pythagoreans. It is the foundation of the whole scheme for training the souls of the young 'guardians' of *Republic* II–III into moral beauty by surrounding them with the loveliness which appeals to eye and ear. The main principle of this 'early education', that the soul inevitably grows like, takes on the character of, that which it contemplates, is manifestly Pythagorean.

Even more manifestly Pythagorean is it when it reaches the higher levels and becomes a question of the philosopher growing like the divine object of the most worth-while contemplation of all. We may recall the Pythagorean comparison of life to a festival or fair, at which some are present to take part in athletic or musical contests, others to buy or sell, 'but the best as spectators'.[1] So in life, slavish natures strive for money or glory, but the philosopher seeks the truth. He seeks it with a definite aim. Just as the universe is composed of material elements reduced to an ordered structure because they are pervaded by a divine life and reason, so we are *kosmoi* in miniature, organic structures composed of the same stuff and reproducing the same principles of order. But we shall only reproduce them satisfactorily, so far as in a mortal body one may, if we cultivate the freedom of the divine element of reason of which we too possess a spark, and, by studying the order displayed on a grand scale around us, learn to reflect it in the motions of our own lives. The philosopher who contemplates the *kosmos* becomes *kosmios* in his own soul.[2]

The simile of spectators at a festival might seem to suggest that the Pythagoreans adopted a purely passive attitude to the world.

[1] οἱ δέ γε βέλτιστοι ἔρχονται θεαταί, D.L. VIII, 8. (Cf. also p. 164, above.)

[2] A modern parallel may be found in a perhaps surprising quarter. Cf. Bertrand Russell, *The Problems of Philosophy* (H.U.L. 1912), p. 250: philosophy is to be studied 'above all because, through the greatness of the universe which philosophy contemplates, the mind also is rendered great, and becomes capable of that union with the universe which constitutes its highest good'.

But it was clearly more than that. (*a*) It meant active intellectual study, particularly in the fields of number-theory, geometry, music and astronomy, for those are the studies which will bring understanding of the ordered and lasting movements taking place in the heavens, and of the structure of everything which they contain. (*b*) It involved an actual change in the philosopher's own nature, for it is by this active contemplation (θεωρία) that the aim of assimilation to the divine (ὁμοίωσις θεῷ) is attained.

(2) *Numbers and the cosmos*

(*a*) *Introductory: the musical intervals*

For these people, the natural world was not an object suitable for experiment, analysis, and exploitation. It was not an object at all. It was alive with certain mysterious and powerful forces, and man's life still possessed a richness and a dignity which came from his sense of participation in the movement of these forces.[1]

The book from which the above quotation comes is a study of some modern Greek poets, and the passage refers directly to the Greek peasant of Turkish times, from whom the author is claiming that his poets, and Sikelianos in particular, inherited a living tradition. Elsewhere, however, he makes it clear that this tradition has its roots in antiquity, and in fact the passage could stand without alteration as a description of the Pythagoreans. It might be thought more appropriate to the previous section of our discussion, but it stands here for the same reason as that section was made to precede the present one: to remind us of a characteristic of their philosophy which to a great extent persisted even in their work on number and mathematics, but which in dealing with this aspect it would be easier to forget.

It is a dark and difficult subject, and some general remarks are necessary at the outset to make clear, and to some extent justify, the policy that we shall pursue. There is no doubt that the Pythagoreans were responsible for important advances in the science of mathematics. Nevertheless, as the above quotation was intended to hint and as has, I hope, been made abundantly clear already, their attitude to

[1] Philip Sherrard, *The Marble Threshing Floor* (1956), 128.

it was utterly different from that of a mathematician of today. For them numbers had, and retained, a mystical significance, an independent reality. Phenomena, though they professed to explain them, were secondary, for the only significant thing about phenomena was the way in which they reflected number. Number was responsible for 'harmony', the divine principle that governed the structure of the whole world. Numbers not only explained the physical world, but also symbolized or stood for (but the Pythagoreans said 'were') moral qualities and other abstractions. It was no hard-headed mathematician who declared that justice 'was' the number four (on the grounds that justice was essentially reciprocity and reciprocity was embodied in a square number), and marriage five,[1] and Aristotle had some reason for his complaint (*Metaph.* 986a3): 'Any agreements that they found between number and harmony on the one hand, and on the other the changes and divisions of the universe and the whole order of nature, these they collected and applied; and if something was missing, they insisted on making their system coherent.' There follows his complaint that they invented a non-existent planet to make up the total to the sacred number ten. Again in *De Caelo*, 293a25: they invented the counter-earth 'not seeking accounts and reasons to explain the phenomena, but forcing the phenomena and trying to fit them into arguments and opinions of their own'. Such an attitude to science is no more than the natural consequence of that side of their philosophy which we have already studied.

No reader of Plato can fail to be struck by the solemn and religious tone with which he sometimes speaks of mathematics, and the fact that they have for him a metaphysical as well as a purely mathematical significance. Arithmetic 'draws the soul upwards,...never allowing anyone to offer it for discussion mere collections of visible or tangible bodies' (*Rep.* 525 D). The objects of geometrical knowledge are 'eternal, not subject to change and decay', and it 'tends to draw the soul towards truth and to produce a philosophic intelligence for the directing upwards of faculties which we wrongly turn earthwards' (527B). As to

---

[1] For the equation of such abstractions with numbers see Arist. *Metaph.* 985b29, 1078b21, *MM*, 1182a11 (all in DK, 58B4), and with the last compare *EN*, 1132b23. Cf. pp. 301ff., below.

astronomy, which is to be studied purely as a branch of mathematics 'in terms of pure numbers and perfect figures...perceptible to reason and thought but not visible to the eye' (529D), it too must turn the soul's gaze upwards—not literally to the sky, but to the realm of 'real being and the invisible'. The next study in the philosopher's propaedeutic is harmonics, and here Plato's only criticism of the Pythagoreans (whom he mentions by name) is that they are too much inclined to look for numerical relationships in physical, audible sound. The whole curriculum—arithmetic, geometry, astronomy, harmonics— is plainly Pythagorean, and we need not be afraid to say that the metaphysical view of mathematics here displayed is a legacy from the same school. No one doubts—nor could it well be doubted—that much of the doctrine of the *Timaeus*, which Plato puts into the mouth not of Socrates but of a visitor from Locri in South Italy, is Pythagorean. In this dialogue a 'harmony' made up of series in arithmetical and harmonic progressions is used in the creation of the soul of the world (35 B ff.), and the existence of two mean proportionals between two cubic numbers serves as the reason why the Creator had to provide two elements intermediate between fire and earth. These Platonic passages may justly be used to illustrate the significance of mathematics for the Pythagoreans, for whom, as for Plato, the acquisition of knowledge partook more of the character of a religious initiation than of mere instruction or research.[1]

Our primary source for the more scientific side of Pythagoreanism must always be Aristotle, the best qualified, and for most of it the earliest informant. In his extant works he mentions the school only in the context of an exposition of his own philosophy, and this has consequences which, though they have sometimes been exaggerated, must be taken into account: but whatever he says was based on a special study which had borne fruit in a treatise devoted entirely to their doctrines. That treatise is lost, and we have only a few quotations from it, but its existence in the background may legitimately add to our confidence that in dealing with the Pythagoreans he knew what he was

[1] B. L. van der Waerden, 'Die Arithm. d. Pyth.', *Math. Annalen*, 120 (1947–9), 680ff., Heath, *Thirteen Bks. of Eucl.* II, 294. Even Cornford, who so strongly opposed Taylor's theory that the entire *Timaeus* was a document of fifth-century Pythagoreanism, wrote that much of the doctrine no doubt is Pythagorean (*Plato's Cosmol.* 3).

talking about.[1] It should be added that the quotations that we have are sufficient to refute the suggestion, based on the extant works, that Pythagoreanism as Aristotle knew it was purely a scientific system.

Moreover, while the different generations of pre-Platonic Pythagoreans may prove almost impossible to separate, we must do all we can to distinguish between Pythagoreanism up to Plato's time and the philosophy of Plato himself, which certainly owed much to it, and which tended to be read back into Pythagoreanism by its contemporaries and successors. For this purpose no guide can be as good as Aristotle, since the man who was a member of the Academy for twenty years of Plato's lifetime certainly knew the difference between the two and refers to it more than once. Here again we must allow for a certain amount of philosophical prejudice, though without going so far as those who speak of a perpetual desire on Aristotle's part to belittle the originality of Plato.[2] There is no need to accuse of hypocrisy the man who said that it was hard for him to criticize the Platonic doctrine of forms because those who espoused it were his friends (*EN*, 1096a12). That would be out of keeping with his high regard for two things, friendship (one thinks of the poem in honour of his murdered friend Hermias, which was made the occasion of his own exile) and truth. If he 'passes so rapidly' over the features which distinguish Plato's philosophy from that of the Pythagoreans, it must be remembered that he was simply making notes for the instruction of members or ex-members of the Academy to whom such matters would be perfectly

---

[1] A few examples of ancient references to this treatise may be of interest.

(*a*) After a brief account in *Metaph.* A of the Pythagorean derivation of the world from numbers and their respect for the number ten, with a reference to their astronomy including the counter-earth, Aristotle himself concludes (986a12): 'But I have dealt with this more fully elsewhere.'

(*b*) Alex. *in Metaph.* 986a3 (p. 41.1 Hayd.): 'He deals with this more fully in *De Caelo* and in the work on the opinions of the Pythagoreans.'

(*c*) *Ibid.* 75.15: 'Of the order in the heavens, which the Pythagoreans constructed numerically, he writes in the second book on Pythagorean doctrine.'

(*d*) Stob. *Ecl.* 1, 18, 1c (DK, 58B30): 'In the first book of the treatise on the philosophy of Pythagoras he writes....'

(*e*) Simpl. *De Caelo*, 386.22 Heib.: 'As Aristotle himself records in the second book of his collection of Pythagorean beliefs.'

(*f*) *Ibid.* 511.30: 'For so he himself says in the treatise on Pythagoreanism.'

Others could be quoted. See Rose's ed. of the fragments, nos. 190–205. There is also evidence of a treatise on the philosophy of Archytas (Rose fr. 207).

[2] Raven, *P. and E.* 186. See also Cherniss, *ACP*, 392.

familiar. From our point of view the brevity is to be regretted, but it is not attributable to malice. That his own philosophical point of view should colour his accounts, whether of the Pythagoreans or Plato, is of course inevitable, but to make allowance for this is not difficult, and when that is done, his personal criticism or way of putting the matter may sometimes reveal, rather than conceal, some characteristic feature of the earlier philosophies. While prepared to read him critically, one may still regard his information as invaluable. His date and the circumstances of his life guarantee that what he says about the Pythagoreans will be free from contamination not only with all Hellenistic or Neopythagorean notions but also with Platonism; his intellectual stature justifies considerable confidence (due allowance being made for known factors) in the accuracy of his reports; and his knowledge of the Pythagorean school goes back at least to the first half of the fifth century, that is, to within at the most fifty, and perhaps fewer, years of the death of Pythagoras.[1]

Perhaps the first thing to ask of such an authority is how far it seemed to him that Pythagoreanism changed during its history, or split into sects holding mutually inconsistent views. He most frequently speaks of the school as a whole, though sometimes he limits a doctrine to 'certain Pythagoreans' and occasionally (all too seldom) to an individual by name. The conclusion to be drawn has been put as well as it can be by Mr Raven (*P. and E.* 157):

There can, I think, be little doubt that in this as in other passages concerned with Pythagoreanism Aristotle is content for the most part to lump the whole of it together, but occasionally inserts into his generalizations a remark or criticism, such as that about Eurytus, which applies only to a particular individual or group....It is perfectly reasonable to maintain simultaneously that Aristotle regarded the succeeding generations of Pythagoreans as sufficiently akin to be usually grouped together, and that he yet included in his remarks some that were not capable of universal application. Only so, it seems to me, can we do his testimony the justice it deserves.

This procedure of Aristotle's seems even more likely to reflect the facts when we take into account the conservatism and respect for tradition which were a natural consequence of the religious character of Pytha-

[1] *Metaph.* 985b23, p. 232, below.

Pythagoras and the History of Mathematics

goreanism. Even the *mathematici*, we are told, admitted that those who clung to the older, more primitive side of the teaching were true Pythagoreans (p. 192, above). Modern scholarship with its exacting standards is unwilling to accept any doctrine as being earlier than the earliest period, or individual, to whom it is explicitly ascribed in a source considered trustworthy. This clinging to certainties is of course infinitely preferable to an uncritical confusion. Nevertheless κατὰ τὴν ὕλην οἱ λόγοι ἀπαιτητέοι—one can only demand proof in so far as the subject admits of it—and if we are to speak of Pythagoreanism at all, we must at many points remain content with probabilities. It is therefore permissible to remark that the known character of Pythagoreanism must lead us to expect the greatest possible continuity of doctrine. Failing definite evidence that it would be impossible, the earlier existence of a tenet attested, say, for the late fifth century is more probable than not.

It is commonly held that the Pythagoreans laid the foundations of Greek mathematics. Undoubtedly they made remarkable contributions, but in assessing their originality two considerations must be borne in mind: the state of mathematics in countries further East at and before the time of Pythagoras, and the contribution of the Ionians. Progressive decipherment of cuneiform inscriptions has put the mathematics of the Babylonians in a new light. The traditional ascription to Pythagoras of the famous theorem about the square on the hypotenuse of a right-angled triangle was long doubted on the grounds that it was difficult to assign it to so early a stage of mathematical development. Now, however, that it has been found on a tablet of the time of Hammurabi, the case is different.[1] According to later tradition, Pythagoras spent some time both in Egypt and in Babylonia. Strabo (xiv, 638) says simply that observing the growing tyranny of Polycrates, he left Samos and went on a voyage of study to these two countries. In the *Theologumena Arithmeticae* attributed to Iamblichus (p. 53 de Falco, DK, 1, p. 100), we find the more circumstantial story that he was in

---

[1] On the attribution of the theorem to Pythagoras see Heath, *The Thirteen Books of Euclid*, I, 350–2. Heath 'sees no sufficient reason to question the tradition'. Also B. L. van der Waerden, 'Die Arithm. d. Pyth.', *Math. Annalen*, 120 (1947–9), 132.

Egypt when Cambyses invaded the country and was brought as a prisoner to Babylon, where he 'was initiated into the mysteries of the barbarians'. These statements, made 500 or 800 years after his death, are by modern standards of little or no historical value in themselves, but we know that in the conditions of the mid sixth century B.C. such journeys on the part of an active Samian were neither improbable nor difficult. Assuming then an acquaintance on Pythagoras's part with the achievements of the peoples to the east and south of his native Ionia (and the same was also asserted of Thales earlier), we may say with Neugebauer that the Greeks come not at the beginning but rather in the middle of mathematical science. They did not invent it, though they did much to systematize and put it on an exact and universal basis. As in astronomy, they adopted the most valuable achievements of Mesopotamian culture, but developed and indeed transformed them.[1]

Next, the Ionians. There is a temptation to speak of Pythagoras as if he were a figure of great antiquity, even of doubtful historicity, a shadowy seer like Abaris or Hermotimus. Considering the religious reverence in which he was held, and the rapid growth of an aura of legend about his name, this is by no means surprising; but it must not obscure the fact that he was not only a historical person but one who lived later than Thales and Anaximander, and between whose death and that of Socrates little more than a hundred years had passed— admittedly a momentous century in the history of thought. So far as the evidence goes, Pythagoras had serious predecessors in mathematics not only in the East but among the Ionian Greeks, for Thales was credited with a number of geometrical theorems (p. 53, above). Apparently Aristotle's pupil Eudemus, when he wrote his history of geometry, felt no difficulty in ascribing them to an earlier thinker than Pythagoras, and indeed it must be confessed that none of the mathe-

---

[1] Cf. van der Waerden, *Arithm. d. Pyth.* 132. According to him (131) the Pythagoreans introduced Babylonian algebra into Greece, and turned it into geometrical form, the reason for the transformation being the discovery of irrationals. The relative antiquity of Pythagorean mathematical discoveries could not be exhaustively discussed here, even were the present writer competent to do so. It must be sought in such works as those of Heath, *Greek Math.*; K. Reidemeister, *Die Arithm. d. Griechen*; O. Becker, *Die Lehre vom Gerade u. Unger. im IX. Buch der Eukl. Elemente.* For the relationship of Greek mathematics to Babylonian see Neugebauor, *Stud. z. ant. Algebra* and *The Exact Sciences in Antiquity.*

matical knowledge of Pythagoras himself is attested by so good an authority. W. A. Heidel, who drew attention to these facts,[1] also pointed out with justice that this interest in number and geometry always remained alive in the Ionian tradition. The arrangement of Anaximander's universe, like that of the Pythagoreans later, had a numerical basis, being expressed in multiples of three (p. 95, above). The tunnel of Eupalinus, which was constructed on Samos just about the time that Pythagoras left the island, presupposes definite geometrical propositions. The map-making of Anaximander and Hecataeus points in the same direction, as does the symmetrical town-planning of Hippodamus of Miletus in the mid fifth century. The oldest extant Greek mathematical passage of any length is Eudemus's account of the quadrature of the lune by Hippocrates of Chios, another fifth-century Ionian.[2] Even the Pythagoreanizing Iamblichus says (*V.P.* 88, DK, 18.4) that after the legendary punishment of Hippasus it was Theodorus of Cyrene and Hippocrates who did most to advance mathematical studies in Greece, and Theodorus's brilliant pupil Theaetetus was an Athenian. Proclus in his commentary on Euclid (p. 61 Friedl.) gives a list of Euclid's precursors in the composition of geometrical hand-books, of whom Hippocrates was the first and the others are largely Ionians. There are no good reasons for supposing that all these men learned from the Pythagoreans, and, as Heidel noted, Archytas the friend of Plato is the first Pythagorean whom we can name with confidence as having made notable contributions to mathematics. Pythagoras himself, in spite of the absence of positive early evidence, was no doubt responsible for considerable advances, but he was after all a Samian, and quite old enough to have studied mathematics before he left the East; and it seems certain that a strong mathematical tradition continued in Ionian lands no less, if not more, than in the brotherhood which he founded in the West. It would be in the spirit of Ionian thought to be less bemused by the religious associations of number and more purely rational in approach.

Rostagni said with justice that for the Pythagoreans cosmology,

[1] *AJP*, 1940, 1–33.
[2] Quoted verbatim by Simpl. *Phys.* 61. On the date of Hippocrates cf. Heidel, p. 18, n. 33, Freeman, *Companion*, 217 (*fl.* probably *c.* 430). Ar. *Meteor.* 342b35 clearly implies that he was not a Pythagorean, whatever may have been said to the contrary.

understood as the study of what was for them a *kosmos* in the full Greek sense, embraces and unites together theology, anthropology, ethics, mathematics and any other 'branch' of their philosophy. It is the key to the whole. There is some force also in his additional inference that whatever developments may have occurred later on, their intimate relationship within an all-embracing cosmic *philosophia* gives good grounds for supposing that the fundamentals of the system—the numerical explanation of reality as well as transmigration, universal kinship, and the assimilation of man to god—all belong to it in its original form as taught by the Master himself.

We know (pp. 209 ff., above) that the motive for studying the *kosmos* is to bring our own selves into closer conformity with its laws. We have now to ask what such study reveals. What is the nature of the *kosmos* and on what principles is it constructed? What *archai* did the Italian school have to set over against the *archai* of the Milesians? The answer lies in the implications of the doctrine so often attributed to them by Aristotle that 'things themselves are numbers', or that they 'imitate' or 'represent' numbers, or again that 'they supposed the elements of numbers to be the elements of all things and the whole heaven to be a *harmonia* and a number'.[1]

The word *harmonia*, a key-word of Pythagoreanism, meant primarily the joining or fitting of things together, even the material peg with which they were joined (Homer, *Od.* v, 248), then especially the stringing of an instrument with strings of different tautness (perhaps thought of as a method of *joining* the arms of the lyre, see Kirk, *HCF*, 208), and so a musical scale. Its musical meaning was established by the early fifth century B.C., as we see from Pindar (*Nem.* IV, 44 f.) and fragments of the lyric poets Pratinas (4 *b* Diehl) and Lasus (1). That the *harmonia* which the Pythagoreans equated with number had this musical connotation we know from Aristotle's explanation of their theory of the harmony of the spheres (*De Caelo*, 290 b 12), and may assume also from the statement of Plato that they 'look for numerical relationships in audible concords' (*Rep.* 531 A).

There has been general agreement among scholars that the numerical

---

[1] *Metaph.* 987 b 28, 11; 986 a 1.

explanation of the universe was a generalization from a notable discovery made by Pythagoras himself. So for instance Burnet (*Gr. Phil.* 1, 45): 'It may be taken as certain that Pythagoras himself discovered the numerical ratios which determine the concordant intervals of the scale.' Taylor (*Comm. on Tim.* 164 and 489) speaks of 'the discovery of Pythagoras that the fundamental musical intervals correspond to simple numerical ratios' and 'the success of Pythagoras in finding numerical laws for the relations of the notes of the octave', and from Cornford we have (*CQ*, 1922, 144 and 145):

the original source of the theory, Pythagoras's discovery that the concordant intervals of the musical scale or *harmony* could be expressed exactly in terms of the 'simple' ratios.... Pythagoras was capable of abstracting this complex of conceptions from the particular case of sound. It must have been by a flash of inspired insight that he saw in it a formula of universal application.

Brunet and Mieli exhibit slightly more caution (*Hist. des Sciences*, 1. *Antiquité*, 121, quot. Farrington, *Greek Science*, 1, 48): 'It is to Pythagoras himself that tradition ascribes this discovery, and in this case one may, with all probability, admit the attribution', and Ross is more cautious still (*Ar. Met.* vol. 1, 145): 'Pythagoras is said to have discovered the elements of the theory of musical harmony, and Burnet is inclined to credit this.'

None of the scholars quoted give authority for their categorical statements, and in spite of Taylor's further assertion that the determination of the ratios was 'unanimously ascribed in antiquity to Pythagoras', it must be admitted, first, that none of the extant evidence is very early, and secondly, that antiquity was *not* unanimous in seeing in this discovery the origin of the numerical explanation of the world. Aristoxenus, the friend of fourth-century Pythagoreans, wrote in his treatise on arithmetic that Pythagoras derived his enthusiasm for the study of number from its practical applications in commerce. This is by no means an improbable supposition. The impact of monetary economy, as a comparatively recent phenomenon, on a thoughtful citizen of mercantile Samos might well have been to implant the idea that the one constant factor by which things were related was the quantitative. A fixed numerical value in drachmas or minas may 'represent' things as widely different in quality as a pair of oxen, a cargo of wheat and a gold drinking-cup.[1]

The earliest attribution of the musical discovery to Pythagoras occurs in the following passage from Porphyry's commentary on the *Harmonica* of Ptolemy (p. 31.1 Düring):

> Heraclides in his *Introduction to Music* writes as follows: Pythagoras, so Xenocrates says, discovered that the musical intervals also owe their origin of necessity to number, because they consist in a comparison of one quantity with another. He further investigated in what circumstances the intervals are concordant or discordant, and in general the origin of all harmony and disharmony.

The whole passage is a Chinese-box arrangement of quotation within quotation in which it is by no means always easy to see exactly who is being cited. Some have even expressed doubts whether the Heraclides mentioned is Heraclides Ponticus or another, though Düring is no doubt right in dismissing them.[2] But in any case the statement is quoted from Plato's pupil Xenocrates by (in all probability) one of his contemporaries,[3] and was thus current belief in Plato's time. This together with the brilliant nature of the discovery itself may well justify the confidence that it was due to the genius of the founder. In later centuries of course, when writers freely substituted Pythagoras for the Pythagoreans of their predecessors, the attribution was usual. Theo Smyrnaeus will serve as an example (*Math.* p. 56 Hiller): 'It appears [or is generally believed, δοκεῖ] that Pythagoras was the first to discover the concordant notes in their ratios to one another.' There follows a statement of what the ratios were.

The relevance of number to contemporary music has been simply explained by Burnet (*Gr. Phil.* I, 45–9). In the seven-stringed lyre, four strings were tuned to fixed intervals, namely the outer two, which

---

[1] See p. 177, above. G. Thomson, *The First Philosophers* (263), makes this point without reference to the single ancient passage which supports it. Aristoxenus also believed that Pythagoras gave the Greeks their weights and measures (D.L. VIII, 14, DK, 14.12).

[2] See his discussion of the passage in *Ptol. und Porph. über die Musik*, 154ff. It is fair to mention that according to him 'Pythagoras ist natürlich bei derartigen Zitaten ein Sammelnamen'.

[3] According to D.L. IV, 13 Xenocrates wrote a Πυθαγόρεια. Heraclides might also have been quoting something that he heard him say.

spanned an octave, and two of those between them, of which the
middle string was tuned to a fourth above the lowest (and hence a fifth
below the highest), and the one next above it to one tone higher. These
four strings thus provided the three intervals which the Greeks regarded
as 'concordant' (σύμφωνα, συμφωνοῦντες φθόγγοι): octave, fifth and
fourth. In addition the interval between the two middle strings was
a tone.[1] The tuning of the remaining strings varied according to the
type of scale required.

Until Hellenistic times, as Burnet notes, there was no such thing as
harmony in our sense. *Harmonia* meant (*a*) tuning, (*b*) scale and
(*c*) octave, and classical Greek music was melodic, without the use of
chords. In calling certain intervals concordant, therefore, the contemporaries of Pythagoras referred to melodic progression. The
essential point, however, is that the three intervals of octave, fourth
and fifth were regarded as primary, as the elements out of which
any musical scale or composition was built. To Pythagoras went the
credit of perceiving that this basic framework depended on fixed
numerical ratios 1:2 (octave), 3:2 (fifth), 4:3 (fourth).

These numbers, of course, represent the rate of vibration of a string,
or of the column of air in a pipe. It is doubtful whether Pythagoras
knew this, and in any case he had no means of measuring the rate (see
pp. 226 ff.). Apocryphal stories were current in later antiquity of how he
made the discovery by listening to the varied notes produced by
blacksmiths' hammers ringing in turn on an anvil, and then comparing
the relative weights of the hammers; or producing different tensions in
strings by suspending them and attaching various weights. Nicomachus
reports that weights of 12 and 6 units produced the octave, of 12 and 8
or 9 and 6 the fifth, of 12 and 9 or 8 and 6 the fourth, and weights of
9 and 8 units gave the tone. These stories are repeated by several
writers, but cannot be true. Beating a piece of iron on an anvil with
hammers of different weights produces little or no difference in the
pitch of the sounds, and the vibrations of strings would be propor-

---

[1] There is a reference to these ratios in Aristotle, *Metaph.* 1093 a 29. Cf. also *An. Post.* 90 a 18
(Oxford trans.): 'What is a concord? A commensurate numerical ratio of a high and a low note.'
They are set out in full in Philolaus, fr. 6, which uses συλλαβά for the fourth (later διὰ τεσσάρων),
δι' ὀξειᾶν for the fifth (later διὰ πέντε) and ἁρμονία for the octave (later διὰ πασῶν). On the
fragments of Philolaus see below, pp. 330 ff.

tional, not to the number of units of weight attached but to their square-roots.[1]

Theo, however (p. 57 H.), after briefly listing these and similar, more or less dubious, methods ('tension induced by turning the pegs or more informatively by attachment of weights; in wind instruments the width of the cavities or variation in the force of the breath; or by means of size and weight as with gongs and vessels'), dismisses them with the words: 'For present purposes let us be content to illustrate it by the lengths of string on the *kanon*, as it is called.' The *kanon* was the monochord, an instrument of one string which could be stopped by a moveable bridge,[2] and if the discovery is indeed Pythagoras's, it was no doubt on this that he carried out his experiments. Tradition credited him with its invention (D.L. VIII, 12). The rate of vibration being inversely proportional to the length of the string, if two strings at the same tension are plucked, then if one is twice as long as the other it will vibrate at half the speed, and this produces the musical interval of an octave, and so on with the other 'concordant' intervals.

Since the native Greek stringed instruments, the *lyra* and *cithara*, had strings of equal lengths, the existence of these numerical ratios would not be obvious. It would not naturally occur to the maker, or to the player as he picked out the notes, turning the pegs by a method of trial and error. Even the makers of pipes may have proceeded empirically, without a mathematician's reflexion on the relative distances between the holes.[3] The discovery of Pythagoras, that the basic intervals of Greek music could be represented by the ratios 1:2, 3:2 and 4:3, made it appear that *kosmos*—order and beauty—was imposed on the chaotic range of sound by means of the first four integers 1, 2, 3 and 4.

[1] See e.g. Nicom. *Harm.* in Jan's *Mus. Script.* 245 ff., Iambl. *V.P.* 115, Boethius, *Inst. Mus.* I, 10, and for comment W. H. Stahl's translation of Macrobius, *Somn. Scip.* (Columbia, 1953), p. 187, n. 6, where also are collected further ancient references.

[2] If the string was stretched over an open box, as in the medieval form of the instrument (see Th. Gérold, *La Musique au moyen âge* (Paris, 1932), 387), the contact of the bridge would not noticeably disturb the tension. That the instrument was not perfect, however, was noted by Ptolemy, who devoted a chapter of his *Harmonica* to its disadvantages (II, 12, περὶ τῆς δυσχρηστίας τοῦ μονοχόρδου κανόνος). He describes a form of it in I, 8.

[3] The opposite view has been held, but it does not seem necessary to agree with a writer like E. Frank that the discovery of the mathematical relationships must have been familiar to every Greek instrument-maker, still less with G. Junge that 'every piper or lyre-player must have known them' (Frank, *Plato u. d. sog. Pyth.* 11; Junge, *Classica et Mediev.* 1947, 184). There were twenty-four notes on the *aulos* (Ar. *Metaph.* 1093 b 2–4; see Ross *ad loc.*).

These add up to 10, which provided striking confirmation, if it was not the actual ground, of the Pythagorean belief that the number ten 'was something perfect, and contained in itself the whole nature of number' (Arist. *Metaph.* 986a8). This number they represented graphically by the figure known as the tetractys, which became a sacred symbol for them. The followers of Pythagoras were said to swear by him (thereby acknowledging his superhuman status) in a formula whose antiquity it is difficult to doubt: 'By him who handed down to us the tetractys, source and root of everlasting nature.'[1] Certainly a primitive element of number-mysticism survived, along with genuine mathematical advances, to give to the Pythagorean system its peculiar character. It goes back to the difficulty which men feel at an early stage of culture in mentally separating objects numbered from numbers themselves as abstractions, in forming the concept of a number 3 as distinct from its visible manifestations in groups of three trees or three stones. This outlook is reflected in language, and the criticism of it which we should be inclined to make ourselves is exactly that which was levelled against the Pythagoreans by a more advanced Greek thinker like Aristotle.

If, however, we must allow for a certain survival of primitive modes of thought, we must remember also what irrefutable confirmation, on purely rational grounds, they must have seemed to acquire in the minds of these early Pythagoreans from such discoveries as that of the independent existence of a numerical scheme behind the musical scale. The existence of an inherent order, a numerical organization within the nature of sound itself, came as a kind of revelation. It is not too far-fetched to compare the feelings of a modern physicist when confronted with similar phenomena:

The ideal element in nature consists in the fact that mathematical laws, which are laws of our own thought, really hold in nature. And that deep amazement which we often feel over the inner order of nature is connected above all with the circumstance that, as in the case of crystals, we have already

---

[1] Quoted, with slight variations, by Porph. *V.P.* 20, Iambl. *V.P.* 150, in the *Golden Verses*, 47f., and elsewhere. Cf. A. Delatte, 'La tétractys pythagoricienne', in *Ét. sur la litt. pyth.* 249–68.

By 'number-mysticism' in the next sentence is meant the attribution to numbers not only of a sacred character but also of a substantial, even physical, reality.

recognized the effects of this 'mathematics of nature' long before our own mathematical knowledge was sufficiently developed to understand its necessity.[1]

In the sphere of music, the Greek was in exactly the same position of having been long familiar with the effects of the 'mathematics of nature' before his own knowledge was sufficiently developed to understand it; and if today it still fills the observer with a 'deep amazement', it is not surprising that its effect on him was even greater.[2] Might it not be that in number lay the key, not only to musical sounds, but to the whole of nature? It must be remembered that what the Pythagoreans were trying to find out was not the basic material stuff of the universe, nor yet primarily the physical changes by which it had come into being, but first and foremost the explanation of the order, the *kosmiotes*, which to their eyes it displayed and to their minds, for reasons in large part religious, was the most important thing about it.

Additional Note: 'Speed' and pitch

A relationship between the pitch of a note and its 'speed' was assumed from the time of Plato and Archytas onward, and no doubt earlier. Some of the language used is, however, very vague, and it is not always easy to know exactly what the writers supposed themselves to be describing. The most important passages are these.

(*a*) Theo Sm. p. 61 Hiller (Archytas, A 19 *a*): 'The school of Eudoxus and Archytas posited a numerical ratio between the concordances. They agreed with others that the ratios lay in movements, a swift motion being high-pitched since it produces a continuous succession of blows and stabs the air more sharply, and a slow motion low-pitched because more sluggish.'

(*b*) Archytas, fr. 1: 'The mathematicians seem to me to have shown true insight.... First of all they considered that there can be no sound without the striking of one thing against another, and that a blow occurs when moving bodies meet and collide.... Many of these sounds are imperceptible to us,

---

[1] C. F. von Weizsäcker, *The World-view of Physics*, 21.

[2] The physicist's choice of crystals as an example acquires a certain incidental interest from a conjecture made a good many years ago about the origin of Pythagoras's number-doctrine. Sir Wm. Ridgeway suggested that since Pythagoras was the son of a gem-engraver, and therefore in all probability a gem-engraver himself, it would most naturally arise from his observation of the regular geometrical forms of minerals (*CR*, 1896, 92–5). Pyrites crystals in the form of dodecahedra are found only in S. Italy, where he lived, and on Elba (*RE*, 2. Reihe, V A 2, 1364).

either because of the feebleness of the blow or because of their distance from us, or even because of their excessive strength; for the loudest sounds do not penetrate our hearing, just as if one pours a liquid in great quantity over the mouth of a jar, none of it goes in. Of those which we hear, the sounds which reach us quickly and ⟨strongly⟩ from the impact give the impression of high pitch, but those which come slowly and weakly seem low. If a stick is taken and moved slowly and gently, the sound made by its impact is low, but if swiftly and violently, high....Again, in playing a pipe the breath from the mouth when it falls on the holes near the mouth gives out a higher note on account of the strength of the pressure, but on the further holes, a lower note. This makes it obvious that the swift motion produces a high note, slow motion a low one. The same thing happens with the *rhomboi* [bull-roarers] used in the mysteries. When swung gently they give a low note, when violently a high one....' Finally Porphyry, who quotes this passage, adds: 'After further remarks on the notion of sound as made up of intervals, he sums up his argument thus: "It is clear then from many proofs that high notes move more quickly and low notes more slowly."'

(c) Plato in the *Republic* (530D) speaks of 'harmonic motion' (ἐναρμόνιος φορά), and in the *Timaeus* goes into detail.

Tim. 67B (trans. Cornford): 'Sound we may define in general terms as the stroke inflicted by air on the brain and blood through the ears and passed on to the soul; while the motion it causes, starting in the head and ending in the region of the liver, is hearing. A rapid motion produces a high-pitched sound; the slower the motion, the lower the pitch.'

(d) 80A: 'This principle [i.e. the principle of the "circular thrust"] will also explain why sounds, which present themselves as high or low in pitch according as they are swift or slow, are as they travel sometimes inharmonious because the motion they produce in us lacks correspondence, sometimes concordant because there is correspondence. The slower sounds, when they catch up with the motions of the quicker sounds which arrived earlier, find these motions drawing to an end and already having reached correspondence with the motions imparted to them by the slower sounds on their later arrival. In so doing, the slower sounds cause no disturbance when they introduce a fresh motion; rather by joining on the beginning of a slower motion in correspondence with the quicker which is now drawing to an end, they produce a single combined effect in which high and low are blended.'

(e) One may compare [Arist.] *De audibilibus*, 803b40 (Oxford trans.): 'The same thing happens, too, when two notes form a concord; for owing to the fact that the two notes overlap and include one another and cease at the same moment, the intermediate constituent sounds escape our notice. For in all concords more frequent impacts upon the air are caused by the shriller note, owing to the quickness of its movement; the result is that the last note strikes upon our hearing simultaneously with an earlier sound produced by the slower impact. Thus because, as has been said, the ear cannot perceive all the constituent sounds, we seem to hear both notes together and continuously.'

The *Timaeus* extracts (of which a full explanation is given by Cornford, *Plato's Cosmology*, 320 ff.) are very likely to be dependent on Archytas, and bear out the verdict that he 'confused the velocity of the motion which produces a sound with the velocity of the sound itself, which leads him to conclude, from observations correct in themselves, that higher tones are propagated more rapidly than lower ones' (van der Waerden, *Science Awakening*, 152). The passage from Archytas himself suggests that he was also not very clear in his own mind about any distinction between 'speed' and 'violence' of movement. Adrastus (second century A.D., quoted by Theo, p. 50 H.), in a very lucid account of the Pythagorean theory, clears up this latter obscurity, which may have been only due to carelessness of expression: 'The Pythagoreans give the following account. Every melody and every note are sounds, and a sound is a blow inflicted on air which is prevented from dispersing. Therefore there can be no sound, and hence no note, where the air is undisturbed. But when a blow and a movement occur in the air, then if it is swift the note produced is high, if slow it is low; if violent the noise is loud, if gentle, soft. The speed and violence of the motions may or may not stand in a relationship of rational proportion to one another. If they do not, the sounds are disproportionate and discordant, not to be called notes but mere noises, whereas motions that stand in a simple numerical relationship, or such that one is a multiple of the other or superparticular to it [i.e. containing the whole plus a fraction with 1 for its numerator], produce genuine and mutually compatible notes. Some deserve to be called only this, but those constructed according to the primary, commonly recognized and most fundamental ratios are actually called concordant.'

The currency, in the fourth century, of the confusion between the velocity of the motion producing a sound and that of the sound itself made it possible for Theophrastus to deny the whole idea of a connexion between pitch and velocity, and hence of a numerically expressible ratio between high and low sounds. The high-pitched sound, he says (fr. 89, p. 189 Wimmer), does not differ in speed from the lower: if it did, it would reach our hearing sooner. He argues therefore that differences of pitch are qualitative, not quantitative, in character.

(b) Numbers and things: Aristotle's evidence for the general nature of the doctrine

Aristotle refers to the Pythagorean number-doctrine in three forms (p. 220, above): things are numbers, things 'imitate' or 'represent' numbers, the elements of numbers are the elements of things. Relevant passage (all from the *Metaphysics*) are, in translation:

(a) 987b28: 'They say that things themselves are numbers.' This is stated more fully in book N (1090a20): 'The Pythagoreans, because they saw many of the attributes of numbers belonging to sensible bodies, assumed existing things to be numbers—not separately existing numbers, but that things are actually composed of numbers. Their reason was that numerical properties are inherent in the musical scale, in the heavens, and in many other things.'

(b) 987b11: 'The Pythagoreans say that existing things owe their being to imitation (*mimesis*) of numbers.'

(c) 985b32: 'Since the nature of everything else seemed to be entirely assimilated to numbers, and numbers to be primary throughout the world of nature, they assumed the elements of numbers to be the elements of all that exists, and the whole universe to be a *harmonia* and a number.'

On the first two passages it should be noted (i) that they occur close together in the same context, (ii) that this context is a criticism of the Ideas of Plato, in the course of which Aristotle says that when Plato spoke of the 'sharing' or 'participation' (*methexis*) of individual things in the being of the changeless Ideas, he meant to indicate the same relation as that expressed by the Pythagorean term *mimesis*, which is commonly translated 'imitation'.

Unnecessary difficulty has been introduced by the assumption that these three statements of Aristotle are mutually contradictory.[1]

[1] So especially Cherniss, *ACP*, 386: 'The distinctive feature of the school according to Aristotle was its assumption of number as the principle; but the account he gives of this doctrine is, as has been seen, self-contradictory, for he represents it as identifying numbers and physical objects, as identifying the *principles* of number with the *principles* of existing things, and as making things *imitate* number.' See also the other views summarized in ZN, 454, n. 1.

To take the first and third statements first, it is surely obvious that if an object x consists of y, and y itself is further analysable into elements, then the elements of y are also the elements of x. If a statue is made of bronze, and the bronze is an alloy of copper and tin, then one may speak either of bronze or of copper and tin (the elements of bronze) as being the elements of the statue. Aristotle's own philosophy provides an exact parallel. All physical bodies are made of the four simple bodies earth, water, air and fire. These, though the simplest of independently existing substances, can themselves be analysed further into the elements of prime matter and form. Consequently he can speak, without fear of self-contradiction, either of things consisting of the four simple bodies or equally of matter and form, the elements of the simple bodies, as the ultimate elements of everything.

In comparing the first and second statements, the fact that Aristotle was able to equate Pythagorean *mimesis* with Plato's notion of physical objects as 'sharing in' the Ideas (which Plato himself elsewhere describes as 'patterns' for the world of sense) should put us on our guard against the simple translation 'imitation'. The fact is, of course, that even Plato, and still more the Pythagoreans, were struggling to express new and difficult conceptions within the compass of an inadequate language. We may take a hint first from K. Joel (*Gesch. d. ant. Philos.* 364), who points to the trouble that the Pythagoreans must have experienced in clearly differentiating the concepts of similarity and identity, 'a defect which still plagued Sophistic thought and which Plato's Ideal theory and Aristotle's logic only overcame with difficulty because it is rooted deep in the Greek consciousness: even their language has only one word for "same" and "similar" (ὅμοιος)'. He continues (I translate): 'Are things imitations of numbers or numbers themselves? Aristotle ascribes both views to the Pythagoreans, and whoever is alive to the mind of Greece will also credit them with both and agree that for them numbers served alike as real and as ideal principles.'

Mimesis meant acting as much as imitation, *mimetes* was often and *mimos* always an actor. The relation between an actor and his part is not exactly imitation. He gets inside it, or rather, in the Greek view, it gets inside him, and shows forth through his words and gestures. There is more to it than that. Drama began as, and remained, a religious ritual, and we cannot hope to understand Pythagorean thought if we allow ourselves to forget that it too was primarily religious. In the earliest and simplest dramatic representations men impersonated gods or spirits for religious ends, and what they supposed to be happening can be best illustrated from contemporary ecstatic worship like that of Dionysus. The leader of his *thiasos*, the band of god-intoxicated worshippers, impersonated, or imitated, the god. So we might put it, but to him and his fellow-worshippers what happened was that the god himself entered into him, took possession and acted through him. Hence he was called by the god's name Bacchus, and all who genuinely felt the divine afflatus were Bacchoi or Bacchae. They were *entheoi*, the god was in them, or from another point of view *ekstatikoi*, outside themselves. This is only one example of what was repeated in a large number of cults of the same ecstatic kind. In myth the god was attended by a band of *daimones*, and in performing the ritual the worshippers not only acted the parts of, but for the moment *were*, the god himself and his divine attendants—Bacchoi, Kuretes, Korybantes or whatever the name might be.

Pythagoras and his school, with their belief in universal kinship and the underlying notion of magical relationships, in transmigration and in assimilation to god as the end of human life, were in the full stream of these religious ideas. (Euphorbus was a previous incarnation of Pythagoras. Was Pythagoras now Euphorbus, did he in some way 'imitate' or represent him, or how was the relationship to be expressed?) Pythagoras himself quickly achieved the status of a *daimon*, intermediate between man and god, or even an incarnation of the Hyperborean Apollo.

These are the kind of men who claimed to have made the tremendous discovery that the world of nature was constructed on a mathematical plan. It need cause no surprise that they expressed this by saying at one time that things were numbers, at another that they existed by *mimesis* of numbers. To Aristotle with his instinct for rational classification, and the contempt for religious or superstitious ways of thinking which went naturally with a newly-won emancipation from them, it was all exasperatingly illogical. The modern scholar or scientist may view it more sympathetically.

Before we go on to see what Aristotle made of these strange doctrines, something may be said of the probable date of the theories to which he refers. The best evidence for this is his repeated statement that the Pythagoreanism with which he was familiar went back beyond the time of the atomists Leucippus and Democritus. His general account of Pythagoreanism in chapter 5 of the first book of the *Metaphysics* follows immediately on a description of the theories of these two, and begins (985 b 23) with the words:

Contemporaneously with *and before* these men, the Pythagoreans (as they are called), who were the earliest to apply themselves to mathematics, at the same time were making advances in this subject and, because of their absorption in it, assumed the principles of mathematics to be the principles of everything.

Similarly in a later book (M, 1078 b 19) he says, speaking of the virtual introduction of general definitions into philosophy by Socrates:

Of the natural philosophers Democritus barely approached the conception with his quasi-definition of the hot and the cold, and *before him* the Pythagoreans applied it to a few things, which they defined with reference to numbers.

The chapter in the first book affords some further evidence of date in connexion with the table of ten pairs of contraries (on which see below, p. 245). This table Aristotle ascribes to some, but not all Pythagoreans (986 a 22: 'Others of the same school say...').

Alcmaeon of Croton [he continues] appears to have had the same idea, and either he borrowed it from them or they from him, for he gave a similar exposition to theirs: he says that most of the things affecting human beings go in pairs, though he does not draw up a specific list of contraries as these men do, but mentions any chance pairs such as white and black, sweet and bitter, good and evil, great and small. He made vague remarks about the other contraries, but the Pythagoreans laid down how many and what they were.[1]

Heidel remarked (*AJP*, 1940, 5) that a general doctrine of opposites in nature was shared by the Pythagoreans with the Ionians and Greek

---

[1] I have omitted (with Ross and others before him) the words descriptive of Alcmaeon's date, that 'he was in his prime in the old age of Pythagoras', which are missing from the Laurentian MS. and absent from the ancient commentators. Heidel in *AJP*, 1940, 5 gives further reasons for rejecting them. If, however, they are a later addition, one may nevertheless agree with Ross that 'the statement is likely enough to be true'. Cf. also ZN, 597, n. 2, and see pp. 341 ff., 357 ff. below.

thought in general, and it therefore appeared to him to be 'a profound mystery' why Aristotle should have thought it necessary to suggest that they borrowed it from Alcmaeon or *vice versa*. The universality of the view as Alcmaeon taught it is not easy to assess on the meagre information given here by Aristotle, but if what Heidel says is true, this seems to be strong circumstantial evidence that Aristotle in fact knew of a connexion between Alcmaeon and the Pythagoreans, though he was uncertain which should be credited with the priority. (It is worth noting in passing that, according to the list of his works in D.L. v, 25, Aristotle had studied Alcmaeon sufficiently to write a treatise in criticism of his thought.) The least we can say is that Aristotle regarded the Pythagoreans who put forward the ten pairs of opposites as having been contemporary with Alcmaeon, so that it was possible for either to have borrowed a doctrine of contraries from the other, Alcmaeon generalizing from the Pythagorean list or the Pythagoreans selecting certain items from those mentioned haphazard by Alcmaeon: and if, as Heidel says, 'the consensus of scholars' has tended to regard the Pythagorean table as relatively late,[1] an equally strong consensus has tended with reason to believe that Alcmaeon was a younger contemporary of Pythagoras himself.

We may conclude, then, that Aristotle's knowledge of the Pythagoreans in general goes back to before the time of the atomists, say to the middle of the fifth century when Philolaus was a leading representative, and that he knows of some Pythagorean doctrines which belong to an earlier period than that.[2] Nor is it impossible that those whom, in his general account, he calls 'earlier than the atomists' belong to the same period as these 'some'.

I turn now to the Pythagorean explanation of the world in terms of numbers, as it appeared to the best informed extant authority. Remembering that he was in one way too near, and in another too far off

[1] In fact Raven (*P. and E.* ch. 3) gives strong reasons for supposing that it was already known to Parmenides.

[2] This conclusion accords with that of Raven (*P. and E.* 11): 'When we pass...to the views of "others of this same school", Aristotle's surmise that these Pythagoreans borrowed their doctrine of the opposites from Alcmaeon, or else he his from them, strongly suggests that the transition is from a later to an earlier generation.' As Raven also notes, it is only very rarely that Aristotle explicitly recognizes a distinction between one school or generation of Pythagoreans and another.

from them to achieve a full and sympathetic understanding, we may find that his very puzzlement and irritation throw considerable light on their mentality.

In addition to his statements that the elements of number were the elements of all things, that things were numbers, and that they 'imitated' numbers, the following generalizations have first to be considered:

(*a*) *Metaph.* 1080b16: 'The Pythagoreans also [*sc.* as well as Speusippus] recognize a single type of number, mathematical number, but not as existing apart from sensible things [*sc.* which was the view of the Platonists in general], which they regard as being composed of it. They in fact construct the whole universe out of numbers, not however truly monadic numbers, for they suppose the units to possess magnitude.'

By 'monadic' Aristotle means, as his commentator Alexander says, unextended and incorporeal. The notion of incorporeal reality was not yet grasped by the Pythagoreans or any of their contemporaries.

(*b*) *Metaph.* 986a15 (this and passage (*d*) are from the chapter on the Pythagoreans): 'Evidently they too regard number as a principle both in the sense of matter and of temporary or permanent states.'

By 'too' Aristotle can hardly mean that other Presocratic thinkers had regarded numbers as principles, but more probably that the Pythagoreans were like the others in confusing material and formal causes. With this passage may be compared one in book Z. The purpose of the chapter in which it occurs is to distinguish the material from the formal aspects of a concrete object. This is easy enough, says Aristotle, when the same form is realized in different materials, as the form of circle in bronze or stone or wood. It is less easy when the form is always found in the same matter, as for example the form of man in flesh, bones, etc. The theoretical possibility of the distinction is recognized, but there are cases where it is difficult to pin down. He continues (here Alexander states, and the content shows, that he is thinking of the Pythagoreans):

(*c*) *Metaph.* 1036b8: 'Some are even in doubt about the circle and the triangle, surmising that it is not right to define them by lines and continuous space [i.e. to regard these as their *formal* characteristics], but that these are adduced in the same capacity as the flesh and bones of a man and the bronze or stone of a statue.'

(*d*) *Metaph.* 987a13: 'The Pythagoreans similarly posit two principles, but add something peculiar to themselves, namely that the finite and the infinite are not attributes of other natural substances like fire or earth or something similar. Rather they hold that the infinite itself and unity itself are the substance of that of which they are predicated, and this is why they say that number is the substance of all things.'

(*e*) Similarly in the following chapter on Plato he writes (987b22): 'But in saying that the one was substance, and not something else which was called one, he was speaking like the Pythagoreans, and it was also in agreement with them that numbers should be for other things the cause of their reality.'

Cf. 996a6. It must be remembered that for Aristotle the word 'cause' had a wider meaning than it has today, for instance the matter of which something is made is one of its 'causes'.

(*f*) *Metaph.* 990a12: 'Moreover, if it be granted them, or demonstrated, that spatial magnitude is derived from these principles [*sc.* limited and unlimited, odd and even, which in Pythagorean theory, as we shall see, are the elements of number], even so how can some bodies be light and some heavy? To judge by their assumptions and statements, they are speaking of sensible bodies no less than mathematical. Hence they tell us nothing about fire or earth or other bodies of this kind because, unless I am mistaken, they have nothing to say about perceptible bodies as such.'

(*g*) *Metaph.* 1090a30: 'In this respect [*sc.* in denying that numbers have an existence separate from things] the Pythagoreans are in no way at fault, but when they construct physical bodies out of number—things which possess lightness and weight out of elements which possess neither—they appear to be talking about some other universe and other bodies, not those that we perceive.' (A similar complaint occurs in *De Caelo*, 300a16.)

(*h*) *Metaph.* 1083b8: 'The Pythagorean way of thinking in one way presents fewer difficulties than those previously considered, but in another it adds fresh difficulties of its own. Their denial that number has separate existence removes many impossibilities, but the statement that bodies are composed of numbers, and that this refers to mathematical number, is incredible. It is false to say that there are indivisible magnitudes, and even if there were, units do not have magnitude. And how could a magnitude consist of indivisibles? But arithmetical number is monadic [*sc.* consists of abstract, incorporeal units]. They on the other hand identify real things with number. At any rate they apply their speculations to bodies as if they consisted of numbers of this kind.'

Pythagoras and the Pythagoreans

From Aristotle's point of view, then, Pythagoreanism had the following characteristics:

(1) All things consist of number, in the literal sense that physical bodies themselves are made of numbers; or, since numbers themselves are not ultimate, it may be said that the elements of numbers are the elements of everything.[1]

(2) Units for the Pythagoreans possess magnitude.

(3) Instead of saying that things are numerically characterized, they spoke as if number were the actual matter of which things are composed.

(4) We think of unity and limit as predicates applied to certain, generally physical, objects, saying '*it* is one' or '*it* is finite'—'it' being substantially something else like wood or metal. The Pythagoreans on the other hand regarded unity and limit as substances forming the basic element of everything else.

Aristotle's objections to this as to other previous systems of thought were formulated on the basis of his doctrine of the 'four causes'. To understand the nature of reality, the philosopher must be able to analyse any class of objects into its logical components, of which the primary pair were matter and form, and to account for their existence by detecting the efficient cause and (since for him nature acted teleologically) the purpose of their being. In nature the formal, final and efficient causes usually coincided, for instance in the male parent which engenders the offspring and also provides the pattern according to which it will grow. Thus the primary opposition remains that between matter and form—in a bronze disc the bronze and the circular shape, in a man the material components of the human body on the one hand and on the other (at the highest level, on which 'form' is a very wide conception) that which makes the difference between a living man and a corpse.

Obviously number, whether thought of arithmetically, geometrically or as manifested in musical intervals, is a formal component; hence Aristotle's chief complaint against the Pythagoreans is that they confused formal and material causes. More specifically they imagined that

---

[1] In one place (*De Caelo*, 300a16) Aristotle says: 'Certain people, like some of the Pythagoreans, make the natural world out of number.' The phrase 'some of the Pythagoreans' has been made the basis for theories of a division within the school, particularly between an earlier and a later generation (Raven, *P. and E.*). But in view of its isolation among the numerous passages which ascribe the belief to the Pythagoreans without qualification, it is unlikely to have any significance (ZN, 450f. suggest explanations of it, and cf. Raven, *P. and E.* 55).

physical bodies could be constructed out of what were in fact abstractions, or, as he puts it still more concretely, things with weight out of what has no weight.

In studying the Presocratics, one often has the feeling that they lived in a different world of thought from our own. When we come to Aristotle, we find that he thinks along lines much closer to those which most of us (though not the most scientifically advanced) follow today. His basic outlook is one which we should still regard as that of common-sense. If there is a curtain dividing our minds from those of the Presocratics, he, though a Greek himself and almost their contemporary, is already on our side of it. Failing someone equally at home in both worlds, this makes him probably the most sympathetic informant that we could hope for. He finds them difficult and irritating, and sometimes fails to understand them. So may we, and for reasons astonishingly similar. In all probability he has drawn conclusions from their utterances which they did not explicitly draw themselves, and given as actual Pythagorean statements what are in fact inferences, in his eyes inescapable, but no more. Yet on his and other evidence it seems certain that they saw no difficulty in making a mental leap from an abstraction like a geometrical solid to the concrete physical bodies of the world of nature, and it is with a mentality which saw this continuity as natural that we, like him, have to come to terms.

As we have seen (pp. 225 f., above), it was in all probability the discovery of the 'mathematics of nature' doing its hidden work in the formation of the musical scale that led them, by an audacious stroke of generalization, to explain the whole of reality in mathematical terms. On a mind like that of Pythagoras, not only mathematically but also mystically inclined, to which 'all nature was akin', the impact of this discovery of an independent numerical order inherent in the nature of things must have been tremendous. In the inchoate state of contemporary science, it is no wonder that it sought expression in such phrases as 'Things are number', 'Things represent numbers', 'Whatever numbers are made of is what all things are made of'.

Our understanding is helped when Aristotle objects, in his own terminology, that for the Pythagoreans numbers were at the same time the material and formal causes of things. The Milesians had sought to explain things by their matter—water or air or the *apeiron*—and its behaviour. What the Pythagoreans had really done was to leave the matter aside and define things in terms of their form. Provided the numerical proportions were right, it did not matter whether notes were produced by the motion of a stretched string or of air in a pipe: they were the same notes. This in itself was a great advance, both from Aristotle's point of view and in general. Aristotle always upholds the primacy of form, insisting that to define a thing properly it is necessary to give its *logos* or formal structure: and this opinion would presumably be shared by a modern mathematical physicist. The trouble about Pythagoras and his followers was that they were not quite aware of what they had done. The distinction between form and matter had as yet received no clear formulation. Consequently, though they were in fact describing only the structural scheme of things—in itself a perfectly legitimate procedure—they believed that they were describing their material nature too: that it was possible to speak of things as made up entirely of numbers, regarded in a threefold way as arithmetical units, geometrical points, and physical atoms.

In their excitement at having discovered the importance of the quantitative aspect of things, they ignored entirely the qualitative, which had hitherto had all the emphasis laid upon it, and to which Aristotle—by temperament a naturalist rather than a mathematician—returned. Thus he demanded petulantly (*Metaph.* 1092 b 15): 'How indeed can qualities —white, sweet, hot—be numbers?' Looking back, it seems as if it was Aristotle who was leading science on to the wrong track. Today the scientific description of everything in the physical world takes the form of numerical equations. What we perceive as physical qualities—colour, heat, light, sound—disappear and are replaced by numbers representing wave-lengths or masses. For this reason a historian of science has claimed that Pythagoras's discovery changed the whole course of history.[1] We may accept this, and yet not be surprised that at that early stage of thought, unprovided with any system of logic or even of grammar, he and his school announced their great idea by saying that 'things are numbers'.

[1] Wightman, *Growth of Scientific Ideas*, 20.

(c) Numbers and things: the generation of things from numbers

So far we have learned from Aristotle that there are two stages in the process of generation, that of numbers from certain prior elements and that of 'things' from numbers.[1] It soon appears, however, that there are in fact three: generation of numbers from limit and unlimited, odd and even; of geometrical figures from number; and of physical objects from geometrical solids.

It might well be asked whether in speaking of generation the Pythagoreans thought of an actual process in time, or simply of logical priority, *A* being regarded as logically prior and elemental to *B* simply because the existence of *B* is inconceivable without *A* whereas *A* can be thought of as existing without *B*. Is their description simply an analysis cast into the form of a temporal process, as many suppose the account of the creation in Plato's *Timaeus* to be? The question can only be answered, if at all, in the light of the scanty references to the physical aspect of their cosmogony, which must come last in this exposition. There is no doubt that Aristotle, at least, supposed their references to generation to be intended literally (*Metaph.* 1091a13, 989b34; below, pp. 266, 276). He may, however, have been unperceptive in such a matter, and on one occasion, in a context which must certainly include the Pythagoreans,[2] he puts very clearly, on their behalf, the argument of logical priority. The passage, which is of considerable interest, is from *Metaphysics* B, in which he sets forth dialectically the arguments for and against the chief metaphysical theses (1001b26). Those here given do not represent his own view:

A related problem is whether numbers, bodies, surfaces and points are substances or not. If they are not, there is no saying what is reality and what are the substances of existing things, for attributes, motions, relations, states and ratios do not appear to indicate the substance of anything: they are all predicated of a subject, and none of them is an individual thing. And if we take what would most properly appear to indicate substance—water, earth, fire and air, of which composite bodies are made—their heat, coldness and

---

[1] 'Things' for the Pythagoreans includes both the physical world and its contents and also abstractions such as justice, marriage, etc. (Ar. *Metaph.* 985b29, 990a22, 1078b21; *MM*, 1182a11).

[2] Ross *ad loc.* follows Alexander in thinking that both the Pythagoreans and Plato are meant; Bonitz wished to confine the reference to the Pythagoreans.

other attributes are not substances; it is the body which undergoes these changes that has permanence like a real thing or substance.

On the other hand body is less substantial than surface, surface than line, line than unit or point; for by them the body is bounded, and it would appear that whereas they can exist without body, it cannot exist without them. Hence earlier philosophers, like the man in the street, equated reality and substance with body, and the principles or elements of body with those of real things; but later and reputedly more subtle thinkers saw reality in numbers.

The most likely answer to our question is that Pythagoreans before Plato had no clear conception of the distinction between logical and chronological priority, which was first formulated by Plato and Aristotle. They would not be fully conscious of a shift from one to the other. On the other hand all the emphasis of their work was on the analysis of things into elements logically prior, and at least we need not suppose them to have seriously imagined that there was a time when odd and even existed but not numbers.

(i) *First stage: generation of numbers from their elements: the first principles of the Pythagoreans*. The elements of numbers are, ultimately, the limited and the unlimited, and secondarily the odd and the even and the unit. In this scheme the unit was regarded as the starting-point of the number series, but not as itself belonging to it, because every actual number must be either odd or even and the unit, curiously enough, was conceived as combining in itself both oddness and evenness. The reason why the unit occupies such an anomalous position in Greek thought is no doubt that zero was unknown. Consequently the unit-point was made to fulfil a double function: 'It was both one-dimensional unit of construction and non-dimensional point of contact between two sections.'[1]

(*a*) Aristotle, *Metaph.* 986a17: 'The elements of number are the even and the odd, and of these the latter is limited and the former unlimited. The One is composed of both of these (for it is both even and odd) and number springs from the One; and numbers, as I have said, constitute the whole universe.'

(*b*) 987a15 (quoted above, p. 235) says that for the Pythagoreans the limited, the unlimited, and the One are the actual substance of things, and not simply attributes. This statement is repeated in several places by Aristotle.

[1] Sambursky, *Physical World of the Greeks*, 28.

The Elements of Number

(c) *Phys.* 203a4. At the beginning of his own discussion of the word *apeiron* (unlimited) and its various uses, Aristotle says that all philosophers worthy of the name have had something to say about it, and all regard it as a first principle. But whereas others treat it as an accident or attribute of a physical substance like water or air, 'some, like the Pythagoreans and Plato, speak of it in itself, not as inhering in something else but as being itself a substance. But the Pythagoreans (*a*) place it among sensible things (for they do not reckon number separate from these), and (*b*) say that what is outside the heaven is unlimited.' After pointing out that in these respects they differ from Plato, he continues: 'They say moreover that the unlimited is the even, for this when it is enclosed and limited by the odd provides the unlimited element in existing things. This is illustrated by what happens when gnomons are placed around numbers: when they are placed round the one, and without the one, in the one case the figure produced varies continually, whereas in the other it is always the same. Plato on the other hand considered the unlimited as a duality, the great and small.'

(*d*) At *Metaph.* 990a8 Aristotle, criticizing the Pythagoreans for their inadequate explanation of motion, asks how it can be accounted for 'when the only things assumed are limit and the unlimited and odd and even'— further evidence that, for the theorists he is considering, these were the only ultimates.

The obscurities in the sentence about the gnomons will be discussed in a moment. Heidel cast doubt on Aristotle's accuracy in claiming that the Pythagoreans regard the One and the unlimited as substances and not as attributes, though he offers no reason for this beyond remarking: 'Possibly he was transferring Platonic expressions to them' (*AJP*, 1940, 12, n. 22). To say this about a passage in which Aristotle is with the greatest care *distinguishing* between the Pythagoreans and Plato is astonishing, apart from the inherent unlikelihood that he of all men should make such a mistake. This does not mean that he had a full understanding of what went on in their minds. He looked back from the point of view of one who could take his stand on certain basic distinctions such as those between substance and attribute, abstract and concrete (compare for instance his lucid description of mathematical procedure in *Metaph.* K, 1061a28ff.), and tried to apply these clear-cut categories to the thought of men who were as yet by no means fully conscious of them. Hence his bewilderment and irritation at their 'ascribing magnitude to numbers' and so forth. In saying that things were numbers, as Ross has remarked (*Ar. Phys.* 541), they did not reduce reality to an abstraction, but rather failed to recognize the abstract nature of numbers.

The Greek idiom of adjective-plus-article (the unlimited, the hot, the cold, the dry, the moist, etc.) probably tended to perpetuate this lack of distinction between abstract and concrete. Anaximander in positing the 'unlimited' was mainly aware of it as something material, whereas a Pythagorean saw rather its formal characteristics. But neither could put to himself, or have put to him by a contemporary, the question whether he meant by the phrase something which was without limit or the quality of being unlimited.

Limit and the unlimited are the ultimate notions, as being wider genera within which fall the odd and the even. The first passage quoted seems to make this clear, even though elsewhere Aristotle's language suggests that odd and even were identical with limit and unlimited. No doubt the language of the Pythagoreans themselves left room for ambiguity. In any case the connexion does not seem to us to be obvious. It is explained by Aristotle in terms of certain figures formed with gnomons and numbers, wherein the numbers must be thought of visually as dots. To represent numbers thus in the form of geometrical patterns was regular Pythagorean practice, as it was probably the earliest practice among both the Greeks and other peoples.[1] The gnomon here referred to takes its name from the carpenter's square,[2]

---

[1] Cf. Burnet, *EGP*, 101, Cornford, *P. and P.* 8 (Nicomachus), and the statement of D.L. (VIII, 12) that Pythagoras studied especially the arithmetical aspect of geometry.

[2] The essential characteristic of a gnomon appears to have been that of making or containing a right angle. Thus in Herodotus it is the upright pointer on a sundial, which must be at right angles to the surface. Secondly it was used for a carpenter's set-square, from which came its meaning in the above passage of Aristotle. Again in the *Categories* (15a30) Aristotle says: 'A square when a gnomon is put round it is increased in size, but does not alter' (i.e. in shape: it remains a square). The gnomon here is of the shape of the accompanying diagram. Cornford is not quite accurate when he says (paraphrasing a sentence of Heath's with reference to 15a30): 'The gnomon is defined by Aristotle as the figure which when added to a square increases its size but does not alter its form' (*P. and P.* 9, n. 1). Aristotle's sentence does not exclude, as it would if it were a definition, the possibility of oblong gnomons. That the gnomon was essentially right-angled is illustrated by the terminology of Oenopides of Chios (mid fifth century: see DK, 41.13) as quoted by Proclus: 'He calls the perpendicular in the ancient fashion "gnomonwise", because the gnomon also is at right angles to the horizon.' Euclid (Bk. II, def. 2) extended it to all parallelograms, and his language suggests that he was the first to do so. Later its use was even more widely extended. For fuller details see Heath, *The Thirteen Books of Euclid*, I, 171.

and the figures in question can in all likelihood be represented by the following:[1]

The problem of what Aristotle meant by the words περὶ τὸ ἕν καὶ χωρίς ('round the one and without'—what? Or 'when the gnomons are placed round the one, and in the other case') will probably never be solved with certainty,[2] but they can at any rate be construed in a way not inconsistent with this. When the series of odd numbers is put round the unit in the form of gnomons, the resulting figure is always a square (remains 'the same'); when the even numbers are set out in the same way, the relation between the sides of the figures formed offers infinite variation. We notice that in the Pythagorean table of opposites (*Metaph.* 986a22, p. 245, below), 'square' and 'oblong' appear under the headings of 'limit' and 'unlimited' respectively. Later writers offer other explanations of the Pythagorean association of odd with limit and even with unlimited, for example that even numbers can be divided into equal parts leaving, as it were, a blank in the middle,[3] whereas any attempt at halving an odd number is baulked by coming up against a unit.[4]

The precise reason for the association is of interest to historians of mathematics, who may follow it up in the references here given, but is perhaps no longer to be ascertained with certainty. In any case it originated in the visual, geometrical representation of numbers which was natural to the Pythagoreans. We may proceed from the fact itself. Since every number partakes of the nature of odd or even, these are the basic elements of number and in their turn exemplify

[1] For ancient and modern views see the discussions in Ross (references in next note), noting especially the divergent opinion of Taylor, *CR*, 1926, 150–1.

[2] For a summary of the various interpretations offered see Ross's notes on *Metaph.* 986a18 and *Phys.* 203a13, and cf. Cornford, *P. and P.* 9f.

[3] κενὴ λείπεται χώρα, see ps.-Plutarch quoted by Burnet, *EGP*, 288, n. 4.

[4] In the light of other texts this seems to be the most likely explanation of the superficially absurd statement preserved by Simplicius (*Phys.* 455.20) that what can be divided into equal parts can be bisected *ad infinitum*. For texts and discussion see Burnet, *EGP*, 288–9 and Taylor, *CR*, 1926, 149f.

16-2

limit and the unlimited. They give rise first of all to the unit, which is regarded as standing outside the number-series of which it is the 'principle' (*arche*), and as combining in itself the nature of odd and even. Theo (p. 22 Hiller) quotes from Aristotle's book on the Pythagoreans the explanation that when added to an even number it makes it odd, but when added to an odd number makes it even—hardly a satisfactory explanation, since it applies to every odd number as much as to the unit.[1] It does not seem possible to extract from Aristotle's words at *Metaph.* 986a17 the meaning sought by Cornford, that 'the Monad is prior to, and not a resultant or product of, the two opposite principles, Odd or Limit, and Even or Unlimited'.[2] Cornford quotes Theo's description of the monad as 'the principle of all things and the highest of all principles... that out of which come all things but which itself comes out of nothing, indivisible and potentially all things'. But Theo's testimony can hardly stand against Aristotle's. He was a Platonist, and elsewhere describes the monad in plainly Platonic terms as 'the intelligible form of the one'. The primacy of the One is asserted by other late writers, notably Eudorus (first century B.C., *ap.* Simpl. *Phys.* 181.10) and Alexander Polyhistor (D.L. VIII, 24), but their testimony on the point has been shown to be more than doubtful.[3] The Platonists and Neopythagoreans of their time were, under Stoic influence, much inclined to monism; this can be as definitely asserted of Eudorus as of Theo.[4] With but a little subtracted, the later origin

---

[1] Rostagni in *Il Verbo di Pitagora* (9ff.) makes great play with a fragment of Epicharmus (2 in DK), which in his submission implies a knowledge on the part of the comic poet of every detail of this Pythagorean scheme, thus vouching for its existence in the first half of the fifth century. The lines in question run: 'But if to an odd number, or if you like an even one, someone chooses to add a pebble, or to take one away from those that are there, do you think the number would remain the same?' To draw such far-reaching inferences from this bare sentence is hardly permissible, yet the existence of the doctrine at that time is not improbable.

[2] *CQ*, 1923, 3 with n. 1. He translates ἐξ ἀμφοτέρων εἶναι τούτων '*consists* of both of these', not '*proceeds* from both', while admitting that 'proceeds' is appropriate to the immediately following words, τὸν δ' ἀριθμὸν ἐκ τοῦ ἑνός. But even if this translation were possible, the One would still be a *product* of the Odd and the Even, and could in no sense be prior to them.

[3] By Raven, *P. and E.* 14f. Iamblichus claimed to have found it in Philolaus (DK, 44B8), but his authority in such a matter is very doubtful. It was prominent in the Neopythagorean Nicomachus.

[4] On Eudorus see H. Dörrie in *Hermes*, 1944, 25–39. His value as a source for pre-Platonic Pythagoreanism may be judged by the following extracts from this article: (p. 33) 'Much of what Eudorus reports concerning Pythagorean doctrine comes directly from the *Timaeus*.... Many Platonic features appear in this account, much of it even reads like an anticipation of actual Neoplatonism.' On the next page the author contends that underlying the passage is 'a Pytha-

of which is more than likely ('highest of all principles', 'itself out of nothing'), Theo's account becomes consistent with Aristotle's; for since all things are made of number, and the principles of number are the principles of all things, the unit, as the immediate principle of number, may certainly be described as 'the principle of all things' and 'that out of which all things come'. That there are even more ultimate principles does not affect this, any more than Aristotle's statement that things are made of numbers conflicts with his statement that the elements of numbers are the elements of all things.

In this connexion, however, we find in Aristotle a reference to two divergent Pythagorean theories. Immediately after the passage we have been considering, he continues (986a22):

Others of this same school say that there are ten principles, which they arrange in twin columns, namely:

limit	unlimited
odd	even
one	plurality
right	left
male	female
at rest	moving
straight	crooked
light	darkness
good	bad
square	oblong

...How these principles may be brought into line with the causes we have mentioned [sc. Aristotle's own four causes] is not clearly explained by them; but they appear to class the elements (στοιχεῖα, presumably referring to the pairs of principles enumerated) as matter, for they say that substance consists of and is formed from them as from internal constituents.

In this scheme the unit is ranked with limit and oddness. It is certainly not prior to them, nor yet obviously posterior, though other

gorizing exegesis of the Phaedrus-myth'. One has also to take into consideration Eudorus's attempt to read an esoteric meaning into Plato (Alex. *in Met.* p. 59 Hayduck, Dörrie 34–6).

In general scholars would do well to heed the warning of H. D. Saffrey (*Le* π. Φιλ. *d'Aristote*, etc., 1955, p. xi): 'J'avoue que je suis sceptique sur la connaissance que nous pouvons avoir de l'ancien pythagorisme; en tout cas je ne crois pas que l'on puisse se fonder sans d'infinies précautions sur les écrits pythagoriciens des premiers siècles de notre ère: ce sont tous d'inextricables mélanges de néoplatonisme, de néopythagorisme, de néoorphisme etc., et comment distinguer le bon grain de l'ivraie!'

information (for example *Metaph*. 990a8 quoted earlier) suggests that the position of limit and the unlimited (*peras* and *apeiron*) at the head of their respective lists was probably intentional and implies a certain priority or inclusiveness. An interesting point which must always be kept in mind, though one cannot pursue all sides of Pythagorean thought at once, is that there are in a sense only two opposites, of which the ten listed by Aristotle are no more than different aspects or manifestations. For instance, Pythagoreanism unlike the Ionian philosophies is rooted in values; unity, limit, etc. appear on the same side as goodness because they are good, whereas plurality and the unlimited are bad. The religious belief in the essential unity of nature, and the religious ideal of a unity of the soul with the divine *kosmos*, are present in every part of the system. So Aristotle wrote in the *Ethics* (1096b5): 'The Pythagorean account of the good is more plausible,[1] in that they place the one in the column of goods', and again (1106b29): 'As the Pythagoreans surmised, evil is a form of the unlimited, good of the limited.' One may go further and say that limit and unity are to be equated with the male, the unlimited and plurality with the female element in nature. It is thus possible, when the time comes to describe the making of the universe in physical terms, for the unit to appear in the form of a *sperma* (*Metaph*. 1091a16) reminiscent of the *gonimon* of Anaximander (see p. 278, below).

It would appear then that the ultimate principles are the two contraries limit and the unlimited. With these are equated numerical oddness and evenness respectively, and they thus form the principles of the number-series which in turn is to provide the elements of all existing things. Of the treatment of the unit there are two accounts known to Aristotle: some Pythagoreans derived it from a combination of limit-odd with unlimited-even, whereas others constructed two columns of contraries in which the unit appeared alongside limit, goodness, etc. These columns contain all their principles (in contrast to Alcmaeon, the Pythagoreans 'laid down how many and what they were'), and therefore include the principles of numbers, which all exemplify oddness

---

[1] *Sc.* than the Platonic: everywhere Aristotle distinguishes with assurance between the two, which is only to be expected and would not be worth mentioning were he not so often accused of confusing them.

and evenness. It is not to be doubted that for all Pythagoreans alike the unit stood for what is limited in opposition to the infinite or un-defined (*apeiron*). The only difference between the two schools of thought is that whereas one of them identified it with the active principle of limit itself, the other saw it as the first product of that principle imposing itself on the undifferentiated mass of the *apeiron* and so initiating the introduction of order and limit which was necessary to produce a *kosmos* within it. It has been thought (e.g. by Cornford) that the Pythagoreans believed simultaneously in two distinct grades of unit or monad, the One which was a first principle and regarded as divine, and the unit which began the number-series and was a product of higher principles. This is the view of Neopythagorean and Platonic writers of Augustan and later times, like Eudorus who writes:[1] 'Evidently the One which is the origin of everything is one thing, and the one which is opposed to the dyad is another, which they call the monad.' (Aristotle uses 'one' and 'monad' indifferently when speaking of the Pythagoreans.) But since there is no warrant for this in Aristotle, for whom the varying status of the one reflected a difference of opinion between different branches of the school, its application to the Pytha-goreans of Plato's time and earlier is very dubious. The way in which Aristotle brings the table of contraries into connexion with Alcmaeon shows that the view which it represents was an early one, probably formulated within the lifetime of Pythagoras or very soon after; and his introduction of the main account, from which this is a divergence, as that of men 'contemporary with and earlier than' Leucippus and Democritus gives some ground for supposing that that account represents a slightly later phase.

In what sense the entities mentioned were principles, causes or constituents was something which baffled Aristotle (pp. 237 f., above). The best illustration is provided by music, from which most probably the whole idea originated. The general principle applied by the Pythagoreans to the construction of a *kosmos* is that of the imposi-tion of limit (*peras*) on the unlimited (*to apeiron*) to make the limited

---

[1] *Ap.* Simpl. *Phys.* 181.28. The introductory δῆλον ὅτι betrays an inference of his own. He uses the Platonic term 'dyad' for what earlier Pythagoreans would have called *apeiron*. On Eudorus see p. 244, n. 4, above.

(*to peperasmenon*). Owing to the brilliant exposition by Pythagoras (if I have said enough to justify giving him the credit) of the numerical, proportional structure of the 'concordant' notes of the scale, music now provided the paradigm of this principle at work. The whole field of sound, ranging indefinitely in opposite directions—high and low—represents the unlimited. Limit is imposed on this continuum when it is divided according to the relevant system of ratios, which reduces the whole to order, starting from the octave (*sc.* 1:2, the unit and the first even number, both of which have their places in the table of *archai*). 'The infinite variety of quality in sound is reduced to order by the exact and simple law of ratio in quantity. The system so defined still contains the unlimited element in the blank intervals between the notes; but the unlimited is no longer an orderless continuum; it is confined within an order, a *cosmos*, by the imposition of Limit or Measure.'[1]

That the Pythagoreans, as later sources affirm, reverenced the One as God, or divine, is very probable. There would be no inconsistency in believing in two contrasting principles, both ultimate, but one good and the other bad, and bestowing this dignity on the good one. That they did so is the verdict of the doxographic tradition (Aët. 1, 7, 18, *Dox.* 302): 'Of the principles, Pythagoras said that the Monad was God and the good, the true nature of the One, Mind itself; but the indefinite dyad is a *daimon* and evil, concerned with material plurality.' The juxtaposition of good and evil principles in this passage affords some positive evidence for rejecting the version of a first-century Platonist like Eudorus that the One was sole principle and the Unlimited secondary.[2] At this point, it is true, one begins to ask what precise sense of 'primary' and 'secondary' one has in mind. Hitherto we have meant that what is primary is underived, and what is secondary or posterior is derived from it or from some intermediate. In this sense the one is not primary if we trust our earliest authority. Since, however, it stood for all that the Pythagoreans held in highest esteem—limit, form, goodness, etc.—and in all probability was even at this period accounted divine, it certainly took the primary or highest place in the hierarchy,

[1] Cornford, *CQ*, 1922, 145.
[2] Pointed out by Raven, *P. and E.* 18. Eudorus naturally connected the divinity of the One with its primacy among the principles (Simpl. *loc. cit.* l. 19). The statement that it is divine is repeated by Hippolytus (*Ref.* 1, 2, 2).

and the unlimited, evil, material principle with which it combined in the creation of numbers and the physical universe, though coexistent, was of secondary value and importance. This would make all the easier the later modification of the doctrine in the direction of a sole transcendent Monad-god from which all else was derived, the doctrine which finds its culmination in the inexpressible first principle of a Plotinus.

On the interpretation here offered, Pythagoreanism before the time of Plato was frankly dualistic in its account of ultimate principles, unlike the Milesian systems, which were in intention monistic, although as we have seen the monism of this early stage of rational thought could not bear a critical scrutiny. The opposite view was taken by Cornford. He saw the Pythagoreans as believing in an ultimate One behind all else. From this were derived limit and the unlimited themselves, although this ultimate One or Monad must be distinguished from the unit which is the first number, point or physical atom, since that is clearly described as a product of these two opposite principles. Cornford depended largely for this interpretation on the account compiled by Alexander Polyhistor from certain 'Pythagorean commentaries' and excerpted by Diogenes, the dating of which has been the subject of prolonged controversy (see p. 201, n. 3, above). The conclusion reached here, which is essentially that of Mr Raven in his *Pythagoreans and Eleatics*, has the advantage of relying exclusively on Aristotle, with whose statements the idea of a fundamental monism is indeed hard to reconcile. Raven has shown that it is by no means necessary to see it even in Alexander's account (*P. and E.* 134f.). The monistic theory, involving as it does a distinction between the ideal One and the unit which begins the number-series, is surely Platonic in character. Can we not point to its author, namely Speusippus, the Pythagorizing nephew and successor of Plato? In paraphrasing what Aristotle says about him at *Metaph.* 1028 b 21, his Greek commentator[1] attributes to him a 'One-itself' (αὐτοέν) at the head of the scale of reality. In this connexion it is of interest that a tradition going back to Aristoxenus[2]

---

[1] [Alex.] *in Metaph.* 462.34. (See p. 257 n. 1, below.)

[2] And hence doubtless to Aristotle, whose pupil he was. Aristotle not only wrote books on Pythagoreanism, but was also interested in Persian religion. He wrote that according to the Magi there are two *archai*, a good *daimon* and an evil, the name of the one being Zeus and Oromasdes, and of the other Hades and Areimanios (Aristotle, fr. 6 Rose, p. 79 Ross, D.L. 1, 8).

associated Pythagoras with Zoroaster. It may be, as is generally thought, without historical foundation, but at least it is evidence that a resemblance between the Greek and Persian systems was remarked by the fourth century; and in the latter the powers of good and evil, light and darkness, Ormuzd and Ahriman, were certainly coexistent and independent. As the matter has a certain intrinsic interest, some data on the strength of the tradition are appended in a note below.

Something must be added here to do justice to Cornford's point of view, based as it was on a singular insight into the minds of early thinkers which can best be described as the gift of a poetic imagination. He instinctively, and rightly, felt that there could not at any period have been a real inconsistency between the scientific or rational side of the Pythagorean system and its religion. And as he says (*P. and P.* 4): 'As a religious philosophy Pythagoreanism unquestionably attached central importance to the idea of unity, in particular the unity of all life, divine, human and animal, implied in the scheme of transmigration.' Unity was exalted and revered as the highest and best in the cosmos and the supreme object of human aspiration. Therefore, he argued, in their cosmogony also it must have been the sole starting-point, just as the single *arche* of the Milesians was also the divine element in their world: and he looked to see how this could be so.

Now in contrasting this primal unity of the Italian school with that of the Milesians, he once said of it (in an unpublished lecture): 'The antagonism of the Many is harmonized and held together by *philia* (that is, the bond of kinship) in this unity.' Here his own words set one wondering whether the unity which the Pythagoreans exalted as divine, and held forth as an example for men to follow, was perhaps not an *arche* in the full Milesian sense but rather—as indeed he seems to be saying—the unity of the complete and perfect *kosmos*, which because it is a *harmonia* deserves above all things the name of God. We are here in the realm of conjecture, trying to fill for ourselves the gaps in our knowledge of this early period, nor is it easy to express what is meant in our own terms. But my suggestion is that for these people the principle of limit did indeed exist in the beginning, but was opposed by the formless and evil principle of the unlimited. By imposing itself on this, in a way which I shall try to explain later (pp. 266 ff.), it produces out of unorganized chaos an organic unity or *kosmos*. There are regions of the universe in which the unlimited still maintains its undesirable haphazard character, but in its main structure, as displayed to man by the harmonious motions of the heavenly bodies, it has achieved the unity of a perfect organism. The *kosmos*, by virtue of its ordered and beautiful (that is cosmic) nature, is divine. The good is in the end, the *telos*, not the *arche* in the sense of the beginning. The point seems to be clinched by Aristotle, when we read (*Metaph.* 1072b30): 'The Pythagoreans suppose that supreme beauty and goodness are not present in the beginning: for, although the beginnings of plants and animals are causes, beauty and perfection are rather in their outcome.'[1] In this way the religious need to identify unity with goodness and divinity is satisfied without positing a unity ἐν ἀρχῇ, if we take those words to mean 'in the beginning'. The goodness of the living universe does lie in its unity or order, and that order is only possible because a unifying and harmonizing *principle* (*arche*) has existed alongside the unlimited from the beginning; but it is only when its work is done that unity is achieved.

Additional note: Pythagoreanism and Persian religion

The possibility of Oriental elements in Pythagoreanism has always excited interest, and attempts have been made to establish connexions not only with Persia but also with India and even China (see ZN, 590, n. 2 and Ueberweg–Praechter, 26f.). Concerning these latter countries the remarks of Zeller (589–92) have not lost their force: the positive evidence is weak or non-existent, and the resemblances in doctrine are too general to warrant any definite conclusions, and were certainly current in Greece from a period which makes the hypothesis of borrowing from the further East unlikely. In India some have been impressed by the occurrence of transmigration, abstinence from flesh, and number-mysticism, and as for China, no one can fail to be struck by the superficial resemblance of the Yin–Yang doctrine to the Pythagorean table of opposites. All phenomena are produced by

---

[1] Curiously enough, this translation is Cornford's, which he gives on p. 5 of *P. and P.* He uses it in the course of an argument about unity as the sole original principle in which it is difficult to follow him, for the religious need for unity in the beginning seems to vanish as we read it.

the interaction of the two cosmic principles or forces Yang and Yin, whose characteristics are listed thus (Fung Yu-Lan, *Short History of Chinese Philosophy*, 138, 140):

YANG	YIN
Sunshine or light	Darkness or shadow
masculinity	femininity
activity	passivity
heat	cold
dryness	wetness
hardness	softness
odd	even

Later members of the Yin–Yang school tried to connect the five elements (water, fire, wood, metal, soil) with the Yang and the Yin through numbers. The numbers of Yang are odd, of Yin even, and the elements are produced from numbers. Dr Fung notes the remarkable resemblance to Pythagorean theory, but emphasizes that this feature of the Chinese doctrine did not appear till later. G. Thomson (*The First Philosophers*, 266) has pointed out that there are differences as well as resemblances.

Whether the parallels with Indian thought originate from a common Indo-European heritage is a question which, if it admits of any answer at all, lies far beyond the scope of this study.

The case for Persian influence must be taken more seriously, though the danger lies in overstating it rather than the reverse. The Greeks of later days were strongly inclined to represent their early philosophers as the pupils of the Orient, partly from the sense of age-old and mysterious wisdom with which it has always allured its western neighbours, and partly because in their own, Hellenistic or Graeco-Roman, times a syncretism between Greek and Oriental, in which philosophy tended to lose itself in religion and mysticism, was in fact the order of the day. Consequently it was common form to attribute oriental voyages of study to a Thales or a Pythagoras. At the same time, since the sixth century B.C. was an enterprising age in which communications were well developed and lengthy voyages freely undertaken for commercial and other purposes, such stories cannot be dismissed as improbable. For Pythagoras we may add to this general credibility the fact that his connexion with Zoroaster, or at least with Persia and the Magi, recurs in the tradition with remarkable persistence as compared with the wilder references to Indians, Iberians, etc. Apart from this tradition about Pythagoras, some acquaintance with the principles of the Mazdaean religion of Zoroaster is traceable in Greece to the fourth century, not only, as we have seen, in Aristotle, but also in Eudoxus (W. J. W. Koster, *Mythe de Platon*, etc. 25 f.). But let us turn to the ancient sources.

(1) *References to Zoroaster in person*

(*a*) Hippol. *Ref.* 1, 2, 12 (DK, 14. 11): 'Diodorus of Eretria [an otherwise unknown author] and Aristoxenus the writer on music say that Pythagoras went to Zaratas the Chaldaean.'

A little later in the same chapter Hippolytus says: 'Pythagoras is said to have forbidden the eating of beans because Zaratas taught that in the original formation of the universe the bean was produced when the earth was still in the course of solidifying and still putrid.' This statement presumably does not go back to Aristoxenus, since he denied that Pythagoras forbade beans (p. 189, above). It seems to be an unintelligibly mutilated version of the tenet that beans and men had a common origin (Porph. *V.P.* 44, p. 184, above).

(*b*) Clem. Alex. *Strom.* 1, 69 (II, 44 Stählin): 'Pythagoras was an admirer of Zoroastres the Persian Magus.' (A little earlier at 1, 66 (II, 41) we have: 'Pythagoras consorted with the best of the Chaldaeans and Magi.')

(*c*) Plut. *De An. Procr.* 2: 'And Zaratas the teacher of Pythagoras called this [*sc.* the indefinite dyad] the mother of number and the One its father.'

We may compare the presence of male and female in the Pythagorean table of contraries on the side of the one and of plurality respectively. Whether Plutarch had any warrant for attributing this to Zaratas is another question.

(*d*) Apuleius, *Flor.* 15 (p. 21 Helm): 'Some say that when Pythagoras was taken to Egypt among the prisoners of Cambyses, he had as his teachers the Persian Magi and in particular Zoroastres, the master of all secret religious lore.'

(*e*) *Id. Apol.* 31 (p. 36 Helm): 'Most people believe that Pythagoras was a disciple of Zoroaster and correspondingly versed in magic.'

(*f*) Porph. *V.P.* 12: 'Besides consorting with the other Chaldaeans he went to Zaratas, who purified him of the defilements of his previous life and taught him the means whereby good men maintain purity and the explanation of nature and what were the first principles of all things.'

(2) General references to Magi and Persia

(a) Cic. *Fin.* v, 29, 87: 'Pythagoras...went to the Persian Magi.'

(b) D.L. VIII, 3: 'He also journeyed among the Chaldaeans and Magi.'

(c) Porph. *V.P.* 41: Pythagoras taught above all things to speak the truth, for this was the one way to resemble God: 'for as he learned from the Magi, the body of the god, whom they call Oromasdes, resembles light, and his soul truth'.

One is reminded of the importance of speaking the truth in Persian education according to Herodotus.

(d) Iambl. *V.P.* 19: 'Taken prisoner by Cambyses's men he was brought to Babylon. There he spent his time with the Magi to their mutual satisfaction, was instructed in their sacred teaching and learned how to worship the gods in the most perfect way. In their company he also mastered the science of number and music and other subjects of study.'

(e) *Ibid.* 154: 'He forbade burning the bodies of the dead because as a follower of the Magi he did not wish what is mortal to have any part in anything divine.'

One may compare further Pliny, *N.H.* xxv, 5, xxx, 2; Porph. *V.P.* 6; Lydus, *De Mens.* p. 21 Wünsch; Iambl. *V.P.* 151 (in which Chaldaeans and Magi are mentioned along with Celts, Iberians and Latins, as well as more homely contacts like Orphics, Eleusis, Samothrace, etc.).

There was then a strong tradition, in origin going back almost certainly to Aristotle, that Pythagoras was directly instructed in religion by Zoroaster or some of the Persian Magi. Nevertheless any details are known only from writers of Graeco-Roman date, and create a distinct impression that the belief was no more than a conjecture based on real or fancied resemblances of doctrine. In fundamental principles there is a certain resemblance, if we are not disturbed by the fact that the two ultimates in Zoroastrianism are personal gods, not impersonal principles like those of the Pythagoreans. We even find an uncertainty whether the Persian cult should be strictly described as monotheistic or dualistic, reminding us how some have upheld the monism of the Pythagoreans and we have ourselves concluded that the principle of unity or limit was at least of higher value and importance than the other. Similarly J. Duchesne-Guillemin writes of the Persian system:[1] 'Ce

[1] In his short but most useful book, *Ormazd et Ahriman*, 32f.

système est-il avant tout un dualisme, ou un monothéisme? D'un certain point de vue, c'est un monothéisme: Ahura Mazdah est supérieur aux deux Esprits qui s'affrontent. Il est le créateur de toute chose.... D'un autre point de vue, le système apparaît comme un dualisme: Ahura Mazdah est déclaré identique à son Esprit Bénéfique, et c'est en effet celui-ci qui crée; mais il crée seulement un ordre bon, un bonheur possible qu'a dérangé la rébellion des méchants. Ce sont les hommes qui sont responsables du malheur...c'est aussi l'Esprit Mauvais.... Ainsi donc, le monde a deux maîtres, deux créateurs.' In his conclusion there is a still stronger resemblance to Pythagoreanism, that is, in the subordination of theory to practice: 'Mais, plutôt que de disputer du monothéisme ou du dualisme de Zarathustra, il faut constater l'ambiguïté de son système—et se rappeler qu'il avait d'autres soucis que théoriques. Sa mission est d'agir et de faire agir: il réforme les rites, il proclame des mythes nouveaux.'

We find also in the religion of Zoroaster, either contributed by him or taken over from his heritage, the conception of Arta the 'just order', the opposition good–bad exemplified by light–darkness, and the taboo on killing and animal sacrifice (*op. cit.* 23, 24, 27, 28, 35 ff.). On the other hand an essential belief of Pythagoras is lacking—'La préexistence des âmes n'est attestée en Iran que tardivement' (*op. cit.* 101)—and there is a fundamentally Hellenic character about Pythagorean philosophy which makes it unlikely that it owed much to Oriental sources. As Duchesne-Guillemin justly says, it had its own contribution to make to the formulation of that problem which the Greeks above all bequeathed to later Europe: the problem of reconciling the rational and the sensible worlds, the realms of being and of becoming. This problem arose from the incompatibility of two modes of cognition, 'qui, tous deux, étaient des inventions grecques, bien étrangères à l'Iran: la connaissance mathématique (Pythagore) et la connaissance physique (les Ioniens). C'est parce qu'ils avaient développé ces deux sciences que les grecs, seuls dans l'histoire du monde, ont pu, à un certain moment, apercevoir la différence qui sépare la connaissance sensible et la connaissance rationnelle' (p. 98).

So far as concerns mathematics, the statement that they were a Greek invention is, as we have seen, an exaggeration. In this respect the influence of eastern neighbours is undeniable; but it did not come from Persia.

(ii) *Second·stage: generation of geometrical figures from numbers.* In his account from 'Pythagorean commentaries' Alexander Polyhistor describes the whole process of genesis by saying that from the monad combining with the unlimited spring numbers, from numbers points, from points lines, from lines plane figures, from plane figures solids; and finally, from solid figures are made sensible bodies. The production of numbers from the prior elements limit and unlimited, as exemplified especially in oddness and evenness, and the unit, has now been dealt with. Leaving until later the final stage, we have next to see whether the generation of geometrical figures from numbers can be traced back to the form of Pythagoreanism which Plato knew, and whether anything can be said to make it more intelligible. Understanding is assisted if we remember the early habit, which lasted long with Greek mathematicians, of representing numbers in visible form, by rows of dots, letters or pebbles arranged in regular patterns.[1] It gave their arithmetic a geometrical flavour, and ensured that arithmetic and geometry were for long more closely allied than they are today. Even now, the fact that a formula or equation can be represented geometrically as well as algebraically is often an aid to the mathematician, for whose understanding the double representation no longer digs the pitfalls which beset the pioneers of rational thought.

I shall continue on the assumption that it is sufficient for our purpose if a belief is attested for the Pythagoreans in Aristotle, since he has proved perfectly capable of distinguishing non-Platonic Pythagoreanism from the teaching of his master. (See in particular pp. 241, 246, n. 1, above.)

We may start by considering a passage which has already been quoted in part (p. 234). At *Metaph.* 1036b8 Aristotle says:

Some are even in doubt about the circle and the triangle, surmising that it is not right to define them by lines and continuous space, but that these are

---

[1] 'Calculation with pebbles' (presumably on some sort of board or abacus) is mentioned by Herodotus as the normal method (II, 36). We still talk this language when we speak of numbers as 'figures', and 'calculation' conceals the Latin word for pebble.

adduced in the same capacity as the flesh and bones of a man and the bronze or stone of a statue. They refer everything to numbers, calling two the formula of the line.

The Greek commentator who wrote under the name of Alexander of Aphrodisias[1] says that this refers to the Pythagoreans, as is indeed plain, for the only other possibility is the school of Plato, and Aristotle distinguishes this in the immediately following lines with the words: 'But those who posit the forms....' The same commentator gives a clear and sober explanation:

Some—he means the Pythagoreans—are doubtful even about the circle and the triangle. They hold it wrong to define these in terms of lines, saying 'A circle is a surface bounded by a single line', or 'A triangle is that bounded by three lines', or again, 'A line is a continuous length extended in one dimension'. For a line is to a circle or triangle as underlying matter, and so is continuity to a line, just as flesh and bone are to a man and bronze to a statue. If then we do not define a man in terms of bone and flesh, because these are his material parts, neither must we define a circle or triangle in terms of lines nor a line in terms of continuity. For this reason, viz. that the line and the continuous are as matter in the triangle, etc., they reduce all these to numbers, which are not material nor have any substratum analogous to matter, but exist independently. Thus they say that the formula of the line is that of the number two; for seeing that two is the first product of division (i.e. the unit first divided into two, then into three and the numbers after that), if, they maintain, we are defining a line, we must say, not that it is 'a quantity divided [or extended] in one dimension' but that it is 'the *first* product of division'; for 'the first' is not so to speak a material substratum for the line, as continuity is.

According then to Aristotle, the Pythagoreans had a dim idea that things must be defined in terms of their essence, form or structure, and not of the material in which they were embodied: a statue is not properly described in terms of bronze or stone but of its design and what it represents. To them extension or space was the *matter* of geometrical figures, and the *form* could only be expressed in terms of numbers. Allowing for Aristotle's preoccupation with his own scheme of causation, this means that for the Pythagoreans space or

---

[1] Alex. *in Met.* 512.20 Hayduck. Only the commentary on books A to E is genuine, but in any future references the name of Alexander will be used for the whole work.

extension in itself belonged to the realm of the unlimited, and limit was imposed on it when it was marked out according to a geometrical, that is numerical, pattern.

I take next one of the passages in which Aristotle professes himself baffled by the confusions in Pythagorean thought (*Metaph.* 1092b8):

> We find no clear distinction of the sense in which numbers are causes of substance and being. It might be (1) in the sense of boundaries,[1] as points are of magnitudes. In this sense Eurytus fixed the number of each entity, one for man and another for horse, by imitating the forms of living things with pebbles, in the manner of those who attribute numbers to shapes like triangle and square; or (2) because musical harmony, man, and everything else consist of a ratio of numbers.... That numbers are not substance, nor the cause of form, is obvious: substance lies in the ratio, whereas number is the material constituent, e.g. number is the substance of bone or flesh only in the sense in which one says 'three parts of fire to two of earth'. Again, a number, whichever it is, is always the number *of* things—portions of fire or earth, or units—whereas substance is the ratio of one quantity to another in a mixture. This however is no longer a number but a ratio or mixture of numbers, whether corporeal numbers or others.

As we have seen, in their enthusiasm over the discovery of the numerical (that is proportional) basis of the recognized musical intervals, the followers of Pythagoras tried to make numbers the essential basis of everything. According to Aristotle here, this might mean that all physical things consist of elements combined in a certain proportion. This was the method followed in the first half of the fifth century by Empedocles, who though certainly in the Pythagorean tradition, especially on the religious side, was a philosopher of considerable originality. In his fr. 96 he describes bone as being formed of a *harmonia* of two parts of earth, two of water and four of fire. But then, Aristotle objects, it is this proportion (e.g. the whole formula 2:3) that is the essence or form, not the numbers two or three themselves. This is an unfair distortion of the Pythagorean view, but although he tries here to score a point by maintaining that numbers are the material constituents of a ratio, he doubtless has in mind his more general and oft-repeated criticism of the Pythagoreans, that they speak of numbers

---

[1] The obvious meaning of ὅροι in the context. If it needs defence, this has been provided by Raven, *P. and E.* 104.

as if they were matter in the physical sense, endowed with size and weight.

A second method known to Aristotle of establishing the doctrine that things are numbers was to suppose the structure of things to be dependent on geometrical shapes, which in their turn could be described in terms of numbers, each figure being assigned the minimum number of points required to contain it (two for a line, three for a triangle, etc.). He mentions the attempt of the Pythagorean Eurytus[1] to apply this type of description to living creatures, which he characterizes explicitly as an extension of the association of numbers with geometrical figures like triangle and square.

By the use of his own terminology, Aristotle imports an unnecessary confusion into the thought of the early Pythagoreans. It is no use his putting the question whether they employ numbers as the material or the formal causes of things, since they were innocent of the distinction. Their more primitive meaning is clear. Things are numbers, or, if you like, the basis of nature is numerical, because solid bodies are built up of surfaces, surfaces of planes, planes of lines and lines of points, and in their geometric view of number the Pythagoreans saw no difference between points and units.[2] The essential concept is *limit*. In a number of other passages of the *Metaphysics* Aristotle tells us this plainly:

(*a*) 1028b16: 'Some[3] think that the limits of bodies, such as surface and line and point or unit, are substances, rather than body and the solid.'

(*b*) 1090b5: 'There are some who, because the point is the limit and end of a line, the line of a surface and the surface of a solid, hold it to be inescapable that such natures exist.'

(*c*) See also 1002a4 (second paragraph of quotation on pp. 240f.), noticing how, as in the first passage here, unit and point are treated as synonymous when the Pythagoreans are in question.

Having established as already known to Aristotle the facts (i) that for the Pythagoreans the unit-point came first, from it the line, from line surface and from surface solid, and (ii) that they equated these with numbers, one being the number of the point and two of the line, we

---

[1] For whom see pp. 273 ff., below.

[2] Or, indeed, between unit-points and particles; but that must wait until later (Stage 3 of the exposition).

[3] *Sc.* the Pythagoreans. As Ross *ad loc.* notes, their view is once again distinguished from the Platonic a few lines later. Alex. (*in Met.* 462.16) is mistaken.

may allow ourselves to consider other texts which by themselves might be thought to have less authority than Aristotle but do not in fact go beyond him, though they may show up further details of the scheme.

The tenth chapter of the *Theologumena Arithmeticae* attributed to Iamblichus deals at length with the Decad, and contains, as might be expected, much mystical and theological matter of Neopythagorean type.[1] In it we find, however, one passage which is carefully assigned to its source, namely Speusippus, 'the son of Plato's sister Potone, who succeeded him in the Academy before Xenocrates'. He is said to have composed 'an elegant little work which he called *Pythagorean Numbers*, incorporating the choicest parts of Pythagorean doctrine and especially the writings of Philolaus'. The entire second half of this work was devoted to the properties of the number ten, with the object of showing that it thoroughly deserves its Pythagorean title of the full and perfect number (cf. p. 225, above), and in the course of his account Speusippus wrote that it contains in itself, besides all the basic ratios (this seems to refer to the ratios of the 'concordant' musical notes), 'the formulae of the line, surface and solid; for one is a point, two a line, three a triangle and four a pyramid, and all these are primary and fundamental to the other figures in each class'. A little later he put it thus: 'The point is the first principle leading to magnitude, the line the second, surface third and solid fourth.'[2] Aristotle gives us ample warrant for saying that this doctrine did not originate with Speusippus; in all probability he found it in the writings of his favourite author Philolaus, who like any Pythagorean would embody much older lore in his work. Another possible source might be Archytas, for whom a work on the Decad is actually recorded (by Theo Smyrnaeus, DK, 44B11). The scheme described, represented graphically as the Pythagoreans thought of it, is this:[3]

---

[1] F. E. Robbins (writing in the introduction to d'Ooge's translation of Nicomachus's *Introd. Arith.* 1926, 82f.) argued that it is based almost entirely on Nicomachus.

[2] *Theol. Arith.* pp. 84 and 85 de Falco.

[3] As is more fully explained by Sextus, *adv. Math.* x, 280 (trans. Bury, with slight alterations): 'When three points are set down, two at an interval opposite to each other, and the third midway

Points and Magnitudes

The same correlation between numbers and geometrical figures is described by the Neopythagorean writer Nicomachus of Gerasa (*c.* A.D. 100) in his *Introduction to Arithmetic.* In bk. II, ch. 6 he writes:[1]

Unity, then, occupying the place and character of a point, will be the beginning of intervals and of numbers, but not itself an interval or a number, just as the point is the beginning of a line, or an interval, but is not itself line or interval. Indeed, when a point is added to a point, it makes no increase, for when a non-dimensional thing is added to another non-dimensional thing, it will not thereby have dimension....Unity, therefore, is non-dimensional and elementary, and dimension first is found and seen in 2, then in 3, then in 4, and in succession in the following numbers; for 'dimension' is that which is conceived of as between two limits. The first dimension is called 'line', for 'line' is that which is extended in one direction. Two dimensions are called 'surface', for a surface is that which is extended in two directions. Three dimensions are called 'solid', for a solid is that which is extended in three directions.

And in the next chapter:

The point, then, is the beginning of dimension, but not itself a dimension, and likewise the beginning of a line, but not itself a line; the line is the beginning of surface, but not surface, and the beginning of the two-dimensional, but not itself extended in two directions. Naturally, too, surface is the beginning of body, but not itself body, and likewise the beginning of the three-dimensional, but not itself extended in three directions. *Exactly the same in numbers*, unit is the beginning of all number that advances unit by unit in one direction; linear number is the beginning of plane number, which spreads out like a plane in more than one dimension; and plane number is the beginning of solid number, which possesses a depth in the third dimension besides the original ones.

In the first passage Nicomachus emphasizes that the unit-point has no magnitude at all, just as the line (or two) has no breadth and the surface (three) no depth. This was certainly a refinement on the belief of Pythagoras and his earliest followers, who clung to the more naive notion that a point was the smallest magnitude, and therefore that two

in the line formed from the two, but in another dimension, a plane is constructed. And the solid figure and body, like the pyramid, are classed under the number four. For when the three points are placed as I said before, and another point is placed upon them from above, there is constructed the pyramidal form of solid body; for it now possesses the three dimensions length, breadth and depth.'

[1] Trans. d'Ooge.

261

points in juxtaposition were sufficient to constitute the shortest line. Raven suggests (see especially *P. and E.* 161) that this too was a pre-Platonic development, and that the advance was the outcome of the criticism directed against the more naive view by Zeno of Elea. If this is so, Aristotle would be aware of both views, and in his annoyance with what he considered to be in any case an illogical philosophy would not be too scrupulous in keeping them apart. Referring to the Pythagorean statement that 'two is the formula of the line',[1] he says that continuity is the matter of geometrical figures and number the formal element. Probably this is his interpretation of men who already believed that a line was that which stretched between two points, not that two points placed side by side in themselves constituted a line.

In the view, or views, so far described the progression has been arithmetical (1, 2, 3, 4). We read also of another method of building up geometrical figures, which leads rather to a geometrical progression (1, 2, 4, 8, i.e. point, line, square, cube). This too was known to Aristotle, but there must always remain a slight element of doubt whether it is of genuinely Pythagorean origin, as has been assumed with little or no argument by recent English scholars.[2] The context in Aristotle does not suggest this, Sextus Empiricus (*adv. Math.* x, 282) calls the method Pythagorean but a later one than the other, and Proclus (*Eucl.* p. 97 Friedl.) describes the other as 'more Pythagorean'; and it must be admitted that any modification of Pythagorean doctrine made in the Academy would have been freely accepted as Pythagorean by most Neopythagorean or later writers. Since, however, its pre-Platonic origin remains possible, it must be examined more closely.

In the first book of the *De Anima*, as part of the preliminary review of the theories of his predecessors on the nature of the soul, Aristotle criticizes the theory that it is 'a self-moving number', which he not unreasonably stigmatizes as 'much the most absurd'. After pointing out in a sentence or two the chief difficulties which he sees, he proceeds (409a3): 'Moreover since they say that a moving line generates a surface, and a moving point a line, the movements of units will also be lines, for the point is a unit having position.' Now although Aristotle

---

[1] *Metaph.* 1036b12, quoted above, p. 257.
[2] Cornford, *P. and P.* 12; Raven, *P. and E.* 106.

does not mention it, the theory of the soul as a self-moving number is well attested as having been that of Plato's pupil and successor Xenocrates,[1] and it would therefore be natural to suppose that the subject of φασι ('they say') is Xenocrates and those who agreed with him. On the other side it may be argued (i) that in view of the disjointed, non-literary character of the treatises (lecture-notes, etc.) that form the Aristotelian corpus this assumption is by no means necessary, (ii) that believing as he did in indivisible lines, Xenocrates could not without fundamental self-contradiction have held the doctrine here described. Rodier (*De An.* 1900, II, 141) sees this difficulty, but suggests that possibly Xenocrates may have got over it by admitting at the same time indivisibles of time and movement, a theory referred to in Arist. *Phys.* 263 b 27. His translation, however, seems to reflect a continuing doubt in his mind ('En outre, puisqu'*on dit* que...').

The theory here touched on by Aristotle is generally known as the fluxion theory, and is so referred to by Proclus (*loc. cit.* p. 262, above) in the words: 'Others have different ways of defining a line, some as the fluxion of a point, others as magnitude extended in one direction.' After a brief comment on these, he returns to what he calls the 'more Pythagorean account' according to which the point is compared to the unit, the line to the number two, the surface to three and the solid to four. Sextus refers to fluxion in a number of places.[2] He also describes the earlier method, and twice he seems to confuse the two. His reference to fluxion in *Math.* VII, 99 is: 'We imagine a line (which is a length without breadth) as the flowing of a point, and breadth (i.e. surface without depth) as the flowing of a line; and by the flowing of a surface, body is generated.' At X, 281, after a description of the point–line–triangle–pyramid sequence, we read:

But some say that body is formed from one point. This point by flowing produces a line, the line by flowing makes a surface, and this when moved (κινηθέν, the same verb as is used by Aristotle in the *De Anima*) into depth generates body in three dimensions. *But this scheme of the Pythagoreans*

---

[1] Heinze, *Xenokrates*, pt. IV; see e.g. Plut. *An. Procr.* 1012 D, Andronicus of Rhodes *ap.* Themist. *in De An.* p. 59.8.
[2] *Pyrrh.* III, 19 and 154, *Math.* IV, 4 f., VII, 99, X, 281. Raven (*P. and E.* 105 f.) notes that all these passages seem to rely on the same source.

differs from that of the earlier ones. The earlier created numbers from two principles, the one and the indefinite dyad,[1] then from numbers points, lines, plane figures and solids. But these build up everything from a single point.

The fluxion theory gives the sequence, not point–line–triangle–pyramid, but point–line–square–cube.

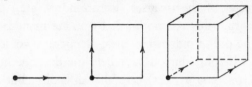

That it came later than the other is only what we should expect, since it is clearly a refinement on it. Cornford (*P. and P.* 12) saw in this refinement the immediate answer to the criticisms of Zeno of Elea, which were directed against the primitive Pythagorean conception of magnitudes as formed by the juxtaposition of discrete points which must themselves have been conceived as having extension. In Mr Raven's view, the immediate answer to Zeno consisted in positing continuity, 'the unlimited', as what Aristotle would call 'matter' for the line, surface, etc., and regarding the points simply as boundaries or limits. It is the advance from the conception of the minimum line as consisting solely of two points in contact to the conception of it as that which stretched between two points. This advance he puts down to the generation of Philolaus and Eurytus. It is not yet the fluxion theory, which he would attribute to 'a generation of Pythagoreans approximately contemporary with the Platonists who borrowed it from them' (*P. and E.* 109). We have perhaps seen grounds for admitting yet another possibility, namely that it was elaborated in the Academy of Plato's time, possibly by Xenocrates. Like much other Platonic doctrine, it would be appropriated as Pythagorean by later generations,

---

[1] The Platonic term for what the Pythagoreans called the unlimited (Ar. *Metaph.* 987b25).

It may be of some interest to compare a view of Isaac Newton, who wrote: 'I consider mathematical quantities in this place not as consisting of very small parts, but as described by a continuous motion. Lines are described, and thereby generated, not by the apposition of parts, but by the continued motion of points; superficies by the motion of lines; solids by the motion of superficies; angles by the rotation of the sides; portions of time by a continual flux; and so on in other quantities.' 'These geneses', Newton adds, 'really take place in the nature of things, and are daily seen in the motion of bodies.' (*Two Treatises on the Quadrature of Curves, and Analysis by Equations of an Infinite Number of Terms*, trans. John Stewart (London, 1745), 1. Quoted by M. G. Evans, *Journ. Hist. Ideas*, 1955, 556.)

for whom Platonic and Pythagorean were almost one system. They are not to be blamed for this, for on the one hand Plato's thought is steeped in Pythagoreanism, and on the other he and his immediate successors made their own modifications to it. The only extant author who was in a position to know the true state of affairs is Aristotle, and in his single reference to the fluxion theory he not only does not attribute it to the Pythagoreans but strongly suggests that it is due to Xenocrates and his fellow-members of the Academy.

What seems certain is that the fluxion theory of the generation of geometrical figures, whether or not Zeno's arguments had anything to do with it, is designed as a solution of the problem of incommensurable magnitudes.[1] This arose from the discovery of the incommensurability of the diagonal of a square with its sides, which would follow on the 'theorem of Pythagoras' (whenever that was first enunciated by Greeks) and dealt a blow to the earlier Pythagorean view that 'things are numbers', i.e. that geometrical figures, and hence ultimately the physical world, were based on a series of integers. No proportion between integers can be the basis for the construction of a right-angled triangle.[2]

---

[1] Cornford apparently attributed the development *both* to Zeno's criticisms *and* to the difficulties created by the discovery of irrationals, which inevitably raised questions of continuity and infinite divisibility such as are involved in Zeno's arguments. Owen on the other hand (*Proc. Ar. Soc.* 1958, 214) is emphatic that the paradoxes of Zeno can have had nothing to do with the substitution of the fluxion or motion of a point for the summation of unitary parts as the model of a line, and attributes it solely to the discovery of incommensurables. Whatever the truth about this, it has been well remarked by N. B. Booth (*Phronesis*, 1957, 100) that awareness of the problem of incommensurability does not necessarily carry with it an appreciation of the problem of irrational numbers and infinite divisibility. Cf. also A. Wedberg, *Plato's Philosophy of Math.* 24: 'Although the existence of incommensurable geometrical magnitudes was known by the Greek mathematicians of Plato's time, they never created a corresponding theory of irrational numbers. The incommensurability was confined to the field of geometry', and van der Waerden, *Math. Ann.* 1941, 156.

[2] The date of the discovery of irrationals has been long and inconclusively discussed. A firm *terminus ante quem* is provided by Plato, *Theaet.* 147D, where Theodorus is said to have proved the irrationality of $\sqrt{3}, \sqrt{5} \ldots, \sqrt{17}$, that of $\sqrt{2}$ being already known before his time. Most probable is the conclusion of van der Waerden (*Math. Annalen*, 1948, 152–3) that the proof of the irrationality of $\sqrt{2}$ was made before 420, perhaps about 450, by Pythagoreans, on the basis of their theory of odd and even numbers. (Cf. the proof given by Aristotle, *An. Pr.* 41a26, that if the diagonal were commensurable the same number would have to be both odd and even.) The late dating of E. Frank (not before 400, *Plato u. d. sog. Pyth.* 228ff.) is now generally discredited.

For any interested in following up the question of irrationals in Greek thought, the following additional references may be useful: Heath, *Hist. Gr. Maths.* I, 154–5; Taylor, *Timaeus*, 366f.; O. Becker, *Gnomon*, 1955, 267; E. Bréhier, *Études de Phil. Antique*, 48f. (discussing the views of P.-H. Michel); G. Junge, *Class. et Med.* 1958, 41–72; A. Wasserstein, *CQ*, 1958, 178f.

(iii) *Third stage: generation of physical bodies from geometrical figures* (*cosmogony*). 'From solid figures come sensible bodies', said the Pythagorean notebooks used by Alexander (p. 201, above). The solids themselves were imagined as built out of numbers, and so, as Aristotle says, the Pythagoreans conceived of number not, like the Platonists, 'as existing apart from sensible things, which they regard as being composed of it. They in fact construct the whole universe out of numbers, not however truly monadic numbers, for they suppose the units to have magnitude' (*Metaph.* 1080b16, quoted above, p. 234).

Aristotle cannot conceal his contempt for this misguided and illogical procedure. How can it be right to treat numbers and their elements as if they had magnitude? Even granted this, how could they produce bodies with physical properties like weight? Or again, how does their explanation account for motion and change? 'They tell us nothing about fire or earth or the other bodies of this kind because, unless I am mistaken, they have nothing to say about perceptible bodies as such.'[1]

It is easy to share Aristotle's irritation. So far, we have seemed to be dealing with a world of Euclidean abstractions, in which one may legitimately speak of the *construction* of solids out of points, lines and surfaces, or the *progression* of points into lines, surfaces and solids. If we could as easily grant the next step—'from solid figures sensible bodies'—we could see plainly how, for the early Pythagoreans at least, 'things were numbers'. How was it done?

There is not the evidence to put together a full and coherent account of Pythagorean cosmogony. Moreover, inadequate as the sources are, they leave no doubt that (as might be expected in the circumstances) there was no single, consistent system to discover. Different people, not necessarily at different periods, offered different accounts of the relation between the physical world and numbers (geometrical figures). One way of accomplishing the transition was by assigning to each of the four elements (that is, presumably, to elementary particles of them) the shape of one of the regular solids. The fifth of these, the dodecahedron, was assigned to the enveloping cosmos or *ouranos* itself. It has

---

[1] *Metaph.* 990a16. Since there is no doubt that the Pythagoreans did say something about fire and the other physical elements, I take Aristotle to mean that they had nothing to add to our knowledge about them, because in his view to relate each one to a mathematical solid threw no light whatever on their real nature. One may compare the common use of the phrase οὐδὲν λέγειν.

been thought unlikely that this theory could have been held by Pythagoras or his immediate followers, on the grounds that the regular solids were probably not all recognized until later and that the four elements appear to have been first explicitly distinguished by Empedocles.[1] The geometrical structure of the elements is not mentioned as a Pythagorean doctrine by Aristotle, though he criticizes it at length as it is given by Plato in the *Timaeus* (*De Caelo*, III, chh. 7 and 8), and knowledge of it doubtless lies behind his strictures on the Pythagoreans for giving only mathematical accounts of physical bodies. Even if the date of the doctrine cannot be finally settled, to discuss it raises some problems of considerable interest in themselves. Aëtius (based on Theophrastus) ascribes it to Pythagoras as follows (II, 6, 5, DK, 44A15): 'There being five solid figures, called the mathematical solids, Pythagoras says that earth is made from the cube, fire from the pyramid, air from the octahedron, and water from the eicosahedron, and from the dodecahedron is made the sphere of the whole.' The attribution to Pythagoras himself is common form and can be ignored. But the doctrine recurs in words attributed to Philolaus, and since it is undoubtedly Pythagorean, known to Plato and yet hardly primitive, it must be accepted as his unless this can be shown to be impossible. (To accept it need not prejudge the question of the authenticity of other fragments.) The fragment of Philolaus runs: 'The bodies in the sphere are five: fire, water, earth, and air, and fifthly the hull (?) of the sphere.'[2] It implies the regular solids of the Aëtius passage, and *prima facie* at least would seem to correlate them with five elements. The question is, therefore, whether either of these conceptions could have been known to, or introduced by, Philolaus.

The regular solids are employed by Plato in the cosmogony of the *Timaeus*, where, as in the passage quoted above, four of them are equated with the four elements and the fifth with the universe as a

---

[1] On this point, however, cf. the remarks on pp. 122f., above.

[2] Fr. 12, text as in Burnet, *EGP*, 283, n. 3. The normal meaning of ὁλκάς was a cargo-boat. LSJ interpret it as passive ('a ship which is towed'), but DK think its meaning here is active, that which *carries* the cosmic sphere, comparing ὢ γῆς ὄχημα in Eur. *Tro.* 884. Wilamowitz (*Platon*, II², 91) emended to ὁλκός, which can mean a coil (*volumen*), and so the rounded mass of the sphere itself. Perhaps cf. rather *Orph. Hymn* 87, 3 ψυχὴν...καὶ σώματος ὁλκόν, in the sense of 'the body's bulk' (*not*, as Rostagni takes it, as a synonym for ψυχή).

It is of course a peculiarity of the five solids that they can be inscribed in a sphere.

whole. Some have therefore thought that the scheme was Plato's invention, falsely ascribed by later compilers to the Pythagoreans. It is more probable that Plato was here, as in so much else, adopting and elaborating Pythagorean notions. The statement in Aëtius must go back to Theophrastus (though with 'the Pythagoreans' in place of 'Pythagoras', Burnet, *EGP*, 292, n. 2), who is unlikely to have been mistaken on this point. Simplicius, too, who had Aristotle's treatise on the Pythagoreans to draw on, notes that according to them fire is composed of pyramids.[1] The elaboration with which Plato works out the scheme, and the immense authority of the *Timaeus*, would naturally lead to the appellation 'Platonic figures' in later antiquity.

Proclus says that Pythagoras himself 'discovered the construction of the five cosmic figures' (*Eucl.* 65 Friedl., DK, 14,6a). Their theoretical construction must have come much later, and that of the octahedron and eicosahedron is credited to Theaetetus, the brilliant mathematician and friend of Plato who was killed in 369 B.C. A scholiast on Euclid book XIII says that the so-called five Platonic bodies did not originate with Plato, but that the cube, pyramid and dodecahedron came from the Pythagoreans, the other two from Theaetetus (Eucl. v, 654 Heiberg). The tradition is difficult to evaluate, since the construction of the octahedron is a less advanced mathematical feat than that of the dodecahedron, and could certainly have been carried out on principles known long before Theaetetus.[2] The latter is, however, elsewhere placed earlier in Pythagorean history by the story of the punishment of Hippasus because he 'first drew the sphere constructed out of twelve pentagons' (Iambl. *V.P.* 88, DK, 18, 4). Both Plato and Philolaus (if the doctrine of the fragment be rightly attributed to him) equate the dodecahedron and the sphere, and this passage is more explicit about the connexion between the two. One is inevitably reminded (with Proclus) of the phrase in the *Phaedo* in which Plato compares the spherical earth to 'the balls made of twelve pieces of leather'. They are brought in as something familiar, so it was evidently common practice in Plato's time to make balls by stitching together twelve pentagonal pieces of leather in the form of a dodecahedron, which when stuffed would fill

[1] Simpl. *De Caelo*, 621.9. On the rest of his sentence see Cornford, *P. and P.* 23 f.
[2] Cf. on this Burnet, *EGP*, 284, n. 1.

out to spherical shape. The context suggests that the patches were of different colours. Using the same phrase as Plato, Plutarch brings the two figures together when he describes the dodecahedron as being, with its blunt angles, 'flexible, and becoming by distention round like the balls made of twelve pieces of leather' (*Qu. Plat.* 1003 c).

Much discussion has been devoted to the question of the date at which the theoretical construction of the regular solids was achieved.[1] But to equate them with the elements no more is absolutely necessary than a knowledge of their existence. This might have been gained in the first place from observation of their occurrence in nature in the form of mineral crystals.[2] To construct them geometrically may have been a gradual achievement which was at least partially accomplished before Theaetetus. One objection, admittedly, might be raised against the claim that the 'Philolaic' scheme need imply no more than a knowledge of the existence of the solids: they are referred to in the fragment as 'the bodies in the sphere', and if this is a reference to the regular solids at all, it presumably implies an awareness that they can all be inscribed in a sphere. In Euclid, however (XIII, 13), the construction of the solids and their inscription in a sphere are treated as one and the same problem. The objection is perhaps not fatal (though it does suggest that the actual wording is not Philolaus's), and on balance the evidence inclines us to believe that the correlation of solids and elements was not impossible for Philolaus. More than that it does not allow us to say.

The Philolaic fragment speaks of five bodies in the sphere, four of which are the four elements as recognized since the time of Empedocles. It looks therefore as if its author recognized the existence of a fifth element, and one would naturally suppose that the Pythagorean doctrine described by Aëtius did the same. Is this so, and if so, what is its bearing on the ascription of the doctrine to Philolaus?

To base a cosmogony on the five regular solids, it was not absolutely

[1] For a full mathematical discussion see K. von Fritz in *RE*, *s.v.* 'Theaetetus', 2. Reihe, v A 2, 1363 ff. More briefly Raven, *P. and E.* 151. Note also that, in the opinion of Heath, the method by which Plato constructs the solids in the *Timaeus* contains nothing that would have been beyond Pythagoras or the Pythagoreans provided that they knew the construction of the regular pentagon. See also discussion in *Manual of Gk. Math.* 106 ff.

[2] P. 226, n. 2, above. Moreover a regular dodecahedron of Etruscan origin, discovered in Italy near Padua, is thought to date from before 500 B.C. (Heath, *Manual of Gk. Math.* 107).

necessary to believe in five elements. Plato in the *Timaeus* reproduces the Philolaic scheme so exactly as to have given grounds for the suspicion that it originated with him and was falsely credited to earlier Pythagoreanism. Yet he does not in this dialogue associate the dodecahedron with a separate element, although he says that it was used by the Creator not for any of the four elements but as the shape of the whole cosmos which contains them all. The earliest unambiguous mentions of the fifth element in extant literature are in the *Epinomis* (which if not by Plato himself is by an immediate pupil) and of course in Aristotle; and both of these writers identify it with *aither*. In the *Timaeus* on the other hand *aither* is classified as a species of air.[1]

The 'fifth body' (πέμπτον σῶμα) is usually associated with Aristotle, who in the second and third chapters of Book I of *De Caelo* argues for its existence and describes its nature. It is the substance of the stars, which had earlier been thought to consist of fire. For Aristotle the elements were distinguished by having different natural places and motions. The natural place of *aither* is at the circumference of the spherical universe and its natural motion is not, like that of fire, rectilinear in an upward or outward direction, but circular. This is the earliest reasoned case for a fifth body, but in the *Epinomis* (*loc. cit.*) we read: 'There are five bodies, which we must call fire and water, thirdly air, fourthly earth, and fifthly *aither*.'

Can we take this teaching even further back? Apart from the possibility, not wholly disproved, that the *Epinomis* itself, which has come down to us under Plato's name, might actually be a work of his old age, there is excellent evidence that, in spite of what he said in the *Timaeus*, he himself came to believe in a fifth element. It consists of a direct quotation from his pupil Xenocrates in Simplicius's commentary on Aristotle's *Physics* (p. 1165.27):

Why then does he [Aristotle] call it a fifth substance? Surely because Plato too declares the substance of the heaven to be distinct from the four sublunary elements, since he assigned to it the dodecahedron and delineated each of the four elements by a different shape. He too therefore says that the substance of the heaven is a fifth one. This is put even more clearly by Xenocrates, the most trustworthy of his pupils, who in his life of Plato

[1] *Epin.* 981 C, Ar. (e.g.) *De Caelo*, 270 b 21, *Tim.* 58 D.

The Fifth Element

writes: 'Thus then he classified living creatures into genera and species, and divided them in every way until he came to their elements, which he called five shapes and bodies, *aither*, fire, water, earth, and air.' So for Plato too the *aither* is a separate fifth simple body apart from the four elements.

Simplicius himself seems to argue that because in the *Timaeus* Plato employs the five solids, he must necessarily have posited five elements. This would indeed be reasonable, if only the text of the *Timaeus* did not seem to deny it, and it is difficult to believe that Plato remained to the end of his days in the uncomfortable position of having five elementary solids and only four elementary bodies to relate to them. Here Xenocrates, who ought to have known, steps in with the positive information that at some time Plato himself distinguished the *aither* from the other elements. It is not usually remarked that the doctrine of the five elements in the *Epinomis* is not identical with that of Aristotle, but comes closer to what is said in the *Timaeus*. For Aristotle, *aither* is at the top of the scale, the divine substance of which the stars are made. In the *Epinomis*, the 'visible gods' who constitute the highest class of divine being have bodies of fire. *Aither* is the substance of the *daimones*, a slightly inferior class of divinity intermediate between those made of fire and those of air, and very close to the latter. Indeed one and the same description is made to do for both of them (984 E–985 A). Although five kinds of body are distinguished, this is not far from the point of view of the *Timaeus*, where *aither* is 'the brightest and clearest kind of air', which in its lower reaches tails off into fog and murk. In earlier thought *aither* had of course been identified both with air (we find the words used interchangeably by the poets) and with fire, as by Anaxagoras.

The truth is that the emergence of a fifth element in Greek thought was a gradual process. In bare outline, a common conception of the universe seems to have been shared by most religious and philosophical thinkers in the centuries before Plato. The cosmos, a sphere bounded by the sky, contains the conflicting 'opposites' (that is primarily the hot, the cold, the wet and the dry), which in the more developed thought of Empedocles became the four root-substances earth, water, air and fire. The mutually destructive nature of these elements ensures that the creatures compounded of them shall be mortal. But this cosmic sphere is not the whole of existence. It floats, as it were, in a circumambient substance of indefinite extent. This 'surrounding' (περιέχον) was of a purer and higher nature, everlasting, alive, and intelligent—in fact divine (θεῖον). This description applies to the *apeiron* of Anaximander, the air of Anaximenes and Diogenes of Apollonia, perhaps also to the logos-fire of Heraclitus (pp. 470ff., below). The Pythagoreans held that the cosmos 'breathed in' from an infinite breath outside it (pp. 277ff., below), and there are grounds for thinking that the dogmatic basis for Orphic or similar religious systems of a mystical tendency was the same.[1] Thus the Italian scholar Rostagni was justified in writing, with reference to the opinion of Eva Sachs:

Now if it is a question of doctrine in the true and proper sense, something formal and schematized as the doxographers understood it, the author is certainly right in saying that this is the fruit of Platonic and Aristotelian experience. But the underlying concepts for this doctrine were all in existence, under varying formulations, among the primitive Pythagoreans, inasmuch as they answered to a universal mystical intuition. In fact the περιέχον ('surrounding') and the ἄπειρον ('infinite') of Anaximander, the ἀήρ ('air') of Anaximenes, the ἄπειρον πνεῦμα ('infinite breath') of the Pythagoreans and so forth were essentially one and the same thing—that which sooner or later was called *aither* and the fifth element.[2]

When therefore we read in Aëtius that Pythagoras said that the universe began 'from fire and the fifth element' (II, 6, 2, *Dox.* 333), we need not dismiss the statement as wholly anachronistic in substance, because the Pythagoreans before Plato's time would not have used the phrase 'fifth element'. They probably spoke rather, as Aëtius a little later in his epitome (II, 6, 5) makes Pythagoras speak, of the four bodies and the sphere of the whole. This no doubt implies that the sphere is of a substance different from the four, as do the words of Plato also. When Plato says that the Creator made the four elements respectively out of four of the regular solids, and used the fifth for 'the whole', then whatever he may subsequently say about the nature of *aither*, we

[1] For further evidence on this matter see Guthrie, *Harv. Theol. Rev.* 1952, 87ff. It is perhaps worth remarking that *Phaedo*, 109A–110B contains as vivid an expression as one could wish of the distinction between *aer* and *aither* as different substances.
[2] *Verbo di P.* 58, n. 1 (translated).

cannot suppose him to mean that 'the whole' is made out of any of the four elements already described.[1]

From this rather tangled evidence we may conclude that the correlation of the physical elements with the regular solids was known to Theophrastus as a genuine Pythagorean doctrine, and that his information was correct. It may have originated with Philolaus himself, but on that one can hardly be positive.[2]

Most of the Presocratic world-systems proceeded from their ultimate *arche* to the infinite variety of nature by two stages. From the *arche*, or original 'everything together', there evolved first the primary opposites, or in later systems the four elements; and from them again the world of organic and other natural substances. For the Pythagoreans further stages were involved, since their *archai* went back even beyond number to the elements of number; but relatively to the physical world numbers were the *archai*, and, like their contemporaries, they derived from these *archai* first of all, through the medium of geometrical figures, the primary forms of matter, or physical elements. One at least of them tried to apply the numerical framework further, to organic creatures like men and horses. This was Eurytus, who according to our sources (which go back to Aristoxenus) was a Pythagorean from South Italy and a pupil of Philolaus. The last generation of Pythagoreans, including Echecrates to whom in Plato's dialogue Phaedo recounts the last hours of Socrates, were said to have been disciples of these two.[3] Theophrastus learned of the theory of Eurytus from Plato's contemporary Archytas of Tarentum, who was presumably Aristotle's source also. In one of his numerous complaints about the Pythagoreans, Aristotle says (*Metaph.* 1092b8):

They do not even make it clear in what way numbers are the causes of substances and of existence, whether as boundaries, in the way that points are of magnitudes, and after the manner of Eurytus, who laid down which

[1] Cf. Plutarch's interpretation, *De E*, 390A.
[2] Some may even yet remain unconvinced that the whole thing was not an invention of Plato. Cornford seems to have wavered. See *Plato's Cosmology* (1937), 210, 'So far as we know, the assignment of these figures to the primary bodies is due to Plato and had not been anticipated by any earlier thinker', and *P. and P.* 15, n. 2, 'It is not impossible that the shapes of the regular solids may have been associated with the elements before Plato'.
[3] Iambl. *V.P.* 148, D.L. VIII, 46 (DK, 45, 1, 44 A 4).

number belongs to which thing—e.g. that this is the number of a man and that of a horse—by representing the forms of living things with pebbles (like those who reduce numbers to triangular and square figures) or....

Theophrastus makes a similar statement in his brief essay on *Metaphysics* (ed. Ross and Fobes, p. 13). When people have laid down a first principle or principles, he says, one might expect them to go on to explain all that follows from them, and not to proceed a certain way and then stop; 'for this betokens a competent and sensible man, to do what Archytas once said Eurytus did by arranging certain pebbles: he said (according to Archytas) that this is the number of man, this of horse, and this of something else'.

This curious procedure is explained in more detail (though scarcely made less curious) in pseudo-Alexander's comment on the passage of Aristotle just quoted (DK, 45, 3):

Assume for the sake of argument that the number of man is 250 and of plant 360. Having put this forward he would take 250 pebbles, some black, others red, and in general of a great variety of colours. Then he coated the wall with whitewash and, having made a shaded drawing[1] of a man or a plant, he stuck pebbles in it, some in the face, others in the hands, and others in other parts. Thus he finished off the sketched-in representation of a man with pebbles equal in number to the units which in his view defined a man.

As a pupil of Philolaus, Eurytus must have been living and working about the end of the fifth century. He seems to have attempted an extension to natural species of the particular Pythagorean doctrine which explained geometrical figures numerically by equating the line with 2, triangle with 3 and pyramid with 4 because these are the minimum number of points required to define their structure. The projection of this doctrine into the physical world by the construction of the physical elements out of regular solids would encourage the belief that a simple counting of boundary-points could explain organic nature also. Hence his demonstration of the 'number of man' by the minimum number of points necessary to ensure that the surfaces formed by joining them would represent a man and nothing else. Admittedly

---

[1] Usage shows that σκιαγραφία was a method of drawing which at a distance produced the illusion of solid reality, but when looked at close up was unintelligible. It was occasionally used for an outline-drawing, but that is much the less likely meaning here.

this is a slightly less childish procedure than that of which he has sometimes been accused, namely drawing pictures with pebbles and claiming
that thereby he was determining the number of unit-atoms that they
contained. That this was not the way he worked is proved by Aristotle's
association of him with those who treat numbers as boundaries (ὅροι).[1]
At the same time, the arbitrary and subjective nature of the method
(even granted the use of different-coloured pebbles) shows the *naïveté*
of which a Pythagorean was capable, even in the late fifth or early
fourth century, when it came to applying his mathematical explanations
to the nature of the physical world.

Aristotle very seldom mentions an individual Pythagorean by name,
which suggests that Eurytus's demonstration of how 'things' could be
numbers was peculiar to him. Immediately after it he mentions an
alternative explanation, that the differences between qualities like white,
sweet and hot are attributable to different ratios of numbers. He
illustrates this in the careless manner with which he is often content
when these, to him, rather ridiculous beliefs are in question: 'The
essence of flesh or bone is number in this way: three parts of fire to
two of earth.'[2] For Pythagoreans the essential difference between
different kinds of body lay in the *harmonia* or *logos* in which the elements were blended. The elements themselves were put together from
mathematically defined figures, and so 'the whole universe is a *harmonia* and a number'. This is how the *limit* is composed which makes it
a *cosmos* and so *good*, and in so far as the elements are *not* mixed in
mathematical proportion we have a residue of chaos, evil, ugliness, ill-
health and so forth. It is a view of the world of which the best extant
exposition is Plato's *Timaeus*. We need not concern ourselves with the
objections felt by Aristotle to such a way of looking at things—that
number and ratio are not the same thing, that everything could turn

---

[1] The interpretation given here agrees with that of J. E. Raven. See KR, 315. That those of
whom Aristotle is speaking did indeed think in this way he makes clearer elsewhere. See *Metaph.*
1028b16 and 1090b5 (quoted above, p. 259).
[2] So Ross. Jaeger's version of the text is οἷον σαρκὸς ἢ ὀστοῦ ἀριθμός· ἡ δ' οὐσία οὕτω, τρία
πυρὸς γῆς δὲ δύο, which I find difficult to translate. Whether the ratio mentioned is that for flesh
or bone Aristotle does not deign to make clear, but since Empedocles is nowadays often brought
in at this point, it should be noted that the formula which he gives for bone is not this, but 4 of
fire to 2 each of earth and water. (See fr. 96.)

into everything else,[1] that the good in a mixture has nothing to do with its being in a strict arithmetical or geometrical proportion: 'honey-water is no more wholesome if mixed in a proportion of three times three, in fact it is better if it is in no particular ratio but well diluted'. These only help us to form an opinion of what the doctrine is likely to have been. In essentials it is a view which was basic to Pythagoreanism from its beginnings, even if the correlation of elements with regular solids was a later refinement.

Of a Pythagorean cosmogony expressed in more physical terms there are some valuable hints in Aristotle, which can be supplemented to a certain extent from later writers. He has said (*Metaph.* 989b 34) that they 'speak of the generation of the universe, and pay close attention to the actual course of events', mistakenly confusing physical with abstract, numerical reality. Elsewhere he says a little more about this process.

The following passages are relevant:

(*a*) *Metaph.* 1091a12: 'It is absurd, too, or rather impossible, to suppose the generation of numbers, for they are eternal. Yet the question whether or not the Pythagoreans suppose it admits of no doubt. They say plainly that when the unit had been constructed—whether from planes or surfaces or seed or they cannot say what—the nearest parts of the infinite at once began to be drawn in and limited by the limit. However, since they are making a world and wish to be understood in a physical sense, we must examine them in that connexion and dismiss them from the present inquiry' [*sc.* which is concerned with abstract principles].

(*b*) *Phys.* 203a6: 'But [*sc.* in distinction from Plato] the Pythagoreans place the infinite among perceptible things—for they do not reckon number separate from these—and say that what is outside the heaven is infinite.'[2]

(*c*) *Metaph.* 1092a32: Here, in the course of considering, and rejecting, a number of ways in which numbers might be thought to be generated from prior principles, Aristotle says: 'Should we think of it as from seed? But nothing can emerge from that which is indivisible.'

(*d*) To the mentions of seed in two of the above passages may be added

---

[1] Raven suggests (*P. and E.* 162) that the mutual transformation of the elements may in fact have been already a feature of Pythagorean theory. It is ascribed to it by Alexander Polyhistor in terms which some have thought to smack of Stoicism: τὰ στοιχεῖα...ἃ μεταβάλλειν καὶ τρέπεσθαι δι' ὅλου (D.L. VIII, 25).

[2] Or 'that the infinite is what is beyond the heaven'. τὸ before ἄπειρον F, Simpl.; retained by Carteron and Wicksteed and Cornford.

Theon of Smyrna, p. 97 Hiller. Here in his list of different interpretations of the Pythagorean tetractys Theon says: 'The sixth tetractys is that of growing things. The seed is analogous to a unit and a point, growth in length to 2 and a line, in breadth to 3 and a surface, in thickness to 4 and a solid.'

(*e*) Aristotle, *Phys.* 213b22 (during a general discussion of the opinions of his predecessors on the subject of void): 'The Pythagoreans also said that void exists, and that it enters the universe from the infinite breath, the universe being supposed to breathe in the actual void,[1] which keeps different kinds of things apart; for they define void as that which separates and divides things that are next to each other. This happens first in numbers; the void divides their nature.'

(*f*) Simplicius in his commentary paraphrases the passage of the *Physics* thus (651.26): 'They said that the void enters the cosmos as if it breathed in a sort of breath from that which lies outside.'

(*g*) In illustration of the same passage Stobaeus quotes from Aristotle's own lost treatise on Pythagoreanism (Stob. *Ecl.* I, 18, 1c (DK, I, 460, 3)): 'In the first book on the philosophy of Pythagoras he writes that the universe is unique, and that from the infinite it draws in time, breath, and void which distinguishes the places of separate things' (Ar. fr. 201 Rose).

(*h*) Aët. II, 9, 1 (*Dox.* 338): 'The followers of Pythagoras say that outside the cosmos there is void, into which and out of which the cosmos breathes.'

The prime elements of the world are numbers. These, as we know, are themselves constituted of prior elements—limit and unlimited, odd and even—but from the point of view of cosmogony 'in the beginning was the One'. 'They suppose their monads to have magnitude,' Aristotle grumbles elsewhere (*Metaph.* 1080b19), 'but how the first unit with magnitude was constructed they seem at a loss to explain.' Their accounts did not satisfy him, but he is not likely to have invented those that he mentions and dismisses. On one suggestion it was formed of planes, in which case it must have been a solid, at least as complex as a pyramid. On Pythagorean principles this might be expected to be the number 4, not 1, and Theon may have been more correct in equating it with the point. Aristotle is obviously speaking carelessly, but the Pythagoreans themselves were highly arbitrary and inconsistent in their equation of entities with particular numbers.[2] At some

---

[1] I follow Ross in retaining the MS. reading πνεύματος. Diels's πνεῦμά τε and other emendations seem unnecessary, as well as having no authority (for the '*fort.* E' of *apparatus critici* amounts to nothing; see Ross's note *ad loc.*).
[2] Cf. p. 304, below.

date no doubt the unit was equated with the simplest elemental solid, that is the pyramid or unit-atom of fire.

The next suggestion known to Aristotle is interesting. The first unit consisted of a seed, the seed of the world, like the *gonimon* attributed to Anaximander. What follows in passage (*a*) above, as well as what is said about number in (*b*) and elsewhere, shows that this is how the unit is to be understood, as both a number and the nucleus of the physical world. The old poetic analogy between the world and a living creature can be traced from the anthropomorphic Ouranos of Hesiod through the Presocratic philosophers down to the *Timaeus* of Plato, and lingers on in the animate stars of Aristotle. Here it is a reminder of the religious side of Pythagoreanism and their belief in the kinship of all life. The idea is well put by Sextus in a statement which, as Cornford and Delatte recognized, preserves the genuine spirit of early Pythagoreanism. 'The followers of Pythagoras and Empedocles, and most of the Italian philosophers, say that there is a certain community uniting us not only with each other and with the gods but even with the brute creation. There is in fact one breath pervading the whole cosmos like soul, and uniting us with them.'[1] Nothing could be more natural than that the world should grow from seed like any other living creature. The formation of a cosmos was seen as the imposition of Limit on the Unlimited, but equally as the impregnation of female matter by the form-giving sperm of the male. One may compare the inclusion of male with limit and female with unlimited in the table of opposites.[2]

How the unit-seed was sown in the Unlimited we know no more than Aristotle. Once there, it grew by drawing in the Unlimited outside it and assimilating it, that is, conforming it to limit and giving it numerical structure. The physical side of this process (which mathematically considered is the generation of the number-series) resembles breathing, the Unlimited being called *pneuma* as well as *kenon* (emptiness, void). As the first act of the newly-born universe, this has some resemblance to the account of animal birth given by the Pythagorean Philolaus.[3]

---

[1] *Math.* IX, 127. Cf. p. 200, n. 2, above.

[2] P. 245, above. See Cornford, *P. and P.* 19f. for the importance of the image of father, mother and seed in early philosophy.

[3] Preserved in the extracts from the medical doxography of Aristotle's pupil Menon which we have in the papyrus *Anon. Londinensis* (ed. Diels, Berlin, 1893, W. H. S. Jones, Cambridge, 1947). See col. 18.8ff.

Both seed and womb are hot, and so therefore is the whole body of the new-born creature. Hence 'immediately after birth the animal draws in breath from outside, which is cold, and then again discharges it like a debt'. This is done in order that the heat of the body may be cooled 'by the drawing-in of this imported breath'.[1] The parallel in all probability extends to the heat, the unit-seed of the world being imagined as fire (p. 281, below). In cosmogony too, therefore, one purpose of the breathing of the nascent cosmos may have been to cool this fire in order to generate the other elements; but of this the sources say nothing.

In detail, the cosmogony that we are now considering was probably more primitive than that of Philolaus, though in its beginnings his was no doubt sufficiently similar to exhibit the same parallel with his ideas on animal birth. Some features of the present accounts seem to belong more nearly to the beginning than the end of the fifth century, thus bringing us fairly close to the lifetime of Pythagoras. The failure of the earlier natural philosophers to distinguish empty space from some form of corporeal substance was one of the things which laid them open to devastating criticism from Parmenides, who argued that space or void is 'not what exists', i.e. does not exist, and that without it there can be no movement. The atomists were the first to distinguish explicitly between body and space, in fact Empedocles reiterated Parmenides's denial that empty space could exist (fr. 14); but the idea of 'infinite breath' surrounding the universe can hardly have been maintained after Empedocles had taught that air was only one of four elements all on the same level of existence, and not even the outermost of them (which was fire, fr. 38, 4). It is nearer to Anaximander and Anaximenes, both of whom believed in an unlimited basic stuff in which, by its differentiation at a certain point, the cosmos had its origin. For Anaximenes that stuff was air or breath, which not only surrounded the universe but gave it life. The originality of Pythagoras did not lie here, but in his mathematical ordering of the chaotic mass of unformed matter, which for him meant not so much the imposition of numerical organization *upon* it as the turning of it *into* numbers. Numbers (as we

---

[1] τῇ ἐπεισάκτῳ τοῦ πνεύματος ὁλκῇ. Cf. the language of Arist. fr. 201 ἐπεισάγεσθαι δ' ἐκ τοῦ ἀπείρου χρόνον καὶ πνοὴν καὶ τὸ κενόν and *Metaph.* 1091 a 17 εὐθὺς (as above '*immediately* after birth') τὰ ἔγγιστα τοῦ ἀπείρου ὅτι εἵλκετο...ὑπὸ τοῦ πέρατος.

see from Aristotle's next words in the *Physics*) are spatially extended, and the void keeps them apart. What keeps things apart must be *something*, and the only form of existence so far conceivable is bodily substance; hence it is thought of as a particularly tenuous form of matter. The unlimited, ubiquitous and animate air was of course a tacitly accepted inheritance rather than a concept expressly defended.

Aristotle in passage (*e*) above, and Simplicius in his comment on it (*f*), seem to say unmistakably that the Pythagoreans in question identified void, breath, and the Unlimited. This has been doubted, partly through uncritical acceptance of a modern alteration in Aristotle's text and partly on the ground that it would be inconsistent with the quotation from Aristotle's lost treatise (passage *g*).[1] Linguistically there is no difficulty. The repeated καί in the Greek can serve to join different descriptions of the same thing. But can we really say not only that void and breath are identified but that both are identified with time? Yes, for that too (or strictly speaking the raw material of time) was to a Pythagorean only another aspect of the Unlimited. As physical matter, it was that on which the nascent cosmos fed and by which it grew; as space, or extension, it was that which could submit to the imposition of mathematical form; but it had also a temporal aspect, as anything *apeiron* had. Until the middle of the fifth century the different senses of this word 'unlimited' or 'endless' were not distinguished, and the Pythagoreans would not be the first to distinguish them. As mere duration also, or chaotic movement, it was waiting to be taken into the cosmos and limited, that is divided up into the nights, days, months and years which in Greek eyes alone deserved the name of *chronos* (time), and which were unimaginable without the ordered and recurrent motions of sun, moon and stars.[2]

---

[1] Cf. Raven, *P. and E.* 49: 'Nobody would venture to maintain that time, the relation of which to the unlimited was clearly the same as that of the void, was actually identified with it.' Admittedly Cornford's translation in *P. and P.* (p. 21, 'time and breath *or* the void') seems to take something for granted, but since Raven nowhere tackles the question of the Pythagorean conception of time, his abrupt denial also calls for justification.

It is interesting that Alcmaeon of Croton, who according to ancient tradition had connexion with the Pythagoreans and in any case was a contemporary and fellow-citizen of the earlier among them, identified κενόν with ἀήρ in his explanation of hearing. (Beare, *Gk. Theories of Elem. Cognition*, 93f.)

[2] Since this is perhaps an unfamiliar idea, I have dealt with it more fully in an appendix, pp. 336 ff., below.

The Breathing Universe: Eternal Recurrence

It is evident (and passages still to be considered will confirm it) that the growth of the cosmos proceeded from the centre outwards. We also find, as we go on from cosmogony to cosmology, or the structure of the completed universe, that for the Pythagoreans the centre was occupied by fire. The unit-seed, then, physically considered, was of the nature of fire, and we can see what lay behind the brief doxographic statement in Aëtius that 'Pythagoras derived the world from fire and the fifth element'. The active or formative element was the fiery unit;[1] the living material on which it fed was identified by the Pythagoreans with air or breath, but was in fact that substance embracing or cradling the world (τὸ περιέχον) in which most of the Presocratics believed, and which later cosmologists distinguished as a separate fifth element (pp. 271 f., above).

Once in being, the cosmos was in all probability believed to be ever-lasting. We have no direct statement of the fact, but Zeller was justified in inferring it from the doctrine of the exact repetition of history which is vouched for as Pythagorean by Eudemus, in a quotation from the third book of his *Physics* which Simplicius has preserved.[2] It is cited to illustrate the distinction between merely specific recurrence, as of one spring or summer after another, and the recurrence of actual individual events. The relevant sentence is: 'But if one may believe the Pythagoreans, that the same events will recur individually, and I shall be talking to you holding my stick as you sit here, and everything else will be as it is now, then it is reasonable to say that time repeats itself.' Porphyry also, in the brief list of dogmas which in his opinion may safely be referred back to Pythagoras himself (probably taken from Dicaearchus, see p. 186, above), cites the belief 'that past events repeat themselves periodically and nothing is new in an absolute sense'.

Taylor (*Comm. on Tim.* 87) went astray in connecting this with the theory, characteristic of the Ionians, of the alternate creation and dissolution of the world. Eudemus's illustration includes a reference to

---

[1] Cf. Simplicius's remark that according to the 'more genuine' Pythagorean doctrine fire was at the centre as a 'creative power' (δημιουργικὴν δύναμιν, *De Caelo*, 512.9ff., quoted below, p. 290). Further considerations are in Burnet, *EGP*, 109.

[2] ZN, I, 550, followed by Cornford, *P. and P.* 18. See Eud. *ap.* Simpl. *Phys.* 732.26 (fr. 88 Wehrli).

reincarnation, and in general the doctrine of the everlasting repetition of history (which is a common one in Greek thought) is linked with that of the indestructibility of the world.[1] The Pythagoreans were doubtless among those censured by Aristotle for believing that the world could have a beginning and yet be everlasting (*De Caelo*, 279b12), and their notion of a cyclical repetition of history would accommodate itself naturally to that of a Great or Perfect Year. This was the period (variously estimated in antiquity) required for the sun, moon and planets to reach again the same positions in relation to each other as they occupied at a given moment. Plato defines it in that most Pythagorean of his dialogues, the *Timaeus* (39D), and a version of it was attributed in later times to Philolaus.[2]

(d) Cosmology

The most remarkable feature of the Pythagorean cosmology recorded by Aristotle is that it displaced the earth from the centre of the universe and made it into a planet circling the centre like the others. This idea was unparalleled in pre-Platonic thought, and called for a bold leap of the scientific imagination which proved too great for Plato himself. It was not, however, an anticipation of the heliocentric theory, even if it be right to say with Burnet that 'the identification of the central fire with the sun was a detail in comparison' with setting the earth to revolve in an orbit. The centre of the whole system the Pythagoreans believed to be occupied by a 'fire' which we do not see because the side of the earth on which we live is turned away from it. The same system included, along with sun, moon and the other known planets, a 'counter-earth' invisible to us for the same reason. The relation of the sun, as a

---

[1] See Guthrie, *In the Beginning*, 63ff. This theory of *retour éternel* has been held in more modern times also. M. Capek in *J. Philos.* 1960, 289–96, writes of its appearance in Nietzsche, Poincaré and C. S. Pierce, and shows how it has only been put out of court by the most recent developments in physics.

[2] By Censorinus, DK, 44A22. But although we are told nothing of the basis on which it was calculated, this cannot have been a full Great Year as described above, since it consisted of a mere 59 years with 21 intercalary months. The Great Year of which Plato speaks, though variously estimated by ancient astronomers, was an affair of 10,000 years or more. There was also a cycle as brief as eight years, correlating the solar and lunar years only. See further p. 458, below, and Guthrie, *In the Beginning*, 64f. and 134, n. 2.

On the connexion of the Great Year with the exact repetition of events in sublunary history see B. L. van der Waerden, *Hermes*, 1952, 129ff.

heat- and light-giving body, to the central fire is not explained by Aristotle in his extant works, but according to later sources it was a case of reflexion like that of the moon's light from the sun.

That is the system in outline. I shall take first the passages of simple description, and afterwards (p. 287) consider what Aristotle and others have to say about the reasons which led these men to it and any other questions to which it may give rise.

(*a*) Aristotle, *De Caelo*, 293a17: 'Concerning the position of the earth there is some divergence of opinion. Most of those who hold that the whole universe is finite say that it lies at the centre, but this is contradicted by the Italian school called Pythagoreans. These affirm that the centre is occupied by fire, and that the earth is one of the stars, and creates night and day as it travels in a circle about the centre. In addition they invent another earth, lying opposite our own, which they call by the name of 'counter-earth', not seeking accounts and explanations in conformity with the appearances, but trying by violence to bring the appearances into line with accounts and opinions of their own....'

(*b*) *De Caelo*, 293b15: 'This then is the opinion of some about the position of the earth, and on the question of its rest or motion there are conformable views. Here again all do not think alike. Those who deny that it lies at the centre suppose that it moves in a circle about the centre, and not the earth alone, but also the counter-earth, as we have already explained. Some even think it possible that there are a number of such bodies carried round the centre, invisible to us owing to the interposition of the earth. This serves them too as a reason why eclipses of the moon are more frequent than those of the sun, namely that it is blocked by each of these moving bodies, not only by the earth.'[1]

(*c*) Aët. II, 29, 4 (Stobaeus's version, DK, 58B36): (On eclipses of the moon.) 'Some of the Pythagoreans, according to the investigations of Aristotle and the statement of Philip of Opus, say that they occur by the interposition sometimes of the earth, sometimes of the counter-earth.'

(*d*) Simplicius in his commentary on *De Caelo* (511.25) quotes a slightly fuller account taken from Aristotle's own lost work on the Pythagoreans, but this adds little. The counter-earth, he says, is so called because

[1] Aristotle does not say who are the 'some' who accounted for the frequency of lunar eclipses by inventing a number of extra bodies circling round the centre, but, according to Simplicius (515.25), Alexander of Aphrodisias identified them as being among the Pythagoreans. We may assume that he knew, especially as the explanation seems to be linked with the idea of a planetary earth, which so far as we know was not held outside the school. Probably the information came from Aristotle's own work on the Pythagoreans.

it is opposite to this earth. It lies nearest the central fire, the earth taking the second position and the moon the third. The earth in its revolution round the centre creates night and day 'according to its relation to the sun'.

A number of later passages refer this system by name to the Pythagorean Philolaus.

(*e*) Aët. III, 11, 3 (DK, 44A17): 'Philolaus the Pythagorean says that the fire is at the centre, calling it the hearth of the universe; second comes the counter-earth, and third the inhabited earth which in its revolution remains opposite the counter-earth, wherefore the inhabitants of this earth do not see those of the other.'

(*f*) Aët. III, 13, 1–2 (DK, 44A21): 'Unlike other philosophers, who say that the earth is at rest, Philolaus the Pythagorean says that it revolves about the fire in an inclined circle like the sun and moon.'

(*g*) Aët. II, 7, 7 (On the order of the cosmos) (DK, 44A16): 'Philolaus teaches that there is fire in the middle lying about the centre, and he calls it the hearth of the whole, the home of Zeus, the mother of the gods, the altar and sustainer and measure of nature. Moreover there is another fire surrounding the universe at the uppermost limit. The middle is primary in the order of nature, and around it dance ten divine bodies: the heaven and the planets,[1] after them the sun, under it the moon, under that the earth, and under the earth the counter-earth. After all these comes the fire which occupies the position of hearth at the centre.

'The uppermost region of the surrounding heaven, where the elements are at their purest, he calls Olympus; *kosmos* he uses for the region below the circuit of Olympus, in which the five planets, the sun and the moon have their positions; and *ouranos* for the sublunary region beneath these and surrounding the earth, the home of change and becoming.'[2]

(*h*) Aët. II, 20, 12 (On the nature of the sun) (DK, 44A19): 'Philolaus the Pythagorean taught that the sun is like glass. It receives the reflexion of the fire in the cosmos and filters through to us both the light and the heat, so

---

[1] Unfortunately there is some difficulty about the reading of the manuscripts here. Diels (*Dox.* 337) prints οὐρανόν †τε πλανήτας, the reading of F, noting that C omits τε. He suggests that these at least slightly incorrect texts may conceal a reference to the five planets (τοὺς ε̅ πλανήτας) which are mentioned as such a little lower down, and notes that in Philolaus's terminology as given here οὐρανός did not refer to the outermost heaven of the fixed stars but to the sublunary world. On the other hand a reference here to the fixed stars seems necessary if the bodies mentioned are to total ten, and it seems preferable to assume (with Zeller) that the doxographer is using οὐρανός in the way natural to himself.

[2] The author of the *Epinomis*, when he writes εἴτε κόσμον εἴτε ὄλυμπον εἴτε οὐρανὸν ἐν ἡδονῇ τῷ λέγειν, λεγέτω (977B), seems to show himself aware that such distinctions had already been made, and to be protesting against their pedantry.

The Philolaic Cosmology

that in a sense there are two suns, the fiery substance in the cosmos and that which is reflected from the sun owing to its mirror-like character; unless one wishes to distinguish as a third the beam which is scattered in our direction by reflexion from the mirror.'[1]

(i) Aët. II, 30, 1 (DK, 44A20): 'Some of the Pythagoreans, among whom is Philolaus, explain the earth-like appearance of the moon by saying that it is inhabited like our own, with living creatures and plants that are bigger and fairer than ours. Indeed the animals on it are fifteen times as powerful and do not excrete, and the day is correspondingly long.'

The authorities so far cited present a single coherent system, which is either described anonymously or assigned to Philolaus. At the centre is the fire, and our earth moves in the second orbit from the centre, the nearest being traversed by the counter-earth. Next come moon, sun, the five planets, and lastly the sphere of the fixed stars which bounds the whole and is fiery like the centre. It is known that the moon's light is borrowed, and, with the notional fire to provide a central source of light, this derivative character is extended to the sun.[2] Eclipses of the moon are already attributed to the earth's shadow, though it is supposed that sometimes the cutting-off of its light may be due to the counter-earth or even (in the view of some) to one of several unrecognized planetary bodies. The moon is of similar substance to the earth, and has life on it of a larger, more powerful and more beautiful type.[3] This is

---

[1] I.e. using 'sun' in the sense of 'sunlight', as when we speak of 'sitting in the sun'. Greek idiom allowed this too. Burnet rightly says that this is not a part of the doctrine, but only a captious criticism on the part of Theophrastus from whom the report comes. So also ZN, note on pp. 371f.

[2] The phrases τὸ ἐν τῷ κόσμῳ πῦρ and τὸ ἐν τῷ οὐρανῷ πυρῶδες must both be intended to refer to the central fire (Burnet, *EGP*, 298, n. 1), in spite of the doubts felt by Heath (*Aristarchus*, 116f.). The use of διηθοῦντα in Aët. II, 20, 12, as well as ἰσοπτροειδές, may seem to imply that the sun is simultaneously being described as a kind of burning-glass through which rays pass and also as a reflecting mirror. What Philolaus himself said is scarcely recoverable with certainty, but if the sun collected the heat and light from the central fire, and not from the circumference of the heavens, I think that he can only have intended to imply reflexion.

[3] The statement attributed to Philolaus has a curiously exact parallel in that quoted by Athenaeus (II, 50, 57f., see DK, I, p. 404, n.) from Herodorus of Heraclea that 'the women of the moon are oviparous and those born there are fifteen times our size'. Philolaus and Herodorus must have been contemporaries, and it would be interesting to know if either learned this from the other or both were relying on an earlier source. There is no other certain evidence of so early a belief in an inhabited moon. According to D.L. II, 8 Anaxagoras said it had 'dwelling-places' (οἰκήσεις), but on this see Guthrie, *Orph. and Gk. Rel.* 247, n. 10.

The theory that the moon-animals are fifteen times as strong as those on earth was no doubt also connected in the minds of its advocates with the fifteen-day lunar day, on which see Heath, *Aristarchus*, 118f.

doubtless due to its position at the limit of the sublunary region. The placing of fire at the centre as well as the circumference is a Pythagorean innovation, but otherwise the system follows current philosophico-religious belief in teaching that the further 'up' one goes in the spherical universe, the 'purer', and hence nearer to the divine and more nearly immune from change and decay, are the substances which one finds.

The Milesians and Heraclitus had highly fanciful notions on the subject of eclipses of the moon. Isolated claims in late writers on behalf of Thales and Anaximenes cannot stand against the evidence that down to the time of Anaxagoras and Empedocles no one (with the doubtful exception of their near-contemporary Parmenides) knew that it was lit by the sun. This seems to have been a discovery of Anaxagoras,[1] though he like the Pythagoreans whom we are considering retained the more primitive belief of Anaximenes (p. 134, above) in 'earthy bodies' revolving with the stars, seeing in it a possible part-cause of the moon's eclipses. The same truth was known to Empedocles (fr. 42), who also had a curious theory about the sun which may possibly have assisted the Pythagoreans in forming their own (Aët. II, 20, 13, DK, A 56; cf. A 30). Unfortunately we do not have it in an actual quotation from his poem, and some points in the account are obscure; but he said that there were two suns, because the sun that we know is the reflexion of fire filling the other hemisphere of the universe. Though not identical with the Pythagorean, this theory makes the points that there may be said to be two suns and that our own has its light and heat by reflexion. It is the more bizarre, which suggests that the Pythagoreans adapted it rather than the other way round, though there can be no certainty about this.

All this amounts to sufficient evidence that the cosmology attributed by Aristotle to the Pythagoreans, and by later authorities to Philolaus in particular, was evolved by philosophers who were already acquainted with the work of Anaxagoras and Empedocles, that is, in the latter half of the fifth century. It can well be a part of the same scheme which related the structure of the physical elements to the regular mathe-

[1] Admittedly it is a question of balancing evidence, but Plato, *Crat.* 409A may be taken as decisive. Cf. Heath, *Aristarchus*, 78 f., 75 f.

286

matical solids, and there is no reason why the whole should not have been the work of Philolaus himself.[1]

What are likely to have been the motives and arguments which led to the adoption of so remarkable a scheme? We turn again to the authorities. Some of the following passages are direct continuations of descriptive extracts already cited.

(*a*) Aristotle, *De Caelo*, 293 b 1: 'The Pythagoreans make a further point. Because the most important part of the universe—which is the centre—ought more than any to be guarded, they call the fire which occupies this place the Guardroom of Zeus.'

Aristotle makes fun of this idea, pointing out that the mathematical centre of anything is not necessarily the most important part (line 8):

'For this reason there is no need for them to be alarmed about the universe, nor to call in a guard for its mathematical centre; they ought rather to consider what sort of thing the true centre is, and what is its natural place.'

(*b*) Simpl. *De Caelo* 512.12 (on the above passage of Aristotle): 'Some [*sc.* of the Pythagoreans] call the fire the Tower of Zeus, as Aristotle says in his work on the Pythagoreans, others the Guardroom of Zeus as here, and others the Throne of Zeus.'

Aristotle, *Metaph.* 986 a 3 (after the statement that the Pythagoreans supposed the elements of number to be the elements of everything, and the whole universe to be a *harmonia* and a number):

(*c*) Any agreements that they found between number and harmony on the one hand, and on the other the changes and divisions of the universe and the whole order of nature, these they collected and applied; and if something was missing, they insisted on making their system coherent. For instance,

---

[1] Van der Waerden (*Astron. d. Pyth.* 53 ff.) would have it that the 'Philolaic' system is actually post-Platonic. He argues (*a*) that to conceive of the revolution of the heavens as only apparent ('Der Fixsternhimmel steht nämlich nahezu still') is 'a very bold idea' which could only have ensued upon an advanced and carefully elaborated geocentric astronomy on the lines of the *Timaeus*; (*b*) that in the *Phaedo* Plato portrays Philolaus as a 'wandering prophet', not an astronomer, and one who did not make his meaning clear (the implication is rather that Simmias and Cebes were not his brightest pupils, and there is no reason why he should not have combined, like Pythagoras, astronomical and mathematical genius with mystical beliefs about the soul. These, not astronomy, happen to be the subject of the *Phaedo* passage); (*c*) that the fragments of Philolaus (which may or may not be genuine) indicate a second-rate and muddled mind. None of these arguments compels us to deny the possibility that Philolaus may have hit upon a brilliant and audacious idea, and his motives show just the mixture of intellectual acumen and religious mysticism which one would expect of a Pythagorean.

they regarded the decad as something perfect, and as embracing the whole nature of number, whence they assert that the moving heavenly bodies are also ten; and since there are only nine to be seen, they invent the counter-earth as a tenth.

(*d*) Alexander on this passage (p. 40 Hayduck) says: 'Because they thought the decad the perfect number, but the phenomena showed them that the revolving spheres were nine (seven for the planets, eighth the sphere of the fixed stars, and ninth the earth, which they believed to travel in a circle also round a stationary hearth, which according to them is fire), they added in their own doctrine what they called the counter-earth, which they supposed to be situated opposite the earth and for that reason to be invisible to its inhabitants. He [Aristotle] goes into this in more detail in the *De Caelo* and in his work on the Pythagoreans.'

Of this criticism, that the counter-earth was invented in order to bring the number of revolving bodies up to ten, Burnet says that it is 'a mere sally, and Aristotle really knew better', and Heath was of the same opinion. The explanation of eclipses, they say, was the true reason. If, however, our account of Pythagoreanism up to this point has been even remotely correct, it has shown that in the minds of Pythagoras and his followers the preservation of mathematical *harmonia* must always take the first place.[1] Nor must it be forgotten that their science was pursued with a religious aim, to discover the perfect *kosmos* of the world in order to reproduce it in one's own soul. This is borne out by the religious titles lavished on the central fire, and leads to the conclusion that all the arguments with which the Pythagoreans are credited did in fact carry weight with them. The reasons, then, for the cosmological system which posited a central fire, a planetary earth, and a counter-earth were threefold: (1) the number of revolving bodies must show forth the perfection of the decad; (2) fire was regarded with religious awe and had therefore to be assigned the central place, where it was honoured with such titles as Throne of Zeus, etc.; (3) the system could be supported by an appeal to phenomena in that it could be said to afford the explanation of eclipses.

The fact that their ultimate motives were religious does not detract

[1] We may remind ourselves that prominent among the meanings of *harmonia* was 'octave', that the octave for the Pythagoreans was constructed out of the first four integers, whose sum is ten, and that the decad (in the form of the tetractys) thereby acquired supreme significance as a religious symbol.

from the scientific character of much of their thought. For instance they tried to answer the objection that, if the earth were displaced from the centre, the phenomena of the revolving heavens as we see them could not in fact be accounted for. This is attested by their critic Aristotle himself, in the continuation of a passage of the *De Caelo* already quoted (p. 283, above), at 293 b 25:

Since the earth's surface is not in any case the centre, but distant by its whole hemisphere [i.e. radius] from the centre, they do not feel any difficulty in supposing that the phenomena are the same although we do not occupy the centre as they would be if the earth were in the middle. For even on the current view there is nothing to show that we are distant from the centre by half the earth's diameter.

We have seen that the 'Philolaic' world-system could not well have been evolved before the time of Empedocles, and is likely to have been due to Philolaus himself. It may be asked, are there traces in our authorities of an earlier scheme which may have been that of Pythagoras or his immediate followers? One would naturally expect such a scheme to be geocentric, and in the 'Pythagorean notebooks' summarized by Alexander Polyhistor we read:[1]

And [the Pythagoreans say] that there arises from them [*sc.* the four elements] a living, intelligent, spherical cosmos, containing the earth at the centre, spherical like itself and inhabited; and that there are antipodeans who call 'up' what we call 'down'.

The features of Alexander's account are difficult to date, but we may assume that the geocentric system originated earlier than that which made the earth a planet, not necessarily because to our own ideas it is 'more primitive' or 'less sophisticated' (that might be a dangerous criterion), but rather because this is in line with what we know of the history of early Greek thought. For Anaximander the earth was certainly at rest in the centre of a spherical universe, and neither Thales nor Anaximenes, Heraclitus, Parmenides nor Empedocles can be supposed to have believed in a planetary earth. A reading of Aristotle's *De Caelo*, book II, chapter 13 leaves no doubt that a geocentric universe was universally believed in until the Philolaic system was promulgated.

---

[1] D.L. VIII, 25. For these ὑπομνήματα see p. 201, n. 3, above.

This does not of course imply that the Philolaic system replaced the geocentric, even within Pythagoreanism. The notion of a planetary earth was a short-lived aberration, and firmly associated in tradition with the name of Philolaus.[1] (Aristotle's own reluctance to mention a name accords with an idiosyncrasy which may be observed elsewhere in his works.) Eudoxus, Heraclides Ponticus, and Aristotle himself placed the earth firmly back in the centre, from which it was not moved again until Aristarchus suggested the heliocentric theory. No doubt, then, Alexander refers to a Pythagorean system which was still current in the fourth century.

There is no other direct statement of a geocentric Pythagorean view, but certain passages have plausibly been taken to refer to it. Simplicius, after his own explanation of the Aristotelian text describing the revolution of the earth about a central fire, goes on like this (*De Caelo* 512.9):

This then is Aristotle's account of the Pythagorean view, but the more genuine adherents of the school mean by fire at the centre the creative power which animates the whole earth from the centre and warms that part of it which has grown cold. Hence some call it the Tower of Zeus, as Aristotle says in his work on the Pythagoreans, others the Guardroom of Zeus as here, and others the Throne of Zeus. They called[2] the earth a star as being itself an instrument of time, for it is the cause of day and night. Day it creates by being lit up on the side which is turned towards the sun, and night through the cone of its shadow. 'Counter-earth' was the name given by the Pythagoreans to the moon (as also 'heavenly earth'), both because it blocks the sun's light, which is a peculiarity of earth, and because it marks the limit of the heavenly regions as does earth of the sublunary.

Simplicius then, who is deriving at least part of his information from Aristotle's lost work, knows of a 'more genuine' type of Pythagoreans who do not believe in the system just described by Aristotle in *De Caelo*. Yet they still spoke of 'fire at the centre', and the only reasonable interpretation of the following words is that they meant a core of fire at the heart of an earth which is itself (save for having this fiery centre) in the middle of the cosmos. Doubtless these were 'more genuine' because their view remained closer to that of Pythagoras

---

[1] For the doubtful exception of the shadowy Hicetas of Syracuse see pp. 326 ff., below.

[2] The change of tense (cf. 'mean' above) is Simplicius's.

himself.[1] It is of course only what we should expect that both types share the same religious terminology. Similarly Proclus (*In Tim.* III, 141, 11 Diehl; 143, 26), after mentioning that the Pythagoreans called the centre of the cosmos 'the Tower of Zeus', goes on to say that this Tower of Zeus is inside the earth. The fact that they called the earth a star, and the phrase with which they defended this appellation, suggest that they were post-Philolaic. *Astron* seems to be used polemically. ('You may call the earth *astron* if you like, but without supposing it to be one of the revolving bodies.') The phrase 'instrument of time', and the statement that in spite of being central and stationary it may be said to create day and night, recall Plato's language in the *Timaeus* (41 E 5, 40 B–C) too strongly for coincidence; but we hardly have the evidence to decide whether Plato was here (as in so much) following the Pythagoreans, or the Pythagoreans in question were already acquainted with the *Timaeus*, or, finally, Simplicius was confusing the Pythagoreans and Plato or regarding the *Timaeus* as a legitimate source of Pythagorean doctrine.

Most expositors slide rather quickly over the application of the term 'counter-earth' to the moon. It seems incredible that this was its original reference, and it is best explained on the same lines as the designation of the earth as a star: these more conservative members of the school took the words out of the mouth of Philolaus (if it was he), but applied them to the older scheme.

The belief that there is fire in the interior of the earth is a natural inference from observation of volcanos and hot springs. The Greeks had also a more potent reason for it. It was commonly believed among them that all life, animal and human as well as vegetable, originated from within the earth. Going back to the immemorial worship of earth as the Great Mother, this belief survived to be rationalized and clothed in scientific terms by the philosophers.[2] At the same time the essential elements of life were universally held to be heat and moisture, the former the active agent which animates a passive, moist material. In one form of the theory (exemplified by Anaximander) the only source

---

[1] Two other examples of γνήσιος in this sense: Xenocrates is called ὁ γνησιώτατος τῶν Πλάτωνος ἀκροατῶν by Simplicius (*Phys.* 1165.34), whereas Diogenes Laertius accords this place to Aristotle in the words ὁ γνησιώτατος τῶν Πλάτωνος μαθητῶν (v, 1).

[2] For a full treatment see Guthrie, *In the Beginning*, chh. 1 and 2.

of heat mentioned is the sun, but both myth and philosophy preserve traces of the idea that the heat as well as the moisture came from inside the earth, where the first living creatures were formed and whence they thrust themselves to the light. This was the teaching of Empedocles, though for him, in the period of Strife's ascendancy which he is describing, the fire within the earth must be thought of as trapped there, and striving to join its like at the periphery. So fr. 62:

Come now, hear how fire, as it was separated, raised up the darkling shoots of miserable men and women. Not erring nor ignorant is the tale. Whole-natured forms first arose from the earth, having a portion both of water and of heat. These the fire sent up, wishing to come to its like.

That is, under the influence of Strife, which represents the tendency of like to join its like and shun foreign substances, the heat in the earth was drawn towards the main mass at the circumference of the cosmos.

Empedocles speaks again of a fiery core to the earth in fr. 52: 'Many a fire burns beneath the earth' (cf. A68). He was a Western philosopher whose thought, especially on its religious side, had much in common with Pythagoreanism, and in his native Sicily both volcanic eruptions and hot springs were familiar phenomena. Plato, who in the *Phaedo* (111D) asserts likewise that there are 'great rivers of fire' as well as liquid mud within the earth, explicitly compares this state of things with Sicilian Etna.

This arrangement of a central earth with fiery core is by no means inconsistent with the generation of the cosmos from a fiery seed or unit in the centre of an undefined mass of air or vapour. Moreover the generative power of the fiery unit-seed of the Pythagoreans links naturally, in the geocentric scheme, with the universal belief in the generative power of the earth, in which the activating principle was always heat. Early Pythagorean cosmogony and cosmology can perhaps be dimly seen united in an admittedly superficial and confused account of the late mathematical writer Anatolius:[1]

Moreover the Pythagoreans said that at the centre of the four elements there lies a fiery monadic cube. . . . In this respect the followers of Empedocles and Parmenides and indeed most of the ancient sages appear to follow the Py-

---

[1] Third century A.D. From his treatise *On the Numbers up to Ten*, ed. Heiberg (1900), p. 30.

thagoreans, for they say that the unitary substance is situated in the middle like a hearth and maintains the same position on account of its even balance. Euripides, too, like the disciple of Anaxagoras which he had become, refers to the earth in these terms: 'Wise mortals deem thee hearth.'

The 'fiery monadic cube'[1] suggests the generative fiery unit, and by the comparison with Empedocles and Parmenides, whose cosmologies were certainly geocentric, the author is presumably conveying that all alike gave a fiery interior to the earth. The unmetrical misquotation from Euripides[2] is only one of a number of instances of the name 'Hearth' (*Hestia*) applied to the earth in Greek literature, which perhaps attests the same belief in fire at its centre, just as we are told that Philolaus, having displaced the earth from the centre of the cosmos, transferred the name to the central fire. Sophocles gave earth that title in his *Triptolemus*, and it may be taken as certain that the goddess Hestia who in Plato's *Phaedrus* 'abides alone in the gods' dwelling-place', while the other gods circle the heavens, personifies the central and stationary earth.[3] Plutarch speaks of Cleanthes the Stoic asserting that Aristarchus deserved punishment because with his heliocentric theory he 'displaced the hearth of the universe'.

The evidence collected in the last few pages suffices to show (*a*) that, besides the Philolaic cosmos, there was also in vogue among the Pythagoreans a geocentric scheme in which the earth was believed to have a core of fire, (*b*) that this belief agreed with one already current in popular thought and shared by certain other philosophers.

A question that naturally arises at this point is that of the shape of the earth in relation to the history of Pythagoreanism. The date of the discovery of its sphericity has been the subject of much discussion, which cannot be fully considered at the moment, but the soundest

[1] Why a cube, it would be hard to say. There is no evidence that the Pythagoreans equated fire with any other figure than the tetrahedron, and for the atomists an atom of fire was spherical. The idea may have originated with someone who held the fluxion theory of the generation of solids, according to which the first, or simplest, solid was not a tetrahedron but a cube.

[2] ἑστίαν δέ σ' οἱ σοφοὶ βροτῶν ὀνομάζουσιν. The correct version is given by Macrobius (Eur. fr. 944 N.):
καὶ Γαῖα μῆτερ· ἑστίαν δέ σ' οἱ σοφοὶ
βροτῶν καλοῦσιν ἡμένην ἐν αἰθέρι.

[3] Soph. fr. 558 N. (615 Pearson), Plato, *Phaedrus*, 247A. Cf. Hackforth, *Plato's Phaedrus*, 73.

conclusion seems to be that it was not put forward until the late fifth century.[1] There are certainly no good grounds for attributing it to Pythagoras himself. For this the only evidence is (*a*) a doubtful passage of Diogenes Laertius (VIII, 48, quoting Favorinus, a polymath of the second century A.D.) which uses the ambiguous word 'round' (στρογγύλην) and in the same sentence quotes Theophrastus as giving the credit not to Pythagoras but to Parmenides; and (*b*) a statement in Aëtius (III, 14, 1, *Dox*. 378) which credits Pythagoras with having divided the earth into five zones on the analogy of the sky. But even if these writers categorically attributed the discovery to Pythagoras, that would mean no more than that it was known as a Pythagorean tenet. (According to Diogenes, even Anaximander said the earth was spherical, which must be false; cf. the evidence on p. 98, above.) It is probable, though not certain, that Parmenides and Empedocles believed the earth to be flat,[2] as did Diogenes of Apollonia, Anaxagoras, and Democritus. The retention of this view by the last-named (vouched for by Aristotle, *De Caelo*, 294b14) is especially significant, for he was one of the scientific giants of the second half of the fifth century. Strictly speaking, he seems to have taught that the earth was a disc with a concave surface (Aët. III, 10, 5, DK, A94), presumably in an attempt to explain the observable changes in the horizon as one's own position changes (which finally of course became a proof of its sphericity; see Aristotle, *De Caelo*, 297b30ff.). This reason is explicitly attested for his approximate contemporary Archelaus (DK, 60A4), and the view of the earth as a 'kneading-trough' gets a contemptuous mention from Plato (*Phaedo*, 99B). Aristotle provides evidence that the flat-earth theory still had lively defenders in his own time (see *De Caelo*, 293b33ff.).

Thus the balance of the evidence leads us to believe that the Pythagoreans of whom Aristotle and Alexander Polyhistor spoke, who taught that the earth is spherical, belonged to the last two generations of the school, in the late fifth and early fourth centuries. This points

---

[1] Herodotus mentions tales of men who sleep for six months and of Phoenicians who circumnavigated Africa and found the sun on their right while sailing westward. Both stories he dismisses as incredible (Hdt. IV, 25 and 42). Dreyer (*Planetary Systems*, 39) says they show that already 'some people must have been able to perceive the consequences of the earth being a sphere'; but all they show is that these phenomena were observed. It does not follow that they were correctly explained.

[2] Against Burnet, *EGP*, 190 see Morrison, *JHS*, 1955, 64, and Heidel, *AJP*, 1940, 14f.

particularly to Philolaus, the probable author of the planetary theory of the earth and counter-earth. The earliest mention of a spherical earth in extant literature is in the *Phaedo* of Plato.[1] Plato however, like the Pythagoreans of whom Alexander spoke, puts it in the centre of the cosmos.

The cosmology of the Pythagoreans includes of course their extraordinary theory of the 'harmony of the spheres', which so caught the fancy of later generations in the ancient world and at the Renaissance, not least among the English Elizabethan writers. Its details varied in accordance with changing theories of planetary motions—*quae* (to quote Censorinus) *si vellem in unum librum separatim congerere, tamen in angustiis versarer*.[2] But the idea itself is of immense importance as perhaps the supreme example of the Pythagorean attempt to explain the whole vast cosmic plan by reference to the basic discovery of the founder: the all-pervading influence of, and intimate connexion between, the laws of mathematics and of music. As Plato approvingly expressed it: 'Just as our eyes are made for astronomy, so are our ears for harmonious motion, and these two sciences are sisters, as the Pythagoreans say and we agree.'

Plato's agreement went so far that he incorporated the melody of the stars in his own myth at the end of the *Republic*, and that is the first exposition of it in extant Greek literature.[3] Since he cannot touch such a theme without adorning it, he adds, as a picturesque embroidery to his myth, that the sounds are produced not by the moving stars themselves, but by the voice of a Siren stationed on the circle of each; but a clear and critical account is given by Aristotle in *De Caelo* (290b12ff. That the theory is Pythagorean he does not explicitly state at this point, but only later when he has passed to criticism of it and speaks, at

[1] 110B ὥσπερ αἱ δωδεκάσκυτοι σφαῖραι. Mr J. S. Morrison (*Phronesis*, 1959, 101 ff.) argues that even here the earth is not described as spherical. I am not convinced. In particular it seems unlikely that in the comparison with the balls we are meant to think only of their colours to the exclusion of their shape.
[2] Readers interested in the finer points of Greek astronomy may be referred to the still standard work of Heath, *Aristarchus*, and to B. L. van der Waerden, *Die Astronomie der Pythagoreer*, 29–37. The speculations of G. Junge in *Class. et Medievalia*, 1947, 183ff. are best avoided.
[3] The suggestion of G. Junge (*Class. et Med.* 1958, 66) that the whole theory might have originated in Plato's mind assumes an incredible ignorance on the part of Aristotle, even if our other authorities are ignored.

291 a 8, of 'what puzzled the Pythagoreans and made them postulate a musical harmony for the moving bodies'):

It follows that the theory that music is produced by their movements [*sc.* the movements of the planets and the outer heaven], because the sounds they make are harmonious, although ingeniously and brilliantly formulated by its authors, does not contain the truth. It seems to some that bodies so great must inevitably produce a sound by their movement: even bodies on the earth do so, although they are neither so great in bulk nor moving at so high a speed, and as for the sun and moon, and the stars, so many in number and enormous in size,[1] all moving at a tremendous speed, it is incredible that they should fail to produce a noise of surpassing loudness. Taking this as their hypothesis, and also that the speeds of the stars, judged by their distances, are in the ratios of the musical consonances, they affirm that the sound of the stars as they revolve is concordant.

To meet the difficulty that none of us is aware of this sound, they account for it by saying that the sound is with us right from birth and has thus no contrasting silence to show it up; for voice and silence are perceived by contrast with each other, and so all mankind is undergoing an experience like that of a coppersmith, who becomes by long habit indifferent to the din around him.

Set beside this part of the comment of Alexander of Aphrodisias on the passage of the *Metaphysics* (985 b 32 ff.) in which Aristotle characterizes the Pythagoreans as having reduced all things to numbers or the elements of numbers, and described the whole universe as 'a *harmonia* and a number' (p. 39.24 Hayduck):

They said too that the whole universe is constructed according to a musical scale (this is what he means to indicate by the words 'and that the whole universe is a number'), because it is both composed of numbers and organized numerically and musically. For (i) the distances between the bodies revolving round the centre are mathematically proportionate; (ii) some move faster and some more slowly; (iii) the sound made by the slower bodies in their movement is lower in pitch, and that of the faster is higher; hence (iv) these separate notes, corresponding to the ratios of the distances, make the resultant sound concordant. Now number, they said, is the source of this harmony, and so they naturally posited number as the principle on which the heaven and the whole universe depended.

[1] Plato, or an immediate pupil, says in the *Epinomis* (983 A) that the sun is larger than the earth.

The Harmony of the Spheres

Apart from Aristotle's straightforward account and the imaginative adaptation of Plato, we have only descriptions from the Graeco-Roman period. Of these one is especially worth quoting, that of Cicero in the *Dream of Scipio*:[1]

I gazed in amazement at these wonders; but when I had recovered, I said: 'What means this great and sweet sound that fills my ears?' 'That', replied he, 'is a sound which, sundered by unequal intervals, that nevertheless are exactly marked off in due proportion, is produced by the movement and impulse of the orbs themselves, and, commingling high and low tones, causes varying harmonies in uniform degree; for such swift motions cannot be produced in silence, and nature ordains that the extremities sound low at one end, high at the other. Hence the course of the starry heaven at its highest, where the motion is exceedingly rapid, moves with a sharp, quick sound; while the moon in its course (which is the lowest of all) moves with a heavy sound; for earth, the ninth of these bodies, biding immovable in one place, ever holds fast in the centre of the universe.

Now these eight revolutions (whereof two possess identical powers)[2] form seven sounds, distinguished by their intervals; and this number seven is the bond of well-nigh all things. Learned men, imitating this with strings and with songs, have opened for themselves a way back to this region, even as others have done, who, thanks to outstanding genius, have all their lives devoted themselves to divine studies.'

Cicero goes on to give the Pythagorean explanation of why we do not hear this music, substituting for Aristotle's simile of the coppersmith that of people living their lives within sound of the cataracts of the Nile.[3]

Cicero affords a reminder of the overriding religious purpose of this

---

[1] Ch. v, trans. E. H. Blakeney. The others are conveniently collected (references and German translation) in van der Waerden, *Astronomie der Pyth.* 29–34. See also Heath, *Aristarchus*, 105–15, and T. Reinach in *REG*, 1900, 432ff.

[2] Mercury and Venus.

[3] It is curious that Shakespeare's explanation, that

> whilst this muddy vesture of decay
> Doth grossly close us in, we cannot hear it,

should manage to be so genuinely Pythagorean in sentiment, and yet, according to these authorities, not in fact the explanation which the Pythagoreans offered. But cf. Plut. *Qu. Conv.* 745 E ⟨τὰ δ' ὦτα τῶν⟩ μὲν πλείστων περιαλήλιπται καὶ καταπέπλασται σαρκίνοις ἐμφράγμασι καὶ πάθεσιν (to which my attention was drawn by Mr F. H. Sandbach).

It was a Pythagorean belief that Pythagoras himself, that semi-divine being, could hear the heavenly music. See Porph. *V.P.* 30 and Simpl. *De Caelo* 468.27 τοῖς Πυθαγορείοις...τὸν Πυθαγόραν ἱστοροῦσιν ἀκοῦσαί ποτε τῆς τοιαύτης ἁρμονίας.

mathematical–musical–cosmological synthesis. By understanding and in our own fashion reproducing it, we may 'open for ourselves a way back' to the divine.

Hippolytus, generally a good doxographical source in spite of his heresy-hunting, gives a simple statement of the doctrine (*Ref.* 1, 2, 2, *Dox.* p. 555): 'In this way Pythagoras showed the monad to be god, and having made a profound study of the nature of number he asserted that the cosmos sings and is harmoniously constructed, and he was the first to reduce the motion of the seven planets to rhythm and melody.'

The Pythagoreans, said Eudemus, were the first to investigate the positions of the planets relative to one another.[1] It is clear also that they believed the ratios of their relative distances to correspond to recognized musical intervals, and that according to the most commonly received form of the theory the intervals in question were those that made up a complete octave of the diatonic scale. This is the general burden of the post-Aristotelian evidence, in which the cosmos is most frequently compared to the seven-stringed lyre which had this compass, and as Zeller says in his long note on the doctrine,[2] by the 'ratios of the consonances' of which Aristotle himself speaks we can hardly understand anything else but these intervals. Although in the later sources variants occur which make the notes cover more than an octave, these, as Heath says (*op. cit.* 115), must have been later than Plato's time. In Plato himself there are eight circles,[3] each carrying a body or bodies which can be identified both from their descriptions and from the names supplied in the *Epinomis* as follows: moon, sun, Venus, Mercury, Mars, Jupiter, Saturn, fixed stars. The scheme is of course geocentric. Plato continues: 'The spindle turned on the knees of Necessity. Upon

---

[1] Simpl. *De Caelo* 471.5 τὴν τῆς θέσεως τάξιν. The sentence, in which the Pythagoreans are contrasted with Anaximander, is translated on p. 93, above.

[2] ZN, I, 538, n. 1. The cumulative effect of this late evidence can be gauged from this note, where it is conveniently summarized. To the Pythagoreans the word ἁρμονία itself meant 'octave'. Zeller (*ibid.* 463, n. 2) quotes Aristoxenus, *Mus.* II, 36 τῶν ἑπταχόρδων ἃ ἐκάλουν ἁρμονίας and Nicom. *Harm.* p. 252 Jan. οἱ παλαιότατοι... ἁρμονίαν μὲν καλοῦντες τὴν διὰ πασῶν. See further n. 1 on next page.

[3] Or spheres. Plato's description is not evidence on this point, since they have to be circles to conform to the purely mythical image of the composite whorl turned on the knees of Necessity. In the case of the fixed stars, at least, the circle must presumably symbolize a sphere. In fact they are the circular rims of a nest of hemispherical bowls, but only the rims are taken into account and κύκλοι is the word used.

each of its circles stood a Siren, who was carried round with its movement, uttering a single sound on one note, so that all the eight made up
the concords of a single scale.'[1]

To a modern mind the most pertinent question that arises over this
is one which, unfortunately, it is impossible to answer satisfactorily:
how could the Pythagoreans have supposed that all eight notes of an
octave sounding simultaneously would produce a concordant and
pleasing effect, *tantus et tam dulcis sonus* as Cicero calls it? The question
was raised by Martin in his *Études sur le Timée de Platon* as long ago as
1841, and it was useless for Burnet to pretend (*EGP*, 307, n. 1) that
'there is no force in Martin's observation that the sounding of all the
notes of an octave at once would not produce a harmony. There is no
question of harmony in the modern sense, but only of attunement
(ἁρμονία) to a perfect scale.' It may be true, as Burnet has said elsewhere (*Gr. Phil.* 1, 45), that 'when the Greeks called certain intervals
concordant (σύμφωνα) they were thinking primarily of notes sounded
in succession', and that 'the word "harmony" (ἁρμονία) means, in the
Greek language, first "tuning" and then "scale"'. Nevertheless in the
present instance it is obvious that (*a*) the notes *are* sounded simultaneously, since the heavenly bodies are all revolving all the time, and
(*b*) we are supposed to believe that the combined effect would be
musical and pleasant if we could hear it. Yet no explanation is offered,
nor is this particular objection raised by even the most unsympathetic
of ancient critics. It is true that classical Greek music was melodic,
not harmonic, and this in itself may have entailed the consequence that
they were not so alive as we should be to the effect of sounding as

[1] Late authorities frequently compare the Pythagorean cosmos to the heptachord or instrument of seven strings. This should take into account only the 'seven planets', omitting the sphere
of the fixed stars, yet some even retained the simile while increasing the number of singing bodies
to nine by giving a note to the earth. Others again criticized them for doing so. See e.g. Alexander 'of Aetolia' quoted and censured by Theo Smyrn. pp. 140f. Hiller. Yet he still kept
within the octave (τὸ πᾶν ἐννεάχορδον συνίστησιν, ἓξ μέντοι τόνους περιέχον). The allotting of
the same *vis* to two of the planets by Cicero seems to be a way of overcoming this difficulty.

The heptachord and octachord alike spanned an octave, but in the heptachord either the two
tetrachords of which it was composed were joined by a string common to both (συναφή), or,
where they were separated by a tone (διάζευξις), one of them was defective by one string. This
was the instrument in use in Terpander's time (seventh century), but the octachord was introduced by the early fifth century at latest, and was familiar to Plato and Aristotle, both of whom
obviously have it in mind in their exposition of the heavenly *harmonia*. The attempts to retain a
seven-stringed scheme were probably prompted by the ancient sacredness of the number seven.

chords what they were only accustomed to hear as a progression of single notes. In any case one can only conclude, with Zeller and Heath, that 'the Pythagoreans did not allow themselves to be disturbed in their fancies (*Dichtung*) by this consideration any more than by the other difficulties which confronted them, most of which are already raised by Aristotle'.[1]

It may be, however, that in its origin the theory was simpler, and that the manner of its growth helped to obscure for the followers of Pythagoras what seems to us such a serious difficulty. W. Kranz has argued with some cogency that the application of the rational musical intervals to the distances between the cosmic circles or spheres was due to Pythagoras himself.[2] With Anaximander's scheme before him, he transformed its equality of distances into a dynamic mathematical relationship. In this scheme only three orbits are in question, those of the moon, sun and stars, the planets not being distinguished in respect of their orbits from the fixed stars (p. 94, above). The intervals could therefore be identified with the three primary consonances, the octave (1:2), fifth (2:3), and fourth (3:4), which would be supposed to correspond to the distances from the earth of the three most anciently recognized orbits. The existence of such a scheme at some time is vouched for by Sextus when he says of the Pythagoreans:

This is how they imagine the bodies and the whole cosmos [*sc.* as made up out of points, lines, surfaces and solids]. They also say that the cosmos is arranged according to ratios of harmony: the fourth, which is epitrite, i.e. as 8 is to 6; the fifth, or one-and-a-half, as 9 to 6; and the diapason (octave), which is a double ratio, as 12 to 6.[3]

Because this is a scheme of only three intervals, in which the sphere of the fixed stars is not distinguished from the orbits of the planets as in fifth-century Pythagorean teaching, therefore (argues Kranz), it is a form of the doctrine which must go back to the sixth century.[4]

---

[1] ZN, I, 539, n. Cf. Heath, *Aristarchus*, 115.

[2] *Philologus*, 1938–9, 437f.   [3] *Pyrrh.* III, 155; also *Math.* I, 95.

[4] In essence this view was already put forward by Burnet, *EGP*, 110. Heath (*Aristarchus*, 107) contradicts it, maintaining that Pythagoras 'certainly distinguished the planets from the fixed stars' and that 'the original form of the theory of the "harmony of the spheres" no doubt had reference to the seven planets only'. One may at least query the word 'certainly'. Few things are certain about Pythagoras, and this is not one of them. Heath's only evidence appears to be Theo Smyrn. p. 150 Hiller (cf. his article on astronomy in the *OCD*, 110), but the words καθὰ πρῶτος ἐνόησε Πυθαγόρας in a writer of this date have little or no value.

The Harmony of the Spheres

This is a very probable suggestion. Not only was Pythagoras's discovery concerned with these three basic concords, which together made use of the first four integers forming the sacred tetractys, but in the seven-stringed lyre only these were marked by strings of fixed tuning. They were the stationary (ἑστῶτες) strings. The others were adjustable to the type of scale required and hence were called movable (κινούμενοι).[1] It is therefore highly likely that in the first attempt to fit his musico-mathematical discovery to the cosmic frame, Pythagoras himself should have had the 'concordant intervals' in mind, the simultaneous sounding of which is at least less obviously discordant to our ears than that of the seven or eight strings of a complete diapason.

Another thing of which we have no certain knowledge is how Pythagoras and his followers calculated the relative distances between the heavenly bodies. Plato, by allowing varying breadths to the rims of the whorls on Necessity's spindle, appears to be stating an order of magnitude governing the distances between the various heavenly bodies; but he offers no statement of actual ratios.[2] Some writers of Graeco-Roman date, for example Pliny and Censorinus, offer definite numerical schemes, which, however, obviously belong to a later epoch. Alexander of Aphrodisias, in continuation of the passage quoted on p. 296, above, seems to feel that he can do no more than offer a few figures by way of illustration: 'For *suppose* (φέρε εἰπεῖν) the distance of the sun from the earth was double that of the moon, that of Venus triple and that of Mercury quadruple, they assumed that for each of the others also there was an arithmetical ratio, and that the movement of the cosmos was harmonious.'

(e) Abstractions as numbers

To the Pythagoreans *everything* was an embodiment of number. They included what we should call abstractions like justice, mixture, opportunity,[3] and this led them into all sorts of difficulties which cannot

---

[1] Burnet, *Gr. Phil.* I, 46; *OCD*, 587.

[2] See *Rep.* 616E in Cornford's translation and the notes thereto; also Cornford's *Plato's Cosmology*, 79: 'Probably Plato intentionally left the meaning vague. He would not commit himself to any estimates that had actually been made on very insufficient data.'

[3] This is of course an inadequate translation of καιρός, but its exact meaning makes no difference here, and it may be allowed to stand as a more convenient term than, say, 'the right time'.

be said to have been counterbalanced by any advantages for the development of human thought. 'Unmethodical and capricious', said Zeller severely, and one must agree with Mr Raven when he writes (*P. and E.* 57): 'It is true that for a certain type of mind this number-symbolism has always had an attraction; but there is little to be learned, from the Pythagorean addiction to it, of the scientific system with which—to judge from Aristotle's criticisms—they somehow attempted to reconcile it.'

It was indeed a scientific blind alley, and not worth lengthy treatment; but if the interest of a historian of philosophy is not simply in the progress of scientific thought but in the human mind and its vagaries (and this book is written on that assumption), it will be worth while setting down some of the evidence and seeing what can be made of it.

Aristotle refers to this practice at several places in the *Metaphysics*. At 1093a1 he makes the general criticism that 'if everything must partake in number, many things will turn out to be the same'. Since 4 is equated both with the tetrahedron and with justice, there seems to be some substance in this objection, at least for a strictly rational mind. At 985b29 he says that for the Pythagoreans 'such-and-such a disposition of numbers was justice, another was soul and mind, another opportunity and so on'. At 1078b21 he is discussing how far his predecessors sought universal definitions: 'The Pythagoreans did in a few cases, the formula of which they linked with numbers, as when they asked what is opportunity or justice or marriage.' The *Magna Moralia* (probably the work of an early follower of Aristotle) states at 1182a11: 'Pythagoras was the first to treat of virtue, but erroneously; in reducing the virtues to numbers he made his researches irrelevant to their subject, for justice is *not* a square number.' To return to the *Metaphysics*, at 990a18 Aristotle has been criticizing the Pythagoreans by asking how numbers can be the causes of things and events in the universe and at the same time the constituents of the material cosmos. He then (l. 22) puts the question differently: how can numbers be opinion, opportunity, etc. and at the same time the substance of the material universe?

For the Pythagoreans, opinion and opportunity are located in a certain quarter, and injustice, separation [perhaps 'decision'], or mixture a little above or below. But they demonstrate this by saying that each of these is a number, and there happens to be already in this area a multitude of magnitudes so constructed (because these modifications of number belong to the several regions).[1] Is, then, the number which one must suppose to constitute each of these abstractions the same as the one which is in the physical universe, or a different one?

This passage suggests that the difficulties of the Pythagoreans arose in part from their inability to draw a clear distinction between abstract and concrete: to Aristotle their language suggested that they allotted the same number to (say) air and opinion without making it clear that they existed on quite different ontological planes, and even spoke of moral qualities as situated in space.

Aristotle has other matters to pursue, and wastes little time over what was to him a manifest absurdity: but his commentator Alexander of Aphrodisias gives a further glimpse into their minds. He also reveals that the actual number to be assigned to a given quality was sometimes a matter of dispute (*in Met.* 38.10 Hayduck):

Because they assumed, as a defining property of justice, requital or equality, and found this to exist in numbers, therefore they said that justice was the first square number;[2] for in every kind the first instance of things having the same formula had in their opinion the best right to the name.[3] This number some said was 4, as being the first square, divisible into equal parts and in every way equal, for it is twice 2. Others, however, said that it was 9, the first square of an odd number, namely 3 multiplied by itself.

Opportunity,[4] on the other hand, they said was 7, because in nature the times of fulfilment with respect to birth and maturity go in sevens. Take man for instance. He can be born after seven months,[5] cuts his teeth after

---

[1] 'Constructed' (συνισταμένων) probably means constructed out of numbers like the abstractions opinion, mixture, etc., and the reference will be to the physical elements which were also equated with numbers by way of the geometrical solids (pp. 266ff., above; cf. Ross's commentary *ad loc.*).

[2] Cf. Aristotle, *EN*, 1132b21: 'Some think justice is simply requital, as the Pythagoreans said: they defined justice simply as requital to another.'
Note that τὸ ἀντιπεπονθός (requital or reciprocity) was in use as a mathematical term meaning 'reciprocally proportionate', e.g. at Eucl. VI, def. 2 and probl. 14.

[3] Cf. Aristotle, *Metaph.* 987a22 ὡρίζοντό τε γὰρ ἐπιπολαίως, καὶ ᾧ πρώτῳ ὑπάρξειεν ὁ λεχθεὶς ὅρος, τοῦτ' εἶναι τὴν οὐσίαν τοῦ πράγματος ἐνόμιζον.

[4] Or 'the fit and proper season'. For a criticism of this type of reasoning with respect to the number 7 see Aristotle himself, *Metaph.* 1093a13ff.

[5] Cf. the Pythagorean Hippon as cited by Censorinus, VII, 2 (DK, 38A16): *Hippon Metapontinus a septimo ad decimum mensem nasci posse aestimavit; nam septimo partum iam esse maturum,* etc. The reckoning of human life in multiples of seven was a commonplace of Greek thought. Cf. Solon, fr. 19 Diehl, Alcmaeon, A15 (DK), Hippocr. *De Hebdom.* 5 (IX, 436 Littré).

another seven, reaches puberty about the end of his second period of seven years and grows a beard at the third. Moreover they say that the sun, because (so he tells us)[1] it appears to be the cause of the seasons,[2] is situated in the region of the number 7 which they identify with opportunity, that is, it occupies the seventh place among the ten bodies which move around the central hearth....Marriage they identified with 5, because it is the union of male with female and according to them male is odd and female even,[3] and the number 5 arises from the first even number (2) and the first odd number (3)....Mind and being they identified with the unit, for soul he [presumably Pythagoras] classified with mind.

It becomes even more difficult to take this aberration of the Pythagoreans seriously when we learn from other late authorities that besides the numbers 4 and 9, mentioned by Alexander, 8, 5 and 3 were also identified by some of them with justice. As to marriage, the *Theologumena Arithmeticae* gives its number as 3, Nicomachus as 10.[4] Cornford wrote (*P. and P.* 26):

These 'resemblances' (ὁμοιώματα) between things like Justice and the properties of numbers explain why Aristotle sometimes says things represent (μιμεῖσθαι) numbers, rather than simply *are* numbers. A sensible body, as we have seen, can be said to *be* the unit-atoms composing it; but if a man says that 'Justice is a square number', he cannot mean that Justice is a plane figure composed of four unit-points; obviously he means that the square figure is a symbol which represents or embodies the nature of fairness, just as when an honest man was called 'four-square without reproach' no one imagined that his figure really had four corners. The two modes of describing the relation of things to numbers are perfectly compatible, being respectively appropriate to different orders of 'things'.

This, however, is probably to take an unwarrantably favourable view of Pythagorean rationality. The explanation of the equation of justice

[1] φησί, if correct, might just possibly mean 'Pythagoras says'. Much more probably it refers to Aristotle, and is an indication that Alexander (as is in any case likely) is taking all this information from Aristotle's lost treatise on the Pythagoreans. Note the different tense of εἶπε at 39.14 below.
[2] καιρῶν, i.e. the same word as is translated 'opportunity'. This is the reading of Asclepius and Hayduck; καρπῶν MSS., Bonitz.
[3] See the table of opposites, p. 245, above.
[4] The correspondences alleged between numbers and physical bodies were scarcely less capricious, if we allow any truth to the statement of [Alex.] *in Met.* 767 Hayduck that body in general was equated with 210, fire with 11, air with 13 and water with 9, and try to fit in these statements with some of the Pythagorean doctrines already considered.

with a square number by the notion of reciprocity or requital does indeed show, if that were necessary, that the equivalence is in part symbolic; but it does not account for the conception of justice as extended in space. It is not even true that Aristotle uses the language of resemblance rather than identity when speaking of the relationship of these abstractions to numbers. More helpful at this point in elucidation of the mode of thought of fifth-century Pythagoreans is a comparison with the Love and Strife of Empedocles, which he conceived as sharing the cosmic sphere with the four elements, 'equal in length and breadth' to them (fr. 17, 20), and capable of direct physical action. The alternation of language between 'identity' and 'resemblance' is rather to be accounted for, as we have already seen, by an ambiguity inherent in the Greek word ὅμοιος, which in common usage corresponded both to 'similar' and 'same'.[1]

Perhaps the most useful outcome of drawing attention to these numerical fantasies is that it reveals how much specific Pythagorean teaching lay behind the curiously mathematical approach to ethics which we find in Plato. In the ethical discussion of the *Gorgias*, where Socrates is upholding the ideals of justice and self-restraint against the drive for power and personal gratification advocated by Callicles, he adduces as an important part of his argument the following (507E):

Wise men say that heaven and earth and gods and men alike are held together by community, friendship, orderliness, self-control and justice, which is why they call this universe a world-*order* (*kosmos*)—not disorderliness or intemperance. But I fear you ignore them, wise though you are yourself, and fail to see the great power that is wielded among both gods and men by geometrical equality. Hence your defence of selfish aggrandisement: it arises from your neglect of geometry.

Here, as on some other topics, the absurdity of Pythagoreanism is the result of carrying to its logical extreme, within the limitations of con-

---

[1] P. 230, above. Cf. F. H. Sandbach, quoted by Raven, *P. and E.* 57: the confusion between the different types of proposition involved in the equation of, say, the moon and opinion with a number would be facilitated by the use of the Greek word ὅμοιος, '" the ambiguity of which between absolute and partial similarity"—the senses, that is to say, of ὁ αὐτός or ἴσος on the one hand and προσφερής on the other—"is responsible for many fallacies and logical puzzles in Greek thought"'.

temporary thinking, a sound and fruitful idea, in this instance the value of preserving a sense of proportion, in conduct as in artistic design or elsewhere.

(3) *The nature of the soul*

To determine what the Pythagoreans believed about the nature of the soul might seem to belong to the earlier section dealing with their religious views and the relation of man to the cosmos. We can indeed make use of much information already gained; but one problem in particular remains which we were not in a position to tackle until we had investigated the number-doctrine. Nor is it a bad thing to let the wheel come full circle as a further reminder that in Pythagorean philosophy the religious and scientific sides cannot be considered in isolation from each other without grave distortion of its outlook and aims.

We have seen (pp. 157, 186) that Pythagoras himself taught transmigration, and may also be safely credited with the complex of ideas with which transmigration is bound up: the doctrine that the human soul is immortal, that it owes its immortality to its essential kinship with the divine, universal soul, and that it may hope to return to its divine source when purified. We may also quote Aristotle for the Pythagorean belief in transmigration, although this is one of the rare cases where he is not our earliest informant:

De An. 407 b 20: 'All that these thinkers [Platonists and others] try to do is to state the nature of the soul; of the body that is to receive it they add no description, just as if it were possible, as in the Pythagorean stories, for any soul to be clothed with any body.'[1]

A little earlier in the *De Anima* (404a17) Aristotle attributes to 'some Pythagoreans' the opinion that the motes in the air constitute soul, whereas others said that it was 'that which moves them'. As with primitive people in general, the phenomenon of apparent self-motion immediately suggested to the early Greeks the presence of life, and so the reason for this crude notion was no doubt what Aristotle goes on to suggest: 'because the motes are always seen in motion, even when the air is completely still: all who define soul as that which moves itself show the same tendency'. The belief is mentioned by Aristotle in close

[1] That this remark could have been made, as has been suggested, without reference to the doctrine of transmigration is impossible.

connexion with the similar doctrine of the atomist Democritus, who, however, used the motion of the motes as a *simile*. The motes were not the soul-atoms—soul-atoms were the smallest and finest of all, and far below the level of perception—but they must be assumed to be like them and to have a similar motion, self-caused as that of the motes appeared to be.

The first form of the Pythagorean view mentioned by Aristotle sounds the more primitive, and the second a refinement on it in a spiritual direction, though 'what moved them' was no doubt still thought of in what we should call material terms as the air (which indeed it is), identified with *pneuma* or the breath-soul.[1]

Since we have no further information on this view, little more can be said about it. In either of its forms it fits in with the almost universally-held belief, adopted by the Pythagoreans as by their near relations the Orphics (Arist. *De An.* 410b27), that the soul was of the nature of air or breathed in with the air;[2] and we have already seen (p. 129, above) how this general belief could be pressed into service by materialists and religious mystics alike. In itself it does not seem to have affected the question of the soul's immortality either one way or the other.

Another doctrine mentioned by Aristotle, in his review of previous theories, was that the soul is a *harmonia*. Although he does not here mention the Pythagoreans, the word *harmonia* itself is sufficient guarantee of its authorship.[3] What Aristotle says is (*De An.* 407b27): 'There is yet another theory about the soul....Its supporters say that the soul is a kind of harmony, for harmony is a blend or composition

---

[1] Dodds (*Greeks and the Irrational*, 174) notes that the view of the soul as a tiny material particle has plenty of primitive parallels, and goes on to say that this is the persistent, 'occult' soul and is 'quite distinct from the breath-soul which is the principle of life on the ordinary empirical level'. As will appear later, the distinction which Dodds draws between the 'occult' and the 'empirical' soul is true and important; but it is difficult to understand why the view at present under discussion should refer to the occult one.

[2] Cf. the closely related opinion of 'some of the Pythagoreans' that 'some animals are nourished by smells' (Arist. *De Sensu*, 445a16).

[3] In fairness one must quote the opinion of Cherniss (*ACP*, 323, n. 1), to which others would probably assent: 'Aristotle never suggests that the doctrine was Pythagorean; it was most probably a late reinterpretation of some Pythagorean doctrine of the soul as number worked out by physicians or musicologists...in the late fifth or early fourth century and not ascribed to the Pythagoreans until even later.' J. Tate (*CR*, 1939, 2–3) thought it belonged to no philosophical school but was simply a widespread and popular view, that of 'anyone and everyone who thinks that the soul begins and ends with the organic union of the bodily parts'.

of contraries, and the body is compounded out of contraries.' In the course of criticizing this view he makes the interesting point that it might mean one of two things (both of which he himself thinks absurd):

Further, in using the word 'harmony' we have one of two cases in mind; the most proper sense is in relation to spatial magnitudes which have motion and position, where harmony means the disposition and cohesion of their parts in such a manner as to prevent the introduction into the whole of anything homogeneous with it, and the secondary sense, derived from the former, is that in which it means the ratio between the constituents so blended.[1]

In another brief reference to the view he again distinguishes between two forms in which it was held (*Pol.* 1340b18): 'There seems to be in us a sort of affinity to musical modes and rhythms, which makes many philosophers say that the soul is a *harmonia*, others that it possesses *harmonia*.' That the soul should be a *harmonia* seems a very natural belief for the Pythagoreans; indeed one can scarcely suppose that they viewed it otherwise, and it would cause no misgivings were it not for the use to which it is put by Plato in the *Phaedo*. There the doctrine that the soul is a *harmonia* is used as an argument that it cannot be immortal but must perish with the body. That is the problem that we have to face.

If we leave the *Phaedo* aside for the moment, everything fits happily together. The ultimate elements of everything are numbers, and the whole cosmos owes its character as something perfect, divine and permanent to the fact that the numbers of which it is made up are combined in the best possible manner according to the rules of mathematical proportion as Pythagoras's studies had revealed them. In short the cosmos owes all these desirable qualities to the fact that it *is* a *harmonia*, and this *harmonia* is therefore found above all in the majestic movements on a cosmic scale of the sun, moon, planets and fixed stars. The heavens do not *declare* the glory of God, they *are* the glory of God; for the cosmos is a living god, welded into a single divine unity by the marvellous power of mathematical and musical harmony.

If then our individual souls are essentially of the same nature, though separated by impurity in our incarnate state, then surely our identity

[1] 408a5 (Oxford translation).

with the divine must consist essentially of numbers in harmony, and in so far as we are still in need of the purification of philosophy it must be right to call the element of impurity, in other terms, an element of discord, a jarring note caused by a flaw in the numerical order of our souls—or, to put it in yet another Pythagorean way, an element of the Unlimited as yet unsubdued by the good principle of Limit.

This is genuine Pythagorean doctrine. Now let us see what is said in the *Phaedo* (86B, trans. Hackforth):

(Simmias speaks): And in point of fact I fancy that you yourself are well aware, Socrates, that we mostly hold a view of this sort about the soul: we regard the body as held together in a state of tension by the hot, the cold, the dry and the moist, and so forth, and the soul as the blending or attunement [*harmonia*] of these in the right and due proportion. Now if the soul really is a kind of attunement, plainly when our body is unduly relaxed or tautened by sickness or some other trouble, the soul, for all its divine nature, is bound forthwith to be destroyed, just as much as any other attunement or adjustment—in musical notes, for instance, or in a craftsman's product; whereas the bodily remains will last for a considerable time, until they are burned or rot away. So see what answer you can find for us to this argument, which insists that the soul, being a blending of the bodily constituents, is the first thing to perish in what is called death.

There are many opinions about this passage, and it is no doubt impossible to bring irrefutable proofs of any one of them; but one may try to give a probable account, and indicate the arguments in its favour. What is difficult to believe *without* irrefutable proof, knowing what we do about Pythagoras and the general conservatism of his followers in religious matters, is that any who claimed him as master were prepared to say that the soul was mortal.

As a refutation of immortality the soul-harmony was put forward by Simmias, a Theban who was said at the beginning of the dialogue to have listened to Philolaus when he was in Thebes. Burnet therefore thought that it must reproduce the teaching of Philolaus.[1] Against

---

[1] *EGP*, 295, *Gr. Phil.* I, 92f. Wilamowitz (*Platon*, II, 90) was also inclined to think that Philolaus denied the immortality of the soul on the ground that it was an attunement of the bodily parts, though he could not quite make up his mind. For Cornford, on the other hand, 'there is no doubt that Philolaus held both that the soul is, in some sense, a *harmony* and that it is immortal' (*CQ*, 1922, 146). 'It is probable', he thought, 'that the objection was first raised by Plato.'

this one may make two points. In the first place, Simmias and Cebes do not seem to have been very assiduous or understanding disciples. Earlier in the dialogue Socrates has expressed surprise that they are not familiar with the idea that suicide is contrary to religion, since it was something taught by Philolaus. Have they not heard it from him? (61 D.) 'Nothing at all clear', says Cebes; and a moment later, 'Yes, to answer your question, I have heard, both from Philolaus and from others, that one ought not to do this; but no one has ever made it clear to me.' Secondly, these views on suicide, which are expressly attributed to Philolaus, are said by Socrates to depend on the idea contained in a 'secret doctrine' (ἀπόρρητος λόγος) that we are put into the world by the gods and looked after by them; that therefore we must not leave it until they give the word; but that when they do permit it, death is comparable to a release from bondage or imprisonment. It is hardly likely that these are the beliefs of a man who believed that the soul was immediately dissolved at death.

We may note also the attitude to Simmias's objection of Echecrates, a Pythagorean from Phlius and pupil of Philolaus[1] to whom Phaedo is relating this conversation of the day of Socrates's death. It is one of great uneasiness (88 D):

This doctrine that the soul is a kind of attunement of us has always had and now has a strong hold upon me, and when you uttered it I was, as it were, reminded that I too had believed in it. And now, as if I were starting from the beginning again, I am terribly in need of another argument to persuade me that the souls of the dead do not die with them.[2]

Here is a Pythagorean who is attracted (as what Pythagorean could fail to be?) by the idea that the soul is an attunement, yet believes in its immortality and wishes to be reassured by other considerations that this one is (as presumably he has hitherto regarded it) not fatal to his belief.

As to the position of Philolaus himself, we know from the *Phaedo* that he forbade suicide, and why should he do this if not for the characteristically Orphico-Pythagorean reasons which follow in the

---

[1] *Phaedo*, 57 A, Aristoxenus, fr. 19 Wehrli (*ap.* D.L. VIII, 46).
[2] The translation is that of A. Cameron, *Pythagorean Background*, 45 f. His remarks on this question are worth reading.

dialogue?[1] The value of our other evidence is diminished by its late date, but for what it is worth we have the following:

(a) Clem. Alex. *Strom.* III, 17 (DK, 44B14): 'The words of Philolaus are also worth quoting. This Pythagorean says: "The ancient theological writers and prophets also bear witness that the soul is yoked to the body as a punishment, and buried in it as in a tomb."'

(b) Claudianus Mamertus (Christian writer of fifth century A.D.), *De Statu Animae*, II, 3, ed. A. Engelbrecht, 1885, p. 105 (DK, 44B22): 'Before deciding on the substance of the soul, he [Philolaus] discourses marvellously on measures, weights and numbers in conjunction with geometry, music and arithmetic, proving that the whole universe owes its existence to these... (p. 120). Concerning the human soul he says this:[2] the soul is set in the body by means of number and an immortal and incorporeal harmony. And a little later: the soul loves the body, because without it it can make no use of the senses. But when separated from it by death, it leads a disembodied life in the world.'

(c) Macrobius, *Somn. Scip.* I, 14, 19 (DK, 44A23): 'Pythagoras and Philolaus called the soul a harmony.'

The doctrines attributed to Philolaus in Clement are paralleled in detail not only in the *Phaedo* but also elsewhere in Plato, where we find references to incarnation as a punishment and to the body as both a prison and a tomb (*Gorg.* 493A, *Crat.* 400C). In the *Cratylus* these notions are ascribed to 'Orpheus and his followers', that is, to 'ancient *theologoi*' as by Philolaus. In view of all this we may agree with Nestle (ZN, 442) that the coincidence with the *Phaedo* affords no ground for regarding the quotation from Philolaus, at least in substance, as a forgery.[3] Similarly the passage from Claudianus Mamertus, in spite of its traces of later Greek terminology in Latin dress,[4] contains

---

[1] 61E, 62B. 'No ancient author who wrote about Philolaus ever questioned his attachment to the religious background of his order' (Cameron, *Pyth. Background*, 45). One can do no more than state what seems sensible and then in honesty report the fact that other scholars can disagree. Thus Hackforth (*Plato's Phaedo*, 35, n. 3); 'It would be unsafe to deduce from this οὐδὲν σαφές (cf. 61A8) anything as to Philolaus's religious views.'

[2] The word 'humana' is accidentally omitted by DK.

[3] Wilamowitz (*Platon*, II, 90) was more suspicious, mistrusting the word καθάπερ as he may well have been right to do. But his view is coloured by the belief that the doctrine of ψυχή–ἁρμονία attributed to Philolaus by Macrobius is necessarily inconsistent with belief in immortality. Since, however, Macrobius assigns it at the same time to Pythagoras, this is obviously not so.

[4] F. Bömer has discussed this passage in detail in *Der latein. Neuplat. u. Neupythagoreismus*, 143–54, where references to many other modern opinions will be found. Bömer, however, who regards the doctrines here ascribed to Philolaus as Neopythagorean, goes astray in several places,

no doctrine that cannot be paralleled in pre-Aristotelian Pythagorean-ism. Its chief fault is that it is fragmentary and leaves serious gaps. Points to note are that according to this account Philolaus elaborated his cosmology, with its demonstration that everything in the world is dependent on number, before approaching psychology. He then showed that the soul is no exception, but even when incarnate is organized according to number and to an attunement which is immortal and incorporeal. That the soul in this life loves or clings to the body, seduced by sensual gratification, is something that we learn also in the more Pythagorean parts of Plato's dialogues. One thinks in particular of the soul in the *Phaedo* (81 B) which 'has always associated with the body and tended it, filled with its lusts and so bewitched by its passions and pleasures as to think nothing real save what is bodily, what can be touched and seen and eaten and made to serve sexual enjoyment'. Death, we are told finally, is not extinction of the soul. It lives on in a disembodied state 'in the world' (*in mundo*), that is, until its next incarnation. The soul in question here is not the fully purified one, but the soul that has loved the body, of whom Plato says that it is compelled to wander about the visible world until once more fettered to a body (*Phaedo*, 81 D).

Of the brief statement in Macrobius all that need be said is that since he couples the name of Philolaus with that of Pythagoras, this Neo-platonist evidently did not think the doctrine of soul as harmony to be incompatible with belief in its immortality. Putting together our scattered evidence from Plato onwards, it seems that Philolaus was a true follower of Pythagoras in holding that the soul was both a *harmonia* or attunement (as was everything else of real worth in the world) and also immortal.[1]

particularly in his interpretation of the clause 'diligitur corpus ab anima' and the words 'in mundo'. As to the terminology, Claudian doubtless chose the words 'de mensuris ponderibus et numeris' for their correspondence with the words of scripture to which he compares them: 'Mensura pondere et numero omnia disposuisti.' (See Wisdom of Solomon xi. 20.) But this casts no doubt on the obvious truth that Philolaus, like any true Pythagorean, *did* explain the cosmos by number and measure. Again, the word 'incorporalem' (ἀσώματον) would probably not have been used by Philolaus himself, but describes well enough the kind of *harmonia* that he must have had in mind. H. Gomperz in *Hermes*, 1932, 156 does indeed defend the fragment, ἀσώματον and all, but is criticized by Bömer, 153.

[1] It may be true that the best authenticated of Philolaus's views are those contained in the papyrus which records extracts from Menon's history of medicine. But the argument which

The Soul a 'Harmonia'

What then of the argument brought forward by Simmias? The view of the soul which he propounds, hoping to have it refuted by Socrates, has been generally recognized to have a strong affinity with the theories of the medical writers of Magna Graecia, and in particular with the chief of them, Alcmaeon of Croton. With Simmias's language may be compared Alcmaeon, fr. 4 (Aët. v, 30, 1):

Alcmaeon said that what preserves health is the equilibrium of the powers—wet, dry, cold, hot, sweet and so forth—whereas the unchecked rule of any one of them engenders disease: the rule of a single contrary is destructive.... Health is a balanced (σύμμετρον) mixture of opposites.

So far as it concerns the causes of health and disease, Alcmaeon and Simmias are clearly describing the same theory; yet Alcmaeon does not go on to identify the equilibrium or balanced mixture of the opposites with the soul, nor argue that as the one can be destroyed so can the other. In spite of his views on health and disease, he believed the soul to be immortal. So Aristotle, *De An.* 405 a 29 (see DK, 24 A 12 for this and supporting passages from Cicero, Clement and Aëtius): 'He says that the soul is immortal because it resembles the immortal beings in that it is always in motion; for all the divine bodies likewise are in continuous and unceasing motion—the moon, sun, stars and the whole heaven.'[1]

Empedocles in Sicily held similar physiological views. In him for the first time the ancient 'opposites' were given more concrete form as the four imperishable 'root-substances' earth, water, air and fire, and he defined each separate organic substance in terms of a mixture of these in a certain ratio (fr. 96, Arist. *De An.* 408 a 18 ff.). At the same time, in obedience to the principle that 'like is known by like', he taught that the soul, at least in its empirical aspect as that with which we perceive the world around us, was composed of the material elements themselves

Nestle based on this fact is absurd: 'Der echte Philolaos liegt in den neuerdings bekannt gewordenen Auszügen aus seinen medizinischen Schriften in Menon's *Iatrika*. Darnach war *Philolaos weniger Philosoph als Arzt*, und zwar gehörte er zur Krotoniatischen Artztschule' (ZN, 437: my italics). If nothing of Aristotle had been preserved save part of the *Poetics* in another man's history of literature and a few fragments on other subjects of doubtful authenticity, it would have been as reasonable to argue that he had been 'not so much a philosopher as a literary critic'. We know at least enough about Philolaus from other sources to save us from this mistake.

[1] Alcmaeon must of course be more fully treated later. See pp. 341 ff., below.

(fr. 109, *De An.* 404b11). In his criticism of the soul-as-attunement theory (408a18ff.), Aristotle succeeds only too well in his attempt to make Empedocles appear illogical and confused, and we have not the relevant parts of his poem as a check; but he does seem to have described the soul as a particular tension or equilibrium of the bodily parts and also said something which might be construed as meaning that it vanished when this balance was upset. Aëtius too (v, 25, 4, DK, 31A85) says that according to Empedocles death is caused by the coming apart of the elements of which man is a composition, 'so that to this extent (κατὰ τοῦτο) death is common to body and soul'.

In spite of all this Empedocles, deeply imbued as he was with the general Italian tradition, wrote a religious poem whose theme was the immortality, transmigration and ultimate apotheosis of the human soul. He therefore affords an interesting parallel to Alcmaeon, although the question of how, if at all, he reconciled the two sides of his doctrine must be left until later.[1] Burnet himself regards the soul-as-attunement theory as evidence that the Pythagoreanism of the end of the fifth century was an adaptation of older doctrine to the new principles introduced by Empedocles.

The problem is certainly difficult, and it can hardly be wrong to detect here a certain tension existing within the school. Scattered as they were by the fifth century in Italy, Sicily and Greece, the Pythagoreans did not all develop the doctrine of their master along identical lines. For medical men, such as Alcmaeon was,[2] the body and its states tended naturally and rightly to occupy the centre of the field. Their aim was to combat disease and produce health in particular bodies, and they tend to be impatient with the more metaphysical pronouncements of philosophers. Their business was with the physical opposites of which the body was composed, for their practice was founded on the belief—surely a Pythagorean one—that health depended on a due and rightly proportioned mixture of these opposites in the body—hot and cold, wet and dry, bitter and sweet and others. Inevitably they would be led to the belief that physical life at any rate depended on these

---

[1] See, however, Kahn in *Arch. f. Gesch. d. Philos.* 1960, 3–35, especially 28, n. 70.

[2] Of course, like any serious thinker of his time, he was more than this, but we may perhaps say with Diogenes Laertius (VIII, 83) τὰ πλεῖστά γε ἰατρικὰ λέγει, ὅμως δὲ καὶ φυσιολογεῖ ἐνίοτε.

things, and could not outlast the dissolution of the attunement between the physical elements of the body. And the identification of *psyche* with the physical life was deeply rooted in the Greek mind, so that the temptation lay close at hand to say that the *psyche* could not outlive the dissolution of the body. Dicaearchus the pupil of Aristotle, who though not a Pythagorean himself was the friend of Pythagoreans and acquainted with their teaching, went the whole way and called the soul explicitly 'an attunement *of the four elements*'. It could not therefore exist in separation from the body, for it had no substance of its own but was simply a way of describing a characteristic of the body (namely life, or the power to act and feel) when constituted in a certain way.[1] It is legitimate to suppose that this was something that could gnaw at the mind of a Simmias, even though he was the disciple of a Pythagorean teacher, but it does not follow that it represented the full depth of true Pythagorean teaching. What that was I have already stated, but lest it be thought to be merely a personal opinion I should like to quote other authorities. Cornford wrote:

As Zeller points out, it is only Plato (in the *Phaedo*) and Aristotle (who, at *De An.* A, iv, is clearly thinking of the *Phaedo* and is moreover assuming his own doctrine of the *synthesis* of simple bodies in compounds, Hicks *ad loc.*) who speak of the soul-*harmony* as a *harmony of the bodily opposites*. We are nowhere told that the Pythagoreans so defined it, and it is this definition that entails the inconsistency with immortality. Zeller accordingly infers that Philolaus cannot have meant a *harmony* of bodily opposites, but more probably the view attributed to him by Claudianus Mamertus, that the soul is *connected* with the body by means of number and *harmony*.[2]

Not the mortality but the immortality of the soul depended on its being a harmony, but a harmony in the sense in which the cosmos was a harmony. That is, a harmony not ultimately of physical opposites but of numbers. Not that the Pythagoreans in the fifth century drew a clear distinction between the material and the non-material. We have already seen that they were not in a position to do so. But there were degrees in these matters. Numbers were nearer to the ultimate, and therefore to the divine, than physical opposites like hot and cold.

[1] See Dicaearchus, frr. 7–12 Wehrli.
[2] *CQ*, 1922, 146. Cf. ZN, 553.

It is a general principle of early Greek thought, common to both the Ionian and the Italian traditions, that the primary nature, the *arche* of things, stands in the same relation to the world of experience as soul does to body.[1] And in the Pythagorean system the primary nature is not the physical opposites or a more primitive form of body like the air of Anaximenes: it is number. We may compare Plato's description of the world-soul in the *Timaeus*, which certainly has a Pythagorean foundation. It is described as 'invisible and having part in *harmonia* and reason' (36E), and is constructed according to the numerical intervals of a musical scale based on one form of the Pythagorean tetractys. At the same time its priority and superiority to the body of the cosmos are emphasized in every way (cf. 34B–C). As Taylor said (*Comm. on Tim.* 136), 'the cosmic soul is not (as it would be according to the formula of those Pythagoreans who are refuted in the *Phaedo*) a *harmonia* of the corresponding body, but, being wise and good, it of course exhibits a *harmonia* in its own structure, has music in itself'.

That the soul was for the Pythagoreans a state or arrangement of *numbers* is what Aristotle says in the *Metaphysics*. After explaining that they were the first to make considerable advances in mathematics, and as a result became absorbed in the subject and assumed that mathematical principles underlay everything, he continues (985 b 26):

Numbers are the simplest of these, and it was in them that they thought they saw resemblances to the things that are and come to be, rather than in fire and earth and water. Thus such-and-such a disposition of numbers is justice, and another is soul and mind....

On this view the soul is a harmony of *its own* parts, not of the parts of the body, just as music is a harmony of the numbers 1, 2, 3 and 4, and not of the frame and strings of the lyre; so that Simmias's analogy, even if some Pythagoreans were taken in and disturbed by it, was in fact by genuine Pythagorean reasoning a false one. In Pythagoras's experiment, perhaps, the numbers 1, 2, 3 and 4 happened to be embodied in, or represented by, strings of varying lengths; but this is accidental, as is shown by the fact that they may just as well be represented by columns

---

[1] See under Anaximenes, pp. 128 ff., above.

of air passing through a pipe which is stopped at various intervals. The genius of Pythagoras, even though he could not have so expressed it in words, lay in his concentration on the formal element as real and permanent, and dismissal of the physical and individual as accidental.

We are of course approaching Plato's view of the soul as he expounds it in the *Republic*, and can see how much he owed to his Pythagorean friends. There (431 ff.) the virtue of 'temperance' (*sophrosyne*) is said to be the virtue of the soul as a whole, the result of the smooth working together of all its parts. But Plato speaks in Pythagorean language of it 'singing together through the whole octave', and calls *sophrosyne* straight out a *harmonia*. The man who possesses it is 'well-tuned' (ἡρμοσμένος; note that this has nothing to do with his state of health), and it is achieved 'by bringing three parts into accord, just like the three fixed intervals in the scale—highest, lowest and middle'[1]—that is, as a musical harmony is achieved. In the case of the soul, the three parts that have to be brought into accord are of course reason, passion (θυμός) and desire. The soul *is* a *harmonia*, but not a *harmonia* of bodily parts or physical opposites. Neither therefore does its well-being (*arete*) consist in bodily health. Its parts are psychical faculties like desire, courage and intellect, and its *arete* is a moral virtue, temperance. For the physical *psyche*, if I may use that term to connote mere animal life, *euharmostia* of the bodily parts results in health, *anharmostia* in disease or death. But for the divine and immortal *psyche* which it was the object of the Pythagorean to cherish and purify, *euharmostia* was of its own parts and resulted in moral virtue, *anharmostia* in vice. This, one may suggest, has the true Pythagorean flavour. It will not be forgotten that for the Pythagoreans moral virtues too, like justice, were equated with numbers, so that this conclusion is not inconsistent with believing that it is numbers of which the soul is a *harmonia*.

Were there then for these people two kinds of soul? There are good grounds for supposing that there were, and that in this they were only adapting to their own purposes a widespread primitive belief. The

---

[1] To appreciate the full Pythagorean, musical flavour of the language it must be read in Greek: 431 Ε ἐπιεικῶς ἐμαντευόμεθα ἄρτι ὡς ἁρμονίᾳ τινὶ ἡ σωφροσύνη ὡμοίωται...432 Α δι᾽ ὅλης ἀτεχνῶς τέταται διὰ πασῶν παρεχομένη συνᾴδοντας τούς τε ἀσθενεστάτους ταὐτὸν καὶ τοὺς ἰσχυροτάτους καὶ τοὺς μέσους...ὥστε ὀρθότατ᾽ ἂν φαῖμεν...κατὰ φύσιν συμφωνίαν. 443 D συναρμόσαντα τρία ὄντα, ὥσπερ ὅρους τρεῖς ἁρμονίας ἀτεχνῶς, νεάτης τε καὶ ὑπάτης καὶ μέσης.

existence of such a belief has long been recognized. R. Ganszyniec in 1920 characterized the two souls of early Greek thought as (*a*) breath-soul (ψυχή) and (*b*) image- or shadow-soul (εἴδωλον), and quoted parallels from Africa.[1] The breath-soul he also called the 'life-soul'. The duality comes out very clearly in Empedocles, and a comparison with this Italian philosopher of the first half of the fifth century should throw some light and excuse a brief anticipatory summary at this point. So far as the empirical world was concerned, Empedocles was a thorough materialist, even extending this outlook to the psychic functions of sensation and thought. Aristotle (*De An.* 427a21) says that he looked on sensation and thought as the same and both alike as corporeal, and this is borne out by the remains of Empedocles's own writings (frr. 105, 109). None the less he believed in a divine self alien to the body—which he calls not *psyche* but *daimon*—an exile from the gods to whom it longs to return (fr. 115). For its release knowledge is necessary, but not the knowledge of the empirical part of us, whose objects, like its foundation, are physical, confined to the lower parts of the cosmos. But 'blessed is the man who has gained the riches of *divine* wisdom' (fr. 132). Like is known by like, so to know the divine is to become divine, and the divine is not something which we perceive with any of the bodily senses (fr. 133). Evidently we have other means of attaining knowledge, means more like those described by Socrates in the *Phaedo* when he speaks of the soul of the philosopher seeking the truth 'all by itself', leaving the body behind.

The faculty by which we do this is not the *psyche* in the earlier and popular sense of mere animal life. It can be called a *daimon*, and there was much earlier lore about *daimones*, on which Pythagoras and Empedocles could build. Sometimes the word is used interchangeably with *theos*, god. Where there is a distinction, as in Plato's *Symposium*, *daimones* are a race of intermediate beings dwelling in the elements between heaven and earth (compare Empedocles, fr. 115). Hesiod knows of how they go up and down over the earth clad in mist or darkness (i.e. invisible), and he says they are the souls of the men of the Golden Race. It is evidently this part of us which in stories of strange

[1] *Arch. Gesch. d. Naturwiss. u. d. Technik*, IX, 13 ff. He refers to Ankermann, *Totenkult u. Seelenglaube bei afrikanischen Völkern, Zeitschr. f. Ethnol.* 1918, 89–153.

seers like Abaris, Epimenides and Hermotimus could leave the body temporarily in search of divine knowledge. It is the image of life or time (or whatever αἰῶνος εἴδωλον may mean) of which Pindar speaks when he says the body of every man goes the way of death, 'but there is yet left alive this image, for it alone is from the gods. It sleeps when the limbs are active, but to men asleep it reveals in many a dream the pleasant or painful issue of things to come.'[1]

Two different notions of soul, then, existed in contemporary belief, the *psyche* which 'vanished like smoke' at death, and which medical writers (including no doubt some sceptical and therefore heretical Pythagoreans) rationalized into a *harmonia* of the physical opposites that made up the body; and the more mysterious *daimon* in man, immortal, suffering transmigration through many bodies, but in its pure essence divine. This too could be called *psyche*, as it was by Plato. Both survived side by side in the general current of religious thought, and both also survived in the curious combination of mathematical philosophy and religious mysticism which made up Pythagoreanism.

E. INDIVIDUAL PYTHAGOREANS

After Pythagoras himself the history of Pythagoreanism is, for us, to a large extent anonymous. For this reason it has seemed best to treat it generally, although certain individuals—Philolaus in particular, also Hippasus, Eurytus, Hicetas—have found a place in the exposition. Others are shadowy figures, little more than names, like Cercops and Brontinus (or Brotinus) who were said to have written poems in the Orphic corpus, Paron the Pythagorean who called time 'stupid' because it makes us forget (Arist. *Phys.* 222b18), or Xuthus, of whom Aristotle reports (*Phys.* 216b24) that in his opinion there must be void to allow of compression, without which either there could be no motion or 'the universe would heave like a wave'. Simplicius in his comment says that this Xuthus was a Pythagorean.

Some, however, whether already mentioned or not, deserve a closer look, which has been reserved for this section.

[1] Pindar, fr. 131 Schroeder, 116 Bowra. Cf. the language of Hippocr. *De Victu*, IV, init. (VI, 640 Littré), which may, however, be later than the middle of the fourth century (Kirk, *HCF*, 26f.).

Pythagoras and the Pythagoreans

(1) *Hippasus*

What we have already seen of Hippasus of Metapontum suggests that as a Pythagorean he was something of a rebel. There were the stories of his punishment for revealing mathematical secrets (pp. 149 and 268, above), and the allegation by one of the two divergent types of Pythagorean that the other owed its origin not to Pythagoras himself but to Hippasus (p. 192). There are other indications that he overlapped the lifetime of Pythagoras and was by no means a docile pupil. In the events leading up to the democratic conspiracy of Cylon and Ninon (pp. 178f.) he is mentioned as having, with others, urged the adoption of democratic measures at variance with the oligarchic policy of the school. Again, to stir up popular feeling against the Pythagoreans Ninon is said to have read from a pretended 'sacred *logos*' of Pythagoras which proved them to be the enemies of the popular cause.[1] It is significant of Hippasus's reputation that in later times a similar forgery, from similar motives, was attributed to him, probably by transference from the story of the conspiracy with which he evidently had some sympathy: a tradition going back to Sotion's *Successions* (*c.* 200 B.C.) says that the 'Mystical Logos' of Pythagoras was really written by Hippasus to defame him (D.L. VIII, 7).

His adoption of fire as first principle led to a story that Heraclitus had been his pupil (Suda, DK, 18, 1*a*). Such assumptions of a master-pupil relationship have no historical value, but the fact that it is put this way round indicates at least a traditional date for Hippasus which is compatible with his having been a personal rival of Pythagoras.

Whatever be the truth about the authorship of the 'Mystical Logos', Demetrius of Magnesia in the first century B.C. says that Hippasus left no writings (D.L. VIII, 84, DK, 18, 1), so presumably none existed in Hellenistic times. The teaching traditionally attributed to him supports the belief that he did not simply follow an orthodox Pythagorean line, since from Aristotle onwards (*Metaph.* 984a7) he is regularly coupled with Heraclitus as a proponent of the doctrine that the *arche* is fire. Theophrastus (*ap.* Simpl., DK, 18, 7) enlarged on this by saying in addition that both men held the universe to be unique and finite, and

---

[1] Iambl. *V.P.* 257 (DK, 18, 5), 260. Cf. Minar, *Early Pyth. Pol.* 56ff.

both produced existing things out of fire by condensation and rare-faction and resolved them into fire again. Since this standard Peri-patetic description of a monistic cosmogony misrepresents Heraclitus (pp. 455ff., below), we cannot well trust it for Hippasus, but must content ourselves with the knowledge that he gave the primacy to fire: but seeing that for all his independence of mind he is regularly agreed to have remained a Pythagorean, it may be supposed that he meditated on the creative power residing in the original fiery unit, and the divine status assigned by the Pythagoreans to the fire still burning at the centre.[1]

The doctrines of Hippasus and Heraclitus seem to have been much confused in later ages. We are told by Diogenes that Hippasus said the cosmos completed its changes in a limited time. The same phrase occurs in Simplicius's version of Theophrastus, where however the words 'by some necessity of fate' are added and it appears to be referred to Heraclitus and connected with his saying that 'everything is an exchange for fire'.[2] Now as an interpretation of Heraclitus's notion of 'exchange' the statement is inappropriate. It does, however, describe very well the Pythagorean doctrine of the cyclical repetition of history (p. 281, above), and so was probably intended by Theophrastus to refer to Hippasus.

Later authorities also claim to impart Hippasus's teaching about the soul, but their information even if trustworthy (which is doubtful) contains nothing original. Naturally he is coupled with Heraclitus as teaching that the soul was of a fiery nature, but being a Pythagorean he also thought of it as a number. Claudianus Mamertus also ascribes to him the ideas that one would expect from a Pythagorean: he said that soul and body were very different things, that soul is active when the body is inactive and alive when it is dead.[3]

Other information about Hippasus concerns discoveries in music.

---

[1] Pp. 281, 288, above. Clement explicitly says that Hippasus and Heraclitus (coupled as usual) believed fire to be god. His authority is usually considered dubious, but to name something as the *arche* was in Hippasus's time (and particularly for a Pythagorean) itself tantamount to belief in its divinity. And in this case the statement is correct for Heraclitus, whose λόγος–πῦρ was certainly a divine principle.

[2] D.L. VIII, 84, DK, 18, 1 ἔφη δὲ χρόνον ὡρισμένον εἶναι τῆς τοῦ κόσμου μεταβολῆς. Cf. Theophr. *ap.* Simpl. *Phys.* 24.4 (DK, 22 A 5, continuation of DK, 18, 7 already quoted).

[3] Clement, Aëtius and Claudianus Mamertus. See DK, 18, 8–10. DK say that the passage of Claudianus Mamertus is from a Neopythagorean forgery, but even if so, it contains no doctrine that could not be paralleled in the fifth century B.C. With *corpore torpente viget* cf. Pindar, fr. 131 Schroeder (p. 319, above).

Rivalry with Pythagoras is again suggested by a story of Aristoxenus (fr. 90 Wehrli, DK, 18, 12) that he produced the concordant intervals by striking four bronze discs whose thicknesses were in the proportions 4:3, 3:2, and 2:1. (Compare the story of Pythagoras in the black-smith's shop, p. 223, above.) Iamblichus (DK, 18, 15) says that Pythagoras and the mathematicians of his time recognized the arith-metical, geometrical, and harmonic means, but called the last-named *hypenantia*: it was Archytas and Hippasus who re-named it *harmonic*. There is no suggestion in the passage that Hippasus was a contemporary of Archytas.

(2) *Petron*

All that we know of Petron is that he said there were 183 worlds arranged in a triangle. This is a striking enough statement, and might be of great interest if we knew anything of the arguments or evidence on which he based it: but we do not. We do not even know that he was a Pythagorean; in fact the main object in giving space to him must be destructive rather than constructive.

Our sole authority is Plutarch in the treatise *De Defectu Oraculorum*. At 422B one of the speakers in the dialogue tells how he met in the neighbourhood of the Persian Gulf a mysterious stranger, not a Greek, who was a kind of desert prophet. This man told him, together with a great deal of mythology about the gods, that there are 183 worlds (*kosmoi*) arranged in the form of a triangle. Each side of the triangle has 60 worlds and the remaining three are placed at the corners. They are in contact with one another and revolve steadily as in a dance. To this another of the company retorts that the stranger was a fraud, a pilferer of other men's thoughts and obviously a Greek well versed in the literature of his country.

The number of his worlds convicts him, for it is not Egyptian or Indian but Dorian from Sicily, in fact the theory of a man of Himera called Petron. I have not actually read his book, nor do I even know if it is still preserved. But Hippys of Rhegium, mentioned by Phanias of Eresus, says that this opinion and account are Petron's, namely that there are 183 worlds in contact with one another according to element—though what is meant by being 'in contact according to element' he does not explain further, nor does he add anything else to make it more plausible (422D, DK, 16).

Petron: Ecphantus

On the strength of this sole passage Burnet described Petron as 'one of the earliest Pythagoreans' and 'much older than the atomists'.[1] That he was a Pythagorean may perhaps be conjectured from the mathematical character of his highly individual theory, and his Sicilian origin would be in keeping. The early dating depends on accepting a guess of Wilamowitz (in *Hermes*, 1884, 444) that when Plutarch mentions Hippys of Rhegium he means Hippasus of Metapontum, because both Petron and Hippasus were Pythagoreans. On this one cannot do better than quote Cornford (*CQ*, 1934, 14f.):

Against this conjecture there is the evidence of Demetrius Magnes[2] (D.L. VIII, 84) that Hippasos left nothing in writing. Further, Jakoby (*s.v.* Hippys of Rhegium, PW, VIII, 1929) points out that, if Plutarch or Phanias did not mean Hippys, it is more likely that he meant Hipparchides of Rhegium (Iambl. *Vit. Pyth.* 267), who has at least the advantage over Hippasos of coming from Rhegium. I cannot myself see why Phanias, who may have lived far on into the third century, should not have quoted Hippys (whom Jakoby places in the first half of that century), or why Hippys should not have mentioned Petron's eccentric view. It was not unusual for historians to refer to cosmological speculations. There is no better evidence than this for ranking Petron among the 'earliest Pythagoreans'. He may have been a contemporary of Leucippus or Democritus or Plato.

(3) Ecphantus

The very existence of this philosopher has had to be defended. Voss in 1896, followed by Tannery in 1897 and later, put forward a theory that he and Hicetas (no. 4, below) were imaginary characters in a dialogue by Heraclides Ponticus, later mistaken for historical figures as was the Timaeus of Plato. The thesis rests on the known fact that Heraclides wrote dialogues, together with a certain similarity between the doctrines attributed to the three men. In the case of Hicetas, this applies only to the theory that the earth rotates. In addition Ecphantus shared with Heraclides an atomic theory of matter. Voss and Tannery were followed by Heidel in 1909 (though by 1940 he had become more cautious and would only say that 'perhaps' Ecphantus was an imaginary person),

[1] *EGP*, 60f., and cf. 109.
[2] Contemporary of Cicero and friend of Atticus. The work of his which Diogenes Laertius cites was one devoted to distinguishing between writers of the same name, a very necessary task in the confusion of Greek nomenclature.

Heath in 1913, and Frank in 1923. More recent scholars have on the whole followed Diels, Wellmann and Daebritz in rejecting this scepticism, e.g. Praechter (1923), Taylor (1928) and Vlastos (1953).[1]

The theory can hardly stand. Against it may be said first that both Hicetas and Ecphantus were mentioned by Theophrastus in his doxographical work, apparently as real persons. Cicero names him as his authority for Hicetas, and for Ecphantus we have statements from both Aëtius and Hippolytus, whose common source can have been no other. And as Vlastos says, 'it seems most unlikely that Theophrastus would present the view of a fictitious character in a dialogue of his own contemporary Heraclides in a form that would lead the doxographers to mistake these views for those of a historical thinker. There is no parallel for such a mistake in the doxographic tradition; the case of Timaeus is surely evidence to the contrary.'

Apart from this, the supposed resemblance in doctrine between Heraclides and Ecphantus is only partial. Heraclides was known for having given up the term 'atoms' and substituted 'disjoined particles'. These were said to differ from Democritean atoms by being subject to change.[2] We hear nothing like this of Ecphantus, and his belief that the atoms move 'not by weight nor impact but by a divine power which he calls mind and soul' is not noticeably the same as the one attributed by Cicero to Heraclides, who, he says, 'applies the epithet divine now to the cosmos, now to mind, and again attributes divinity to the planets, deprives his god of perception and conceives him as changeable in form'.

The ancient evidence for Ecphantus's views is slender in amount, and worth translating in full. (It is collected in DK, 51.)[3]

(*a*) Hippol. *Ref.* I, 15: 'Ecphantus a Syracusan claimed that it was not possible to get true knowledge of the things that exist, but only to define them as we believe them to be. He said that the primary realities are indi-

---

[1] Some references on both sides: Voss, *De Heracl. Pont. vita et scriptis* (diss. Rostock, 1896), 64; Tannery, *Arch. Gesch. Phil.* 1898, 266, *REG*, 1897, 134–6, *Rev. de Philol.* 1904, 233 ff.; Heidel, *TAPA*, 1909, 6, *AJP*, 1940, 19, n. 36; Frank, *Plato u. d. sog. Pyth.* 138 f.; Heath, *Aristarchus*, 251. Contrast Wellmann, *s.v.* 'Ekphantos' in *RE*, v, 2215; Daebritz, *s.v.* 'Heracl. Pont.' in *RE*, VIII, 477; Ueberweg-Praechter, 345, n. 1; Taylor, *Timaeus*, 239; Vlastos, *Gnomon*, 1953, 32, n. 1. See also ZN, 606, n. 3. As Nestle points out, even the appearance of these two as characters in a dialogue by Heraclides would be no evidence against their historical existence.

[2] ἄναρμοι ὄγκοι frr. 118–20 Wehrli, παθητά as opposed to ἀπαθῆ fr. 120.

[3] The fragments of a work *On Kingship* attributed to Ecphantus by Stobaeus (not in DK) are a production of late Hellenistic times. See Skemp, *Plato's Statesman*, 62, and references there.

visible bodies which differ in three respects—size, shape, and power.[1] Out
of them arise perceptible things, and their number is limited, not infinite.[2]
These bodies owe their movement not to weight or external impact but to a
divine power which he calls mind and soul. The cosmos is a form [or manifestation, ἰδέα] of this[3] for which reason it has become, by divine power,
spherical. The earth is the middle of the cosmos and moves about its own
centre in an eastward direction.'

(*b*) Aët. I, 3, 19: 'Ecphantus of Syracuse, one of the Pythagoreans, held
that the principles of all things were indivisible bodies and the void, for he
was the first to declare that the Pythagorean monads were corporeal.'

(*c*) Aët. II, 1, 2 includes Ecphantus in a list of philosophers who believed
the cosmos to be unique.

(*d*) Aët. II, 3, 3: 'Ecphantus held that the cosmos was composed of atoms,
but was ruled by providence.'

(*e*) Aët. III, 13, 3 (immediately after the sentence describing Philolaus's
theory of a planetary earth, p. 284, above): 'Heraclides of Pontus and
Ecphantus the Pythagorean make the earth move, not in the sense of changing
its location but turning about an axis like a wheel: it revolves round its own
centre from West to East.'

There is no positive evidence for the date of Ecphantus, but if the
reports of his beliefs are in general trustworthy, he must have been at
least late enough to come under the influence of the atomists, and probably belonged to the last generation of Pythagoreans who were contemporaries of Plato. He was a Pythagorean who saw the possibilities
of combining the Pythagorean evolution of a world from numbers with
genuine atomism as taught by Democritus. The words 'he was the
first to declare the Pythagorean monads to be corporeal' have been
taken, on the assumption that Ecphantus is a fourth-century figure, as
invalidating Aristotle's view that the Pythagorean numbers had magni-

---

[1] *Dynamis*. From meaning force or power, this word was sometimes watered down so as to
signify little more than quality, but always in an active sense. That is to say, in using the word a
writer would always be thinking of what it described in terms of producing an effect, e.g. of a
colour the effect which it produces on the eye. In the medical writers it was frequently applied
to the characteristics of a disease, which in an obvious sense are active powers at the same time.
Cf. the note of W. H. S. Jones, 'Δύναμις in scientific writings', in *Anon. Londinensis*, 9–10.

[2] Roeper's emendation καὶ οὐκ ἄπειρον (for the nonsensical καὶ τοῦτο ἄ.) gives the most probable sense. It was accepted by Zeller (ZN, 605, n. 2) and more recently by Kranz in *Convivium*,
28. Fortunately the first words of the clause establish the material point that for Ecphantus the
number of atoms was limited.

[3] The translation follows Roeper's emendation (printed by DK) τούτου μὲν οὖν τὸν κόσμον εἶναι
ἰδέαν for the MS. τοῦ μὲν οὖν τ. κ. εἰδέναι ἰδεῖν.

tude in earlier times. In fact, however, they only show (if Aëtius's statement is to be trusted) how at this time the distinction between corporeal and incorporeal was beginning to be appreciated, as it is by Plato. Aristotle's complaints make it perfectly clear that the earlier Pythagoreans were not aware of the inconsistency involved in building a universe out of numbers. They *treated* numbers as if they were corporeal ('had magnitude'), but they did not say to themselves 'numbers are corporeal', having neither the words in which to say it nor a grasp of the dichotomy which the words imply. Numbers for them could exist on both the mathematical and the physical planes at the same time. Ecphantus, one may suppose, belonged to the period when the distinction was emerging into consciousness, and having therefore to make the choice he declared the monads to be corporeal, thus giving Pythagoreanism a push in the direction of atomism of the Democritean type. The first sentence of passage (*a*), about the impossibility of true knowledge of real things (i.e. atoms), is based directly on Democritus (frr. 7–9); but the addition of *dynamis* to size and shape as a differentiating property of the atoms was a striking and original contribution. For the 'weight and external impact' of the atomists he substituted life and mind as the cosmogonic force, possibly borrowing from Anaxagoras the idea of *nous* as primary motive cause, though passages (*a*) and (*d*) suggest that he allowed it a more continuous role. In Anaxagoras's system mind simply set the wheels going and then withdrew, leaving the cosmos to continue under its own momentum, subject to purely mechanical laws. For Ecphantus the Pythagorean the cosmos itself is divine and rational, and the way in which the text (as emended) links its divinity causally with its sphericity is strongly reminiscent of Plato's *Timaeus*. In view of the textual uncertainty we cannot attach much weight to this, and even if it is correct there is not the evidence to account for it with certainty. It might be a Platonic reinterpretation of Ecphantus's own doctrine and due to the doxographer, but the give-and-take between Plato and contemporary Pythagoreanism was such that the debt might have been Plato's, or again a debt owed directly or indirectly to Plato by Ecphantus himself.

The atomic theory of Ecphantus also differed from that of Democritus in that he maintained the cosmos to be unique, and the number of the atoms finite. In the view of Democritus the void was infinite and contained an infinite number of worlds scattered about the vastness of space. Once again Ecphantus has modified atomism into something more in keeping with the religious requirements of Pythagoreanism.

Philolaus, it seems, was the first to make the momentous suggestion that the apparent daily rotation of the heavenly bodies is affected by the actual movement of the earth from which we observe them.[1] He explained this, however, as a planetary revolution about an invisible central fire. A little later Ecphantus and Heraclides (there is not the evidence to assign priority between them), and probably also Hicetas, brought the new idea more into line both with earlier philosophy and with common sense by restoring the earth to the centre and supposing it to rotate about its own axis.

It is interesting to note that Copernicus, in the preface to *De Revolutionibus Orbium Coelestium*, quotes Aët. III, 13, 1–3 (the theories of Philolaus, Heraclides and Ecphantus about the movement of the earth) as having given him the courage to consider seriously (*quamvis absurda opinio videbatur*) the question whether the heavenly revolutions might be explained *posito terrae aliquo motu*. Kranz (*Convivium, loc. cit.*) suggests that the indivisible bodies of Ecphantus, possessed of *dynamis* and activated by divine power, may have been a direct influence on the monads of Giordano Bruno (themselves containing their own kind of cosmogonic spiritual power) and through him on the monads which Leibniz posited as 'forces primitives'. Not only would Bruno have read Copernicus, but Hippolytus's *Refutation* was also well known in the Renaissance period. Little as we know of Ecphantus, it does seem that his Pythagorean version of atomic theory was an original and effective contribution to the development of cosmological thought.

(4) *Hicetas*

Of Hicetas we know even less than of Ecphantus. The testimonies are as follows:

(*a*) D.L. VIII, 85 (DK, 44 A 1): 'Philolaus is also supposed to have been the first to maintain that the earth moves in a circle, though some say it was Hicetas the Syracusan.'

---

[1] Cf. pp. 286f., above.

(*b*) Cicero, *Ac. Pr.* II, 39, 123 (DK, 50, 1): 'Hicetas of Syracuse, so Theophrastus says, held the view that the heavenly vault, the sun, moon and stars, in fact everything in the sky, was motionless. Nothing in the universe moved except the earth, which, by turning upon itself and rotating about its axis at high speed, produced the same effects as if the earth were stationary and the heavens in motion.'

(*c*) Aët. III, 9, 1–2 (DK, 50, 2): 'Thales and those who followed him said that there was one earth, Hicetas the Pythagorean two, our own and the counter-earth.'

The statement which Cicero makes on the authority of Theophrastus is full and explicit. Against it the vague allusion in Diogenes to a minority who credited Hicetas with an anticipation of the Philolaic system can carry no weight. Van der Waerden (*Astr. d. Pyth.* 55) has, it is true, attempted to find the theory of a planetary earth in the words of Cicero, which he translates not 'about its axis' but 'about the axis of the universe'. There is, as he points out, no word for 'its', but only *circum axem*, 'i.e. "about an axis", or, in my opinion, "about *the* axis" (of the universe)'. But this argument is more naturally reversed. In the absence of any qualifying word at all, it is much easier to suppose that *circum axem...se convertat* means 'turns around its own axis' than to supply *mundi* from the previous clause. To imagine that Cicero would make things so difficult for his readers is to offer an undeserved insult to a master of lucid prose.

There remains passage (*c*), which is irreconcilable with Cicero's statement. It is highly suspicious. The compiler has practically condensed his Theophrastus (or an intermediate source) to nonsense, for it is absurd to confine belief in the uniqueness of the earth to Thales and his followers. It is also most improbable that in a brief enumeration like this, where only the chief representatives of a theory are being mentioned, the name of Philolaus should not occur in connexion with the counter-earth with which he was so generally associated. Boeckh went so far as to suppose that the name of Philolaus had fallen out in transcription, and his conjectural emendation was accepted as probable by Zeller.[1] Whatever the explanation, it is safest to trust to Cicero's version of Theophrastus, and to group Hicetas with Ecphantus and

---

[1] ZN, 530, n. 1. Boeckh's suggestion was that the sentence originally ran Θ. καὶ οἱ ἀπ' αὐτοῦ μίαν εἶναι τὴν γῆν, Ἱ. ὁ Πυθαγόρειος ⟨μίαν, Φιλόλαος δὲ ὁ Πυθαγόρειος⟩ δύο, κτλ.

Heraclides as one of those who simplified the Philolaic system by supposing the earth to rotate 'not in the sense of changing its location'.

Nothing is known of Hicetas's life, but if the above interpretation is
right, there is, as Zeller remarked (ZN, 530, n. 1), much to be said
for Boeckh's conjecture that he was a younger man than Philolaus.
Boeckh thought it also probable that Ecphantus was his pupil.

(5) *Philolaus*

Philolaus was a Pythagorean of South Italy, according to some a
Crotoniate, to others a Tarentine. The best evidence for his date is the
mention of him in Plato's *Phaedo*. The words of Cebes at 61 E, 'I heard
Philolaus say, when he was living in our city...', indicate that Philolaus
had been living in Thebes but left it before the death of Socrates in
399 B.C. The upheavals in South Italy, which were the cause of Philolaus's exile to Thebes, are dated by Minar on good grounds to about
454, and tradition going back to Aristoxenus (the friend of some of his
pupils) said that he was then a young man.[1] The statement of Diogenes
that Plato met Philolaus, as well as his pupil Eurytus, when he visited
the West about 388, rests on no good authority, but is not impossible
on this reckoning. Other evidence (cited by Raven, *P. and E.* 94) is in
accord, and we may take it that Philolaus was born about 474, that is,
perhaps no more than 20 to 25 years after the death of Pythagoras.

Aristotle, like Plato, mentions Philolaus once only, and in a rather
uninformative context. In the *Eudemian Ethics* he is discussing voluntary and involuntary action, and suggesting that one must take into
consideration what a man's nature is able to bear. For some the
compulsion of anger or desire may be so strong that acts committed
under its influence cannot be said to be voluntary, 'but, as Philolaus
said, there are *logoi* which are too strong for us'.[2] By itself this does not
even tell us that Aristotle knew a book of Philolaus, for sceptical
minds have not failed to point out that so brief and gnomic a saying

[1] E. L. Minar, *Early Pyth. Pol.* 77, 82, 92.
[2] 1225 a 30. I am accepting the now prevailing view that *EE* is an early work of Aristotle
himself.

For the exact interpretation of the saying, it is unfortunate that such a maid-of-all-work among
words as *logos* should have been used. Diels, approved by Wilamowitz and followed by Mondolfo,
rendered it 'motives', which is perhaps as near as one can get.

may have been handed down as one of his *obiter dicta*. But one may agree with Mondolfo (see below) that doxographical testimonies going back to Aristotle's pupils Theophrastus and Menon (p. 278, above) are sufficient evidence for the currency in Aristotle's time of writings under his name on a variety of subjects.

The statement that Philolaus 'wrote one book' is quoted from Hermippus, the Alexandrian scholar of the third century B.C., but it has shared the disrepute attaching to the obvious invention with which it is linked in our source: that is, the malicious tale told against Plato in various forms, the essence of which is that he got hold of this work of Philolaus and wrote the *Timaeus* out of it without acknowledgment.[1] Demetrius of Magnesia also refers to a treatise on Pythagorean doctrine by Philolaus, and quotes its opening sentence (D.L. *ibid.*, Philolaus, fr. 1 DK): 'Nature in the cosmos was constructed out of unlimited and limiting factors, as was the whole cosmos and all things in it.' Bywater, however, emphasizes that Demetrius was a writer of the first century B.C., the time of the revival of Pythagoreanism in which Cicero's friend Nigidius Figulus played a leading part, a revival notable for its credulity and eager acceptance of spurious writings. A number of authors and compilers of the Christian era claim to quote verbatim extracts from Philolaus, and it is primarily around these 'fragments' that controversy has raged in modern times for almost a century and a half. In this century the chief proponents of opposing views have been E. Frank and R. Mondolfo, and anyone wishing to trace the history of the argument in detail will find full references to date in their accounts.[2] Short of an unlikely discovery of fresh evidence, the question will no doubt never be settled in a manner which all scholars can accept as final. Here we can only pause for a few observations which make no claim to decide it.

[1] D.L. VIII, 85. The growth and variations of this legend are set forth by Bywater in *J. Philol.* 1868, 27. It is a pity that their well-founded indignation at this calumny has led some scholars to deny that Pythagoreanism had any considerable influence on Plato at all. The wording of Diogenes suggests that Hermippus knew the book, but would by no means go bail for the story (βιβλίον ἕν, ὅ φησιν Ἑ. λέγειν τινὰ τῶν συγγραφέων Πλάτωνα τὸν φιλόσοφον...ὠνήσασθαι).

[2] Frank, *Plato u. d. sog. Pythagoreer*, esp. 263–335; Mondolfo in his Italian translation of Zeller–Nestle (1938), 1, 2, 367–82. Of recent discussions in English one may mention A. Cameron, *Pyth. Background*, 46, n. 29, and Raven, *P. and E.* 92–100. A lively defence of the fragments has been undertaken by de Santillana and Pitts, *Isis*, 1951, 112–20. For the latest conspectus of the controversy see Thesleff, *Pythagorean Literature*, 41–5.

Those who impugn the fragments do not seem to be at their best on the subject. The early full-scale attack of Bywater (*J. Phil.* 1868, 20–53) employs arguments which are hardly worthy of that great scholar. The question, he says, 'resolves itself into a somewhat narrower one: are the Philolaic fragments on number metaphysical rather than arithmetical, that is to say, Platonic in their origin rather than Pythagorean?' The examination of Pythagorean philosophy which we have now made suggests that this criterion is somewhat artificial and hardly likely to be workable. But Bywater was of those who resent the suggestion that a genius like Plato could have owed anything considerable to his predecessors. 'We have in Aristotle (*Met.* A 5)', he writes, 'a general assertion of Plato's debt, *if such it can be called*, to his Pythagorean predecessors.' What Aristotle says at the beginning of ch. 6, after describing the Pythagorean philosophies, is: 'To the philosophies described there succeeded the work of Plato, *which in most respects followed these men*, though it had some features of its own apart from the Italian philosophy.'

Again, in fr. 14 Philolaus attributes Orphic doctrines about the soul to 'ancient theological writers and seers'. To speak in this way of 'the Orphic societies of the fifth century B.C.', says Bywater, would have been natural to a writer of the age of Cicero, but not to a writer who himself lived in that century. Apart from the fact that the existence of anything called 'an Orphic society' in the fifth century is doubtful, the doctrines got their name because they were enshrined in verses ascribed to Orpheus and Musaeus, who were certainly ancient and venerable in fifth-century eyes. Equally absurd is the argument that to say that the body is the soul's tomb is 'diametrically opposed' to the description of it as linked by way of punishment to the body, because in one case the soul must be supposed to be dead, and in the other alive! The doctrine expressed is simply that to be confined in a body is a grim business for the soul and prevents it from enjoying its true life. There is no contradiction in the fact that different metaphors were used to illustrate the same religious truth.

In conclusion Bywater says that forgeries of this sort were easily acceptable in antiquity, but not now, because 'criticism has learned to see continuity even in the world of thought; we assume that ideas do not spring up fortuitously or out of due season, but in the intellectual soil and atmosphere prepared for them'. But he does not seem to apply this salutary principle to Plato, whose philosophy, it may with equal plausibility be argued, could not have been what it was had not the soil and atmosphere been prepared for him (as his pupil Aristotle tells us that it was) by the Pythagoreans.

The position maintained by Frank is a difficult one. Those who (like Bywater) suppose the spurious work of Philolaus, from which our fragments are taken, to be a Neopythagorean production of the era of 'Timaeus on the World-Soul', 'Ocellus Lucanus' and other similar forgeries, have an easier time;[1] but the thesis of Frank is that the forgery was perpetrated in the immediate circle of Plato's own disciples. This leaves a limited field, from which his own choice is Speusippus, Plato's nephew who succeeded him in the headship of the Academy and evolved a system closer in type to the Pythagorean than to Plato's own.[2] He makes much of what he calls 'the contemporary literary fashion' of ascribing what one wrote to somebody else (p. 277), which was 'the well-known practice' of the Academy. Yet the fact that it was established practice, it would seem, was not enough to save even Speusippus's own contemporaries like Theophrastus from falling into the trap of supposing that Philolaus had really written what Speusippus put forward in his name. When Frank goes so far as to entertain the possibility that Philolaus may be no more than a fictional character in Plato's *Phaedo* (p. 294), he overreaches himself and raises grave doubts of his capacity to handle evidence.[3]

None of this affords any positive evidence for the genuineness of the fragments. They have been strongly assailed on grounds both of

[1] Though of course the knowledge of a book of Philolaus on the part of Hermippus has to be explained away. See Bywater, p. 28.

[2] P. 334: 'Also haben wir wohl in Speusipp den wahren Verfasser unserer Fragmente zu erkennen.'

[3] The passage of the *Theol. Arithm.* from which comes our information about the relation of Speusippus's work to Philolaus's has been translated on p. 260, above. Wilamowitz, who also believed the fragments to be spurious, nevertheless argued in a way directly contrary to Frank: 'In the *Theol. Math.* [*sic*] is an extract from a work of Speusippus π. Πυθ. ἀριθμῶν, which according to the anonymous writer (or rather Nicomachus) is taken largely from Philolaus. *There is not the slightest ground for attributing this statement to Speusippus*' (*Platon*, II, 88). Contrast Frank, p. 277: 'But out of all these [*sc.* the disciples of Plato] only one had represented his number-speculation as drawn from the writings of Philolaus, namely Speusippus.'

language and of content, and a detailed reply on both counts is offered by Mondolfo, to whom a reader must be referred for the best defence possible. Here the aim has been to reconstitute as far as possible the flexible structure of Pythagorean philosophy up to the time of Plato, and it has been described (for reasons stated at the beginning) in general terms rather than as a series of separate achievements by individual philosophers. In this reconstruction we have relied largely on a critical use of the information supplied by Aristotle. The opinions of Philolaus have been introduced only where they were necessary contributions to the same end, and in each case as it arose I have tried to justify the attribution. Following this procedure we have credited him with belief in the soul as an immortal *harmonia* (309–12), and have seen him as the authority of Speusippus in constructing solids out of points, lines and surfaces (260), as probable author of the cosmology of planetary earth and central fire (284–7, 327), and as the teacher of Eurytus (273). We have discussed his relation to the construction of the regular solids and the question of a fifth element (267–73) and considered his embryology particularly for the light it throws on the micro–macrocosm analogy in Pythagorean thought (278f.). The rest of the testimonies and fragments (which would in any case add little to our sketch of fifth-century Pythagoreanism) have been left out of account owing to the continuing doubt of their authenticity.

(6) *Archytas*

Archytas of Tarentum brings Pythagoreanism down to the time of Plato and the Academy. More than that, with him Pythagoreanism makes a direct and personal impact on Plato himself, for the two men formed a lasting friendship. He may well have contributed to the central thesis of the *Republic* that philosophers should rule, for he seems to have been a most successful statesman and general, with a position at Tarentum comparable to that of Pericles at Athens. We are told that the law against holding the supreme office of *strategos* for more than one annual term was waived in his favour, and that he held it seven times; also that as a commander he was never defeated in battle. Several authorities stress the mildness of his character, and if Strabo is to be believed, his politics were exceptional for a Pythagorean, for he says that during the ascendancy of Archytas Tarentum enjoyed a democratic constitution.[1] We have no precise indications of his date, but he cannot have been much older or younger than Plato.

Plato made three visits to the West, first at the age of about forty (*c.* 388/7), then again after an interval of twenty years, and thirdly six years after that. On his first journey he visited the Italian cities before going on to Sicily, and in all probability made the acquaintance of Archytas then. At any rate by the second visit he had established relations with him and the Tarentines as well as with the tyrant of Syracuse, Dionysius II:[2] in his efforts to persuade Plato to come to Sicily a third time Dionysius sent a trireme with one Archedemus, whose opinion he thought Plato would value as that of an associate of Archytas. On this last visit, after he had incurred the hostility of the tyrant and had reason to fear for his life, he got word to Archytas and his other friends in Tarentum, and they sent a ship to Syracuse and persuaded Dionysius to let him go.

So much we know from Plato's seventh letter. It says nothing of any interchange of philosophical ideas, but the statements of later writers, used by Cicero, that one of Plato's motives in visiting the Western centres of Pythagoreanism had been to learn more of that philosophy, have everything in their favour.[3] Discussion of this point will be more appropriate in connexion with Plato, but it is likely that the shock of Socrates's death, and further reflexion on his methods, was leading him to the view that the simple ethic of his master could not stand unless defended and supported by a metaphysic and a psychology which Socrates himself had been neither able nor concerned to provide. In his search for these he was immensely attracted by the Pythagorean outlook on mankind and the cosmos.

Our information about the intellectual achievements of Archytas

---

[1] D.L. VIII, 79, Strabo, VI, 280 (DK, 47A1 and 4). Diogenes at least was using the work of Aristoxenus, who was born at Tarentum and wrote a life of Archytas. His father Spintharus seems to have known Archytas personally (Iambl. *V.P.* 197, DK, A7). In general our information about Archytas should be well founded, for in addition to Aristoxenus Aristotle himself wrote a work on him in three books (DK, A13) and for his mathematics our authorities quote the history of Eudemus.

[2] In *Ep.* VII, 338C, he claims to have acted as a successful intermediary in bringing about ξενίαν καὶ φιλίαν between these parties.

[3] See the passages quoted by Field, *Plato and his Contemporaries*, 223f.

relates chiefly to the advances which he made in certain rather special-ized branches of knowledge. He was an outstanding mathematician, who in addition to other successes solved the problem of the dupli-cation of the cube, as formulated by Hippocrates of Chios, by an elegant construction which excites the admiration of modern historians of mathematics.[1] In harmonics he carried on the work of Pythagoras by determining the numerical ratios between the notes of the tetra-chord in three types of scale: diatonic, chromatic, enharmonic.[2] He was also said to have been the first to apply mathematical principles to the study of mechanics (D.L. VIII, 83 and Vitruvius, *praefatio* VII, 14, DK, B7) and to have been an inventor of mechanical toys. One of these was a wooden dove which could fly (DK, A10*a*), and 'Archytas's rattle' became proverbial and is already mentioned by Aristotle (*Pol.* 1340b26, DK, A10), who describes it as a toy 'which they give to children so that by using it they may refrain from breaking things about the house; for young things cannot keep still'. This goes with other stories about his consideration for children and slaves (DK, A8).

Although the testimonies, and any fragments that are likely to be genuine,[3] deal chiefly with the topics mentioned, we need not share Field's doubts (*op. cit.* 186) whether his interests extended beyond these

---

[1] For convenient descriptions see K. Freeman, *Comp. to Presoc. Phils.* 236f., or Heath, *Manual of Gk. Math.* 155-7. Fuller information about Archytas's mathematics will be found in Heath's *Hist. of Gk. Math.* vol. I. Van der Waerden in his article on Pythagorean arithmetic (*Math. Annalen*, 120, 1947/9) gives an interesting appraisal. Archytas, he concludes, was 'an inventive geometer and outstanding in mechanics and musical theory, with an unlucky love of logic and exact arithmetical calculation' (p. 150).

[2] Freeman, *op. cit.* 238. His theories on the nature of sound have already been mentioned (pp. 226f., above).

[3] The prevailing opinion is that the mathematical fragments are genuine, the rest spurious. Cf. the opinions of Zeller (ZN, I, 375-7), Wellmann in *RE*, II, *s.v.* and Ross, *s.v.* in the *OCD*. Frank was less sceptical about Archytas than about Philolaus: he regarded the 'fragments' in the 'A' section of DK as authentic because vouched for by authorities like Aristotle and Eudemus (contrast his arguments about Philolaus, p. 332, above), but considered the authenticity of the 'B' section (actual quotations in Doric) a question that cannot be decided. He admitted, however, that in this case a resemblance to Plato is no bar, 'because here Plato evidently follows Archytas closely' (*Plato u. die sog. Pyth.* 384, n. 413).

A. Delatte defended the fragments in Stobaeus of the work *On Law and Justice*, which had been rejected on the grounds that they presuppose the peculiarly Platonic theory of Forms (*Essai sur la politique pythagoricienne*, 107f.); but doubts are cast on his arguments by Rivaud (*Mél. Glotz*, 1932, II, 779-92) and Theiler (*Gnomon* I (1925), 146-54). (In general, however, Rivaud's argumentation concerning the extent of Pythagorean participation in politics is perverse.) Minar on the other hand strongly supports Delatte (*Early Pyth. Pol.* 111).

special sciences. There is evidence that, as a follower of Pythagoras, he not only gave chief place to mathematics and music but also related them to wider themes. In fr. 1 we find him repeating the Pythagorean claim that mathematics is the key to all nature, both as a whole and in detail. He supported the Pythagorean belief in infinite extension beyond the cosmos by asking the pertinent question: 'If I were at the extremity, say at the heaven of the fixed stars, could I stretch out my hand or staff or could I not?'[1] The Aristotelian *Problemata* (DK, A23a) show him interested in biology, but in a typically abstract and Pythagorean way, for the question that it occurs to him to ask is: Why are all the parts of plants and animals, other than the organs, round?

One passage from his mathematical works (generally agreed to be genuine) deserves at least partial quotation in a general history of Greek thought. It illustrates admirably his adherence to the full Pythagorean belief that number and calculation are the ruling force not only in the natural world but also in human relations and morals, and only in so far as they are heeded can society be harmoniously organized. At the same time we are reminded how much of the thought of Plato is formed in the Pythagorean mould, for it is precisely this mathematical conception of the ordering of human affairs which impresses, and sometimes disturbs, us in his works.

The discovery of calculation ends faction and promotes unanimity. Where it has entered, unfair advantage is impossible and equality established, since it is what enables us to agree over our contracts with one another. Through it the poor receive from the powerful, and the rich give to those in need, for both are confident that thus they will have their rightful share.[2]

APPENDIX

Time and the Unlimited

'The universe is unique, and from the Unlimited it draws in time, breath, and void which distinguishes the places of separate things' (from Aristotle's treatise on the Pythagorean philosophy, cited by Stobaeus, *Ecl.* 1, 18, 1. See pp. 277, 280.).

---

[1] A24 (from Eudemus). The answer to the question as given by Eudemus contains Aristotelian terminology, but Archytas must certainly have asked the question, and no doubt Eudemus gives the gist of his reply.
[2] From B3. Cf. Minar, *Early Pyth. Pol.* 91 f.

Time and the Unlimited

In dealing with Anaximander (p. 86, above) I had occasion to remark that the drawing of distinctions between different meanings of the same word belongs to a fairly advanced stage of thought. When he spoke of the *arche* of all things as the *apeiron*—the Unlimited, or Infinite—he meant by this not only that there was an indefinitely large amount of it but also that (in contrast to the cosmos which was formed within it) it had no beginning in time. The same confusion can be seen in the middle of the fifth century in Melissus. This follower of Parmenides, who like him denied the possibility of any process of becoming, stated first that what exists, 'since it did not come into being, is and always was and always will be, and has no beginning or end but is *apeiron*'. Not only does he here use *apeiron* in a temporal sense; he goes on to argue openly from this to the spatial, in the words: 'But just as it exists for ever, so it must be for ever *apeiron* in magnitude.' To his way of thinking, all that has to be shown is that it 'has neither beginning (*arche*) nor end'. If this is shown in one respect, it holds good in the other also. 'Nothing which has a beginning and end is either everlasting or *apeiron*'—a proposition which he treated as convertible.[1]

We may be sure that the Pythagoreans of the same period drew no clearer distinctions, and therefore that 'the Unlimited' outside the nascent cosmos was unlimited in duration as well as in extent. But then it must also be true that the limiting of the Unlimited by the imposition on it of number (regularity, measure, or due proportion), which is what is meant by the generation of a *kosmos*, applies in both spheres. In the sphere of extension, this means the imposition of geometrical proportion whereby the formless 'Unlimited' becomes differentiated into the several distinct forms of matter which we know; in duration, it means that by the creation of the heavenly bodies and their regular, recurrent and harmonious motions, time becomes subject to measure and in place of mere succession we have the orderly and predictable series of days, nights, months and years.

A reference to the *Timaeus* of Plato will make this clearer. Since Plato made use of much Pythagorean material in this dialogue, there

---

[1] Melissus, frr. 2, 3 and 4. These quotations have been interpreted differently (e.g. by Cherniss, *ACP*, 67–71), but I cannot myself see that Melissus is to be absolved from the confusion. His thought will be discussed in detail in vol. II.

need be no anachronism involved. If that is too bold a claim, it will at least demonstrate that it is possible to think in this way, that is, to distinguish time (χρόνος) from mere succession (τὸ πρότερον καὶ ὕστερον) and so to speak without absurdity of a time before time existed. For Plato 'time came into existence together with the heavens' (38B). 'By ordering the heavens, the Creator made an everlasting image, *moving according to number*, of the eternity which abides in unity. This image it is which we call time; for there were no days, nights, months or years before the birth of the heaven, but by putting it together he contrived to bring them into being' (37D, E). 'So from the god's intention to create time, in order that time might be started, sun, moon, and five other stars called "wanderers" were created to mark off and maintain the number of time' (38C). There follows immediately the description of their intricate circular paths.

Earlier in the dialogue Plato has said that to create the cosmos, the supreme god took over the whole realm of the visible 'not at rest, but in discordant and disorderly motion, and brought it from disorder into order' (30A). Summarizing at a later stage, he says that there were Being (the ideal model of the future cosmos), Becoming (the disorderly mass) and Space, these three, *even before the generation of the heavens* (καὶ πρὶν οὐρανὸν γενέσθαι, 52D).

Putting these statements together, A. E. Taylor used them as an argument in favour of dismissing the whole temporal element in the *Timaeus* as mythical, on the ground that 'no sane man could be meant to be understood literally in maintaining that time and the world began together, and also that there was a state of things *before* there was any world' (*Commentary on the Timaeus*, p. 69). How far Plato's account of creation is to be understood literally is not a question to be decided here, but we need have no hesitation in dismissing this particular objection as irrelevant. We translate χρόνος by 'time', but it is not surprising that two words belonging not only to different languages but to different civilizations do not coincide exactly. Time for us embraces the whole field of 'before and after', but Aristotle says: 'Before and after are involved in motion, but time is these in so far as they are numbered' (*Phys.* 223a28). Elsewhere he defines time as 'the *number* of motion in respect of before and after', and he can seriously discuss the question whether there could be time without conscious and thinking beings; 'for if there could be no one to count, there could be nothing counted.... If nothing can count but soul, and within soul mind, there cannot be time without soul, but only the substratum of time' (*ibid.* 219 b 2, 223 a 22). To put it another way, we speak of a clock as an instrument for measuring time. In Plato's and Aristotle's scheme of things, time (χρόνος) is itself a kind of clock, not just the passage of events but a standard by which that passage can be measured. At one point, Plato notes that whereas the revolutions of sun and moon are universally recognized as time-keepers and given the names of day, month and year, those of the other planets, being less conspicuous, are not made use of in this way. 'Indeed', he continues, 'men scarcely realize that the journeyings of these planets *are* time.'[1] One could not wish for a clearer indication that for Plato time is actually to be *identified* with the planetary motions.

Time then is movement, or the measure of movement,[2] when regular and recurrent, and it is obvious that there can be movement when there is not time. After Plato, the distinction has perhaps been most clearly expressed by Plutarch, who in his *Platonic Questions* writes (1007 c): 'Hence Plato said that time came into being together with the heavens, but there was motion before the generation of the heavens. There was not then time, for there was no order or measure or distinction, only indefinite motion which was as it were the shapeless and unformed raw material of time.'

Our return to the Pythagoreans may be helped by two further statements of Aristotle. In the *Physics* (218 a 33) he writes that 'some say time is the movement of the whole, others that it is the sphere itself'. The first view is obviously Plato's, and it is hardly necessary for Simplicius to cite, as he does, eminent authorities for the attribution. The second can be none other than Pythagorean, as some ancient authorities also said, though Simplicius rather obscurely suggests that 'perhaps' these have misunderstood a sentence of Archytas. According to Aëtius 'Pythagoras [that is the Pythagoreans] said that time was the

---

[1] 39 c ὡς ἔπος εἰπεῖν οὐκ ἴσασιν χρόνον ὄντα τὰς τούτων πλάνας.

[2] Arist. *Phys.* 223 b 21 διὸ καὶ δοκεῖ ὁ χρόνος εἶναι ἡ τῆς σφαίρας κίνησις, ὅτι ταύτῃ μετροῦνται αἱ ἄλλαι κινήσεις καὶ ὁ χρόνος ταύτῃ τῇ κινήσει.

enclosing sphere'.[1] Aristotle continues (218b5): 'The reason why the sphere of the whole seemed to be time to those who took that view is that everything is in time and everything is in the sphere of the whole; but the statement is too childish for us to go into its impossibilities.' The tone is that which Aristotle habitually adopts towards the Pythagoreans, and the theory itself bears their characteristic mark of a fusion between concrete and abstract, the cosmic sphere and the measure of cosmic motion.

We may now go back to our original statement from Aristotle's treatise on the Pythagoreans, that according to them the universe (οὐρανός) draws in from the Unlimited time and breath and the void. The cosmic nucleus starts from the unit-seed, which generates mathematically the number-series and physically the distinct forms of matter. To do this it feeds on the Unlimited outside and imposes form or limit on it. Physically speaking this Unlimited is unformed matter, imagined as breath or air;[2] mathematically it is extension not yet delimited by number or figure. But it had a temporal aspect too. As *apeiron* in the full sense, it was movement or duration without beginning, end or internal division—not time, in Plutarch's words, but only the shapeless and unformed raw material of time, just as it was the unformed matter of the universe and of mathematical figure. As soon, however, as it has been drawn or breathed in by the unit, or limiting principle, number is imposed on it and at once it is time in the proper sense. Thus in saying that 'the nearest portions of the Unlimited were drawn in and limited by the Limit' the Pythagoreans were describing what to us might seem three unrelated processes, though to them they were only three aspects of a single process: the Limit, that is the growing cosmos, breathed in matter for its physical growth, it imposed form on sheer extension, and by developing the heavenly bodies to swing in regular, repetitive circular motion around their harmoniously related orbits it took in the raw material of time and turned it into time itself.

[1] 1, 21, 1, DK, 58B33: Πυθαγόρας τὸν χρόνον τὴν σφαῖραν τοῦ περιέχοντος εἶναι.

[2] Self-moving, no doubt, and therefore animate, soul as well as body. This is an important point for Pythagorean doctrine as a whole, but not for the present limited discussion.

V

ALCMAEON

Alcmaeon of Croton was by some late writers called a Pythagorean.[1] Aristotle, however, who thought him of sufficient importance to compose a work in refutation of him (πρὸς τὰ Ἀλκμαίωνος, D.L. v, 25), expressly distinguishes him from the Pythagoreans, and is borne out in this by some of the doctrines attributed to him. His citizenship of Croton, together with his belief in the immortality of the soul and its kinship with the divine, and in the divinity of the stars, and a general emphasis on the role of opposites in nature, would be sufficient, in the opinion of uncritical Neopythagorean and Neoplatonic writers, to warrant the Pythagorean label. In fact, however, he seems to have displayed considerable originality of thought, 'without', as Heidel put it, 'recognizable affiliation with any special group of natural philosophers'.

This comparative independence makes it difficult to determine his date by assigning him a probable place, on internal testimony, in the succession of Presocratic philosophers. Of positive evidence we have only one sentence of Aristotle's *Metaphysics*, which is, however, missing from the Laurentian MS. A[b]. In ch. 5 of the first book, Aristotle lists the ten Pythagorean pairs of opposites (p. 245, above), and continues (986a27): 'Alcmaeon of Croton appears to have spoken in the same way, and either he took this doctrine from them or they from him;[2] for as to his period, he lived in the old age of Pythagoras.' Admittedly the Greek of the last clause is vague (cf. Wachtler, *op. cit.* n. 1 on p. 342), but at least it means that the lifetimes of Pythagoras and Alcmaeon overlapped. On the other hand the words long ago came under suspicion of being a later interpolation, though the editors of

[1] D.L. VIII, 83 says Πυθαγόρου διήκουσε, Iambl. *V.P.* 104, 267 includes him in a list of Pythagoreans. So also Philop. *De An.* p. 88 Hayduck, schol. on Plato, *Alc. I*, 121 E. Simpl. (*De An.* 32.3) reports objectively that ὑπὸ μὲν ἄλλων ὡς Πυθαγόρειος παραδέδοται but that Aristotle denies this.

[2] This is the evidence for saying that in Aristotle's eyes Alcmaeon himself was not a Pythagorean. Three lines lower down he goes on to say that Alcmaeon did not in fact conceive of the opposites in the same way as the Pythagoreans (οὐχ ὥσπερ οὗτοι).

341

Aristotle admitted them until Ross, who writes (note *ad loc.*) that they 'are omitted by A^b, and there is no trace of them in Alexander; they are probably a later addition, though the statement is likely enough to be true'. Since then the first clause of Ross's sentence has been accepted more readily than the last, and there has been a tendency to put the lifetime of Alcmaeon later and later, until L. Edelstein wrote in 1942:

Generally speaking, Stella's essay increases the suspicion that Alcmaeon cannot possibly have been a man of the sixth century. One must probably go still further than did those who contested this date and assume that Alcmaeon belonged to the Pythagoreans [*sic*] of Socrates's time or even later; all the convictions ascribed to him seem indicative of such an attribution. Certainly, had Alcmaeon lived at the end of the fifth century B.C. instead of the sixth, his views as outlined by Stella according to the testimonies preserved would be more plausible though far less original. Whether this traditional picture itself will have to be modified as a result of an inquiry into the genuineness of the fragments, nobody can as yet say.[1]

In favour of the genuineness of the words in the *Metaphysics* it may be said (1) that, on the general authority of A^b, Ross's own researches have altered the balance of the evidence. Of his opponents Wachtler wrote in 1896 (*op. cit.* 4): 'suo iure codicem A^b optimum metaphysicorum testem esse contendunt'. Contrast Ross (*Metaph.* clxv):

It is perfectly clear that neither EJ nor A^b should be followed exclusively. But the weight of the Greek commentators and of the medieval translation is decidedly on the side of EJ, and I have accordingly followed this group of manuscripts, except where the evidence of the Greek commentators, or the sense, or grammar, or Aristotelian usage...turns the scale in favour of A^b;

---

[1] *AJP*, 1942, 372.

Before Ross, Brandis, Zeller (ZN, 597, n. 2) and others had suspected the words in Aristotle, but like Ross, Zeller had thought them an accurate approximation to Alcmaeon's date. J. Wachtler, in what is still the best monograph on Alcmaeon (*De Alcmaeone Crotoniata, ad init.*), defended their genuineness, as also in recent times does Skemp (*Theory of Motion in Plato's Later Dialogues*, 36), and they are retained in DK, 24A3 (with Diels's conjectural addition of νέος). But many modern writers reject them, as does Jaeger in his Oxford text of 1957.

As to Alcmaeon's date, Wellmann (*Arch. f. Gesch. d. Medizin*, 1929, 302) suggested the first half of the fifth century, and Deichgräber (*Hippokr. über Entstehung u. Aufbau des Menschl. Körpers*, 37) the middle, as also does Heidel in *Hippocr. Medicine*, 43 f. ('Judging by his opinions, one would naturally take [Alcmaeon] for an unusually intelligent physician living about 450 B.C.'). Mr G. E. R. Lloyd in an unpublished thesis has written that 'all lines of evidence would point to a date about the middle or end of the fifth century'. But the remarks of Edelstein, Heidel and Lloyd are all made *en passant*, and the evidence itself is not cited.

(2) that the silence of Alexander means little (see Wachtler, 5 f.), and Asclepius includes the words in his commentary (39.21 Hayduck); (3) that the reference to Alcmaeon's date undoubtedly gains point from Aristotle's next sentence, in which he expresses uncertainty whether Alcmaeon or the Pythagoreans can claim priority for the particular doctrine in question. Zeller's remark that the words 'stand there rather idle' is unjustified. Moreover we must reject one argument advanced by Ross and repeated by Jaeger, namely that the words are suspect because they mention Pythagoras by name, and Aristotle only does this once elsewhere and nowhere claims any knowledge of his date. This ignores the fact that Aristotle wrote treatises on the Pythagoreans which are lost, but which certainly gave some account of Pythagoras himself. However, since the genuineness of the remark is by no means universally admitted, the best hope of assigning an approximate date to Alcmaeon must lie in the nature of his views, and so cannot well be discussed until the evidence for these views, such as it is, has been considered. For the moment we may simply say that if the mention of his date is not Aristotle's, that is not in itself evidence that his lifetime did *not* overlap that of Pythagoras, but only that we can no longer claim Aristotle himself as a witness to the fact.

Favorinus the friend of Plutarch (quoted by Diogenes, VIII, 83) said rather absurdly that Alcmaeon had the reputation of being the first to write a natural philosophy (φυσικὸν λόγον). Galen twice mentions him along with Parmenides, Melissus, Empedocles and others as author of a book which passed under the title *On Nature*. This work was no longer available to commentators of the Christian era,[1] who were dependent on Aristotle and Theophrastus for their information about Alcmaeon. Aristotle presumably had the book in order to write his polemic against it, and Theophrastus summarizes at length its account of sensation, obviously at first hand. Wachtler (*op. cit.* 32f.) has argued that it probably survived in the Hellenistic library at Alexandria. With Alcmaeon as with Philolaus, Diogenes (VIII, 83 and 85, following Demetrius of Magnesia) quotes the first few words of his book, and this seems to go back to the practice of Callimachus, who

---

[1] Probably not to Galen himself, Wachtler, p. 32. For the Aristotelian commentators cf. esp. Simpl. *De An.* 32.6 and Philop. *De An.* 88.11 Hayduck.

in his catalogue of the library regularly gave title followed by opening words.

Diogenes writes of Alcmaeon (VIII, 83): 'Most of what he says concerns medicine, though he sometimes treats of natural philosophy, saying, "The majority of human things go in pairs".' This farrago is typical of the compiler, who could have illustrated the 'physical' side of Alcmaeon's thought very much better than by tearing this particular sentence from its context in Aristotle. Alcmaeon had indeed an intense interest in medicine and physiology, which influenced the whole tendency of his thought, but he lived before the age of specialization. The study of the human body was still only a part of philosophy as a whole, and he did not hesitate to pronounce also on the nature of knowledge, on cosmology and astronomy, and on the immortality of the soul.

The opening words of his treatise were: 'Thus says Alcmaeon of Croton, the son of Peirithous, to Brotinus, Leon, and Bathyllus. Concerning things unseen, and concerning mortal things, the gods see clearly, but so far as men may judge....'[1] Many Presocratic philosophers are sublimely certain that they have the key to knowledge. Alcmaeon opens on a humbler note: certainty is only for the gods. They know the truth directly, but men can only follow the signs[2] given to them in the visible world and by interpreting them feel their way towards the unseen. Cornford has shown in *Principium Sapientiae* that in his certainty the early philosopher shows himself the successor of the seer-poet, speaking under divine inspiration, whereas the humbler attitude towards knowledge was inculcated by the nascent science of medicine with its detailed observation of particular cases and its awareness of fallibility in diagnosis. Alcmaeon is already writing in the spirit

---

[1] Fr. 1 (D.L. VIII, 83). The asyndeton in the first six words of the second sentence is awkward, and περὶ τῶν θνητῶν may well conceal a corruption (see *app. crit.* to DK, 24в 1 for suggestions), but the general contrast between divine and human knowledge is unaffected.

The 'dedication' (Burnet's word is not too unsuitable) to the Pythagoreans Brotinus, Leon, and Bathyllus affords some slight confirmation of Alcmaeon's early date, since Brotinus is only spoken of as an early Pythagorean, either father-in-law or son-in-law of Pythagoras, or married to a woman who was one of Pythagoras's pupils (authorities in DK, 17). The dates of the other two, who appear in Iamblichus's list of Pythagoreans, are unknown.

[2] τεκμήρια. On τεκμαίρεσθαι in this sentence Professor T. B. L. Webster says rightly that it means 'to use the signs that are given to us to interpret what is unseen' (*Acta Congr. Madvig.* II, Copenhagen, 1958, 36). Cf. Thuc. I, 1, 3 σαφῶς μὲν εὑρεῖν ἀδύνατα ἦν, ἐκ δὲ τεκμηρίων....

of the Hippocratic treatise *On Ancient Medicine*, the writer of which deprecates the study of 'unseen and doubtful matters' like 'what goes on in the sky and under the earth'. Philosophers who do this may claim to know the truth, but are in fact relying on baseless suppositions. The truth of these is not 'clear' either to the speaker or to his audience, for there is no standard of verification.[1]

All that we know of Alcmaeon's views points to this preference for the concrete, a solid basis of observation, and dislike of airy hypotheses and over-simplification. He had no use for the contemporary fixation on a single *arche* to which everything could be reduced. If the doxographers could have fastened such a notion on to him, we may be sure they would have done so. But though they tell us in their schematic way of the *arche* of even minor and imitative thinkers—the water of Hippon or the fire of Hippasus—of Alcmaeon we read nothing of the sort. Like the Pythagoreans he made great use of opposites, and applied them to human nature and destiny. Aristotle's evidence on this is as follows (*Metaph.* 986a31):

Alcmaeon says that most human things go in pairs, but he speaks of the oppositions not, like the Pythagoreans, as limited in number but haphazard, e.g. white–black, sweet–bitter, good–bad, large–small. He threw out indefinite suggestions about the rest, but the Pythagoreans specified how many and what the contraries were. From both therefore we may understand that the opposites are principles of existing things, but their number, and which they are, we learn only from the Pythagoreans.

One way in which he applied his doctrine of pairs of opposites to mankind is shown in a doxographic paragraph, printed by Diels–Kranz as an actual fragment or quotation. In fact it is in indirect speech, and Diels himself noted (*Dox.* 223 f.) that some Peripatetic and Stoic terms have crept into the expression. Also the text is by no means perfect. All this enjoins a certain caution, yet the thought and much of the language have an archaic tone, especially perhaps the use of the political terms *isonomia* (equality of rights)[2] and *monarchia* to describe equilibrium between the physical 'powers' and the preponderance of

---

[1] *VM*, p. 2 Festugière (vol. 1, 572 Littré) οὐ γάρ ἐστι πρὸς ὅ τι χρὴ ἀπενέγκαντα εἰδέναι τὸ σαφές—a complaint with a remarkably modern ring.

[2] G. Vlastos discusses the political significance of this term in his article 'Isonomia' in *AJP*, 1953.

one of them. These are foreign to later medical writers, but would spring to the mind of one who lived when rivalry between popular and despotic factions was a familiar feature of city-state life. There is no reason to doubt that the theory was Alcmaeon's own. The text of Diels–Kranz may be rendered thus (B4):

Alcmaeon taught that what preserves health is equality between the powers—moist and dry, cold and hot, bitter and sweet and the rest—and the prevalence of one of them produces disease, for the prevalence of either is destructive. The active cause of disease is excess of heat or cold, the occasion of it surfeit or insufficiency of nourishment, the seat of it blood, marrow or the brain.[1] Disease may also be engendered by external causes such as waters or local environment or exhaustion or torture or the like. Health on the other hand is the blending of the qualities in proper measure.

This passage, together with other more striking instances of Alcmaeon's empirical approach to the study of physiology, sensation, and kindred subjects, explains why in his treatment of contrary qualities he differed from the Pythagoreans in the way indicated by Aristotle. They could specify a rigid and exclusive list of opposites because they were constructing a theoretical system on predominantly mathematical lines. He was a practical physician and scientist, who saw that there went to the making of a natural body an indefinite number of physical qualities rather than a set of semi-abstractions like odd and even, left and right, limited and unlimited. The world of experience, which the doctor cannot ignore, is less tidy, less cut-and-dried, than the *a priori* system of the mathematical philosopher.

Croton was from an early date famous for its medical men. Herodotus (III, 125 ff.) tells the story of Democedes son of Calliphon, a Crotoniate and 'the best physician of his day', who practised first in Aegina and Athens, then was employed by Polycrates of Samos until the latter's death at the hands of Oroites the Persian in 522 B.C. Brought to Sardis as a prisoner, Democedes cured Darius of a dislocated ankle and his wife Atossa of a growth on the breast, and finally managed to return to his native city, where he married the daughter of Milo (the athlete and friend of Pythagoras). Of this man Herodotus says that 'he was mainly responsible for the high reputation of the medical men of

[1] In this sentence Alcmaeon is of course speaking *exempli gratia*.

Croton'. There was, then, a recognized school of physicians at Croton of which Alcmaeon was one. It went back into the sixth century and was independent of Pythagoras and his followers, although after Pythagoras's arrival in the same city the two could not have remained without mutual contact or influence.

The character of Alcmaeon's physiological science may be judged from a summary in Theophrastus's *De Sensu* (25 f., DK, A 5):

Among those who explain sensation by dissimilars, Alcmaeon begins by clarifying the difference between men and the lower animals. Man, he says, differs from the others in that he alone has understanding, whereas they have sensation but do not understand:[1] thought is distinct from sensation, not, as it is for Empedocles, the same.

He then proceeds to each sense separately. Hearing is through the ears because they contain void, which resounds. Sound is produced in the cavity [*sc.* of the outer ear—Beare], and the air [of the intra-tympanic ear—*id.*] echoes it. A man smells with his nostrils, as he draws the breath up to the brain in the act of breathing. Tastes are distinguished by the tongue, which being warm and soft melts the object by its heat, and owing to its porous and delicate structure receives and transmits the flavour. The eyes see through the water surrounding them. That the eye contains fire is evident, for the fire flashes forth when it is struck,[2] and it sees by means of the bright element and the transparent[3] when the latter gives back a reflexion, and the purer this element is, the better it sees.

All the senses are in some way connected to the brain, and for this reason they are incapacitated if it is disturbed or shifted, for it obstructs the passages through which the sensations take place.

Concerning the mode or the organs of touch he has nothing to say. This then is the extent of his explanations.

This account (to which the doxographers, naturally enough, add nothing material) is not altogether easy to translate, and no doubt it is inevitable that the inchoate physiology of Alcmaeon should at certain points appear obscure. Our knowledge can, however, be supple-

[1] The word used, ξυνιέναι, means literally 'to put together', and traces of this basic meaning probably survived in the mind of a Greek writer of the fifth century. All animals have sensation, but only man can make a synthesis of his sensations.

[2] The subject of ἐκλάμπειν is πῦρ. Cf. Arist. *De Sensu*, 437a24.

[3] I.e. the fire and the water both play their part (Wachtler). Beare, rather against the sentence-construction, refers both epithets to water on the ground that στίλβειν applies more appropriately to it than to fire (*Gk. Th. of Elem. Cogn.* 11, n. 3). This seems to make the introduction of fire improbably otiose, but that of course may be a fault in Theophrastus's epitomizing.

mented a little by descriptions in other medical writers, and criticisms in Aristotle, of theories which are probably Alcmaeon's or similar. Those interested in the details may be referred to J. I. Beare's *Greek Theories of Elementary Cognition* and Wachtler's monograph previously cited. From Empedocles, the nearest writer in time and space whose views on these subjects have survived, he differed in several ways. In general he thought of sensation as resulting from the interaction of unlikes, whereas Empedocles explained it by a belief in the natural affection of like by like: 'With earth we see earth, with water water', and so on (fr. 109). For Empedocles, as for Aristotle later, psychical activity was centred in the heart (fr. 105), for Alcmaeon in the head. For this reason, according to Aëtius, he held that the head was the first part of the embryo to be formed (DK, A13: there are several testimonies to his interest in reproduction and embryology: see A13–17, B3).

One of the most remarkable signs of independence from his contemporaries is the drawing of a clear line (though we do not know where or how) between sensation and thought: 'Thought is distinct from sensation, not, as it is for Empedocles, the same', and this for Alcmaeon provided a criterion of distinction between man and the other animals. In *De Anima*, II, 3, Aristotle says that the other view was general among earlier thinkers, but is himself emphatic that the line taken by Alcmaeon is right (427a19ff.):

Intellect and thinking are believed to be a sort of sensation...and the older philosophers maintain that thought and sensation are the same, as Empedocles when he says 'the wisdom of men grows with reference to what is before them'....All these regard intellect as a bodily function just like sensation.... But that sensation and thinking are *not* the same is obvious, for the first is common to all animals, the second shared by a few only.[1]

Aristotle not only sides with Alcmaeon, but like him cites as evidence the superiority of man to the other animals. That he does not mention Alcmaeon by name may be accidental (he is in general annoyingly parsimonious with references to particular predecessors) or possibly due to a feeling that Alcmaeon, though he made the distinction, had

---

[1] Contrast Emped. fr. 110, 10 πάντα γὰρ ἴσθι φρόνησιν ἔχειν καὶ νώματος αἶσαν *et al.*

not understood the basis of it correctly. For Aristotle it is a distinction between corporeal and non-corporeal functions, and Alcmaeon was not yet capable of speaking or thinking in these terms.

The explicit recognition of the brain as the central organ of feeling and thought was another striking contribution of Alcmaeon.[1] In connexion with the sense of sight we have the information in Chalcidius's commentary on the *Timaeus* (DK, A 10) that Alcmaeon was the first to undertake the scientific excision of an eye. This would make it possible for him to see the nerves running from the eye to the brain, an achievement which Chalcidius pretty certainly attributes to him, though he mentions two later writers in the same sentence. From Theophrastus we know that he spoke of 'passages' (πόροι) leading from sense-organs to the brain, and by these he may have intended nerves, inferring from those which he could see the existence of those which he could not. Plato refers to Alcmaeon's discovery (though without naming him) in the *Phaedo* (96 B), where Socrates, running through a list of various physical philosophers, says ('whether it is the blood with which we think, or air, or fire, or none of these, but) the brain is what provides the sensations of hearing, sight and smell'. In the *Timaeus* Plato himself followed Alcmaeon's example, unlike Aristotle, who less wisely retained the heart as common sensorium.

Another indication that Alcmaeon's ideas were uncommonly influential is provided by the subject of sleep. Aëtius reports (DK, A 18): 'Alcmaeon says that sleep is brought about by the retirement of the blood to the larger blood-vessels, whereas waking is their rediffusion', and in Aristotle's own haematology we find this (*H.A.* III, 521 a 15): 'When living creatures are asleep, the blood becomes less plentiful near the surface, so that if they are pricked it does not flow so copiously.' It looks as if he rated the authority of his predecessor higher than the evidence of observation and simple experiment.

It is of some general interest that in his account of hearing Alcmaeon identified void (κενόν) with air. This emerges from Theophrastus, and he must have been one of those whom Aristotle had in mind when he

---

[1] Aëtius (A 13), using Stoic terminology (but cf. Plato, *Tim.* 41 C), says that for Alcmaeon τὸ ἡγεμονικόν was in the brain, and that semen was a part of it. Cf. also the words of Chalcidius (A 10): ...*a cerebri sede, in qua est sita potestas animi summa et principalis.*

wrote in *De Anima* (419b33): 'Void is rightly said to be the basic condition of hearing, for by void is meant air, which is indeed the cause of hearing when it is moved in a single continuous mass.' This identification of air with void is of course a link between Alcmaeon and the Pythagoreans (p. 280, above).

On the soul Alcmaeon had an important contribution to make.

He says that its immortality follows from its resemblance to the immortal beings, a resemblance which it possesses by virtue of being in everlasting motion; for all the divine things also move continuously and for ever, to wit the moon, sun and stars, and the heaven as a whole (Aristotle, *De Anima*, 405a30).

Cicero and Clement repeat Alcmaeon's belief in the divinity of the heavenly bodies (DK, A12), and Aëtius reproduces the argument for the soul's immortality, adding to the everlastingness of its motion the fact that it is self-caused. These are all dependent on Theophrastus for their information, and elsewhere in *De Anima* (404a20) Aristotle himself speaks of 'those who define the soul as that which moves itself', no doubt with Alcmaeon in mind as well as Plato and Xenocrates.

A vague belief in the animation of nature at large, based on its eternal and apparently self-caused motion, was ancient and not confined to philosophers.[1] In Anaximenes and the Pythagoreans this becomes the basis of a close relationship between macrocosmic and microcosmic life. The divinity of the heavenly bodies was firmly established in popular religion, which also brought men and stars together in the belief that the latter were the souls of dead men (Aristophanes, *Peace*, 832f.). But Alcmaeon had thought these ideas out and went a step further towards presenting them in a rational way. Starting from the observable fact of movement, we may suppose him to have inferred the everlasting and self-caused motion of *psyche* from the assumption that the ultimate cause of motion must be the presence of life. Life then in some form or other must have existed uninterruptedly from all time or no motion could have been either started or maintained. Aristotle divides his predecessors in psychology into two classes, according as they saw the essential characteristic of soul in

---

[1] Cf. remarks on Ionian hylozoism, esp. pp. 63ff., 127ff., above.

movement or in sensation. Of the former he says (*De An.* 403b28):
'Some maintain that soul is eminently and primarily the mover; and
assuming that what does not move itself is incapable of moving anything else, they conceive of soul as something in motion.' And a little
later (404a21): 'All those who define the soul as self-mover seem to
think that movement is the most essential characteristic of soul, and
that everything else is moved by soul, but soul by itself, for they
observe no agent of motion which is not itself in motion.'

This argument for the immortality of the soul was developed by
Plato in a famous passage of the *Phaedrus* (245 c, trans. Hackforth):

All soul is immortal; for that which is ever in motion is immortal. But that
which while imparting motion is itself moved by something else can cease to
be in motion, and therefore can cease to live; it is only that which moves
itself that never intermits its motion, inasmuch as it cannot abandon its own
nature; moreover this self-mover is the source and first principle of motion
for all other things that are moved.

Plato has taken Alcmaeon as his starting-point, but has refined the
argument and set it forth more logically. The ever-moving is immortal, the self-moving is the ever-moving, therefore the self-moving is
immortal. Soul is the self-moving, therefore soul is immortal.[1]
Alcmaeon (to judge by the reports) relied more naively on the analogy
with the heavenly bodies, which (as everybody believed) were divine
and immortal, and could be observed to be in perpetual motion. More
of his premisses are suppressed or half-suppressed, because he is nearer
to the unquestioned assumptions of pre-philosophical thought.

There is a saying attributed to Alcmaeon in the Aristotelian *Problemata* which at first sight looks puzzling (fr. 2 DK): 'Alcmaeon says
that the reason why men die is that they cannot join the beginning to
the end.' The language—'unable to make ends meet'—is a little
startling from its familiarity, but in fact the image behind Alcmaeon's
phrase is one of great weight and remarkably wide application in early
Greek thought: it is the image of circular motion.[2] The outer shell of
the whole cosmos, and all the heavenly bodies, appeared to revolve

---

[1] Cf. *Laws*, 895 E ᾧ δὴ ψυχὴ τοὔνομα, τίς τούτου λόγος; ἔχομεν ἄλλον πλὴν τὸν νυνδὴ ῥηθέντα, τὴν δυναμένην αὐτὴ αὑτὴν κινεῖν κίνησιν;

[2] Cf. with Alcmaeon's phrase Arist. *Phys.* 264b27: motion other than that of a complete circle cannot be continuous, οὐ γὰρ συνάπτει τῇ ἀρχῇ τὸ πέρας.

visibly in a complicated pattern of circles that has continued with regular recurrences from time immemorial, as was known from the records of Babylonian astronomers. It was equally obvious that these celestial revolutions were the cause of a circular repetition of events on earth. Summer gives place to winter but will return inevitably as the sun completes his circuit of the ecliptic, and this seasonal recurrence brings about a cycle of birth, growth, dying and new birth among individual things. The seed grows into the plant, which flowers, fades and dies, but not before it has dropped new seed from which the cycle of life will be repeated. Philo of Alexandria was perpetuating a very ancient idea when he wrote:

It was God's will to prolong the existence of nature by immortalizing the kinds and allowing them a share in eternity. Hence he brought, indeed hastened, the beginning to the end and caused the end to return to the beginning; for from plants comes the fruit, as it were from the beginning the end, and from fruit the seed which contains within itself the plant, that is, from the end the beginning.[1]

End and beginning meet in the seeding of the dying plant, just as end and beginning are the same point on the sun's annual journey or anything else which traces the shape of a circle. 'On a circle beginning and end are common' (Heraclitus, fr. 103).

The ramifications of this thought in the Greek mind are multifarious—geometrical, astronomical and chronological, as well as physiological—and this is not the moment to trace them all out.[2] But let us look at the context in the *Problemata* in which Alcmaeon's remark is introduced. The subject is the circular character of time, and the question whether 'before' and 'after' have any absolute meaning. If time is circular and recurrent, we may just as well be described as living before the Trojan War as after it. The analogy from the circling heavens to the history of living things is explicitly drawn (916a24):

As the path of the heaven and of each star is a circle, why should not the birth and death of perishable creatures be similar, so that the same things come into being and decay? 'Human life is a circle', as the saying is. To suppose

---

[1] Philo, *De Opif. Mundi*, XIII, 44, quoted by Kahn (see next note), 27, n. 13.
[2] Much may be learned on the subject from the illuminating article of C. H. Kahn, 'Anaximander and the arguments concerning the ἄπειρον'.

indeed that those who come into being are always individually identical[1] would be foolish, but a specific identity is more acceptable. Thus we our-selves would be the earlier, and one may assume the series to be arranged so as to turn back again to the beginning, to act continuously and always follow the same course. Alcmaeon says that the reason why men die is that they cannot join the beginning to the end—a clever saying, if we take it that he is speaking in a general sense and not with strict accuracy. If life is a circle, and a circle has neither beginning nor end, none can be earlier by being nearer the beginning, neither they earlier than we nor we than they.

The connexion of thought between the circular paths of the heavenly bodies and the eternal recurrence of history was made by means of the concept of the Great Year (p. 282, above). But the notion of circu-larity was applied in particular to the human body, whence it occurred that 'the coincidence of beginning and end was a theme of special interest to doctors'.[2] The Hippocratic *De Victu*, in a series of far-fetched parallels designed to show that in the arts man imitates the natural functions of the body, says (1, 19): 'Weavers work in a circle, starting from the beginning and finishing at the beginning: in the body we find the same circular progression; whence it began, to that it comes in the end.' Another example from medical literature is at the beginning of *De Locis in Homine*: 'In my view the body has no beginning (*arche*), but everything is beginning and end alike; for when a circle has been drawn, its beginning cannot be found.' To recapture as far as possible the thought behind Alcmaeon's dictum we must, as Kahn has noted, bear in mind not only the eternal celestial motions to which the *Proble-mata* refer, but also the Hippocratic statements about the cycle (περίοδος) of the body. 'In the human subject, which is of primary concern for a doctor like Alcmaeon, the maintenance of life depends upon the circular knitting-together of all parts into one continuous whole. When this link is snapped, death occurs' (Kahn, *op. cit.* 26). The individual human soul, in its action on the body, is trying to repro-duce in its own way the eternal circular motions of the divine stars, for, as Alcmaeon himself said, 'all divine things also move continuously and for ever, the moon, sun and stars, and the heaven as a whole'.

---

[1] As some at least of the Pythagoreans did, p. 281, above.
[2] Kirk, *HCF*, 114, who quotes the Hippocratic examples.

Alcmaeon

It is difficult not to believe that Plato was deeply influenced by Alcmaeon. We have already seen the similar proof of the soul's immortality of which he made use in the *Phaedrus* and *Laws*. The *Timaeus* teaches that the activity of the soul of the living cosmos consists of circular motions. In a human being, whose soul is essentially of the same nature as the world's soul though of inferior quality, 'the circuits of the immortal soul' are confined 'within the flowing and ebbing tide of the body'. The shock of submitting to the exigencies of bodily nourishment and rapid growth distorts the circles of the soul, which were originally constructed by the Creator according to strict laws of geometrical and musical proportion. By the assaults of matter they were 'twisted in all manner of ways, and all possible infractions and deformations of the circles were caused, so that they barely held together' (43 D–E), and this accounts for the irrational behaviour of infants. In adult life a certain equilibrium and calm are attained, and the revolutions proceed more regularly.

What then did Alcmaeon really believe about the nature of the soul? There is no further evidence, and to suggest a coherent doctrine one must resort to inference. This may be worth attempting, for it will shed some light on Greek ways of thinking, even if only dubiously on Alcmaeon's. Since soul is immortal, it evidently outlasts physical death; and if men die 'because they cannot join the beginning to the end', it follows that the soul, which is immortal, does join them. Thus we have already implicit (and for all we know explicit) in Alcmaeon's philosophy the doctrine that the soul imitates the divine stars and heavens not only in self-caused motion but in circular motion.[1] So far we may follow Rostagni (*Verbo di P.* 136). But when he goes on to say that the circle in question is the circle of births or cycle of reincarnation known from Pythagorean and Orphic lore, he goes beyond the reach of legitimate inference. There is no hint that Alcmaeon believed in transmigration, and it has more than once been pointed out that the radical distinction which he draws between men and animals tells rather against it. It may not be easy to imagine how he conceived of

---

[1] This conclusion has been reached here independently of the arguments of Skemp in *The Theory of Motion in Plato's Later Dialogues* (Cambridge, 1942), ch. 3. I do not think the objections of Festugière (*REG*, 1945, 59–65) to Skemp's arguments are fatal.

the soul's circular motion, but Plato, a much more advanced thinker, saw no difficulty in describing its revolutions as going on inside our heads, a procedure unconnected with the belief in transmigration, although he held that also. A further conjecture of Rostagni's, that the soul is only subject to motion—only 'moves itself' at all—when it enters the world of incarnate being, and is in its own nature unmoved, not only outruns the evidence but contradicts it.

The testimonies might suggest that Alcmaeon had a double conception of the soul like that of Empedocles which has been discussed in connexion with the 'soul-harmony' doctrine on pp. 317ff. Sensation and thought both belong to the body, being dependent on the brain: yet the soul is immortal, and must therefore be not the 'empirical' soul but the divine *daimon* temporarily incarcerated in a human body and having knowledge not of the world around it but of things divine. This too is maintained by Rostagni, in whose eyes Alcmaeon owed his belief in the soul's immortality to 'the mystical currents pervading the sixth century B.C.' (*op. cit.* 102ff.). 'The immortal soul that he concedes is the mystical soul, very different from the body and from the soul of the body centred in the brain' (p. 154). On the other hand (*a*) there is no evidence for it, nor any hint that Alcmaeon like Empedocles used the word *daimon* or any other second word when speaking of the human soul; (*b*) it seems to have been a cardinal point of difference between Alcmaeon and Empedocles that Empedocles said that thought and sensation were 'the same', so that even the lower animals possessed some faculty of thinking (Aët. IV, 5, 12, DK, 28A45). He therefore insisted at every turn on the Pythagorean belief in the close kinship of men and the lower animals, whereas Alcmaeon distinguished between mind and the senses and regarded the possession of intelligence as marking off humanity from the beasts.

Perhaps the most likely supposition is this. *Psyche* for a thinker of the fifth century meant not only *a* soul but soul; that is, the world was permeated by a kind of soul-stuff which is better indicated by the omission of the article. Soul animates the cosmos, and its characteristic manifestation is the unceasing and self-caused motion which it performs and imparts to the heavenly bodies. Portions of this soul-substance, Alcmaeon thought, inhabit the human body, and in particular the brain, where they naturally attempt to carry out the same circular motions, but are hampered by the crasser material in which they are now implicated. In the end the uneasy partnership breaks down, the composite creature as a whole can no longer preserve the integrity of the circle, and the immortal soul deserts the body, which thereupon perishes. A doctor's task is, in detail, to maintain or restore the equilibrium in the body of the physical opposites wet, dry, cold, hot, bitter, sweet and the rest; but in general terms his aim may be described as the establishment of conditions in which the soul may be least impeded by the body from carrying out its natural revolutions. So long as physical equilibrium is preserved, the soul is able to impart to the body, by means of its own regular motions, movement and the powers of sensation and thought.

Our sources do not tell us what Alcmaeon supposed to happen to a soul after death. Probably, however, it was released to join the pure soul-substance among the stars—'spirit to the *aither*, body to the earth' (Euripides, *Suppl.* 533 f.)—a notion which in one form or another was popular in the fifth century and not confined to any one religious or philosophical school.

The analogy between the regularity of motion in a circle and psychic functions, especially reason, must be accepted as natural to Greek thought. It had an important place in Plato's philosophy and still haunted the cosmology and theology of Aristotle. It is argued at length in the tenth book of the *Laws*, where at 898 A we read that 'motion performed in one place must always be about a centre, like a well-turned wheel, and is in every way so far as possible closest and most similar to the revolution of intelligence'. In the *Timaeus* the intelligence of the world-soul is synonymous with its revolution, that 'supreme' outermost revolution of the Same which affects all interior motions of the cosmos: and at 40 A, describing how the Creator set the stars in this outermost sphere, Plato actually says that he set them 'in the *intelligence* of the supreme... to keep company with it, distributing them all round the heaven'. The word 'intelligence', instead of sphere or circuit, comes as a shock, but for Plato the two were interchangeable. As he says a few lines later of the axial rotation of the stars, they 'have one motion in the same place, *as each always thinks the same thoughts about the same things*. Evidently this analogy (or symbolism; it is difficult to say how far Plato meant his language in the *Timaeus* to be taken literally) did not begin with Plato, and so far as we know Alcmaeon was the first to give it philosophical expression.

In the details of his astronomy (so far as the doxographers tell us anything about it, which is very little; see A4) Alcmaeon is credited with a repetition of the crudities of Anaximenes and Heraclitus: the sun is flat, the moon is eclipsed because it is bowl-shaped and the bowl sometimes turns at an angle to us. Nevertheless he followed the Pythagorean rather than the Ionian line in regarding the stars as living and divine, and Aëtius says of him that he 'agreed with the *mathematici*' in teaching the independent movement of the planets from West to East. According to the typical Ionian view (Anaxagoras, Democritus) they were lifeless masses of earth or stone carried passively round by the universal vortex, whereas the possibility of independent and contrary movement was closely bound up with their divinity. Both were taught by the Pythagoreans, of whom *mathematici* is an appropriate description,[1] and Alcmaeon could have picked up the doctrines from them at Croton. The phrase in Aëtius does not suggest originality, and if the other reports of his astronomy are true, he is not so likely to have been original in this as in his special fields like physiology and psychology.

Can anything be usefully added about Alcmaeon's date? First, that the disputed clause in Aristotle's *Metaphysics* does not make him out to be so early as some think. Edelstein suspects that he 'cannot possibly have been a man of the sixth century', but no one is asking us to believe that he was. Aristotle says nothing more definite than that he existed in the old age of Pythagoras. Pythagoras probably died about 490, perhaps even a little later, and whether or not we concur in Diels's conjectural addition of the word *young* (νέος) in the text, the statement does not demand that Alcmaeon be born any earlier than 510. He may

---

[1] For the divinity of the heavenly bodies we have seen plenty of evidence. The contrary movement of the planets is taught by Plato in some of his most Pythagorizing passages, and attributed to them in later times ([Geminus], [*Eisagoge*], p. 11 Manitius; see van der Waerden, *Astron. d. Pyth.* 22).

have written his book at any time between the ages of thirty and seventy, i.e. between 480 and 440. The dates of the Presocratic philosophers are no more than approximately known, but this would make him considerably younger than Heraclitus, and give him a working life roughly contemporary with those of Empedocles and Anaxagoras. He would be older than Democritus, nor do we find any trace of the atomic viewpoint in his remains. The identification of void and air suggests that he was earlier.

If we accept this date, there is nothing in his medical and physiological science to cause surprise, especially considering the antiquity of the Crotoniate school of physicians. Comparison with the Hippocratic treatises is a dubious aid, in view of their own uncertain date. But some who have sifted the question most thoroughly would date *On Ancient Medicine* (*VM*) between 450 and 420,[1] and its view of the role of opposites in disease (see especially *ad init.* and ch. 15) reflects a maturer science than Alcmaeon's: it is all very well (it says) to prescribe 'the hot' or 'the cold' as a remedy, but these do not exist in isolation, and whatever one gives the patient to eat or drink will inevitably contain other qualities as well—e.g. astringency—which will also have their effect. Similarly with *VM*'s denunciation of the philosophical school of doctors who think it necessary to make assumptions about what goes on in the sky and under the earth. Alcmaeon is already imbued with this spirit, he has the mind and method of a true physician, yet he still studies 'the things in the sky' and relates them to human life: he is only half-way towards the strict empiricism of the Hippocratic writer.

He has something in common with the Sicilian Empedocles, as well as differing from him in ways already noted. Resemblances and differences alike suggest that they belonged to the same period, and perhaps exchanged ideas, rather than that either followed the other. Both made use of 'passages' (πόροι) in their explanations of sensation, but in quite different ways. It is perhaps to be noted that not even the doxographers, to whom such language is natural, describe Alcmaeon as

[1] See in particular Festugière, *De l'anc. méd.* XIII, and W. H. S. Jones, introd. to Loeb ed. p. 5. G. E. R. Lloyd (unpublished) thinks the author a contemporary of Plato on the grounds of his use of εἶδος and ὑπόθεσις, but there remain objections to this dating.

working with the concept of the four elements introduced by Empedocles: we read only (as already with Anaximander) of the hot, the cold, etc., not of fire, air, water and earth, which e.g. the later physician Philistion mentions (fr. 4 Wellmann) when he is treating of the causes of disease. Much the same may be said about the relation of Alcmaeon's remains to those of Anaxagoras.

As we have seen, Alcmaeon also introduces ideas which were later developed by Plato—the soul as self-mover, the analogy of circular motion—but it became clear that these ideas were present in the thought of the fifth century or earlier, and needed only the application of an intelligent and perceptive mind to give them more definite form. All in all, it is more reasonable to believe that Alcmæon, as we are told, was already alive in the old age of Pythagoras, and was a thinker of considerable power and influence, than to push his lifetime down into the manhood of Plato in order to show (on little evidence) that he was not original at all.

VI

XENOPHANES

This is the way to speak around the fire
In winter, on a soft couch, belly full,
Drinking sweet wine, and crunching hazelnuts:
'Now tell us, sir, your name and home and age.
How old were you the year the Mede appeared?' (fr. 22)

Now is the floor swept, hands and cups washed clean;
Fresh-woven garlands crown our heads, and now
The fragrant unguent-bottle makes its rounds.
The bowl stands waiting brimful of good cheer,
And here's another wine that will not fail—
Soft-tasting, flower-scented in its jars.
Incense distils the scent of holiness,
And there is water, cold and sweet and clean.
See the brown loaves, and on a worthy table
A load of cheeses and rich honey lies.
As centre-piece an altar, thickly strewn
With flowers. Song and revel fill the hall.
    First it is meet for righteous men to hymn,
With pious stories and pure words, the god.
Then, due libations paid, with prayers for strength
To act aright (our plainest duty this),
It is no sin to drink—so much, that all
Not weak from age may come safe home alone.
Praise him who after drinking can relate
Fine deeds, as memory serves and lust for good.[1]
Give us no fights with Titans, no nor Giants
Nor Centaurs, which our fathers falsely told,
Nor civil brawls, in which no profit is.
But to be mindful of the gods is good.   (fr. 1)

---

[1] Translating the text in DK:

ἀνδρῶν δ' αἰνεῖν τοῦτον ὃς ἐσθλὰ πιὼν ἀναφαίνῃ,
    ὡς οἱ μνημοσύνη καὶ τόνος ἀμφ' ἀρετῆς.

ἐσθλ' εἰπὼν H. Fränkel, ἐσθλ' ἐπιὼν Untersteiner.   τὸν ὃς for τόνος Kaibel (Athen. 462 F), Bowra.

Poet and Teacher

It may well be asked why the writer of these cheerful lines is to be included among the philosophers. The first quotation recalls a scene familiar to travellers in Greek lands from the time of the *Odyssey* to our own. All possible personal information is to be extracted from the stranger, but the duties of hospitality come first. Only when he is fed, over the nuts and wine, is it proper for the questions to begin. The second sets the scene in vivid detail for a typical symposium, at which the Greek would always give the gods first place, and liked to mingle serious and elevating conversation with the entertainment of song and dance that was also provided. This poem conforms to a type, and what is laid down in the latter part scarcely goes beyond the limits of conventional piety. The stories of the gods are to be purged of their more unseemly or unprofitable elements, but this was equally insisted on by Pindar in his odes.

Xenophanes is indeed a reminder of the artificiality of the barriers which the need for selection forces us to set up between other Greek writers and those whom at this early period we choose to call philosophers. He is a poet, the only one whose genuine writings find a place both among the Presocratic philosophers of Diels and in the lyric anthology of Diehl; and like every Greek poet he was a teacher with a message to convey. Poetic form is no bar to philosophy. Though the Milesians used prose, we shall find Parmenides and Empedocles embodying highly complex intellectual systems in verse, as in the Roman world did Lucretius. But from the passages quoted it looks as if philosophy was not his only or his chief concern. Thoroughly at home in social gatherings, he loves to depict them and, as singer and honoured guest at the same time, to prescribe some of the rules according to which they were customarily conducted. Yet among later Greeks he had the reputation of being the founder of the Eleatic school, to which we owe the first attempt to base an ontology on strict deductive logic. The opinions of modern scholars vary widely: 'A poet and rhapsode who has become a figure in the history of Greek philosophy by mistake'; 'On le regarde trop comme un véritable philosophe, alors qu'en réalité c'est bien plutôt un poète humoriste'; 'Represents the only true monotheism that has ever existed in the world'; 'Clearly recognized a plurality of gods'; 'Only as a theologian can he be really understood'; 'He would have smiled if he had known that one day he was to be regarded as a theologian'; 'A link between Ionian investigations and the Eleatic doctrine of pure Being'. The list could be lengthened.

Perhaps we can make up our own minds. At least he is the first Greek philosopher (if we may account him such) of whose undisputed writings we can still read an appreciable quantity. There may be textual errors, but thanks to the verse-form we are in no doubt whether a passage is direct quotation or paraphrase (that bugbear in particular of the study of Heraclitus), and the quotations amount to about 118 lines.

(1) *Date and life*

About the actual date of Xenophanes there is a certain conflict of evidence. Timaeus the historian of Sicily (p. 170, above), an island which Xenophanes certainly visited, described him (according to Clement of Alexandria) as contemporary with Hieron and Epicharmus (A8). Hieron reigned in Syracuse 478–467 and Epicharmus was there at the time. Diogenes Laertius (IX, 20) gives his *floruit* as Ol. 60, i.e. 540–537, suggesting a birth about 575. This is not impossible to reconcile with Timaeus (whose actual words we do not know), since we have the invaluable information from one of Xenophanes's own poems that he was alive and writing at the age of ninety-two (fr. 8; a late source says that he lived to over a hundred—see A7).

Diogenes does not mention his source, but it is almost certain to have been the chronicler Apollodorus. On the other hand Clement (A8) quotes Apollodorus against Timaeus as having put the birth of Xenophanes in Ol. 40 (620–617) and added that he survived 'to the time of Darius and Cyrus'. This is a strange phrase, since Cyrus died in 529 and Darius succeeded to power in 521, and it gives ground for suspicion that sources have become distorted.[1] Clement (like Sextus, A8) has probably copied a mistaken report of Apollodorus's estimate, which we are fortunate to be able to correct through Diogenes. It would be like Apollodorus to connect the *floruit* with the foundation-

---

[1] Diels, it is true, explained the order of the names as due originally to exigencies of metre. (Apollodorus wrote in iambic trimeters.) See Zeller, 640, n. 1.

Life

date of Elea,[1] a city with which the name of Xenophanes was closely connected in later times.

We may therefore assume, as the most likely dates for his long life, approximately 570–470. He would then have been born about the same time as Pythagoras (of whom he writes in fr. 7), but probably outlived him for twenty or thirty years. Heraclitus, who criticizes him by name, will have been some thirty years younger, and Parmenides perhaps sixty. Since we do not know at what age he wrote his various poems, his exceptionally long life makes it impossible to place them within any narrow limits.[2]

He was born in the Ionian city of Colophon, which fell to Harpagus the Mede after Cyrus's conquest of Lydia in 546. 'The coming of the Mede', which he recalls in fr. 22, drove him from his native land to seek, like Pythagoras, a new home among the Western Greeks.[3] In some autobiographical lines he says (fr. 8):

> Now seven and sixty years have tossed my cares
> Throughout the length and breadth of Hellas' land.
> To these add five and twenty from my birth,
> If I can know and truly speak of that.

Fr. 3, too, shows experience of the way of life of the Colophonians before their downfall. That he was twenty-five at the time of the conquest fits well enough with the approximate date here assumed for his birth.

'Exiled from his country,' says Diogenes (IX, 18), 'he lived in Sicily at Zancle[4] and Catana.' His name also became associated with Elea, which lies some way up the west coast of the Italian mainland, owing to the common assumption that he founded the 'Eleatic school' of philosophy; for Parmenides of Elea, its undoubted founder, was thought to

---

[1] I.e. about 540 and not later than 535 (*RE*, 2. Reihe, VIII, 2400).

[2] Bowra has pointed out that fr. 2 was probably written before 520. It seems to mention all the main events of the Olympic games, yet omits the race in armour which was introduced at that time. H. Thesleff, *On Dating Xenophanes*, probably puts him too late. See G. B. Kerferd in *CR*, 1959, 72, and for a brief summary and appraisal of the evidence for Xenophanes's dates von Fritz, *CP*, 1945, 228, n. 25.

[3] That this was the occasion of his migration is certainly the most reasonable conclusion. Cf. H. Fränkel, *Dichtung u. Philos.* 421, n. 2 and *Hermes*, 1925, 176, n. 1.

[4] I.e. Messana. The older name Zancle was in use until *c*. 480 (*RE*, XV, 1221), and its use here may mean, as Burnet pointed out, that the information is from a poem of Xenophanes himself.

have been taught or inspired by him. In fact the only positive evidence connecting him with Elea is the inclusion among his reputed works of an epic poem on its foundation, along with one on that of his native Colophon; but it is of course possible that he spent some time there soon after its foundation, or even that he arrived in time to take part in it. One may sum up by saying that he was an Ionian who lived many years among the Western Greeks, that on his own testimony his life was a wandering one, and that according to tradition his sojourn included Messana, Catana, Elea, and, late in his life, the court of Hieron at Syracuse.

(2) *Social and political outlook*

His surviving poems reveal something of his social and political position and outlook. Fr. 1 shows him at home in circles of traditional good living. The singer of the elegiac song which opened a symposium in archaic or classical times was by no means necessarily the hired rhapsode of Homer who performed at rich men's feasts to earn his meal and a present. A phrase in Diogenes that he 'recited his own poems' (ἐρραψῴδει, IX, 18) has been thought to hint at this, but wrongly. There seems to have been a class of elegiac poems sung at the beginning of symposia and including advice to the guests on behaviour or deportment,[1] and the singers were at least the equals of their fellow-drinkers. Xenophanes indeed, as a man with a message of his own, speaks with a special air of authority, but without overstepping the bounds of contemporary aristocratic taste.

In another poem (fr. 2) he attacks the excessive honours paid to athletes, claiming that their physical feats are of far less worth than 'my art': they contribute neither to the good government of the city nor to its material prosperity—both of which we must therefore suppose to be furthered by the poet. This claim is characteristic of a poet of the time, and would have been made equally by Solon or Theognis. The disparagement of physical prowess has been seen as anti-aristocratic, evidence already of the 'inevitable clash' between the old ideals and nascent philosophy with its more humanistic, democratic and even revolutionary outlook. But the cult of success at the games

---

[1] See C. M. Bowra, 'Xenophanes on Songs at Feasts'.

was neither traditional nor peculiarly aristocratic. It had gained immense popularity with all classes, and tyrants courting the favour of the poor regarded it as of political importance to compete and win themselves. In a well-reasoned article Sir Maurice Bowra argues that Xenophanes 'looks back to a past when words were more honoured than athletic success, and his language, though not specifically political, belongs to an aristocratic order of society in which any far-reaching change which seemed to promote the unworthy was regarded as ἄδικον'. He concludes: 'He was a high-minded member of a society which was conscious of social and moral obligations. In the sixth century Greek aristocrats were neither all so reactionary as Alcaeus nor so homogeneous in their opinions as some social historians have thought, and the intellectual vigour and range of a class which produced Pythagoras and Heraclitus found a characteristic voice in Xenophanes.'[1] Moderation, an enjoyment of the good things of life without any ostentatious display of wealth, was a part of the same ideal, and it was quite in accord with it that Xenophanes should condemn the luxurious habits of his countrymen on the eve of their downfall (fr. 3):

> And they learned dainty, useless Lydian ways
> While they were still from hated tyrants free.
> In robes all scarlet to the assembly went
> A thousand men, no less: vainglorious,
> Preening themselves on their fair flowing locks,
> Dripping with scent of artificial oils.

(3) *Writings*

Xenophanes wrote his poems in hexameters, elegiacs and iambics (D.L. IX, 18). The extant fragments are in hexameters and elegiacs, with one example (fr. 14) of an iambic trimeter followed by a hexameter. He is credited with epics on the foundation of Colophon and Elea, which if true makes him the earliest Greek poet to treat of contemporary and recent history. (D.L. IX, 20; but cf. Burnet, *EGP*, 115, n. 2.) He was also famous for his Silloi, a title (probably bestowed on them later) indicating poems of mockery or parody. They are no doubt

---

[1] 'Xenophanes and the Olympian Games', 28, 37. For the opposite view see Jaeger, *Paideia*, 1, 171 f.

the same that Athenaeus referred to as 'the parodies' (Xenoph. fr. 22). His example was followed (and the name perhaps invented) by the sceptic Timon of Phlius in the first half of the third century B.C., an admirer of Xenophanes who dedicated to him his own satirical criticism of earlier philosophers (Sextus in A35). Part of this he cast into the form of a Nekyia, a parody of the visits to the underworld related in the *Odyssey* and elsewhere, in which Xenophanes played the role of Homer's Tiresias, the wise guide to the land of shades. Late writers mention a fourth and a fifth book of the Silloi of Xenophanes (frr. 21*a* and 42), which could have contained hexametric as well as elegiac pieces, and it is likely that most of our fragments come from the collection so named. Writers of the Christian era refer also to 'Xenophanes in his work on nature', and it is disputed whether our hexametric quotations come from a separate work with this title, or formed part of the Silloi.[1] One must at least admit justification for Deichgräber's statement that 'in the Hellenistic age there was a poem of Xenophanes with the title "On Nature" (περὶ φύσεως), in other words a poem which in the judgment of the grammarians and librarians deserved this title as much as the didactic poems (*Lehrgedichte*) of other philosophers of earlier times'. When, however, he goes on to argue at length whether this or that fragment belongs to the Silloi or the περὶ φύσεως, the exercise seems to have little point.

(4) *Tradition*

It is impossible to say how long the complete works of Xenophanes survived, but certain that many of our authorities for his teaching possessed no more than extracts, or even depended entirely on the reports of others. Since Theophrastus and hence the later doxographers who copied him took their cue from Aristotle, it is unfortunate that Aristotle himself felt some contempt for Xenophanes as a naive and confused thinker, and consequently did not devote much attention to him.[2]

---

[1] A separate hexametric work on natural philosophy was assumed by Zeller, Diels and Reinhardt, and strongly upheld by K. Deichgräber, *Rh. Mus.* 1938, 1–31. The contrary view has been favoured by Burnet and Jaeger (*TEGP*, 40, and n. 11, p. 210). KR comment (p. 166) that a formal work on physical matters 'seems questionable, though not so impossible as Burnet would have us believe'.

[2] At least in the treatises which became canonical after the edition of Andronicus in the time of Cicero and so have survived until today. It should not be forgotten that he probably wrote a

Theophrastus followed this lead in refusing to recognize him as a serious student of the physical world, 'admitting that the record of his views belongs to some other study rather than to that of nature' (Simplicius, A31). This rejection may have hastened the lapse of his more serious poems into obscurity or rarity. From Cicero onwards no one shows unmistakably by his comments that he had the actual poems in his hand, and in the second century A.D. both Sextus Empiricus and Galen use expressions indicating that they had not. Simplicius in the sixth century was a learned and careful commentator to whom we owe much of our knowledge of early Greek philosophy, and who always went back to primary sources if he could and castigated those who neglected to do so. But for Xenophanes he relies on Theophrastus and the treatise *On Melissus, Xenophanes and Gorgias* (*MXG*), and at one point professes himself unable to explain the exact meaning of a line of Xenophanes about the earth (fr. 28, *v.* 2) 'because I have not come across the actual verses of Xenophanes on this subject'.[1] So far as cosmology is concerned, it is probable that the complete poems had become difficult if not impossible of access by the beginning of our era. Short quotations were of course handed down, some of which are still available to ourselves.

A special problem is created by the existence of the treatise *MXG*, which is included in the Aristotelian corpus but was certainly not written by Aristotle and probably not before the first century B.C.[2] The section on Xenophanes professes to give a full exposition of his arguments, which if it could be relied on would be an extremely valuable source. It does, however, make him out to be a systematic

short work (in one book) 'Against Xenophanes', the title of which appears in Diogenes's list. On the other hand the spurious *On Melissus, Xenophanes and Gorgias* exists to remind us that later productions could borrow the illustrious name (see P. Moraux, *Les Listes anciennes des ouvrages d'Aristote*, 106).

[1] Simpl. *De Caelo*, 522.7, A47; Sext. *Math.* VII, 14 (A35) has ὡς φασί τινες. Other expressions of doubt in Sextus (*Math.* VII, 110 and 49) refer rather to different interpretations of extant lines, but this one is difficult to accept as such. See also Galen in A36 καὶ Θεόφρ. ἂν ἐν ταῖς τῶν φυσικῶν δοξῶν ἐπιτομαῖς τὴν Ξ. δόξαν, εἴπερ οὕτως εἶχεν, ἐγεγράφει. His reliance on Theophrastus is plain. The question of the survival of the poems was well treated by Ch. A. Brandis in *Comm. Eleat.* 1 (*de Xenoph.*), 10 ff. and S. Karsten, *Xen. Coloph. Carm. Rell.* 27 ff.

[2] So Diels in his ed. of the treatise (Berlin Academy, *Abhandl.* 1900) and most modern scholarship. Untersteiner, however, in his *Senofane*, considers it not a Peripatetic work at all, but written towards the end of the fourth century by a member of the Megarian school, possibly a former pupil of Theophrastus.

thinker using logical argument of a type impossible before Parmenides, and anything else that is known about him makes it extremely unlikely that the picture is a true one. Diels's assessment of it is generally accepted, that the writer had no first-hand knowledge of the poems: his primary interest was in the Eleatic school, and as the name Eleatic had stuck to Xenophanes he has simply read into a few words of Aristotle a great deal more than they said. It will be best to get this point out of the way before starting our own account (as proper method demands that we should) by approaching Xenophanes himself in the surviving remains of his own writings.

The earliest extant reference to him is a contemptuous remark of Heraclitus (fr. 40) that though he had much learning it did not teach him sense. The next is in Plato's *Sophist* (242 C–D). The chief speaker in the dialogue, an unnamed visitor from Elea, complains that philosophers who have professed to determine the nature and number of real sub-stances (among whom he singles out Parmenides) treat their audience like children who can be put off with stories. One says there are three real things fighting with each other and making it up, marrying and begetting like human beings; another that there are two. 'But our own Eleatic tribe, starting from Xenophanes and even earlier, relates its stories on the basis that what are called "all things" are really one.' The words 'even earlier' show that the remark is rather casual, and not seriously intended to mark out Xenophanes as the historical founder of the school. All one can conclude is that in some sense he asserted the unity of reality.

Aristotle, in the review of his predecessors which occupies the greater part of the first book of the *Metaphysics*, speaks (986b 10ff.) of a group of thinkers who taught that reality is one in a different sense from the Milesians who 'positing the unity of reality nevertheless produce things out of it as out of a material'. Such a theory necessitated movement and change, whereas the thinkers in question denied move-ment, and so by Aristotle's criterion disqualified themselves from being classified as philosophers of nature at all. He proceeds:

Yet so much it is relevant to note at present. Parmenides seems to be concerned with logical unity, Melissus with material. That is why the former says it is finite, the latter infinite. But Xenophanes, the first of these unifiers,[1] whose disciple Parmenides is said to have been, in no way made himself clear, neither does he seem to have had a grasp of either of these conceptions.[2] He simply considered the whole world and said that the one exists, namely the god. These men therefore, as I said, may be omitted from our present inquiry, two of them—Xenophanes and Melissus—altogether, as being somewhat primitive, though Parmenides indeed speaks with more insight.

This, as one would expect from Aristotle, is a careful and informative statement, to which we shall have to return. But it is utterly different from what is said about Xenophanes in the treatise *MXG*, although one can see at the same time how a not very perceptive writer, bent on making Xenophanes an Eleatic in the full sense, could have evolved it out of an unintelligent reading of the present passage. Aristotle tells us, cautiously disclaiming certain knowledge, that Parmenides was 'said to have been' Xenophanes's pupil—chronologically a perfectly possible relationship. In an age which loved clear-cut 'successions' among the philosophers, this would strengthen the impression gained from Plato that Xenophanes was the real founder of the Eleatic school. Again, Aristotle's negative verdict that Xenophanes did not distinguish between material and non-material, nor (as is implied) between finite and infinite, is absurdly twisted by the later writer into a positive statement that the divine unity of Xenophanes was *both* moved *and* unmoved, both finite and infinite. He then produces sophisticated arguments from Eleatic and even later logic in favour of each thesis in turn. This distortion may have been based not directly on Aristotle but on Theophrastus, who, though in fact only repeating his master's opinion in different words, did put it in a form more liable to misunderstanding.[3]

---

[1] πρῶτος τούτων ἑνίσας, a neat phrase difficult to match in English. It is explained by Alexander as ἓν εἶναι τὸ ὂν εἰπών. The context shows that by τούτων Aristotle means those who described the sum of things as a unity now and always, in distinction from those who assumed an original state of unity out of which a plurality has been generated.

[2] I.e. logical and material unity, not finitude and infinity as Burnet thought (*EGP*, 124), though that also follows from the previous sentence. What Aristotle says here is true: only after Parmenides could the distinction between abstract and concrete, logical and numerical unity, begin to emerge.

[3] See Simplicius in A 31: μίαν δὲ τὴν ἀρχὴν ἤτοι ἓν τὸ ὂν καὶ πᾶν, καὶ οὔτε πεπερασμένον οὔτε ἄπειρον οὔτε κινούμενον οὔτε ἠρεμοῦν, Ξενοφάνην τὸν Κολοφώνιον τὸν Παρμενίδου διδάσκαλον ὑποτίθεσθαί φησιν ὁ Θεόφραστος. Note that Xenophanes has now become 'the teacher of Parmenides' *sans phrase*. This whole nexus between Aristotle, Theophrastus and the writer of *MXG* affords an illuminating insight into the growth of a myth of philosophical history.

Karl Reinhardt in his book *Parmenides* raised a lone voice in vigorous defence of the trustworthiness of *MXG*. Admitting that its arguments must be post-Parmenidean, he solved this difficulty by reversing the order of precedence between Xenophanes and Parmenides and making Xenophanes the follower, a conclusion which, since it demands the rejection of every scrap of ancient testimony, it is impossible to accept. His strongest argument in favour of *MXG* is the accuracy with which it records the teaching of Melissus. This is confirmed by comparison with the extant fragments of Melissus's work. Why then, demanded Reinhardt, should the same man report Melissus faithfully and Xenophanes with wild inaccuracy? The answer is perhaps not very far to seek. He was a keen student of the Eleatics—Parmenides and his followers Zeno and Melissus—and steeped in their tradition. Consequently when he was dealing with genuine Eleatic thought he reported it correctly. When, however, he was writing of a man whom legend had made into an Eleatic though in fact he was a thinker of far less sophistication, his acceptance of the legend made it inevitable that he should misinterpret him in accordance with Eleatic logic; and seeing that Parmenides brought about one of the most fundamental revolutions in philosophical thinking, the misinterpretation was naturally far-reaching.

(5) *Destructive criticism*

Xenophanes was chiefly known to the ancient world as a writer of satirical criticism and denunciation, and the extant verses provide ample evidence that such was indeed his attitude to poets, philosophers, and the ordinary run of men. His passion for reform has appeared already in the social and autobiographical pieces. He recommends expurgation of theological myths at the drinking-party, fulminates against the cult of athleticism, and denounces the luxurious habits of his former countrymen. Among philosophical and religious teachers Thales, Pythagoras and Epimenides are specially named as having aroused his opposition (D.L. IX, 18), and we can still read his satirical lines about Pythagoras and his doctrine of reincarnation (fr. 7; see p. 157, above).

But the fullest weight of his displeasure was reserved for Homer and Hesiod, the two poets who as Herodotus said had determined for the

Greeks the nature of their gods.[1] The extent of their influence is nowadays difficult to appreciate, especially when we read Homer, for we enjoy the *Iliad* and *Odyssey* as marvellous poems and exciting tales of warfare and travel showing great insight into human nature, but it may not occur to us that they can ever have been regarded as much more. Yet in Greece, whatever may have been the intentions of the bards who had created them, they became at an early date the foundation of religious and moral, as well as literary, education. Herodotus was justified in his remark, and so was Xenophanes when he wrote (fr. 10): 'What all men learn is shaped by Homer from the beginning.'

Both in Homer and Hesiod the gods play a prominent part, and it is on religious grounds that Xenophanes launches his attack. His main charges are two: that they portray the gods as immoral and that they cast them in human shape.

Homer and Hesiod have ascribed to the gods all deeds that among men are a reproach and disgrace: thieving, adultery, and mutual deception (fr. 11).[2]

The second charge is, for its time, even more remarkable in its perception and objectivity:

Ethiopians imagine their gods as black and snub-nosed, Thracians as blue-eyed and red-haired (fr. 16).

But if oxen and horses or lions had hands, or could draw and fashion works as men do, horses would draw the gods shaped like horses and lions like lions, making the bodies of the gods resemble their own forms (fr. 15).

Men suppose that gods are brought to birth, and have clothes and voice and shape like their own (fr. 14).

Aristotle presumably had these last lines and their context in mind when he wrote in his handbook of rhetoric (1399 b 6, not out of any interest in Xenophanes's views, but solely as an example of a particular form of argument): 'As for instance Xenophanes used to argue that to

---

[1] Hdt. II, 53: 'It is they who created a theogony for the Greeks, gave the gods their names, distributed their privileges and skills, and described their appearance.'
[2] The indifferent verse into which the fragments have so far been translated was intended to fix in a reader's mind that it is in fact poems that are in question throughout. From now on the precise wording of a translation may be more important, and prose will usually be adopted.

say the gods are born is as impious as to say that they die; for either way it follows that there is a time when they do not exist.' This may be accepted as confirmation of the statements made by much later writers that Xenophanes upheld the eternity of God.

Another line from the Silloi runs: 'And fir-trees as Bacchi stand around the well-built hall.'[1] It is quoted by a scholiast on the *Knights* of Aristophanes in the following context: 'Not only Dionysus is called Bacchus but also those who perform his rites, and the branches carried by the initiates. Xenophanes mentions this in his Silloi. . . .' This is not the occasion to expound the psychology of the Bacchic religion, but it may be said, first, that the purpose of its orgiastic rites was to become *entheos*, filled with, and so at one with, the god. (See also p. 231, above.) This stage once reached, then as the initiate cries in the *Cretans* of Euripides (fr. 472 N.): 'I was sanctified and called Bacchus.' The worshipper could have his life taken up into that of the god who stood for the essence of life itself. Bacchus, god of the grape, was god also of all life-giving juices. He made the difference between a pliant, green and sappy bough and a dead, dry and brittle one, as also between the living creature with blood coursing through its veins and the stiff and lifeless corpse. As such his spirit was in the trees as much as in his human worshippers. Classical art shows columns of foliage with the god's mask hanging on them, and it is not at all surprising that fir-trees which decorated a scene of Bacchic rites should have been given the name of the god.[2] Although the line of Xenophanes has no context of its own to help us, we may be sure that its purpose was to heap further ridicule on popular forms of religion. Gods with human clothes and bodies, gods with snub noses or red hair, and now a god in vegetable form!

The discrepancies between the religious beliefs and customs of different people began to make a deep impression in the fifth century, as appears especially in the pages of Herodotus, and from then on gave

---

[1] Fr. 17 (Schol. Ar. *Eq.* 408) ἑστᾶσιν δ' ἐλάτης ⟨βάκχοι⟩ πυκινὸν περὶ δῶμα. So DK. Lobeck (*Aglaophamus*, I, 308, note (i)) emended more freely to ἑστᾶσιν δ' ἐλατῶν πυκινοὶ περὶ δώματα βάκχοι. Fortunately the sense is assured by the context in the scholiast (quoted in full by Lobeck *loc. cit.*).

[2] The fir had particular associations with Dionysus. The thyrsi carried by bacchants were tipped with its cones, and in the story of Pentheus the ἐλάτη plays a significant part (see Eur. *Bacchae*, 1064).

a powerful impetus to scepticism. But to find this dispassionate and critical appraisal in a contemporary of Pythagoras is remarkable, and says much for the genius of its author. Fr. 16 seems to mark the foundation of social anthropology, with a power of observation and inference that is matched in the study of nature by the same philosopher's remarks on fossils (pp. 387f., below). His condemnation of the poets for ascribing immoral acts and unworthy sufferings to the gods was particularly influential, not least through the ready response which it aroused in the questing mind of Euripides, as in the following lines from the *Heracles*:

That the gods enjoy illicit love I do not believe, nor have I ever thought it right nor counted it true that they should go in chains, nor that one god should lord it over another; for the god, if he be truly god, lacks for nothing. Those are the wretched tales of singers.[1]

This passage is so obviously modelled on Xenophanes that we may use the latter part as confirmation of yet a third charge which he brought against the poets: deity must be self-sufficient, and can admit no hierarchy within it. Though perhaps implied by a line like fr. 25 (see next page), this is nowhere stated explicitly in the extant fragments, but Euripides vindicates the dubious authority of the *Stromateis* in Eusebius, where we read (A 32): 'Concerning the gods he shows that there is no government among them, for it is impious that any of the gods should have a master; and that none of them lacks anything in any respect.' Cicero (see A 52; also in Aëtius) mentions yet a fourth way in which he showed himself well ahead of his contemporaries, namely in denying the reality of divination or prophecy.

(6) *Constructive theology*

Taken together, these charges exhibit a surprisingly high level of religious thought for the sixth century B.C. in Greece. They show that if Xenophanes believed in a god at all, this divinity must be non-anthropomorphic, morally good, everlasting, completely self-sufficient and independent. One might well ask whether a rejection of so much

[1] Eur. *H.F.* 1341 ff. The lengthy outburst against athletes in fr. 282 N. (DK, vol. I, p. 139) is an even more obvious imitation of Xenophanes.

in the beliefs of his contemporaries carried with it the abandonment of religious belief altogether. Did he believe in any kind of god? He did, and our respect is hardly diminished when we turn to the constructive side of his message. The extant verses in which he describes the nature of god may be translated as follows, if we sacrifice poetic expression in the attempt to portray the thought more accurately:

Fr. 23: 'God is one,[1] greatest among gods and men, in no way like mortals either in body or in mind.'

Fr. 24: 'He sees as a whole, perceives as a whole, hears as a whole.'[2]

Frr. 26 and 25: 'Always he remains in the same place, not moving at all, nor indeed does it befit him to go here and there at different times; but without toil he makes all things shiver by the impulse of his mind.'[3]

Xenophanes is still thinking of Homer. In the last line (fr. 25) κραδαίνει means literally 'makes to shake', which recalls the way that Olympus shook when Zeus nodded his head (*Il.* 1, 530): the true god does not even need to nod. Homeric gods, in order to affect the course of events on earth, were constantly flying down from Olympus to intervene personally; but the true god remains always in the same place. Aeschylus, another whose conception of deity was ahead of most of his time, appreciated these thoughts and took them over in the *Supplices* (100–3): 'All divine action is without toil. Sitting still he

---

[1] εἷς θεός, often translated simply 'One god'. But the couplet was certainly in Xenophanes's mind a complete sentence, and Greek omits the copula as naturally as English inserts it. One could also translate 'There is one god', but with a risk of diminishing the great emphasis placed on εἷς by its position.

[2] Reporting this line in *oratio obliqua*, Diogenes says (IX, 19, DK, A 1): ὅλον δὲ ὁρᾶν καὶ ὅλον ἀκούειν, μὴ μέντοι ἀναπνεῖν. This omits ὅλον νοεῖν, and KR would seem to be wrong in saying (p. 170) that it 'implies that the concluding words were not οὖλος δέ τ' ἀκούει but οὐ μέντοι ἀναπνεῖ'. From his use of the term σφαιροειδής, one may assume that Diogenes was one of those who equated Xenophanes's deity with the cosmos, and his last words must be meant to contrast it with the breathing world of the Pythagoreans. One cannot be certain whether the actual words were in Xenophanes's poem, but it is probably not accidental that they form the ending of a dactylic hexameter. (Cf. also Kahn, *Anaximander*, 98, n. 2: 'The accurate paraphrase of fr. 24 shows the hand of Theophrastus, and thus guarantees the concluding reference to breathing.') He may have been making the point that the one divine spherical universe contains all that there is: there is nothing besides the One, therefore no 'infinite breath' outside for it to absorb. (For a contrary view, with which I disagree, see Heidel, *AJP*, 1940, 2. Heidel argues that because *Xenophanes himself*—as he believes—did not identify god with the cosmos, therefore this cannot be directed against the Pythagoreans. He supposes it to refer to popular anthropomorphism: god needs no eyes or ears, so why should he need lungs?)

[3] On νόου φρενί cf. *Il.* IX, 600 νόει φρεσί (KR, 171); also Snell, *Discovery of Mind*, 316, n. 16, von Fritz, *CP*, 1945, 229 f. To bring out the full meaning of the words, von Fritz would translate: 'by the active will (or impulse) proceeding from his all-pervading insight'.

somehow accomplishes his intent just the same there and then, from his sacred throne.' Frr. 23 and 24 are complementary to the criticisms of anthropomorphic divine beings in frr. 11, 14, 15, 16: god is not in any way like man, he needs no separate organs of perception.[1]

God is one. The emphatic opening of fr. 23 leaves no doubt that to Xenophanes this was important and essential. Nevertheless to see it in perspective it must be understood that the question of monotheism or polytheism, which is of vital religious importance to the Christian, Jew or Moslem, never had the same prominence in the Greek mind. (For that matter, even Jehovah was not always without his divine rivals and foes.) Immediately after his emphatic proclamation of the unity of god, we have the phrase 'greatest among gods and men'. This is dealt with nowadays by the device of giving it a label: it is merely a 'polar expression'. Nevertheless its use by one for whom monotheism was a religious dogma would argue at the least a surprising carelessness.[2]

It is often said that in other places also Xenophanes allows himself to speak of gods in the plural in the conventional Greek way. Looked at individually, however, these passages amount to little. In fr. 1 he is the genial *arbiter bibendi*, and naturally sees no harm in conforming to the traditional custom which indeed it is his function to enforce. Consequently he speaks at the end of being 'mindful of the gods', and when in line 13 he mentions *theos* in the singular, that is no doubt explained by the mention of the altar two lines earlier. It would be an altar set up to a particular god—Dionysus or some other—in whose honour therefore the hymns are sung. Whichever it is, he has nothing to do with the 'one god' of fr. 23, nor should we look for serious theology in this drinking-poem.

[1] In fr. 23 οὔτε δέμας θνητοῖσιν ὁμοίιος seems worded to contradict such Homeric descriptions of human beings as δέμας εἰκυῖα θεῇσι (*Il.* VIII, 305), δέμας ἀθανάτοισιν ὁμοῖος (*Od.* VIII, 14). So Deichgräber, *Rh. Mus.* 1938, 27, n. 45.

[2] The idea is that such 'polar expressions' are simply clichés used for emphasis and not intended to be taken literally. KR, 170 compare Heraclitus, fr. 30, where 'no god or man made this cosmos' is only a way of saying that it was not created at all. A difference would seem to be that in Heraclitus the polar expression, if it were taken literally, would still state what its author wants to say. In Xenophanes it contradicts it. 'Neither god nor man made it' is as much as to say 'No one made it, it was not made'. 'Greatest among gods and men', if there is only one god, becomes strictly nonsense.

Kahn (*Anaximander*, 156, n. 3) suggests that 'in all probability the plural "gods" of Xenophanes are the elements and the sun, moon and stars; the greatest deity is the world itself, or its everlasting source'.

The critical fragments are all negative. Homer and Hesiod were wrong to depict gods as thieves and adulterers; it is wrong to believe that they are born and die, that they have human bodies, voices and clothes. From all this the message of fr. 23—that there is one god only, and he in no way resembles man—may follow without contradiction. The same may be said of fr. 34: 'No man has known or will know the plain truth about the gods and about all that I speak of.' Fr. 18 is equally negative: 'The gods did not reveal to men all things in the beginning, but in course of time, by searching, they find out better.' This is tantamount to saying that the advance of knowledge depends on man's own efforts and not on any divine revelation (p. 399, below). In no other extant fragment does Xenophanes refer to gods in the plural. Fr. 38 begins: 'If God (*theos*) had not made yellow honey....' This is not evidence either way. It is a conventional phrase in which a Greek might use either singular or plural, and means no more than 'if honey had never existed'.

Doubtless Xenophanes did not condemn the worship of gods outright, provided men's notion of them was stripped of anthropomorphic crudities and immorality. He is emphatic that god is essentially one, but if this one god was, as will be argued here, the living and divine cosmos, then he probably thought that the spirit of this universal being manifested itself to the imperfect perceptions of man (fr. 34) in many forms.

It is usually assumed that the words of fr. 23—'in no way like mortals in body'—prove that the god of Xenophanes was not incorporeal but had a body of his own, only not of human shape. Even if this inference is perhaps not certain, there is nothing in his remains or the tradition to suggest that he was so far ahead of his time as to have advanced to the notion of incorporeal being, an inherently unlikely supposition. His one god, then, had a body. What was this body, and of what shape? No relevant quotation has survived from Xenophanes himself, but most ancient authorities say that it was spherical. Texts are:

(*a*) D.L. IX, 19 (DK, A 1): 'The being of the god is spherical, with no resemblance to man. He sees as a whole and hears as a whole', etc. We may note in passing that where Diogenes's description can be checked against the extant fragments, it tallies with them exactly.

(*b*) *MXG*, 977 b 1 (A 28): 'Being similar in all directions he is spherical.'

(*c*) Simplicius (A 31) repeats the substance of *MXG*, and adds that according to Alexander the *arche* of Xenophanes was finite and spherical.

(*d*) Hippolytus (A 33): 'He says that the god is eternal and one and similar in all directions and finite and spherical and sentient in all his parts.'

(*e*) Cicero (A 34): *deum...conglobata figura.*

(*f*) Sextus (A 35): 'Xenophanes asserted...that the all is one, and god consubstantial with all things,[1] and that he is spherical, impassible, unchanging, and rational.'

(*g*) Theodoret (A 36): 'He said that the all was one, spherical and finite, not generated but eternal, and altogether unmoved.' Here the spherical shape elsewhere ascribed to god is given to the total sum of things. Comparison makes it obvious that Theodoret is referring to the same being as the others: he is so sure that Xenophanes identified god with the universe that it is a matter of indifference to him which term he uses.

Between them these passages make two points: the god of Xenophanes was spherical, and he was identical with the universe. Let us take them one by one. With such a strong consensus of ancient evidence for sphericity, one might suppose that even though we do not possess the relevant words of Xenophanes, it could be taken for granted. In fact, however, modern opinion is sharply divided.[2]

A slight difficulty is caused by the occasional intrusion of the word 'infinite' or 'indefinite' (*apeiron*)[3] into the accounts. Galen,

---

[1] συμφυῆ. The translation is R. G. Bury's (Loeb). συμφυής (lit. 'growing together') is used with the dative in various ways, meaning 'adapted to' (Arist. *De An.* 420 a 4), 'attached to' (*id. P.A.* 660 b 28), or 'coalescing with'. In the last sense Plato speaks of the visual ray that shoots forth from the eye coalescing or not coalescing with the air around it (*Tim.* 45 D), and Plutarch says that Lycurgus taught the Spartans to live not for themselves but τῷ κοινῷ συμφυεῖς, *integrated* or *identified* with the community (*Lyc.* 25). Only the last sense is possible in the present context. The meaning therefore is the same as when ps.-Galen says (A 35) that Xenophanes 'asserted only that all things are one and this is god (εἶναι πάντα ἓν καὶ τοῦτο ὑπάρχειν θεόν), finite, rational, unchanging'. The source is clearly a common one (cf. also ἐδογμάτιζε Sext., δογματίσαντα Gal.) which stated that Xenophanes identified god with the universe.

[2] A few recent opinions. Sphericity 'goes beyond the fragments and is highly dubious' (KR, 170); 'obviously due to a later interpretation of B 23 under the influence of Parmenides' (Jaeger, *TEGP*, 211, n. 23); 'Peut-être faut-il aller plus loin et dire que, déjà, cette unité cosmique et divine est conçue comme sphérique' (Diès, *Cycle Mystique*, 75 f.); 'Dass Xenophanes seinem Gott die Kugelgestalt gab, scheint mir sicher schon im Hinblick auf B 23' (Deichgräber, *Rh. Mus.* 1938, 27, n. 45); 'He regarded his god as a sphere' (Snell, *Discovery of Mind*, 142). Reinhardt also accepted sphericity.

[3] The uses of this word have been discussed under Anaximander, pp. 83 ff., above.

Hippolytus and Theodoret all combine with the epithet 'spherical' that of 'finite'. Simplicius, however, after quoting the statement of Alexander also that the *arche* of Xenophanes was finite, adds that Nicolaus of Damascus (first century B.C.) said it was *apeiron* and unmoved. Aëtius (II, 1, 3, DK, 12A17) puts him among those who posited an infinite number of *kosmoi*, in an undiscriminating list which certainly contains some errors and admits only the two divisions 'innumerable *kosmoi*' or 'a single *kosmos*', and Diogenes (IX, 19) credits him with the same belief (a most unlikely one in view of what we know of him).[1] Finally an Epicurean in Cicero's dialogue *De Natura Deorum* (DK, A34), in a cursory survey of early theologies designed to show that they are all wrong-headed, speaks of Xenophanes's god as *infinitum*.

The doxographers commonly drew on Theophrastus, either directly or indirectly, but for Xenophanes there is the complication of *MXG*, whose writer had a particular interest in the Eleatics and put forward interpretations of his own.[2] Fortunately Simplicius quotes a relevant sentence from Theophrastus himself (A31): 'Theophrastus says the hypothesis of Xenophanes was that the *arche* was one, or the universe (τὸ πᾶν) was one, and neither finite nor infinite, nor moving nor at rest.' Here as often Theophrastus is doing little more than paraphrase Aristotle, to whom we shall return in a moment. He is certainly not the authority for saying that Xenophanes believed in an infinite universe nor an infinite god, nor, as I have tried to show, is there any solid evidence that this was the truth. All the soberer accounts have 'spherical and finite', and they must be believed. Neither the unintelligent classification of Aëtius[3] nor the contemptuous remarks of Cicero's Epicurean deserve credit against them, and this leaves Nicolaus of Damascus the only one out of step. One instance of the word *apeiron* in Xenophanes's own remains must be mentioned. He says of the earth that it 'goes downward indefinitely' (εἰς ἄπειρον). This will be discussed later, but I would venture the opinion that it does not involve

---

[1] With the addition of the obscure words οὐ παραλλακτοὺς δέ ('not overlapping in time', Hicks) or ἀπαραλλακτοὺς δέ (a Stoic term meaning 'precisely similar': the MSS. differ).

[2] That the elaborate logic which he attributes to Xenophanes did not come from Theophrastus emerges clearly enough from Simpl. *Phys.* 22.26ff. (DK, A31).

[3] On which see Cornford, 'Innumerable Worlds', *CQ*, 1934, especially 9–10.

a strictly infinite universe, though when once, through the work of Aristotle, the concept of infinity had been isolated and grasped, it may well have suggested such an idea to one or two anachronistic interpreters.

Those who, like Jaeger and Kirk, deny any authority to the description of Xenophanes's god as spherical do not propose any alternative. They rightly insist that this god had a body, and the body a shape,[1] but suppose that beyond this Xenophanes only described him in negative terms. This is unsatisfactory. If Xenophanes was positive enough to state that his god had a body, he probably indicated its shape. The only argument produced against this is that Parmenides compared his One Being to a sphere and owing to the tendency, from Plato onwards, to number Xenophanes among the Eleatics, Greek historians were apt to assimilate his doctrine to that of Parmenides. Therefore the sphere is an illegitimate importation from Parmenides into Xenophanes. But does this conclusion follow? It is true that *MXG*, which carries the assimilation of Xenophanes to the Eleatics to absurd lengths, is one of the sources for sphericity; but it is much more likely that this was one of the initial similarities which must have existed to make the tradition possible at all.[2]

We have still to consider our earliest witness. Aristotle's remarks on the one god of Xenophanes have been seen in their context on p. 369. To translate the central sentence slightly differently: 'He

---

[1] Note particularly this from Jaeger (*TEGP*, 43): 'It never occurs to Xenophanes to suggest that God may be without form altogether. It is significant that all the time that the Greeks gave their philosophical attention to these matters, the problem of the form (μορφή) of the divine was one that never lost its importance.'

[2] In this I agree strongly with Deichgräber (*Rh. Mus.* 1938, 27, n. 45): 'Xenophanes muss über die Gestalt des einen Gottes Angaben gemacht haben und gerade in Hinblick auf den ὅλος-Begriff scheint das Prädikat σφαιροειδής das einzig mögliche.'

Those who regard the mention of a sphere as Parmenidean cite the phrases of Timon of Phlius about Xenophanes, that his 'all' (τὸ πᾶν) πάντῃ ἐφελκόμενον μίαν εἰς φύσιν ἵσταθ' ὁμοίην and that θεὸν ἐπλάσατ' ἴσον ἁπάντῃ. These, it is argued, are really a misappropriation of the description of the One in Parm. 8, 44 as μεσσόθεν ἰσοπαλὲς πάντῃ, and gave rise to the idea that the One God of Xenophanes was spherical. This is tortuous reasoning. It is not denied that Parmenides was an Italian Greek who lived later than Xenophanes. Why then reject the more natural supposition that he took something from his predecessor? Timon, who 'repeatedly praised Xenophanes and went the length of dedicating his Silloi to him' (Sextus: see A35), knew his poems better than we do. In any case the idea of a spherical divine universe is hardly surprising for the sixth or early fifth century. There is no suggestion that Xenophanes anticipated the pure intelligible One of Parmenides, though his insistence on unity (which is fortunately attested by actual quotation) represents an advance which no doubt gave an impetus to the even subtler thought of his successor.

concentrated his attention on the whole heaven (*ouranos*) and said that the One exists, the god.'[1]

This sentence suggests to the imagination a rather magnificent picture of the philosopher-poet standing alone in a wide empty landscape on a clear night, flinging out his arms in an all-embracing gesture and crying, 'The One exists, and it is God'; that is, looking up at the heavens and declaring that the world was one and divine. Something like that I believe he must have done, even if we concede that Aristotle's words do not *necessarily* imply it. The verb used, though a compound of 'to look', was commonly used metaphorically of a mental process. Aristotle is saying that by fixing his attention on the nature of the universe Xenophanes came to the conclusion that the One was God. If this does not necessarily mean that he actually identified the universe with the unitary divinity, it at least creates a strong presumption that he did.

Aristotle, we may remind ourselves, characterized Xenophanes as the first to posit a unity in a stricter sense than did the Milesians, but nevertheless a more primitive thinker than the genuine Eleatics Parmenides and Melissus, one who had not yet grasped the distinction between material and logical unity and for this reason did not make his concept altogether clear. That he did in some way advance the notion of unity we may assume both from this and from Plato's mention of him as having given a start to the Eleatic ways of thinking; and Aristotle tells us in what the advance consisted, namely in supposing the cosmos to be ungenerated. He and his successors 'are not like some of the writers on nature who regard reality as one but nevertheless assume generation out of the one as matter. They speak in a different way, for the others, since they generate the universe, add motion, whereas these men say it is unmoved' (*Metaph.* 986b14).[2]

---

[1] εἰς τὸν ὅλον οὐρανὸν ἀποβλέψας τὸ ἓν εἶναί φησι τὸν θεόν. (Alternatively: '...that the One was the god'.) The precise meaning of some of the Greek words is important. It is true that οὐρανός here must be used in the sense of 'universe' rather than merely 'sky'. Nevertheless it has associations quite different from, say, τὸ πᾶν or ὁ κόσμος. Ouranos *was* the sky, and he was also a god, even if the word had come to be used when the sky was being thought of particularly as the envelope of the world and even as that envelope with its contents.

The central idea in ἀποβλέπειν εἰς is that of looking away from all other things and so only at a particular object, to *concentrate* one's gaze. Its classical usage is by no means confined, as Heidel would have confined it here, to treating something as a model.

[2] It may seem odd that in *De Caelo* (279b12) Aristotle should say so emphatically of the world γενόμενον μὲν οὖν ἅπαντες εἶναί φασιν, but the words of *Metaph.* A ἐκεῖνοι μὲν γὰρ προστιθέασι

God and the World

(7) God identified with the world

They say the universe (τὸ πᾶν) is unmoved; and we have it in Xeno-phanes's own words that the One God is unmoved (fr. 26). The world is ungenerated; and in his own words 'gods are not born' (fr. 14). It is some additional confirmation, if that were needed, of the conclusion which has now become inescapable, that Xenophanes identified God and the world and to that extent may be called a pantheist. But one or two difficulties must be faced before attempting to sum up his view.

The pantheism of Xenophanes has been denied on various grounds or none. Cherniss writes (*ACP*, 201, n. 228): 'The fragments give no reason to suppose that he identified God and the world; and it is likely that the notion of a spherical god was inferred for him from the unity which he predicated of God.' This implies that if the god *were* spherical, that would be an argument in favour of the identification. Reinhardt on the other hand (*Parm.* 116f.) accepts his sphericity, and denies the identification on that very ground. He cites the statement of fr. 28, which, he claims, says that the earth (and *a fortiori* the universe) stretches downwards to infinity. This point has been mentioned already. The balance of the evidence is strongly in favour of a finite universe, and *apeiron* need not mean 'infinite'.[1]

A more serious difficulty is the immobility ascribed to the god in fr. 26. H. Fränkel writes (*Dicht. u. Phil.* 428): 'The scope of this pro-nouncement only becomes plain when it is recognized that in Greek philosophy the word "motion" covers every kind of change. Hence in the sphere of God no physical event takes place at all; only when his influence "without toil" reaches our world, is it transformed into

---

κίνησιν, γεννῶντές γε τὸ πᾶν, οὗτοι δὲ ἀκίνητον εἶναί φασιν are unambiguous, and Xenophanes is included among the οὗτοι. Presumably he has only φυσιολόγοι in mind in *De Caelo*, from whom Xenophanes and the Eleatics are expressly excluded owing to the novelty of their conceptions.
[1] Cf. Cornford, *Princ. Sap.* 147, n. 1: 'Frag. 28, stating that the underside of the earth reaches down "indefinitely" (ἐς ἄπειρον) can be explained as denying that the earth floats on water (*Thales*) or on air (*Anaximenes*), or that there is any hollow Tartarus beneath it. The earth extends downwards, unlimited *by anything else*, to the bottom of the sphere (Gilbert, *Meteor. Theor.* 280, 671). The sun, according to Xenophanes, moves in a straight line εἰς ἄπειρον, "indefinitely", not "to infinity"; it burns out in a short time (Zeller, I⁷, 669).' The addition to fr. 28 in the *Stromateis* (A 32), (τὴν γῆν ἄπειρον εἶναι) καὶ μὴ κατὰ πᾶν μέρος περιέχεσθαι ὑπὸ ἀέρος, presumably means that air cannot enclose it all round as it did the free-floating earth of Anaxi-mander. I take it to be a doxographer's gloss.

movement and events.' Kirk (KR, 172) thinks that Aristotle's statement on Xenophanes 'clearly implies that god is identical with the
world', but that Aristotle must be wrong because the god could not be
motionless if identical with a world which is itself implied to move
(in fr. 25).

The right answer to this problem lies, I think, in a challenge to
Fränkel's generalization that 'in Greek philosophy' the word 'motion'
(*kinesis*) covers every kind of change. It did so for Aristotle (which is
probably one reason why he found Xenophanes obscure), and he
methodically divided it into locomotion or change of place, qualitative
change, quantitative change, and birth-and-destruction or change
between being and non-being. But such precision is hardly found
before his time, and certainly not before the time of Parmenides, whose
confrontation of Being and Becoming, with its proofs that what is can
neither become nor perish, neither grow nor diminish, nor yet change
in quality nor move in space, marked a turning-point in Greek thought.
Before that, the word *kinesis* was not a technical term, but used in
relation to its context and most usually in the popular sense of local
motion or disturbance.

The context shows that this is how Xenophanes is using it in fr. 26.
'Not moving at all' means that the god 'remains in the same place'.
He must not be thought of as 'going to different places at different
times'. This is consistent with imagining him as the universe itself in
its aspect as a living and conscious being.[1] Aristotle says that the
universe itself (or sum of things, τὸ πᾶν) was 'unmoved' according to
Xenophanes, but he is not necessarily ignoring the last words of fr. 25,
for he is using the word in the sense of ungenerated. This too Xenophanes believed the world to be, but he is not referring to it here. It
appears rather in fr. 14 ('Gods are not born').

I conclude that for Xenophanes the cosmos was a spherical body,
living, conscious, and divine, the cause of its own internal movements
and change.[2] He was in the Ionian tradition. Anaximander had already

---

[1] 'This is not a denial of any change inside the world. It probably means that, unlike other
animals, which must move about to seek their food, the world, needing no sustenance, stays
where it is' (Cornford, *Princ. Sap.* 147).

[2] Fr. 25. I agree with Cornford again when he says (*loc. cit.*): 'The word "sways" (κραδαίνει)
need mean no more than "moves".' Its choice was doubtless motivated, as has been suggested

taught that the stuff of the universe was alive and divine. But whereas Anaximander was thinking of an indefinite mass of stuff *out of* and *in* which the cosmos came to be, Xenophanes insisted that the cosmos itself was the divinity and therefore had no beginning or dissolution but was everlasting. This gave it unity in a new and more absolute sense which he himself regarded as important ('One god...'), and which in the eyes of Plato and Aristotle justified a view of him as the spiritual father of the Eleatics, whose contribution to philosophy was to be a strict denial of all plurality. Probably his 'unifying' of things went little further than this. He was not only, or even primarily, a natural philosopher, as Theophrastus perceived (p. 367, above), and certainly not a logician like Parmenides. He was a poet who took the didactic function of poetry seriously. What impressed him was that if Ionian hylozoism, or anything like it, were correct, this proved the falsehood of Homeric theology; and since the lessons of that theology were morally undesirable, it provided the intellectual basis for a lesson of which mankind was much in need: they must be shown that their conception of deity was altogether unworthy.

(8) *All creatures born from earth*

The zeal for theological and moral reform was the strongest motive behind the poems. I am not one of those who would dismiss this remarkable figure as a mere rhapsode undeserving of the name of philosopher: we have seen enough already to make that view untenable. Yet his aims were quite different from those of an Anaximander, and it is very possible that this made for a certain lack of precision, even of consistency, in his description of the physical world. We must not press him too hard, nor, while making every effort to understand him, necessarily conclude that our sources or our own reasoning are wrong if they fail to produce an altogether coherent picture.

As an example we may take the line (fr. 27): 'From earth come all things, all things end in earth.' Assuming it to be genuine,[1] we have

here and elsewhere, by hostility to Homer, and its general sense much the same as that of the κυβερνᾷ of Anaximander and later Diogenes of Apollonia (p. 88, above), and the οἰακίζει of Heraclitus (fr. 64).

[1] The genuineness of this line, which comes from no earlier authority than Aëtius (and if known to Theophrastus was not interpreted by him as by Aëtius), has been frequently denied,

no context to guide us in its interpretation. The words were used quite early to classify Xenophanes with the first monists as one who simply chose earth as the *arche* instead of water or air. In the Hippocratic work *On the Nature of Man* (VI, 32 Littré: probably early fourth century B.C.) we already read: 'One of them calls this universal unity air, another fire, another water, another earth.' The last can hardly be anyone but Xenophanes. So in a later age Olympiodorus (DK, A36): 'No one believed earth to be the *arche* except Xenophanes of Colophon.' Even the doxographic tradition, however, as represented by the *Stromateis* and Hippolytus (A32 and 33), suggests that it was not as simple as that. In the collection of opinions which (with little attempt at correlation) they ascribe to Xenophanes, the words 'and everything originates from earth' occur side by side with statements that, unlike Thales, Anaximander and Anaximenes, he denied coming-into-being and passing away, and asserted that 'the whole' was not only one but 'always the same' and 'exempt from change'. Theodoret, bothered by the inconsistency, says simply (A36) that he forgot his statement that 'the whole' was imperishable when he wrote the line 'From earth come all things, all things end in earth'. Sextus (*Math.* x, 313), though he too quotes the line itself, adds only that 'according to some' this meant that earth was the 'origin of becoming' in the same sense as water for Thales or air for Anaximenes.

Sabinus, a commentator of the time of Hadrian, wrote (paraphrasing *On the Nature of Man*): 'I do not say that man is altogether air like Anaximenes, or water like Thales, or earth like Xenophanes in one of his poems.' This is quoted by Galen (see A36), who adds that Sabinus 'villainously traduces' Xenophanes, for 'nowhere can he be found

perhaps most cogently by Gigon (*Heraklit*, 45), though Deichgräber could still write in 1938: 'Ein schlagendes Argument gegen die Echtheit des Verses 27 sehe ich nicht' (*Hermes*, 1938, 16). There are grounds for doubt, and I do not wish to say that it cannot be spurious; but one cannot be sure, and there is at least some interest in following the *via difficilior* of supposing it genuine. Aëtius interpreted it as meaning that earth was an *arche* in the Milesian sense, and, in view of the ultimate dependence of most of the doxography on Aristotle, it would be interesting to know how, if it is spurious, it came to be ascribed to Xenophanes in the face of Aristotle's categorical statement (*Metaph.* 989a5): οὐθεὶς γοῦν ἠξίωσε τῶν ἓν λεγόντων γῆν εἶναι στοιχεῖον. (Also *De An.* 405b8.)

Jaeger's only comment on the line, which he does not reject, is that it 'has indeed nothing to do with natural philosophy' (*TEGP*, 211). It would be more helpful if he had said what it *has* to do with.

making such a declaration...and if this had been his opinion, Theophrastus in his summary of the views of the natural philosophers would have said so'.

Aristotle himself, reviewing earlier philosophers in the *Metaphysics* (989a5), says that 'none of those who posit a unity makes earth the element', and in *De Anima* he repeats (405b8) that all the other elements had been chosen save earth. Of course he is thinking primarily of the Milesians, and might be supposed to exclude Xenophanes for that reason, since he distinguishes him from them. But his reason for making the distinction was that Xenophanes believed the cosmos to be eternal, and so could not have believed in any *arche* at all as the Milesians understood it. We have seen that Aristotle was right in this, so our line must have meant something different, as it easily can.

It is now time to bring two other fragments into the discussion:

> Fr. 29: 'All that is born and grows is earth and water.'
> Fr. 33: 'For we are all born out of earth and water.'

These have been solemnly regarded as offering a different account of origins from fr. 27, so that there is a task of reconciliation to be performed between them. Deichgräber for instance, on pp. 14f. of his *Hermes* article, suggests that 'all things' in fr. 27 means the cosmos as a whole, but in the other lines means the individual things and creatures within it. These are born from earth and water, but water itself derives from earth, which is the ultimate *arche* of the cosmos. This is the reverse of the explanation offered earlier by Freudenthal, who thought it probable that other things had originated from earth alone, but earth itself from water: hence all things could be said to be born, at one remove, from earth *and* water.

When the solutions of two good scholars cancel out so neatly, one may suspect that there is something wrong with the posing of the problem. Now the belief that all living things were originally born from the earth was very common among the Greeks. This was their way of getting over the difficulty of bringing life into being in the first place, when it could not have been produced as it is now, by procreation from already existing animals and men. It was the more easily adopted because to them it seemed a fact of observation that certain small creatures like maggots were still spontaneously generated. To bear the first animals and men, the earth had to be made fertile, and the vehicle of fertility was moisture. The transformation of dry, barren soil by rain or irrigation was an obvious fact of their own day, and could be invoked analogically by the rationalists. For those who preferred religious or mythological explanations, the earth was a person, the goddess Gaia, the Great Mother, and her fertilization took the form of marriage with the sky-god, Ouranos, Aither, or Zeus. He by his rain became the father of men and animals as well as plants, and the Earth was their mother, who brought them to birth when she had received the fertilizing drops.[1]

It was natural and right for those who held this belief to say that all things are born from Earth, the common mother, and so they frequently did. But it was equally correct to say that they are born from earth and water, since assuredly the earth will not be fecund when dry. Neither the mythologists nor Anaximander nor any other philosopher believed that. Hence earth alone may be mentioned, or water and earth, with equal propriety. Lucretius wrote (v, 805):

> Tum tibi *terra* dedit primum mortalia saecla.
> multus enim calor atque *umor* superabat in arvis.

If his poem, like Xenophanes's, had been lost, and an ancient authority had quoted the first line without the second, some literal-minded scholar might have argued from it that mortal creatures were supposed to have been born from dry earth alone, and that therefore any reference to birth from earth and water must apply to something different.

We may conclude, then, that all three lines describe the same thing, namely the origin of organic life from the earth, which, in order to produce it, had to be moist. The *arche* of the cosmos is not in question because, being everlasting, it has no *arche*. In accounting for the origin of life, we may be sure that Xenophanes followed the rationalistic rather than the polytheistic path, and in fact his motive seems to be still the same: to discredit Homer in whatever ways he can. He can hardly have

---

[1] Eur. fr. 839. The subject is treated fully, with authorities, in Guthrie, *In the Beginning*, chh. 1 and 2, where both the mythological and the scientific types of account are discussed.

written fr. 33 without a thought for the curse of Menelaus on the Achaeans who lacked the courage to respond to Hector's challenge (*Il.* VII, 99): 'May you all become earth and water!' 'That is just what we all are', Xenophanes seems to say.[1]

(9) *Alternation of wet and dry ages*

According to the doxographers (there is no mention of it in the fragments) Xenophanes believed that the earth was subject to alternate encroachments of land on sea and sea on land. The evidence is as follows:

(*a*) *Stromateis*, IV (A32): 'He declares also that in the course of time the earth is continuously slipping down and gradually moving into the sea.'

(*b*) Hippol. *Ref.* I, 14, 4–6 (A33): 'He said that the sea is salt because many mixtures flow together in it. Metrodorus accounts for its saltness by the fact that it is filtered through the earth, but Xenophanes thinks that a mingling of earth with sea takes place and that in course of time it is dissolved by the wet element, claiming as proofs that shells are found in the midst of the land and on mountains;[2] and in the quarries at Syracuse, he says, the impressions of a fish and of seaweed[3] have been found, on Paros the impression of a bay-leaf[4] in the depth of the stone, and on Malta flattened shapes of all sea-creatures. These, he says, were formed when everything, long ago, was covered in mud, and the impression dried out in the mud. All men

---

[1] Behind this odd saying in Homer there may well have lain originally the popular belief, illustrated by the Prometheus myth and others, that men are in fact made of these two substances. But I doubt if the poet was very conscious of this. 'Sitting there each one of you like dummies (lifeless, ἀκήριοι)' are the next words, 'inglorious and helpless.' Primarily the phrase seems intended to mention anything inanimate, to mean no more than 'You might as well be stocks and stones'.

[2] Xenophanes was not the only one to observe this. Speaking of Egypt, Herodotus (II, 12) mentions κογχύλια τὰ φαινόμενα ἐπὶ τοῖς ὄρεσι. Xanthus of Lydia (*ap.* Strabo I, 3, 4, p. 64 Meineke), active during the middle part of the fifth century B.C., both observed fossils and drew the same conclusion that the land was once sea. These writers are slightly later than Xenophanes, but probably he was drawing on common knowledge which may even have been available to Anaximander.

[3] Or 'seals'? φωκῶν MSS., DK; φυκῶν Gomperz, Burnet, Heath, KR, etc. Reinhardt rejects Gomperz's suggestion with the typical flourish: 'Wo kämen wir schliesslich hin, wenn wir die Texte nach den Mitteilungen der Fachleute berichtigen wollen?'

[4] The occurrence of plant-fossils on Paros was once thought impossible, and Gronovius wished to emend δάφνης to ἀφύης. Others have thought that other places than the island of Paros were intended (DK *ad loc.*). It now appears, however, that the text offers no palaeontological difficulties (DK, app. to 1956 ed.; F. Casella in *Maia*, 1957, 322–5; KR, 178; M. Marcovich in *CP*, 1959, 121).

are destroyed when the earth is carried down to the sea and turns to mud, then a new generation begins. Such is the foundation[1] of all the worlds.'

The description of fossil remains, of various kinds and in different places, is impressive, and was reasonably taken as evidence that the sea once covered what is now dry land, and that the solid rock was once soft mud, for which the plant-fossil of itself provided adequate testimony. All this, so far as it goes, seems to suggest that the sea is in *retreat*, but Hippolytus makes it clear that the process is a cyclic one, and in fact from his account and the *Stromateis* together we must conclude that we are already in the next stage and the waters are once more gaining on the earth. At their height they flood it sufficiently to destroy life.[2]

Greek mythology was familiar with disasters which had wiped out all or most of the human race. Whether by flood, as in the story of Deucalion, or scorching heat, as in the story of Phaethon, men perish, in Polybius's words, 'as the records tell us has already happened and as reason suggests to us may often happen again'. In Plato's *Timaeus* the Egyptian priest says to Solon (22B–C): 'There have been, and will be hereafter, many destructions of mankind, the greatest by fire and water, though other lesser ones are due to countless other causes.' Philosophers took these stories seriously. Aristotle believed that the 'so-called flood of Deucalion' actually took place, and hazards the theory that 'just as there is a winter among the yearly seasons, so at fixed intervals in some great period of time there is a great winter and excess of rains' (*Meteor.* 352a30); a theory evidently connected with that of a Great Year (pp. 282, above and 458, below).

In Anaximander's cosmogony the earth began by being wet and is gradually drying out, so that the sea is even now continually shrinking and eventually will dry up completely (p. 92, above). Very probably

---

[1] καὶ τοῦτο πᾶσι τοῖς κόσμοις γίνεσθαι καταβάλλειν MSS.; ταύτην...μεταβολήν DK; ταύτην... καταβολήν H. Lloyd-Jones (KR, 177). One might compare Matt. xiii. 35 ἀπὸ καταβολῆς κόσμου, remembering that Hippolytus was a bishop.

[2] Fr. 37 consists of the simple statement: 'And in some caves water drips down.' This has been taken as Xenophanes's own illustration of the transition between earth and water, referring either to the formation of stalactites (water to rock) or to the ooze and dampness so frequently met in caves (earth turning to water). It may well be so, but in the absence of context we can never be sure.

Xenophanes owed something to his predecessor here, though there are important differences. Anaximander was speaking of the origin of the world, and, so far as our evidence goes, there is no trace of a return to the ascendancy of water.[1] Xenophanes is not speaking of the origin or destruction of the cosmos. The cyclical process which he describes is confined to the earth, and even that is never destroyed. We have no details, but it is clear that when the sea has advanced sufficiently to eliminate life and turn the earth to mud, it retreats to allow the re-emergence of dry land and of life. No reason is given for this, but the process will have been a repetition on a larger scale of the annual alternation of wet and dry in summer and winter.

That Xenophanes believed the cosmos as a whole to be ungenerated and indestructible we have already seen. The alternative, in his time and before, was to believe that it took shape at a particular time out of some sort of formless chaos, as described by Hesiod and in more rational terms by the Milesians. Once generated, it might either be destroyed again (so, in all probability, the Milesians, and certainly a little later the atomists) or last for ever as in Pythagoreanism (pp. 281 f., above). With the belief in an everlasting universe, whether generated or not, went normally the idea of a cyclic repetition of history punctuated by disasters. This was the teaching of the Pythagoreans and of Aristotle himself, and evidently also of Xenophanes. The first attested cyclic scheme involving repeated destruction and rebirth *of the whole cosmos* occurs later in the fifth century in Empedocles. Anaximander had probably believed both that the cosmos would be re-absorbed into the *apeiron* and that another would emerge from it later; but there is little positive evidence for this, and it did not occupy the central place in his thoughts that the cycle of worlds had in the elaborate philosophico-religious scheme of Empedocles, to which it was essential.

These alternative views, current in the sixth and fifth centuries, of the destructibility of the cosmos have been briefly set forth here[2] in order to show how easily they might have been confused in later

---

[1] KR remark (p. 178) that the sea was receding round Miletus, but in Sicily was supposed to have engulfed the land-bridge which became the Messina strait.

[2] Some further information about them will be found in Guthrie, *In the Beginning*, ch. 4.

centuries, when the idea of 'innumerable worlds' was familiar. The last sentence of our Hippolytus passage speaks of 'all the *kosmoi*'. This could, of course, at least in earlier Greek, mean only '"world arrangements", i.e. of the earth's surface' (KR, 179), but I have little doubt that the bishop was thinking of the formation of new worlds. If so, it is equally clear that he was mistaken.[1]

Aristotle was emphatic that all the natural philosophers believed the world to have had a beginning in time (*De Caelo*, 279b12), and Xenophanes must have been the first to anticipate his own view that it has always existed, coupling it like him with the theory of a cycle of terrestrial disasters and the periodic renewal of human life and culture. That being so, it was perhaps unfair of Aristotle to dismiss him as summarily as he does. Yet the actual verses in which these notions were embodied may well have been highly fanciful and lacking in anything that Aristotle would recognize as serious philosophical argument.

(10) *Astronomy and meteorology*

The doxographers offer information about the astronomical and meteorological theories of Xenophanes, which however is for several reasons less worthy of attention than the topics already treated. For one thing, practically none of it is supported by actual verses of the poet, so that its reliability is difficult to check, and the language of the reporters does not always inspire confidence. Where Aëtius does quote a few words (A46), it has been argued that they contradict his interpretation of them.[2] Moreover, some of the views described are simply taken over from the Milesians and others are rather nonsensical. If correctly reported, they suggest that Xenophanes did not take these matters very seriously, but was probably chiefly concerned to ridicule religious notions of the heavenly bodies.

In general terms, the view expressed is that all the heavenly bodies, as well as meteors and rainbows, are in fact luminous (or 'fiery') clouds, that clouds are formed by evaporation from the sea, and that therefore all these heavenly phenomena originate from the level of the

---

[1] A different view is taken by Kahn, *Anaximander*, 51f.
[2] So H. Fränkel in *Hermes*, 1925, 181, though Deichgräber (*Rh. Mus.* 1938, 6) thinks differently.

earth and are not far distant from it. 'The clouds', says Diogenes (ix, 19, A1), 'are composed of the vapour from the sun,[1] rising and lifting them up into the surrounding.' One may compare Aët. iii, 4, 4 (A46):

Xenophanes says that the original cause of what happens in the upper regions is the heat of the sun. Moisture is drawn up from the sea and the sweet part owing to its fine texture is separated out and being thickened into a mist forms the clouds and by compression (lit. 'felting') causes dripping showers and by vaporization makes winds.[2] For he says explicitly: 'Sea is the source of water.'

The most noticeable feature of this passage is the meagreness of the direct quotation on which the whole construction is apparently based.

On the importance of the sea some actual verses have survived, though unfortunately mutilated in parts (fr. 30). They are quoted by a scholiast on the lines in the *Iliad* (xxi, 196) which characterize Oceanus as the source of all water—rivers, sea, springs and wells—and they declare that the sea is the source not only of rivers but also of rain, wind and clouds. This does no more than repeat ideas of Anaximander and Anaximenes (pp. 105, 121, above), and the further step of regarding sun, moon and the other heavenly bodies as fires produced from cloud seems to rely particularly on Anaximenes. In his view, as reported by Hippolytus (DK, 13 A7), air 'when dispersed more finely becomes fire. Winds on the other hand are air in process of condensation, and from air cloud is produced by "felting". The continuation of this process produces water....' In the direction of rarefaction this same process accounts in Xenophanes for the production from water of wind, cloud and fire. Anaximenes had also taught that the heavenly bodies originated from the earth, when moisture rising from it was rarefied and became fire (A6 and 7, quoted on pp. 133 f., above).

His reported views on the sun are that it consists of a collection of many small 'firelets' (πυρίδια: 'sparks' may be the best translation)

---

[1] *Sic* (τῆς ἀφ' ἡλίου ἀτμίδος). Why Diogenes wrote of vapour *from* the sun, rather than drawn up from the earth *by* the sun, it would be hard to say. Heidel wished to alter the text; see ZN, 665, n. 7.

[2] With διατμίζειν τὰ πνεύματα cf. Arist. *Meteor.* 353b7ff., describing the views of unnamed early philosophers: τὸ πρῶτον ὑγρὸν...ὑπὸ τοῦ ἡλίου ξηραινόμενον τὸ μὲν διατμίσαν πνεύματα... ποιεῖν, τὸ δὲ λειφθὲν θάλατταν εἶναι.

and at the same time of cloud. The two descriptions were not thought contradictory, for they occur together in the same source. The testimonies are these:

(*a*) *Strom.* IV (A 32): 'He says that the sun is gathered together out of a number of small sparks.... The sun and the stars, he says, are derived from clouds.'

(*b*) Hippol. *Ref.* I, 14, 3 (A 33): 'The sun comes into being daily from small sparks collected together.'

(*c*) Aët. II, 20, 3 (A 40): 'Xenophanes says that the sun consists of ignited clouds. Theophrastus in his *Physics* wrote that it consists of sparks collected from the damp exhalation and composing [lit. collecting or assembling] the sun.'

Still following Anaximenes, Xenophanes evidently held that by a continuation of the same process whereby water was vaporized into cloud, clouds in their turn could ignite and turn to fire. Why these particular clouds should be disintegrated into many little fires, which have to be 'assembled' to form the sun, is not explained.[1] In this account sun and clouds seem to be mutually dependent, which, seeing that the world had no beginning, is not unreasonable. The stars have the same composition (A 32). They are made of ignited clouds, and like the sun are renewed daily: 'being daily quenched they rekindle at night like embers; their risings and settings are ignition and quenching' (Aët. II, 13, 14, A 38). The moon also is cloud 'felted'; it has its own light, and as with the stars, this light is put out each month as it wanes.[2] The same composition is asserted for comets and shooting stars: they are accumulations or movements of ignited clouds, and the phenomenon known as St Elmo's fire is 'little clouds glimmering in virtue of the kind of motion that they have'. Lightning occurs 'when clouds are made bright by the movement'.[3] On the rainbow, alone of celestial phenomena, we have two lines of the poet himself, which bear out what others have said of the cloudy nature of all these things (fr. 32):

> She
> Whom men call Iris also is a cloud,
> Purple and red and yellow to behold.

---

[1] Possibly to account for the tiny, sparklike appearance of the stars.
[2] Aët. II, 25, 4, etc. (A 43). The word πεπιλημένον recalls Anaximenes again.
[3] A 44, 39, 45 (Aët. III, 2, 11, II, 18, I, III, 3, 6).

Since Iris, besides being the rainbow, was a fully anthropomorphic goddess, messenger to the other gods, the familiar motive of discrediting traditional religion is probably at work.[1]

Xenophanes is credited with other beliefs about the heavenly bodies which are strange indeed and scarcely comprehensible. In the absence of the original writings it is practically impossible to judge them. Since the sun is a kind of cloud-formation amassed each morning out of water-vapour and then catching fire, only to die out at night, it is natural (as we are told more than once) that there should be an infinite number of suns. One would suppose them to succeed one another in time, but what is one to make of this (Aët. II, 24, 9, A41*a*)?

Xenophanes says there are many suns and moons corresponding to the regions, sections and zones of the earth,[2] and at a certain time the disc[3] is banished to a section of the earth not inhabited by us, and so stepping into a hole, as it were, produces the phenomenon of an eclipse. He also says that the sun moves forward indefinitely,[4] but seems to go in a circle because of the distance.

[1] Probably. But Ἶρις in Homer more than once means the rainbow without any hint of personification, and the quotation from Xenophanes occurs in a scholiast on *Il.* XI, 27 in which it is actually used in the plural: the serpents of cyanus on Agamemnon's breastplate are Ἰρίσσιν ἐοικότες. Cf. also *Il.* XVII, 547 and 551, where Athena is said to have descended from heaven like a purple rainbow which Zeus 'stretches out' (no personification here), and simultaneously described as covering herself in a purple *cloud*. As with the role of Ocean as source of all other waters, Xenophanes in matters which were not of prime concern to him may have owed something to the same Homer whom for his theological enormities he reviles.

The impression is irresistible that in these physical matters Xenophanes was not bothering his head very much. Anaximenes could certainly have taught him a more sophisticated explanation of the rainbow, as we know from several sources, the fullest being a scholiast on Aratus (DK, 13A18, going back through Posidonius to Theophrastus: see Diels, *Dox.* 231): 'Anaximenes says that the rainbow is produced when the beams of the sun fall on thick close-packed *aer* (air, mist, or cloud; Aëtius calls it νέφος and adds the epithet 'black'). Hence the anterior part of it seems red, being burned by the sun's rays, while the other part is dark, owing to the predominance of moisture.' This can certainly be summed up by calling the rainbow a coloured cloud, but so far as is known the causal detail was omitted by Xenophanes.

[2] Besides the general confusion, this anachronistic reference to κλίματα and ζῶναι of the earth gives further ground for suspecting these sentences as a report of Xenophanes's belief. Those divisions were only possible when the sphericity of the earth had been established, and were probably not made before Eudoxus in the fourth century. See J. O. Thomson, *Hist. of Anc. Geog.* 116. (κλίματα 'expresses the fact that a place is warmed by the sun according to the "inclination" of its horizon to the earth's axis'.)

Fränkel explains the passage by the nearness of sun and moon to the earth (*Dicht. u. Phil.* 431f.): 'Die Sonne- und Mondbahn legte er so nah an unsere Erde heran, dass für die verschiedenen Erdzonen besondere Sonnen und Monde annehmen musste.'

[3] Presumably of the suns, though for all we are told it might equally well be of the moons.

[4] εἰς ἄπειρον. Not 'to infinity', for it burns out each night.

In another passage (II, 24, 4, A 41) Aëtius has classified under eclipses a statement of Xenophanes which must have referred to the sun's daily setting. There may be similar confusion in this one, but there is little hope of straightening it out.[1] On the other hand, the final sentence about the sun's movement is interesting as evidence of observation and of a power to reason from appearances rather than simply accepting them at their face value: objects or creatures travelling through the air in a straight line do appear to descend in the sky as they recede. Here already is a hint of that distrust of the senses which is developed in Heraclitus and reaches its climax when Parmenides denies outright that the senses can ever bring mankind into contact with reality.

Concerning the earth we have the lines of Xenophanes:

> At our feet
> We see this upper limit of the earth
> Coterminous with air, but underneath
> It stretches without limit.

It is therefore unnecessary to consider the paraphrases of Aristotle and those who followed him. The compatibility of this statement with a spherical universe has already been noted,[2] and the only other point of interest is that the lines are obviously describing a flat-topped, not a spherical earth.

---

[1] 'It seems probable that the plurality of suns and moons is simply due to their being renewed each day; that Xenophanes explained eclipses as caused by the sun withdrawing to another region of the earth; and that the two ideas became confused' (KR, 174f.). See the rest of this paragraph in KR for further suggestions about this obscure passage and the possible 'fantasy and humour' displayed by Xenophanes.

It sounds nonsensical to say that when the sun comes to a part of the earth not inhabited by mankind it therefore (καὶ οὕτως) steps into a hole (lit. 'treads on emptiness') and goes out. Tannery, whom Heath follows (*Aristarchus*, 56), said briefly that it is 'un singulier emploi du principe de finalité' (*Pour l'hist. de la sc. hell.* 137). Presumably (though he does not say so) he connected it with Aët. II, 30, 8 (A42): 'The sun is useful in generating the cosmos and the living creatures in it, but the moon is redundant.'

[2] P. 381, n. 1, above. The passage is referred to by Aristotle, *De Caelo*, 294a21. For this and the doxography see DK, A47, 32, 33. Simplicius, confessing honestly that he has not seen the relevant lines, feels a doubt whether Xenophanes meant to say (*a*) that the earth is genuinely at rest because its own lower parts extend indefinitely, or (*b*) that the space beneath the earth extends indefinitely, and therefore, though it appears to be at rest, it is unceasingly moving downwards. Once this strange doubt had entered his mind, the phrase in Xenophanes himself (εἰς ἄπειρον ἱκνεῖται) would hardly have set it at rest.

(11) *Theory of knowledge*

There remains a side of Xenophanes's thought, fortunately attested by actual quotations, which has more interest for the history of philosophy than his cosmological aberrations. The following lines were famous in antiquity (fr. 34):[1]

Certain truth has no man seen, nor will there ever be a man who knows [from immediate experience][2] about the gods and about everything of which I speak;[3] for even if he should fully succeed in saying what is true,[4] even so he himself does not *know* it,[5] but in all things there is opinion.

The Sceptics of the fourth century B.C. and later seized eagerly on these lines as an anticipation of their view that knowledge was unattainable. Sextus mentions two current interpretations. First (*Math.* VII, 49 ff.), Xenophanes was thought to mean that *everything* is incomprehensible (πάντα ἀκατάληπτα):[6] nobody knows the truth, for even if he should hit upon it by chance, he still does not know that he has hit upon it. We are like people searching for gold in a dark room containing many other kinds of treasure besides. Some will lay hands on it, but they will have no means of confirming their discovery. So with philosophers searching for truth the one who lights on it may

---

[1] To our knowledge they were quoted in whole or in part by Sextus Empiricus four times (*Adv. Math.* VII, 49 and 110, VIII, 326; *Pyrrh. Hyp.* II, 18); also by Plutarch (*Aud. Poet.* 17E), Galen, Proclus, Diogenes Laertius, Epiphanius and Origen (full references in Karsten, *Xen. Reliqu.* 1830, 51). H. Fränkel analyses them in detail in *Hermes*, 1925, 184–92. The Greek text as given by DK is:

> καὶ τὸ μὲν οὖν σαφὲς οὔτις ἀνὴρ ἴδεν οὐδέ τις ἔσται
> εἰδὼς ἀμφὶ θεῶν τε καὶ ἄσσα λέγω περὶ πάντων·
> εἰ γὰρ καὶ τὰ μάλιστα τύχοι τετελεσμένον εἰπών,
> αὐτὸς ὅμως οὐκ οἶδε, δόκος δ' ἐπὶ πᾶσι τέτυκται.

[2] For meaning of οἶδε see Fränkel, *loc. cit.* 186f., *Dicht. u. Phil.* 433, n. 14.

[3] Since εἰδὼς is immediately followed by ἀμφὶ θεῶν, the continuation is probably καὶ περὶ πάντων ἄσσα λέγω. Grammatically of course εἰδὼς could take ἄσσα as direct object: 'knowing . . . all that I say about everything'.

[4] τετελεσμένον, a typically Homeric word.

[5] The contrast is between οἶδε and δόκος: no *knowledge* but only *seeming* or opinion. This 'seeming' may be close to the truth, or it may not. The sense is unlikely to be what the Sceptics later assumed (i.e. 'he does not know when he is speaking the truth and when he is not'), but simply that though he may hit upon the truth his conviction cannot be absolutely certain, though he may have good grounds for believing that his opinion is near the truth. The Sceptics' version makes Xenophanes anticipate the sophistic dilemma posed in Plato's *Meno* (80D): 'How will you look for something when you don't know what it is? Even if you come right up against it, how will you know that what you have found is the thing you didn't know?'

[6] According to D.L. IX, 20, this was in particular the interpretation of Sotion.

well not believe his luck. Secondly (ch. 110), Sextus speaks of 'those
who expound him differently'. They claim that he is not abolishing all
comprehension (κατάληψιν) and every criterion, but substituting
opinion for knowledge as a criterion of judgment. The possibility of
error cannot be dismissed, but it is right to accept what is probable.

There is little doubt that the second, less completely sceptical interpretation is correct; indeed the first depends to some extent on a misunderstanding of certain words which had acquired a different shade of
meaning by the time they were quoted.[1] Yet the difference between
them is only one of emphasis. His observation of the widely differing
beliefs of mankind had led Xenophanes to the conclusion that none of
them could be right. In their place he puts forward what he personally
feels is the truth, yet in all modesty and honesty he must confess that
as all men are fallible, so may he be. He firmly believes in his one god,
whole, eternal, unchanging, non-anthropomorphic; but he cannot
claim to have reached the complete and certain truth. This position he
states in an isolated line which Plutarch quotes: 'Let these things be
believed (or opined) as resembling the truth.'[2]

Later writers supply the information that the four lines of fr. 34
give the first half of an antithesis: men can only surmise, but God
knows the truth.[3] When Alcmaeon made the same distinction between
human conjecture and divine certainty (fr. 1, p. 344, above), his words
are sometimes interpreted as distinguishing between the subject-matter
of the two. There certainly seems to be, in the probably corrupt text,
a reference to two classes of things, 'mortal' and 'non-evident', and

[1] See H. Fränkel, *locc. citt.* and the contemporary and earlier parallels which he quotes: e.g. εἰδώς
in line 2 is closely connected with ἴδεν in line 1, and its meaning still closer to 'see for oneself'
than to 'know'. It means to be acquainted with something from personal experience or investigation, from which Fränkel concludes that οἶδε in line 4 cannot mean οἶδεν ὅτι τετελεσμένον
εἶπεν. Again, by τύχοι...εἰπών Xenophanes probably meant 'succeeds in saying', without
intending to introduce any notion of chance.
[2] Fr. 35. The mood of δεδοξάσθω is due to Wilamowitz: δεδοξάσθαι Plut., δεδόξασται Karsten.
The line is perhaps deliberately aimed at Hesiod, whose ἐτύμοισιν ὁμοῖα are in fact ψευδέα
(*Th.* 27). It is used in Plutarch to encourage a bashful speaker.
[3] (a) Arius Did. *ap.* Stob. *Ecl.* II, 1, 17 (DK, A24): Ξ....τὴν αὑτοῦ παριστάντος εὐλάβειαν, ὡς
ἄρα θεὸς μὲν οἶδε τὴν ἀλήθειαν, δόκος δ' ἐπὶ πᾶσι τέτυκται (presumably taking πᾶσι as masc.: it is
more probably neuter). (b) Varro *ap.* Aug. *Civ. Dei*, VII, 17: scribam...ut Xenophanes
Colophonius scripsit...hominis est enim haec opinari, Dei scire.
The dichotomy which Fränkel introduces into these passages ('aber Gott hat ein echtes Wissen
auch von den transzendenten Dingen', *loc. cit.* 190) is not in the originals.

in this Fränkel supposes Alcmaeon to be dependent on Xenophanes. Yet fr. 34 contains no suggestion that there is a class of things which is plain to men and another of which they can only surmise; he explicitly extends the realm of seeming to 'the gods *and everything of which I speak*'. It is true that Sextus introduces the distinction into his paraphrase of the fragment,[1] but it was a familiar one to the Sceptics who had adopted Xenophanes, and his witness on the point has no weight. Perhaps the strongest evidence in favour of this division between the objects of divine and human knowledge is the line (fr. 36): 'As many things as are evident to mortal view.'[2] Though the context is lost, it seems natural to take it as pointing a contrast with other things which are not so experienced by mortals. It has been accepted as evidence that Xenophanes drew a distinction between direct sensible experience, which gives certainty, and other objects of cognition about which none can be certain save God. These would include theology itself, and perhaps also (in view of 'everything of which I speak' in fr. 34) all theory, speculation or inference; e.g. one might suppose that the visible presence of fossils in certain localities was something 'known', but the theory of wet and dry eras which Xenophanes himself based upon it was for a human being only opinion.

Yet one cannot say with confidence, as Fränkel does, that Xenophanes 'separates cleanly and fundamentally from one another' the two realms of the Absolute and the Earthly, still less that he regarded empirical data, and those alone, as certain, trustworthy, and exhaustive.[3] If what he said about the path of the sun has been correctly reported, he was one of the first to suggest that the sense of sight may be deceptive. The optical illusion to which he referred forms a parallel to the

[1] Though not mentioned in this connexion by Fränkel. See *Math.* VII, 51: τὸ μὲν οὖν ἀληθὲς τό γε ἐν τοῖς ἀδήλοις πράγμασιν. Similarly in VIII, 325 ff. he contrasts τὸ πρόδηλον and τὸ ἄδηλον. Deichgräber (*Rh. Mus.* 1938, 20) takes the opposite view to that taken here.

[2] For εἰσοράασθαι as covering the whole field of personal experience and investigation see Fränkel, *loc. cit.* 186.

[3] Fränkel adduces (*loc. cit.* 191) in favour of this that Xenophanes's own theological conclusion, that God bears no resemblance to man, was reached on purely empirical grounds, i.e. from personal observation of the fact that different human groups formed different gods in their own images. Surely this gives an improbable twist to his train of thought. On the contrary, the fact that Africans believed in black gods and Thracians in red-haired must have led him to the conclusion that the immediate perceptions of an individual or a limited group of human beings were likely to lead to error. His own conception of deity can hardly be said to have an empirical basis, yet he regarded it as, to say the least, more probable than those of other men.

notorious straight stick (or oar) appearing bent in water which was made so much of by later writers in their attacks on the truthfulness of sense-perception.

Taking all the evidence together, but relying particularly on the actual fragments, we cannot affirm that Xenophanes posited two realms of existence, of one of which men could have certain knowledge, and of the other only opinion. He said that men could have no certain knowledge at all: that was reserved for God. They may discover the truth, but, even so, such are their limitations that they can say no more than 'I believe this to be true'. This does not mean that all beliefs are equally probable. Such a wholesale abandonment of criteria was not for the man who said to his fellows: 'All your conceptions of the god-head are wrong; it is not like that but like this.' We must not take appearances at their face value, but penetrate as near to the reality behind them as our wits will allow. When we feel that we have reached what at least resembles the truth, we must hold fast to the belief which we have won (fr. 35).

It was already a commonplace of poetry, expressed in invocations to the Muses and elsewhere, that mankind had no sure knowledge unless the gods chose to reveal it.[1] But Xenophanes was more than a poet, and may fairly be said to have introduced this antithesis into philosophy. Gone are the all-too-human gods of the poets. God is not like man either in shape or in mind: he thinks, sees and hears 'as a whole', without the aid of separate bodily organs. This is a product not of poetic imagination, but of rational thought, and its influence on later philosophers is plain. 'Human nature has no insight, but divine nature has', said Heraclitus (fr. 78). Parmenides speaks of 'mortals who know nothing' (6, 4); and when he wishes to discover not only 'the beliefs of mortals in which is no true conviction' but also 'the unshaken heart of truth', he has resort to a goddess as his informant. Empedocles,

---

[1] Among invocations see especially Hom. *Il.* II, 485–6. Perhaps the most striking expression of the belief, and the closest to Xenophanes, is Theognis, 141–2:

ἄνθρωποι δὲ μάταια νομίζομεν εἰδότες οὐδέν·
θεοὶ δὲ κατὰ σφέτερον πάντα τελοῦσι νόον.

For further treatment of this topic see Snell, *Discovery of the Mind*, ch. 7: 'Human knowledge and divine knowledge among the early Greeks.' Among prose-writers, Herodotus puts the sentiment into the mouth of Xerxes (VII, 50, 2): εἰδέναι δὲ ἄνθρωπον ἐόντα κῶς χρὴ τὸ βέβαιον; δοκέω μὲν οὐδαμῶς.

musing on the limitations of the senses and the brevity of human life, concludes (2, 7): 'Thus these things are not to be seen or heard by men, nor grasped by the mind.' 'We know nothing truly,' said Democritus later in the fifth century, 'for truth is in the depths', and Ecphantus the Pythagorean, who was probably under his influence (p. 325, above), echoed this, we are told, in the form that 'it is not possible to obtain true knowledge of existing things, but only to define them as we believe them to be'.[1]

One thing in particular emerges from Xenophanes's lines on human cognition, and especially from the last line of fr. 34, which was of tremendous consequence for the development of Greek thought: the first explicit confrontation, as two separate things, of knowledge and seeming. No doubt the distinction had been latent in philosophy from the beginning. The earliest philosophers in Miletus determined the direction of subsequent thought when they first tried to set aside the seeming variety of the world and reach the true and single nature (*physis*) which underlay it; and as a result this has been the quest of European philosophy and science ever since. But it is just the explicating of the implicit, the conscious realization of what philosophy has up to now been trying to do, which makes possible the next step forward. Heraclitus owed something to it, in spite of his belittlement of his predecessor (fr. 40), but above all it paved the way for Parmenides, whose whole doctrine is based on an assertion of the antithesis between knowledge and opinion, truth and seeming; and through Parmenides it had an indirect part in shaping the thought of Plato himself. Plato was not devoid of historical sense when he saw in Xenophanes the beginning of the Eleatic tradition, however much his casual remark to that effect may have been exaggerated later by less perceptive writers.

Two more quotations from the poems complete the evidence for his views on human knowledge. Fr. 18 says: 'The gods did not reveal to men all things in the beginning, but in course of time, by searching, they find out better.' The emphasis on personal search, and on the need for time, marks this as the first statement in extant Greek literature of the idea of progress in the arts and sciences, a progress dependent on human

[1] Democr. fr. 117. Cf. also frr. 7–9. Ecphantus, DK, 51, 1.

effort and not—or at least not primarily—on divine revelation. It foreshadows the praise of human ingenuity and perseverance in Sophocles's *Antigone* (332 ff.). Here and in the *Prometheus Vinctus* of Aeschylus the progressive achievements are enumerated in detail. In Aeschylus mankind is said to have been taught by Prometheus, whose name means 'Forethought' and who declares that the first thing he taught them was to use their own minds.[1] The fiction of divine intervention is becoming transparent, and it may be assumed that Aeschylus was consciously drawing on sources which ascribed scientific and technical progress to human ingenuity alone.[2] This is done openly by Protagoras in the account of the origin and development of human life put into his mouth by Plato. On the very existence of the gods Protagoras declared himself an agnostic, and the account must be supposed to represent the substance of his real views.[3]

Two conflicting views of human development were current in classical Greece. The first, that it represented a degeneration from an original 'golden race' in the distant past, was given its standard form by Hesiod (*Works*, 109 ff.). These early men were both good in themselves and happy in their circumstances, for nature produced its fruits in abundance with no toil on their part. According to the second, more realistic view the earliest men were ignorant and brutal in character, and at the mercy of wild beasts and all the forces of a hostile nature. Gradually learning by bitter experience, they improved both morally and in their conditions of life, as one by one the arts of building, weaving, domestication of animals, agriculture, and above all of combining in communities for mutual protection, were discovered and mastered. This less mythical version rapidly gained ground at the expense of the other during the fifth century. Besides the authorities already mentioned, we find it in Euripides, Critias and Moschion. In spite of the lack of detail, fr. 18 of Xenophanes seems to give the same

---

[1] ἔννους ἔθηκα καὶ φρενῶν ἐπηβόλους, line 444.

[2] E.g. the account reproduced in Diodorus, 1, 8, in which men's only teacher is said to have been 'expediency' (τὸ συμφέρον). This account probably goes back to pre-atomistic fifth-century thought (p. 69, n. 1, above.)

[3] Plato, *Prot.* 320 cff. On the question of its authenticity see Guthrie, *In the Beginning*, 140, n. 8, and, for an analysis of the account itself, ch. 5 of the same work. Protagoras chooses to put it in the form of a μῦθος as being more agreeable to listen to, but says that it could just as well be explained in a λόγος, i.e. without the divine apparatus.

idea in a nutshell, and affords good reason for attributing it in the first instance to him.[1]

Finally there is fr. 38: 'If God had not made yellow honey, men would think figs were much sweeter.' This too is presumably intended to emphasize the limitations of human judgment, but introduces incidentally its *relative* character: men's assessment of a particular sensation depends on the sensations which they already happen to have experienced. Here again we have the first hint of an idea which was taken up and developed philosophically by later writers. Heraclitus, for whom the relationship of contraries was central, noted (fr. 111, p. 445, below) that we only appreciate the things we call pleasant—health, satiety, rest—in relation to their contraries disease, hunger and weariness. Protagoras generalized the idea in his famous dictum that man is the measure of all things, their existence or non-existence, by which he meant that each man's sensations are true for him and for no one else.[2] Since no two men can have precisely the same sensations and experiences, this doctrine can be regarded as a conclusion following logically from the statement in Xenophanes, however unlikely it may be that Xenophanes drew it himself.

(12) *Conclusion*

To sum up, Xenophanes was not the rhapsode misnamed philosopher whom some have thought him in the past. Apart from the details of cosmology, which probably interested him only as a stick with which to beat Homeric theology, he definitely points forward rather than back. The mistake made by some ancient critics was to accept as fully-fledged doctrines what were no more than pointers, germs brought to fruition under other hands, and their manifest exaggeration has led to a belittlement of his genuine originality. Regarded as seminal, his philosophical importance is great, and its influence was immediately felt. He provided cogent arguments against anthropomorphism in

---

[1] Eur. *Suppl.* 201 ff., Critias fr. 25 DK, Mosch. fr. 6 Nauck. On the idea of progress in classical Greece see further Guthrie, *op. cit.* chh. 5 and 6.

[2] Plato, *Theaet.* 152A, *Crat.* 386A. I am aware that these passages have aroused interminable discussion, but see no reason to doubt that Plato had understood Protagoras correctly. As Lewis Campbell said in his edition of the *Theaetetus* (p. 37), the repetition of the same language in both passages affords a presumption that the explanation, as well as the original saying, is Protagoras's own.

theology. Though not 'an Eleatic', he abandoned the Milesian tradition for a stricter notion of unity which excluded the possibility of a generated cosmos, taught of a single god who worked by intellection alone, and posited an essential connexion between divinity, eternity, reality, and spherical shape. For all this the Eleatics, and Heraclitus as well, are much in his debt, as also for the distinction between knowledge and seeming or opinion and the idea that all sensations are relative. Popular thought may have had an inkling of some of these things, but Xenophanes put them in a more philosophical setting and ensured that they were taken seriously. The effect of his conception of knowledge as progressing steadily and gradually from small beginnings, through men's own powers of discovery and invention, may be seen in many fifth-century authors, both philosophers and poets. In short, with him philosophy breaks new ground in more than one direction, and sows new seed, from which a fruitful crop of ideas was soon to be reaped.

VII

HERACLITUS

(1) *Difficulties and policy*

A discussion of the thought of Heraclitus labours under peculiar difficulties. His own expression of it was generally considered to be highly obscure, a verdict fully borne out by the surviving fragments. Both in the ancient and the modern worlds he has provided a challenge to the ingenuity of interpreters which few have been able to resist. Perhaps not altogether unfortunately, most of the ancient commentaries have perished, but the amount written on him since the beginning of the nineteenth century would itself take a very long time to master. Some of these writers have been painstaking scholars, others philosophers or religious teachers who found in the pregnant and picturesque sayings of Heraclitus a striking anticipation of their own beliefs.[1] If the interpretations of the latter suffer from their attitude of *parti pris*, the former may also be temperamentally at a disadvantage in penetrating the thoughts of a man who had at least as much in him of the prophet and poet as of the philosopher.

There is, then, an army of commentators, no two of whom are in full agreement. Nor are the doubts confined to the elucidation of a given body of writing. Diels–Kranz present 131 passages as fragments of Heraclitus, but it is a matter of lively argument how far they reproduce his actual words and how much is paraphrase or addition by the ancient writer in whose works they are found or a previous writer in whom he found them. Given an established fragment, there may remain to be resolved a doubt of its grammatical syntax, before one can proceed to wider questions of interpretation. This is an inevitable consequence of Heraclitus's intentionally oracular style, and was

---

[1] Justin Martyr included him, with Socrates, Abraham and others, among those who had lived with the Logos and must be regarded as Christians, and I have personally known a man who claimed to have been converted by reading the fragments. Lenin on the other hand wrote of one fragment: 'A very good account of the elements of dialectical materialism' (see G. Thomson, *The First Philosophers*, 280). The admiration of Nietzsche for Heraclitus is well known.

noticed as early as Aristotle (*Rhet.* 1407b11, quoted below, p. 407). The difficulty of expounding the fragments in translation needs no further emphasis: to translate is sometimes to have taken sides already in a disputed question of interpretation.

To take account of all previous scholarship, even if possible, would be undesirable here. What will be attempted is a fresh exposition in continuous form, relegating as far as possible to footnotes any necessary references to other opinions. Since any interpretation of this paradoxical thinker must be to some extent a personal one, the footnotes in this section will be more extensive than usual, and a reader may be well advised to read the text through without them, in order to keep track of a necessarily complex situation and seize the general picture that is being drawn.

I shall try to achieve a convincing account out of both fragments and *testimonia*, that is paraphrases, summaries and criticisms of Heraclitus in later writers. I shall not hesitate to quote a *testimonium* before a fragment bearing on the same point if this leads to a clearer and better order of exposition, although naturally if *testimonia* actively contradict any certainly or highly probably attested fragments, they must be discarded in favour of Heraclitus's own words.

The common assumption of recent scholars is that philosophers and others from Plato onwards, when it is a question of stating their predecessors' views clearly, must be adjudged guilty unless they can prove their innocence. This assumption, at least for Aristotle and his successors, rests on an impressive amount of study of their own outlook and the questions in their minds, which were inevitably different from the habits of mind and problems of earlier and less sophisticated thinkers. The Aristotelian outlook imposed itself and made certain assumptions almost second nature in those who came later.[1] In the case of Heraclitus we have the further complication that some of his ideas were adopted and remoulded by the Stoics, so that in later sources there is always the possibility of Stoic colouring creeping into what purports to be an original thought of Heraclitus.

While these considerations must be constantly kept in mind, there is

---

[1] For a clarification of the Peripatetic approach to Heraclitus and its effects Jula Kerschensteiner's article in *Hermes*, 1955, is particularly to be recommended.

something to be said for following the prevailing legal principle and requiring proof of guilt. In view of the compensating advantages which the ancient writers enjoyed, notably their possession of a greater amount of first-hand evidence, this seems both more modest and methodically sounder. Their known philosophical prejudices may or may not be relevant in a particular instance.

The procedure adopted here, and doubtless the results attained, will not commend themselves to all. This need trouble us less when we consider that no account of Heraclitus yet put forward has won universal approval as a faithful reflexion of his mind.

(2) *Sources*

The sources of our knowledge of Heraclitus have been enumerated and appraised by G. S. Kirk in his *Heraclitus: the Cosmic Fragments*,[1] and this may exempt us from a separate preliminary treatment which would largely repeat his careful work. Something may be added, however, on one particular source, the Christian apologist Hippolytus, bishop of Rome in the third century, who is not singled out by Kirk in his introduction. The account of Heraclitus forms a part of his *Refutation of all Heresies*, in which he seeks to show that the chief Christian heresies are in fact resuscitations of pagan systems of thought. At the beginning of Book IX he deals with the opinions of Noetus, who taught that since Father and Son were identical, the Father suffered and died in the person of the Son ('patripassianism'). This heresy Hippolytus claims to be rooted in the philosophy of Heraclitus, so that his account of the latter obviously has a particular tendency and purpose. Nevertheless he is our richest single source of actual quotations, and his approach was methodical enough. 'My next purpose', he writes (IX, 8, 1, p. 241 Wendland), 'is to expose the erroneous teaching in the beliefs of the Noetians, *first* explaining the tenets of Heraclitus the Dark, and *then* demonstrating that the details of their system are Heraclitean.' This two-

---

[1] Cambridge, 1954: Introd. §III, 'The Ancient Evidence on Heraclitus's Thought'. Although the main body of this book deals in full only with fragments 'describing the world as a whole rather than men in particular', many others are mentioned incidentally, and the introduction on date, life and sources is a model introduction to Heraclitus as a whole. Kirk's book is, within its chosen scope, the most detailed, factual and sober study that has yet appeared, and will be made use of frequently in the succeeding pages.

Heraclitus

fold division of his scheme is adhered to, and in the course of the first part he gives so many actual quotations that even so cautious a critic as Kirk considers he 'had access to a good compendium, if not to an actual book by Heraclitus' (p. 185, cf. 211). Kirk could not go further, since he does not believe that Heraclitus himself wrote a book, but the Italian Macchioro argued (more plausibly than he did on many topics) that Hippolytus had the actual work of Heraclitus before him, and that all his quotations are taken from a single chapter or section of it. Macchioro placed considerable reliance on the statement of Hippolytus at IX, 10, 8 (p. 244 Wendland): 'In this section he revealed all his real mind at once', and claimed that the quotations are full enough to allow a reconstruction of the all-important chapter referred to.[1] At the least Hippolytus supplies a number of indisputably genuine statements of Heraclitus, instead of only a second- or third-hand version of Theophrastus's epitome filtered through a Stoic mesh; and even if Stoicism and Christianity enter into his interpretation of them, it is based on these texts which he has been conscientious enough to allow us to read for ourselves.

(3) *Writings*

It is not even agreed that Heraclitus wrote a book at all. Such a book is indeed referred to in antiquity from Aristotle onwards,[2] but some have guessed it to be no more than a collection of his sayings, made perhaps after his death. Most sceptical is Kirk, who writes (p. 7):

I hazard the conjecture that Heraclitus wrote no book, in our sense of the word. The fragments, or many of them, have the appearance of being isolated statements, or γνῶμαι: many of the connecting particles they contain

---

[1] V. Macchioro, *Eraclito*, ch. 1 (see, however, Kirk, 349–51, 184f.). W. Kranz also emphasizes Hippolytus's accuracy in citation, and agrees that 'ganz ohne Zweifel benutzt er hier... eine vollständige Heraklitausgabe' (*Philologus*, 1958, 252f.).

[2] The words used are σύγγραμμα (first in Arist. *Rhet.* 1407b16) and βιβλίον. Examples: D.L. IX, 1 'He grew up haughty and supercilious, as his book itself shows'; IX, 5 'The book of his which is in circulation (τὸ φερόμενον αὐτοῦ βιβλίον: perhaps only "the book which circulates as his") is from its general subject-matter a work on nature, but has been divided into three parts'. The parts are then named, and conform to a Stoic classification, and there follows the story that he deposited the book in the temple of Artemis; IX, 15 'The commentators on his book are numerous'.

belong to later sources. In or perhaps shortly after Heraclitus's lifetime a collection of these sayings was made, conceivably by a pupil. This was the 'book': originally Heraclitus's utterances had been oral, and so were put into an easily memorable form.

This is of course, as Kirk says, pure conjecture. Gigon (*Untersuchungen zu Heraklit*, 8) argued that the carefully composed fr. 1 must from its style have been the prooemium of a formal (*redigierten*) book, on which Kirk comments (p. 45): 'It is the longest continuous piece of Heraclitus's prose which we possess, and Gigon may be justified... against the opinion of Diels and others that the "book" was simply a collection of γνῶμαι or aphorisms. Nevertheless, I incline to Diels's view.' The fact that many ancient authors wrote commentaries on Heraclitus's work leaves Kirk unmoved, since, as he points out with justice, the lack of anything but a random collection of sayings attributed to him has in no way deterred modern scholars from doing the same thing.

Many have taken the opposite view. K. Deichgräber wrote (*Philologus*, 1938/9, 20):

We know nothing of a *florilegium*, nor is there any suggestion of such as the source of the existing fragments. The work of Heraclitus will not have been so extensive as to create an urgent need for a separate anthology, as for instance in the case of Epicurus, where, in view of the extent of his *Physics* and its practical tendency, we can well understand his writing an epitome.

Regenbogen (*Gnomon*, 1955, 310) says that both Plato and Aristotle had the whole book of Heraclitus in their hands. Mondolfo (*Phronesis*, 1958, 75), after quoting Cherniss, a highly critical scholar, for the statement that 'Aristotle had the books of [the Presocratics] presumably in their complete form', goes on to say that 'where Heraclitus is concerned, Aristotle himself declares his full and direct knowledge of the text'. The passage in Aristotle is *Rhet.* 1407b11, translated by Rhys Roberts as follows:

It is a general rule that a written composition should be easy to read and therefore easy to deliver. This cannot be so where there are many connecting words or clauses, or where punctuation is hard, as in the writings of Heraclitus. To punctuate Heraclitus is no easy task, because we often cannot tell whether a particular word belongs to what precedes or what follows it. Thus at the outset of his book[1] he says. . . . (There follows fr. 1; see p. 424, below.)

This is cogent evidence, and even if Kirk can write (p. 7): 'Of course it cannot be proved that Heraclitus wrote a book, or that he did not', the onus must, in face of a passage like this, rest on those who would maintain that he did not.

(4) Date and life

The absolute date of Heraclitus of Ephesus is difficult to determine with precision, but, in spite of his dubious methods, Apollodorus may have been approximately correct in estimating that he 'flourished' (i.e. was aged forty) about 500 B.C. (Ol. 69 = 503–500; Apollodorus will have been the source of D.L. IX, 1). Kirk, to whose introduction the interested reader may be referred for discussion of the evidence and previous views, concludes that his philosophical work was probably completed by 480, when according to this reckoning he would be in his sixties. This conforms with his mentions of Pythagoras, Hecataeus and Xenophanes, and the probability that his work was already known to Parmenides, who would be his junior by about twenty-five years. Some of the language used by Parmenides seems only explicable on the assumption that he is deliberately echoing phrases of Heraclitus in a spirit of criticism.[2]

Except perhaps for his membership of the royal clan at Ephesus we know nothing of the externals of his life. All else must be regarded as apocryphal anecdote arising for the most part out of his sayings.[3] Some have thought that the familiar label of 'the weeping philoso-

[1] ἐν τῇ ἀρχῇ αὐτοῦ τοῦ συγγράμματος.

[2] The most striking passages are fr. 6, 8–10, fr. 8, 57–8, fr. 4, 3–4. Diels adduced a number of other fragments (see ZN, 685, n.), but some of his comparisons are far-fetched and weaken his case. Though many have argued to the contrary (e.g. Zeller, ZN, 926 with n., Reinhardt, *Parm.* 155 ff., Gigon, 33, Raven, *P. and E.* 25 f.), I find it impossible to deny that there is an intentional allusion to Heraclitus in at least one of these passages. See especially G. Vlastos, *AJP*, 1955, 341, n. 11, and Kranz, *Hermes*, 1934, 117 f. Kirk's views are on pp. 2, 211. Among nineteenth-century commentators Bernays, Schuster, Steinhart and Patin considered that fr. 6 was aimed at Heraclitus, as also did Burnet (*EGP*, 130). The controversy to date is summarized by Nestle, ZN, 684, n. 1, 688, n. See further N. B. Booth, *Phronesis*, 1957, 93 f., and most recently G. E. L. Owen, *CQ*, 1960, 84, n. 1. The question will be dealt with more fully in the next volume in connexion with Parmenides, but in any case no one now believes Reinhardt's contention that Parmenides was the earlier.

[3] D.L. IX, 3–5. The stories are discussed by Kirk, 3 ff.

pher' arose from a misinterpretation of the *melancholia* attributed to him by Theophrastus, which in medical parlance meant not 'melancholy' but rather 'impulsiveness'. Yet this seems an improbably slender foundation for the story so well known in later antiquity which couples his name with Democritus, saying that whereas the one wept, the other laughed at the follies of mankind.[1]

Strabo (XIV, 632) tells the legend that Ephesus was founded by Androclus son of Codrus the King of Athens. Hence it became the centre of the Ionian kingdom, and in Strabo's own time the family supposed to be of this royal descent were still called kings and entitled to certain privileges, in part religious. Heraclitus was of this family, and presumably its head, since he was entitled to the 'kingdom', but ceded it to his brother out of pride.[2] Whether or not the story is true (and, unlike other stories about him, it betrays no obvious motive for invention), it sets the tone for all that we know about his character, including the evidence of his own writings: an aristocrat of the highest rank and ancient lineage, whose pride was so exceptional that he saw no value in the privileges bestowed by his own people, for whom he had a lively contempt, as indeed for the general run of mankind everywhere. An anecdote in the same vein says that when he was found playing dice with the children, and the citizens asked him why, he replied: 'Why are you surprised, you good-for-nothings? Isn't this better than playing politics with you?' (D.L. IX, 3). Such anecdotes do no more than indicate his reputation, but he himself declared (fr. 49): 'One man is to me ten thousand, if he be the best', and (fr. 33): 'It is law, too, to obey the counsel of one.' Equalitarian ideas roused him to fury. 'Every grown man of the Ephesians', he said, 'should hang himself, and leave the city to the boys; for they banished Hermodorus, the best man among them, saying, "Let no one of us excel, or if he does, be it elsewhere and among others".'[3] Again: 'Insolence

---

[1] μελαγχολία of Heraclitus, Theophr. *ap.* D.L. IX, 6. See also Kirk, 8, quoting Aristotle, *EN*, 1150b25 for the meaning of μελαγχολία. References to the weeping Heraclitus and the laughing Democritus occur e.g. in the π. ὀργῆς of Sotion (the teacher of Seneca, quoted in Stob. *Ecl.* III, 20, 53), Seneca, *De Tranqu.* XV, 2, Juv. X, 28ff. See also Lucian, *Vit. Auct.* 14.

[2] Antisthenes of Rhodes (second century B.C.), *Successions*, quoted by D.L. IX, 6.

[3] Fr. 121, attested by a number of ancient writers: Strabo, Cicero, Diogenes. This Hermodorus is said to have gone to Rome and assisted in drawing up the laws of the Twelve Tables (Burnet, *EGP*, 131, n. 1).

must be quelled more promptly than a conflagration' (fr. 43). His conception of *hybris* must have been much the same as that of Theognis, namely a failure by the lower orders to keep their proper station. A right-minded people will defend the law as they would their city's walls (fr. 44), that law which is the counsel of one man. This follows inevitably from a higher principle, for all human laws are derived from the one divine law (fr. 114), and few men show themselves capable of understanding that. His political views were clearly the reverse of democratic, and though his character was highly complex it is not out of place to begin by emphasizing his austere aloofness from his fellow-men.

(5) *Obscurity and contempt for mankind*

His reputation for obscurity was practically universal throughout antiquity. He delighted in paradox and isolated aphorisms, couched in metaphorical or symbolic terms. This love of paradox and puzzle, without the genius, was inherited by a school of followers, and Plato has an amusing account of their exaggerations of their master's idiosyncrasies. Socrates has remarked that the doctrine that everything is in continuous motion has led to considerable controversy. Theodorus agrees, and adds:

In Ionia indeed it is actually growing in violence. The followers (ἑταῖροι) of Heraclitus lead the quire of this persuasion with the greatest vigour.... There is no discussing these principles of Heraclitus—or, as you say, of Homer or still more ancient sages[1]—with the Ephesians themselves, who profess to be familiar with them; you might as well talk to a maniac. Faithful to their own treatises, they are literally in perpetual motion; their capacity for staying still to attend to an argument or a question...amounts to less than nothing.... When you put a question, they pluck from their quiver little oracular aphorisms to let fly at you; and if you try to obtain some account of their meaning, you will be instantly transfixed by another, barbed with some newly forged metaphor.... There is no such thing as a master or pupil among them.... Each one gets his inspiration wherever he can, and not one of them thinks that another understands anything.[2]

[1] Socrates has humorously suggested that the doctrine of universal flux has an early champion in Homer, on the ground that he made the water-gods Oceanus and Tethys the origin of all things. This does not affect the seriousness with which, as a philosophical doctrine, it is here ascribed to Heraclitus and his followers.

[2] *Theaet.* 179 D ff., trans. Cornford. As Zeller says (ZN, 936f.): 'Heraclitus's school continued long after the death of its founder. Plato is our witness that at the beginning of the fourth

This is caricature, but in many respects (e.g. the individualist claim to be no man's pupil but self-inspired) they were only aping their leader. The obscurity of his style was already remarked on by Aristotle (p. 407, above), and a sentence of Diogenes which can safely be referred to Theophrastus says, after mentioning some of his beliefs: 'But he sets out nothing clearly.'[1] In later antiquity this obscurity became proverbial. The title of 'the Riddler' was bestowed on him by Timon of Phlius early in the third century B.C., and another favourite epithet was 'the Dark'.[2] To Lucretius (I, 639) he was 'clarus ob obscuram linguam', and Plotinus complained (*Enn.* IV, 8, p. 468): 'He seems to speak in similes, careless of making his meaning clear, perhaps because in his view we ought to seek within ourselves as he himself had success-fully sought' (cf. fr. 101). Certainly in reading the fragments one is sometimes tempted to agree with the Cotta of Cicero's dialogue that he hid his meaning intentionally, and even to follow his advice and give up: 'qui quoniam quid diceret intelligi noluit, omittamus' (*N.D.* I, 26, 74; III, 14, 35). But there is another side to the picture, not inconsistent with the first, which impressed at least one of the ancients. In Diogenes IX, 7 we find: 'Occasionally in his treatise he fires off[3] something of brilliant clarity, such that even the dullest can easily grasp and experience an elevation of spirit; and the brevity and weight of his expression are incomparable.' As he said himself (fr. 22): 'Those who seek gold dig much earth and find a little.' The gold is there for the persevering, even though we may occasionally sympathize with the feelings ascribed to Socrates in a doubtless apocryphal story (D.L. II,

century it enjoyed a considerable vogue in Ionia, and especially at Ephesus.' Wellmann agrees (*RE*, VIII, 507), though his added qualification is probably wise: 'But we hear nothing of any pupil worthily representing or developing the master's system.' Indeed Plato's satirical remarks suggest that they were all most *un*worthy followers, but there is nothing in them to suggest that his references to a Heraclitean sect at Ephesus were not intended to be taken literally at all, as Kirk believes (p. 14).

[1] Since this corresponds both to the universal verdict of antiquity and to the impression made by the extant fragments, there seems no reason at all why Kirk should take this 'to mean primarily that Theophrastus's sources were inadequate' (p. 27).

[2] αἰνίκτης Timon *ap.* D.L. IX, 6; σκοτεινός e.g. Strabo, XIV, 25, p. 642 Ἡ. ὁ σκ. καλούμενος, [Ar.] *De Mundo*, 396 b 20 παρὰ τῷ σκ. λεγομένῳ Ἡ., Cic. *Fin.* II, 5, 15 *H. cognomento qui* σκ. *perhibetur, quia de natura nimis obscure memoravit.*

[3] ἐκβάλλει. Cf. ἐκβάλλουσι in Plato, *Theaet.* 180 B. In modern times this praise has been paralleled, significantly enough, by Nietzsche: 'Wahrscheinlich hat nie ein Mensch heller und leuchtender geschrieben' (quoted by G. Burckhardt, *Heraklit*, n.d., p. 15).

22). Asked by Euripides what he thought of Heraclitus's book, he replied: 'What I understood was fine, and no doubt also what I didn't understand; but it needs a diver to get to the bottom of it.'

Conformably with this, he was thought to have held the great majority of mankind in contempt. This is borne out by his own writings, as a few quotations will show.

Fr. 1. Other men are unaware of what they do while awake, just as they forget what they do when asleep.

Fr. 17. Many do not understand such things, indeed all who come upon them, nor do they mark them though they have learned them; but they seem to themselves to do so.[1]

Fr. 19. Rebuking some for their unbelief, Heraclitus says: Knowing neither how to hear nor how to speak.

Fr. 29. The best renounce all for one thing.... But most men stuff themselves like cattle.

Fr. 34. Fools when they hear are like the deaf. The saying describes them: though present they are absent.

Fr. 70. Heraclitus adjudged the opinions of mankind to be 'children's playthings'. (Perhaps a reminiscence of the story quoted on p. 409, above, or conceivably its origin.)

Fr. 104. What sense or mind have they? They put their trust in popular bards and take the mob for their teacher, unaware that most men are bad,[2] and the good are few.

One may safely add frr. 9 and 97, as examples of the 'talking in similes' of which Plotinus spoke.

Fr. 9. Asses would choose rubbish rather than gold.

Fr. 97. Dogs bark at everyone they don't know.

Frr. 2, 56, 72 and 87 may also be compared.

So much for the general run of mankind. Of philosophers and poets he has no better opinion.

Fr. 40. Much learning (*polymathie*) does not teach sense. Otherwise it would have taught Hesiod and Pythagoras, or again Xenophanes and Hecataeus.

---

[1] Whatever the exact text (on which see Wilamowitz, *Glaube*, II, 114, n. 1 and Gigon, *Unters. zu H.* 17), this fragment certainly seems directed against Archilochus, fr. 68 Diehl. Cf. fr. 42, below.

[2] Heraclitus is here making use of a saying attributed to Bias of Priene, one of the 'Seven Wise Men' (see Stob. *Ecl.* III, 1, 172, p. 121 Hense, DK, I, p. 65). In fr. 39 he speaks of Bias in complimentary terms.

Fr. 42. Heraclitus said that Homer deserved to be expelled from the contests and flogged, and Archilochus likewise.

Fr. 57. Most men's teacher is Hesiod. They are sure he knew most things—a man who could not recognize day and night! For they are one.[1]

One or two further fragments sound similar, but in the light of others can be seen to be more probably an illustration of a different side of Heraclitus: his religious sense of the worthlessness of human knowledge in comparison with divine. Such is fr. 28 (text as emended by Diels): 'The knowledge of the most famous of men is but opinion.' This must be read in the light of fragments like these:

78. Human nature has no insight, but divine nature has it.

79. Man is infantile in the eyes of a god, as a child in the eyes of a man.

83. Compared with God, the wisest of men will appear an ape, in wisdom, beauty and all else.

102. To God all things are fair and good and just, but men have assumed some to be unjust and some just.

The cryptic and symbolic style of his sayings is undoubtedly in part due to the contempt that he felt for most of those who were likely to see his work. The truth is something that is there for all men to grasp (in his language it is 'common'), yet most men are too stupid to see it, and live as if they had their own 'private' wisdom (fr. 2). It is not for him to demean himself by using language that fools can understand, nor could the truth be so expressed. He that hath ears to hear, let him hear.[2]

A second reason for obscurity will appear in due course, namely that the content of his thought was itself of a subtlety exceeding that of his contemporaries, so that the language of his time was bound to be inadequate. Symbol and paradox were sometimes his only resource.

(6) Prophetic character

Nor can it be doubted, thirdly, that he believed himself to have come into possession of an absolute truth, a belief which leads naturally to

---

[1] Hesiod made Hemera daughter of Nyx (*Theog.* 124). The criticism of Hesiod in fr. 106 may be a distorted version of this (Kirk, 157–9).

[2] Clement (*Strom.* v, 14, p. 718) actually compares fr. 34 with this saying of Jesus.

a prophetic rather than a dialectical mode of expression. He spoke as one inspired, and it is no metaphor to call his style oracular. One of the few people to whom he refers without contempt is the Sibyl, for all her 'raving mouth' and 'mirthless and unadorned' phrases (fr. 92).[1] More interesting is what he says of the Delphic Apollo (fr. 93): 'The Lord who owns the oracle at Delphi neither speaks nor hides his meaning but indicates it by a sign.' That is, it is a feature of the oracular style to suggest a thing by an image rather than name it outright. We may recall the response given to the Spartans about 'a place where two winds blow by the force of necessity, and there is blow countering blow, and woe lies on woe'—in other words an ironsmith's workshop (Hdt. 1, 61). Equally characteristic is the deliberately ambiguous statement, of which the most famous example is the reply given to Croesus that he would destroy a great empire. Just this imagery and double meaning were a mark of Heraclitus's own style, and he was evidently following the oracle's example.[2] Many things in the fragments suggest the religious rather than the philosophic teacher, for instance his combination of pride and humility. He has seen the truth as no man before, yet he is only its vehicle: 'Listen not to me but to the Logos' (fr. 50).[3]

In spite of his condemnation of poets, whose claims to inspiration he obviously regarded as false, he was convinced that he had an inward inspiration of his own. 'I searched myself' is his boast (fr. 101), and Pindar contrasts favourably the knowledge which comes from a man's inner nature with that which is acquired by learning (the 'polymathy' that Heraclitus despises). He too claimed to speak in a way which only

[1] Exactly how much of Plutarch's sentence here represents Heraclitus's words it is difficult to be sure; but cf. Clem. *Strom.* I, 15, p. 358 (quot. Bywater *ad loc.*, fr. 12) οὐκ ἀνθρωπίνως ἀλλὰ σὺν θεῷ, etc.

[2] The parallel between Heraclitus's style and that of the oracle is developed by U. Hölscher in 'Festschrift Reinhardt', 72f. B. Snell, *Hermes*, 1926, p. 372 brings into connexion with it the story that Heraclitus told about Homer (fr. 56, related p. 443, n. 2, below). Its religious significance is well brought out by P. Merlan in *Proc. 11th Int. Congress of Philosophy*, vol. XII, 56–60.

[3] To this extent one must modify the interpretation by Gigon of fr. 28. He would explain it (p. 128) in the sense of Alcmaeon fr. 1 (p. 344, above) or Xenophanes, fr. 34, as 'an expression of wise self-limitation in knowledge'. When Heraclitus belittles human knowledge in comparison with divine, one cannot, in the light of other fragments, suppose that he would always include his own. To one who looks upon himself as a *prophetes* there is no inconsistency in this. Jesus, who could say 'He that hath seen me hath seen the Father', would at another time say 'The words that I speak, I speak not of myself'.

men of understanding could grasp without an interpreter.[1] Nor is there any contradiction between the idea of being self-taught and that of divine inspiration. Phemius the Homeric bard described himself as *autodidaktos* precisely *because* a god had breathed the lays into his heart (*Od.* XXII, 347). These parallels must not be ignored. It is not merely a question of forms of expression. Heraclitus's language definitely puts him on the side of the inspired: poets, prophets and the teachers of mystery-religions, who like him spoke in symbols not to be understood by the *profani*. We cannot and should not expect such a man to have the rationalistic outlook of the Milesians.

The burden of his complaint against all men is the same. They are blind to the inner significance both of their own nature and of everything around them. 'The many' are aware of these things through the senses, but cannot interpret them. To the passages already quoted may be added fr. 107: 'Eyes and ears are bad witnesses to men if they have souls that understand not the language.'[2] Philosophers and poets are worse, for they have amassed knowledge and still do not understand. These attacks had a new significance, but were couched in familiar terms, for the contrast between much knowledge and true wisdom seems to have been a popular one. There is a line of Archilochus which has a proverbial ring, and indeed is quoted as a proverb and attributed to others as well: 'The fox has many tricks but the hedgehog one big one.' In a similar vein Aeschylus wrote: 'Not he who knows many things is wise, but he who knows what is profitable.'[3]

(7) *Relation to earlier thinkers*

Many have tried to place the thought of Heraclitus in the philosophical succession, seeing it as determined by the influence of this one or that among the other Presocratics. Thus K. Reinhardt thought it an attempt to meet the dilemma posed by Parmenides, and O. Gigon found the

---

[1] Pind. *Ol.* II, 83–6. Pindar's metaphor of arrows in his quiver is the same as that used by Plato to describe the style of the followers of Heraclitus (p. 410, above).

[2] βαρβάρους ψυχὰς ἐχουσιν. The *barbaros* is one who hears the sounds that a civilized (i.e. Greek) man utters, but since he does not know Greek can attach no meaning to them.

[3] Archil. fr. 103 D. πόλλ' οἶδ' ἀλώπηξ ἀλλ' ἐχῖνος ἓν μέγα. Aesch. fr. 390 N. ὁ χρήσιμ' εἰδὼς οὐχ ὁ πόλλ' εἰδὼς σοφός.

key in the direct influence of Xenophanes.[1] Neither attempt has met
with much approval. Heraclitus wrote before Parmenides, whose poem
almost certainly contains a slighting reference to him (p. 408, above).
The statement quoted by Diogenes (IX, 5) from Sotion, that 'some
have said he was a disciple of Xenophanes', is of no value,[2] and when
he mentions Xenophanes it is in a highly critical vein (fr. 40); nor can
Gigon be said to have made out a strong general case on internal
evidence. More recently G. Vlastos (*AJP*, 1955, 354ff.) has pro-
pounded the thesis that to understand him we must link his thought
with that of the Milesians Anaximander and Anaximenes. But no
attempt to link Heraclitus directly and positively with his predecessors
has much chance of success. In all probability he was a far more
isolated thinker than such attempts presuppose. To be so was at any
rate his intention, and the verdict that he learned from no man is
borne out by his own statements,[3] his universal contempt for his
fellow-men, both philosophers and others, and the highly individual
character of his thought.

(8) *Philosophical methods: self-search*

So Heraclitus preached his message, which he regarded as an eternal
truth, from a pinnacle of self-sought isolation. 'He was no man's
disciple,' writes Diogenes (IX, 5), 'but said that he had searched himself
and learned everything from himself.' We have now some conception
of the two great schools of thought which were started in the sixth
century, Ionian and Italian, and the contrast of inspiration and tendency
which they present. Later systems can often be best understood in
relation to these two, either as developments of one or the other, as
attempts to combine them, or again as reactions against them. It is as
the last that the thought of Heraclitus is primarily to be explained, if

---

[1] Reinhardt, *Parmenides*, 155ff.; Gigon, *Unters. zu H.* 1935. See review of the latter by W.
Broecker in *Gnomon*, 1937, 530ff. Reinhardt has been criticized by many, including Gigon
himself.

[2] 'Offenbar schief', ZN, 787, n.; 'not probable', Burnet, *EGP*, 131. See also Kirk, p. 6.

[3] To fr. 101 may be added the advice in fr. 74, not to act 'like children of our parents'. This is
in Heraclitus's Delphic manner, 'not speaking out but indicating by a sign', and Marcus Aurelius,
who quotes the phrase (IV, 46, note to Bywater's fr. 5), was no doubt right in interpreting it to
signify 'following tradition'. Snell also (*Hermes*, 1926, 358) takes the injunction to be that one
should rely on one's own experience, not on tradition or what one has taken over from others.

it is explicable in the light of his predecessors at all. Acquainted with the doctrines of both, he wished to follow neither (as in fact he wished to follow no man), and reacted with particular asperity against Pythagoras. We have seen how he includes Pythagoras in his condemnation of 'polymathy' without understanding (fr. 40). In fr. 129 we have: 'Pythagoras son of Mnesarchus practised inquiry (or research: *historie*) most of all men, and having selected from these writings (?) made a wisdom of his own, a polymathy, a deceit.'[1] Fr. 81, again, implies that Heraclitus called Pythagoras 'prince of cheats', and another fragment (35) runs: 'Men who are philosophers must be inquirers (*historas*) into many things indeed.' In view of his known opinion about *historie*, and his contempt for the knowing of many things instead of the one truth that matters, these words must be heavily ironical. When we take into account also his singling out of Pythagoras as the arch-practitioner of *historie*, and the probability that at this time the word 'philosopher' was applied in particular to Pythagoras and his followers (p. 165, above), it appears pretty clearly who is the target. (On this fragment cf. also p. 204, above.)

From all this disparagement of others we can learn in negative terms what his own method was. It was not *historie*, such as was practised by Hecataeus and a little later by Herodotus; that is, travelling all over the known world, questioning all sorts of people, and amassing factual knowledge, or studying external nature—the heavenly bodies, meteorological phenomena, earthquakes and so forth—as the Milesians had done. Nor was it *polymathie*, learning such as might be obtained from a study of the poets, who in Greece were the recognized teachers of men in theology, morals and other matters including even arts and crafts. The essence of his own procedure is found in the brief sentence already quoted (fr. 101): 'I searched myself.' This pronouncement was quoted by several ancient writers. Plutarch (*Adv. Colot.* 1118c) adds to it that the Delphic saying which he most admired was 'Know thyself'.[2]

---

[1] I agree with e.g. Burnet (*EGP*, 134) and Kirk (390) in seeing no reason to suspect the genuineness of this fragment. The exact translation is doubtful, but it is clearly uncomplimentary in the same sense as fr. 40, with the added charges of plagiarism and imposture. For some attempts at complete interpretation see A. Delatte, *Vie de Pyth.* 159, 161–3.

[2] If Diels's fr. 116 cannot actually be by Heraclitus, it is perhaps more likely to have originated in fr. 101 than in fr. 2 as Kirk thinks (p. 56).

The verb used (δίζημαι) has two main meanings: (1) to look for, as in *Il.* IV, 88 'looking for Pandarus, to see if she could find him anywhere', or Theognis, 415, (2) to question, inquire of somebody, find out. An example of this use is Herodotus, IV, 151: 'They sent messengers to Crete to ask (or find out, διζημένους) whether any Cretan or metic had reached Libya.' But perhaps especially interesting for comparison with Heraclitus is another passage in Herodotus, VII, 142. When the Persian invasion was imminent, the Athenians sent to Delphi for advice and received the famous counsel to rely on a wooden wall. After the messengers had returned with this reply, 'many opinions were expressed as they sought the meaning of (διζημένων) the oracle'.[1] Heraclitus was certainly 'looking for himself' in the sense that he was trying to discover his own true nature. But the pregnant use of the word in Herodotus's seventh book probably illustrates his meaning best. The Athenians were not looking for the oracle; nor were they questioning it: they had done that and received their answer. But like all oracular replies it had a superficial and a hidden meaning, and they were *probing* it to get beneath the surface and discover the underlying truth. Socrates did exactly the same when, having been told of a Delphic response with, on the surface, a much plainer meaning, he immediately asked himself the question: 'What is the riddle behind it?'[2] That there should be such a riddle, or hidden meaning, in the Pythia's answer was only to be expected, for it reflected the oracle's normal practice. To find the explanation of the world, the true nature of reality, was to Heraclitus an analogous process, for 'reality loves to conceal itself'.[3] This explanation moreover was contained in a *logos*

---

[1] Hölscher in *Festschrift Reinhardt*, 76 says: 'δίζησθαι wird im Ionischen vor allem von der Befragung des Orakels gebraucht.' But the examples which he cites (*Od.* XV, 90, XI, 100) do not by any means necessarily bear this out, and he does not quote the Herodotus passage, where the word, though used in connexion with an oracle, does not mean consulting it.

[2] τί ποτε αἰνίττεται; *Apol.* 21 B. Scholars who have thought that the object of Socrates's mission was to 'prove the god a liar' are naturally puzzled and annoyed when he goes on to describe himself as acting 'in obedience to the god' and performing a 'service' to him. But they have misunderstood him. He was only doing what any sensible man did with a Delphic response: looking past the obvious meaning for what was hidden underneath.

[3] Fr. 123 φύσις καθ' Ἡ. κρύπτεσθαι φιλεῖ. Quite enough has been written on the meaning of φύσις in this passage. Kirk, 227–31, has a full discussion of earlier views, and himself concludes that it means the 'real constitution' of things. With this I am in full agreement, but I cannot feel so strongly as he does that, as a consequence, the English word 'nature' is an altogether misleading translation.

(to which we shall come next), that is, a single truth that could be pursued by thought and grasped by insight. It could certainly be seen in external nature, if one had the insight to grasp it, but not by the mere piling up of knowledge; and it was exemplified equally fully in oneself.

Thus by the two words of fr. 101 Heraclitus meant, I suggest, first, 'I turned my thoughts within and sought to discover my real self'; secondly, 'I asked questions of myself'; thirdly, 'I treated the answers like Delphic responses hinting, in a riddling way, at the single truth behind them, and tried to discover the real meaning of my selfhood; for I knew that if I understood my self I would have grasped the *logos* which is the real constitution of everything else as well'. It is not surprising that a man with this outlook made few contributions to what we should call science, and that his conclusions are based on intuition rather than on observation and analysis of data. The later philosophers in the scientific tradition—men like Anaxagoras, Diogenes of Apollonia, and the atomists—ignored him, and the effect of his thought only begins to be seen in a deeper thinker with a religious dimension to his mind, namely Plato.

(9) *The Logos*

Heraclitus believed first and foremost in a Logos. The very opening of his book was a solemn affirmation of the truth, or real existence, of this Logos, which, he says, determines the course of all that comes to pass. It is reasonable to assume (with Gigon) that the other fragments which speak of the Logos in this same sense also belonged to the introductory section of the work. Our first task is to try to understand what this Logos was, but there is a point to be noted in preparation. When he says that 'everything comes to pass in accordance with this Logos' (fr. 1), or speaks of 'the Logos which orders all things' (fr. 72), he appears to be using the word in a specialized sense. On the other hand *logos* was a common word which in current use covered a wide field of meaning, and in other contexts he uses it as anyone else would. Nor is it credible that even when he appropriates it for a concept peculiar to his own philosophy he should divorce it completely from its ordinary uses. In the following sentences there is no difficulty in translating the word: it is used in recognized ways which could be illustrated from other fifth-century writers, indeed all could be found in his fellow-Ionian Herodotus.

Fr. 108: 'None of those whose *logoi* I have heard has achieved this...' ('utterances', sense 1, below).

Fr. 87: 'A fool is excited by every *logos*' ('rumour', 'report'; sense 1, below).

Fr. 39: 'Bias...who was of more *logos* than the rest' ('account', 'worth'; sense 2, below).

Fr. 31: 'Earth...has its measure in the same *logos* as existed before it became earth' ('proportion', sense 6, below).

For these reasons it is as well to begin with a brief outline of the ways in which the word was currently used in and around the time of Heraclitus. *Logos* in the fifth century or earlier meant:[1]

(1) Anything said (or for that matter written). A story or narrative (Hdt. I, 141),[2] whether fictitious or a true history (Thuc. I, 97 of his history of the Peloponnesian War). An account of anything, explanation of a situation or circumstances (Pind. *Ol.* VII, 21, *Pyth.* II, 66, IV, 132, Stesichorus, 11, 1 Diehl). News, tidings (Eur. *Bacch.* 663). A speech (Thuc. I, 22, 1, describing his policy in writing up speeches; perhaps not common till the late fifth century, though Hdt. VIII, 100, 1 comes very near it). Talk, conversation in general (*Il.* XV, 393, *Od.* I, 56, Pind. *Pyth.* IV, 101, Ar. *Wasps*, 472, Hdt. III, 148, 1). Of the response of an oracle, Pind. *Pyth.* IV, 59. Rumour, report (*Batr.* 8, Thuc. VI, 46, 5, Hdt. I, 75, 3), something commonly or proverbially said (frequent in the tragedians, e.g. Aesch. *Ag.* 750, Soph. *Tr.* 1). Mention, notice. Thus the slave Xanthias, standing by with the baggage on his back while his master confers with Heracles, complains: 'But of me and my aching shoulder there's no *logos*' (Aristoph. *Frogs*, 87). So also things are said to be worth *logos*. (In the Scythian winter 'there is no rain worth *logos*', Hdt. IV, 28, 2. 'Greater than *logos*' in Thuc. II, 50 means 'beggaring description'. It is easy to see how we shade off here into the meaning 'worth', 'esteem', which I have separated as (2) below.) Very commonly of *mere* words, as opposed to action or facts. So Soph. *El.* 59: 'What does it harm me if I die in *logoi*, but in fact am safe?' Hdt. IV, 8, 2: 'They say in their *logos* that Oceanus encircles the earth, but do not prove it in fact'; also, among the philosophers, Democritus, fr. 82, Anaxagoras, fr. 7.

[1] No exhaustive philological discussion is attempted here. For something more thorough see H. Boeder in *Arch. f. Begriffsgesch.* 1958, 82 ff.

[2] I give at least one example of each use, although some of course are so common that the examples could run into tens or hundreds.

This may be connected with the fact that in the earliest literature it seems to be used most frequently of *deceptive* talk (*Od.* 1, 56; Hes. *Th.* 229, 890, *Erga*, 78, 789; *H. Herm.* 317; Theogn. 254).

Still under the heading of things said or written, we have the terms of a treaty or agreement (Hdt. VII, 158, 5); a command (Aesch. *P.V.* 40, *Pers.* 363); a section of a written work (Hdt. V, 36, 4, VII, 93, and compare the distinction between one logos and the next in Hesiod, *Erga*, 106, Xenoph. fr. 7, 1 DK, Pind. *Pyth.* X, 54); an account in the financial sense (Hdt. III, 142, 5 'You will render a *logos* of the money which has passed through your hands'), and so generally or metaphorically Hdt. VIII, 100, 3: 'rendering a *logos* of their deeds' (facing the reckoning, paying the penalty).

(2) The idea of 'mention' already noticed leads naturally to that of worth, esteem, reputation; also fame (Pind. *Isthm.* V, 13 and 26, *Pyth.* VIII, 38). In Soph. *O.C.* 1163 the protection of a god is said to be of no small *logos*. This is common in Herodotus, as for example to be of *logos* in someone's eyes (I, 120, 5), in the King's eyes (IV, 138, 1), of much or little *logos* (III, 146, 3; I, 143, 2, etc.). To hold or put a man 'in *logos*' is to honour him (Tyrtaeus, 9, 1 Diehl).

In Aesch. *P.V.* 231 it is said that Zeus had no *logos* of mortals. The same meaning could have been expressed by saying that they were of no *logos* in his eyes, but used as it is the word probably comes under the next heading of 'thought': Zeus had no thought or care for mortals, recked not of them. (So also Pind. *Ol.* VIII, 4, Hdt. I, 117, 1, etc. In I, 62, 2 the Athenians at first 'had no *logos* of Pisistratus', i.e. did not worry about him.)

(3) To the Greeks the notion of taking thought, weighing up pros and cons, commonly presented itself as holding a conversation with oneself. Hence *logos* takes on that meaning too.[1] Eur. *Med.* 872 shows the transition, for Medea's way of saying 'I have thought it over' means literally 'I had a talk to myself' (cf. *Tro.* 916). As early as Parmenides, *logos* in this sense can be opposed, as thought or reasoning, to mere sensation, though elsewhere the same writer uses it of his true *account* of things (8, 50) or, in the plural, to mean simply 'words' (1, 15).

Close to this is the meaning of 'in their *logos*' (Hdt. VIII, 6, 2), shown by the context to mean 'opinion'. The *logos* (in this case that the Greek fleet should be wiped out) is what they would have said if asked, and did say to themselves.

(4) Another easy development from the spoken or written word is the notion of cause, reason or argument. 'Why did she send libations, from what *logos*?' (Aesch. *Cho.* 515). 'Why do you keep silence for no *logos*?' (Soph. *Ph.* 730). So to have *logos*, of a neuter subject, means to be arguable or

---

[1] Similarly also μῦθοι in Hom. *Il.* 1, 545 means unspoken thoughts.

reasonable (Soph. *El.* 466): from the fourth century at least we find it with a personal subject in the sense of the French *avoir raison* (Plato, *Apol.* 34B). The *Clouds* of Aristophanes has the dispute between the Better and the Worse Logos (argument, case). Presumably because it is basically a *spoken* reason, it is also used of a cause which is only alleged, a pretext (Soph. *Ph.* 352), and sometimes (as indeed in Aesch. *Cho.* 515) it is difficult to be sure whether a genuine or trumped-up cause is intended.

(5) In contrast to the meanings of 'empty words' or 'pretext', we have the phrase 'the real *logos*' (Hdt. 1, 95, 1; 116, 5), meaning the truth of the matter, somewhat as in 1, 120, 2 true kings are 'kings in the true *logos*'.

The meanings so far considered melt easily into and out of one another. Others are a little more specialized.

(6) Measure, full or due measure. Hdt. III, 99, 2: 'Not many of them reach the *logos* of old age.'[1] Cf. Thuc. VII, 56, 4 (the full number).

(7) Correspondence, relation, proportion. Aesch. *Sept.* 517 f.: Hyperbius has Zeus emblazoned on his shield, his opponent's device is Typhon. As Zeus defeated Typhon, so he will give victory to Hyperbius 'according to the *logos* of the blazon' (corresponding, conformably to). Theognis, 417 f.: 'I am as gold rubbed on lead, there is a *logos* of superiority in me.' Hdt. II, 109, 2: If an Egyptian's allotment of land was reduced by the Nile, he paid tax on the remainder 'in (or according to) the *logos* of the tax originally assessed'. In VII, 36, 3 Herodotus speaks of two ropes of flax and four of papyrus. 'Their thickness and quality were the same, but the flaxen were in *logos* heavier.' (In proportion: absolutely the two would weigh less than the four papyrus ropes.) Later, in Plato, this sense is common, and is also generalized so that adverbial phrases with *logos* can mean no more than 'similarly'.

In the sense of strictly mathematical proportion or ratio *logos* is frequent in Plato and Aristotle, but there is perhaps no indubitably attested example surviving from the fifth century nearer than Hdt. VII, 36 just quoted. However, from the accounts in Aristotle of the fifth-century Pythagoreans, it is impossible to believe that they did not use the word in this sense.

Two other senses of the word are particularly relevant to our coming examination of its use by Heraclitus: 'general principle, law, or rule' and 'the faculty of reason'. These do not seem by any means the same thing, yet the same word *logos* occurs in contexts where it is difficult to decide which would be the best translation. Another point to remark is the rarity of instances in the fifth century where either translation is indubitably right.

(8) General principle or rule. *Logos* means this in some fourth-century contexts, as when Aristotle speaks of 'the right *logos*' in the *Ethics*. Some

---

[1] In this case it is the exact equivalent of μέτρον. Cf. Hom. *Il.* XI, 225 ἥβης... ἥκετο μέτρον.

examples from the fifth century seem to have been erroneously so translated. For instance LSJ quote under this heading Pind. *Ol.* II, 22, where it seems to mean 'this saying', and *Nem.* IV, 31. In the latter Pindar says: 'He would show himself a tyro in battle who did not understand the *logos*: achievement is like to bring suffering with it.' The last words are one form of a Greek commonplace, and no doubt it is true that to the Greek mind they represented a general principle, an aspect of the normal workings of the world; but the sense does not require that *logos* should mean anything more than 'saying'. The passage, however, is a good illustration of the important truth that a word may well, to the people who use it, convey at once and as a unity what to others are two distinct ideas because they would use different words to express them. So too in Epicharmus, fr. 2, 12 DK (supposing the fragment to be genuine), λόγος can well be translated 'law' as by Diels, but equally well 'argument' (Hicks). More probably than either, the use of κατὰ λόγον here approximates to Plato's in (7) above: 'You and I are different now from what we were yesterday, and *similarly* in the future we shall be different again' (a sense developed from 'in the same ratio').

The nearest fifth-century instance is no doubt the statement of the philosopher Leucippus that 'nothing comes about at random, but all from *logos* and by necessity'. Burnet translates 'ground', and perhaps Leucippus means little more than that there is a reason for everything; but since the statement has a universal, cosmological significance, it comes very near to saying that everything is governed by general laws.

Possibly Democritus, fr. 53, comes close to the meaning: 'Many live according to *logos* though they have not learned *logos*', but here 'right reason', as in (4) above, seems a better rendering. Similarly in Plato, *Rep.* 500C, the philosopher in studying the Universe is contemplating what is well ordered and according to *logos*, and again one might be tempted to suppose that the word means natural law; but Jowett and Cornford are no doubt right in translating it 'according to reason' and 'where reason governs' respectively.

(9) The faculty of reason. This sense is obviously closely allied to (3) and (4), and is regular in fourth-century writers, for whom man is distinguished from the other animals by the possession of *logos*. We see it also in the passage of the *Republic* just quoted. Yet a clear instance in the fifth century might be hard to find, unless some verses which passed as by Epicharmus belong to that century.[1] Possibly also this meaning is ap-

---

[1] Epicharmus, fr. 57 DK. They are attributed by Athenaeus to a certain Chrysogonus the flute-player, said to be a contemporary of Alcibiades. (See DK, I, p. 194.) Diels described them as 'poor poetry, with Heraclitean and Pythagorean echoes'. At the best they are late in the century.

proached by Democritus, fr. 53, quoted in the previous paragraph. (Heraclitus himself is of course being excluded from this survey.)

(10) Another meaning common in the fourth century which it would be difficult to pinpoint in the fifth is that of definition, or formula expressing the essential nature of anything. This is regular in Aristotle, and is of course only a refinement of an earlier usage: to give an account or description of something approximates to defining it. The important thing to notice here as always is that whatever sense is uppermost when the word is used, shreds of the other uses will be clinging to it and influencing the writer's mind. For example, *logos* as we have seen can mean 'reason, cause', and for Plato or Aristotle the *logos* (definition) of anything is not complete unless it includes the reason for its existence.

(11) The word is one of the commonest in Greek, and it is therefore not surprising to find it sometimes used in certain contexts where there is no idiomatic word-for-word English equivalent. Such are Hdt. I, 141, 4: 'The rest of the Ionians decided by common *logos* to send' (agreed to send); III, 119, 1: 'Darius feared that the Six might have acted by common *logos*' (in concert or conspiracy); VIII, 68: 'those who are said to be in the *logos* of allies' (who are called your allies). So too in the example cited under (5): 'those who are kings in the true *logos*' (who are truly kings).

The above account has tried to bring out what a dictionary article inevitably tends to obscure, that word and thought go together, and notions which the Greeks conveyed by one and the same word were more closely linked in their minds than in those of people who lack a word of the same coverage. In reading Greek it is difficult, and sometimes wrong, to draw a hard and fast line between them. Nor is it always easy to know exactly what was intended by the writer.

The book of Heraclitus began as follows:[1]

Although this Logos [*sc.* which I shall describe] exists (or is true) for ever,[2] men prove as unable to understand it when once they have heard it as before

---

[1] ἐν τῇ ἀρχῇ αὐτοῦ τοῦ συγγράμματος Arist. *Rhet.* 1407b16. Sext. *Adv. Math.* VII, 132 says ἐναρχόμενος γοῦν τῶν περὶ φύσεως.... The words are Heraclitus's introduction of his subject.

[2] Ever since Aristotle (*loc. cit.* pp. 407 f.) noted the ambiguity of ἀεί without resolving it, scholars have disputed whether it should qualify ἐόντος (as Hippolytus thought) or ἀξύνετοι. For the chief names on both sides see Kirk, *HCF*, 34, adding Ritter and Preller (*Hist. Gr. Phil.* 32a) and Cornford (*Princ. Sap.* 113) to those who have taken it with ἐόντος. Kirk himself takes it with ἀξύνετοι. Argument will never settle the question finally. I can only say that I myself find it unnatural and impossible to separate ἀεί from ἐόντος. The difference matters less in that Kirk writes that ἐόντος ἀεί 'certainly expresses something which Heraclitus believed; it is to be

they heard it. For, though all things come to pass in accordance with this Logos, men seem as if ignorant when they experience such words and things as I set forth, distinguishing each thing according to its nature and telling how it is. The rest of mankind are unaware of what they do while awake just as they forget what they do while asleep.[1]

Fr. 50 adds: 'Listening not to me but to the Logos it is wise to agree[2] that all things are one.' These two fragments tell us that the Logos is (a) something which one hears (the commonest meaning), (b) that which regulates all events, a kind of universal law of becoming,[3] (c) something with an existence independent of him who gives it verbal expression.

Fr. 2 takes us a little further. 'One must follow what is common; but although the Logos is common, most men live as if they had a private understanding of their own.' This notion of 'the common' is elaborated in fr. 114:[4] 'One must speak with intelligence[5] and trust in what is common to all, as a city in its law and much more firmly; for all human laws are nourished by one, the divine, which extends its sway as far as it will and is sufficient for all and more than sufficient.'

rejected only on the ground that ἀεί goes with ἀξύνετοι' (p. 35). It is also possible to construe τοῦδε as predicate with ἐόντος and the phrase as a genitive absolute: 'The Logos being as I say it is.'

[1] Cornford (*Princ. Sap.* 113) is no doubt right in detecting allusions to the language of the mysteries here and elsewhere in Heraclitus. With ἀξύνετοι cf. Theo Sm. p. 14 Hiller: debarred from the mystic revelation are those who have unclean hands and are τὴν φωνὴν ἀξύνετοι. This is elaborated in Isocr. *Paneg.* 157: the proclamation of the Eumolpidae and Heralds at Eleusis excludes murderers and βάρβαροι (echoed in Heraclitus, fr. 107 βαρβάρους ψυχὰς ἐχόντων). ἄπειρος (especially in connexion with λόγος) recalls the version of the ritual prohibition in Ar. *Frogs*, 355 ὅστις ἄπειρος τοιῶνδε λόγων. Cf. also the reference to the *kykeon* in fr. 125 (p. 449, below).

[2] ὁμολογεῖν, to bring one's own λόγος into conformity.

[3] I omit here fr. 72, which speaks of λόγῳ τῷ τὰ ὅλα διοικοῦντι, because Burnet rejected these words as an addition of Marcus Aurelius who quotes the fragment. Kirk also (*HCF*, 44) describes the fragment as 'genuine quotation interlarded with Marcus's own comments'. For myself, however, in view of fr. 1 and fr. 64, I see no reason to suppose it a Stoic paraphrase.

[4] Which may have stood in Heraclitus's text between frr. 1 and 2 (Kirk, *HCF*, 48f.).

[5] The pun ξὺν νόῳ...ξυνῷ drives home the identity of what is common with intelligent reflexion (i.e. the Logos). No doubt the connexion is also in his mind when he uses the verb ξυνιέναι as in fr. 51. Heraclitus in many places shows that he is still at the stage of thought when verbal similarity appears fraught with a greater significance than would now be allowed it. Cf. Kirk, *HCF*, 198. Snell (*Hermes*, 1926, 368, n. 2) compares Aesch. *Ag.* 1081 (Apollon–Destroyer), 689 (Helen–ἑλένους), and *Sept.* 405 and 829 (the ὀρθόν or ἐτήτυμον of a name).

Cleanthes recalled this fragment in his hymn to Zeus, 20f.:

οὔτ' ἐσορῶσι θεοῦ κοινὸν νόμον οὔτε κλύουσιν,
ᾧ κεν πειθόμενοι σὺν νῷ βίον ἐσθλὸν ἔχοιεν.

Other Stoic echoes are also quoted by Kirk, *HCF*, 49f. (Considering the methods of some modern scholars, one may be grateful that they have not tried to reverse the relationship.)

The Logos being 'common', it is a virtue to grasp 'the common', and a fault to lay claim to a wisdom peculiar to oneself. Paradoxically, Heraclitus claims to be the only, or practically the only, man to have grasped this common Logos. But that is the fault of the others, for the truth lies there for all to see, but, as he says in fr. 72: 'They divorce themselves from that with which most of all they are in continuous contact' (cf. also fr. 34, p. 412, above).

The Logos is common to all, and what is common is intelligence or insight. This emerged from fr. 114 (with its pun on ξὺν νόῳ...ξυνῷ).[1] It is thus an additional aspect of the Logos that it includes the act of thinking or reflexion.[2]

We have noted Heraclitus's deliberately oracular style, and the disjointed and picturesque character of the pronouncements in which he conveyed his message. To draw from them a consistent world-view or system of thought is inevitably to supply connecting links which are not in the fragments, and to that extent must be speculative. Moreover any connected exposition is so alien to his own habits that it cannot but

---

[1] νοῦς and νοεῖν (though often in Homer the latter can hardly be rendered by anything but 'see': *Il.* III, 21, 30; V, 590, 669, 711, etc.) include the power not only to perceive with the senses but to recognize the identity or significance of what is perceived. On early uses of the words see K. von Fritz in *CP*, XXXVIII (1943), XL and XLI (1945–6). To take one illustration, in *Il.* III Aphrodite has appeared to Helen disguised as an old woman of her retinue. Soon, however, Helen sees through the disguise and realizes that she is in the presence of the goddess. The verb for this is ἐνόησε (*v.* 396). So also Epicharmus wrote (fr. 12 DK): 'It is *nous* that sees and *nous* that hears; the rest are deaf and blind', i.e. the senses by themselves, without the supra-sentient power to interpret their message, tell one nothing. As Heraclitus himself truly says (fr. 40), it is possible to learn many facts without having the *nous* to grasp their significance. Fr. 34 comes even nearer to Epicharmus.

The equivalence of 'the common' to right thinking is repeated in fr. 113 ξυνόν ἐστι πᾶσι τὸ φρονέειν, which, however, Kirk supposes to be nothing but a short and inaccurate version of the general sense of fr. 2 in particular (*HCF*, 56). I do not find his objections conclusive.

[2] Kirk writes (p. 63) that 'the universal Reason, in which men share', is the Stoic interpretation of the Logos, and that 'there is nothing in this which corresponds to what Heraclitus appears to have meant by his λόγος'; for Heraclitus, he thinks, it describes an objective state of things, common to all things and to all men, but with no epistemological implications. The Stoics certainly developed and laid especial emphasis on the concept of Logos as Reason, but this seems to go too far. It is impossible that Heraclitus, for all his originality, should have so rigidly divorced his objective use of λόγος from the usages of the same word current in his own time, especially as he was not a logician, but, to quote Kirk again (p. 396), 'lived, as his language shows, in the tradition of poetical thought'. I doubt whether it can be altogether reconciled with Kirk's remark on p. 396 that 'for him there was no rigid distinction in kind between the Logos as comprehended in a human mind and the Logos operating in nature'. In any case I should say we have seen evidence that for Heraclitus the Logos was not only 'comprehended in a human mind', but included the mind's active power of comprehension.

alter the quality of his message. Nevertheless I share with others the impression that many of the fragments fit together in a way that one would not at first expect, so that what seem to be isolated and meta-phorical utterances are in fact integral parts of a unified conception of the universe and of man as a part of it. It is discouraging, certainly, to note how many different impressions of this world-view have been put forward in the past and continue to be put forward; but one can only give one's own.

Some Presocratic systems seem so much the product of a single central idea that it is difficult to clarify them in a continuous exposition. They are like circles, of which Heraclitus said that 'beginning and end are common' (fr. 103), or as Porphyry paraphrased it: 'Any point you can think of is both beginning and end.'[1] One can break into them at any point, and by following on from there may hope in the end to see the system complete. To pick the best starting-point, the clearest order in which to present these parts of a single whole, is not easy, but we must make our entry and try.

In fr. 1 Heraclitus finds fault with men for behaving in their waking hours as if they were asleep. If we may accept fr. 73,[2] he said elsewhere: 'It is wrong to act and speak like men asleep.' At first sight there does not seem to be much logical connexion between this criticism and the injunction in fr. 2 to 'follow the common'. To be told to *wake up* and pay attention is usual enough, and does not normally give any informa-tion about the doctrine for which our attention is demanded. Yet here it is a part of it. The link is in a passage from Plutarch: 'Heraclitus says that the waking share one common world, but when asleep each man turns away to a private one.'[3] We must now follow a train of thought which will explain Heraclitus's conception of sleep and wakefulness, and their connexion with the principles by which the world is governed. It will also bring out something which is of great importance for an appreciation of his position in the history of Greek thought. Hitherto

---

[1] This peculiarity of their systems was even noted by at least one of the Presocratics them-selves. Parmenides wrote (fr. 5): 'It is all one to me, the point from which I begin; for there I will arrive back again.'

[2] Kirk thinks it more probably only Marcus Aurelius's paraphrase of the end of fr. 1.

[3] *De Superst.*, 166c (Heraclitus, fr. 89), rejected by Kirk as a conflation of the last parts of frr. 1 and 2, but vigorously defended by Vlastos in *AJP*, 1955, 344–7.

the material and spiritual worlds have been united without much misgiving. Later they became clearly distinguished from one another. Much of the obscurity of Heraclitus results from the fact that his more subtle thinking had really brought him to a stage when matter and spirit, or equally the concrete and the abstract, require to be thought of as separate, but he is still too much in the groove of previous thinking to effect the separation consciously. Before this could be achieved philosophy had to suffer the intellectual jolt which it received from Parmenides. As Kirk observes (*HCF*, 53), Heraclitus would have been unable to define any other type of 'being' than corporeal being. It is easy to forget how close to the concrete, material world his conceptions remained, and to interpret them too much in terms of abstractions.

We have seen evidence that the Logos is both human thought and the governing principle of the Universe.[1] It represents in fact the nearest that Heraclitus came to an *arche* like that of his predecessors,[2] which commonly combined both characters. This was true of Pythagorean thought, and appeared in more plainly material terms in the Air of Anaximenes, which was at the same time the divine and living stuff of the Universe and the element of soul and mind in us. In Heraclitus too the Logos had a material embodiment.

Being universal and all-pervading, this Logos—the law by which the world is ordered, and which can be comprehended in human minds—is of course common to all. When Heraclitus says emphatically that we must hold fast to what is common, he means this part-material, part-spiritual force which makes for rational order. In the language of Presocratic thought it 'guides' or 'steers' all things. This metaphor from navigation is used in fr. 64: 'The thunderbolt steers all things'

[1] On the former point Kirk disagrees. His description of it in the latter aspect is worth quoting (*HCF*, 39): "'The organized way in which (as Heraclitus had discovered) all things work''; "plan" (in a non-teleological sense), "rule", even "law" (as in "the laws of force") are possible summaries. "Principle" is too vague; I suggest the less ambiguous if more cumbersome phrase "formula of things" as a translation of λόγος in frr. 1, 2, 50. In this formula the idea of measure is implicit.'

[2] Cf. Gigon, *Unters. zu H.* 3f. Gigon notes the contrast in fr. 1 between the Logos as *being* (ἐών) and the world of *becoming* (γιγνομένων) which follows its pattern. Kirk (p. 41) doubts whether Heraclitus deliberately drew the contrast between εἶναι and γίγνεσθαι, but it was a possible one for his age. Cf. Simonides, 4, lines 1 and 6 Diehl, with the comments of H. D. Verdam (*Mnemos.* 1928, 299–310) and L. Woodbury (*TAPA*, 1953, 153–63).

(that is, the fiery weapon of Zeus the supreme god, used naturally for the power which drives the Universe), and also in fr. 41. Unfortunately text and meaning of the latter fragment are hotly disputed, but Vlastos has made out a reasonable case, against Kirk and others, for keeping to the rendering: 'Wisdom is one thing, to know the Thought by which all things are steered through all things.'[1] The rendering favoured by Kirk runs: '...to be skilled in true judgment, how all things are steered through all things'. The 'steering' is not in doubt, and, as Kirk says (p. 390), one is reminded by it of fr. 64, and 'it must be something akin to fire which "steers all things through all"'.... The *whole* course of each separate thing is the result of "steering", that is, of an operation either dependent on a mind or at least similar to that which a mind would have devised.'[2]

That the divine force which brings rational order into the Universe is at the same time a physical, material entity is only what we should expect from the general climate of early fifth-century thought. It follows that we get our share of it by physical means, which include breathing and the channels (πόροι) of the sense-organs. There is in Heraclitus no wholesale condemnation of sense-perception like that in Parmenides, for whom the mind does better to ignore the senses altogether. They are only 'bad witnesses' to those whose souls have not the insight to understand the message that they convey (fr. 107)— though this, indeed, in his opinion includes the vast majority of mankind. He goes so far as to say (fr. 55) 'Things that can be seen, heard, learned—these are what I prefer', and judges the relative value of first-hand experience and hearsay in the words (fr. 101a) 'Eyes are more accurate witnesses than the ears'. Though he has nothing but contempt for those who can only amass data without the *nous* to draw the right conclusion from them, he sees that accurate perception of phenomena

---

[1] In fr. 64 the verb is οἰακίζειν, in 41 κυβερνᾶν. On the latter see p. 88, above. Plato (*Phil.* 28 D) speaks of οἱ πρόσθεν ἡμῶν, who said that τὰ σύμπαντα...νοῦν καὶ φρόνησίν τινα θαυμαστὴν διακυβερνᾶν.

For reading and translation of fr. 41 see Kirk, *HCF*, 386–90 and Vlastos, *AJP*, 1955, 352 f. Kirk's construction of γνώμην as internal accusative after ἐπίστασθαι instead of direct object (in which he follows Heidel, Reinhardt and Gigon) is based on the conviction which he shares with Heidel that to equate γνώμη with the Logos and make it an independent guiding principle is a Stoic idea.

[2] This seems to give back a good deal of what Kirk has taken away by refusing to equate γνώμη with the Logos and regard it as a divine principle.

is the necessary preliminary to the discovery of the Logos which underlies and explains them (cf. Kirk, *HCF*, 61).

The senses, then, are for human beings the primary channels of communication with the Logos outside. Here we must supplement the actual fragments of Heraclitus from an account of his doctrine by Sextus Empiricus, whose general sense there is no reason to suspect, though it is expressed in later, particularly Stoic terminology.[1] He describes 'the common and divine Logos, by sharing in which we become *logikoi* (capable of thought)'. It is for Heraclitus the standard of truth, 'wherefore', he adds, paraphrasing frr. 1 and 2, which he quotes soon after, 'what appears to all in common is trustworthy, for it is grasped by the common, divine Logos; but what occurs to one alone is not to be believed'.

The senses are channels, through which, as well as by breathing, we draw in the Logos in a literal, physical sense. They are compared to windows through which 'the mind (*nous*) in us' in our waking hours thrusts forward and, making contact with that which surrounds it, 'puts on the power of thought'. In sleep however these sense-channels (αἰσθητικοὶ πόροι) are closed, and so the mind 'is prevented from growing together with what lies outside' (χωρίζεται τῆς πρὸς τὸ περιέχον συμφυίας). Since we still live, the severance is not complete. Respiration is left as sole means of contact with the outside source of life, 'like a root', says Sextus. We are still taking some part in the cosmic activity, which is presumably why 'Heraclitus says' (so Marcus Aurelius tells us)[2] 'that even sleepers are workers and co-operators in what goes on in the world'. Respiration, it seems, is sufficient to preserve life but not rationality, and when thus cut off the mind loses its power of memory. Sextus then quotes fr. 2 and the last sentence of fr. 1 in support of his exposition.

In sleep we each retire into a private world. No one shares our dreams as our waking experiences are shared. And dreams are unreal. Thus for

---

[1] *Math.* VII, 126ff., DK, 22A16. Kirk agrees that the ideas are genuinely Heraclitean, at least to the extent that 'for Heraclitus the soul's efficiency depended on contact with the outside world and with the material Logos, possibly by the medium of breath, as Sextus tells us' (*HCF*, 341).

[2] VI, 42, quoted by DK as fr. 75, but hardly a word-for-word extract from Heraclitus. (DK obscure the sense by omitting the καί before τοὺς καθεύδοντας.)

Heraclitus three ideas are essentially connected: (a) living as if one had a private wisdom of one's own, (b) falsehood, (c) sleep and dreams. To retire into a world of one's own is to starve the rational element by shutting it off from the universal and true Logos on which it should feed.[1] The many who do this are, compared to a man with an insight into the common Logos, like sleepers compared to a man awake. Hence the exhortation to follow the Common, to hold fast to it with all one's might.

If this interpretation is correct, it would seem that Heraclitus already had a dim foreshadowing[2] of the truth which was later to be explicitly formulated by Protagoras, that each man is the judge of his own sensations, for they are his alone and not the same for any two persons. There *is* a common world of truth (here he would differ from Protagoras), but it is only to be attained by going beyond individual and disconnected sensations and drawing conclusions from them by reflexion, or perhaps rather intuition. It is understandable therefore that in certain moods he could praise the senses (since in our bodily state they are the channels through which in the first instance and in an elementary way we are brought into contact with the Logos), and in others, with seeming contradiction, emphasize their limitations or even abuse them. In such a context of thought he could well have said that 'seeing is being deceived' (fr. 46, suspected by Kirk, p. 281 as an improbable statement for Heraclitus). After all, *mere* seeing and hearing are precisely the activities of 'the many' whom he lashes so unmercifully for their refusal to understand the truth (see the examples on p. 412, above).

The physical aspect of these—as we might call them—psychical

---

[1] The word τρέφονται in fr. 114 (τρέφονται πάντες οἱ ἀνθρώπειοι νόμοι ὑπὸ ἑνὸς τοῦ θείου) is probably not entirely metaphorical for Heraclitus. See Kirk, *HCF*, 53 f. and 69: 'The "divine law" which is akin to the Logos is described in material terms which are probably not just due to personification.'

Cornford has pointed out how with his notion of sleep Heraclitus contradicts yet another popular view, namely that in sleep the soul is more open to divine influences and so may have prophetic truth revealed to it in dreams (*Princ. Sap.* 150, referring to Pind. fr. 131 and Aristotle, fr. 10 Rose, p. 84 Ross).

[2] I do not wish to deny what Kirk says on p. 74 of his book, that 'there is no indication in the fragments that Heraclitus based any epistemological conclusions on this view—for him such facts were of interest only because they showed that the opposites were not essentially different, as they appeared to be'.

processes is carried into even further detail, and for the sake of clarity it may be as well to follow up the topic, at the risk of introducing at this point things which will find their proper place for full discussion later on. The doxographers say that Heraclitus's first principle was fire. They speak as if it were the *arche* and *physis* of things in the Milesian sense, e.g. Theophrastus (*ap*. Simpl. *Phys*. 23.33, DK,A5): 'Hippasus of Metapontum and Heraclitus of Ephesus...made fire the *arche*, and out of fire they produce existing things by thickening and thinning, and resolve them into fire again, on the assumption that fire is the one underlying *physis*; for Heraclitus says that all things are an exchange for fire' (cf. fr. 90). Aristotle himself (*Metaph*. 984a7) lists the fire of Heraclitus as his 'first cause' along with the water of Thales, the air of Anaximenes and Diogenes of Apollonia, and the four primary substances of Empedocles. The primacy of fire in Heraclitus seems also to be unmistakably referred to by Plato (*Crat*. 413B–c). We shall have to consider whether these later writers correctly interpreted the role of fire in Heraclitus, but about its primacy there can be no question, and he himself said that the whole world-order is an ever-living fire (fr. 30; see p.454, below). It cannot then be wrong to identify it with the Logos, and agree with the Stoics and Hippolytus when they say that the fire of Heraclitus is 'rational, and responsible for the government of the whole world'.[1] This, clearly, is what in Sextus's account 'surrounds us and is rational and intelligent' (*Math*. VII, 127).

The material aspect of the Logos is fire. It follows that divine reason at its purest is hot and dry. Though not a mere symbol for an abstraction, 'fire' represents for Heraclitus the highest and purest form of matter, the vehicle for soul and mind, or rather soul and mind themselves, which in a more advanced thinker would be distinguished from any matter whatsoever. It must not therefore be imagined as a visible flame or glow, but rather a kind of invisible vapour, as Philoponus says commenting on Aristotle, *De Anima*, 405a25: 'By fire he does not mean flame: fire is the name he gives to the dry exhalation, of which the soul

---

[1] λέγει δὲ καὶ φρόνιμον εἶναι τοῦτο τὸ πῦρ, καὶ τῆς διοικήσεως τῶν ὅλων αἴτιον (Hipp. IX, 10: see fr. 64 DK). The phraseology is Stoic, but the sense Heraclitean, as Kirk agrees (*HCF*, 351 ff., and on 396: 'Unchanged fire is the most active kind of matter and in its purest form or aither (so we may conjecture) it possesses directive capacity, it is the embodiment of the Logos...and it is wise').

also consists.'[1] Thus if Heraclitus is consistent, foolishness and death will be connected with cold and dampness; and so it is. 'The dry soul is wisest and best' (fr. 118). This explains among other things the effects of intoxication: 'A man when he is drunk stumbles and is led by a beardless boy, not knowing whither he goes, for his soul is wet' (fr. 117).[2] Death itself is a turning of the soul to water (fr. 36). It is not rash to infer, though no fragment actually says it, that sleep, like drunkenness, is an intermediate state in which moist vapours have temporarily overcome the soul, which is restored to a drier and warmer state on waking.[3] Since bodily pleasures lead to a moistening, that is a weakening, of the soul, we can understand why Heraclitus should say (fr. 110): 'It is not better for men to get all they want'; for unfortunately 'it is enjoyment for souls to become moist'.[4] The same thought must be behind one of his most striking aphorisms (fr. 85, known to Aristotle; see *Eth. Eud.* 1223b22): 'To fight with desire is hard: whatever it wishes it buys at the price of soul.'

Everything is in continual and cyclic change, and the soul takes its part quite naturally in the mutual conversions of the elements. 'It is death to souls to become water, death to water to become earth, but from earth comes water and from water soul' (fr. 36). By substituting 'souls' for the expected 'fire' Heraclitus has emphasized the substantial identity of the two. Since each element lives by the death of the other, or as we might put it devours the other, it is quite in order that souls, though their proper nature is hot and dry, should live on moisture. Immediately after quoting what all accept as a genuine fragment of

---

[1] 'Recte hunc locum explicat Philoponus' (Ritter and Preller, *Hist. Ph. Gr.* 38b). For a contrary view see Kirk, *HCF*, 275, n. 1. I cannot agree with Gigon that it is wrong to identify the Logos with fire. He writes (*Unters. zu H.* 59f.): 'Dass die Seele aus trockenster Substanz besteht, hat H. zwar gelehrt. Aber dass sie feurig sei, ist damit noch gar nicht gesagt, und überhaupt dürfte das sinnlich-banale Einzelwesen ψυχή nicht mit dem kosmogonischen Urfeuer gleichgestellt werden.' This is very un-Heraclitean language. He also thinks it wrong to identify the Logos with fire (p. 60): 'Dies folgt der Neigung der Stoa.' Is it not evident that in this as in certain other respects the Stoa followed Heraclitus? Gigon's further claim on p. 110 that 'die Trockenheit ist nicht Attribut des Feuers, sondern der Luft' is simply wrong.

[2] Whether Heraclitus ever asked himself the question why one cannot get drunk on water is something we shall never know.

[3] 'Sleep was generally regarded as due to a reduction of organic heat', Vlastos in *AJP*, 1955, 365, with references in note. The obscure fr. 26 seems to bring sleep and death close together.

[4] Fr. 77. Much of this fragment is highly obscure, but so much at least seems certain. As Gigon says (*Unters. zu H.* 109), it is unlikely that so individual a phrase should be spurious.

Heraclitus, Cleanthes[1] says he believed that 'souls are exhaled from moist things' (fr. 12). The plural is probably to be explained, with Gigon, as indicating that Heraclitus, like Thales, had various liquids in mind, not only water but blood and other bodily humours. In the same way some of the 'Heraclitizers' were said to teach that the sun (which occupied a rather special place in Heraclitus's own cosmic system) 'is vaporized from the sea' ([Ar.] *Probl.* 934b35). The sun draws up moisture and feeds on it, but being a hot body converts it into heat, a theory which makes use of elementary observation of the phenomenon of evaporation. The living, waking animal does the same. These later statements of Heraclitus's views (whose complete accuracy one would perhaps not like to vouch for) are only particular applications of the general law enunciated in fr. 36 and also in fr. 31 (p. 463, below); and given the equivalence of souls and fire, the analogical behaviour of the sun and animals is natural and inevitable.

There will be more to say about the soul, but the present excursion into psychology is intended to further an understanding of the complexity of the Logos-conception in Heraclitus. To sum this up, it is first of all the everlasting truth to which he is giving verbal expression, but which is independent of his utterance of it (frr. 1, 50). Next, it is the subject of that truth, the One which is everything (fr. 50). And this One is at the same time the divine, intelligent principle which surrounds us and causes the ordering of the cosmos, and that within us to which we owe whatever intelligence we possess. In us it is adulterated with lower elements and therefore with foolishness. At the same time it is fire, the hot and dry, and what corrupts it in us is its encounter with moisture and cold. Questions (all closely related) which remain to be considered in their due place are: (*a*) What is the content of the Logos, considered as the true explanation of the changing world? What is this 'principle' in accordance with which, says Heraclitus, everything has its becoming? (*b*) In what sense are 'all things one' for him? What is the bond of unity between them? Is it as with the Milesians, that they are all made out of the one material stuff, which remains the permanent ground of their existence? (*c*) What exactly is the role of fire in the life of the cosmos?

---

[1] Cleanthes rather than Zeno, as Kirk perceived (*HCF*, 367).

The Logos: Summary

(10) Three Basic Statements.

Besides the Logos, and intimately connected with it, it would appear that the fundamentals of Heraclitus's interpretation of the world are contained in three general statements. For convenience of exposition we must deal with them one by one, but none can be fully understood without the others, indeed they are only different ways of explaining the same truth. These three statements are: (*a*) Harmony is always the product of opposites, therefore the basic fact in the natural world is strife. (*b*) Everything is in continuous motion and change. (*c*) The world is a living and everlasting fire. Consideration of these statements will make it possible to return to the Logos, as the law of becoming, with better understanding, and grasp the limitations which it imposes on the continuous warfare and change within the Universe.

(a) Harmony is of opposites

The meaning of the word *harmonia* has been discussed in connexion with the Pythagoreans (pp. 220ff., above). We may assume that both its application to music and its general use, as the fitting-together and construction of a complex whole according to rational principles and in due proportion (which is one of the meanings of *logos*), were familiar to Heraclitus. We ourselves use the word 'harmony' in a non-musical sense, as when we speak of living in harmony or of a harmonious effect in architecture, painting or other spheres. It might however be unwise to leave it to stand generally for *harmonia* in a Heraclitean context, even after explaining the Greek word, because it carries psychological overtones which are biased in a Pythagorean direction.[1] Since the *harmonia* of Heraclitus is the very reverse of the Pythagorean, this could not fail to be misleading.

A number of Heraclitus's sayings illustrate his novel interpretation of the 'harmony of opposites', but perhaps the best starting-point is offered by a comparison of two passages in Plato. In the *Symposium*, the doctor Eryximachus is taking his turn to sing the praises of Eros, and puts forward the current view of his craft as that of reconciling

---

[1] Our thought is more influenced by Pythagoreanism than we always realize. The psychological application of the musical concept is seen for instance in the line from the *Merchant of Venice*: 'Such harmony is in immortal souls', which occurs in a definitely Pythagorean context.

the opposites in the body. The good practitioner, he says (186D, transl. W. Hamilton), 'must be able to bring elements in the body which are most hostile to one another into mutual affection and love; such hostile elements are the opposites hot and cold, wet and dry and the like; it was by knowing how to create love and harmony between these that our forefather Asclepius, as our poets here say and as I believe, founded our craft'.

These ideas of health as a harmony of physical opposites belonged to the Western school of medicine, being taught by Alcmaeon the fellow-townsman of Pythagoras and by some at least of the Pythagoreans (pp. 313–15, above). That Eryximachus has learned from the Pythagoreans is confirmed by his development of the musical example in the next few sentences. He continues:

That the same is true of music is plain to everyone who gives the smallest attention to the subject, and this is presumably what Heraclitus meant to say, though he is not very happy in his choice of words, when he speaks of a unity which agrees with itself by being at variance, as in the stringing of a bow or lyre [cf. fr. 51, pp. 439-51, below]. It is, of course, quite illogical to speak of a concord being in discord, or of its consisting of factors which are still in discord at the time when they compose it, but probably what he meant to say was that the art of music produces a harmony out of factors which are first in discord but subsequently in concord, namely treble and bass notes.

It would be very surprising if, after the insults that he hurled at Pythagoras, Heraclitus should be doing his best to say that he agreed with him, only not managing to express it very well. His view was in fact a contradiction of the Pythagorean, and this is a particularly instructive example of something which has constantly happened to Heraclitus: the sharp edge of his teaching has been taken off, and it has been blunted into the similitude of someone else's. Here Plato satirizes the doctor, who is represented as a pompous and not very subtle-minded person, by putting the misunderstanding into his mouth. Elsewhere he shows that he knew perfectly well what Heraclitus meant, indeed he was perhaps the first to appreciate the full boldness of his thought. To say that harmony was produced out of disharmony in chronological succession, and represented a reconciliation of elements formerly hostile but no longer so, was to assert precisely what Heraclitus had denied. This Plato makes clear in the *Sophist* (242D). The chief speaker has been talking about the dispute between those who hold that the world is many and those who maintain it to be one. He goes on:

Later, certain Muses in Ionia and Sicily perceived that safety lay rather in combining both accounts and saying that the real is both many and one and is held together by enmity and friendship. The stricter of these Muses [i.e. the Ionian, by which Plato means Heraclitus] say 'in drawing apart it is always being drawn together'. The milder [i.e. the Sicilian, who stand for Empedocles] relax the rule that this should always be so and speak of alternate states, in which the Universe is now one and at peace through the power of Love, and now many and at war with itself owing to some sort of Strife.

Empedocles, who followed the Italian tradition dominated by Pythagoras, spoke of alternate states of harmony and discord, unity and plurality. (This is fully borne out by his remains.) Heraclitus with his 'stricter Muse' asserted that any harmony between contrasting elements necessarily and always involved a tension or strife between the opposites of which it was composed. The tension is never resolved. Peace and war do not succeed each other in turn: always in the world there is both peace and war. Cessation of struggle would mean the disintegration of the cosmos. Plato's grasp of this essential point, which eluded so many of Heraclitus's would-be interpreters, is an excellent guarantee of his insight, and warrants confidence in anything that he has to say about this difficult thinker.[1]

The boldness of Heraclitus was too much even for Aristotle, indeed his own exceptional powers of clear and logical thinking were themselves an obstacle to his understanding of such an oracular and poetic truth. Heraclitus appeared to be breaking the law of contradiction, therefore he cannot have meant what his words seem to say. And so in *De Caelo*, 279b14, he classes him along with Empedocles, ignoring the distinction which Plato had been at such pains to point out. Some, he says, hold that the world is everlasting, others that it will perish; 'others again that it alternates, being at one time as it is now and at another changing and perishing,...as Empedocles of Acragas and Heraclitus of Ephesus say'. However, he sometimes comes closer to Heraclitus's words,

---

[1] In showing this high respect for Plato's testimony the present account differs from that of Kirk.

Heraclitus

whether or not with full understanding. In the *Ethics* for instance he writes (1155b4, fr. 8 DK): 'Heraclitus says that what is opposed is helpful, that the finest harmony is composed of differing elements, and that everything comes into being by way of strife', a sentence which paraphrases more than one fragment of Heraclitus.[1]

Heraclitus makes free use of picture-language, and it is not surprising that his sayings have been subject to almost as many interpretations as isolated texts of the Bible in the sermons preached on them. Indeed it is impossible not to be struck by the similarity between his use of paradox and parable and that of Jesus. Needless to say, there is no question of any comparison of doctrine, but in spite of the difference in meaning, an expression like 'he that findeth his life shall lose it' (Matt. x. 39) is remarkably Heraclitean in style (e.g. fr. 21), and apart from actual coincidence (compare Mark viii. 18 'Having eyes, see ye not, and having ears, hear ye not, and do ye not remember?' with Heraclitus frr. 19, 34, 1), to convey the heart of his message—the answer to the question: 'What is the Kingdom of God?'—Jesus has to make free use of symbol and comparison. It is like a mustard seed, like seed broadcast on different kinds of ground, like leaven in bread, or hidden treasure, or a candle: or think of a master with an unsatisfactory servant, a vineyard let to criminals, a man hiring labourers, money given in trust, a wedding-feast, bridesmaids and their lamps. Similarly Heraclitus, to bring home his new idea about the workings of nature and the constitution of things, finds himself compelled to say: Think of fire, of the structure of a bow or a lyre, of warfare, of a river, of a road (which is the same road whether it takes you from North to South or from South to North), of sea-water (a healthy element for fishes, death to men), of the track of a writer's pencil, straight and crooked at the same time, of a surgeon who inflicts sharp pain to cure pain.[2]

---

[1] E.g. frr. 51, 80, 10. In the first phrase (τὸ ἀντίξουν συμφέρον), Kirk notes (*HCF*, 220) that the Ionic word ἀντίξουν must be accepted as Heraclitus's own. 'Helpful' is the common meaning of συμφέρον, and the one which the context leads us to suppose was in Aristotle's mind. In the Hippocratic *De Victu*, I, 18 (τὰ πλεῖστα διάφορα μάλιστα συμφέρει) it includes the meaning 'is of use in producing pleasure'. But it recalls also the διαφερόμενον ἀεὶ συμφέρεται of the *Symposium* passage (187A). The play on words is very much in Heraclitus's manner, and in spite of the change to the active mood (for which the word-play would be a motive) the whole brief phrase may well be his. [2] Frr. 30, 51, 53, 60, 61, 59, 58.

Paradox and Parable

The teaching of Heraclitus was not something essentially indescribable in literal terms like the religious message of Jesus; but it was something which could at no time have been easy to express, and in his own day was so novel as to outrun the resources of contemporary language. This made the resort to a variety of symbols inevitable. It is for us to see whether we have the 'ears to hear', that is, the ability to grasp the single truth underlying this parable or that.

The doctrine of the 'harmony of opposites' has three aspects: everything is made of opposites and therefore subject to internal tension,[1] opposites are identical, and (mainly as a consequence of the first) war is the ruling and creative force and a right and proper state of affairs.

(i) *Everything is made of opposites, and therefore subject to internal tension.* After quoting fr. 50 Hippolytus continues: 'And that all men do not understand or admit this, he complains in terms of this sort (fr. 51): "They do not grasp how by being at variance it agrees with itself,[2] a backward-turning adjustment[3] like that of the bow or lyre."'

---

[1] I use 'tension' in its widest sense. Vlastos complains (*AJP*, 1955, 349) that 'there is much talk of "tension" in Kirk's and others' interpretations of Heraclitus, but none of it is grounded textually on anything beyond the disputed παλίντονος in B 51'. But how can it be claimed that the idea of universal tension is absent from such phrases as διαφερόμενον συμφέρεται or δίκην ἔριν?

[2] Or more literally (if we accept the reading συμφέρεται for ὁμολογέει, see crit. n. in Kirk, 203): 'in being drawn apart it is drawn together'. As here translated the verb has no expressed subject, but this is more probable than that Heraclitus intended the same sense as if the definite article had stood before διαφερόμενον. (So Burnet: 'What is at variance agrees with itself.')

[3] Or alternatively 'an adjustment of opposite tensions'. 'Adjustment' (Vlastos, *AJP*, 1955, 350) is a good rendering of ἁρμονίη in a context like this. The variant readings παλίντροπος and παλίντονος for the epithet with ἁρμονίη go back to ancient times, and modern scholarship shows an impressive array of champions on either side. For a summary of the controversy see Kirk, 210ff. Since Kirk wrote, and himself came down on the side of παλίντονος, Vlastos (*AJP*, 1955, 348–51) and Kranz (*Philologus*, 1958, 250–4) have both argued in favour of παλίντροπος. The question cannot be finally settled. The fact that Homer uses the epithet παλίντονος of a bow certainly makes that the *lectio facilior*, as Vlastos says, but is also an argument in favour of Heraclitus having used it, just as he borrows Homeric language in calling war ξυνός in fr. 80. (Cf. *Il.* xviii, 309.) Nor is it more difficult to apply it to the ἁρμονίη of a bow than to the bow itself.

But the arguments on both sides are endless. For my part I believe that whichever epithet Heraclitus used, his image is that of a bow which is strung but not actually being drawn, and a lyre tuned but not actually being played. This (the fitting-together or structure of something) is after all what ἁρμονίη means. If he wrote παλίντονος he was thinking of the ἁρμονίη of the bow or the lyre as consisting in the opposed pulls of the string or strings and the wooden frame: if παλίντροπος, which means 'turning in opposite directions' (Vlastos, *loc. cit.* 350), he had chiefly in mind, so far as the bow is concerned, the tendency of the springy framework to turn away from the string. In the lyre, the word seems an excellent description of the relation between the strings

The reference is evidently general as in the abbreviated version given by Plato in the *Sophist* (242E). Everywhere there are forces pulling both ways at once. *Apparent* harmony, rest, or peace is in the real constitution of things (*physis*) a state of precarious equilibrium between these forces. Look at a strung bow lying on the ground or leaning against a wall. No movement is visible. To the eyes it appears a static object, completely at rest. But in fact a continuous tug-of-war is going on within it, as will become evident if the string is not strong enough, or is allowed to perish. The bow will immediately take advantage, snap it and leap to straighten itself, thus showing that each had been putting forth effort all the time. The *harmonia* was a dynamic one of vigorous and contrary motions neutralized by equilibrium and so unapparent. The state of a tuned lyre (or for that matter violin) is similar, as any player whose string has broken knows to his chagrin. And the point is that the functioning of both instruments, their very nature as a working bow or lyre, is dependent on this balance of forces, which is therefore *good*, as will emerge below in the fragments considered under (*c*). For Heraclitus bow and lyre symbolize the whole cosmos, which without such constant 'warfare' would disintegrate and perish.[1]

Well may he say (fr. 54): 'Invisible *harmonia* is stronger than (or

and the pegs used to tighten them. The pegs are turned in one direction, which is the opposite to that in which the strings are (as one might say) trying to turn them. This will be evident if a peg should work loose, when its string will turn the peg back until it has slackened itself. This destroys the ἁρμονίη, which was dependent on the balance of the opposite-turning forces and may appropriately be described as a παλίντροπος ἁρμονίη.

Efforts to explain the image in terms of the 'opposite tensions' created when the bow is being drawn or the lyre plucked have always led to difficulties. Vlastos is definitely wrong when he says (*loc. cit.* 351) that the bow and lyre only yield a dynamic image if we assume that ἁρμονίη refers to their *modus operandi*. (See text.)

[1] The phrase συμφερόμενον διαφερόμενον occurs yet again in the exceedingly difficult fr. 10, and with other contrasting pairs is ultimately generalized in the sentence ἐκ πάντων ἓν καὶ ἐξ ἑνὸς πάντα. I can add nothing useful to the careful and perceptive work of Snell and Kirk on this fragment, and I agree with them that the last sentence need imply no successive temporal stages in the formation of the cosmos, which would contradict the denial of cosmogony in fr. 30 (p. 454, below). One point in Kirk's interpretation makes me slightly uneasy. He regards the passive sense of συλλάψιες (which he adopts in preference to the συνάψιες of DK's text) as made probable by the plural and 'justified by the very close analogy of συλλαβή' (*HCF*, 173). Since these are two different verbal formations from the same root, there seems to be little valid analogy between them. Verbal forms ending in -σις commonly indicate an action or process (ἀμφίβασις, κίνησις, etc.; and the plural κινήσεις is common enough). There are of course exceptions (ἄροσις in Homer, φάσις and others), but the passive sense is much less frequent, and (perhaps more important) σύλληψις itself seems elsewhere to connote only the action of grasping, apprehending or arresting.

superior to) visible.' As far as visible connexion goes, the bow might be naturally bent and the string simply tied to it at either end; the invisible connexion between them is the element of struggle, of dynamic opposition. So it is that 'Nature loves concealment' (fr. 123).[1]

There is a standing temptation to interpret Heraclitus's statements as a description of alternating change, now in this direction, now in that. It is not surprising therefore that he is represented in most ancient authorities as having believed that the whole cosmos arose from a different initial state, exists for a while and will then be resolved once more into its *arche*, especially since this was familiar to his readers as the stock conception from the Milesians onwards, which had been developed into an elaborate periodic scheme by Empedocles. But his own words put us on our guard against any such simple and unoriginal explanation. In view of all this one is justified in paying especial attention, not to the accounts which make him a conformist, but to any hint in our authorities that he was struggling, against the limitations of his language, to express something new and different. His thought was so difficult and to later antiquity unexpected, and his expression at times so ambiguous, that it would have been no surprise if his ancient interpreters had missed the point entirely. But Plato grasped it, and from later antiquity there is a passage of Plutarch which although it is for the most part only a paraphrase of Heraclitus, and makes use of the philosophical terminology of a later age, reveals in contrast to most contemporary testimony the true Heraclitean conception (*De E*, 392 B–C; given by DK as fr. 91 of Heraclitus). Plutarch's speaker is drawing the Platonic contrast between the permanence of being and the ceaseless flux of becoming, and cites Heraclitus in support of the latter:

One cannot, according to Heraclitus, step twice into the same river, nor lay hold twice of any mortal substance in one permanent state. Owing to the impetuosity and speed of change, it scatters and brings together again, *or rather, not again, nor later, but at the same time* it comes together and flows away, approaches and retreats.

---

[1] Or as Kirk more accurately renders it (*HCF*, 227): 'The real constitution of things is accustomed to hide itself.' It is, however, a real loss if we give up the pithy, Delphic style of Heraclitus's sayings, and the element of personification which was probably present.

Heraclitus did not of course deny the occurrence of internal temporal changes within the universe—hot becoming cold, age following on youth and death on life and so forth. As we shall see, he cited them as part of the evidence for the identity of opposites. But in themselves they were something of which even 'the many' were aware. To grasp the simultaneous operation of opposed tendencies was both more difficult and more essential.

(ii) *The identity of opposites.* Hesiod in his *Theogony* called day the offspring of night. This earned him the censure of Heraclitus, who hits both at him and at his favourite target, the unenlightened multitude, in the words (fr. 57): 'Teacher of most men is Hesiod. They are sure he knew most things, a man who could not recognize day and night; for they are one.'[1] Again, Porphyry, possibly making slight changes in Heraclitus's wording (see Kirk, 180f.), attributes to him the statement that 'to God all things are good and fair and just, but men have assumed some to be unjust and others just' (fr. 102). This statement has several sides, including obviously a theological and a moral one, but for the moment let us note simply that, here again, what men habitually separate and contrast are to be identified. Hippolytus mentions a number of contrasting pairs, of both nouns and adjectives, whose identity he claims to have been asserted by Heraclitus, including 'good and bad'. He produces no actual quotation with these words, but cites instead Heraclitus's illustration of cautery and the surgeon's knife, as being both bad (painful) and good (curative).[2] The identity of good and bad was earlier attributed to Heraclitus by Aristotle (*Top.* 159b30, *Phys.* 185b20). It is unlikely that he stated it in so many words (cf. the Simplicius passage quoted by Kirk, p. 95), but it is a reasonable inference from a fragment like 102. To argue that on these grounds he had no right to criticize 'the many' or to tell them to follow the Logos, because if good and bad are the same no kind of behaviour would be better than any other, would be, as Kirk justly says, 'to show a grave lack of historical sense as well as an over-literal interpretation of Heraclitus's language'.

---

[1] On the authenticity of fr. 106, which may be as Kranz thought a criticism made in the same context as fr. 57, see Kirk, 157–61.

[2] So much may be said with confidence about fr. 58, though in detail its text and interpretation both raise many thorny problems. See Kirk's exhaustive treatment, *HCF*, 88ff.

The Identity of Opposites

These examples of the identity of opposites are paradoxical in the full sense that they remain difficult to credit even when made explicit. To buttress their credibility he also gave illustrations in which the identity of what is commonly contrasted might seem admissible to the ordinary man, once it is pointed out. Up and down are opposites, but, he says (fr. 60), 'The road up and the road down are one and the same'. Since the meaning in this example is especially plain, we may use it to help our understanding of what he meant by 'the same'. What was for him an exciting discovery was only possible at a stage of thought when many logical distinctions, now obvious, had not yet become apparent. By baldly stating the absurd consequences of neglecting them, he unintentionally paved the way for their recognition. From *A* to *B* one traverses the same ground as from *B* to *A*, but this does not mean that to go in one direction is the same as to go in the other. The material road of earth and stones is the permanent substratum of both journeys, as philosophers would say from Aristotle on, and it is sometimes difficult to explain Heraclitus without resorting to that 'anachronistic but convenient term' (*HCF*, 197).

A second example of this type is fr. 59: 'The track of writing is straight and crooked.'[1] The pen or stylus follows a straight line across the page or tablet, but yet in the course of it traces out all sorts of convolutions in forming the letters. Once again a statement is seen to be (*a*) only an apparent paradox, and (*b*) to our minds only a very loose and equivocal use of language. One of Heraclitus's ancient nicknames was 'The Riddler', and some of his statements do indeed bear a resemblance to children's riddles and are solved in a similar way. ('What is it that is both straight and crooked at the same time? A line of writing.')[2]

[1] Retaining as the first word the γραφέων of the MSS., which has been convincingly defended by Kirk (97 ff.). In any case, as Kirk says (p. 104): 'Even if the reading γναφέων or γναφείῳ (DK) were right and the reference were to a carding-roller or even a screw-press, the import of the fragment would remain roughly the same.'

[2] Evidently he did like actual riddles. One that Hippolytus says he related is amusing enough to quote (fr. 56, and for the riddle in full see ps.-Plut. *De Vita Hom.* 4, quot. Walzer *ad fr.*). Homer, it runs, saw some children fishing, and asked them what luck they had had. They replied: 'What we have caught we left behind, and what we didn't catch we take with us.' The answer was that having got bored with catching no fish, they had been delousing each other. To Heraclitus the whole of nature was a riddle, in which the hidden meaning was more important than what appeared on the surface (frr. 123, 54).

In the fragments so far quoted, Heraclitus teaches that two apparently contradictory things or epithets in the same genus are in fact identical: day and night, just and unjust, up and down, straight and crooked. Fr. 67 is more comprehensive and takes us further: 'God is day and night, winter and summer, war and peace, satiety and hunger—"all the opposites: that is the meaning"[1]—but he changes just as fire,[2] when it is mingled with perfumes, is named according to the scent of each.' Just what Heraclitus understood by God must be left till later. For present purposes we may accept Kirk's remark (p. 187) that here at least he is 'somehow identified with or inherent in the whole world'. The fragment shows that not only are the extremes in a single genus to be identified with each other, but the whole apparently disparate collection of phenomena displays to the discerning mind an essential unity. This is the true Logos, listening to which 'it is wise to agree that all things are one'. The question which Kirk thinks worth raising on one of the pairs mentioned, namely (p. 187): 'How can God be described as "peace" when fr. 53 asserted that "War is the father and king of all", and Homer was rebuked for his prayer that "strife may perish from gods and men"?' does not really arise. Heraclitus uses words in his own sense, a sense which 'the many' do not grasp. If God is both war and peace, that is because war and peace are identical. This is not the peace that men in their ignorance long for: rather is war itself the true peace. The man who said 'In changing it is at rest' (fr. 84a) would not have hesitated to say 'In war it is at peace'. On the level of common-sense, of course, war and peace succeed one another as do the other pairs in this saying; so however, on that level, do change and rest.

---

[1] The words in parenthesis are a comment, and a sensible one, by Hippolytus who quotes the fragment.

[2] The noun is missing in the MSS. 'Fire' is the suggestion adopted by Diels. Another attractive one is H. Fränkel's 'olive-oil'. Plato in the *Timaeus* (50E) describes how the makers of unguents took care to see that the liquid base to which the perfumes were to be added should be as free as possible from all scent of its own. Whichever noun we choose, the lesson of the fragment is the same. (Discussion and references in Kirk, 191 ff.) The notion of a permanent substratum which can assume different qualities is not far off in this sentence of Heraclitus.

Fr. 7 ('If all existing things were to become smoke, the nostrils would distinguish them') may have a similar sense to fr. 67 and others indicating identity in difference. If all things turned to smoke, we should see only one thing (smoke), but the nose would distinguish their different scents. So Reinhardt, *Parm.* 180, n. 2, Gigon, 57.

The Identity of Opposites

The 'identity' of opposites includes for Heraclitus several different relationships, all of which he is aware of and explains or illustrates, without thereby losing faith in his discovery that they are all 'the same'. These are:

(a) Reciprocal succession and change, as of qualities or things which are at opposite ends of the same continuum like day and night, summer and winter, hunger and satiety. Relevant also is fr. 126: 'Cold things grow hot, hot things cold, moist dry, dry wet.' That this reciprocal change was to him evidence of identity is brought out by fr. 88: 'The same thing in us (?) is living and dead, and the waking and the sleeping, and young and old; for these things when they have changed are those, and those when they have changed are these.'[1]

(b) Relativity to the experiencing subject. So fr. 61: 'The sea is the purest and most polluted water, drinkable and salutary for fishes, undrinkable and deadly to men.' In this sense also Aristotle interprets fr. 9: 'Asses would choose rubbish rather than gold', namely as indicating that different species of animals take pleasure in different things, though he does not of course draw Heraclitus's ultimate conclusion that there is no essential difference between pleasant and unpleasant.[2]

(c) In the sphere of values, opposites are only appreciated in relation to their opposites. Hence although men commonly call the one good and the other bad, neither would be good without the other. So fr. 111: 'It is disease that makes health pleasant and good, hunger satiety, weariness rest.' That this relationship amounted in Heraclitus's eyes to identity we may conclude from the identification of hunger and satiety in fr. 67, and possibly also, with reference to weariness and rest, from the paradox of fr. 84a: 'In changing it is at rest.'[3] What is said here adds point to the assertions of frr. 110 and 102—that it is not good for men to get all they want and that, whereas

---

[1] It is not absolutely certain that the last, explanatory clause belongs to Heraclitus himself, but it is accepted after careful discussion by Kirk (139 ff.).

[2] Arist. EN, 1176a5. Kirk, 81–6 treats the fragment in detail, though in view of his own conclusion about its purport (83–4) it seems a little hard to say that Aristotle's use of it has no bearing on its original context. Cf. also fr. 13: 'Pigs take pleasure in mud rather than in clean water', which Sextus (Pyrrh. Hyp. I, 55, Bywater on fr. 54) brings also into relation with fr. 61.

[3] 84b (κάματός ἐστι τοῖς αὐτοῖς μοχθεῖν καὶ ἄρχεσθαι) is taken by Kirk (p. 252) and others to be the converse of this: as change is rest, so lack of change is weariness. But like Gigon I find the saying puzzling. What is to be made of μοχθεῖν καὶ ἄρχεσθαι? One would rather expect him to say (on the lines of 'war and peace, hunger and satiety, etc. are the same') that toil is rest rather than weariness. If lack of change is the only point, then one must stress τοῖς αὐτοῖς almost to the exclusion of the following words, and it would have been more to the point if Heraclitus had said ἐν τῷ αὐτῷ μένειν, ἠρεμεῖν or the like. Perhaps indeed the vagary is to be explained (as Kirk tentatively suggests) by the existence of a popular saying about the weariness of working always for the same master. This would be quite in Heraclitus's manner, but we know of no such saying.

men call some things just and others unjust, to God all things are just and good. This is probably also the significance of the vaguely-worded fr. 23, i.e. 'They [*sc.* men in general] would not have known the name of right if these things [*sc.* wrong things] did not exist.' So Kirk (p. 129): 'Men only recognize a "right" way because of the examples that they have of the existence of a "wrong" way.'

(*d*) Fourthly there are the opposites which are 'identical' because only different aspects of the same thing, the point at which Heraclitus gets nearest to the later distinction between permanent substratum and mutable characteristic. Up and down are opposites—but not really so, because it is one and the same road that you go up and down. Straight and crooked are opposites, but one and the same line of writing is both at the same time.[1]

In the philosophers of Greece one can often detect not so much a completely original idea as the effect of a powerful, analytical mind on a mode of thought typical of the age. The Heraclitean doctrine of the simultaneity of opposites and its paradoxical consequences is the result of intense concentration on a mental phenomenon common in the early Greek world, to which the name 'polarity' has been given. Thus for example H. Fränkel writes of 'a thought-form which after Homer, in the archaic period of Greece, was the dominant one, namely the polar mode of thought: qualities cannot be conceived otherwise than together with their contraries'.[2]

(iii) *War (struggle, tension) is the universal creative and ruling force.* This is an obvious consequence of much that we have seen already, and is stated in fr. 53: 'War is father of all and king of all, and some he reveals as gods, others as men, some he makes slaves, others free.' By calling War 'father and king of all', Heraclitus deliberately recalls Homer's titles for Zeus, and so suggests that War, not Zeus, is the supreme god. It has been thought that here he has only in mind the limited, literal sense of war, though of course using it as an illustration of the universal conflict which for him constitutes the Universe. This fits well with the statement that it makes some slaves and others free, but leaves the mention of gods and men more difficult to explain.[3]

---

[1] This is probably the point of fr. 48: 'The name of the bow (βιός) is life (βίος), but its work is death', if we grant (as we must) that for Heraclitus a name was an essential attribute of the thing named. See Kirk, 116–22. [2] *Dichtung u. Philos. des frühen Griechentums*, 77.

[3] See Kirk, 246 ff. To read into this brief phrase a reference to the apotheosis of those killed in battle, even if Heraclitus believed in this, seems a little far-fetched.

Whatever the reason, the statement does look as if it were confined to gods and men and their affairs. Apart from the second half of the fragment, the reminiscence of the Homeric Zeus, 'Father of gods and men', suggests that the word 'all' is masculine. But he may yet be thinking of war in its wider aspect, as creating opposition and tension between opposed classes everywhere, of which gods–men, slaves–free are only examples. In any case the general principle is stated in fr. 80: 'One must know that war is common, and justice strife, and that all things come about by way of strife and necessity.' With this must be taken a passage from Aristotle (*EE*, 1235a25, DK, 22A22) which runs: 'And Heraclitus rebukes the poet who wrote "Would that strife might perish from among gods and men";[1] for there would be no melody without high and low, nor living creatures without male and female, which are opposites.' Simplicius adds the comment, after the line from Homer, 'For he [Heraclitus] says that everything would disappear.'[2]

By saying that war is 'common' Heraclitus immediately links it (more probably actually identifies it) with the Logos (p. 425, above). At the same time he gets in another covert attack on Homer, who had also called war 'common'. Homer's line[3] says that war strikes down all alike: 'he that hath slain shall himself be slain'. It is no respecter of persons, but deals its blows impartially all round. 'Common', as we now know, has a deeper meaning for Heraclitus, and by alluding to Homer's use of the same word he hints that its profundity had escaped him. War is common because the Logos that is the law of all becoming (fr. 1) is a law of strife, of simultaneous opposite tensions. 'That strife is universal follows from the assumption that whatever exists is in change with the added assumption that all change is strife.'[4] In saying that justice (or right) is strife he probably shows himself aware also of Anaximander's teaching (pp. 76ff., above), which branded the warfare of the opposites as a series of acts of injustice. On the contrary,

---

[1] Hom. *Il.* xviii, 107.

[2] For later versions of Heraclitus's rebuke, which omit the reference to high and low, male and female, see Kirk, 243.

[3] *Il.* xviii, 309 ξυνὸς 'Ενυάλιος καί τε κτανέοντα κατέκτα. The phrase was copied by Archilochus (fr. 38 Diehl). Possibly this is one reason for the censure of Homer and Archilochus together in fr. 42—that they could utter such words and yet remain ignorant of the true Logos.

[4] Vlastos, *AJP*, 1955, 357.

retorts Heraclitus, it is the highest justice. Once again an erring predecessor is tacitly corrected.[1]

The kernel of Heraclitus's quarrel with other thinkers seems to lie in his revolt against their ideal of a peaceful and harmonious world. This was in particular the ideal of Pythagoras, of whom, it is relevant to remember, he speaks more than once with particular harshness (see especially p. 417, above). For Pythagoras the best state was one in which opposite qualities were so blended by a law of proportion that their oppositions were neutralized and they produced, for example, euphony in music, health in the body, *kosmos*—order and beauty—in the Universe as a whole. These states of peace between elements which had been at war, brought about by the imposition of limit (*peras*) on a chaotic *apeiron*, he and his followers called *good*. Their opposites—discord, disease, strife—were *evil*.[2]

Heraclitus rejects all these value judgments, which seem to him pusillanimous. 'Rest and quiet? Leave them to the dead, where they belong' (Aët. I, 23, 7, DK, 22A6). Health, peace, rest, he says, are in themselves no more good than their opposites, and their goodness only appears when set against these opposites. The co-existence of what a Pythagorean would regard as good and bad states is necessary and right. 'To God all things are good and fair and just.' In fact it is all a matter of point of view, and good and bad are entirely relative notions. Sea-water is pure and good to fishes, foul and poisonous to men.

The Pythagoreans spoke as if the opposites exhibited no reluctance to be blended in a *harmonia*, but found rest[3] and, as one might say, contentment when they were contributing to a perfect *krasis*, as in a

---

[1] This possibility is strengthened by the addition of the words καὶ τὸ χρεών at the end of the fr., if (*a*) this is the correct text and (*b*) the words κατὰ τὸ χρεών in Anaximander's fr. I genuinely belong to him.

[2] Some scholars will say that we know too little of the opinions of Pythagoras to make statements like this. That the ideas are Pythagorean they might admit, but would argue that we cannot know whether they were current before the late fifth century. However, unless we are going to deny any original ideas to Pythagoras himself (in which case it is a little difficult to account for his reputation), his teaching must have been on these lines. The full justification for attributing them to Pythagoras (or at least an early generation of his followers, contemporary with Heraclitus) lies of course in the earlier chapter on the Pythagoreans, where each reader must assess it for himself. For a contrary view to that here given see Kirk, *HCF*, 218 f.

[3] In the Pythagorean table of opposites (p. 245, above), 'resting' (ἠρεμοῦν) is to be found on the 'good' side, along with πέρας, φῶς, ἀγαθόν, etc.

448

musical scale or a healthy body. But that is nonsense, says Heraclitus. By the very fact of being opposites, they must be pulling opposite ways, resisting all the time. Heat and cold, wet and dry, do not co-operate, they are mutually destructive. From their constant strife there may result a temporary *harmonia*, but equally well a disharmony like disease. The causal factors are the same in both cases. If there is a perfectly proportioned blend, it is only because the warring opposites have reached a state of equal tension or balance of power in which neither has the upper hand. Rest, cessation of effort, would mean the opposite of *kosmos*, for it would result in the falling apart of the opposites, whose union in an 'adjustment of opposite tensions'—locked, as it were, in an internecine struggle—is what keeps in being the world as we know it.

b) Everything is in continuous motion and change

The doctrine that 'harmony is of opposites' has already led to this conclusion, which Heraclitus drives home once again with a familiar illustration. A well-known drink or posset in Greece from Homer's time onwards was the *kykeon*, made by taking a cup of wine and stirring into it barley and grated cheese. These of course would not dissolve, so that the mixture had to be kept in motion until the moment it was drunk. 'The *kykeon*', he said, 'falls apart if it is not being stirred.'[1] Kirk's comment on this fragment cannot be improved on: 'The fragment is of greater importance than at first appears: it is the only direct quotation that asserts, even though only in an image' (but this was Heraclitus's declared way of announcing the most fundamental truths, p. 414, above), 'the consequences of an interruption in the reciprocity of opposites.' The illustration itself was not so entirely homely as it might seem, for in addition to other uses the *kykeon* was drunk at the Eleusinian mysteries in commemoration of the myth of Demeter, who would accept no other refreshment during her sad search for the lost Persephone. This would give it a special significance in Heraclitus's eyes.[2]

---

[1] Fr. 125. On the text see Kirk, 255 f.
[2] *Hom. Hymn Dem.* 210, Clem. Al. *Protr.* 1, 16 St., Nilsson, *Gesch. Gr. Rel.* 1, 622 f. For Heraclitus and the mysteries cf. p. 425, n. 1, above.

One of his most famous sayings is: 'You cannot step into the same river twice.'[1] Plutarch (*Qu. Nat.* 912C) adds the explanation, which may have been given by Heraclitus himself:[1] 'for fresh waters are flowing on'. Concerning the meaning of this parable our authorities are pretty well agreed. Plato (*Crat.* 402A) says that it is an allegory of 'existing things' in general, and its lesson is 'that everything moves on and nothing is at rest'. That this was Heraclitus's belief he has already stated (401D), and in the *Theaetetus* (160D) he repeats that in the view of 'Homer and Heraclitus and all that crowd' all things move 'like streams'.[2] Plato, says Aristotle, while still a young man, became familiar with Cratylus and 'the Heraclitean theories that all sensible things are for ever flowing';[3] and reflexion on these theories led him to the conclusion that knowledge of the sensible world was impossible. Since he could not tolerate abandoning the possibility of knowledge altogether, this gave rise to the characteristically Platonic doctrine of transcendent Forms.

This Heraclitean doctrine of the flux of sensible things is mentioned

---

[1] See Appendix, pp. 488 ff., below. The statement of the flux-doctrine which has become almost canonical in later ages, πάντα ῥεῖ, occurs in the ancient authorities only in Simplicius (*Phys.* 1313.11), and is unlikely to have been a saying of Heraclitus.

[2] Plato was fond of calling Homer the ancestor of certain philosophical theories because he spoke of Oceanus and Tethys, gods of water, as parents of the gods and of all creatures (*Il.* XIV 201, 246; see *Crat.* 402B, *Theaet. loc. cit.*, 152E, 180C–D). Aristotle followed him (*Metaph.* A 983b30), and neither of them can be supposed to have been very serious in this. Plato, as Ross remarks on the *Metaphysics* passage, 'jestingly suggests that Heraclitus and his predecessors derived their philosophy from Homer, Hesiod and Orpheus', and he adds that Aristotle himself admits that the suggestion has no great historical value. (This is an understatement. See also p. 56, n. 1, above.) The reference to Ὅμηρον καὶ Ἡράκλειτον καὶ πᾶν τὸ τοιοῦτον φῦλον suggests a similar levity, but the nature and frequency of Plato's allusions to the 'flux' theory of Heraclitus and his followers are a guarantee of his sincerity. Admittedly he liked to make game of them for it (e.g. *Theaet.* 179E κατὰ τὰ συγγράμματα φέρονται; at 181A he calls the philosophers themselves οἱ ῥέοντες), but there was a basis for his jibes. Moreover we have the testimony of Aristotle that he took it seriously, and indeed that it was a formative influence on his own philosophy.

[3] *Metaph.* 987a32. Cratylus, Aristotle tells us (*ibid.* 1010a13), carried the views of Heraclitus to their logical extreme by correcting the sentence 'You can't step into the same river twice' to 'You can't step into it once'. Between the instant when your foot touched the surface and the instant when it reached the bottom the river at that point had already changed. Cratylus was a Heraclitean heretic (one of τῶν φασκόντων ἡρακλειτίζειν as Aristotle calls them) who was so carried away by the idea of uninterrupted change that in the end he thought it best not to speak (presumably because to make a statement about anything would give a spurious impression of permanence: by the time the statement was out of his mouth its object would have changed), but only waggled his finger! Although the continuous motion and change of sensible things *was* a dogma of Heraclitus, it was not the whole story. On Cratylus and the reliability of Aristotle's account see D. J. Allan in *AJP*, 1954, 271–84.

more than once by Aristotle (e.g. *Metaph.* 1063a22, 35), but some of his remarks are vitiated by his mistaken assumption that Heraclitus's system was essentially Milesian, as he says in *De Caelo*, 298b29:

They [*sc.* the earliest natural philosophers] held that in general everything is in a state of becoming and flux, and that nothing is stable, but that there is one substance which persists, out of which all these things have evolved by natural transformations. This seems to have been the meaning both of Heraclitus of Ephesus and of many others.

(How Heraclitus would have wept to find himself included with the *oolloi* after all that he had done to cut himself off!) In the *Physics* he says (253b9): 'Some assert, not that some things are in motion and others not, but that *everything* is *always* moving, though this escapes our perception.' Here we have the doctrine in its more strict and particular form, which we must refer (with Simplicius) to the Heracliteans, and, as Kirk says (p. 376), to Heraclitus in particular. Trying to explain their meaning, Aristotle says it is like the argument (which he thinks fallacious) about a stone being worn away by drops of water or split by the roots of a plant. According to this argument, if we notice that over a period of months the drops have made a visible dint in the stone, it follows that each drop must have removed an infinitesimal fraction too small to be seen. It is plain from Aristotle's language, including his complaint that the thinkers in question 'do not define the kind of motion they are talking about', that this illustration was not used by Heraclitus. Nevertheless it seems to represent just what he had in mind, although strictly speaking one must imagine a continuous stream of water flowing over the rock rather than separate drops. That the rock is changing every instant we cannot see with our eyes, but it is what their evidence suggests if we apply 'minds that understand the language'. To supplement their evidence we need that understanding (νόος) which few men have but which is essential if the senses are not to lead us astray, for by itself the eyesight is deceptive (frr. 107, 46, 40; and cf. 104). The continuous imperceptible change is a natural inference from the observation. Heraclitus did not use this simile, but he said the same thing by means of the image of the bow and lyre. The strung bow appears static to the eyes, but if the string should snap, that would be only the consequence of what the man whose mind was not 'barbarian' would have known all the time: that its true condition had been a *continuous* putting forth of effort in contrary directions, corresponding to the abrasive action of the water and the resistance offered by the hardness of the stone.[1]

The doctrine of the continuous change of physical things is closely linked with that of the identity of opposites, as appeared in particular from fr. 88 (p. 445, above). This is because the change is *cyclic*, from *a* to *b* and back to *a* again, and to Heraclitus's mind what could apparently change into something else and then back into what it was before must have been in a way the same all the time. He is drawing fresh conclusions from a common Greek conception on which the Milesians had already relied, the circularity of time, based on observation of the recurrence of seasonal changes year after year. Cold prevails over hot as summer gives way before winter, but nothing is

[1] I am truly sorry to adopt an interpretation which in the eyes of Kirk is 'very far indeed from the truth' and 'entirely contrary to what Heraclitus tells us in the fragments' (pp. 376f.). 'Our observation', he says, 'tells us that this table or that rock are *not* changing at every instant; there is nothing in nature to persuade us that they are so changing; the very idea would be repulsive to Heraclitus.' The fragments that he cites in support of this are 107, 55, 101*a*, and for comparison 17 and 72. 55 must, however, be read in the light of the important proviso in 107, and 17 and 72 seem to support the interpretation given here. The whole misunderstanding, Kirk thinks, arose from Plato's assertion that according to the Heracliteans 'everything is undergoing every motion all the time', which he considers a disastrous misinterpretation.

To speak of 'every motion' is no doubt to import distinctions which Heraclitus had not consciously made: thinkers like him, says Aristotle, did not define the kind of motion they had in mind. But with that trivial qualification I believe that Plato was right. This would seem the place to say also that I believe not only that the flux doctrine was true for Heraclitus, but also that it occupied a central position in his thought: in short that Plato, as knowledge of him would lead one to expect, had a pretty good insight into Heraclitus's mind, and did not go seriously astray even in the matter of emphasis.

I know that this will seem reactionary to more than one scholar for whom I have great respect. Snell for instance writes (*Hermes*, 1926, 376; I translate): 'Only now will it become quite clear how Heraclitus is misinterpreted when he is made the teacher of πάντα ῥεῖ.' I can only say that it has not become clear to me. Of course πάντα ῥεῖ is not the whole of his message, but, as I hope to show, the other side of the picture is the confining of change within measures, not (at least in the sensible world) the exaltation of stability (for there is none) at the expense of change. 'The dominating idea in Heraclitus is rest in change, not change in apparent stability.' So Kirk paraphrasing Reinhardt's view. But what Heraclitus says in fr. 84*a* is that for this world change *is* rest, which, as I hope I have shown already, is something different.

To put it briefly, I find that from Plato onwards all our authorities attribute to Heraclitus the doctrine ὡς ἁπάντων τῶν αἰσθητῶν ἀεὶ ῥεόντων. Those who take the *prima facie* improbable line that Plato grossly misunderstood him and every subsequent Greek interpreter meekly followed his lead, in spite of possessing either Heraclitus's book or at least a much more comprehensive collection of his sayings than we have, may be expected to produce incontrovertible evidence from the fragments that their conclusion is inescapable. But in fact the extant fragments offer no challenge to the universal ancient view.

more certain than that the hot will have its turn again in the following year. Anaximander spoke of the warfare and mutual 'injustice' of the opposites, followed inevitably by reparation, and in Heraclitus it takes a new turn.[1]

Three passages in Stoic sources attribute to him a statement that each of the four elements, as they were called later, 'lives the death' of another, or that the death of one is birth for another. Marcus Aurelius puts it that 'it is the death of earth to become water, and the death of water to become *aer*, and of *aer* to become fire, and the reverse'. In Maximus of Tyre we have: 'Fire lives the death of earth and *aer* lives the death of fire, water lives the death of *aer*, earth that of water.' These statements are rejected by most modern scholars, chiefly on the ground that they include *aer* among the 'elements', and it is generally believed that this was first done by Empedocles. Its absence from frr. 31 and 36 is taken as confirmation of their inaccuracy, though this point has been countered by Gigon.[2] Without necessarily sharing these doubts, we may leave the statements in question in view of the impressive consensus of opinion against their authenticity, and turn to another set of passages in which the cycle of natural changes is described, in particular frr. 31 and 36.

However, we cannot well approach these fragments immediately. At this point one feels acutely the difficulty of reducing the 'barbed

---

[1] A reference, devoid of context, to 'the seasons which produce all things' may be an indication that Heraclitus explicitly acknowledged the source of the general conception (see fr. 100, discussed in detail by Kirk, 294 ff.).

[2] Gigon, *Unters. zu H.* 99. The three passages (the third is from Plutarch) are grouped together by DK as fr. 76. The mention of ἀήρ was held to condemn them by Zeller (ZN, 850 f.), and although Nestle disagreed (851, n. 1), most scholars have followed Zeller, including in recent times Snell (*Hermes*, 1926, 361, n.) and Kirk (see his full discussion, 342 ff.), but not Gigon. The three versions are differently worded, and there is no means of knowing whether any one of them reproduces Heraclitus with complete verbal accuracy. Probably not, but I do not think the mention of ἀήρ is necessarily a blunder. Heraclitus had no theory of 'elements', whether three or four. Only fire had a certain primacy, and in describing its transformations he may just as well have mentioned ἀήρ as earth or water. His description of change is based on observation, and in particular on the phenomenon of evaporation, in which ἀήρ has a natural place as an intermediate stage between water and fire. The word need not, indeed most frequently does not, mean 'air'. The Loeb translator of Plutarch in the relevant passage (*De E*, 392 C) translates it with some plausibility as 'steam'.

Since this note was written Kahn's *Anaximander* has appeared. I agree with his defence of the fragment on p. 152, n. 1, where he writes: 'The ἀήρ is not Stoic, but Milesian, and the word is used in the regular sense by Xenophanes, Anaxagoras, and Empedocles.' See the whole note and its context.

arrows' of Heraclitus to an exposition in continuous prose, which of necessity deals with points successively, one at a time, when what is wanted is a simultaneous advance on several fronts at once. I spoke earlier of three tenets, the second of which was that everything is constantly changing, while the third described the cosmos as fire. In fact these are different aspects of the same truth, but to state them together calls for the style of the Delphic oracle or Heraclitus himself. It will therefore be best to introduce now the notion of the cosmic fire, in terms of which the further statements of the law of change between opposites are made.[1]

(c) The world an ever-living fire

Fr. 30 is a pronouncement 'solemn, elaborate, and portentous, which reveals its origins in heroic verse.... The monumental style probably indicates that the pronouncement was considered by Heraclitus an especially important one' (Kirk, 311). It may be translated thus:

This world-order [*kosmos*], the same for all,[2] none of the gods nor of men has made,[3] but it was always and is and shall be:[4] an ever-living fire, which is being kindled in measures and extinguished in measures.

[1] Cf. Walzer, *Eraclito*, 71: 'Soltanto mercé la dottrina delle cose opposte il fuoco diviene una entità equivalente al cosmo.'

[2] τὸν αὐτὸν ἀπάντων. Rejected by Reinhardt, whom Kirk follows, but Vlastos (*AJP*, 1955, 345 with n. 18) believes the words genuine. For the genitive cf. ξυνὸν ἀπάντων in fr. 114. Drawing attention to this fragment, Vlastos takes ἀπάντων as masculine. The real world is 'the same for all', as opposed to the dream-worlds which most men make up for themselves (pp. 430f., above). Gigon (*Unters.* 55) understood the phrase more widely: this order is 'the same for everything' (*alle existierende Wesen*), i.e. for all the things comprehended in it. Kirk (309) asks what then will be the point of τὸν αὐτόν. I think myself that this translation quite probably represents Heraclitus's mind, and it is the one which occurred to me independently. The 'order' in question is, as we know, an arrangement of opposite and warring tensions, a 'harmony of opposites' which is universal (τὸν αὐτὸν ἀπάντων). To emphasize its universality is not superfluous because the ordinary man perceives it only in a few things and is quite unaware of it in others. He cuts himself off from 'the common'.

[3] κόσμον...ἐποίησε = διεκόσμησε (Walzer, p. 70, n. 4), as in Anaxagoras, fr. 12 πάντα διεκόσμησε νοῦς. What is denied here is not of course creation *ex nihilo*, an idea quite foreign to Greek thought, but only the creation of κόσμος out of previous disorder. The denial is no doubt primarily aimed at the parcelling out of the world into sky, sea and earth, symbolized by the distribution (δασμός) between the chief gods, of which the old poets spoke (*Il.* xv, 187 ff., Hes. *Th.* 74, 885). This is the kind of thing that the masses believe because they have no more sense than to listen to the popular bards (fr. 104).

Kirk (311) rightly notes that the addition of ἀνθρώπων is formulaic and has no significance.

[4] The reasons adduced by Kirk (310f.) for punctuating with a colon after ἔσται seem convincing.

The World an Ever-living Fire

The meaning of *kosmos* has been discussed earlier (p. 208, n. 1). It is 'the natural world and the order in it' (Kirk, 317). The notion of order or arrangement is still essential, and that is one reason why this fragment seems decisive against the Stoic assumption, derived from Theophrastus and pervading all later accounts of Heraclitus, that he believed in a periodic destruction of the world by a general conflagration. The formulation of Diogenes Laertius (IX, 8) may be taken as typical: 'The cosmos is born out of fire and again resolved into fire in alternate periods for ever.' It could be argued that the essential substance of the universe, which Heraclitus after all called 'fire', was not destroyed or brought into being by the alternation of conflagration and renewal of the world, but only altered in its manifestations. Of this type of cosmogony Aristotle wrote (*De Caelo*, 280a11): 'As for the view that the world is alternately put together and dissolved, that is just the same as making it eternal, only changing its shape. It is as if one were to regard the coming-to-be of a man from a child and a child from a man as involving at one stage destruction and at another existence.' Yet however true that may be of the primary substance, once that substance is equated with the *kosmos* of the existing world it becomes impossible to call it 'ever-living' and at the same time speak of a cosmic conflagration, which, whatever it did to the *arche*, would certainly destroy 'this cosmos'.

Although the question whether Heraclitus believed in a periodic *ecpyrosis* (destruction of the cosmos by fire) is a difficult one, on which universal agreement will never be reached, the view will be taken here that fr. 30 is decisively incompatible with *ecpyrosis* and must override all later testimony, and that certain obscurer fragments, which have been thought to imply *ecpyrosis*, must be interpreted in its light. Such are fr. 65, which says that Heraclitus called fire 'want and satiety', and 66: 'For fire, he says, will come and judge and convict all things.' There is also the phrase 'from all things one and from one all things' in the difficult fr. 10. Fr. 65 seems to be no more than another statement of the identity of opposites, like the list in fr. 67, where 'the god' (who may be safely equated with the living fire) is identified with satiety and hunger among many other pairs. Fr. 66 was with some reason suspected by Reinhardt of being an addition of Hippolytus (see Kirk,

359–61). Its language is in any case figurative, and if Heraclitus wrote it he need only have meant to emphasize the primacy of fire and the truth that at some time everything must become fire, which shows up the impurities of other states of matter. (Plato in the *Cratylus*, 413 B, speaks of an unnamed thinker, who must be Heraclitus, equating fire with justice.) In the same way Aristotle, when he wrote (*Phys.* 205 a 3) that Heraclitus 'said that everything at some time becomes fire', need not have had *ecpyrosis* in mind.[1]

The originality of Heraclitus (I would repeat) was such, and his expression of it so difficult, that any hint of a less usual interpretation may be given extra prominence against the mass of later testimony which would make him conform to the expected. Such a hint is Aët. II, 4, 3 (DK, 22 A 10): 'Heraclitus says that the cosmos is subject to generation not in time but conceptually.' The later phrasing reflects the controversy over the genesis of the world in Plato's *Timaeus*— whether Plato intended it literally or figuratively—and the difference between chronological and logical generation belongs of course to a more sophisticated philosopher than Heraclitus. But it is interesting that, in spite of the general opinion from Aristotle onwards, Heraclitus's words did suggest to someone at least that the cosmos was not at any time brought into being from a different state of things. Plutarch, too,

---

[1] Whether or not Cherniss is right (*ACP*, 29, n. 108) in taking πῦρ as subject and ἅπαντα as predicate, there is no necessary reference to *ecpyrosis*, for even without it everything at some time becomes fire (note the present) in the course of the constant change that is going on in the cosmos. That Aristotle did, however, adopt the *ecpyrosis* view of Heraclitus is very probable. Cf. Kirk, 321 f. Certainly that view was taken by Theophrastus and after him by the Stoics, who adopted it as their own (Kirk, 318 ff.). On pp. 335 ff. Kirk summarizes the arguments for and against it. He himself believes it impossible. Since he wrote, *ecpyrosis* in Heraclitus has been defended once again by Mondolfo in *Phronesis*, 1958, 75–82. One of the strongest pieces of evidence against it has always been Plato, *Soph.* 242 D (p. 437, above, and see Burnet, *EGP*, 158 f.). Mondolfo endeavours to argue that even this passage is consistent with *ecpyrosis*, on the ground that fire is in itself a unity of opposites for Heraclitus, therefore the simultaneous convergence and divergence insisted on by Plato would in fact be maintained even if fire had absorbed all other states of matter in a literal conflagration. The interpretation is subtle, but does not quite convince. Part at least of the evidence for the contradictions inherent in fire, in Heraclitus's eyes, was the everlasting maintenance of balance (μέτρα) in its changes, whereby an absorption into literal fire in one part of the cosmos is inevitably counteracted by a quenching of it into vapour or water in another part. A destruction of this balance would be incompatible with the unity of opposites in fire, and is therefore unthinkable for Heraclitus. (Kirk has replied to Mondolfo in *Phronesis*, 1959, 73–6.)

That Heraclitus believed in a temporal beginning and end of the present cosmos has been most recently argued by Kahn (*Anaximander*, 225 f.). He, however, is convinced that the eternity of the world-order is a purely Aristotelian invention, a thesis that is difficult to sustain.

makes a character in a dialogue say: 'I see the Stoic *ecpyrosis* spreading over the works of Hesiod as over those of Heraclitus and Orpheus' (*Def. Or.* 415 F).

Moreover, Theophrastus and the writers who followed him would have quoted supporting statements from Heraclitus himself if they could; but what they do quote seems rather to weaken their view. In Simplicius for instance we find this:[1]

'Hippasus of Metapontum and Heraclitus of Ephesus also believed the substance of the universe to be single, in motion, and finite; but made fire the *arche*, and out of fire they produce existing things by thickening and thinning, and resolve them into fire again, on the assumption that fire is the one underlying *physis*; for Heraclitus says that all things are an exchange for fire'.

The statement that all things are an exchange for (or exchanged for) fire is quoted as Heraclitus's by other authorities (see fr. 90, discussed below, pp. 460f.), and would hardly be adduced today to support the view that Heraclitus believed in an alternate destruction and rebirth of the universe.

On general grounds also it is unlikely that anyone devising a cosmology on Milesian lines would have chosen as *arche* an *extreme* like fire. The *arche* of the Milesians was always something intermediate between two opposites, owing to their assumption that it contained and concealed both members of the pairs of opposites which could therefore subsequently emerge from it and develop in opposite directions. Such were water and air, and the *apeiron* of Anaximander was described by later writers as 'something rarer than water but denser than air'.[2] Whether or not he thought of the *apeiron* in this way (and it seems a rather naive objectification of what was in fact a remarkably subtle conception), it must be true that Anaximander regarded the initial state of things as something neutral and therefore mediate: he seems to have seen even more clearly than the others that it could not be qualified by any one of the opposites in actuality.

Fire on the other hand is an opposite itself, an extreme, which does not contain its own opposite, and could not, *if it ever existed solely in*

---

[1] *Phys.* 23.33–24.4, quoted *Dox.* 475 f. as from Theophr. *Phys. Opinions.*
[2] E.g. Alexander, *in Metaph.* 60.8 Hayduck: τὴν Ἀναξιμάνδρου δόξαν, ὃς ἀρχὴν ἔθετο τὴν μεταξὺ φύσιν ἀέρος τε καὶ πυρὸς ἢ ἀέρος τε καὶ ὕδατος· λέγεται γὰρ ἀμφοτέρως.

the form of physical fire, divide into two opposites. Here our surmises of what Heraclitus could or could not have thought are reinforced by his own statements of the inevitable coexistence of opposites.[1]

Some, of whom Zeller was one, have connected the *ecpyrosis* with the idea of a Great Year, mentioned earlier in connexion with the Pythagoreans (p. 282, above). It is attested for Heraclitus by more than one authority, and his estimate of its length is said to have been 10,800 years.[2] In giving this estimate of the Great Year along with those of others, Censorinus also gives its definition as the time in which the sun, moon and planets return together to the same positions as they occupied at a given previous time.[3] He then introduces into his account the Stoic *ecpyrosis*, saying that in the summer of the Great Year the universe is burned up, and in the winter it is destroyed by flood.[4]

It is likely enough that Heraclitus himself connected the astronomical cycle with a cyclic renewal of the universe, as did the Pythagoreans with their disturbing notion of an exact repetition of history. If so, he most probably had in mind, as Vlastos has put it, 'the time required for every part of the fire which takes the "downward" turn at any given moment to return to its source, or, to look at it the other way round, the interval after which every part of water and earth existing at any given time will have been replaced'.[5] Such a cycle can of course be imagined

---

[1] That fire 'is' the opposites does not invalidate this view, as I have argued against Mondolfo on p. 456, n. 1. The cosmic fire, equated with divinity, is day and night, summer and winter, etc., precisely because it appears in these contrasting forms, 'kindled in measures and extinguished in measures'. To equate it with physical fire alone is impossible.

[2] Censorinus, *De Die Nat.* XVIII, 11 and Aët. II, 32, 3 (latter as emended by Diels, DK, 22 A 13).

[3] *cum ad idem signum ubi quondam simul fuerunt una referuntur.* Even though Censorinus be muddled in his examples, there is really no evidence at all for separating Heraclitus's Great Year from the majority by giving it a human rather than a cosmic reference. See Kirk, 300 f. and Vlastos, *AJP*, 1955, 311.

[4] The connexion of the Flood with the winter of a Great Year occurs already in Aristotle, *Meteor.* 352a28 ff.

[5] *AJP*, 1955, 311. The suggestion is a variant of an earlier one, made e.g. by Burnet. In general I find Vlastos's account here of the Great Year in Heraclitus and the origin of the *ecpyrosis* interpretation the most satisfactory, and readers may be referred to it for further details as to the composition of the number 10,800. He thinks that the ease with which this cycle of world-renewal could be mistaken for the commoner cycle of world-creation and destruction is probably what led Aristotle astray. That Theophrastus was also misled he doubts, quoting as the only words to be attributed to him on the subject these from Simpl. (*Phys.* 24. 4): ποιεῖ δὲ καὶ τάξιν τινὰ καὶ χρόνον ὡρισμένον τῆς τοῦ κόσμου μεταβολῆς. This could indeed be a statement of what we have just put forward as the actual belief of Heraclitus, but its context gives a rather different impression. J. B. McDiarmid has also expressed the opinion that Theophrastus did not share Aristotle's mistake (*Th. on the Presoc. Causes*, n. 28, pp. 137 f.).

as starting and finishing at any moment that one likes to choose, a feature which it shares with the astronomical parallel to which it was tied.

Returning to fr. 30, we notice first that the fire which is the cosmos is not only everlasting, but ever-*living*, which prepares us for its identification with *psyche*, the life-principle. The last clause of the fragment shows how the paradoxical expressions of Heraclitus resulted from the difficulty of the ideas he was trying to express. Fire in its normal acceptation exists when it is kindled: extinguish it and there is no longer fire. But fire in the generally accepted sense is not what Heraclitus intends by the word: the verbal paradox tells us that he is not asking us to accept a factual paradox, or flat contradiction of the evidence of our senses, by supposing the world to be a perpetual bonfire like the burning bush of Moses. The ever-living fire of the cosmos is being kindled (the present participle is used) *and extinguished* in measures. I agree with Kirk against Gigon (to mention only two of the latest partisans in a long controversy) that the general sense of the fragment is all against understanding these measures temporally as successive periods affecting the whole world. Heraclitus is describing the cosmos in its present state, which is sustained in two ways, to which we have already been introduced as aspects of the identity of opposites. First, in different parts of the world it is being alternately kindled (becoming fire in the popular sense, or an even hotter vapour) and extinguished (taking the form of water or earth), and all within fixed measures or limits which ensure the balance of opposites necessary to the maintenance of universal cosmic order. Secondly, it is maintained in the subtle way which Heraclitus found so difficult to express and which is his peculiar contribution to cosmological theory: by the simultaneous interaction of contrary forces tending in opposite directions, as in the structure of the bow or lyre, or the 'pain-curing pain' of the surgeon's knife.

(11) *Final explanation of the theory of change: fire and soul*

We must now grapple finally with Heraclitus's description of the process of change. To Theophrastus it was parallel to the Milesian scheme. He took the words 'all things are an exchange for fire' to mean that fire was the *arche* or element (στοιχεῖον; I am following the version of D.L. IX, 8), out of which other substances were formed, as in Anaximenes, by condensation and rarefaction. Since he immediately adds: 'But he explains nothing clearly', we may feel justified in departing from this interpretation if we will. Diogenes Laertius does however reproduce some of Heraclitus's terminology, and we learn from him that the 'way up and down', which Hippolytus tells us was 'one and the same', was the name given by Heraclitus to the process of change.[1] Putting together these two references to the way up and down, we find them echoed by Plato in the words: 'Everything is always flowing upwards and downwards.'[2] In the light of other fragments (especially 51), and Plato's further testimony about the 'stricter Muses' in *Soph.* 242D ('in drawing apart it is drawing together'), this must mean just what it says—not simply, as the prosaic and rational minds of some later Greeks thought, that some things are on the upward path while some are on the downward, but that *all* things are moving both upwards *and* downwards. It is not surprising that Aristotle accused Heraclitus of breaking the law of contradiction; or rather (since to his logical mind such a thing seemed impossible) said that some people supposed him to be doing so. 'It is impossible for anyone to suppose that the same thing is and is not, as some people think Heraclitus said' (*Metaph.* 1005b23).[3]

The way up and down is that of the transformation of the various forms of matter, and presumably things made by their mixture, into one another. Heraclitus did not of course use the word 'element' (στοιχεῖον) of fire, but the way in which he expressed its primacy is also quoted by Diogenes, and more fully by Plutarch (fr. 90): 'All

---

[1] καλεῖσθαι...τὴν μεταβολὴν ὁδὸν ἄνω κάτω. I see no good evidence to make us reject this statement as Kirk would have us do, though he says himself (p. 328) that 'the specific physical application of these terms would not, it is true, be unsuitable'.

[2] *Philebus*, 43A (not assigned by name to Heraclitus, but impossible to attribute to anyone but him or his true followers). Kirk in his discussion of this sentence says that in its context it refers to changes of fortune, but this is not correct: the reference is purely general. I have given reasons already for trusting what Plato says about Heraclitus. The strongest is that from Aristotle onwards most writers do their best to make him into a rather conventional thinker, whereas Plato's remarks, casual though they are, give the clue to his originality; and that he was original stares us in the face from every fragment.

[3] Aristotle perhaps had in mind fr. 49a: 'We step and do not step into the same rivers, we are and are not', on which see Appendix, p. 490.

things are an exchange for fire and fire for all things, as goods for gold
and gold for goods.'[1] Once more he can only express himself by a
simile, and hence to some degree imprecisely, but if he had wanted to
describe fire as simply the basic substance which changed its shape or
appearance in becoming earth or water he would have used a different
comparison. (He could easily have said, for example, 'as gold is
fashioned into coins, necklaces or cups'.) In mercantile transactions
the essential thing is parity of value: a certain quantity of gold will buy
a certain quantity of goods. This is no doubt the primary thought,
though he probably had in mind, as Kirk says, the single homogeneous character of gold (fire) as opposed to the manifold kinds of
goods (physical things) for which it can be exchanged.

We need not expect Heraclitus's thought to be by our standards
completely logical or self-consistent. From what we know of him that
would be surprising. He seems to be saying that although in the
cosmos as he sees it fire has a definite primacy, grounded in its divinity
and perpetual life, yet it is not a permanent substratum which, in
Aristotle's later formulation, remains essentially the same though
changing in its modifications. Such a permanent *physis* would contradict the law of flux, and introduce rest and stability into a world from
which he thought they should be banished. There was law in the
universe, but it was not a law of permanence, only a law of change, or,
in something more like his own picturesque phraseology, the law of the
jungle, since everything comes into being 'by way of strife' and War is
lord of all.

Fire was particularly well suited to embody this law. A flame may
appear steady and unchanging, as in a candle, but it is constantly re-
newing itself by the destruction of the fuel, and giving off heat and
sometimes smoke. The river-statement expresses the same truth, of apparent, or formal, stability coupled with continuous change of material.[2]

Heraclitus also expresses his conception of change by saying that

---

[1] See on this fr. Kirk, 345–8.

[2] It is interesting that Aristotle, in what sounds like a reminiscence of Heraclitus, links the flow
of water and of flame together in a comparison expressive of continuous change within the limits
of the same form and quantity: ἀεὶ γὰρ ἄλλο καὶ ἄλλο γίγνεται τούτων ἕκαστον [*sc.* air, fresh water,
and fire], τὸ δ’ εἶδος τοῦ πλήθους ἑκάστου τούτων μένει, καθάπερ τὸ τῶν ῥεόντων ὑδάτων καὶ τὸ τῆς
φλογὸς ῥεῦμα, *Meteor.* 357b30 (Kirk, 379f.).

each form of matter makes its appearance by the death of another (a natural result of the rule of War). We have seen this statement in the various forms of the suspected fr. 76, and repeated in fr. 36, with 'souls' substituted for the expected 'fire'. None of the Milesians spoke in this way of the death of the elements, although they contrasted the eternal nature of the *arche* with the arising and passing away of the transitory things which were formed by its modifications. Heraclitus was clearly groping after something different, though to say 'groping' is to betray the modern demand for rational and intellectual justification. To himself he was one who had discovered the divinely-appointed truth, and was therefore divinely charged to proclaim it. He had not Aristotle's severe eye for the law of contradiction, and uttered his paradoxes with relish.

We know that fire was living and rational, and that there is consequently a parallel throughout the cycle of change between physical and psychical elements. When warm and dry the soul is at its most intelligent and vital. The encroachment of moisture brings a dimming of the flame of life, and these two threads—of the physical elements and of life—are twisted together in fr. 36. Aristotle hits the mark (save in his misconception of the *arche*) when he says that for Heraclitus the *arche* was not only fire, but *psyche*, and that he described *psyche* as an exhalation (*De An.* 405 a 25). This last word is prominent in later accounts of Heraclitus's physical theory, e.g. fr. 12 (p. 434, above): 'Souls are exhaled from moist things.'[1] According to Diogenes, Heraclitus 'reduces nearly everything to exhalation from the sea', and this, he says, is the upward way.[2] The sun, which Heraclitus believed to be quenched every night and renewed the next day (fr. 6), and also the stars, consist of 'bright exhalations' from the sea collected in certain 'bowls' or cavities in the sky, where they turn to flame (D.L. IX, 9). If we may trust this, it gives us some idea of the process involved in the 'death and birth' of the elements mentioned in fr. 36, which seems to

---

[1] Whether Heraclitus used the word ἀναθυμίασις is doubtful. See Burnet, *EGP*, 151, n. 2 and Kirk, 274. Kirk thinks ἀτμίς a more probable word for him.

[2] Diogenes continues with a reference to the theory (expounded by Aristotle) of two kinds of exhalation, a bright one from the sea and a dark one from the land. Kirk (272f.) suggests that Heraclitus's theory was of a single exhalation (from the sea), and that Aristotle was responsible for its expansion into a two-exhalation scheme. Deichgräber (*Philol.* 1938/9, 24f.) supports the two exhalations for Heraclitus.

be based (as in Anaximenes, and perhaps not independently) on a theoretical extension of the observed process of evaporation. On the one hand moist vapours are drawn up from the sea by the heat at the world's circumference, become dry and bright themselves and renew the heavenly bodies. On the other hand soul too arises out of moisture, and is fed in the same way by exhalations from the watery element.

Fr. 36 showed the double nature of the way, up as well as down. This entails that the death of anything, though it implies complete loss of its character as that thing—fire dies[1] and becomes mist or vapour, soul dies and turns into water—is nevertheless not complete extinction. Nothing is permanent, not even death. Everything must continue to move on the upward and downward path. Philo rightly comments on fr. 36: 'What he calls death is not utter annihilation, but change into another element.'[2]

One can understand a circular path of becoming on which fire changes to steam, then to water, then to earth, then back to fire through the same stages reversed; and soul pursues a parallel series of transformations manifested in sleep and death. Anaximenes took a not dissimilar view. But Heraclitus is obviously struggling to say something more, something harder. He ignores the law of contradiction, he insists that opposites are identical. The way up and down is one and the same, everything flows upwards and downwards *simultaneously*. This is why (fr. 32) 'the one wise thing', i.e. the Logos which is also fire, 'is both unwilling and willing to be called Zen', a name which means both Zeus, the supreme god, and life; for life and death, Hades god of the dead and Dionysus god of life, are one and the same (fr. 15). Another important statement of the law of change, a part of fr. 31, may help here: 'The turnings of fire are: first sea, and of the sea half is earth and half burning.'[3] Sea is never *just* water, indeed there is no such *thing* as

---

[1] Vlastos (*AJP*, 1955, 366) thinks that Heraclitus's choice of the word ἀείζωον (ever-living) rather than ἀθάνατον (deathless) in fr. 30 was motivated by his belief that 'the condition of life ever-lasting is not deathlessness but life endlessly renewed by death in a process where youth and age are "the same" (B88)'. If so, this illustrates once more the extreme difficulty of putting into words his novel conception of change.

[2] P. 480, n. 1, below.

[3] Half earth and half πρηστήρ. This word has aroused much discussion. Burnet calls it 'a hurricane accompanied by a fiery water-spout' (*EGP*, 149), referring to Hdt. VII, 42 and Sen. *Q.N.* II, 56 *igneus turbo*. Kirk considers this 'absurd', and doubts whether Heraclitus would have chosen an uncommon phenomenon as a regular means of change between water and fire, or

Heraclitus

water. That would introduce rest (*stasis*) and contradict the law of flux and struggle. Water is only a momentary stage on the upward and downward path, and, by saying that sea is half earth and half a burning substance, Heraclitus seems to be telling us, in his Delphic manner, that it is being transformed upward and downward at the same time, 'drawn apart and drawn together'.

In the light of this, fr. 62 may be assumed to refer to this continuous transformation, a transformation of the physical bodies and of soul in one and the same process. It is quoted in various forms, but, assuming with Kirk (p. 144) that Hippolytus's version is the most accurate, it runs: 'Immortal mortals, mortal immortals (or 'Immortals are mortal, mortals are immortal'), living the death of the others and dying their life.' It reads like an echo of fr. 36. It has, however, been interpreted, both in ancient and in modern times, as implying the whole Pythagorean and Orphic doctrine of the soul as an immortal being for which this earthly life is a kind of death and the body a tomb, because it only enjoys full life when discarnate. Men may be described as mortal immortals, gods or *daimons* temporarily incarcerated in mortal bodies. Undoubtedly the language is impressive, especially considering the equivalence of 'immortal' and 'god' in Greek usage, but the question of the nature and fate of the human soul must be considered separately later. (See pp. 473 ff., below.)

(12) *Change and stability: the concept of measure*

We have not yet done justice to the presence of 'measures' in the account of change. The reference in fr. 30 to the measures in which the cosmic fire is kindled and extinguished is amplified by the second quotation made by Clement of Alexandria in the passage cited as fr. 31. (Clement interprets both as descriptions of the formation of a cosmos

even a symbol of such change. He thinks it simply a synonym for fire, like κεραυνός in fr. 64. On the other hand Heraclitus seems to have been interested in πρηστῆρες, and thought them worthy of an explanation ('ignition and quenching of clouds') alongside such common phenomena as thunder and lightning (Aëtius, III, 3, 9, DK, A 14). Moreover a man is more likely to be impressed by a rare phenomenon, and regard it as significant, if it happens to support his own views; and, as Diels saw, a waterspout accompanied by lightning ('Windhose mit elektrischer Entladung', and so LSJ) was ideal as ocular demonstration of the link binding fire and water in the process of reciprocal change (Diels, *Herakleitos*, 24, quot. Reinhardt, *Parm.* 178, n. 1). In any case Heraclitus means that half the sea is reverting to fire.

n time and its subsequent destruction by fire; and their inappropriate-
ness to such a conception inclines one still further to reject it.) 'Earth
is liquefied as sea, and is measured in the same proportion'—the word
is *logos*—'as existed before it became earth.'[1] The last sentence has been
well explained by Vlastos. Any part of earth which becomes water
retains throughout all its changes a pre-existing *logos*, it is measured in
that *logos*. In other words, though it changes in appearance it is equivalent throughout in quantity or value, judged by an independent
standard, which is that of fire; for all things are an exchange for fire,
as goods for gold (fr. 90). This 'identifies fire as the thing that remains
constant in all transformations and implies that *its* measure is the same
or common measure in all things'. 'Each member of the whole series
represents the same amount of fire, which is the common thing—τὸ
ξυνόν—in all the different things that compose the series.... The in-
variance of *its* measures is what accounts for the observance of the
metron in all things, and fire is therefore that which "governs" or
"steers all things"' (frr. 41 and 64).[2]

The idea of measure is introduced also in fr. 94: 'The sun will not
overstep his measures; otherwise the Erinyes, servants of Justice, will
find him out.' 'Measures' should be taken here in a general sense (cf.
Kirk, 285) so that to overstep them means to deviate in any way
from the normal course. The sun is set to follow a measured path in
the sky in a measured time, giving out a measured amount of heat.
If he were to depart from it in any way (as for example in the
myth of Phaethon, when he came too near the earth), the cosmic
balance would be upset, and this is never allowed to happen.[3]

The emphasis laid in this account on Heraclitus's doctrine of flux
and contrary motions ('strife' or 'warfare') has been disallowed by
Kirk, who writes (p. 370) that 'Heraclitus did *not* deny stability to the
natural world; on the contrary, his main purpose seems to be to assert
such a stability, which according to him underlies all change, and most
notably change between opposites.... Reinhardt is right in em-

---

[1] Accepting DK's text, with ⟨γῆ⟩ inserted before θάλασσα, on which see Kirk, 331 f., Vlastos,
AJP, 1955, 359, n. 46. Vlastos adopts a suggestion of Cherniss that the last three words of the
fragment are a gloss (*ibid.* 360, n. 47).   [2] Vlastos in *AJP*, 1955, 359–61.
[3] For the difficult fr. 120, which Kirk connects with the measures of the sun, see his pp. 289–93.

phasizing that there never was anything approaching a *Flusslehre* in Heraclitus himself.'[1] That the change was always contained within limits, the battle swaying to and fro so that the global balance is always preserved, is of course essential to the maintenance of the cosmos. Nevertheless his main purpose seems to be to show that all stability in the world is merely apparent, since if observed with understanding as well as with the senses it proves to be only a resultant of unremitting strife and tension. This is the tenor both of the fragments and of other testimony, in particular that of Plato, whose remarks consort well with the fragments themselves. Perhaps the strongest evidence of all is the primacy given to fire. Since it becomes all things, one might ask why one of the others—water or earth—might not serve equally well as the standard of measurement and the ruling force. Heraclitus, who is seeking for poetical or religious as much as logical truth, gives a twofold answer. First, as Aristotle said (*De An.* 405 a 5), fire is the most subtle element, which most nearly approaches the incorporeal, is itself in motion and imparts motion to other things. Secondly (a consequence of the first, as Aristotle knew), it is the same as *psyche*, the vehicle of life. 'Heraclitus says the *arche* is soul, i.e. the exhalation out of which he composes other things. It is the least corporeal of substances and is in constant flux' (*ibid.* 25). For soul we may read fire.

In the identification of soul and fire he was perhaps at his least original. It was a popular Greek belief that *aither*, the substance which filled the upper heaven above the less pure *aer* about the earth and of which the celestial bodies were made, was alive and divine; and until the time of Aristotle, or a very little before him (pp. 270ff., above), *aither* and fire had not been clearly distinguished. Moreover in the fifth century, and no doubt earlier, there was a widespread idea that the soul was immortal because it consisted of an imprisoned spark of *aither*, which at death would rejoin its like. Seeing that *aither* was believed to fill all the upper regions, it was not only the visibly fiery substance of the sun and stars, and this doubtless helped Heraclitus in his supposition that the 'fire' of his own system was not flame but a hot dry vapour.[2]

---

[1] Reinhardt's view (*Hermes*, 1942, 18) has been contested by Nestle in ZN, 798, n.

[2] *Aither* is divine in Aesch. *P.V.* 88 and Eur. fr. 839 N. In Eur. fr. 877 it is equated with Zeus. Cf. also other passages adduced by Kirk and Raven, 200, n. 1. For the connexion between soul and *aither* see Eur. *Hel.* 1014ff., *Suppl.* 533f., fr. 971 (Guthrie, *Greeks and their Gods*, 262f.).

The Flux-Doctrine and its Significance

An observation may be permissible on the wider significance of Heraclitus's doctrine of change. A fundamental distinction in speculation about the reality of things has always lain between those who see it in matter and those who see it in form. This distinction is very obvious in Greek thought, but is of course by no means confined to it. Now Heraclitus's statement about the river, that it is not the same river the second time you step into it, illustrates the culmination of materialist belief. We speak of a river as the same river from day to day, although we know that if we stand on its banks tomorrow we shall be looking at entirely different water from that which we see there today. Similarly we commonly regard our bodies as having continuity even though we may be told, and believe, that their material constituents are constantly changing and will have renewed themselves entirely within a period of seven years. Our justification for this habit of thought is that the form remains the same: the water or other matter as it comes in is poured, as it were, into the same mould, by which token we recognize it as having the same identity.

Through their mathematical studies, Pythagoras and his school achieved with remarkable suddenness a rational conception of the significance of form, and were much blamed by their successors for ignoring the material side. For them reality lay in form, for others in matter. Both views have persisted, and whatever may be their respective merits, in anything like a developed scheme of thought only those who see reality in form can find any permanence in the world. The logical outcome of materialism is the doctrine of uninterrupted flux, as Heraclitus had the intelligence to perceive and the courage to assert; for the matter of things is in fact always changing, and the only permanent thing is form, which can be expressed in the timeless language of mathematical equations.

The logical outcome of form-philosophy, on the other hand, is Platonism or something resembling it: a belief in absolutes, or 'forms' of things, existing eternally in a region beyond the reach of space or time. On the nature of the physical world Plato agreed with Heraclitus. He makes the wise Diotima say to Socrates:

Even during the period for which any living being is said to live and retain his identity—as a man, for example, is called the same man from boyhood to old age—he does not in fact retain the same attributes, although he is called the same person: he is always becoming a new being and undergoing a process of loss and reparation, which affects his hair, his flesh, his bones, his blood and his whole body. And not only his body, but his soul as well. No man's character, habits, opinions, desires, pleasures, pains and fears remain always the same: new ones come into existence and old ones disappear.[1]

In what way the flux of becoming was for Heraclitus limited or qualified by the existence of a permanent and stable reality is a question that needs further consideration.

Aristotle, as we know, represented Plato's doctrine of immutable forms as having been the outcome of, among other things, 'the Heraclitean opinions that all sensible things are continually flowing and there is no knowledge of them'. Impressed by this, but unwilling to accept the impossibility of knowledge, Plato posited a permanent reality outside the physical world. It is usually assumed (*a*) that these opinions were Heraclitus's own (although Aristotle mentions Cratylus by name as Plato's informant), and (*b*) that although they are explicitly confined to the sensible world, this for Heraclitus constituted the total sum of reality.

Cratylus carried the consequences of the flux-doctrine to absurd lengths. Nevertheless we have seen evidence in the primacy of War and Strife, in the similes of the bow and lyre and elsewhere, that for Heraclitus the essence of wisdom lay in recognizing unceasing motion, unceasing struggle and effort in the exertion of contrary tensions, as necessary conditions for the continuance of the physical world-order. It seems accurate enough to describe this, with Plato, as a doctrine of the everlasting flux of physical things, and to illustrate it by the simile of the river into which one cannot step twice.

Over against this, however, stands the Logos, whose permanence Heraclitus emphasizes in fr. 1 by the use of the word *is* or *exists*, in contrast to the changing phenomena which *become* according to its laws. Because of these laws, the order and balance (*kosmos*) of the world are also constant and everlasting (fr. 30), though no particle of its internal components—earth, sea or visible flame—is the same for two instants together. It is here that a would-be interpreter is most acutely

[1] Plato, *Symp.* 207 D, trans. W. Hamilton.

embarrassed by the curious stage of thought represented by Heraclitus, which at this point is likely to have led him into what from our point of view is an illogical and inconsistent position. Spiritual and material forces are still united as aspects of one and the same entity, although in fact they are becoming so far distinguished as to demand complete separation. Hence the mysterious conception of a 'rational fire', of a Logos, a law of limit, measure or proportion, which takes a physical form. In that aspect, as fire, it would seem to be itself subject to the all-pervading flux, yet in the eyes of Heraclitus there was a difference. It was in some way a standard by which all things were measured and evaluated (fr. 90, pp. 460 f., above). In its aspect as Logos, the same point is made by its appellation of 'the common' (pp. 425 f., above).

(13) *The complete world-picture: theology*

Although not all will agree,[1] there seems no other way of explaining this puzzling feature of Heraclitus's thought than by relating it to the prevalent religious and philosophical world-picture of his time. In spite of important differences in detail, it may be said that most thinkers of the sixth and fifth centuries shared, in outline, a common

---

[1] Vlastos thinks that for Heraclitus there is no περιέχον, but the whole sum of existence is contained within the cosmos (*AJP*, 1955, 366). His reason is that according to the doxographers Heraclitus said that the *arche*, or fire, is finite. He cites Arist. *Phys.* 205 a 1–4, Theophr. *ap.* Simpl. *Phys.* 23 . 21 ff. (*Dox.* p. 275), and D.L. IX, 8. In the context I do not find it certain that Aristotle's words κἂν ἦ πεπερασμένον ascribe limitation of the primary substance to Heraclitus himself, though since Theophrastus did so it is probable that Aristotle did also. Theophrastus (who is the source of Diogenes as well as Simplicius) divided the natural philosophers into two classes, those who believed the *arche* to be infinite and those who believed it finite, and put Heraclitus in the latter class. It may seem an easy way out of a difficulty to say that Theophrastus was simply wrong, and I have at other times deprecated such a course. Heraclitus is, however, a rather special case, and that he was misunderstood in antiquity is agreed by all. It is fair to point out that in the immediate context Diogenes attributes the following statements to Heraclitus as well: (*a*) fire was the element (στοιχεῖον) out of which all things were formed by rarefaction and condensation; (*b*) the cosmos emerged from fire and will be reduced to fire again, and so on alternately for ever, the way from fire to cosmos being called by Heraclitus war and strife, and the way to *ecpyrosis* agreement and peace. Vlastos would not accept the truth of either of these statements. Why then should we rely on their author for the finite extent of the *arche* in Heraclitus? We know that in other respects Theophrastus wrongly assimilated this *arche* (his word for it, not Heraclitus's) to those of other Presocratic thinkers. He even admits himself that he does not understand it, for it is in this same passage that he makes the rather despairing comment: σαφῶς δ' οὐδὲν ἐκτίθεται. Apart from all this, even if it is true that Heraclitus denied the infinity of fire, it would not necessarily follow that he limited it to this cosmos.

I cannot say that my suggestion about Heraclitus's conception of τὸ πᾶν is certain: there is a great deal of uncertainty about this unique and obscure thinker, and Vlastos may be right. But I give what seems to me the most probable hypothesis.

notion of the universe.[1] Heraclitus would accept this scheme just as even an original and rebellious thinker in the Middle Ages would take for granted the Aristotelian universe with the earth immobile at its centre. There is the cosmic sphere, bounded by the sky, with the earth at its centre, the fixed stars at the circumference, and the sun, moon and planets circling in between. The contents of this cosmos are subject to change and dissolution, being mainly composed of elements or qualities which conflict, and prey upon each other. But the cosmos is not the whole of reality. There is also 'that which surrounds', a quantity of the untransformed primal substance or *arche* which for some at least of the Presocratics was infinite or indefinite in extent. This was of a purer, higher nature than the 'opposites' within the cosmos, which had in some way been 'separated out' or 'condensed' from it. It was ever-lasting, alive and active, itself the initiator of the changes which formed the cosmos, which it not only surrounded but directed or 'steered'. It was in fact divine. Aristotle describes it thus (*Phys.* 203b10): 'It appears to be the originator of all things, to surround and to direct them.... And this, it seems, is the divine, for it is immortal and indestructible, as Anaximander and most of the natural philosophers say.' That this is a fair description of the *apeiron* of Anaximander we have already seen. The living, sentient character of the *arche* was especially emphasized by Anaximenes. Claiming that it was air, he not only said that this surrounded the universe, but drew an explicit parallel between it and the human soul (fr. 2, p. 131, above), as in the fifth century did his follower Diogenes of Apollonia. The Pythagoreans also spoke of the universe taking in breath from the surrounding void (pp. 277ff., above).

Although the *arche* only existed in purity and perfection outside or at the circumference of the cosmos, it penetrated and was mingled with its creatures, while inevitably suffering in the process some degree of assimilation to their degraded character. This was the basis of the Pythagorean belief in the kinship of all nature (pp. 200ff., 278, above). It can be seen also in those passages, philosophical or other, which describe the fixed stars as made of *aither*, the incarnate soul as *aer*, and

[1] For a fuller account see Guthrie, 'The Presocratic World-picture', *Harv. Theol. Rev.* 1952, 87–104.

say that the soul may become a star (as in Aristophanes, *Peace*, 832–3), or plunge into the *aither*, after death; for *aer* is an impure form of *aither*-fire. It was commonly believed that the souls of living creatures were portions of the surrounding divine substance sullied by entry into contact with the lower elements, an idea exploited a little later by Empedocles. The prevalence of this nexus of beliefs in other than philosophical circles makes it probable that it was part of the common background of the philosophers rather than the individual and reasoned theory of any one of them.

If we suppose that Heraclitus had not emancipated himself from this general conception which was common to the philosophical and popular religious thought of his time, it is a little easier to make sense of his cosmology and the part played in it by the Logos-fire. In fr. 30, the ever-living fire that is 'kindled in measures and extinguished in measures' (i.e. involved in warfare and the 'way up and down') is with some emphasis identified with 'this world-order of ours' (κόσμον τόνδε), which suggests the possibility that there exists something else not so designated. This will be the Logos-fire (or *aither*) surrounding the cosmos in its purity, inextinguishable and invisible, mind and soul in their highest form (though not yet conceived as wholly incorporeal). Like the *arche* of other thinkers it 'steers all things' (fr. 64).[1] It determines the 'measures' which limit the extent of the 'ups and downs' within the cosmos and ensure the persistence of the inconclusive battle between its constituent parts, the guarantee of its continued life. For Heraclitus as a child of his time it would be not illogical but natural to think of the divine principle as immanent as well as external, the standard or measure of change within the cosmos appearing in physical form as cosmic fire. He would be quite likely to emphasize at one time the all-pervading character of this principle and at another its

---

[1] Perhaps 'all these things'. Dr H. Boeder has suggested (unpublished) that the fragment begins τάδε πάντα (not, as usually printed, τὰ δέ), corresponding to the κόσμον τόνδε in fr. 30. By calling the universal guiding principle 'thunderbolt' (κεραυνός) in this fragment, Heraclitus presumably means to 'indicate', in the symbolic language of prophecy which was his vehicle, that it is both fiery and the supreme divinity; for the thunderbolt was the weapon of the chief of the gods, who was even identified with it. Kirk (p. 354) quotes a fifth-century inscription from Mantinea ΔΙΟΣ ΚΕΡΑΥΝΟ and later evidence. He notes that in all these identifications the name of Zeus is attached to κεραυνός, but to omit it is entirely in keeping with the obliquity of Heraclitus's Delphic style.

transcendence. The latter may be the purport of fr. 108, where it is asserted that 'wisdom is separate from all things'.[1]

When Heraclitus spoke of 'god' or 'the divine', he clearly had in mind the Logos-fire; but a final brief consideration is wanted of his pronouncements containing the words. Frr. 5, 24 and 53 show that he recognized gods in the traditional sense of Greek polytheism, and such a pluralization is not surprising or difficult to understand. That he had his own conception of divinity emerges from one or two of his many rebukes to mankind: 'Divine things for the most part escape recognition because of unbelief' (fr. 86). Again, in fr. 5, he condemns the practice of praying to images, saying that the worshipper 'does not understand what gods and heroes really are'. Divine wisdom and excellence are contrasted with human lack of these qualities in frr. 78 and 79. There is one divine law from which all human laws draw their sustenance (fr. 114). God does not recognize the distinctions drawn by man between just and unjust; to him all things are fair and good and just (fr. 102, p. 442, above). In the light of fr. 67 (p. 444, above) we can go further and say that this is because he comprehends all contraries in himself. There was a sense in which the *apeiron* of Anaximander and the air of Anaximenes also 'were' the opposites, since the opposites were produced from them. The inherent paradox of this conception was made explicit by Heraclitus, though the identity of his Logos-fire with the opposites was much more subtly conceived. In so far as it is explicable, it has been explained earlier: the parallel shows only that this identity is for a Presocratic thinker no hindrance to belief in a primary, living and directive principle which exists both outside and within the cosmos. 'Zeus is all things *and* what is beyond them all.'[2]

The theology of Heraclitus included the notion of divine judgment. 'Justice', he says (fr. 28), 'will convict those who fabricate and testify to lies.' Justice is a person, as the sentence in fr. 94 about 'the servants of Justice' shows, and in that fragment it is infringement of due

---

[1] The omission of the article is not impossible for Heraclitus. See Kirk, 398. Walzer translates it 'la sapienza'. For τὸ σοφόν as the god or divine principle cf. fr. 32.

For the 'inconsistency' one may compare Anaxagoras on the point. The divine Mind (νοῦς), he insists, is 'mingled with no thing, but is alone and by itself', and he gives reasons for this (fr. 12). Nevertheless there is a qualification. 'In everything there is a portion of everything except Mind; but in some things there is Mind also' (fr. 11).

[2] Aesch. fr. 70 Ζεύς τοι τὰ πάντα χὦτι τῶνδ' ὑπέρτερον.

measure which they chastise. Justice again is equated with the cosmic strife in fr. 80, and of this strife fire is the symbol. If fr. 66 is genuine,[1] its assertion that '*fire* will come and judge and convict all things' bears out this identification. As others associated Zeus with Justice, so Heraclitus identified it with the divine fire that had taken the place of Zeus, the War which is 'father and king of all' (fr. 53; cf. Plato, *Crat.* 413C, to be quoted shortly). For those who believe Heraclitus taught *ecpyrosis*, fr. 66 refers to the final conflagration of the world, but it can equally well apply to individuals. At any rate it is clear that although he may have said 'good and evil are one' (p. 442, above), this did not signify that no kind of behaviour was preferable to any other. (The equivocal ways in which contraries 'are one' have been explained on pp. 445 f.) The particular sins that call down vengeance are denying the truth (fr. 28) and exceeding the appointed measure (fr. 94).

How, if 'everything at some time becomes fire', this same fire can *judge*, i.e. discriminate between the sinner and the just, is a question which will be faced in the next section.

(14) *Religion and the fate of the soul*

What attitude did Heraclitus adopt to popular religious cults, and what were his beliefs about the soul and its fate after death? The answers to these two questions are closely linked, but I start with the evidence for the first. Clement of Alexandria in his *Protrepticus* treats the Greek mysteries to some heavy sarcasm. They reached their climax at night, by the light of torches. Yes, he says, 'worthy of night-time are the rites, and of fire, and of the great-hearted (or rather empty-headed) sons of Erechtheus, and the other Hellenes too, whom there awaits, when they die, what they do not expect' (an allusion to Heraclitus, fr. 27). 'To whom does Heraclitus of Ephesus direct his prophecies? To night-wanderers, magi, bacchants, maenads, initiates. It is they whom he threatens with the things after death, to whom he prophesies fire. For impious is the initiation into the mysteries practised by men.'[2]

---

[1] It is rejected by Reinhardt and Kirk (see Kirk, 359–61), but has been defended against them by M. Marcovich (paper to 3rd Internat. Congr. of Class. Stud. 1959, publ. by Univ. of Mérida, Venezuela). Marcovich, however, adds that 'of course the fragment cannot be an argument in favour of the ecpyrosis-interpretation'.

[2] See fr. 14 DK; the full text in Bywater, no. 124.

It is doubtful whether, in referring to Heraclitus's 'prophecies of fire', Clement had anything more to go on than fragments 16 and 66. For the former he himself is our only authority. It runs: 'How could anyone escape the notice of that which never sets?' In all these quotations from Heraclitus Clement is doing his best to see a Judaic or Christian meaning. This one he brings into connexion with Isaiah xxix. 15: 'Their works are in the dark, and they say, Who seeth us? and who knoweth us?' It is vague enough, but probably does refer to the divine fire, which is always present, as opposed to the sun which, ever since the time of Homer, was regarded as the 'mighty eye' (Soph. *Tr.* 101), Helios who sees and hears everything (*Il.* III, 277). With his customary pleasure in showing up the stupidity of others, Heraclitus points out that the actions of men after sunset are *not* carried out under the eye of Helios. Some confirmation of this is found in Plato's *Cratylus* (413 B–C), where the reference can hardly be to anyone else. Socrates says that, in his search for justice, someone has told him it is the sun. Someone else, however, pours scorn on this, asking whether justice disappears when the sun sets. 'And when I ask him what he in his turn calls justice, he says it is fire.'[1] Fr. 66 has been quoted on the previous page. Its context in Hippolytus is this: 'And he calls it [fire] want and satiety [fr. 65]. Want is in his view the ordering of the cosmos, and the universal conflagration is satiety, for he says that fire will come and judge and convict everything.' The sentence 'fire is want and satiety' has a genuine ring, for Heraclitus believed that fire embraced all the opposites, but it is far from supporting the *ecpyrosis*-interpretation of the eschatologically-minded Christian bishop.

Clement's references to prophecies of fire demanded a slight digression, but at present our concern is to note that according to him Heraclitus uttered threats against the practitioners of mysteries and of bacchic and kindred rites.[2]

Further criticism of established cult occurs in a fragment referred to by several writers of late antiquity, which runs something like this

---

[1] Cf. R. Mondolfo in *Phronesis*, 1958, 76. On fr. 16 in general see Kirk, 362–6.

[2] It is impossible to be certain that the last sentence, introduced by an explanatory γάρ, and saying that initiations are 'impiously carried out' (ἀνιερωστὶ μυοῦνται), should be attributed to Heraclitus; but the οὖν at the beginning of the following sentence suggests that it is, and that only in that sentence does Clement resume the thread of his own argument.

(fr. 5): 'They vainly purify themselves with blood when defiled with it,[1] as if a man who had stepped into mud were to wash it off with mud. He would be thought mad,[2] if anyone marked him acting thus.' Here he expresses disapproval of the general belief that a homicide, whose hands were stained with blood, could be purged of the pollution of the act by a ritual including animal sacrifice.[3]

Fr. 15 further criticizes Dionysiac religion, though with an important qualification. 'If it were not for Dionysus that they hold processions and sing hymns to the shameful parts [phalli], it would be a most shameless act; but Hades and Dionysus are the same, in whose honour they go mad and celebrate the bacchic rites.'[4] This is a hint that the acts performed are only reprehensible when the performers do not understand the significance of what they are doing. Here as usual it is lack of insight that Heraclitus blames. It calls to mind a passage in the Neoplatonist Iamblichus: 'Thus I hold that of sacrifices also there are two kinds: first, those of men completely purified, such as might occur in one instance, as Heraclitus says, or among an easily-counted few; secondly material, corporeal sacrifices, grounded in mutability, such as befit those who are still in the grip of the body.'[5] Iamblichus is drawing his own distinctions on familiar Neoplatonic

---

[1] καθαίρονται δ' ἄλλως αἵματι μιαινόμενοι MSS. of Aristocritus and Origen; ἄλλως om. Elias and Bywater; ἄλλῳ conj. H. Fränkel; ἄλλως⟨αἷμα⟩ αἵματι D. S. Robertson (Kirk and Raven, 211). M. Marcovich (*CP*, 1959, 259) defends the traditional text, with a comma after αἵματι. He says: (*a*) μιαινόμενοι is absolute, containing the notion of αἵματι within it; cf. μίασμα as t.t.; (*b*) μιαινόμενοι is perfect in sense; cf. *De Morb. Sacr.* 1 *ad fin.* (VI, 364 Littré) ἐσιόντες τε περιρραινόμεθα οὐχ ὡς μιαινόμενοι and Xen. *An.* III, 2, 17 οἱ...πρόσθεν σὺν ἡμῖν ταττόμενοι νῦν ἀφεστήκασιν. This interpretation has been followed in the translation above.

[2] We know that word-play had significance for Heraclitus, and here it is probably double: (*a*) a pun on μαίνεσθαι–μιαίνεσθαι, (*b*) a play on the religious and non-religious uses of the former. It meant to be out of one's senses, but to the worshipper of Dionysus it was the desired climax of his religious experience, when the god had entered and taken possession of his soul. Dionysus himself was called μαινόμενος (*Il.* VI, 132). The reference to washing in mud or clay (πηλός) may contain another hit at current religious practices, for certain ritual purifications actually did involve smearing the person with clay. See Dem. *De Cor.* 259, Guthrie, *Orph. and Gk. Rel.* 212.

[3] Whatever the reading of the first clause, this seems to be its reference. Cf. the purifying of Orestes by the sacrifice of a pig at Delphi after the killing of Clytemnestra. Apollonius of Tyana alludes to the saying as if it covered animal sacrifice in general.

[4] Most scholars accept Schleiermacher's εἴργαστ' ἄν for the MS. εἴργασται. Wilamowitz suspected further corruption, but does not attempt a translation (*Gl. d. Hell.* II, 209), and the sense can hardly have been other than is normally supposed. For phallic processions in honour of Dionysus see Hdt. II, 48, Nilsson, *Gr. Feste*, 263ff.

[5] *De Myst.* V, 15, 219.12 Parthey. See Heraclitus, fr. 69.

lines, but he evidently knew of a saying of Heraclitus that there was a right and a wrong way of offering worship, and that very few men chose the right way. Elsewhere he hints at a more favourable attitude to purificatory and other religious rites. 'Such things then', he writes,[1] 'are introduced for the tendance of the soul in us and to keep within bounds the evils which birth has caused to grow about it, to set us free and release us from bonds. Hence Heraclitus rightly called them "cures", as tending to cure our troubles and the disasters attendant on generation.'

The upshot is that Heraclitus was not hostile to initiations and Dionysiac *orgia* as such, but deplored the fact that they were carried out without any understanding of their true significance. This made their performance wrong and impious, reducing phallic rites to mere obscenity. Of the esoteric lesson to be learned from them we have learned this much, that Hades and Dionysus—the god of death and the god of life—are the same.

The mysteries, whether Eleusinian or other, taught of life after death, not the colourless shadow-existence of the Homeric *psyche*, but one in which full individuality was retained and rewards and punishments were possible. The emphasis on these was especially strong in Orphic and Pythagorean circles (pp. 195 ff., above). Whether Heraclitus believed in the immortality of the soul and in posthumous rewards and punishments, or whether such ideas must be excluded as incompatible with the process of flux, is an almost insoluble question on which diametrically opposite views have been held. Soul, it has been said, is subject to continuous change into the other elements, and at death turns to water (fr. 36). How then can it have the permanence necessary for the preservation of identity after death, still less through several lives as the Pythagoreans taught?[2]

Whatever his views about the soul and its fate, we may be sure that they will not be purely rational or without religious overtones. He himself prepares us for this in fr. 45: 'The limits of soul wouldst thou not discover though thou shouldst travel every road: so deep a *logos*

---

[1] *Ibid.* I, 11, 40.8 Parthey. In so far as τὰ τοιαῦτα has a definite antecedent, it is τὰ ἐν τοῖς ἱεροῖς θεάματα καὶ ἀκούσματα: 'the things seen and heard in sacred rites'.

[2] This view was put most strongly and persuasively by Rohde in *Psyche*, Eng. tr. 392-4.

has it.'[1] We are not much helped by fr. 27: 'When men die there awaits them what they do not expect or think', though it certainly suggests survival (and is interpreted by Clement as a threat of punishment). So does the equally mystifying 'Souls smell [i.e. use the sense of smell] in Hades.'[2]

Other fragments must also be passed over if we are looking for a positive doctrine of immortality, on the grounds that, although they may seem to suggest it, it is impossible to say what precisely Heraclitus meant by them. Such is fr. 21: 'What we see when awake is death, what we see asleep is sleep.' Clement thought this an admission that birth to earthly life is in reality death ('the body a tomb' as the Pythagoreans said), but the apparent lack of real contrast between the two clauses, when contrast is obviously intended, leaves the meaning obscure. Sleep as a cognitive state seems to be condemned as at the end of fr. 1, but then one would expect the waking state to be contrasted with it as better. Fr. 24—'Gods and men honour those slain in war'— has also been adduced as evidence for posthumous survival and reward, but need mean no more than that death in battle is thought glorious, and the memory of the slain respected, by gods as it undoubtedly is by their fellow-mortals.[3]

Somewhat in favour of an 'Orphic' strain in Heraclitus is a further criticism of customary rites not yet mentioned: 'Corpses are more fit to be cast out than dung' (fr. 96). In thus dismissing all funerary practices and exhibiting the utmost contempt for the body, he might be thought to imply the complementary belief in the eternal value of the soul. The two certainly went together in Orphic and similar religious teaching. In a medieval source he is quoted as saying (fr. 4):

---

[1] Having treated of λόγος fairly exhaustively, I will not add to the many meanings proposed for it here: 'ground' (*Grund*, Diels), 'meaning' (*Sinn*, Kranz), 'cause' (Hicks), 'essence' (E. Weerts), 'measure' (Burnet, Gigon, Kirk). Kirk thinks it refers to the soul as a representative portion of the cosmic fire, 'which, compared with the individual, is obviously of vast extent' (KR, 206); but βαθὺν λόγον ἔχει would seem a rather recherché phrase to express simply 'so extensive is it'.

[2] Fr. 98. Kirk suggests a possible explanation at KR, 211.

[3] Cf. the κλέος ἀέναον θνητῶν of οἱ ἄριστοι in fr. 29. Fr. 26 is also best left out of the discussion. The text is most uncertain (contrast e.g. Bywater's version (fr. 77) with DK's), and however settled leaves the sense highly obscure. The same may be said about fr. 20, in which Clement understood Heraclitus to be κακίζων τὴν γένεσιν. For modern interpretations see Snell, *Hermes*, 1926, 369; Gigon, *Unters. zu H.* 121f.

'If happiness lay in the delights of the body, we should call cattle happy when they find vetch to eat', and this ascetic attitude towards bodily pleasures (reflected again in fr. 29?) finds a parallel in the same circles. However, these sayings cannot be said to offer certainty.

One fragment however is much more positive (fr. 63): 'They arise and become vigilant guardians of the living and the dead.'[1] There is no reason to doubt its genuineness, of which its very unsuitability to bear the reference Hippolytus gives it (to the Christian doctrine of the resurrection of the body) is itself a guarantee. The words are a plain allusion to Hesiod's *Works and Days* (121–5), where it is said that the heroes of the Golden Race after their death became 'good spirits, guardians of mortal men, roaming everywhere over the earth clad in darkness'. In the light of this, fr. 62, which is in his best oracular style, may also be thought to contain a promise of immortality: 'Immortal mortals, mortal immortals, living the death of others and dying their life.' V. Macchioro indeed interpreted the fragment in terms of the complete Orphic doctrine of man: the immortal mortals are human beings who are partly divine and may become wholly so, and 'mortal immortals' refers to Dionysus who though a god was killed by the Titans.[2] The reference to the myth is highly unlikely, but the passage could be a cryptic statement of the Orphic and Pythagorean doctrine of the body as a tomb and the cycle of births. This receives some support from Sextus Empiricus (*Pyrrh. Hyp.* III, 230): 'Heraclitus says that both life and death are in both our living and our dying; for when we live our souls are dead and buried in us, but when we die our souls revive and live.' It is difficult to know how much is Sextus's own interpretation, and by itself the fragment might only be giving another

---

[1] I omit the first letters ενθαδεοντι, the division and meaning of which are quite uncertain. They cannot affect the sense of the rest. No definite subject is expressed.

[2] Macchioro, *Eraclito*. Heraclitus's thought is also brought into close relation with the mysteries by A. Delatte, *Les Conceptions de l'enthousiasme*, 6–21.

As evidence for Orphism in Heraclitus, Macchioro also adduces fr. 52: 'Aion (Time?) is a child playing, playing draughts: the kingdom is a child's.' Aion is identified with Dionysus in Christian and Neoplatonic writers, and in the Orphic story the Titans who killed him beguiled him with playthings (including ἀστράγαλοι which Macchioro mistakenly identifies with πεσσοί). But there are no pre-Christian references to Dionysus as Aion, and the interpretation is altogether hazardous. (Philo seems to have taken Aion to be Chance, playing draughts with human lives. There must surely be an echo of both this fragment and fr. 60 in his *De Vita Mos.* I, 6, IV, 107.9 Cohn: τύχης γὰρ ἀσταθμητότερον οὐδὲν ἄνω καὶ κάτω τὰ ἀνθρώπεια πεττευούσης.) Of this fragment I can only say with Gigon that it is one of those 'vor denen wir kapitulieren müssen'.

instance of the identity of opposites. One may compare fr. 88: 'Living and dead are the same, and waking and sleeping and young and old; for these when they have changed are those, and those, changing once more, are these.' Assuming that the last clause is genuine (p. 445, n. 1, above), identity here implies no more than reciprocal succession, as in fr. 67 (cf. fr. 126). That the change is reciprocal, however, is difficult to explain without invoking the soul's survival after death and rebirth into a new life. A die-hard sceptic might argue that 'living comes from dead' means only that creatures are formed of what was previously inanimate matter, but it is not so easy to explain away 'old changes and becomes young'. On the whole therefore this fragment favours immortality and palingenesis, though by itself it would perhaps not be conclusive.

The fragments provide no more direct statements on immortality. What follows is inference, and lays no claim to certainty. I start from the fact that Heraclitus was more of a religious prophet than a rationalist, as the tone of his utterances abundantly proves. From such a man one should not look for perfect consistency of thought on the subject of the human soul. It is there if anywhere that he will be influenced by unconscious presuppositions arising from the traditions of his people, and the position taken here will be that his beliefs about the soul derive from the general world-picture which has been tentatively ascribed to him. In that picture, macrocosm and microcosm were integral parts of the same system, in which the world itself was a living creature. Where in the following summary it is necessary to repeat points previously made, this will be done as briefly as possible.

To exclude all permanence from his scheme of things is clearly wrong. He believed in 'the divine'. The Logos is eternal, and there is emphasis on the related concepts of law and measure. That he did teach a doctrine of flux, and regarded it as one of his prime discoveries, I have maintained against some recent interpretation, but to call that the whole of his teaching is a serious misunderstanding, which in antiquity may have arisen from confusion with his followers. Flux and impermanence were kept within the strict limits of the 'way up and down', and moreover stopped, spatially, short of the confines of the cosmos. He shared with popular belief the following ideas.

The outermost part of the universe is made of fire. It is the substance of the sun and stars, and fire in our part shows an upward tendency. The heavenly bodies are alive and divine. So therefore is fire when pure. Divinity to a Greek mind was synonymous with everlasting life, therefore fire, the substance of divinity, is the principle of everlasting life. In varying degrees of impurity this life-substance pervades our own world and gives life to us and the animals. In its pure form it was also called *aither*. When the Orphics and other early thinkers (cf. e.g. Aristotle, *De An.* 410b27 and Aristoph. *Clouds*, 227–30) said that soul and mind were breathed in from the air, this is consistent, because *aer* is the less pure form of the same thing, filling the lower atmosphere. (In Heraclitean terms, the fire-soul suffers a certain degree of moistening by the time it reaches mortal bodies.) The statement of Sextus that according to Heraclitus 'we draw in the divine Logos by breathing' belongs to this early scheme of thought, and need not be supposed a Stoic distortion. In the same passage he compares the soul to coals or embers which glow when brought near the fire but fade when removed from it. This too may be a genuine Heraclitean reminiscence. Being in its purest form *aither*, a soul, if it has cherished the flame of life, may hope to join the heavenly *aither* at death (see the references on p. 466, n. 2, above).

These beliefs were worked up by the Orphic sectaries and other religious teachers in Greece into an elaborate doctrine of the 'wheel of birth', but they arise naturally out of a background of folklore, seen at its simplest in the 'we become stars in the sky when we die' of the slave in Aristophanes. Now in Heraclitus souls, like everything else, are subject to the way up and down; they are encroached on by the other elements (fr. 36). But their real nature is fiery (hot and dry), and death is due to the encroachment of the cold and moist. 'It is death to souls to become water'; 'the dry soul is wisest and best'. Death, however, is not complete extinction,[1] for that would contradict the law of unending and reciprocal change, and so we have '...but from earth comes water, and from water soul'.

The parallel with Orphic notions is striking. Souls caught in the

---

[1] As Philo saw, *De Aet. Mundi*, 21 (77.8 Cohn–Reiter, on fr. 36): θάνατον οὐ τὴν εἰς ἅπαν ἀναίρεσιν ὀνομάζων, ἀλλὰ τὴν εἰς ἕτερον στοιχεῖον μεταβολήν.

cosmic 'way up and down' are in the position of those in the 'weary wheel' of birth and rebirth of which the religious teachers spoke.[1] Just as they taught that a soul which had wholly purified itself by the proper rites and the right kind of life could escape from the wheel and unite itself permanently with the divine, so also, we may conjecture, did Heraclitus. If a soul lives a foolish, 'wet' life, neglecting the opportunities to nourish itself by contact with its source, the fiery Logos,[2] it goes the way of water and its circulation in the cosmic flux may be endless. The wise soul on the other hand keeps itself dry, cherishes the fiery element in it by worshipping the gods in the proper way (that is, with understanding), listens to the Logos and grasps the truth that wisdom is one thing and all opposites subsumed in a higher unity. It would be in keeping with all the habits of early Greek thought that such a soul should at the death of the body be assimilated to that Logos, becoming pure fire, and escape from the cosmic cycle of becoming; and if we may believe Macrobius, Heraclitus described the soul as 'a spark of the substance of the stars' (DK, A15 *scintillam stellaris essentiae*). Burnet and others have seen evidence in the fragments of a 'fiery death' as opposed to the death whereby souls become water. It is supposed to be the death of those killed in battle, full of courage and virtue as well as vigour, as opposed to those whose souls have been weakened by disease (or, presumably, dissipation; cf. frr. 117, 77).[3] Such a view finds perhaps its strongest support not in any actual saying of Heraclitus but in its consonance with the general picture. The nearest to confirmation in Heraclitus himself is the gnomic assertion of fr. 25: 'Greater deaths win greater portions.'

This seems a reasonable account. But 'the limits of soul thou wouldst not discover though thou shouldst travel every road'. Heraclitus himself would certainly scorn the notion that a twentieth-century barbarian could fathom the depths of its *logos*, and would doubtless refer us to

---

[1] The purified soul is taught to say, when it meets the guardians of the other world, κύκλου δ' ἐξέπταν βαρυπενθέος ἀργαλέοιο (gold plate from tomb at Thurii, see Guthrie, *Orph. and Gk. Rel.* 173). It adds: 'I am a child of earth and starry heaven, but my lineage is heavenly.'

[2] In one fragment (115) Heraclitus says that soul has a λόγος ἑαυτὸν αὔξων, a *logos* which increases itself.

[3] KR, 209f. Direct evidence consists mainly of the metrical imitation of Heraclitus ψυχαὶ ἀρηίφατοι καθαρώτεροι ἢ ἐνὶ νούσοις (136 among the frr. in DK). This can be brought into relation with frr. 24 and 25.

481

his own advice: 'Let us not make random conjectures about the greatest matters' (fr. 47).

Some of his sayings are so good as they stand, and have so clearly the character of isolated epigrams, that the attempt to fit them into a general framework seems not only hazardous but misguided. Such is the scarcely translatable fr. 119: ἦθος ἀνθρώπῳ δαίμων—'A man's individuality is his *daimon*'. The *daimon* was the personal genius or guardian angel which looked after an individual both in life and after death (for which see especially Plato, *Phaedo*, 107D); the man with a good *daimon* would be happy (εὐδαίμων). This superstitious belief Heraclitus reinterprets in a highly enlightened, rational, and ethical way.[1]

It is, however, tempting to speculate further. *Daimon* was a word of more than one use, with a whole world of popular beliefs behind it. Sometimes it was simply a synonym for a god. But as we have seen, from the time of Hesiod at least the immortal spirits of good men were also *daimones*, and since he gives them the function of 'guardians', it looks as if the *daimones* who looked after individual men were thought of in this way. Heraclitus alludes to Hesiod in fr. 63 (p. 478, above), and must have accepted this. Moreover in those religious circles which taught that the soul survived the body, and underwent many incarnations, it was looked upon as a fallen *daimon* which might rise again to its proper godlike form. (This comes out most clearly in Empedocles, fr. 115.) There is thus a further depth to this saying. It links up with the belief in transmigration and means: 'A man's character is the immortal and potentially divine part of him.' This lays a tremendous emphasis on human responsibility and adds to the ethical content of the sentence. (On *daimon* see also p. 318 above.)

(15) *Astronomy and meteorology*

We are now acquainted with the most important and interesting parts of Heraclitus's message, but may add some details for the sake of completeness. He had some rather strange ideas on astronomy and

---

[1] B. Snell has some valuable remarks on this fragment in *Hermes*, 1926, 363f. It seems to be directed (at least in part) at the old belief, common to Homer and early lyric poetry, that idiosyncrasies and failings, particularly emotional outbursts, are the work of the gods. If Helen leaves her husband for Paris, she is not to blame, for her infatuation was the work of Aphrodite: Zeus can cause a man to act wrongly by making him angry or 'taking away his wits'.

meteorology, which are thus summarized by Diogenes Laertius (IX, 9–11):

Exhalations arise from both land and sea, the one sort bright and pure, the other dark. Fire is increased from the bright, and moisture from the others. The nature of the surrounding substance he does not explain, but says that there are in it bowls with the inside turned towards us, in which the bright exhalations are collected and produce flames which are the heavenly bodies. Brightest and hottest is the flame of the sun; for the other stars are further from the earth and for that reason give less light and heat, whereas the moon, though near the earth, does not move through a pure region. The sun on the other hand is in a brilliant and uncontaminated region and at a suitable[1] distance from us, and therefore gives more heat and light. The sun and moon are eclipsed when the bowls are turned upwards, and the monthly phases of the moon are due to the gradual turning of its bowl.[2] Day and night, months, seasons and years, rain, winds and the like are brought about by the various exhalations. The bright exhalation catching fire in the circle of the sun causes day, whereas the predominance of the contrary one produces night: summer is caused by an increase of heat from the bright one, winter by a preponderance of moisture from the dark. His explanation of the other phenomena follows the same lines. On the other hand he offers no explanation of the nature of the earth, or even of the bowls.

This account does not seem very percipient, and throws together a surprisingly diverse collection of phenomena under a single general cause. Yet it would be characteristic of Heraclitus to be somewhat impatient of detail, and he may himself have dismissed a number of astronomical and other natural phenomena in a few aphorisms of the sort with which we are familiar. His interest lay, not like that of a Milesian *physikos* in explaining all possible natural phenomena, but solely in using them to support the doctrine of universal reciprocal change (cf. Reinhardt, *Parm.* 181). Beyond a few remarks about the sun, we have nothing but the late compiler's version of his views to go by.

That the sun will not and must not 'overstep his measures' we have already seen (fr. 94, p. 465, above). He also said: 'If there were no

[1] Kirk (271) translates 'commensurate' and thinks the word is evidence of Peripatetic expansion. But 'commensurate' does not fit the context, and the sense required is not Peripatetic. Cf. rather Soph. *O.T.* 84 ξύμμετρος γὰρ ὡς κλύειν.
[2] Literally 'to the bowl gradually turning in it'. I confess I cannot understand ἐν αὐτῇ: the only antecedent for the pronoun seems to be σελήνη.

sun, with all the other stars it would be night',[1] a fragment whose interpretation, says Kirk, 'remains somewhat precarious'. That is, of course, if one expects a symbolic meaning, for there is no obscurity about the factual commonplace which it states. With or without the phrase about the stars, it is probably a straightforward statement. Though as it stands it hardly seems worth making, it may have found its place in an account of the comparative brightness of sun, moon and stars which went on to offer an explanation, on the lines paraphrased by Diogenes, in terms of relative distance from the earth and purity of atmosphere. Heraclitus may also have wished to emphasize that day and night are the product of the same cause (the sun) according as it is present or absent, thus emphasizing their essential unity as expressed in fr. 57; but this seems a lot to get out of a very simple sentence.

'The sun is new every day' (fr. 6), and Plato in the *Republic* (498A) says of those who have abandoned philosophy that 'they are much more truly extinguished than the sun of Heraclitus, for they are never rekindled'. Later commentators expand this. The sun passes below the earth, and is extinguished either because the western regions are cold (Olympiodorus) or because it plunges into the sea (scholiast on the *Republic*): when it rises the next morning it is rekindled in the east.[2] It consists of vapour collected in a 'bowl', which ignites when in a fiery region, and no doubt acquires fuel from further vapours or 'exhalations' which its heat sucks up from the earth. The doxography records it as a belief of Heraclitus that 'the heavenly bodies are nourished by the exhalation from the earth'.[3]

[1] Fr. 99. Kirk (162 ff.) thinks it probable that the words ἕνεκα τῶν ἄλλων ἄστρων (which occur in Plut. *De Fortuna*, 98 c but are omitted when Plutarch quotes the saying again in *Aqu. et Ign. Comp.* 957 A) are an insertion by Plutarch.

[2] For texts see Kirk, 267, and in general cf. his long discussion of this fragment, 264–79.

[3] Aët. II, 17, 4, DK, 22 A 11. It is hardly necessary to go into the troubled question of whether Diogenes was right in attributing to Heraclitus a theory of two exhalations, bright from the sea and dark from the earth, which Kirk (271 ff.) regards as an Aristotelian theory read back into Heraclitus. A single-exhalation theory would certainly be adequate for his system, and seems more probable. It would of course be dark and moist, or bright, dry and fiery, according to the law of constant change, partaking in the 'way up and down'. This does not mean that the description of Aëtius (τῆς ἀπὸ γῆς ἀναθυμιάσεως) is wrong: it may quite well be general. The sun draws up an exhalation from the earth, whether it comes from sea or land.

Kirk seems to go too far in saying (in KR, 204, n.): 'The explanation of night and day (as well as winter and summer) as due to the alternating prevalence of the dark and bright exhala-

The Sun

Heraclitus's conception of the sun evidently owes much to Xenophanes's description of it as formed of ignited clouds, or a collection of sparks from the moist exhalation; but since we are told that his sun travels during the night beneath the earth from its setting-place in the west to its rising-place in the east, he cannot have intended the daily newness of the sun to be taken in the same radical sense. According to Xenophanes the sun shot off into space in a straight line, and the appearance of a circular course was illusory (p. 393, above). Heraclitus speaks rather of renewal of the sun than of an entirely new sun, probably with two points in mind: (*a*) as a heat- and light-giving body it is new every day, since its flame is quenched at night, (*b*) like any other flame (and indeed like everything else in the cosmos, which for that reason he characterized as itself a fire), it is *constantly* being renewed by the absorption of new matter. Aristotle complains (*Meteor.* 355a12) that if the sun were 'nourished' like a flame, as 'some' say, then it would not only be new every day, as Heraclitus asserts, but always new at every moment. This of course is what Heraclitus did believe. He did not, however, use the precise language of philosophy but the isolated 'barbed arrows' of prophetic utterance, leaving his hearers to interpret them. For his purpose, 'new every day' was an adequate phrase, which those with civilized souls might understand.

The 'bowl' of the sun cannot be unconnected with the traditional and poetic idea that at night the sun sailed in a golden bowl round the rim of the world on the encircling stream of Oceanus from west to east (Mimnermus, fr. 10, Stesichorus, fr. 6 Diehl). Heraclitus has simplified things by making the bowl the vehicle of the sun in its daily journey through the sky as well, thus getting rid of the obviously mythical apparatus of chariot and horses; and the extension of the notion of bowls to the moon and stars is an innovation. It looks, however, as if, in a matter so remote as the heavenly bodies, he had been content with a superficial rationalization which (as Kirk has noted) does not even fit the phenomena; for the turning of the bowls which he

tions,...is absurd: Heraclitus knew as well as anyone that day is due to the sun.' Since the sun itself consists of 'the bright exhalation catching fire', there is no inconsistency in attributing day both to the sun and to the bright exhalation; and whether or not Heraclitus said it, it is at least reasonable that the quenching of the sun's fire, which produces night, should be due to the victory of the dark (cold, moist) exhalation.

invokes to explain eclipses and the phases of the moon would produce an ellipse of light, not the 'bite' out of the solar and lunar circles, leading ultimately to a crescent shape, which in fact appears. (It is slightly amplified in Aët. II, 24, 3, DK, A 12: 'Eclipses are accounted for by the turning of the bowl-shaped so that its hollow is turned upwards and its convex part downwards towards our sight.') As for the composition of the bowls themselves, we know no more than Diogenes and must take his word for it that Heraclitus did not explain them further.

The subsequent account of seasonal and meteorological events is too vague to make comment worth while.[1] Nor is it easy to see the significance of the only other pronouncement of Heraclitus about the sun which has come down to us, namely that 'its breadth is the length of a human foot' (fr. 3) or alternatively 'it is of the size that it appears to be' (D.L. IX, 7). The first statement, though included in the actual fragments by DK, reads like the second half of a hexameter and may have been from a late metrical version of Heraclitus such as we know to have existed.[2] By itself, and without context as it is, it might be supposed to refer only to appearances, as a reinforcement of the thesis that the senses are misleading unless interpreted by the mind. But the version in Diogenes expressly denies this. It is directly contradictory to the example used by Aristotle in the *De Anima* (428b3) when he wishes to illustrate the deceptiveness of appearances even in cases where we know better, 'as the sun appears to be a foot wide, though it is recognized to be larger than the inhabited world'. It is hardly possible that Heraclitus believed his statement to be literally true, and its significance must remain mysterious.[3] The same thing was said later by Epicurus, for whom however it is the outcome of his peculiar doctrine of the infallibility of sense-perception.

(16) *Conclusion*

Here we may leave this astonishing figure, in his proud isolation. The thoughts in his mind were ahead of his time and language. In his own

---

[1] It is amplified by what is said of thunder, lightning and πρηστῆρες in Aët. III, 3, 9, DK, A14, which, however, is hardly more satisfying.

[2] It occurs in ordinary doxographical form in Theodoret, IV, 22 Ἡράκλειτος δὲ ποδιαῖον (Kirk, 280).

[3] Attempted explanations are listed in Kirk, 281f.

estimation he was a prophet, bearer of the divine law which the mass of men were incapable of grasping. He could only set it before them in image and paradox. Practically all his language is metaphorical, and only seldom does he attempt a brief train of argument. What is the use of arguing with the self-satisfied many?

The truth that has flashed on him has two sides. First, we conceive of the world of our experience as containing objects, possessed of a certain stable and relatively permanent character. This seems to us also a desirable state of affairs, so that we commend as good any apparently harmonious arrangement which enables its product to stay quietly as it is, and stigmatize disruptive forces as bad. The truth is far otherwise. What we take for stability and rest is the outcome not of any harmonious agreement of parts but of an incessant struggle of opposing forces which has happened to reach an equilibrium of tension. Exertion, motion, change are constantly though invisibly going on; strife is the condition of existence: there is no rest, only unremitting change. 'Thunderbolt is at the helm', War is father and king, War is the true peace; and all these things are good, for peace as popularly conceived is death.

On the other side, however, this constant warfare is not allowed to go on unregulated. If it were, it might some day cease. The cosmos has existed for ever and will go on existing, and this could not be guaranteed if there were a possibility of one of the contraries ever gaining a permanent advantage. In fact no contrary can exist if its contrary should disappear. Pre-eminent in the Heraclitean universe stands the Logos, the divine law of measure and proportion. Everything is always moving up and down the path of change, driven thereto by the attacks of its opposites or its own attacks upon them, but all within strict limits. The path is a circular one, on which 'beginning and end are the same'.

In the unity of the Logos all opposing forces are contained and transcended. It is the 'one wise', the god who is day and night, winter and summer, war and peace: personal, then, and intelligent above all else. At the same time, since nothing is yet divorced from matter, this god is of a fiery nature, and in some degree pervades the whole world like the Zeus-*aither* of Aeschylus. The world is a living organism, as it remained to Plato, and later to the Stoics. We too have our share in it, we are knit into the cosmic unity; for the Logos is common to all, our own souls are fiery and through the intermediate stage of air we are in direct contact with the cosmic reason by breathing. Not even when asleep can we be entirely cut off. We still live, though our bond with 'the common' has become so tenuous, in the absence of sense-perception to serve as material for our thought, that we are shut in a private world of illusion. Heraclitus exhorts us not to carry over this shameful condition into our waking hours. We must cultivate the fiery nature of the soul so that when released from the damp fumes of the body it may be ready to rejoin the Logos-fire. The road to this goal is the road of understanding. Whether or not we carry out the recognized rites of communion is immaterial. Performed without understanding they are merely disgusting, but if they help us to grasp the unity behind the flux and multiplicity of phenomena they can do good.

NOTE. No mention has been made in this chapter of any possible connexions of Heraclitus's thought with Persia, in particular with Zoroastrianism. His Logos has sometimes been compared with the Zoroastrian concepts of *Ahuna Vairya* (as divine Word) and *Vohu Mana* (as universal Mind), and it has been thought possible to find in Heraclitus (as Plutarch did) the same dualism as in the Persian religion. All this has been omitted because in fact there is no sure evidence of contact or affinities, but only a field for speculation and conjecture. At the same time it is true that Heraclitus was a subject of King Darius and was traditionally believed to have been his friend; that one of his fragments provides the earliest occurrence in Greek literature of the title Magus; and that he accorded a supreme and divine status to fire. Those interested may be referred to the brief and sober summary, with bibliography, of S. Wikander in *Éléments orientaux dans la religion grecque ancienne*, 57–9.

APPENDIX

The river-statement (see p. 450)

The evidence that Heraclitus said (in whatever exact Greek words), 'You cannot step twice into the same river', is perhaps stronger than that for the genuineness of any other fragment. There would be no need to rehearse it again, were it not that a few scholars have questioned it in favour of the un-paradoxical and uncharacteristic form of words which occurs only in Arius Didymus as quoted by Eusebius (DK, 22B12): 'Upon those who step into the same rivers different and again different waters flow.' Since the claim that this sentence reproduces the original words of Heraclitus has received the support of Kirk (whose translation of it I have given), the evidence had better be set forth. But since Kirk's arguments have already been countered by Vlastos (*AJP*, 1955, 338–44), I shall content myself with doing little more.

(*a*) Plato, *Crat.* 402A: 'I believe Heraclitus says that everything moves on and nothing is at rest, and comparing existing things to the flow of a river he says that you cannot step into the same river twice.'

λέγει που Ἡράκλειτος ὅτι πάντα χωρεῖ καὶ οὐδὲν μένει, καὶ ποταμοῦ ῥοῇ ἀπεικάζων τὰ ὄντα λέγει ὡς δὶς ἐς τὸν αὐτὸν ποταμὸν οὐκ ἄν ἐμβαίης.

(*b*) Aristotle, *Metaph.* 1010a13: 'Cratylus criticized Heraclitus for saying that it is impossible to step into the same river twice: in his opinion you could not do so even once.'

Κρατύλος... Ἡρακλείτῳ ἐπετίμα εἰπόντι ὅτι δὶς τῷ αὐτῷ ποταμῷ οὐκ ἔστιν ἐμβῆναι· αὐτὸς γὰρ ᾤετο οὐδ' ἅπαξ.

(*c*) Plutarch, *De E*, 392B: 'According to Heraclitus it is not possible to step into the same river twice, nor to lay hold twice of any mortal substance in one permanent state.'

ποταμῷ γὰρ οὐκ ἔστιν ἐμβῆναι δὶς τῷ αὐτῷ καθ' Ἡράκλειτον, οὐδὲ θνητῆς οὐσίας δὶς ἅψασθαι κατὰ ἕξιν.

(*d*) *Qu. Nat.* 912A: 'You cannot step twice into the same rivers, as Heraclitus says, for fresh waters are flowing on.'

ποταμοῖς γὰρ δὶς τοῖς αὐτοῖς οὐκ ἄν ἐμβαίης, ὥς φησιν Ἡράκλειτος· ἕτερα γὰρ ἐπιρρεῖ ὕδατα.

(*e*) *Ser. Num. Vind.* 559C: 'Before we know where we are, we shall have thrown everything into Heraclitus's river, into which he says one does not step twice, because nature in its changes moves and alters everything.'

ἥ λήσομεν εἰς τὸν Ἡρακλείτειον ἅπαντα πράγματα ποταμὸν ἐμβαλόντες, εἰς ὃν οὔ φησι δὶς ἐμβῆναι, τῷ πάντα κινεῖν καὶ ἑτεροιοῦν τὴν φύσιν μεταβάλλουσαν.

Plutarch quotes Heraclitus frequently, and clearly did not get his quotations from Plato; and he leaves us in no doubt, as he himself was in no doubt, of what Heraclitus said.

(*f*) Simplicius, *Phys.* 77.31 speaks of 'the continuous flow which interchanges all things, which Heraclitus described in riddling terms in the

sentence "You could not step twice into the same river", comparing becoming to the continuous flow of a river, as having more of not-being than
of being'.

τὴν συνεχῆ ῥοὴν τὴν πάντα ἐναλλάσσουσαν, ἣν ὁ Ἡράκλειτος ἠνίξατο διὰ
τοῦ 'εἰς τὸν αὐτὸν ποταμὸν δὶς μὴ ἂν ἐμβῆναι', τῇ ἐνδελεχεῖ τοῦ ποταμοῦ
ῥοῇ τὴν γένεσιν ἀπεικάζων πλέον τὸ μὴ ὂν ἔχουσαν τοῦ ὄντος.

(*g*) *Ibid.* 1313.8: 'The natural philosophers who follow Heraclitus, con-
centrating on the continuous flow of becoming, . . . say naturally enough that
everything is always in flux and you cannot step twice into the same river.'

τοὺς δὲ περὶ Ἡράκλειτον φυσιολόγους εἰς τὴν ἐνδελεχῆ τῆς γενέσεως ῥοὴν
ἀφορῶντας. . .εἰκός ἐστι λέγειν ὅτι ἀεὶ πάντα ῥεῖ καὶ ὅτι εἰς τὸν αὐτὸν
ποταμὸν δὶς οὐκ ἂν ἐμβαίης.

This, it will surely be admitted, is impressive evidence that in the eyes
of those most likely to know, whose testimony to the words of Heraclitus we are inclined to accept on other occasions, he said 'You cannot
step (*or* it is impossible to step) into the same river twice'. What is the
evidence that he put it differently?

The first-century A.D. writer of a book on Homeric allegories (also
called Heraclitus but otherwise unknown), after seriously misquoting
fr. 62, proceeds: 'And again he says: "We step and do not step into
the same rivers, we are and are not"' (Heracl. Homer. *Qu. Hom.* 24,
fr. 49*a* DK: ποταμοῖς τοῖς αὐτοῖς ἐμβαίνομέν τε καὶ οὐκ ἐμβαίνομεν,
εἶμέν τε καὶ οὐκ εἶμεν). With this may be compared Seneca, *Ep.*
58, 23: 'As Heraclitus says, into the same river we step and do not
step twice; for the name of the river remains the same, but the water
has flowed past' (*hoc est quod ait Heraclitus: in idem flumen bis descendimus et non descendimus. manet enim idem fluminis nomen, aqua
transmissa est*). In the first passage some editors suppose that 'twice'
(δίς) has fallen out of the MSS. In any case the words τοῖς αὐτοῖς show
that the meaning is the same, for apart from the nonsensical 'we step
into the same rivers' (i.e. each of us steps into the same rivers as the
others), 'the same' can only mean the same rivers as we have stepped
into before. Since our authorities agree that this allegory stood for an
essential of Heraclitus's thought, he himself may well have stated it
more than once in slightly different terms. It is certainly tempting to
suppose that what Vlastos has called the 'yes-and-no' form is his own
(cf. 'is not willing and is willing' in fr. 32, 'wholes and not wholes' in

fr. 10). Seneca, a little heavy-footedly, improves on the explanation given elsewhere, which may have been Heraclitus's own: one can step twice into the same river—say the Thames or the Cam—but in another sense it is not the same, for the water you step into the second time was not there before. In this form therefore the saying is essentially the same as in the other, in which it is regularly quoted from Plato onwards, and which I believe to represent more exactly what Heraclitus himself said.

The words 'we are and are not' are irrelevant to this discussion, save as they do or do not tend to discredit the preceding sentence. I agree with Vlastos that, taking the verb in the full existential sense, they express a thoroughly Heraclitean sentiment. They have been thought to make an abrupt transition, and it is not improbable that Heraclitus's unscholarly namesake should have thrown together two utterances which did not come together in the philosopher himself. But he had his reason for doing so, for they both illustrate the same Heraclitean doctrine, that so-called natural entities or substances have no permanent being but undergo a constant flux of change and renewal.

Finally there is the form cited by Arius Didymus, which it is advisable to quote in its full context (fr. 12 DK, *Dox.* 470f.):

Concerning the soul, Cleanthes, putting the views of Zeno beside other natural philosophers for comparison, says that Zeno calls the soul a sensitive exhalation, like Heraclitus. For he, wishing to make the point that souls continuously become intelligent by being vaporized,[1] compared them to rivers, putting it like this: upon those who step into the same rivers different and again different waters flow. And souls are exhaled from moist substances.

περὶ δὲ ψυχῆς Κλεάνθης μὲν τὰ Ζήνωνος δόγματα παρατιθέμενος πρὸς σύγκρισιν τὴν πρὸς τοὺς ἄλλους φυσικούς φησιν ὅτι Ζήνων τὴν ψυχὴν λέγει αἰσθητικὴν ἀναθυμίασιν, καθάπερ Ἡράκλειτος. βουλόμενος γὰρ ἐμφανίσαι ὅτι αἱ ψυχαὶ ἀναθυμιώμεναι νοεραὶ ἀεὶ γίνονται, εἴκασεν αὐτὰς τοῖς ποταμοῖς λέγων οὕτως· ποταμοῖσι τοῖσιν αὐτοῖσιν ἐμβαίνουσιν ἕτερα καὶ ἕτερα ὕδατα ἐπιρρεῖ, καὶ ψυχαὶ δὲ ἀπὸ τῶν ὑγρῶν ἀναθυμιῶνται.

Whether the last sentence is being directly attributed to Heraclitus is doubtful, but as fr. 36 shows ('...from water comes soul'), it repre-

---

[1] Or 'are continually renewed'. J. D. Meewaldt in *Mnemos.* 1951, 53–4 suggested νεαραί for νοεραί, which makes excellent sense.

sents his belief. The obvious difference between this passage and the others is that here the saying about rivers is applied specifically to souls, whereas in the others the reference is to everything alike. The best solution is probably to accept Meewaldt's emendation (n. 1 on previous page), in which case we see that the comparison is applied to souls in respect of a characteristic which they share with everything else, namely that they are continuously being renewed, never substantially the same. The words 'different and again different waters flow' occur also in slightly shorter form in Plutarch (see above), and perhaps in this form the explanation was added by Heraclitus himself (as possibly also in fr. 88, p. 445, above). As to the statement as a whole, I can only say (against Kirk) that the balance of the evidence is strongly in favour of its being a condensed form of the quotation first, and correctly, given us by Plato.[1]

[1] Whether Heraclitus actually wrote οὐκ ἂν ἐμβαίης or οὐκ ἔστιν ἐμβῆναι (as Aristotle gives it) is a trivial question, nor can we decide it. It must be admitted that none of our ancient sources had the passion for verbal accuracy which possesses the modern scholar. At least Vlastos has shown that the potential form which Plato quotes was perfectly possible for Heraclitus (*AJP*, 1955, 338f.).

BIBLIOGRAPHY

The following list contains full particulars of books or articles mentioned (often with shortened titles) in the text or notes. In addition, a selection of titles has been included which may be useful for reference although there has not been occasion to mention them in the course of the work.

Source-collections (other than those of individual philosophers) precede the general list. (On the sources of our knowledge of early Greek philosophy see pp. xiii–xiv.)

The Greek commentators on Aristotle (most frequently Simplicius and Alexander of Aphrodisias) are referred to in the text by page and line in the appropriate volume of the Berlin Academy's edition (*Commentaria in Aristotelem Graeca*, various dates).

COHEN, M. R. and DRABKIN, I. E. *A Source-book in Greek Science.* New York, 1948 (2nd printing, Cambridge (Mass.), 1958).

DE VOGEL, C. J. *Greek Philosophy: a collection of texts with notes and explanations.* 3 vols., Leiden, 1950–9.

DIELS, H. *Doxographi Graeci.* Berlin, 1879.

DIELS, H. and KRANZ, W. *Die Fragmente der Vorsokratiker* (Greek and German). 6th ed., 3 vols., Berlin, 1951–2 (or later editions; the pagination remains the same).

FREEMAN, K. *Ancilla to the Presocratic Philosophers* (translation of the texts in Diels–Kranz). Oxford (Blackwell), 1948.

KERN, O. *Orphicorum Fragmenta.* Berlin, 1922.

KIRK, G. S. and RAVEN, J. E. *The Presocratic Philosophers.* Cambridge, 1957 (selected texts with translation and commentary).

RITTER, H. and PRELLER, L. *Historia Philosophiae Graecae.* 9th ed., Gotha, 1913 (selection of texts with Latin notes).

ALLAN, D. J. 'The Problem of Cratylus', *AJP*, 1952, 271–87.

BACCOU, R. *Histoire de la science grecque de Thalès à Socrate.* Paris, 1951.

BAILEY, C. *The Greek Atomists and Epicurus.* Oxford, 1928.

BALDRY, H. C. 'Embryological Analogies in Presocratic Cosmogony', *CQ*, 1932, 27–34.

BEARE, J. I. *Greek Theories of Elementary Cognition.* Oxford, 1906.

BECKER, O. 'Die Lehre vom Gerade und Ungerade im IX. Buch der euklidischen Elemente', *Quellen und Studien zur Geschichte der Mathematik*, 3 (1936), 533–53.

BERGER, H. *Geschichte der wissenschaftlichen Erdkunde der Griechen.* Leipzig, 1903.

BERTHELOT, M. *Les Origines de l'alchimie.* Paris, 1885.

BOEDER, H. 'Der frühgriechische Wortgebrauch von Logos und Aletheia', *Archiv für Begriffsgeschichte*, 1958, 82–112.

Bibliography

BOEHM, F. *De Symbolis Pythagoreis*, diss. Berlin, 1905.

BÖMER, F. *Der lateinische Neuplatonismus und Neupythagoreismus*. Leipzig, 1936.

BOOTH, N. B. 'Were Zeno's arguments directed against the Pythagoreans?', *Phronesis*, 1957, 90–103.

BOWRA, C. M. 'Xenophanes fr. 3', *CQ*, 1941, 119–26.

BOWRA, C. M. 'Xenophanes and the Olympian Games', *Problems in Greek Poetry*, 1953, 15–37.

BOWRA, C. M. 'Xenophanes on Songs at Feasts', *Problems in Greek Poetry*, 1953, 1–14.

BOYANCÉ, P. 'Note sur la Tétractys', *L'Antiquité Classique*, 1951, 421–5.

BRANDIS, C. A. *Commentaria Eleatica pars 1: Xenophanis Parmenidis Melissi doctrina e propriis philosophorum reliquiis exposita*. Altona, 1813.

BRÉHIER, E. *Études de philosophie antique*, Paris, 1955.

BROAD, C. D. *The Mind and its Place in Nature*, London, 1925.

BRUGMANN, C. 'Der griechische ἐνιαυτός', *Indogermanische Forschungen*, 15 (1903–4), 87–93.

BRUNET, P. and MIELI, A. *Histoire des sciences, I. Antiquité*. Paris, 1935.

BURCH, G. B. 'Anaximander the First Metaphysician', *Review of Metaphysics*, 3 (1949–50), 137–60.

BURCH, G. B. 'The Counter-Earth', *Osiris*, 1954, 267–94.

BURCKHARDT, G. *Heraklit*. Zürich, n.d. (after 1922).

BURNET, J. *Greek Philosophy: Part I, Thales to Plato* (all published). London, 1924.

BURNET, J. *Early Greek Philosophy*. 4th ed., London, 1930.

BUSSE, A. 'Der Wortsinn von λόγος bei Heraklit', *Rheinisches Museum*, 1926, 203–14.

BYWATER, J. 'On the Fragments attributed to Philolaus the Pythagorean', *Journal of Philology*, 1868, 20–53.

BYWATER, J. *Heracliti Ephesii Reliquiae*. Oxford, 1877.

CAMERON, A. *The Pythagorean Background to the Theory of Recollection*. Menasha (Wisconsin), 1938.

CAPEK, M. 'The Theory of Eternal Recurrence', *Journal of Philosophy*, 1960, 289–96.

CAPPARELLI, V. *La sapienza di Pitagora*. 2 vols., Padua, 1941 and 1945.

CAPPARELLI, V. *Il contributo pitagorico alla scienza*. Padua, 1955.

CASELLA, F. 'Hippolyti Refutationes 1.14', *Maia*, 1957, 322–5.

CHAIGNET, E. *Pythagore et la philosophie pythagoricienne*. Paris, 1873.

CHERNISS, H. *Aristotle's Criticism of Presocratic Philosophy*. Baltimore, 1935.

CHERNISS, H. 'Characteristics and Effects of Presocratic Philosophy', *Journ. of the Hist. of Ideas*, 1951, 319–45.

COOK, R. M. 'Ionia and Greece in the Eighth and Seventh Centuries B.C.', *JHS*, 1946, 67–98.

CORBATO, C. 'Studi Senofanei', *Annali Triestini*, 1952, 179–244.

CORNFORD, F. M. 'Mysticism and Science in the Pythagorean Tradition', *CQ*, 1922, 137–50, and 1923, 1–12.

Bibliography

CORNFORD, F. M. 'Innumerable Worlds in Presocratic Cosmogony', *CQ*, 1934, 1–16.

CORNFORD, F. M. *Plato's Cosmology*. London, 1937 (repr. 1948).

CORNFORD, F. M. *Plato and Parmenides*. London, 1939 (repr. 1950).

CORNFORD, F. M. *The Unwritten Philosophy and Other Essays*. Cambridge, 1950.

CORNFORD, F. M. *Principium Sapientiae: the origins of Greek philosophical thought*. Cambridge, 1952.

DARSOW, W. 'Die Kore des Anaximandros', *Jahrb. d. Deutsch. Archaeol. Inst.*, 1954, 101–17.

DEICHGRÄBER, K. *Hippocrates über Entstehung und Aufbau des menschlichen Körpers*. Leipzig, 1935.

DEICHGRÄBER, K. 'Xenophanes περὶ φύσεως', *Rheinisches Museum*, 1938, 1–31.

DEICHGRÄBER, K. 'Bemerkungen zu Diogenes' Bericht über Herakleitos', *Philologus*, 93 (1938/9), 12–30.

DEICHGRÄBER, K. 'Anaximander von Milet', *Hermes*, 1940, 10–19.

DELATTE, A. *Études sur la littérature pythagoricienne*. Paris, 1915.

DELATTE, A. *Essai sur la politique pythagoricienne*. Liège, 1922.

DELATTE, A. *La Vie de Pythagore de Diogène Laerce: édition critique avec introduction et commentaire*. Brussels, 1922.

DELATTE, A. *Les Conceptions de l'enthousiasme chez les philosophes présocratiques*. Paris, 1934.

DICKS, D. R. 'Thales', *CQ*, 1959, 294–309.

DIELS, H. 'Über Anaximanders Kosmos', *Archiv für Geschichte der Philosophie*, 1897, 228–37.

DIELS, H. 'Über Xenophanes', *Archiv für Geschichte der Philosophie*, 1897, 530–5.

DIELS, H. *Herakleitos von Ephesos, griechisch und deutsch*. 2nd ed., Berlin, 1909.

DIELS, H. 'Wissenschaft und Technik bei den Hellenen', *Neue Jahrbücher für das klassische Altertum*, 1914, 1–17.

DIELS, H. 'Anaximandros von Milet', *Neue Jahrbücher für das klassische Altertum*, 1923, 65–75.

DIÈS, A. *Le Cycle mystique*. Paris, 1909.

DIRLMEIER, F. 'Der Satz des Anaximandros von Milet', *Rheinisches Museum*, 1938, 376–82.

DIRLMEIER, F. 'Nochmals Anaximandros von Milet', *Hermes*, 1940, 329–31.

DODDS, E. R. *The Greeks and the Irrational*. California Univ. Press, 1951.

DÖRING, A. 'Wandlungen in der pythagoreischen Lehre', *Archiv für Geschichte der Philosophie*, 1892, 503–31.

DÖRRIE, H. 'Der Platoniker Eudoros von Alexandreia', *Hermes*, 1944, 25–39.

DREYER, A. *History of the Planetary Systems from Thales to Kepler*. Cambridge, 1906.

DUCHESNE-GUILLEMIN, J. *Ormazd et Ahriman: l'aventure dualiste dans l'antiquité*. Paris, 1953.

DUNBABIN, T. J. *The Western Greeks*. Oxford, 1948.

DUNBABIN, T. J. *The Greeks and their Eastern Neighbours*. Hellenic Society, 1957.

Bibliography

DÜRING, I. *Ptolemaios und Porphyrios über die Musik.* Göteborg, 1934.

EDELSTEIN, L. Review of L. A. Stella's *L'Importanza di Alcmeone*, in *AJP*, 1942, 371–3.

EVANS, M. G. 'Aristotle, Newton and the Theory of Continuous Magnitude', *Journ. of the Hist. of Ideas*, 1955, 548–57.

FARRINGTON, B. *Greek Science.* London (Penguin Books), 2 vols., 1944 (repr. 1949).

FESTUGIÈRE, A. J. *De l'Ancienne Médecine.* Paris, 1948.

FESTUGIÈRE, A. J. 'Les Trois Vies', *Acta Congressus Madvigiani*, vol. 2, Copenhagen, 1958, 131–78.

FIELD, G. C. *Plato and his Contemporaries.* London, 1930.

FRANK, E. *Plato und die sogenannten Pythagoreer.* Halle, 1923.

FRÄNKEL, H. 'Xenophanesstudien I und II', *Hermes*, 1925, 174–92 (I: 'X. als Geschichtsquelle', II: 'Die Erkenntniskritik des X.').

FRÄNKEL, H. 'A Thought-pattern in Heraclitus', *AJP*, 1938, 309–37.

FRÄNKEL, H. *Dichtung und Philosophie des frühen Griechentums.* New York (American Philol. Soc.), 1951.

FRÄNKEL, H. *Wege und Formen frühgriechischen Denkens.* 2nd ed., Munich, 1960.

FRANKFORT, H. (ed.). *Before Philosophy.* London (Penguin Books), 1949 and later reprints (originally published as *The Intellectual Adventure of Ancient Man* by Chicago University Press, 1946).

FREUDENTHAL, J. *Über die Theologie des Xenophanes*, Breslau, 1886.

FRITZ, K. VON. *Pythagorean Politics in South Italy: an analysis of the sources.* New York, 1940.

FRITZ, K. VON. 'νοῦς, νοεῖν and their derivatives in Homer', *CP*, 1943, 79–93.

FRITZ, K. VON. 'νοῦς, νοεῖν and their derivatives in Pre-Socratic philosophy excluding Anaxagoras', *CP*, 1945, 223–42 (Part I: from the beginnings to Parmenides) and 1946, 12–34 (Part II: the post-Parmenidean period).

FUNG YU LAN. *A short History of Chinese Philosophy.* London, 1950.

GANSZYNIEC, R. 'Die biologischen Grundlagen der ionischen Philosophie', *Archiv für die Geschichte der Naturwissenschaften und der Technik*, 1920, 1–19.

GIGON, O. *Untersuchungen zu Heraklit.* Leipzig, 1935.

GIGON, O. *Der Ursprung der griechischen Philosophie, von Hesiod bis Parmenides.* Basel, 1945.

GIGON, O. 'Die Theologie der Vorsokratiker', Fondation Hardt, *Entretiens*, 1 (1952), 127–55.

GILBERT, O. *Die meteorologischen Theorien des griechischen Altertums.* Leipzig, 1907.

GOETTLING, C. W. 'Die Symbole des Pythagoras', *Gesammelte Abhandlungen*, vol. 1, Halle, 1851.

GOMPERZ, H. "Ασώματος', *Hermes*, 1932, 155–67.

GOMPERZ, H. 'Problems and Methods of early Greek Science', *Journal of the History of Ideas*, 1943, 161–76.

GOMPERZ, H. 'Heraclitus of Ephesus', *Philosophical Studies*, Boston, 1953.

Bibliography

GOMPERZ, T. *Greek Thinkers: a history of ancient philosophy.* 4 vols., London, 1901–12 (vol. 1 transl. L. Magnus, vols. 2–4 transl. G. G. Berry).

GRÉGOIRE, F. 'Héraclite et les cultes enthousiastes', *Revue néoscolastique de philosophie*, 1935, 43–64.

GRIFFITHS, J. G. 'Herodotus and Aristotle on Egyptian Geography', *CR*, 1952, 10–11.

GUTHRIE, W. K. C. *The Greeks and their Gods.* London, 1950/54.

GUTHRIE, W. K. C. *Orpheus and Greek Religion,* corrected ed., London, 1952.

GUTHRIE, W. K. C. 'The Presocratic World-Picture', *Harvard Theological Review*, 1952, 87–104.

GUTHRIE, W. K. C. 'Anaximenes and τὸ κρυσταλλοειδές', *CQ*, 1956, 40–4.

GUTHRIE, W. K. C. 'Aristotle as a Historian of Philosophy', *JHS*, 1957 (i), 35–41.

GUTHRIE, W. K. C. *In the Beginning: some Greek views on the origins of life and the early state of man.* Methuen, 1957.

HACKFORTH, R. *Plato's Phaedrus.* Cambridge, 1952.

HACKFORTH, R. *Plato's Phaedo.* Cambridge, 1955.

HEATH, T. L. *Aristarchus of Samos, the Ancient Copernicus: a history of Greek astronomy to Aristarchus together with Aristarchus's treatise on the sizes and distances of the sun and moon.* Oxford, 1913.

HEATH, T. L. *A History of Greek Mathematics,* 2 vols., Oxford, 1921.

HEATH, T. L. *The Thirteen Books of Euclid's Elements.* 2nd ed., 3 vols., Oxford, 1926.

HEATH, T. L. *A Manual of Greek Mathematics.* Oxford, 1931.

HEIDEL, W. A. 'Qualitative Change in Presocratic Philosophy', *Archiv für Geschichte der Philosophie*, 1906, 333–79.

HEIDEL, W. A. 'The δίνη in Anaximenes and Anaximander', *CP*, 1906, 279–82.

HEIDEL, W. A. 'The ἄναρμοι ὄγκοι of Heraclides and Asclepiades', *TAPA*, 1909, 5–21.

HEIDEL, W. A. 'περὶ φύσεως: a study of the conception of nature among the Pre-Socratics', *Proceedings of the American Academy*, 1910, 77–133.

HEIDEL, W. A. 'The Antecedents of Greek Corpuscular Theories', *Harvard Studies in Classical Philology*, 1911, 111–72.

HEIDEL, W. A. 'On Anaximander', *CP*, 1912, 212–34.

HEIDEL, W. A. 'On Certain Fragments of the Presocratics', *Proceedings of the American Academy*, 48 (1913), 681–734.

HEIDEL, W. A. 'Anaximander's Book the Earliest Known Geographical Treatise', *Proceedings of the American Academy*, 1921, nr. 7.

HEIDEL, W. A. 'The Pythagoreans and Greek Mathematics', *AJP*, 1940, 1–33.

HEIDEL, W. A. *Hippocratic Medicine: its spirit and method.* New York, 1941.

HEINIMANN, F. *Nomos und Physis.* Basel, 1945.

HEINZE, R. *Xenocrates: Darstellung der Lehre und Sammlung der Fragmente.* Leipzig, 1892.

HENDERSON, ISOBEL. 'Ancient Greek Music', *New Oxford Dictionary of Music*, 1957, 336–403.

Bibliography

HÖLSCHER, U. 'Der Logos bei Herakleitos', *Festschrift Reinhardt*, Münster/ Cologne, 1952, 69–81.

HÖLSCHER, U. 'Anaximander und die Anfänge der Philosophie', *Hermes*, 1953, 257–77 and 385–417.

JAEGER, W. *Paideia: the ideals of Greek culture*, transl. G. Highet. 3 vols., Oxford, 1939–45 (vol. I, 2nd ed.).

JAEGER, W. *The Theology of the Early Greek Philosophers*. Oxford, 1947.

JAEGER, W. 'On the Origin and Cycle of the Philosophic Ideal of Life.' First published in *Sitzungsberichte der preussischen Akademie der Wissenschaften, philosophisch-historische Klasse*, 1928; Eng. transl. in Jaeger's *Aristotle*, 2nd ed., Oxford, 1948, 426–61.

JOEL, K. *Geschichte der antiken Philosophie*. Tübingen, 1921.

JONES, W. H. S. *The Medical Writings of Anonymus Londinensis*. Cambridge, 1947.

JUNGE, G. 'Die Sphärenharmonie und die pythagorisch-platonische Zahlenlehre', *Classica et Medievalia*, 1947, 183–94.

JUNGE, G. 'Von Hippasos bis Philolaos: das Irrationale und die geometrischen Grundbegriffe', *Classica et Medievalia*, 1958, 41–72.

KAHN, C. H. 'Anaximander and the Arguments concerning the ἄπειρον at *Phys.* 203 b 4–15', *Festschrift Ernst Kapp*, Hamburg, 1958, 19–29.

KAHN, C. H. *Anaximander and the Origins of Greek Cosmogony*. New York, 1960.

KAHN, C. H. 'Religion and Natural Philosophy in Empedocles' Doctrine of the Soul', *Archiv für Geschichte der Philosophie*, 1960, 3–35.

KARPINSKI, L. C. 'The Sources of Greek Mathematics' (in M. L. d'Ooge's translation of Nicomachus, *Introductio Arithmeticae*, 1926).

KARSTEN, S. *Xenophanis Colophonii carminum reliquiae*. Amsterdam, 1830.

KERFERD, G. B. 'The Date of Anaximenes', *Museum Helveticum*, 1954, 117–21.

KERFERD, G. B. Review of Thesleff 1957 (*q.v.*) in *CR*, 1959, 72.

KERN, O. *De Orphei Pherecydis Epimenidis theogoniis quaestiones criticae*. Berlin, 1888.

KERSCHENSTEINER, J. 'Der Bericht des Theophrastos über Herakleitos', *Hermes*, 1955, 385–411.

KIRK, G. S. 'Natural Change in Heraclitus', *Mind*, 1951, 35–42.

KIRK, G. S. *Heraclitus: the Cosmic Fragments*. Cambridge, 1954.

KIRK, G. S. 'Some Problems in Anaximander', *CQ*, 1955, 21–38.

KIRK, G. S. 'Logos, ἁρμονίη, lutte, dieu et feu dans Héraclite', *Revue philosophique*, 1957, 289–99.

KIRK, G. S. 'Men and Opposites in Heraclitus', *Museum Helveticum*, 1957, 155–63.

KIRK, G. S. 'Ecpyrosis in Heraclitus: some comments', *Phronesis*, 1959, 73–6.

KOSTER, W. J. W. *Le Mythe de Platon, de Zarathoustra et des Chaldéens*. Leiden, 1951.

KRANZ, W. 'Vorsokratisches I und II', *Hermes*, 1934, 114–19 and 226–8.

KRANZ, W. 'Kosmos als philosophischer Begriff in frühgriechischer Zeit', *Philologus*, 1938–9, 430–48.

KRANZ, W. 'Die Entstehung des Atomismus', *Convivium* (*Festgabe für Konrat Ziegler*), Stuttgart, 1954, 14–40.

Bibliography

KRANZ, W. 'Παλίντροπος ἁρμονίη', *Philologus*, 1958, 250–4.

KRAUS, W. 'Das Wesen des Unendlichen des Anaximandros', *Rheinisches Museum*, 1950, 364–79.

KUCHARSKI, P. 'Les principes des pythagoriciens et la dyade de Platon', *Archives de Philosophie*, 1959, 175–91 and 385–431.

LEVY, A. 'Sul pensiero di Senofane', *Athenaeum*, 1927, 17–29.

LEVY, I. *Recherches sur les sources de la légende de Pythagoras*. Paris, 1926.

LINFORTH, I. M. *The Arts of Orpheus*. Berkeley, California, 1941.

LOBECK, C. A. *Aglaophamus sive de theologiae mysticae Graecorum causis*. 2 vols., Koenigsberg, 1829.

LUKAS, F. *Die Grundbegriffe in den Kosmogonien der alten Völker*. Leipzig, 1893.

LUMPE, A. *Die Philosophie des Xenophanes von Kolophon*, diss. Munich, 1952.

LUTZE, F. *Über das Apeiron Anaximanders: ein Beitrag zu der richtigen Auffassung desselben als materiellen Prinzips*, diss. Leipzig, 1878.

MACCHIORO, V. *Eraclito: nuovi studi sull'Orfismo*. Bari, 1922.

McDIARMID, J. B. 'Theophrastus on the Presocratic Causes', *Harvard Studies in Classical Philology*, 1953, 1–156.

MACDONALD, C. 'Herodotus and Aristotle on Egyptian Astronomy', *CR*, 1950, 12.

MADDALENA, A. *I Pitagorici: raccolta delle testimonianze e dei frammenti pervenutici*. Bari, 1954. (Italian translation of the texts in DK, with introductory essays and notes.)

MARCOVICH, M. 'Note on Heraclitus', *CP*, 1959, 259.

MARCOVICH, M. 'On Heraclitus fr. 66 DK' (paper to 3rd International Congress of Classical Studies). Mérida (Venezuela), 1959.

MARCOVICH, M. 'Was Xenophanes in Paros (Greece), Pharos (Dalmatia), or Pharos (Egypt)?', *CP*, 1959, 121.

MARÓT, K. 'Die Trennung von Himmel und Erde', *Acta Antiqua Academiae Hungaricae*, 1951, 35–63.

MARTIN, H. *Études sur le Timée de Platon*. 2 vols., Paris, 1841.

MATSON, W. I. 'Cornford on the Birth of Metaphysics', *Review of Metaphysics*, 8 (1954–5), 443–54.

MÉAUTIS, G. *Recherches sur le Pythagorisme*. Neuchâtel, 1922.

MERLAN, P. 'Ambiguity in Heraclitus', *Proceedings of the XIth International Congress of Philosophy*, vol. XII, Brussels, 1953, 56–60.

MINAR, E. L. 'The Logos of Heraclitus', *CP*, 1939, 323–41.

MINAR, E. L. *Early Pythagorean Politics in Practice and Theory*. Baltimore, 1942.

MONDOLFO, R. *See also* ZELLER–MONDOLFO.

MONDOLFO, R. *Problemi del Pensiero Antico*. Bologna, 1936.

MONDOLFO, R. *L'Infinito nel pensiero dei Greci*. Florence, 1934; 2nd enlarged edition, under the title *L'Infinito nel pensiero dell'antichità classica*, 1956.

MONDOLFO, R. 'The Evidence of Plato and Aristotle relating to the ekpyrosis in Heraclitus', *Phronesis*, 1958, 75–82.

MORAUX, P. *Les Listes anciennes des ouvrages d'Aristote*. Louvain, 1951.

MORRISON, J. S. 'Pythagoras of Samos', *CQ*, 1956, 135–56.

Bibliography

MORRISON, J. S. 'The Shape of the Earth in Plato's *Phaedo*', *Phronesis*, 1959, 101–19.

NESTLE, W. *See also* ZELLER–NESTLE.

NESTLE, W. Review of Rathmann (*q.v.*) in *Philologische Wochenschrift*, 1934, 407–9.

NEUGEBAUER, O. 'Studien zum antiken Algebra', *Quellen und Studien zur Geschichte der Mathematik*, 3 (1936), 245–9.

NEUGEBAUER, O. *The Exact Sciences in Antiquity*. Princeton and Oxford, 1951.

NILSSON, M. *Griechische Feste von religiöser Bedeutung, mit Ausschluss der attischen.* Leipzig, 1906.

NILSSON, M. *Geschichte der griechischen Religion*, vol. I. Munich, 2nd ed., 1955.

OLMSTEAD, T. A. *A History of the Persian Empire*. Chicago, 1948.

ONIANS, R. B. *The Origins of European Thought*. Cambridge, 1951.

OŚWIECIMSKI, S. *Thales: the ancient ideal of a scientist, Charisteria T. Sinko.* Warsaw, 1951, 229–53.

OWEN, G. E. L. 'Zeno and the Mathematicians', *Proceedings of the Aristotelian Society*, 1957–8, 199–222.

PIAGET, J. *The Child's Conception of the World*. London, 1928.

PIAGET, J. *The Child's Conception of Causality*. London, 1930.

POHLENZ, M. 'Nomos und Physis', *Hermes*, 1953, 418–38.

RAMNOUX, C. *Vocabulaire et structures de pensée archaïque chez Héraclite*. Paris, 1959.

RATHMANN, W. *Quaestiones Pythagoreae Orphicae Empedocleae*, diss. Halle, 1933.

RAVEN, J. E. *Pythagoreans and Eleatics*. Cambridge, 1948.

REIDEMEISTER, K. *Die Arithmetik der Griechen*. Leipzig, 1940.

REINACH, T. 'La musique des sphères', *REG*, 1900, 432–49.

REINHARDT, K. *Parmenides und die Geschichte der griechischen Philosophie*. Bonn, 1916.

REINHARDT, K. 'Herakleitos' Lehre vom Feuer', *Hermes*, 1942, 1–27.

REYMOND, A. *Histoire des sciences exactes et naturelles dans l'antiquité grecque et romaine*. Paris, 2nd ed., 1955.

RICHARDSON, HILDA. 'The Myth of Er (Plato, *Republic*, 616B)', *CQ*, 1926, 113–33.

RIDGEWAY, W. 'What led Pythagoras to the doctrine that the world was built of numbers?', *CR*, 1896, 92–5.

RIVAUD, A. 'Platon et la politique pythagoricienne', *Mélanges Gustav Glotz*, vol. II. Paris, 1932.

RIVIER, A. 'L'Homme et l'expérience humaine dans les fragments d'Héraclite', *Museum Helveticum*, 1956, 144–64.

RIVIER, A. 'Sur les fragments 34 et 35 de Xénophanès', *Revue de Philosophie*, 1956, 37–62.

ROBIN, L. *Greek Thought*, transl. M. R. Dobie. London, 1928.

ROHDE, E. 'Die Quellen des Iamblichus in seiner Biographie des Pythagoras', *Rheinisches Museum*, 1871, 554–76 and 1872, 23–61.

Bibliography

ROHDE, E. *Psyche: The cult of souls and belief in immortality among the Greeks*, transl. W. B. Hillis. London, 1925.

ROSTAGNI, A. *Il verbo di Pitagora*, Turin, 1924.

ROUGIER, L. *La Religion astrale des Pythagoriciens*. Paris, 1959. (This is a semi-popular work. For full references to texts cited the author refers readers to his earlier work '*L'Origine astronomique de la croyance pythagoricienne en l'immortalité céleste des âmes*', published by the Institut français d'Archéologie orientale du Caire, 1933. This I have not been able to see.)

SAFFREY, H. D. 'Le περὶ φιλοσοφίας d'Aristote et la théorie platonicienne des idées nombres', *Philosophia Antiqua*, VII, Leiden, 1955.

SAMBURSKY, S. *The Physical World of the Greeks*. London, 1956.

SANTILLANA, G. DE and PITTS, W. 'Philolaus in Limbo: or, What happened to the Pythagoreans?', *Isis*, 1951, 112–20.

SCHIAPARELLI, G. *Scritti sulla storia della astronomia antica*. 3 vols., Bologna, 1925–7.

SELTMAN, C. T. 'The Problem of the First Italiote Coins', *Numismatic Chronicle*, 6th series, vol. IX (1949), 1–21.

SHERRINGTON, C. *Man on his Nature*. Cambridge, 1946 (Penguin Books, 1955).

SKEMP, J. B. *The Theory of Motion in Plato's Later Diologues*. Cambridge, 1942.

SKEMP, J. B. *Plato's Statesman: a translation of the* Politicus *of Plato with introductory essays and footnotes*. London, 1952.

SMITH, G. *Assyrian Discoveries*. London, 1875.

SNELL, B. 'Die Sprache Heraklits', *Hermes*, 1926, 353–81.

SNELL, B. 'Die Nachrichten über die Lehre des Thales und die Anfänge der griechischen Philosophie- und Literaturgeschichte', *Philologus*, 1944, 170–82.

SNELL, B. *The Discovery of the Mind: the Greek origins of European thought*. Oxford (Blackwell), 1953. (A third ed. in German, published in 1955, contains several additional chapters.)

STEBBING, L. S. *A Modern Introduction to Logic*, 2nd ed., London, 1933.

STELLA, L. A. 'L'Importanza di Alcmeone', *Reale Accademia dei Lincei*, Ser. 6, vol. 8, fasc. 4, 1939.

STOCKS, J. L. 'Plato and the Tripartite Soul', *Mind*, n.s. XXIV (1915), 207–21.

TANNERY, P. 'Pseudonymes Antiques', *REG*, 1897, 127–37 (II. Hicetas, 129–33; III. Ecphantus, 133–7).

TANNERY, P. *Pour l'histoire de la science hellène*. 2nd ed. by A. Diès, Paris, 1930.

TAYLOR, A. E. 'Two Pythagorean Philosophemes', *CR*, 1926, 149–51.

TAYLOR, A. E. *A Commentary on Plato's* Timaeus. Oxford, 1928.

THEILER, W. Review of Rostagni (*q.v.*), *Gnomon* I, 1925, 146–54.

THESLEFF, H. *On dating Xenophanes*. Helsinki, 1957.

THESLEFF, H. *An Introduction to the Pythagorean Writings of the Hellenistic Period*. Åbo, 1961.

THOMPSON, D'ARCY W. *A Glossary of Greek Fishes*. Oxford, 1947.

THOMSON, G. *Studies in Ancient Greek Society*. Vol. 2: *The First Philosophers*. London, 1955.

Bibliography

THOMSON, J. O. *A History of Ancient Geography.* Cambridge, 1948.

'UEBERWEG–PRAECHTER'. Ueberweg, F. *Grundriss der Geschichte der Philosophie,* ed. K. Praechter, 13th ed., Basel, 1953 (photographic reprint of 12th ed., 1923).

UNTERSTEINER, M. *Senofane, testimonianze e frammenti: introduzione, traduzione e commentario.* Florence, 1956.

VERDAM, H. D. 'De carmine simonideo quod interpretatur Plato in Protagora dialogo', *Mnemosyne,* 1928, 299–310.

VERDENIUS, W. J. 'Notes on the Presocratics', *Mnemosyne,* 1947, 271–89, and 1948, 8–14.

VLASTOS, G. 'Equality and Justice in the Early Greek Cosmogonies', *CP,* 1947, 156–78.

VLASTOS, G. 'Presocratic Theology and Philosophy', *Philosophical Quarterly,* 1952, 97–123.

VLASTOS, G. 'Isonomia', *AJP,* 1953, 337–66.

VLASTOS, G. Review of J. E. Raven's *Pythagoreans and Eleatics* in *Gnomon,* 1953, 29–35.

VLASTOS, G. 'On Heraclitus', *AJP,* 1955, 337–68.

VLASTOS, G. Review of Kirk's *Heraclitus: the Cosmic Fragments,* in *AJP,* 1955, 310–13.

VLASTOS, G. Review of Cornford's *Principium Sapientiae* in *Gnomon,* 1955, 65–76.

VOSS, O. *De Heraclidis Pontici Vita et Scriptis,* diss. Rostock, 1896.

WACHTLER, J. *De Alcmaeone Crotoniata.* Leipzig, 1896.

WAERDEN, B. L. VAN DER. 'Zenon und die Grundlagenkrise der griechischen Mathematik', *Mathematische Annalen,* 1941, 141–61.

WAERDEN, B. L. VAN DER. 'Die Arithmetik der Pythagoreer', *Mathematische Annalen,* 1948 (I: 127–53; II: 676–700).

WAERDEN, B. L. VAN DER. *Die Astronomie der Pythagoreer.* Amsterdam, 1951.

WAERDEN, B. L. VAN DER. 'Das grosse Jahr und die ewige Wiederkehr', *Hermes,* 1952, 129–55.

WAERDEN, B. L. VAN DER. *Science Awakening.* Groningen, 1954.

WALZER, R. *Eraclito, raccolta dei frammenti e traduzione italiana.* Florence, 1939.

WASSERSTEIN, A. 'Thales's Determination of the Diameters of Sun and Moon', *JHS,* 1955, 114–16.

WASSERSTEIN, A. 'Theaetetus and the Theory of Numbers', *CQ,* 1958, 165–79.

WEBSTER, T. B. L. 'From Primitive to Modern Thought in Ancient Greece', *Acta Congressus Madvigiani,* vol. 2, Copenhagen, 1958.

WEDBERG, A. *Plato's Philosophy of Mathematics,* Stockholm, 1955.

WEHRLI, F. *Die Schule des Aristoteles: Texte und Kommentar* (Basel), Heft I: Dikaiarchos, 1944; Heft II: Aristoxenos, 1945; Heft VII: Herakleides Pontikos, 1953; Heft VIII: Eudemos von Rhodos, 1955.

WEIZSÄCKER, C. F. VON. *The World-View of Physics,* 1952 (transl. by Marjorie Grene from 4th German ed., 1949).

Bibliography

WELLMANN, M. 'Eine pythagoreische Urkunde des IV. Jahrhunderts vor Christus', *Hermes*, 1919, 225–48.

WHITE, M. 'The Duration of the Samian Tyranny', *JHS*, 1954, 36–43.

WIGHTMAN, W. P. D. *The Growth of Scientific Ideas*. Edinburgh, 1950.

WIKANDER, S. 'Heraklit und Iran (résumé). Éléments orientaux dans la religion grecque ancienne', Colloque de Strasbourg, mai 1958, Paris, 1960, 57–9.

WILAMOWITZ, U. VON. 'Hippys von Rhegion', *Hermes*, 1884, 442–52.

WILAMOWITZ, U. VON. *Platon*. 2 vols. Berlin, 1920.

WILAMOWITZ, U. VON. *Der Glaube der Hellenen*. 2 vols. Berlin, 1931–2.

WOODBURY, L. 'Simonides on ἀρετή', *TAPA*, 1953, 135–63.

ZELLER, E. 'Über die ältesten Zeugnisse zur Geschichte des Pythagoras', *Sitzungsberichte der preussischen Akademie*, 1889, 985–96.

ZELLER, E. *Outlines of Greek Philosophy*, transl. S. F. Alleyne and E. Abbott. 13th ed. reprinted, 1948.

'ZELLER–MONDOLFO.' *La Filosofia dei Greci*, I. 1 and I. 2. (Zeller's work translated, edited and enlarged by R. Mondolfo, Florence, 1932 and 1938.)

'ZELLER–NESTLE.' E. Zeller, *Die Philosophie der Griechen*, I. Teil, 1. Hälfte (7th ed., 1923) and 2. Hälfte (6th ed., 1920), edited by W. Nestle (Leipzig).

ZOUMPOS, A. N. *Herakleitos von Ephesos als Staatsmann und Gesetzgeber*. Athens, 1956.

INDEXES

I. INDEX OF PASSAGES QUOTED
OR REFERRED TO

ACHILLES
Isagoge (19), 93 n. 1
AELIAN
V.H. III (7), 75
AESCHYLUS
Ag. (689), 425 n. 5; (750), 420; (1081), 425
n. 5; (1382), 85 n. 2
Cho. (515), 421, 422
Pers. (363), 421
Pr. (40), 421; (88), 466 n. 2; (231), 421;
(444), 400
Sept. (405), 425 n. 5; (517f.), 422; (829), 425
n. 5
Suppl. (100–3), 374–5
fr. (70 Nauck), 472 n. 2; (379), 85 n. 2; (390),
415 n. 3
AËTIUS
I (3, 1), 67; (3, 3), 84, 100, 108; (3, 4), 119,
131; (3, 19), 325; (7), 89 n. 1; (7, 12), 107;
(7, 13), 130; (7, 18), 248; (21, 1), 339–40
and n.; (23, 7), 448
II (1, 1), 208 n. 1; (1, 2), 325; (1, 3), 108,
378; (3, 3), 325; (4, 3), 456; (6, 2), 272;
(6, 5), 267, 272; (7, 1), 136 n. 2; (7, 7),
284; (9, 1), 277; (11, 2, 4), 136 n. 2; (13,
7), 90; (13, 10), 134; (13, 14), 392; (14, 3),
135 and n. 2; (15, 6), 93; (16, 2 and 3),
357; (16, 5), 93 and n. 1; (16, 6), 137; (17,
4), 484 n. 3; (18, 1), 392 n. 3; (20, 1), 93;
(20, 3), 392; (20, 12), 284–5; (20, 13),
286; (21, 1), 93; (21, 5), 49 *bis*; (22, 1),
134, 135; (23, 1), 135; (24, 1), 49; (24, 2),
93; (24, 3), 486; (24, 4), 394; (24, 9), 393;
(25, 1), 93; (28, 1), 94; (25, 15), 136 n. 2;
(29, 1), 94; (29, 3), 357; (29, 4), 283; (30,
1), 285; (30, 8), 394 n. 1; (32, 3), 458 n. 2
III (2, 11), 392 n. 3; (3, 1), 106; (3, 2), 139;
(3, 6), 392 n. 3; (3, 9), 464 n.; (4, 4), 390,
391; (5, 10), 139; (7, 1), 105; (9, 1–2),
328; (10, 3), 133; (10, 5), 294; (11, 3),
284; (13, 1–2), 284; (13, 1–3), 327; (13,
3), 325; (14, 1), 294; (15, 8), 133; (16, 1),
92

IV (3, 4), 321 n. 3; (5, 12), 355
V (1, 1), 373; (3, 3), 348, 349 n.; (16, 3), 349;
(16, 3), 348; (17, 3), 348; (19, 4), 102;
(25, 4), 314; (30, 1), 313
AGATHEMERUS
I (1), 74 n.
ALCMAEON
fr. (1), 344 and n. 1, 396, 414 n. 3; (2), 351;
(3), 348; (4), 313, 346
ALEXANDER POLYHISTOR
ap. D.L. VIII (25), 289, (27), (31), 203 n. 1
ALEXANDER OF APHRODISIAS
In Metaph. (38, 10), 303–4; (39, 14), 304 n.
1; (39, 24), 296; (40), 288, 301; (41, 1),
215 n. 1; (59), 245 n.; (60, 8), 457 n. 2;
(67, 3 ff.), 92, 97; (75, 15), 215 n. 1; (462,
16), 259 n. 3; (462, 34), 249 n. 1; (512, 20),
257 n.; (767), 304 n. 4; (827, 9), 274
In Meteor. (67, 3), 92, 97
ap. Simpl. *De Caelo* (532, 6ff.), 99 n. 3
ALEXIS
ap. Athen. (IV, 161 A–D), 187
AMMIANUS
XVII (7, 12), 139 n.
AMMONIUS
De Interpretatione (249, 1), 203 n. 3
ANATOLIUS
On the Numbers up to Ten (p. 30 Heiberg),
292–3
ANAXAGORAS
fr. (7), 420; (8), 208 n. 1; (11), 472 n. 1;
(12), 143 n., 454 n. 3, 472 n. 1
ANAXIMANDER
fr. (1), 76, 80, 448 n. 1
ANAXIMENES
fr. (1), 124f.; (2), 119, 131, 208 n. 1,
470
ANDRONICUS OF RHODES
ap. Themist. *in De Anima* (59, 8), 263 n. 1
ANONYMUS LONDINENSIS (18, 8ff.), 201
n. 2, 278 n. 3
ANTIPHANES
ap. Athen. (IV, 161 A), 187

Index of passages quoted or referred to

ANTISTHENES OF RHODES
Successions, ap. D.L. IX (6), 409 n. 2
APOLLONIUS RHODIUS
1 (640ff.), 164
APULEIUS
Apology (31), 253
Florida (15), 253
ARATUS
Phaen. (37–9), 51
Σ on Phaen. (p. 515, 27M.), 393 n. 1
ARCHILOCHUS
fr. (38), 447 n. 3; (68), 412 n. 1; (103), 415 n. 3
ARCHYTAS
fr. (1), 162 n. 2, 226, 336; (3), 336 n. 2
ARISTOPHANES
Clouds (227–30), 480; (230), 130; (404–7),
106 n. 1; (627), 130
Frogs (87), 420; (355), 425 n. 1; (1032),
195 n.
Peace (832f.), 158, 350, 471
Wasps (472), 420
ARISTOPHON
ap. Athen. (IV, 161E) and D.L. (VIII, 38), 187
ARISTOTLE
Anal. Post. (90a18), 223 n.
Anal. Prior. (41a26), 265 n. 2
De Anima (403b28), 351; (404a17), 306;
(404a20), 350; (404a21), 351; (404b11),
313–14; (405a5), 466; (405a19), 65;
(405a21), 132 n. 2; (405a25), 462, 466;
(405a29), 313; (405a30), 350; (405b2),
62 n. 1; (405b8), 384 n., 385; (407b20),
306; (407b22), 168 n. 3; (407b27), 307–8;
(408a5), 308; (408a18ff.), 313, 314;
(409a3), 262; (410b27), 307, 480; (410
b28), 129 n. 2; (411a7), 65; (419b33),
350; (420a4), 377 n. 1; (427a19ff.), 348;
(427a21), 318; (428b3), 486
De Caelo (268a10), 193; (268a11), 158 n. 3;
(270b21), 270; (278b9ff.), 111; (279
b12), 282, 380 n. 2, 390; (279b14), 437;
(280a11), 455; (290b12), 220; (290
b12ff.), 295–6; (291a8), 167 n. 2, 296;
(293a18), 283; (293a20), 154; (293a25),
213; (293b1), 287; (293b15), 283; (293
b25), 289; (293b33ff.), 294; (294a21),
394 n. 2; (294a28), 59; (294b13), 133;
(294b14), 294; (295b10), 98; (297b30ff.),
294; (298b29), 451; (300a15), 235; (300
a16), 236; (303b10), 107
Categoriae (15a30), 242 n. 2
Eth. Eud. (1223b22), 433; (1225a30), 329
and n. 2; (1235a25), 447
E.N. (1096a12), 215; (1096b5), 246; (1106

b29), 207, 246; (1132b21), 303 n. 2;
(1132b23), 213 n.; (1150b25), 409 n. 1;
(1155b4), 438; (1176a5), 445 n. 2
G.A. (730a6), 90 n. 3; (752b22), 348; (762
a20), 61
G.C. (333b18), 73 n. 2
H.A. (521a15), 349; (523a25), 90 n. 3; (558
a28), 91; (559b20), 129 n. 1; (560a6),
129 n. 1; (565b1), 104; (565b24), 104;
(581a12), 303 n. 5, 348
Metaph. (981b21ff.), 35 n. 1; (981b23), 33;
(982b12), 30 n.; (982b18), 41 n. 1; (983
b6ff.), 55; (983b7), 82; (983b20), 40;
(983b30), 60, 450 n. 2; (984a2), 45; (984
a5), 120, 123; (984a7), 320, 432; (984
a21), 63; (985b4ff.), 114 n. 1; (985b23),
216 n., 232; (985b26), 316; (985b29),
213 n., 239 n. 1, 302; (985b32), 229;
(986a1), 220 n.; (986a3), 213, 287;
(986a8), 225; (986a12), 215 n. 1; (986
a15), 234; (986a17), 240, 244; (986a22),
232, 243, 245; (986a27), 341; (986a30),
153; (986a31), 345; (986b10ff.), 368–9;
(986b14), 380 and n. 2; (987a13), 235;
(987a15), 240; (987a22), 303 n. 3; (987
a29), 331; (987a32), 450 n. 3; (987b11),
220 n., 229; (987b22), 235; (987b25),
264 n. 1; (987b28), 220 n., 229; (989a5),
63, 384 n., 385; (989b34), 239; (990a8),
241, 246; (990a12), 235; (990a16), 266;
(990a18), 302; (990a22), 239 n. 1, 202–3;
(996a6), 235; (1000a18), 40; (1001b26),
239; (1002a4), 259; (1005b23), 460;
(1010a13), 450 n. 3, 489; (1028b16), 259,
275 n. 1; (1028b21), 249; (1036b8), 234,
256–7; (1036b12), 262 and n.; (1061
a28ff.), 241; (1063a22, 35), 451; (1072
b30), 251; (1074b3), 40; (1078b19), 232;
(1078b21), 213 n., 239 n. 2, 302; (1080
b16), 234, 266; (1080b19), 277; (1083
b8), 235; (1090a20), 229; (1090a30),
235; (1090b5), 259, 275 n. 1; (1091a13),
239, 276; (1091a16), 246; (1091a17),
279 n.; (1092a32), 276; (1092b8), 258,
273; (1092b15), 238; (1093a1), 302;
(1093a13ff.), 303 n. 4; (1093a29), 223 n.;
(1093b2), 224 n. 3
Meteor. (342b35), 219 n. 2; (349a20), 106 n.;
(352a28ff.), 458 n. 4; (352a30), 388;
(353b5), 92; (353b7ff.), 391 n. 2; (353
b8), 97 n. 3; (353b9), 101 n. 1; (354a28),
138; (355a12), 485; (355a25), 97 nn. 3, 4;
(357b30), 461 n. 2; (360a11), 105 n. 2;
(365b6), 139

Index of passages quoted or referred to

ARISTOTLE (cont.)
  De Part. Animal. (642a28), 8; (645a17), 65
    n. 2; (660b28), 377 n. 1
  Phys. (185a18), 73 n. 2; (185b20), 442;
    (187a12), 120; (187a20), 77, 89; (193
    b12), 82; (203a4), 241; (203a6), 276;
    (203b6), 87; (203b7), 84; (203b10), 470;
    (203b11), 85; (203b13, 15), 83; (203
    b20), 84 n. 2; (203b23), 85 n. 1, 114 n.
    2; (204b24), 80; (205a1-4), 469 n.;
    (205a3), 456; (207a2), 85; (207a18),
    88; (208a8), 84; (213b22), 200 n. 2,
    209, 277; (216b24), 319; (218a33), 339;
    (219b2), 339; (222b18), 319; (223a22),
    339; (223a28), 338; (223b21), 339 n. 2;
    (253b9), 451; (263b27), 263; (264b27),
    351 n. 2; (265b24), 7
  Pol. (1259a6), 52; (1340b18), 308; (1340
    b26), 335
  De Respir. (472a8), 129 n. 2
  Rhet. (1398b14), 153; (1399b6), 371-2;
    (1407b11), 404, 407-8; (1407b16), 406
    n. 2, 424 n. 1
  De Sensu (437a24), 347 n. 2; (445a16), 307 n.2
  Top. (159b30), 442
  De Vita et Morte (469b7ff.), 61 n.
  fragments (Numbers refer to the third
    (Teubner) edition of V. Rose. Those
    that occur in the translated selection of
    Ross (Oxford translation of Aristotle,
    vol. XII) can be identified by consulting
    the table given by Ross on p. 155) (6),
    249; (10), 431 n. 1; (75), 154 n.; (190-
    205), 215 n. 1; (190), 154 n.; (191), 149
    n. 1, 154 n.; (192), 149 n. 1, 150, 154 n.;
    (195), 154 n., 188; (201), 200 n. 2, 277,
    279 n.; (207), 154 n., 215 n. 1; (Protr. fr.
    11 Ross, not in Rose), 168 n. 2
[ARISTOTLE]
  De Audibilibus (803b40), 227
  Magna Moralia (1182a11), 209 n. 1, 213 n.,
    239 n. 1, 302
  De Mundo (396b20), 411 n. 2
  MXG (977b1), 377
  Problemata (915a25), 336; (916a24), 352-3;
    (916a33), 351; (934b35), 434; (937a14),
    136 n. 2
ARISTOXENUS
  Mus. II (36), 298 n. 2
  fr. (ed. Wehrli) (1), 169 n. 1; (11a), 173 n. 3;
    (16), 173; (18), 180; (19), 169 n. 1, 310
    n. 1; (23), (24), 177 n. 3; (43), 151 n. 1;
    (90), 322
  ap. Iambl. V.P. (137), 199 n. 2

ARIUS DIDYMUS
  ap. Euseb. P.E. XV (20), 489, 491
  ap. Stob. Ecl. II (1, 17), 396 n. 3; (7), 199
    n. 1
ASCLEPIUS
  In Metaph. (39, 25), 343
AUGUSTINE, S.
  C.D. VIII (2), 44 n., 109, 130
AULUS GELLIUS
  IV (11, 1ff.), 188; (11, 9), 185 n. 1
Batrachomyomachia
  (8), 420
BOETHIUS
  Inst. Mus. I (10), 224 n. 1
CALLIMACHUS
  fr. (9) (Pfeiffer 1923, pp. 43ff.), 51; (128
    Schneider), 185 n. 1
CELSUS
  VII (7, 3), 137 n. 1
CENSORINUS
  De Die Natali IV (7), 103
  V (2ff.), 348
  VI (4), 348
  VII (2), 303 n. 5
  XVIII (8), 282 n. 2; (11), 458 nn. 2, 3
CHALCIDIUS
  In Tim. (279), 349 and n.
CHRYSIPPUS
  ap. D.L. VII (143), 202 n. 1
CICERO
  Ac. I (4, 15), 8
  II (37, 118), 44 n., 122, 377; (39, 123), 328
  De Divinatione I (3, 5), 373; (50, 112), 75
  De Finibus II (5, 15), 411 n. 2
  V (29, 87), 254
  N.D. I (5, 10), 149 n. 2; (10, 25), 109; (10,
    26), 127 n., 130 and n.; (11, 27), 200 n. 2,
    350; (11, 28), 378; (26, 74), 411
  III (14, 35), 411
  De Republica I (14, 22), 74
  Tusc. V (3, 8), 164; (4, 10), 8
CLAUDIANUS MAMERTUS
  De Statu Animae II (3), 311; (7), 321 n. 3
CLEANTHES
  Hymn to Zeus (20f.), 425 n. 5
CLEMENT OF ALEXANDRIA
  Protrepticus (I, 16 Stählin), 449 n. 2, 473; (I,
    49), 321 n. 3; (I, 50), 350; (I, 80), 484 n. 1
  Stromateis (II, 40), 362; (II, 41), 49; (II, 41-
    2), 253; (II, 44), 253, 414 n. 1; (II, 184),
    164; (II, 203), 163, 311; (II, 404), 413
    n. 2
CRITIAS
  fr. (25 DK), 401 n. 1

Index of passages quoted or referred to

DEMETRIUS MAGNES
  ap. D.L. VIII (84), 323
DEMOCRITUS
  fr. (5), 69 n. 1; (7–9), 326, 399 n.; (34), 208
  n. 1; (53), 423, 424; (82), 420; (117), 399
  and n.
DEMOSTHENES
  De Corona (259), 475 n. 2
DERCYLLIDES
  ap. Theon. Sm. (198, 14 H.), 49
DICAEARCHUS
  fr. (ed. Wehrli) (7–12), 315 n. 1; (34), 178
  n. 1
DIODORUS
  I (7), 69; (8), 400 n. 2
  XII (9), 176
DIOGENES OF APOLLONIA
  fr. (2), 208 n. 1; (3), 143; (4, 5), 129; (5), 88,
  382 n. 2
DIOGENES LAERTIUS
  I (3), 115; (8), 249 n. 2; (12), 204; (13), 45;
    (22), 47; (23), 46, 49, 54 n.; (24), 53, 66;
    (25), 51; (27), 51; (120), 158
  II (1), 74, 75, 94 n. 2; (2), 72, 74 and n., 75
    n. 4; (3), 44 n., 115; (8), 285 n. 3; (22),
    411–12; (46), 178 n. 2
  IV (13), 222 n. 3
  V (1), 291 n. 1; (25), 233, 341
  VII (143), 202 n. 1
  VIII (3), 173, 175, 254; (4), 164; (6), 158;
    (7), 320; (8), 158, 211 n. 1; (12), 190, 224,
    242 n. 1; (14), 222 n. 1; (15), 151 n. 1,
    155; (20), 190; (24), 184, 244; (24ff.),
    201 n. 3; (25), 276 n. 1, 289; (28), 201;
    (33), 188; (34), 183, 184 *bis*, 185, 188; (36),
    157; (40), 179; (46), 149 n. 2, 169 n. 1,
    178 n. 3, 273; (48), 208 n. 1, 294; (54),
    161; (54–5), 209 n.; (79), 334 n. 1, 335;
    (82), 335; (83), 314 n. 2, 341 n. 1, 343,
    344; (84), 320, 321 n. 2; (85), 327, 330
    n. 1, 343
  IX (1), 157, 406 n. 2, 408; (3), 409; (3–5),
    408 n. 3; (5), 406 n. 2, 416 *bis*; (6), 409
    nn. 1, 2, 411 n. 2; (7), 411, 486; (8), 455,
    460, 469 n.; (9), 462; (9–11), 483; (15),
    406 n. 2; (18), 363, 364, 365, 370; (19),
    374 n. 2, 376, 378, 391; (20), 362, 365, 395
    n. 6; (32), 91 n. 2; (33), 95 n., 138 n. 3;
    (38), 155
EMPEDOCLES
  fr. (2, 7), 399; (8), 82; (14), 279; (17, 20),
    305; (26, 5), 208 n. 1 *bis*; (28), 85; (38, 4),
    279; (42), 286; (52), 292; (62), 292; (96),
    258, 275 n. 2, 313; (105), 318, 348; (109),

  209, 313–14, 318, 348; (110, 10), 200,
    348 n.; (112, 4), 199; (115), 318 *bis*, 482;
    (127), 200 n. 1; (129), 161, 165; (132),
    318; (133), 209, 318; (134), 203 n. 3; (134,
    5), 111 n., 208 n. 1 *bis*; (137), 195 n.;
    (139), 200 n. 1; (140), 200 n. 1; (141), 185
    n. 2, 200 n. 1
EPICHARMUS
  fr. DK (2), 244 n. 1; (2, 12), 423; (12), 426
  n. 1; (20), 199 n. 1; (57), 423 n.
EPICTETUS
  II (8, 10), 202 n. 1
EUCLID
  II (def. 2), 242 n. 2
  VI (def. 2), 303 n. 2; (probl. 14), 303 n. 2
  XIII (13), 269
  Σ on XIII (v, 654 H.), 268
EUDEMUS
  (fr. 65 Wehrli), 336 and n. 1; (fr. 88), 281
  n. 2; (fr. 133), 52–3; (fr. 134), 51, 53; (fr.
  135), 53 n. 2; (fr. 145), 74, 98; (fr. 186),
  281 n. 2
EUDORUS
  ap. Simpl. *Phys.* (181, 10), 244; (181, 28),
  247 and n.
EUDOXUS
  ap. Porph. *V.P.* (7), 187
EURIPIDES
  Bacch. (663), 420; (1064), 372 n. 2
  Hel. (1014ff.), 466 n. 2
  Heracl. F. (1341ff.), 373
  Hipp. (952f.), 195 n.
  Med. (872), 421
  Or. (25), 85 n. 2
  Rhes. (924), 166 n. 3; (949), 166 n. 3
  Suppl. (201ff.), 401 n. 1; (533f.), 356, 466
    n. 2
  Tro. (884), 267 n. 2; (916), 421
  fr. (282 N.), 373 n.; (472), 372; (484), 69
    and n. 2; (839), 386 n., 466 n. 2; (877),
    466 n. 2; (910), 73 n. 2, 208 n. 1; (944),
    293 and n. 2; (971), 466 n. 2
EUSEBIUS
  P.E. X (14, 11), 74
  XV (20), 489
FAVORINUS
  ap. D.L. II (1), 75
  VIII (83), 343
GALEN
  De Usu Partium X (4), 137 and n. 1
  In Hippocr. de nat. hom. XV (25), 367 n. 1, 384
[GALEN]
  Hist. Phil. (7), 377 n. 1
  In Hippocr. de hum. I (1), 54 n.

Index of passages quoted or referred to

[GEMINUS]
[*Isagoge*] (p. 11 Manitius), 357 n.
Golden Verses
(47 f.), 225 n.
HERACLIDES
fr. (ed. Wehrli) (22), 164; (40), 163; (41),
164; (44), 164, 168; (88), 164, 204; (89),
164; (118–20), 324 n. 2
ap. D.L. 1 (12) (= fr. 87), 204
HERACLITUS (*bold figures denote a main entry*)
fr. (1), 407, 408, 412, 419, **424–5**, 425 n. 3,
427 and n. 2, 428 n. 1, 430, 434, 438, 447,
468, 477; (2), 412, 413, 417 n. 2, **425**, 426
n. 1, 427, 428 n. 1, 430; (3), 486; (4), 477–
8; (5), 472 *bis*, 475; (6), 462, 484; (7), 444
n. 2; (8), 438; (9), 412, 445; (10), 438 n. 1,
440 n. 1, 455, 490–1; (12), 434, 462, 489;
(13), 445 n. 2; (14), 473 n. 2; (15), 463,
475; (16), 474; (17), 412, 452 n.; (19),
412, 438; (21), 438, 477; (22), 411; (23),
446; (24), 472, **477**, 481 n. 3; (25), 481
and n. 3; (26), 433 n. 3, 477 n. 3; (27),
473, 477; (28), 413, 472, 473; (29), **412**,
477 n. 3, 478; (30), 110, 208 n. 1, 375 n. 2,
432, 438 n. 2, **454**, 455, 459, 464, 468, 471
and n.; (31), 420, 434, 453, **463**, 464; (32),
463, 472 n. 1, 490; (33), 409; (34), 412,
413 n. 2, 426 and n. 1, 438; (35), 204, 417;
(36), **433** *bis*, 434, 453, 462 *ter*, 463 *bis*,
476, 480, 491; (39), 412 n. 2, 420; (40),
157, 204, 368, **412**, 416, 417, 426 n. 1, 451;
(41), 88, **429** and n. 1, 465; (42), 412 n. 1,
413, 447 n. 3; (43), 409–10; (44), 410;
(45), 476; (46), 431, 451; (47), 482; (48),
446 n. 1; (49), 409; (49 a), 460 n. 3, 490;
(50), 414, **425**, 428 n. 1, 434 *bis*, 439; (51),
438 nn. 1, 2, **439** and n. 3, 460; (52), 478
n. 2; (53), 438 n. 2, 444, **446**, 472, 473;
(54), 440–1, 443 n. 2; (55), 429, 452 n.;
(56), 412, 414 n. 2, **443** n. 2; (57), 413,
442 and n. 1, 484; (58), 438 n. 2, 442 and
n. 2; (59), 438 n. 2, 443; (60), 438 n. 2,
443, 478 n. 2; (61), 438 n. 2, 445 and n. 2;
(62), 464, 478, 490; (63), 478, 482; (64),
382 n. 2, 425 n. 3, **428**, 429 and n. 1, 432
n., 464 n., 465, 471; (65), 455 *bis*, 474;
(66), 455 *bis*, 473 *bis*, 474 *bis*; (67), **444**
and n. 2, 445, 455, 472, 479; (68), 476 and
n. 1; (69), 475 n. 5; (70), 412; (72), 412,
419, 425 n. 3, 426, 452 n.; (73), 427; (74),
416 n. 3; (75), 430 and n. 2; (76), 453 and
n. 2, 462; (77), 433 and n. 4, 481; (78),
398, 413, 472; (79), 413, 472; (80), 438
n. 1, 439 n. 3, **447**, 473; (81), 417; (83),

413; (84 a), 444, 445, 452 n.; (84 b), 445
n. 3; (85), 433; (86), 472; (87), 412, 420;
(88), 445, 452, 479, 492; (89), 427 n. 3;
(90), 432, 457, **460–1**, 465, 469; (91), 441;
(92), 414; (93), 414; (94), **465**, 472, 473,
483; (96), 477; (97), 412; (98), 477 and
n. 2; (99), 483–4; (100), 453 n. 1; (101),
411, 414, 416 n. 3, **417–19**; (101 a), 429,
452 n.; (102), 413, 442, 445, 472; (103),
352, 427; (104), 412, 451, 454 n. 3; (106),
413 n. 1; (107), **415**, 425 n., 429, 451, 452
n.; (108), 420, 472; (110), 433, 445; (111),
401, 445; (113), 426 n. 1; (114), 410, **425**,
426, 431 n. 1, 454 n. 2, 472; (115), 481
n. 2; (116), 417 n. 2; (117), 433, 481;
(118), 433; (119), 482; (120), 465 n. 3;
(121), 409 n. 3; (123), 83 n., 418 n. 3, 441,
443 n. 2; (125), 449; (126), 445, 479;
(129), 157 and n., 158 n. 2, 417; (136),
481 n. 3
HERACLITUS HOMERICUS
Qu. Hom. (24), 490
HERMEIAS
Irris. (10), 91 n. 4
HERODORUS OF HERACLEA
ap. Athen. 11 (50, 57 f.), 285 n. 3
HERODOTUS
1 (17 ff.), 32; (30), 166, 204; (61), 414; (62,
2), 421; (74), 46; (75), 46, 51, 420; (95, 1),
422; (116, 5), 422; (117, 1), 421; (120, 2),
422; (120, 5), 421; (130), 46; (141), 420,
424; (143, 2), 421; (146), 50; (170), 51
11 (12), 387 n. 2; (25), 67; (48), 475 n. 4;
(53), 371 n. 1; (81), 160, 173 n. 4; (109),
33, 35 n. 1, 74, 422; (123), 160, 173 n. 4
111 (99, 2), 422; (119, 1), 424; (125 ff.), 346;
(131–2), 174 n. 3; (142, 5), 421; (146, 3),
421; (148, 1), 420
1V (8, 2), 420; (14), 159; (25), 294 n. 1; (28,
2), 420; (42), 294 n. 1; (93–4), 158–9;
(95), 148; (138, 1), 421; (151), 418
V (36, 4), 421
VII (36, 3), 422 *bis*; (42), 463 n. 3; (50, 2),
398 n.; (93), 421; (142), 418; (158, 5), 421
VIII (6, 2), 421; (68), 424; (100, 1), 420;
(100, 3), 421; (115), 91 n. 3
HESIOD
Erga (78), 421; (106), 421; (109 ff.), 400;
(121–5), 478; (789), 421
Theog. (27), 396 n. 2; (74), 454 n. 3; (124),
413 n. 1; (126–7), 134; (229), 421; (885),
454 n. 3; (890), 421
HIERONYMUS OF RHODES
ap. D.L. 1 (27), 51, 53

Index of passages quoted or referred to

HIPPOCRATIC WRITINGS
De Hebd. (IX, 436 L.), 303 n. 5
De Loc. in Hom. (VI, 276 L.), 353
De Morb. Sacr. (VI, 364 L.), 475 n. 1
De Nat. Hom. (VI, 32 L.), 58, 132 n. 2, 384
De Nat. Pueri (VII, 488 L.), 61 n., 91 n. 2
De Vet. Med. (I, 572 L.), 345 and n. 1; (I, 620 L.), 73 n. 2
De Victu (VI, 472 L.), 67 n.; (VI, 492 L.), 438 n. 1; (VI, 492–3 L.), 353; (VI, 640 L.), 319 n.
HIPPOLYTUS
Refutatio I (2, 2), 248 n. 2, 298; (2, 12), 173 n. 3, 253; (2, 14), 184 n. 2; (6, 1), 44 n., 83; (6, 2), 91 n. 4; (6, 3), 98; (6, 4), 90, 93; (6, 5), 106 n. 1, 110; (6, 6), 102; (6, 7), 105; (7, 1), 119, 121, 130; (1, 2), 127; (1, 3), 391; (1, 4), 133, 135; (1, 5), 134; (1, 6), 137, 138; (1, 8), 139; (9, 4), 294; (13, 2), 114 n. 3; (14, 2), 377; (14, 3), 384, 392; (14, 4–6), 387; (15), 200, 324–5, 399 IX (8, 1), 405; (9), 439; (10), 432 n., 474; (10, 8), 406
HOMER
Iliad I (530), 374; (545), 421 n.
II (485–6), 398 n.
III (21), 426 n. 1; (30), 426 n. 1; (277), 474; (396), 426 n. 1
IV (88), 418
V (590, 669, 711), 426 n. 1
VI (132), 475 n. 2
VII (99), 387
VIII (305), 375 n. 1
IX (600), 374 n. 3
XI (225), 422 n.
XIV (200), 60; (201), 60, 450 n. 2; (246), 60, 450 n. 2
XV (187ff.), 454 n. 3; (393), 420
XVI (150), 129 n. 1
XVII (547), 393 n. 1; (551), 393 n. 1
XVIII (107), 447 n. 1; (309), 439 n. 3, 447 n. 3; (399), 60
XXI (196), 60, 391
Odyssey I (56), 420, 421
V (248), 220
VIII (14), 375 n. 1
X (303), 82 n. 2; (469), 47 n. 2
XI (100), 418 n. 1
XV (90), 418 n. 1
XIX (246), 99
XXII (347), 415
Σ on *Il.* (XI, 27), 393 n. 1
Homeric Hymns
Demeter (210), 449 n. 2; (480ff.), 197 n. 2

Hermes (317), 421
IAMBLICHUS
De Comm. Math. Sc. (76, 16ff. Festa), 191
De Mysteriis I (11), 476
V (15), 475
In Nicom. (77, 9 P.), 244 n. 3; (109, 9), 322
Protrepticus (9), 154 n., 168 n. 2
V.P. (19), 254; (25), 190; (72), 151; (81), 191–2; (85), 188; (87), 191–2; (88), 150 n. 1, 219, 268; (94), 151; (104), 341 n. 1; (115), 224 n. 1; (137), 199 n. 2; (148), 273 n. 3; (150), 225 n.; (151), 254; (154), 254; (177), 176; (197), 334 n. 1; (199), 155 n. 2; (231ff.), 185 n. 1; (248), 178 n. 3; (249), 179; (251), 179, 180; (252f.), 180; (257), 320 n., 322; (267), 323, 341 n. 1
[IAMBLICHUS]
Theologumena Arithmeticae. See under title of work
ION OF CHIOS
fr. (1), 158; (2), 150, 158 *bis*, 182 n. 2; (4), 158 and n. 1
ISAIAH
xxix (15), 474
ISOCRATES
Busiris (28), 163; (29), 151
Panegyricus (157), 425 n. 1
JUVENAL
X (28ff.), 409 n. 1
LACTANTIUS
De Opif. Dei (17, 6), 136 n. 2
LASUS
fr. (1 Diehl), 220
LEUCIPPUS
fr. (2), 423
ap. D.L. IX (33), 138 n. 3
LUCIAN
De Sacrif. (6), 129 n. 1
Vit. Auct. (14), 409 n. 1
LUCRETIUS
I (639), 411
V (805 f.), 386
LYDUS
De Mensibus (p. 21 W.), 254; (pp. 99–100 W.), 164, 184 n. 2, 185 n. 1
MACROBIUS
S. Scip. (5), 297; (14, 19), 224 n. 1, 311, 481
MARCUS AURELIUS
IV (46), 416 n. 3
V (27), 202 n. 1
VI (42), 430 and n. 2
MARK, S.
viii (18), 438

MATTHEW, S.
  x (39), 438
  xiii (35), 388 n. 1
MELISSUS
  fr. (2; 3; 4), 337 and n. 1
MIMNERMUS
  fr. (10 D.), 485
MNESIMACHUS
  ap. D.L. (8, 37), 187
MOSCHUS
  fr. (6 N.), 401 n. 1
NICANDER
  Alex. (302), 91 n. 3
  Ther. (355; 392), 91 n. 3
NICOMACHUS
  Arithm. II (6 and 7), 261
  Harmon. (245 ff. Jan), 224 n. 1; (252), 298
    n. 2
OENOPIDES OF CHIOS
  ap. Procl. *in Euclid.* (283, 9), 242 n. 2
OLYMPIODORUS
  De Arte Sacr. (24), 384
ONESICRITUS
  ap. Strab. xv (716), 187
Orphica
  fr. (p. 52 Kern), 198 n. 1
  Hymn. 87 (3), 267 n. 2
OVID
  Trist. IV (3, 1–2), 51
PARMENIDES
  fr. (1, 15), 421; (4, 3–4), 408 n. 2; (5), 427
    n. 1; (6, 4), 398; (6, 8–10), 408 n. 2; (8,
    44), 379 n. 2; (8, 50), 421; (8, 57–8), 408
    n. 2; (12, 3), 88
PHILISTION
  fr. (4 W.), 359
PHILO
  De Aet. Mund. (21), 480 n.
  De Opif. Mund. XIII (44), 352
  De Vit. Mos. I (6), 478 n. 2
PHILOLAUS
  fr. (1), 330; (6), 223 n.; (8), 244 n. 3; (12),
    267; (14), 311, 331; (14–15), 163 and n. 1;
    (22), 311
  ap. Anon. *Lond.* (18, 8 ff.), 278–9 and n.
PHILOPONUS
  De Anima (9, 9), 132 n. 2; (87, 11), 432–3;
    (88), 341 n. 1; (88, 11), 343 n.
PINDAR
  Isth. V (13), 421; (14), 196; (26), 421; (28),
    166 n. 3
  Nem. IV (31), 423; (44 f.), 220
  Ol. II (22), 423; (83–6), 415 n. 1
  VII (21), 420

VIII (4), 421
Pyth. II (66), 420
  III (61), 199
  IV (59), 420; (101), 420; (132), 420
  VIII (38), 421
  X (54), 421
  fr. (131 Schr.), 319 n., 321 n. 3, 431 n. 1

PLATO
  Alcibiades I (Σ on 121 E), 341 n. 1
  Apology (21 B), 418 n. 2; (34 B), 422
  Charmides (156 D), 158
  Cratylus (386 A), 401 n. 2; (400 C), 311;
    (401 D), 450; (402 A), 450, 489; (402 B),
    450 n. 2; (409 A), 286 n.; (413 B), 456;
    (413 B–C), 432, 474; (413 C), 473
  Epinomis (977 B), 284 n. 2; (981 C), 270;
    (983 A), 296 n.; (984 E–985 A), 271
  Epistle VII (338 C), 334 n. 2
  Gorgias (493 A), 311; (507 E), 209, 305
  Laws (782 C), 195 n.; (889 A), 144; (895 E),
    351 n. 1; (898 A), 356; (899 B), 65
  Lysis (214 B), 73 n. 2
  Meno (76 A), 209; (80 D), 395 n. 5; (81 A, C),
    209
  Phaedo (57 A), 310 n. 1; (61 D), 310; (61 E),
    311 n. 1, 329; (62 B), 162 and n. 3, 311
    n. 1; (63 E), 204–5; (81 B), 312; (81 D),
    312; (86 B), 309; (88 D), 310; (96 A), 73
    n. 2; (96 B), 349; (99 B), 294; (107 D), 482;
    (108 E), 100; (109 A–110 B), 272 n. 1;
    (110 B), 295 and n. 1; (111 D), 292; (113 B),
    202 n. 1
  Phaedrus (245 C), 351; (247 A), 293 n. 3
  Philebus (24 B), 207 n.; (28 D), 429 n. 1;
    (43 A), 460 n. 2
  Protagoras (320 C ff.), 400 n. 3; (343 A), 50
  Republic (431 ff.), 317; (498 A), 484; (500 C),
    210, 423; (525 D), 213; (527 B), 213;
    (529 D), 162 and n. 1, 214; (530 D), 153,
    162, 227; (531 A), 220; (581 C), 165;
    (600 B), 148, 167
  Sophist (242 C–D), 368; (242 D), 456 n., 460;
    (242 E), 440
  Symposium (186 D), 435–6; (186 E), 88 n. 2;
    (187 A), 438 n. 1; (207 D), 467–8
  Theaetetus (147 D), 265 n. 2; (151 E), 90 n. 3;
    (152 A), 401 n. 2; (152 E), 450 n. 2; (155 D),
    30; (160 D), 450; (174 A), 52; (176 A), 199
    n. 1; (179 D ff.), 410; (179 E), 450 n. 2;
    (180 B), 411 n. 3; (180 C–D, 181 A), 450
    n. 2; (182 A), 79 n.
  Timaeus (22 B–C), 388; (30 A), 338; (34 B–C),
    316; (35 B ff.), 214; (36 E), 316; (37 D, E,

PLATO (*cont.*)
38 B, C), 338; (39 C), 339 and n. 1; (39 D),
282; (40 A), 356; (40 B–C), 291; (41 C), 349
n.; (41 E), 291; (43 D–E), 354; (45 D), 377 n.
1; (47 B–C), 210; (50 E), 444 n. 2; (52 D),
338; (58 D), 270; (67 B), 227; (80 A), 227
PLINY
N.H. II (12, 53), 46; (31), 74; (187), 44 n.
V.(112), 29 n. 2
XVIII (118), 184
XXV (5), 254
XXX (2), 254
XXXV (77), 174 n. 1
XXXVI (82), 53
PLOTINUS
Enn. IV (8), 411
PLUTARCH
Adv. Colot. (1118 C), 417
Aqu. et Ign. Comp. (957 A), 484 n. 1
Conv. (147 A), 53
De Am. Prol. (494 C), 104
De An. Procr. (1012 D), 263 n. 1; (1012 E), 253
De Aud. Poet. (17 E), 395 n. 1
De Def. Orac. (415 F), 457; (422 B, D), 322
De E (390 A), 273 n. 1; (392 B), 489; (392 B–
C), 441; (392 C), 453 n. 2
De Fortuna (98 C), 484 n. 1
De Is. et Os. (34), 58
De Prim. Frig. (947 F), 124
De Pyth. Orac. (402 F), 54 n.
De Ser. Num. Vind. (559 C), 489
De Soll. Anim. (982 C), 104
De Superst. (116 C), 427 and n. 3
Qu. Conv. (727 D), 103 n.; (727–8), 184 n. 1;
(729 C), 194 n. 2; (730 E), 102 f.
Qu. Nat. (912 A), 489; (912 C), 450
Qu. Plat. (1003 C), 269; (1007 C), 339
V. Lyc. (25), 377 n. 1
V. Sol. (2), 51
[PLUTARCH]
Strom. (II), 90, 98, 102, 110; (III), 127 n.,
133 *bis*; (IV), 373, 381 n., 384, 387, 392;
(X), 136 n. 2
De Vita Hom. (4), 443 n. 2
POLYBIUS
II (39, 1–4), 179
PORPHYRY
De Abst. I (15), 194; (23), 194; (26), 163, 194
II (4), 194; (28), 194
III (26), 195
De Antr. Nymph. (19), 184
V.P. (6), 173 n. 3, 254; (7), 187; (9), 173;
(12), 173 n. 3, 253; (15), 190; (18), 175
n. 1; (19), 151, 186; (20), 225 n.; (30) 297

n. 3; (37), 192; (41), 254; (43), 188; (44),
184 n. 2, 253; (54), 178 n. 3; (57), 179;
(57 ff.), 180; (85), 188
Quaest. Hom.
ad *Il.* IV, 4 (I, 69, 6 Schrader), 442
ad *Il.* XIV, 200 (I, 190 Schrader), 427
In Ptolem. Harm. (31, 1 Düring), 222
PRATINAS
fr. (4 *b* Diehl), 220
PROCLUS
In Eucl. (p. 61 Friedl.), 219; (65), 268; (65,
3 ff.), 52, 53; (97), 262, 263; (250, 20 ff.),
54 n.
In Tim. (III, p. 141, 11 Diehl), 291; (III, 143,
26), 291
PTOLEMY
Harmon. I (8), 224 n. 2
II (12), 224 n. 2
RUFUS
ap. Oribasius (III, 156), 348
SABINUS
ap. Galen. *in Hippocr. de nat. hom.* (XV, 25),
384
SENECA
De Tranq. XV (2), 409 n. 1
Epist. (58, 23), 490; (108, 17 ff.), 194 n. 1
Quaest. Nat. II (18), 106 n. 2; (56), 463 n. 3
SEXTUS
Adv. Math. I (95), 300 n. 3
IV (4 f.), 263 n. 2
VII (14), 367 n. 1; (49), 367 n. 1, 395 n. 1;
(49 ff.), 395; (51), 397 n. 1; (65), 73 n. 3;
(99), 263 and n. 2; (110), 367 n. 1, 395
n. 1, 396; (126 ff.), 430 and n. 1; (127),
432; (132), 424 n. 1
VIII (325 ff.), 397 n. 1; (326), 395 n. 1
IX (127), 200 n. 2, 278
X (280), 260 n. 3; (281), 263 and n. 2; (282),
262; (313), 384
Pyrrh. I (55), 445 n. 2; (223–4), 366; (225)
377
II (18), 395 n. 1
III (19), 263 n. 2; (154), 263 n. 2; (155), 300;
(230), 478
SIMONIDES
fr. 4 Diehl (1 and 6), 428 n. 2
SIMPLICIUS
De Anima (32, 3), 341 n. 1; (32, 6), 343 n.;
(68, 10), 275 n. 2
De Caelo (202, 13), 108; (202, 14), 106,
107–8;. (386, 22), 215 n. 1; (468, 27),
297 n. 3; (471, 4), 93; (471, 5), 298
n. 1; (511, 25), 283–4; (511, 30), 215 n.;
(512, 9 ff.), 281 n. 1, 290; (512, 12), 287;

Index of passages quoted or referred to

SIMPLICIUS (cont.)
(515, 25), 283 n.; (522, 7), 367 and n. 1;
(532, 6ff.), 99 n. 3; (557, 10), 73; (615, 15),
107; (615, 20), 123; (621, 9), 268 n. 1
Cat. (412, 26), 447
Phys. (22, 26ff.), 369 n. 3; (22, 29f. Diels),
367; (23, 16), 377; (23, 21ff.), 469 n.; (23,
32), 54 n.; (23, 33), 320, 432; (23, 33-24,
4), 457 and n. 1; (24, 4), 458 n. 5; (24, 13),
76; (24, 14), 43 n. 2; (24, 16), 109; (24,
21), 81 n. 2; (24, 26), 43 n. 2, 121; (25, 11),
64 n. 1; (61), 219 n. 2; (70, 16), 73; (77,
31), 489-90; (149, 32), 120 n.; (150, 20),
89 n. 2; (150, 22), 77; (150, 24), 79 n.;
(181, 10), 244; (181, 28), 247 and n.; (455,
20), 243 n. 4; (651, 26), 277; (732, 26),
186 n. 2, 281 n. 2; (1121, 5), 108; (1165,
27), 270; (1165, 34), 291 n. 1; (1313, 8),
490; (1313, 11), 450 n. 1
SOLON
fr. (19 Diehl), 303 n. 5
SOPHOCLES
Ajax (35), 88 n. 2
Antig. (332ff.), 400
El. (59), 420; (466), 422
O.C. (1163), 421
O.T. (84), 483 n. 1
Phil. (352), 422; (730), 421
Trach. (1), 420; (101), 474; (473), 199 n. 1
fr. (558 N., 615 P.), 293 n. 3
STESICHORUS
fr. (6 Diehl), 485; (11, 1), 420
STOBAEUS
Ecl. I (1, 29b), 107; (18, 1c), 215 n. 1,
277
II (1, 17), 396 n. 3
III (1, 172), 412 n. 2; (20, 53), 409 n. 1
STRABO
I (p. 7 C.), 44 n., 74; (49), 387 n. 2
VI (p. 263 C.), 176; (280), 334 n. 1
XIV (632), 409; (638), 217; (642), 411
n. 2
XV (716), 187
SUDA
47, 73, 320
THEMISTIUS
In de an. (p. 59, 8 Spengel), 263 n. 1
THEO SMYRNAEUS
(p. 14 Hiller), 425 n. 1; (22), 244; (50), 228;
(56), 222; (57), 224; (61), 226; (97), 277;
(106), 260; (140f.), 299 n.; (150), 300
n. 4; (198), 49
THEODORETUS
IV (5), 377, 384; (22), 486 n. 2

THEOGNIS
(141-2), 398 n.; (254), 421; (415), 418;
(417f.), 422
Theologumena Arithmeticae
(p. 53 de Falco), 217; (84; 85), 260, 332 n. 3
THEOPHRASTUS
De Igne (44), 90 and n. 4
De Sensu (25f.), 347; (42), 130
ap. D.L. IX (6), 409 n. 1
ap. Simpl. de cael. (615, 13), 43-4 n.
ap. Simpl. phys. (22, 26), 378; (23, 21ff.),
469 n.; (23, 33), 320, 432; (24, 4), 321
n. 2; (24, 14), 43-4 n.; (24, 26), 44 n.; (24,
31), 127 n.
fr. 89 (p. 189 Wimmer), 228-9
THUCYDIDES
I (1, 3), 344 n. 2; (22, 1), 420; (97), 420
II (50), 420
VI (46, 5), 420
VII (56, 4), 422
TIMAEUS
fr. (133 Jacoby ap. Clem. Str. I, 64), 362
TIMON
ap. D.L. IX (6), 411 n. 2
TYRTAEUS
fr. (9, 1 Diehl), 421
VARRO
ap. Augustin. C.D. VII (17), 396 n. 3
VIRGIL
Geor. III (271ff.), 129 n. 1
VITRUVIUS
praef. VII (14), 335
WISDOM OF SOLOMON
xi (20), 312 n. 4
XANTHUS OF LYDIA
ap. Strab. I (49), 387 n. 2
XENOPHANES (bold figures denote a main entry)
fr. (1), 360, 364, 375; (2), 364; (3), 365; (7),
157, 363, 370, 421; (8), 362, 363; (10), 371;
(11), 371, 375; (14), 365, 371, 375, 381,
382; (15), 371, 375; (16), 371, 373, 375;
(17), 372 n. 1; (18), 376, 399; (21a), 366;
(22), 360, 366; (23), 374, 375 bis and n. 1,
376 bis; (24), 374 and n. 2, 375; (25), 373,
374, 382 bis and n. 2; (26), 374, 381, 382;
(27), 383, 385 bis; (28), 367, 381 n.; (29),
385; (30), 391; (32), 392; (33), 385, 387;
(34), 376 bis, 395 and n. 1, 396, 397 bis,
399, 414 n. 3; (35), 398; (36), 397; (37),
388 n. 2; (38), 376, 401; (40), 399; (42),
366
XENOPHON
Anab. III (2, 17), 475 n. 1
Mem. I (1, 11), 73 n. 2

II. GENERAL INDEX

Bold figures in entries referring to modern scholars denote a main entry.

Abaris, 218, 319

Abraham, 403 n. 1

abstention from animal flesh, Pythagorean, 187ff.; Porphyry's work on, 193f.

abstract, expression of by adjective and article, ambiguity of, 79, 116, 242

abstraction, attained by Greeks, 37f.; of number, not recognized by Pythagoreans, 242

Academic School, 22

Academy of Plato, 10

actuality and potentiality in Aristotle, 12

Acusmata (*Symbola*), Pythagorean, 183ff., 188

acusmatici, 191ff.

Adrastus, on Pythagorean musical theory, 228

aer (ἀήρ): earlier history of word, 126; among elements, reputedly first in Empedocles, 453; as vapour, 81; in Heraclitus, 453 and n. 2; less pure form of *aither*, 471, 480; in Anaximander's cosmology, 92; and *pneuma*, in Anaximenes, 131 and n.; renders invisible but can be seen through, 95 n. 1

Aeschylus, 374f., 400, 415

Aethalides, and Pythagoras, 159 n. 1, 164

Aëtius, as source, xiv

Agathemerus, 74 n.

Ahriman (Areimanios), 250

Ahuna Vairya, 488

Ahura Mazdah, nature of, 254f.

Aion, 478 n. 2

air (see also *aer*), as a god, in Aristophanes, 130; solidified in Empedocles, 136; as *arche* in Anaximenes, 115ff.; as source of life in popular belief, 128f., cf. 480; divine, 130; in Anaximenes, substance both of human soul and divine universe, 131f., 201; parallel with human soul in Diogenes of Apollonia, 470; surrounding air of Anaximenes and Diogenes of Apollonia, 470

aither, 466 and n. 2, 470, 480; in Parmenides, 136; substance of the *daimones* in Plato, *Epinomis*, 271-3; in Aristotle, 271; as a 5th element, 270, 271; equated with Zeus, 487

Alcmaeon of Croton, 232f., 246, 247, 313, 341ff.

treatise on by Aristotle, 233

date, 341-3, 342 n., 344 n. 1, 357ff.; relationship to Pythagoreans, 341; writings, 344; range of interests, 344, 345; originality of, 359

medical interests, 314, 344; empirical approach, 345, 346, 349, 358; his physiology summarized by Theophrastus, 347

account of the senses, 347f.; brain as central organ, 348, 349; hearing, 349; sleep, 349; summary by Theophrastus, 343; distinguished between sensation and thought, 348

doctrine of opposites, 232f., 341; his pairs not enumerated, 247, 345; their application to mankind, 345f.; health depends on balance of opposites, 313, 346, 436

on the soul, 354ff.; in everlasting motion, hence divine, 313, 350; soul-stuff animates the cosmos, 355, with circular motion, 354; motion impeded by crasser material of body, 356; fate after death, 354ff.: no evidence for belief in transmigration, 354f., or in soul as incarnate *daimon*, 355

human conjecture distinguished from divine certainty, 344, 396

astronomy, 357; void identified with air, 280 n. 1, 349f.

relation to Empedocles, 348, 358, 359; to Anaxagoras, 359; to Plato, 354

[Alexander of Aphrodisias], on Aristotle's account of Pythagorean generation from numbers, 257

Alexander the Great, 15

Alexander Polyhistor, 201 and n. 3, 244; and Pythagorean commentaries, 249, 256, 289

Alexandria, 16

Alexis (comic poet), 187, 189

Allan, D. J., 450 n. 3

Allman, G. J., 46 n. 1

ἀλλοίωσις, 89 n. 2

Alyattes, of Lydia, 32, 46

Amasis, 173

amber, 66

General index

ambiguity, of oracles, 414

Anacreon, 174

ἀναθυμίασις, 462 n. 1

Anatolius, quoted, 292f.

Anaxagoras, 5, 6, 88, 89 n. 1, 96, 120, 286, 294, 300, 357; Mind in, 6, 143, 327, 454 n. 3, 472 n. 1; spoke of dwelling-places in moon, 285 n. 3; discovered illumination of moon by sun, 286

Anaximander, 43, 71, 72ff., 120, 279, 294, 337; background, 29; Ionian spirit of *historie*, 43; date, 72; no mention of before Aristotle, 72; taste for travel, 75; reputed statue of, 75 and n. 3

works, 73, 75, 76; his map, 74, 99 n. 2; sundial, 74f.

cosmogonic views, 76ff., 89ff.; on basic stuff of the cosmos, 279; account of *genesis*, 76; the opposites, 78ff., things rather than qualities, 79; heat a first agent of *genesis*, 92; the *gonimon* of, 90, 278; *arche* the Unlimited, 76; in eternal motion, 91; cosmos formed by 'separating off', 89ff.; 'injustice' of elements, 76f., 80, 101; compared with Heraclitus, 447, 453; meaning of *apeiron*, 82, 83ff.; nature of *apeiron*, 109, 272; both indefinitely large and having no beginning in time, 337f.; the *apeiron* material, 242; *apeiron* living and divine, 114, 470; equated with the mixture of Empedocles and Anaxagoras, 77 n. 3; whether in fact a mixture, 87 and n. 2; ultimate prevalence of fire over water, 101; end of the cosmos, 100 and n. 2

cosmology: numerical basis of, 219; astronomical achievements, 74; formation of heavenly bodies, 93f.; dimensions of celestial objects, 95f.; sun, moon and eclipses, 49, 93; shape and position of earth, 98; release from view that earth is supported, 99; alleged view that earth is in motion, 99; origin of sea, 92; sea will dry up eventually, 92, 101, 388; 'innumerable worlds', 106ff.; the ἄπειροι οὐρανοί gods, 112

meteorology, 105; winds and rain, 105 and n. 2

origin of life, 101ff.

Anaximenes, 43, 208 n. 1, 279; background, 29; date and writings, 115; use of simile, 138f.; relation to Anaximander, 115; influence on Xenophanes, 391; deduction of his character, 139f.; no mention of before Aristotle, 72

cosmogony: no detailed working-out of system, 134; influence of mythical cosmogonies, 134; basic stuff of cosmos, 279; his *arche* air, 115f.; *arche* alive, immortal and eternal, 128; *arche* in eternal motion, 127; *psyche* its source of motion, 128; association of air and life (*psyche*), 128; rational motives for choice of air, 119ff.; unconscious and traditional reasons, 127ff., 130; not retrogressive choice, 116; rarefaction and condensation of air, 120ff., 460; accounts by Simplicius and Hippolytus, 121; natural evidences of the process, 124; linked with Anaximander's doctrine of opposites, 124f.; 'offspring' of air the other elements, 122; difficulty of producing fire from air *via* earth, 134; gods arisen from air, 130; analogy between cosmic air and human soul, 131, 201, 428

formation of natural world: evidence lacking, 123; earth, shape and position, 133; heavenly bodies originate from the earth, 133f.; stars of nature of fire, containing earthy bodies, 134; fixed in the crystalline, or like fiery leaves, 135; possible distinction of planets and fixed stars, 135; at great distance from the earth, 138; sun flat like leaf, 135; eclipses, 135; universe in effect a hemisphere, 138; heavenly bodies revolve round earth, not under, 137f.; probably not thought divine, 131; meteorology, 139

contrasted implicitly with pluralists by Aristotle, 120; explanation of change, 119f.; reduces qualitative differences to quantitative, 126

Andronicus, editor of Aristotle, 366 n. 2

animals, criterion of distinction from man, in Alcmaeon, 348

animation of nature, general belief in, 350

anim(at)ism, 64, 66, 350

anthropomorphism, abandoned by Milesians, 44; attacked by Xenophanes, 371ff.

Antiochus, teacher of Cicero, 22

Antiphanes, 187

Antisthenes of Rhodes, *Successions*; on Heraclitus, 409 n. 2

apeiron (ἄπειρον), 77; uses of word analysed by Aristotle, 83; not necessarily 'infinite', 381 and n.; of indistinguishable parts, 85f.; 'having no beginning or end' (Melissus), 337; used of spheres and rings, 85; also temporal aspect, 280; temporal

515

33-2

General index

apeiron (cont.)
    and spatial senses not distinguished,
    337; divine, 87f.; Aristotle's discussion,
    241; in account of Xenophanes's god,
    377f.; εἰς ἄπειρον 'indefinitely', 378, 393
    and n. 4. *See also* Anaximander
Aphrodite, 27, 70
apokrisis or *ekkrisis* (separation), as a cosmo-
    gonic process, 89ff., 105, 119; of seed in
    womb, 91
Apollo, 28, 44; particular patron of Pytha-
    goreans, 203, 205; in Empedocles, 203
    n. 1; Hyperborean, Pythagoras identified
    with, 149, 231; Delphic, characterized by
    Heraclitus, 414
Apollodorus, chronologist, 46; method of fix-
    ing *floruit*, 49f.; on date of Anaximander,
    72; of Xenophanes, 362; of Heraclitus, 408
Apollonia, Milesian colony, 75
Apollonius of Tyana, 169
ἀπόρρητα (or ἄρρητα), Pythagorean, 150
ἀπόρρητος λόγος, in *Phaedo*, 310
Apsu, Babylonian male principle, 60
Aratus, quoted by S. Paul, 24
arche (ἀρχή), early search for, 28f.; term first
    used by Anaximander, 77; senses of, 57;
    divinity of, 88, 89 n. 1, 128; as reservoir
    of all that exists, 82 and n. 1; cause of
    changes in, 63; living and sentient acc. to
    Anaximenes, 128ff., 470; as conscious
    directive force, 88; in Milesians, always
    intermediate between opposites, 457;
    related to world as soul to body, 316; in
    Alcmaeon, none, 345; in Anaximander,
    76f.; in Anaximenes, 115; in Hippasus,
    320; in Pythagoreans, the beginning of
    number-series, the unit, 244; in Xeno-
    phanes, 378
Archedemus, associate of Archytas, 334
Archelaus, on shape of earth, 294
Archilochus, 415; criticized by Heraclitus, 412
    and n. 1, 413, 447 n. 3
Archippus of Tarentum, Pythagorean, 180
Archytas of Tarentum, 147, 162 n. 2, 180, 273,
    322, 333ff.; date, 334; friendship with
    Plato, 333; extent of interests, 335f.;
    public life, 333f.; possible influence in
    Plato's *Republic*, 333; contributions to
    mathematics, 219, 335 and n. 1; on infinite
    extension, 336; on the Decad, 260;
    mechanical applications, 335; theories on
    sound, 226ff.; ratios of musical scales
    determined, 335; biology, 336; genuine-
    ness of fragments, 335 and n. 3; on

calculation as ruling force in nature and
    morals, 336
Areimanios, 249 n. 2
arete (ἀρετή), as well-being of soul, 317
Aristarchus, heliocentric theory, 290, 293
Aristeas of Proconnesus, 159
aristocracy, in literal sense, under Pythagoras's
    constitution, 175
aristocrats, character of in sixth century, 365
Aristophanes, 9, 106 n. 1, 130
Aristophon (comic poet), 187
Aristotelian terminology, 56
Aristotle, survival of early ideas in, 2; philo-
    sophy of, 12ff.; on origin of philosophy,
    30, 31; as historian of philosophy, 41ff.,
    56, 82, 120, 214f., 237; cautious attitude
    on Thales, 54f.; abundance of surviving
    work, 25; classificatory work, 14; scheme
    of causation, 63, 236; classification of
    motion, 382; modernity of outlook, 237;
    definition of time, 338; on sensation and
    thought, 348; *Ethics*, 13; *Protrepticus*,
    154, 171; on Alcmaeon, 341; on Archytas,
    334 n. 1; on Heraclitus, 437, 451; on
    Philolaus, 329; references to Pythagoras,
    153f.; on the Pythagoreans, 42, 154f.,
    183, 200, 214ff., 229ff.; on Xenophanes,
    366–7; relation to Democritus, 12; to
    Plato, 12
Aristoxenus, 150, 169, 178 n 3, 188–9, 191; on
    conformity with the divine, 199, 210; on
    Pythagoras's enthusiasm for the study of
    number, 177, 221; on Hippasus and con-
    cordant intervals, 322; on Philolaus, 329;
    wrote life of Archytas, 334 n. 1
ἄρρητα (or ἀπόρρητα), of Pythagoreans, 150
Arta, in Persian religion, 255
Artemis, 44
Asclepius, 436
assumptions, popular scientific, 3; of philoso-
    phers, unconscious, 116ff.
Astyages, 46
ataraxia, 17
ἀθάνατον, quality of the divine only, 68
Athena, 28
Athens, 7, 8
ἀτμίς, 462 n. 1
atomism, of Leucippus and Democritus, 5, 6f.,
    129, 143; of Ecphantus, 325ff.; innumer-
    able worlds in, 113f.
atoms, motion of, in Democritus and Epicurus,
    18; numbers finite according to Ecphan-
    tus, 326f.
autarkeia, 17

General index

autarkes, of the Stoic Sage, 20
αὐτοέν, in Speusippus, 249

Babylonia, religious governance of practical life in, 35; astronomy of, 34f., 138 n. 2; mathematics, 34f., 36, 217f.; cosmology, 59f.
Bacchoi, 231; in Xenophanes, 372
Bacchus, properties of, 372
Baccou, R., 38 n. 1, 96 n. 1
Bailey, C., 116
Baldry, H. C., xii, 61 n., 62, 90, 133 n. 1
Bathyllus, 344
beans, Pythagorean prohibition on eating: explanations of, 184f.; rationalized politically, 185; denied, 191; taboo elsewhere, 185 n. 1
Beare, J. I., 347 n. 3, 348
Becker, O., 218 n., 265 n. 2
beginning and end, joining of (Alcmaeon), 353
being, potential and actual, in Aristotle, 13; and becoming (Platonic), in relation to Heraclitus, 441
Berger, H., 138 n. 1
Berosus, 94
Berthelot, M., 58 n. 3
Bias of Priene, 412 n. 2
birth, analogous to cosmogony, in Anaximander, 90; in Pythagoreanism, 278f.; interest in, a feature of primitive thought, 62 n. 2
body as tomb or prison, Pythagorean and Orphic view, 311, 331, 464; whether found in Heraclitus, 477, 478
Boeckh, A., 328
Boeder, H., 420 n. 1, 471 n.
Boehm, F., 183 n. 1, 190
Boll, F., 46 n. 1, 48 n. 3, 135
Bömer, F., 311 n. 3
Bonitz, H., 239 n. 2
Booth, N. B., 265 n. 1, 408 n. 2
Bowra, C. M., 363 n., 364 n., 365
brain, as centre of sensation, in Alcmaeon and Plato, 349
Brandis, C. A., 367 n. 1
breath, universal, 200 n. 2, 278. See also *pneuma*, soul
breathing, of cosmos, in Pythagoreanism, 272, 277, 278ff., 340
Bréhier, E., 265 n. 2
Broad, C. D., 57
Broecker, W., 416 n. 1
Bro(n)tinus, 319, 344 and n. 1
Brugmann, C., 47 n. 2

Brunet, P., 221
Burch, G. B., 96 n. 2
Burnet, J. (selected references), 62, 65, 66 n. 1, 84 n. 3, 112, 126, 131, 166 n. 1, 204, 221, 222f., 285 n. 1, 288, 299, 323, 369 n. 2, 481
Bywater, I., 171, **330**ff.

Cadmus, 50 and n.
Callimachus, 185 n. 1, 189, 343
Cambridge Platonists, 24
Cambyses, 218, 253, 254
Cameron, A., 157 n., 161 n. 1, 164 n., **165, 310** n. 2, **311** n. 1, 330 n. 2
Campbell, L., 401 n. 2
Capek, M., 282 n. 1
Carneades, 22
Casella, F., 387 n. 4
Catana, stay of Xenophanes at, 363
cause: Greek interest in causes, 36; in early philosophers, contrasted with Aristotle's scheme, 63f.; Aristotelian senses of, 234, 236; moving cause, problem of, 6f., 89, 145; ultimate cause, as chance or necessity (Atomists, Empedocles), 143f.; as 'nature', mechanical and non-theological, 144; mythological view of, 26ff., 40f., 140f.; *logos* as cause in Stoicism, 21
celature, 174
Celsus, 137
Celts, and Pythagoreans, 254
Cercops, Pythagorean, 319
Ceyx, wedding of, in Hesiod, 103
chance, and nature, Plato quoted on, 144
change, continuous and imperceptible, in Heraclitus, 451
Cherniss, H., **52, 75, 84** n. 3, 87 n. 2, 97 n. 4, **120, 122**f., **155** n. 1, 215 n. 2, **229, 307** n. 3, **381**, 456 n., 465 n. 1
China, and Pythagoreanism, 251f.
Christianity, interaction of with pagan thought, 23f.
Chrysippus, of Soli, 19, 20, 21, 202 n. 1
Chrysogonus, flute-player, 423 n.
Cicero, on Epicurus, 19; on Carneades, 22; on Anaximander, 75 n. 2; on Heraclitus, 411; *De Officiis*, 22; *Somnium Scipionis*, 297
circle, and beginning and end (Alcmaeon), 351ff.; beginning and end common (Heraclitus), 427 (Parmenides), 427 n. 1
circular motion, in Aristotle, 13; the only continuous, 351f.; and psychic functions, 356

circularity, connexion with life, 351 ff.; and reason, 356 f.; special perfection of, in Aristotle, 2; and later, 3, 207; of time, 452; or cycle (περίοδος), of the body, 353

cithara, 224

city, the natural unit for the Greek, 15; combination of cities into leagues, 15

city-states, after Alexander, 15

classification, neglected by early Greek thinkers, 37

Claudianus Mamertus, on Hippasus, 321; on Philolaus, 311

Cleanthes, 293; on soul in Heraclitus, 434, 491

Clement of Alexandria, 24; on mystery cults, in *Protrepticus*, 473

Cleobulina, mother of Thales, 50

coagulation (πάγος), of air in Empedocles, 136

cocks, forbidden to epileptics, 190; to Britons, 190; white cocks forbidden to Pythagoreans as sacred to lunar god, 188

Codrus, 409

Cohen, M. R. and Drabkin, I. E., 53 n. 2

coinage (incuse), in Croton and neighbourhood, 176

Colophon, birth-place of Xenophanes, 363

comic poets, on Pythagoreans, 163 f., 187

common, of Heraclitus's Logos, 425 f.; use of term in Heraclitus, 447 etc.

common sense, reaction to physical speculation, 9

concordance, in Greek music, 223

concordant intervals, *see* intervals

condensation and rarefaction of air, in Anaximenes, 120 ff., 460; alleged of Heraclitus's fire, 460

conflagration. See *ecpyrosis*

Confucius, 175

contradiction, law of, broken by Heraclitus, 460, etc.

contraries. *See* opposites

convention, distinction of from nature, 9, 10

Cook, R. M., 47 n. 4

Copernicus, 207; encouraged by theories of Philolaus, Heraclides, Ecphantus, 327

Cornford, F. M. (selected references), 111 f., 118, 125, 172, 221, 242 nn., 244, 249, 250, 264, 265 n. 1, 273 n. 2, 301 n. 2, 303, 309 n., 315, 323, 344, 381 n., 382 n. 2

corporeality (*see also* matter), emergence of distinct notion of, 326

cosmogony, mythical, xi, 28 f., 60, 68, 119, 141; creative and evolutionary contrasted, 142; design in, 142 f.; Hebrew, 60; Babylonian, 59 f.; Egyptian, 58 f.; in Diodorus,

68 f.; given in terms of organic life in earlier Greek speculation, 90 f.; stages in Presocratics between *arche* and variety of nature, 122 f., 273; alternate creation and dissolution of world, 281 f.

Cosmopolis, in Stoicism, 21

cosmos (see also *kosmos*, world), compared to seven-stringed lyre, 298; in Pythagoreanism, is a harmony, 229, 308; living and intelligent to Pythagoreans, 289; a god to Xenophanes, 381 ff., to Heraclides of Pontus, 324; prevalent scheme of, in sixth and fifth centuries, 470 f.; in Zeno, the work of a providence, 20; views on its destructibility, 389 f.

counter-earth, invented by Pythagoreans, 213, 282 ff., 288; attributed to Philolaus, 284; to Hicetas, 328; meaning the moon, 290 f.

Crates, 93

Cratylus, acquaintance of Plato with, 450, 468; a Heraclitean heretic, 450 n. 3; extreme application of views of Heraclitus, *ibid.*; and the river-statement, 489

creation, and evolution in ancient thought, 142; *ex nihilo*, foreign to Greek thought, 454 n. 3

creator, in Plato, 143; absence of in early Greek philosophy, 142

Critias, on progress in human culture, 400

Croesus, 32, 115; and Thales, 46; and the oracle, 414

Croton, migration of Pythagoras to, 174; home of Alcmaeon, 341; medical school at, 174 n. 3, 346 f.

crystalline, meaning 'viscous and transparent', 137; question of, in Anaximenes, 135 f.

crystals, geometrical forms of, 226 n. 2, 269

cube, duplication of, by Archytas, 335; fiery monadic, 292 f.; connected with element earth by Pythagoreans, 267

cults (*see also* mystery-religions), agrarian, 197

curiosity, source of philosophy, 30

Cyaxares, 46

Cybele, cults of, 23

cycle, of births, Orphic and Pythagorean (*see also* transmigration), 202 f., 354, 478, 480; parallel with Heraclitus, 480, 481 n. 1; of the seasons, 80, 352; astronomical, and cyclic renewal of the universe, in Heraclitus, 458; of world-renewal and of world creation and destruction, 458 n. 5

cyclic change, in Heraclitus, 433

Cylon, conspiracy and revolt of, 178 f., 320

Cynic School, 10, 187

General index

Cyrenaic School, 10
Cyrus, 32, 46, 362, 363

daimon, daimones, meanings of word, 318, 482;
in Hesiod, etc., 318f.; as divine attendants of Dionysus, 291; as divine element
in man, 318f.; in the *Epinomis*, 271
Damasias, archonship of, 47
Darius, 174 n. 3, 346, 362, 488
darkness, as a substance to early Greek mind,
126
Darsow, W., 75 n. 3
dasmos (δασμός), 29, 454 n. 3
death, in Empedocles, common to body and
soul, 314; one element living the death of
another (Heraclitus), 453; due to inability
to 'join the beginning to the end'
(Alcmaeon), 351, 354
decad, 153, 225, 260, 288
definition, 232; general definitions introduced
into philosophy by Socrates, *ibid.*; in
terms of form, not matter (Pythagorean),
257
Deichgräber, K., 342 n., **366, 377** n. 2, **379** n. 2,
384 n., **385**, 390 n. 2, **407**, 462 n. 2
Delatte, A., 151 n. 2, 157 n., 161 n. 1, 164 n.,
173 n. 3, 183 nn. 1 and 2, 184 n. 3, 193 n.,
200 n. 2, 202 n., 203 n. 1, 225 n. 1, **335**
n. 3, 417 n. 1, 478 n. 2
Delian League, 8
Delphic oracle, 414, 417, 418
Delphic precepts, 183
Demeter, 197, 449
Demetrius of Magnesia, 323 and n. 2; on
Philolaus, 330
Demetrius of Phaleron, 16
Democedes, of Croton, court physician to
Polycrates, 174; his career, 346f.
democratic government, in fifth-century
Athens, 8
Democritus, 6f., 69 n. 1, 89 n. 1, 113, 232, 325,
326, 327, 357; book on Pythagoras, 155;
on soul, 129, 201; on shape of earth, 294;
simile of motes in air, 307; atomic system
adopted by Epicurus, 18; 'the laughing
philosopher', 409; notion of microcosm
in, 208 n. 1; on human ignorance, 399
Dercyllides, on Anaximander, 98
design in nature, in Plato's *Laws*, 12, 144;
absence of in early Greek philosophy,
142ff.
destructions, of human race by fire, flood, etc.,
101, 388; of world, whether in Heraclitus,
455

Deucalion, 388
development, human: two conflicting views in
classical Greece, 400; viewed as a progress, 400f.
διακοσμεῖν, 454 n. 3
dialectical method, 9
Dicaearchus, 169; on Pythagoreans, 151, 175,
186 and n. 1; on soul, 315
Diels, H., xiiif., **47** n. 2, 48 n. 3, 107 n., 110,
161 n. 1, 324, **362** n., 366 n. 1, **368**, 377 n. 2,
408 n. 2, 423 n.
Diès, A., 377 n. 2
difficulties of earliest philosophers, 118
dimension, defined by Nicomachus, 261
Dingle, H., 3
Diogenes of Apollonia, 92, 121, 123, 131, 135
n. 1, 294; follows Anaximenes on air and
soul, 129f.; restores unity of matter and
spirit, 143; draws parallel between air and
human soul, 470
Diogenes Laertius, as source, xiv; on Pythagorean *Acusmata*, 183; on meeting of
Philolaus and Plato, 329; on Alcmaeon,
344
Dionysius II of Syracuse, 334
Dionysus, 27, 478 and n. 2; phallic processions
in honour of, 475 n. 4; identified with
Hades by Heraclitus, 463, 475, 476
divinity, to Greeks synonymous with everlasting life, 480; conception of τὸ θεῖον both
rationalist and mystic, 203; assimilation
to, 199, 318, (through knowledge according to Empedocles) 209
of cosmos, in Ecphantus, 326
of primary entity, 4; in Anaximander, 87f.;
in Anaximenes, 128
of primary substance, in Milesians, 88
divisibility, infinite, 265 n. 1
δίζημαι, meanings of, 418
Dodds, E. R., 159 n. 1, 307 n. 1
dodecahedron, in Pythagoreanism, assigned to
enveloping cosmos or *ouranos*, 266; and
Hippasus, 268; date of construction, 268;
equated with sphere, 268f.; Etruscan of
sixth century B.C., 269 n. 2; pyrites
crystals in form of, 226 n. 2
Dörrie, H., 244 n. 4
Drabkin, I. E., *see* Cohen
Dreyer, J. L. E., 93 n., 95 n., 97 n. 2, 98, 136 n. 1,
294 n. 1
Duchesne-Guillemin, J., 254f.
Dunbabin, T. J., 50 n. 1, 174 n. 4, 175f., 178
n. 1
Düring, I., 171 n., 222 and n. 2

519

dyad, indefinite, 202 n., 248, 264
dynamis (δύναμις), usage of the term, 325 n. 1;
of atoms, fresh conception of Ecphantus,
326

earth, shape of: in Anaximander, 98 f.; in
Anaximenes, 133; in Pythagoreans,
293 ff.; evidence of Aristotle on believers
in flat earth, 294; sphericity: date of discovery, 293 ff., 393 n. 2; first mentioned
in Plato's *Phaedo*, 295; position: central,
in early Greek thought, 289; freely suspended (Anaximander), 98, 99 f.; central,
rotating about own axis (Ecphantus,
Heraclides), 327, (Hicetas), 328 f.; central
view adopted by Socrates, 100; a planet,
circling the centre, 282; planetary notion
short-lived, 290; called star by Pythagoreans, because an instrument of time
(Aristotle), 290; earth substance not
taken as element by any who posit unity
(Aristotle), 385; whether so taken by
Xenophanes, 383 ff.; its generative power,
292; as mother of all life, 291, 385 f.; as
Hestia (hearth of universe), 293
earthquakes, predicted by Anaximander, 75
and n. 2; storks give warning of, 75 n. 2;
according to Anaximenes, 139
earthy bodies in sky (Anaximenes), 134,
135
Echecrates, 169, 273, 310
eclipses, and date of Thales, 46–9; in Anaximander, 96; in Anaximenes, 135; in
Leucippus, 138 n. 3; in Xenophanes,
393 f.; in Alcmaeon, 357; according to
Heraclitus, 483, 486; prediction of, 33;
extent of Babylonian prediction, 48; of
moon, 283 and n., 285, 286
ecliptic. *See* zodiac
Ecphantus, 200 and n. 3, 323 ff.; his existence
defended, 323 f.; date uncertain, but
apparently influenced by atomists, 325;
supposed work *On Kingship*, 324 n. 3;
evidence for his views, 324 f.; cosmology
reminiscent of the *Timaeus*, 326; his
cosmos unique, 326 f.; declared Pythagorean monads corporeal, 325 f.; atomic
theory distinct from Democritus's, 326;
his atoms limited in number, 325 and n. 2;
combination of *genesis* from numbers,
and atomism, 325; on impossibility of
knowledge, 399
ecpyrosis (ἐκπύρωσις), 456 n., 473 and n. 1, 474;
spread of idea back into earlier thought,

457; associated with Great Year, 458;
question of, in Heraclitus, 455 f.
Edelstein, L., 342, 357
effluences, Empedocles's theory of, 209
egg, the Orphic, 69, 90; wind-eggs, 90 n. 3,
129
Egypt, journeys to by early Greek philosophers, 32, 48, 217; scientific and tech-
nological achievement of, 30, 32 ff.; its
limitations, 34 f.; cosmogony, 58 f.
Egyptian religion, supposed Greek borrowings from, 160
eicosahedron, connected with water by
Pythagoreans, 267
ekstatikos (ἐκστατικός), 231
Elea, foundation of, 362 f.; association with
name of Xenophanes, 363
Eleatic School, founded by Parmenides, 363;
reputedly by Xenophanes, 361, 363
elements, four explicitly distinguished by
Empedocles, 5, 267; but developing in
earlier thought, 122 f.; geometrical structure, in *Timaeus*, 267; mutual transformation, 276 n. 1; in Anaximander, swallowed
up by their opposites, 81; fifth element:
history of, 270 f.; five elements in Chinese
philosophy, 252
elenchtic methods, 9
Eleusinian mysteries, 197 f., 199, 203, 425 n. 1,
449
embryology: of Anaximander, 103; of Alcmaeon, 348
Empedocles, 5, 6, 120, 136, 165, 172, 177, 199,
200 n. 1, 267, 294; motive cause in, 88;
four elements in, 122 f.; relationship with
Pythagoreans, 160 f., 208 n. 2, 258; verses
on Pythagoras, 160 f.; on proportion of
elements in natural substances, 258, 275,
313; denial of empty space, 279; cosmos,
cyclic destruction and rebirth of, 389;
created by random interplay of elements,
144; cosmology: two suns, 286; shape of
earth, 294; fire at earth's centre, 292;
origin of life from within the earth, 292;
formation of organic substances, 313;
materialistic outlook on sensation and
thought, 318; theories of the soul, 313 f.,
318; Love and Strife in, 305, 437; Apollo
in Empedocles, 203 n. 2; theories of
sensation and thought, 348; relation to
Heraclitus, 437; to Alcmaeon, 348, 358 f.;
physis in, 82; speaks of 'unlimited
sphere', 85; kinship of nature, 186, 208,
278; preached abstention from beans, 185,

Empedocles (*cont.*)
189; from flesh, 195; believed all things had consciousness, 200; god in Empedocles, 203 n. 2; claimed immortality, 206; *kosmos* in, 208 n. 1; theory of effluences, 209

ἐνιαυτός, etymology of, 47 n. 2

entheos (ἔνθεος), meaning of in connexion with Bacchic rites, 231, 372

Enuma Elish, 59f.

Epaminondas, 179

Ephesus, legendary foundation of, 409

Epicharmus, 244 n. 1, 362, 423 n., 426 n. 1

Epictetus, 21

Epicureanism, 17ff.; general later disapproval of, 22

Epicurus, 18f., 25, 130, 407, 486; innumerable worlds of, 108, 109, 113

Epimenides, 319; his *Theogony*, 39

epopteia (ἐποπτεία), at Eleusis, 203

equality, human, in Stoicism, 20f.

Eratosthenes, on Anaximander, 74

Eros, 28, 61, 69, 88 n. 2

eternal recurrence. *See* repetition

eternity of world, 456 n.; in Pythagoreans, 281; in Xenophanes, 380, 389

Etna, 292

Euclid, 53 n. 2; construction of regular solids, 269

Eudemian Ethics, 329 n. 2

Eudemus, pupil of Aristotle, 49, 93, 98, 218; his *Astronomical History*, 74, 334 n. 1; on eternal recurrence, 281; on Pythagoreans' investigations into positions of planets, 95, 298

Eudorus, on pre-Platonic Pythagoreanism, 244 and n. 4, 247, 248 and n. 2

Eudoxus, 187, 253, 290, 393 n. 2

euharmostia, anharmostia, in the *Republic*, 317

Eupalinus, Samian engineer, 174, 219

Euphorbus, and Pythagoras, 159 n. 1, 164, 231

Euripides, 293; on separation of heaven and earth, 69; on progress, 400; imitates Xenophanes, 373 and n.

Eurytus, 258, 273ff.; meeting with Plato, 329

evolution, as opposed to creation, 142

Examyes, father of Thales: a Carian name, 50

exhalations. *See* Heraclitus

experiment, in early Greek philosophy, 37, 66 n. 1, 125f.; lack of, 9

extension, the matter of geometrical figures, 257; *see also* space

eye, Alcmaeon's study of the, 347, 349

Farrington, B., 52 and n. 1, 125

Favorinus, 294, 343

'felting', in Anaximander, 90; in Anaximenes, 121 and n. 3, 133, 139; in Xenophanes, 391

Festugière, A. J., 165 n. 1, **202** n., 354, 358 n.

Field, G. C., 334 n. 3, 335

fifth element. *See* elements

figures, origin of meaning 'numbers', 256 n.

fir, particular associations with Dionysus, 372 and n. 2

fire, itself an opposite, thus unsuited to be Milesian-type *arche*, 457; substance of the heaven in Parmenides and others, 136; as rarefied air (Anaximenes), 121f.; 'nourished' by moisture, 67, 80f., 97; as creative power, 281 n. 1; by Pythagoreans regarded with religious awe, 288; equated with pyramid, 267, 268; related to *aither* in Aristotle, 270; in Heraclitus, *see* Heraclitus; popularly identified with *aither*, 466; power to become frozen or solidified, in Empedocles, 290f.; 'central fire', *see* Pythagoreans; sphere of (Anaximander), 92, 94

fish, and origin of human life, 102f.; eating of, 103 n.; sacred fish not to be eaten, 188

flesh, abstention from enjoined in Orphic writings, 195; Pythagorean prohibition on, 187ff.; eating confined to *some* species, 188; or some parts, . 189; prohibition denied, 188ff.; sacrifice an exception, 195; eating of, and transmigration, Empedocles on, 195 and n.

flood (*see also* destructions), connected with Great Year, 458 n. 4

floruit = 'was aged forty', 408

fluxion theory, of generation of geometrical figures, 262ff.; period of origin, 264; Newton quoted, 264 n.

form, Greek discovery of, 36; study of, in Italian branch of Presocratics, 4; recognition by Pythagoreans of its importance, 238, 317, 467; its permanence, 467f.; outcome of the philosophy of form, 467; form and matter in Aristotle, 12; distinction between them, 234; and teleology, 12; purely actual form, in Aristotle, is God, 12

forms, in Plato, 10f., 210; origins of the doctrine (Aristotle's account), 450, 468

fossils, ancient observations of, 387f., 387 n. 2

Fraenkel, E., 205 n. 1

General index

Frank, E., 53 n. 1, 150 n. 2, **181** n., **201** n. 2, 265 n. 2, **324, 330, 332, 335** n. 3
Fränkel, H., x, 81 n. 1, 363 n. 3, **381** f., 390 n. 2, **393** n. 2, 395 nn., **396** nn. 1 and 3, **397** and nn., **444** n. 2, **446**
Frankfort, Henri, quoted, 28, 40 f., 141
Freeman, K., 219 n. 2, 335 n. 1
free-will and swerve of atoms, in Epicurus, 18
Freudenthal, J., 385
Fritz, K. von, 170 n. 2, **171** n., **180, 202** n., 269 n. 1, **373** n. 3, **426** n. 1
Fung Yu Lan, 177 n. 2, 252

Gaetringen, H. von, 29 n. 2
Gaia, 28, 69, 123, 131, 386
Galen, 137; on Alcmaeon's supposed book *On Nature*, 343; on Xenophanes, 384
galeus, dogfish or shark, 102, 103 and nn. 1, 2
generalization, importance (and dangers) of, 36 f.; in Thales, 54; and universals, necessary for philosophy, according to Aristotle, 40
generation, logical and chronological, 239 f., 456; spontaneous, 59, 102 n. 1, 386
genesis, problem of, 38; by separation according to Anaximander, 76 f.; from numbers, 256
geocentric universe, in pre-Philolaic Pythagoreanism, 289
Gercke, A., 158 n. 1
Getae, Thracian tribe, 158
Gigon, O., 29 n. 1, 73, 131 n., **384** n., **407**, 408 n. 2, **414** n. 3, **415**, 428 n. 2, **433** nn. 1 and 4, 434, 444 n. 2, **445** n. 2, 453, 454 n. 2, **459**, 477 n. 3, 478 n. 2
Gilbert, O., 105, 106 n.
Giordano Bruno, possible influence of Ecphantus on, 327
gnomon, of sundial, 33, 74; Pythagorean use, 241; essential meanings of term, 242 and n.
god (*see also* anthropomorphism; divinity; Heraclitus, theology), concern of gods for human affairs, in early Greek thought, 27; held responsible for human failings, 26 f., 482 n.; neglected by Ionians, 30; assimilation to, *see* divinity; relation of man to God, in Aristotle, 13; all things full of gods (Thales), 65; the air a small portion of, within us (Diog. Apoll.), 130; spherical in Xenophanes, 376 ff., and identified with the world, 381 ff.; in Aristotle, 13
Goettling, C. W., 183 nn. 1 and 3
gold plates, inscribed, of mystic sect in Magna Graecia, 206, 481 n. 1

Golden Race, heroes of, 400, 478
Gomperz, H., 65, 312 n.
gonimon, of Anaximander, 90, 278
good, according to Pythagoreans: in the table of opposites, 245, 246; in the end, not the beginning, 251; a peace produced by imposition of *peras* on *apeiron*, 448; good and bad identified by Heraclitus, 442, 445
goodness, its true nature to be sought (Socrates), 10; question whether it has a true nature, 10; as supreme form in Plato, 10
Gorgias, 73
Great Year (Perfect Year), 282 and n. 2, 353; and periodic destructions of mankind, 101, 388; and *ecpyrosis*, 458
Greek language, later universality of, 23 f.
Griffiths, J. Gwyn, 35 n. 1
γυρός, meaning of, 98 f.
Guthrie, W. K. C., 39 n. 1, 43 n. 1, 69 n. 3, 102 n. 1, 132 n. 1, 137 n. 2, 182 n. 2, 203 n. 1, 206 n., 272 n. 1, 282 nn., 285 n. 3, 291 n. 1, 386 n. 1, 389 n. 2, 400 n. 3, 466 n. 2, 470 n., 475 n. 2, 481 n. 1

Hackforth, R., 293 n. 3, 311 n. 1
Hades: equated with Dionysus (Heraclitus), 463, 475, 476; with Areimanios, 249 n. 2
Halley, Edmund, 47
harmonia, harmonie, harmony: account of the word, 220, 223; as octave, 223, 288 n., 298 n. 2; other senses: 'proportion' (Empedocles), 258; 'adjustment', 439 and n. 3; in Heraclitus, the reverse of the Pythagorean, 435 f., a precarious equilibrium, 440 (*see further under* Heraclitus); soul as *harmonia* (Pythagorean), 307 f.
harmonic mean, 322
'harmonic motion', 227
harmonics, study of, in Plato, 214
harmony of the spheres, in Plato's *Republic*, 295; attested as Pythagorean, 167; critical account by Aristotle, 295 f.; Cicero's account, 297; why not heard by us, 296, 297; heard however by Pythagoras, 297 n. 3; notes simultaneous yet concordant, 299
Harpagus the Mede, 363
head, the seat of intelligence (Alcmaeon), 348
health, as harmony of physical opposites, in Alcmaeon, 346; in Western school of medicine, 436; in Plato's *Symposium*, 435 f.
hearing, Alcmaeon's explanation of, 347, 349 f.

General index

heart, seat of intelligence (Empedocles), 348; common sensorium (Aristotle), 349

heat: connexion with life, 61, 92, 291, (in Anaximander) 101 f., 105; explained by decrease of density (Anaximenes), 121 f., 124 f. *See also* fire

Heath, T., 46 n. 1, **47**, 49, 95 n., 97 nn., 135 and n. 2, 138 n. 1, 218 n., 265 n. 2, 269 n. 1, 285 nn., 286 n. 1, **288**, 295 n. 2, 297 n. 1, 298, **300** n. 4, **324**, 335 n. 1

heaven, separation from earth, 68 f. *See also* Ouranos

heavenly bodies, living creatures in Aristotle, 2; divinity of, 350, 357 and n., 480

Hecataeus, 74, 157, 408

Heidel, W. A., 57 n. 2, 58 n. 1, 67, 72 n. 3, 73 n. 2, **74** f., 77 nn. 1, 3, 4, 80 n., 82 n. 1, 97 n. 1, 100 n. 2, **118**, **161** n. 2, **219** and n. 2, **232** f., **241**, 294 n. 2, **323**, 342 n., **374** n. 2, 391 n. 1

Heinimann, F., 58 n. 1

heliocentric theory, 290, 293

Hellenistic civilisation, 15 ff.

van Helmont, J. B., 71

Hemera, 413 n. 1

Henderson, Isobel, 161 n. 2

Hephaestus, 131

Heraclides of Pontus, 51, 290; on Pythagoras and his school, 163 f.; on Pythagoras and *philosophia*, 204; relation to Hicetas and Ecphantus, 323 f.; cosmological views, 324

Heraclitus, 4, 65 f., 83 n. 1, 145, 403–92; variety of modern interpretations, 403; subject of King Darius, 488; membership of royal clan at Ephesus, 408 f.; date and life, 408 ff.; anecdotes and sayings illustrative of his character, 409 f.; the 'weeping' philosopher, 409 and n. 1; relation to the prevalent world-picture of his time, 469 f., 479 f.

sources, 405 f.

writings, 406–8; doubt of extent of his own actual words, 403; question whether he wrote a book, 406 f. and n. 2; Aristotle's evidence for its existence quoted, 407 f.; a metrical version, 486

social relations: contempt for great majority of mankind, 412; for his own people, 409; in particular, for philosophers and poets, 412 f.; for 'much learning', 412, 414; aristocratic pride and rejection of equality, 409 f.; respect for law, 410, 425; on poverty of human knowledge, 413

relation to earlier philosophers, 415 f.;

censure of Homer, 413, 447; of Hesiod, 412, 413, 443; of Xenophanes, 412; of Archilochus, 412 and n. 1, 413; of Pythagoras, 157, 412, 417, 448; criticized by Parmenides, 408 and n. 2; ignored by later, scientific, philosophers, 419; borrowings by Stoics, 404; misunderstood by Aristotle to be essentially Milesian, 451; his appeal for other philosophers and religious teachers, 403 and n.

style: his obscurity, 403, 410 f.; due to amalgamation of spiritual and material in his expression, 428, 469; the 'Riddler', 411, 443 and n. 2; ancient references to his obscurity, 411; due to contempt for mankind, 410 ff.; anecdote concerning Socrates, 411 f.; oracular style, 414; picture-language, paradox, parable, 410, 438, 461; word-play, 425 n. 5, 475 n. 2; on occasion brilliantly clear, 411 and n. 3

philosophical method: prophetic character of his teaching, 413 ff., 414 and n. 2; self-search, 414, 416, 417 ff.; conclusions based on intuition, 419

'the common', 413, 425 f., 428, 431, 447, 454 n. 2

the Logos, 419 ff.; its existence affirmed at the outset, 419; independent of the speaker, 424 f.; permanent, 468; common, 425 f., 428, 431; includes act of thinking or reflexion, 426 and n. 1; has material embodiment, 428; in fire, 432; drawn in physically through the senses, 430; by breathing, 430, 480; both human thought and governing ('steering') principle of the universe, 428; both outside and within the cosmos, 472; is H.'s nearest approach to an *arche*, 428; the true Logos: 'all things are One', 425, 444; identified with war, 447; the Logos-fire, 471; summary of conception, 434

the senses: H.'s mistrust of, 5; need to be interpreted by the understanding, 415, 429, 451; but primary channels of communication with the Logos, 429 f. (cf. 431); effects of sleep, 427, 430 f.; explanation of sleep, 433 and n. 3

war (strife, tension), the universal creative and ruling force, 446 ff.; common, like the Logos, 447; peace and war identical, 444; Aristotle's account of the doctrine, 437 f.

harmony: is of opposites, 435 ff.; simile of bow and lyre, 439 f., 451 f., 459; invisible

Heraclitus (*cont.*)
  and visible, 440f.; a balance of forces in tension, 440; revolt against idea of peaceful and harmonious world, 448; stability of world only apparent, 466; harmony and discord co-existent, 436f.
  opposites: co-existence of, 437, 441, 458; all things made of them, 439; identity of, 442ff., 445f., 463; qualities valued through their opposites, 448
  way up and way down, the same, 443, 460, 461, 463
  death: elements live by each others', 433, 453, 462f.; for soul means becoming water, 433, 480; in battle, 466 n. 3, 481; relation between life and death, 478f.
  change, 441, 444, 445; continuity of, 449ff., 452, 459ff.; cyclic character of, 452; and the concept of measure, 464ff.; fire the measure of change, 465; cyclic change of elements into each other, 433
  fire: the cosmic fire, 454ff., 459; not flame, but hot, dry vapour, 432, 466; world an everlasting fire, 454ff.; its kindling not temporal, 459; in one sense the outermost part of the universe, 480; alleged to be H.'s *arche*, 432, 457, 459f.; his 'first cause' according to Aristotle, 432; primacy of fire, 456; but not permanent substratum, 461; the constant factor in all transformations, 465; all things exchange for, 457; as gold for goods, 461, 465; law or measure of change, 461, 466; fire everliving, rational, divine, both immanent and external, 432, 459, 462, 469, 471, 474; identified with the Logos, 432, 471; with *psyche*, 459, 462, 466; parallel changes of of fire and soul, 459ff., 463; its opposites, cold and wet, connected with foolishness, 433
  other pronouncements on fire: want and satiety, 455, 474; sea 'half earth and half burning', 463f. and n.; fire as judge or justice, 473, 474
  flux, doctrine of, 450f. and n. 1, 452 n., 461, 468; essential to being, 449; illustration of the *kykeon*, 449; its influence on Plato, 450 and n. 2; denial of the doctrine, 452 n., 465f.
  the 'river-statement', 450, 461, 467, 488ff.; passages bearing on the statement, 489ff.; variant forms of it, 490f.
  cosmology, astronomy, etc., 482ff.; no particular interest in natural phenomena, 483;

  account of his cosmology by D.L., 483; real world 'the same for all', 454 and n. 2; *kosmos* of world everlasting, though components never the same, 468; substance of universe single, moving, finite (Simplicius), 457; subject to generation not in time but conceptually (Aëtius), 456 and n.; question of *ecpyrosis* in H., 455ff., 456 n., 473; no theory of elements, 453 n. 2
  exhalation, from sea, the origin of all things, 462; theory of exhalations, 452f.; two kinds of exhalation, 462 n. 2, 483, 484 n. 3; stars are exhalations from sea, 462; heavenly bodies nourished by them, 484; *psyche* an exhalation, 462
  sun, 484ff.; 'one foot wide', 486; renewed daily, 462, 484f.; will not overstep his measures, 465
  seasons 'which produce all things', 453 n. 1
  estimate of Great Year, 458 and nn. 3, 5
  meteorology vague, 486
  soul, 476f.; equated with fire, 433, 466, cf. 481; at death turns to water, 433, 476, 480; nourished by moisture, 433f., 463; described as exhalation, 462; question of immortality, 476ff.; soul a spirit guardian, 478, cf. 482
  traditional religion and morality: criticism of established cult, 474f.; of mysteries and Dionysiac religion, 474f.; of funeral rites, 478; of praying to images, 472; purificatory rites sometimes approved, 476; right and wrong ways of worship, 475f.; his own ascetic attitude, 478
  justice, 472f.; identified with strife, 447, 473; with fire, 473; Erinyes the servants of justice, 465; just and unjust not distinguished by God, 413, 442, 446, 448, 472
  theology, 469ff.; 'Orphic' strain, 477; gods recognized in traditional sense, 472; God, the divine, 444, 472; comprehends all contraries in himself, 444, 472; our share of divine force, got by physical means, 429
  summary of H.'s scheme of things, 479f.; general summing up, 486ff.
Heraclitus, school of, 410 and n. 2, 434, 451
Hermeias, Aristotle's poem on murder of, 215
Hermes, 164
Hermippus, knowledge of book of Philolaus, 332 n. 1
Hermodorus, of Ephesus, 409 and n. 3
ἡρμοσμένος, of man who has *sophrosyne*, 317
Hermotimus, 218, 319; and Pythagoras, 164
Herodorus of Heraclea, 285 n. 3

General index

Herodotus, 294 n. 1; on Pythagoras, 159 f.; on Greek borrowing from Egyptians, 160

Hesiod, xi, 28, 39, 61, 69, 70, 112, 134, 140 f., 183, 278, 318, 389, 396 n. 2, 400, 442, 478; castigated by Xenophanes, 370 f.

Hestia, 293

ἑταιρεία, 176; ἑταιρεῖαι, Pythagorean, 178

ἑταῖρος, 115 n.

Hicetas, 323 f., 327 ff.

Hiero of Syracuse, 362, 364

Hippasus of Metapontum, 192, 268, 320 ff.; no writings, 320; sympathy with conspiracy against Pythagoreans, 320; connexion and confusion with Heraclitus, 320 f.; on substance of the universe, 432, 457; his first principle fire, 320, 432; discoveries in music, 321 f.; his punishment, 149 f.

Hippias, of Elis, 66

Hippocrates of Chios, 219, 335

Hippocrates of Cos, 8

Hippocratic writings, 8; criticism of philosophers in, 345, 358; *On Ancient Medicine*, 345; *On the Nature of Man*, 58 and n. 2

Hippodamus, of Miletus, 219

Hippolytus, of Rome, his *Refutations* as a source, xiv; on Pythagorean *Acusmata*, 183; on harmony of spheres, 298; on Heraclitus, 405 f.

Hippon, of Samos, Pythagorean, 62 and n.; his *arche* water, 345; on birth after seven months, 303 n. 5

Hippys of Rhegium, 322

historical research, Alexandrian, 16

historie, Ionian spirit of, 43, 71; attitude of Heraclitus to, 417

Hobbes, Thomas, quoted, 31

ὁλκάς, ὁλκός, 267 n. 2

Hölscher, U., 60 n. 2, 77 n. 1, **79** n. 2, 87 n. 2, 138 n. 2, 414 n. 2, **418** n. 1

Homer, 126, 129, 132, 148, 393 n. 1; the foundation of Greek education, 371; gods of, 18, 26 f.; characteristics of Homeric religion, 196 f.; soul in, 196; Homeric religion and the Ionian spirit, 196; a philosophical precursor according to Plato, 450 n. 2; with Hesiod, determined for Greeks the nature of their gods, 370–1 and n. 1; castigated by Xenophanes, 370 f., 374; by Heraclitus, 413, 447; anecdote about, 443 n. 2; *physis* in, 82

ὅμοιος, ambiguity of, 305

hospitality, Greek, 361

humanitas, 23

hybris, 8; Heraclitus's conception of, 410

ὑγρός, meanings of, 61 f.

hylozoism, 21, 63 f., 130, 350; inseparable from evolutionary view of nature, 144 f.

hypenantia, harmonic mean, 322

Iamblichus, Neoplatonist, 177, 475; source for life of Pythagoras, 23, 155 f.; Pythagorean *Acusmata*, 183; *Protrepticus*, 154, 171; treats 'Pythagoreans' as 'Pythagoras', 151; method of compilation, 171

[Iamblichus], *Theologumena Arithmeticae*, on Pythagoreans in Egypt, 217 f.

Iberians, and Pythagoreans, 253, 254

Ibycus, 174

identity, search for underlying, 56 f.

ignorance, remedy sought by Socrates, 9

immortality, Thracian belief in compared with Pythagorean, 159; aspiration of mystic sect in Magna Graecia, 206; denial of, a legacy from Homer, 196; in Heraclitus, 476 f. *See also* cycle of births, divinity, Orphics, Pythagoreans, soul, transmigration

imperceptible, invoked to explain the perceptible, 78

incarnation, as punishment, 311

incommensurability, 149, 265

indefinite dyad, 202 n., 248, 264

India, 187; and Pythagoreanism, 251 f.

'indifference' and position of earth (Anaximander), 99

individual, problem of knowledge of, 41

infinite extension, beyond the cosmos, Archytas on, 336

infinitesimal change, argument of, 451

infinity, concept of (see also *apeiron*), isolated and grasped through work of Aristotle, 379

initiation, at Eleusis, 197 f.; of Orphics, 198; attitude of Pythagoreans to, 149

innumerable worlds, *see* worlds

intelligence, centre of: the heart (Empedocles), 348; the head (Alcmaeon), 348; interchangeable with sphere or circuit, in the *Timaeus*, 356; in connexion with the Logos (Heraclitus), 426

intermundia, Epicurean, 113

intervals, musical, 212 ff.; concordant, 223; discovered by Pythagoras himself, 221 ff., 301; applied by him to cosmology, 247 f.; to distances between planets, 298, 300

Ion of Chios, 158, 182 n. 2

525

General index

Ionia, early seat of philosophy, 3; under rule of Lydia, 32; Ionian mathematics, 218f.; contrast between Ionian and Italian traditions, *see* Italian philosophy

Iris, 139, 393

irrationals, 149, 218 n., 265 and n. 1; date of discovery, *ibid.* n. 2

Isis, cults of, 23

Isocrates, on Pythagoras and Pythagoreans, 151, 163, 173

isonomia, in Alcmaeon, 345 and n. 2

Italian philosophy, 196; contrasted with Ionian, 4, 146, 172, 198, 250

Italians, in Aristotle, in sense of 'Pythagoreans', 154

Jaeger, W., 88 n. 1, **115, 165, 208** n. 1, 275 n. 2, 343, 365 n., 366 n. 1, **379** and n. 1, **384** n.

James, William, 117

Jehovah, divine rivals and foes of, 375

Jesus, 413 n. 2, 414 n. 3, 438, 439

Joel, K., 140 n.

Jones, W. H. S., 358 n.

Jowett, B., 423

judgment, relative character of, 401

judgments, moral, in Stoicism, 20

Junge, G., 265 n. 2, 295 nn.

justice, opposite views of Anaximander and Heraclitus, 447f.; personification of in Heraclitus, 472; equated with a number by Pythagoreans, 301, 302ff.

Kahn, C. H., xiv, **41** n. 3, 44 n., Section III C *passim,* **123** n. 1, 314 n. 1, **352** n. 2, **353, 374** n. 2, 375 n. 2, 390 n. 1, **453** n. 2, **456** n.

καιρός, 301 and n. 3, 304 n. 2

kanon (monochord), 224 and n. 2

Karpinsky, S., 35 n. 2

Karsten, S., 367 n. 1

Kepler, Johannes, 3

Kerferd, G. B., 115 n., 363 n. 2

Kern, O., 40 n. 1

Kerschensteiner, J., 404 n.

kinesis, scope of term, 382

kings, at Ephesus, 409

kinship, of all nature (*see also* microcosm-macrocosm analogy), 186f., 200, 202, 205f., 209, 237, 246, 470; the foundation of Pythagorean beliefs, 200, 205, 208, 250, 278; of all animate nature, in Empedocles, 186, 208; of all animals to man (Porphyry), 195

Kirk, G. S., xii, xiii, 57 n. 2, 82 n. 3, 90 n. 5, 95, **105** n., **114f., 131f.,** 135 n. 1, 157 n., 204 n. 1, **208** n. 1, 353 n. 2, **379, 382, 405** and n. 1, **406ff., 452** n., **489,** and Section VII *passim*

klepsydra, 133 and n. 2

κλίματα, origin of term, 393 n. 2

knowledge, human, limitations of recognized by Xenophanes, 398 and n.; emphasis on personal search, 399; contrasted with divine by Alcmaeon, 344; by poets, Xenophanes, Parmenides, 398; by Heraclitus, 398, 413; true knowledge of real things impossible (Ecphantus), 326, 399; of sensible world impossible: influence of Cratylus on Plato, 450; contrast with true wisdom, 415; knowledge and seeming: importance of the distinction brought out by Xenophanes, 399

Korybantes, 231

kosmiotes, 226

kosmos (*see also* cosmos), 206ff., 448; history of the term, 110f., 131 n. 1, 208 n. 1, 305; used of world first by Pythagoras, 208; construction of in Pythagoreans, 247f.; according to Philolaus, 284 and n. 2; in Heraclitus, 454f.; element of, link between the philosopher and the divine, 210f., 288; *kosmos, kosmoi,* in the *Timaeus,* 211; and adjective *kosmios,* 210f.

Koster, W. J. W., 253

Kranz, Walther, 39, 47 n. 2, 131 n., 157 n., 158 n. 4, 208 n. 1, 300, 327, 406 n. 1, 408 n. 2

krasis, in Pythagoreanism, producing *harmonia,* 448f.

Kronos, 69, 70, 141

κρυσταλλοειδής, 136f.

Kuretes, 231

κυβερνᾶν, in philosophic and religious thought, 88; in Diogenes of Apollonia, 130; in Heraclitus, 429 n. 1

kykeon, 425 n. 1, 449

kyria δόξαι, of Epicurus, 25

Lane, Arthur, 37 n.

language: bilingual philosophers, 21; limitations imposed on philosophers by language, 118 (*see also* words)

Latins, and Pythagoras, 254

Leibniz, possible influence of Ecphantus on, 327

Lenin, 403 n. 1

Lenschau, T., 173 n. 5

Leon, tyrant of Sicyon or Phlius, 164, 204

Leon (Pythagorean), 344
Leucippus, 6, 91 n. 2, 95 n., 113, 138 n. 3, 232
Lévy, I., 161 n. 1, 163 n. 3, 202 n.
life (*see also* soul): in Milesians, stuff of world instinct with life, 201; its essentials, in popular thought, heat and moisture, 291, in Anaximander, 103; and its origin within the earth, *ibid.*; belief in its spontaneous origin, among Egyptians and in Anaximander, 59, 102; as cosmogonic force (Ecphantus), 326; after death, in Eleusinian and other mysteries, 476 (*see also* immortality etc.); the three types of life (Pythagoras), 164f., 211f.; (Plato), 165
like: 'like to like', 3; known by like, 206, 211; Empedoclean doctrine, 209f., 313, 318; in contrast with Alcmaeon's, 348
limit, Greek ideal of, 205f.; see *peras*, Pythagoreans
line, relation to figures in Pythagoreanism, 257
Linforth, I. M., 160 n.
Lloyd, G. E. R., 342 n., 358 n.
Lobeck, C. A., 151, 372 n. 1
Locri, 178 n. 1
lodestone, soul attributed to by Thales, 65 f.
logic, for Aristotle, the tool (*organon*) of philosophy, 14
logical and chronological priority, 239f.
λόγον διδόναι, 38
logos (λόγος), meanings of, 38, 205, 477 n. 1; survey of meanings current in fifth century or earlier, 419–24; in Heraclitus, 5, 272, 419ff.; use of term by Stoics, 21, 426 n. 2; particularly Zeno, 19f.
Love (*see also* Eros) and Strife, in Empedocles, 6
Lucretius, 386; on Heraclitus, 411
Lukas, F., 60 n. 2
Luynes, Duc de, 176 n. 1
Lyceum, 16
Lydia, conquest of by Cyrus, 363
lyre, structure of, 222f., 224, 299 n., 301; cosmos compared to, 298
Lysis, 179, 180

Macchioro, V., 406 n. 1, 478 and n. 2
McDiarmid, J., **41** n. 3, **56** n. 1, **62**, 77 nn. 1, 2, 4, 87 n. 2, **120** n., 121 n. 1, 458 n. 5
Macdonald, C., 35 n. 1
Magi, good and evil *archai* of, 249 n. 2; connexion of Pythagoras with, 173 n. 3, 253 f.
magic, sympathetic, 185 f.
Magna Graecia, philosophers of, 5; connexions with Miletus, 30

magnet. *See* lodestone
Magus, as title, 488
Malta, fossils found on, 387
map, Babylonian, 99 n. 2; of Anaximander, 74, 99 n. 2
Marcovich, M., 387 n. 4, 473 n. 1, 475 n. 1
Marcus Aurelius, 453
marriage, equated with a number by Pythagoreans, 302, 304
Martin, H., 299
Martin, T. H., 49
Mason, S. F., quoted, 36
material and formal, in Aristotle, 233
materialism, leads to belief in flux, 467; term irrelevant to Milesian philosophy, 64
mathematici, division of Pythagoreans, distinguished from *acusmatici*, 191, 217 357,
mathematics, Egyptian, limitations of, 34f.; Greek: its debt to Egypt and Babylon, 33, 218 n.; state of eastern mathematics at and before time of Pythagoras, 217f.; Ionian, 218f.; Pythagorean attitude to, 212f.; religious significance for Plato, 213f.; for Pythagoreans, 152f.; mathematics 'of nature', 226, 237; relevance to morals, (Plato) 305, (Archytas) 336; denied by Aristotle, 209 n.
matter, in early Greek philosophers, not dead and inert, 63f.; notion of, anachronistic, 64, 82, 89; meaning of the term in Aristotle, 12; matter and form, 234, 237, 467; and spirit: relations between them, 6, 88f., 143, 144f., 257f., 428, 468; union with mind in Stoicism (Zeno), 19
Maximus of Tyre, 453
Mazdaean religion, 253
mean, harmonic, so named by Archytas and Hippasus, 322
meat, abstention from. *See* flesh
mechanics: mathematical principles first applied by Archytas, 335
mechanistic theories of cosmogony, 144
medicine (*see also* Alcmaeon, Hippocratic writings): Egyptian, 34; Greek, separately treated by fifth century B.C., x; awareness of fallibility in diagnosis, 344; Western school and health as harmony, 436; quarrel with philosophers, 58, 345, 358
Meewaldt, J. D., 491 n.
Megarian School, 10
melancholia, meaning of word, 409 and n. 1
Melissus, 73, 337, 370
Melissus, Xenophanes, Gorgias (treatise), 367f.

memory, power of lost in sleep (Heraclitus), 430
Menon, pupil of Aristotle, 278 n. 3, 312 n., 330
Mesopotamia, 58, 60; visited by early Greek philosophers, 32
Messana (Zancle), 363 n. 4
Metapontum, 179
meteorites, 135 n. 1
methexis, in Plato, and Pythagorean *mimesis*, 229 f.
Metrodorus of Chios, 93
Meyer, E., 46 n. 1, 60 n. 2
microcosm–macrocosm analogy (*see also* kinship of all nature), 67, 90, 130, 131 f., 201 f., 208 n. 1, 209 ff., 278 f., 316, 350 f., 470, 479
Mieli, A., 221
Milesian philosophers, 3 f., 29 ff.; practical character, 30; moved by curiosity, 30 f.; acquaintance with Eastern countries, 32; mythical predecessors, 39; scientific outlook, 40, 43, 70, 83; questions asked by, 44; how far a school, 43; summary and appraisal, 140 ff.
Miletus, 121 n. 3; account of, 29; geographical situation, 31; materialistic culture, 30
Milky Way, 94
Milo of Croton, 176, 179, 346
Milton, quoted on opposites, 79
mimesis, mimetes, mimos, meaning of, 230 f.
Mimnermus, 30
Minar, E. L., 153 n. 1, **170** n. 1 and n. 2, 173 n. 2, **174** n. 2, 179 and n., 193 n., 329, **335** n. 3
mind, union of with matter in Zeno's Stoicism, 19; cosmogonic in Anaxagoras etc., 143, 326, 454 n. 3; in Ecphantus, 326
Minoans, 50 n. 1
Mnesarchus of Samos, father of Pythagoras, 173
Mnesimachus (comic poet), 187
moisture, connexion with life, 61 f., 67, 71 f., 92, 101, 128, 386; bad for souls (Heraclitus), 433
monad. *See* unit
monarchia, in Alcmaeon, 345
Mondolfo, R., 115, 161 n. 1, **330**, **407**, **456** n., 474 n. 1
monism, 70; in later Platonists and Neopythagoreans, 244
monochord, 224
monotheism or polytheism, question unimportant to Greeks, 375
moon, in Anaximander, 93 f.; moon-rainbow in Anaximenes, 139; moon in Philolaus, 285;

inhabitants of, 285 and n. 3; called 'counter-earth', 290; in Xenophanes, 392; cause of illumination, when discovered, 94 n. 2, 286; white cocks sacred to moon-god, 188; eclipses of, *see* eclipses
Moraux, P., 367 n.
Morrison, J. S., 165 n. 2, 173 n. 1, 294 n. 2, **295** n. 1
mortality, thoughts of, enjoined by Herodotus, tragedians, Pindar, 196, 205 f.; rejected by Pythagoras etc., 206; contrasted with 'assimilation to the god', 198 f.
Moschion, on progress in human culture, 400
motes, in air, constitute soul, 306 f.
motion: methodical classification of its types by Aristotle, 382; in Greek philosophy, 'covers every kind of change', 381; this generalization denied, 382; cause of, 6 f., 88 f., 128, 145; initiation of, a psychic property, 66, 350; eternal, 4, 350; (in Anaximander), 76, 89, 91, 98; (in Anaximenes), 124, 127; continuous motion of everything a doctrine among followers of Heraclitus, 410
movement, denied by Parmenides, 279 (*see also* motion)
mover and moved, not yet distinguished in sixth century, 128
mullet, abstained from by Pythagoreans, 189
Musaeus, 69, 115
Museum, at Alexandria, 16
music (*see also* intervals, pitch, Pythagoreans): Greek music melodic, 162 n. 2, 223, 299; primary intervals, 223; in Pythagoreanism, provides paradigm for construction of a *kosmos*, 247 f.; music and moral state of the soul (Plato), 317
musical sounds, note on speed and pitch, 226 ff.
mystery-religions (*see also* Eleusinian mysteries), 152; in Hellenistic age, 17; and Heraclitus, 425 n. 1, 478 n. 2; sarcasm of Clement of Alexandria, 473
myth, value and danger of, 2; Platonic, *ibid.*; demands particular causes, 40; sudden dissipation of with rise of Milesians, 141
mythology, latent, in early Greek philosophy, 1 f.
μῦθος, 421 n.

Nabonidus, 46
Naster, P., 176 n. 1

General index

natural forces, personal explanation of in early Greek thought, 26 f.

nature. *See physis*

'nature' and convention, 9

Naucratis, 29

Neanthes, 180, 209

necessity, irrational, in the *Timaeus*, 12; in early Greek philosophical thinking, 27

Neoplatonism, 23, 155; and interaction between Christianity and paganism, 24

Neopythagoreans, 23, 330; characteristics of their evidence on Pythagoreanism, 156; their picture of Pythagoras, 175

Nestle, W., **107**, 131 n., 161 n. 1, **313** n., 324 n. 1

Neugebauer, O., 46 n. 1, **47** nn. 2 and 4, **48**, 218 and n.

Nicander, 91 n. 3

Nicolaus of Damascus, on the *arche* of Xenophanes, 378

Nicomachus of Gerasa, Neopythagorean, 169, 180, 244 n. 3; *Introduction to Arithmetic* quoted, 261

Nietzsche, 282 n. 1; on philosophy as autobiography, 117; on Heraclitus, 403 n., 411 n. 3

Nigidius Figulus, 330

Nile, annual floods of, 59

Nilsson, M. P., 183 nn. 1 and 2, 449 n. 2, 475 n. 4

Ninon of Croton, 177, 320

Noetus, and Heraclitus, 405

non-perceptible, notion of, 78

nouns, abstract, relative lateness of, 79

nous, voῦς, vóos, in Anaxagoras, of primary motive cause, 326; unmixed with matter, 6; in Heraclitus, essential to avoid error due to senses, 451; survival of the term in Aristotle, 14; of perceiving and recognizing identity or significance, 426 n. 1

number: soul a self-moving number (Xenocrates), 263; numerical order inherent in world, 237. *See also* Pythagoreans

Nūn, primordial waters, in Egyptian mythology, 59

Nyx, 413 n. 1

occultation of star by moon, 95 n.

Oceanus, 55, 60 f., 123, 131, 391, 410 n. 1

'Ocellus Lucanus', 332

octahedron, connected with air by the Pythagoreans, 267; construction attributed to Theaetetus, 268

Oenopides of Chios, 74; quoted on gnomon, 242 n.

officium, a conception with a Roman history, 22

Olmstead, A. T., 31 n. 2, 60

Olympian religion, 196

Olympic games, 363 n. 2

Olympic gathering, illustrating types of life, 164

Olympus: name for uppermost heaven in Philolaus, 284

One, the (*see also* unit), 'All things come from one', 69, 87 and n. 1, 115; One and Many, problem of, 132

Onesicritus, Cynic philosopher, 187

opinion (or seeming) contrasted with knowledge, 13, 395 n. 5, 399

'Opinions', δόξαι, *Placita*, as source-material, xiii

opportunity (καιρός), equated with a number by Pythagoreans, 301, 302, 303

opposites, 271, 470; evolved directly from *arche* in Presocratic thought, 122, 273; in Anaximander, 76 f., 78 ff., 89 etc.; can originate from each other, 80 f.; in Anaximenes, 112 f.; in Alcmaeon, *see* Alcmaeon; in Pythagoreanism, 232, 245 ff.; *see also under* Heraclitus; health as harmony of opposites, 314 (*and see* Alcmaeon); in medical prescription, 358

oracles, proceed by suggestion, 414

order, notion of, as beginning of philosophy, 26, 29, 44; behind phenomena, grasped by Milesians, 141 f.; of the world (*kosmos*), 206 f.; universal order reproduced in the philosopher, 210 f.; see also *kosmos*

Orestes, 475 n. 3

organization, and the limit, 207

Orient, extent of influence of, on early Greek philosophers, 31 f.; Greek attitude to, 252; Oriental elements in Pythagoreanism, 251 ff.; later syncretism between Oriental and Greek, 252

originality, in philosophic systems, 17

Ormuzd (Oromasdes), 250

Oroites, Persian, kills Polycrates, 346

Oromasdes, 249 n. 2

Orpheus, xi, 150

Orphics, 182, 203, 272, 331; cosmogony, xi, 39; theogonies, 69; relation to Pythagoreans, 150, 198 f., 254; problem of One and Many in, 132; rivalry with Homer, 150; general doctrine, 198; doctrine of man and immortality, 464, 478; the 'wheel of birth', 480; rewards and punishments after death, 476; the soul as breath, 129, 201, 307, 480

General index

Oświecimski, S., 44 n., 66 n.
ouranos, οὐρανός, senses of distinguished, 111; according to Philolaus, 284 and n. 2; as universe, not merely sky, 380 and n. 1
Ouranos, 28, 69, 70, 112, 123, 278, 380 n. 1, 386
Ovid, 79
Owen, G. E. L., 265 n. 1, 408 n. 2

παλίντονος, παλίντροπος, 439 n. 3
Pamphila, 53
Panaetius of Rhodes, 22
πάντα ῥεῖ, probably not words of Heraclitus, 450 n. 1
pantheism, question of in Xenophanes, 381
parable, use of in Heraclitus, 438
Paracelsus, 71
parallax, how disposed of by Pythagoreans, 289
Parmenides, 70, 87, 95 n., 122, 136, 172, 294, 428, 429; on source of moon's light, 94 n. 2, 286; relationship to Xenophanes, 363, 379 and n. 2, 380; probably acquainted with Heraclitus's work, 408 and n. 2; his 'Way of Seeming', 136; denied physical movement and change, 4–5, 9; influence of this denial, 145; denied existence of void, 279; shape of earth according to, 294; contrasted knowledge and opinion, 399
Paron, Pythagorean, 319
Paros, plant-fossils on, 387 and n. 4
patripassianism, claimed to be rooted in philosophy of Heraclitus (Hippolytus), 405
Paul, Saint, 23
peras (*see also* Pythagoreans), 78; and *apeiron*, contrasting Pythagorean principles, 207; and *kosmos*, 206 f.; imposed on *apeiron*, produces *peperasmenon*, in construction of a *kosmos*, 247 f.
περιέχειν, περιέχον, 'surrounding the world', 134 n., 272; in Anaximander, 85; in Pythagoreanism, 281; allegedly none in Heraclitus, 469 n.
Peripatetic School, continuation of, 22; its approach to Heraclitus, 404 n.
Persephone, 197, 449
Persian religion, monotheistic or dualistic?, 254 f.; and Pythagoreanism, 251–6 (*see also* Zoroaster, Zoroastrianism)
Persian Wars, 8
Persians, moral scheme of compared with Pythagoreanism, 250; Persian influence on Pythagoreanism, 252
pessimism, in Homer, 27

Petron, 322 f.
Pfligersdorffer, G., 69 n. 1
Phaethon, myth of, 388
Phanias of Eresus, 322
Phemius, 415
Pherecydes, xi, 29 n. 1, 158
philia, and the primal unity of the Italian school, 250
Philip of Opus, 283
Philistion, physician, 359
Philolaus, 146, 155, 179, 201 n. 2, 233, 260, 268, 329 ff.; place and date, 329; standing, 287 n.; question of writings, 330 ff.; fragments, controversy on genuineness, 330 ff.; and regular solids, 267, 269 f.; and creation from regular solids, 267, 273; as author of a Pythagorean cosmology, 284 f., 286 f.; on the Great Year, 282; Philolaic world-system probably due to Ph. himself, 289; movement of the earth, 327; the counter-earth, 328; on animal birth, 278 f.; on the soul: passages quoted, 311; soul a *harmonia*, 309 f., 312; on wickedness of suicide, 162 f., 167, 310; summary of his views, 333
philosophia, *philosophos*, 31; account of the words, 204 f.; new use of the term by Pythagoras, 164, 165 f., 204; term 'philosopher' applied especially to Pythagoras and followers, 417
philosophy, effect of temperament on, 117; of current thought, 118; wide sense of in early period, x; relation of Greek philosophy to modern thought, 1 ff.; summary of Greek philosophy, 3 ff.; originality of, 31 ff.; European, origin in curiosity, 30; denied, 117; origin of in abandonment of mythological solutions, 29; early Greek, two main streams in, 4, 172
Phlius, Pythagorean centre established at, 164 n., 179
φλοιός, 91, 102 n. 2
Phoenicians, 50 n. 1, 51, 294 n. 1
phosphorescence, 139
physical or 'natural' view of universe, change to with Thales, 43
physici or *physiologi*, 40, 73
physis, φύσις, meaning of term, 82; in Milesians, as actual, material substance, 55, 142; περὶ φύσεως, as title of Presocratic works, 73; in Heraclitus, 418; identified with 'what is', 113
Piaget, J., 64 n. 1
Pierce, C. S., 282 n. 1

πιλίον, in Anaximenes, 121 n. 3, 137, 138 n. 1
Pindar, 319, 414
Pirithous, father of Alcmaeon, 344
pitch of notes, ancient theories of, 226 ff.
Pitts, W., 330 n. 2
Placita, ἀρέσκοντα, as source material, xiii
planets, in Anaximander, 94 f.; in Anaximenes, 135; in Plato: relative positions and distances, 298, 301; function of, 339; independent movement from west to east (Alcmaeon), 357 and n.; orbits etc. in Pythagoreanism, 285, 301; non-existent planet invented by Pythagoreans, 213
Plato (*see also* forms, harmonics, soul), xiv, 5, 10 ff., 25, 27, 86, 100, 189, 209, 334, 368, 395 n. 5, 400, 419, 435 f., 436, 437; on origin of philosophy, 30; relations with Pythagoreanism, 153, 161 ff., 170, 204, 214, 265, 334, cf. 213; harmony of the spheres in, 295 f., 301; teleological and theistic view of nature, 11, 144; on mathematics and morals, 305; religious attitude to mathematics, 213 f.; views on the soul, 308 ff., 311, 316, 317, 351; on knowledge as recollection, 167; on connexion between intelligence and circular motion, 356 f.; *methexis* and *mimesis*, 229; on motion of planets, 357; political theory, 11; dilemma of the *Meno*, 395 n. 5; influence of other philosophers: Alcmaeon, 351, 354; Heraclitus, 436 f., 450, 452 n., 467 f.; doctrine of creation, 239, 456; *Timaeus*, 11, 203 n., 210, 227, 267, 275, 291, 338, 349, 354, 388, 444 n. 2, 456
Platonic figures, or bodies, i.e. regular solids, 268
Platonism, its relation to earlier and later Pythagoreanism, 170
Platonists, Protestant, 24
pleasure, nature of Epicurean, 18 f.
Plotinus, and Neoplatonism, 23; entry of new religious spirit with, 24; inexpressible first principle of, 249; on Heraclitus, 411
pluralism, in Presocratic philosophy, 5
Plutarch, quotations from Heraclitus, 489
[Plutarch], *Epitome*, as source, xiii; *Stromateis*, as source, xiv
pneuma, πνεῦμα, in cosmogony of Anaximenes, 131 n., 132; of the Pythagorean Unlimited, 132 f., 272, 278; of the soul as breath, 307; in Zeno, as material representation of *logos*, 20
Pohlenz, M., 82

Poincaré, H., 281 n. 1
point, according to Pythagoreans the smallest magnitude, 261; graphic representation of dimensions by points, 260
polar expressions, 375 and n. 2, 446
πολιτεία and *res publica*, 23
pollution, by bloodshed, 201 n. 1
polos, time-measuring instrument, 33
Polycrates of Samos, 173 f., 346
polydaemonism, in early Greek thought, 26
polymathie, πολυμαθίη, condemned by Heraclitus, 417, etc.
polytheism, 26; not rejected by Pythagoreans, 203; Xenophanes's attitude to, 375 f.
Pontus, in mythology, 61
Porphyry, 24, 186; *De Abstinentia*, 193 f.; *Life of Pythagoras*, 23, 155 f.; and Pythagorean *Acusmata*, 183
Poseidon, 44, 102
possession, in ecstatic worship, 231, 475 n. 2
potentiality and actuality, in Aristotle, 12
Potone, sister of Plato, mother of Speusippus, 260
Praechter, K., 131 n., 324
praeparatio evangelica, Greek philosophy viewed as, 24
pre-philosophical thought, 26 f., 39
πρηστήρ, 463 n. 3
presuppositions of philosophers, unconscious, 116 ff.
primary (and secondary), senses of, 248
priority, logical and chronological, not properly distinguished by Pythagoreans, 240
progress, in human culture, 400; idea to be attributed first to Xenophanes, 399 f., 401
Prometheus, myth of, 387 n. 1, 400
proof, mathematical, meaning of, 53 and n. 2
proportion, Pythagorean insistence on, 205; in combinations of elements, (Empedocles) 258, (Pythagorean) 275 and n. 2
Protagoras: his account of human origins in Plato's dialogue, 400; autonomy of individual's sensations, 401, 431
psyche, ψυχή (*see also* soul), in Homer, 196, 476; as cause of motion, 65, 67; self-mover, in Anaximander, 128, in Plato etc., 351; closely identified in general with physical life, 315; fifth-century meaning not only *a* soul but soul, 355
Ptolemy I of Egypt, 16
purification, rites of, 188, 475 and nn. 1 and 2; for Pythagoras, dependent on *philosophia*, 204, 205

General index

pyramids, fire composed of (Pythagoreans), 267, 268; height of, calculated by Thales, 53; Great Pyramid, 33

Pythagoras, 4

life, 173–9; no sources before Aristotle, 149; date of birth, 173; evidence of connexion with rising mercantile class, 177; his travels, 173, 217; migration to S. Italy, 4, 174; perhaps responsible for Crotoniate incuse coinage, 176ff.; gives Italians a constitution, 175; banished from Croton, 178f.; death at Metapontum, 179, 357

ancient picture: Aristotle's information on Pythagoras, 154; known to contemporaries as a polymath, 166; mentioned with censure by Heraclitus, 157, 412, 417, 448; in Isocrates, 163; veneration, heroization, canonization, 148; semi-divine attributes, 149, 203, 231; legendary elements: his successive incarnations (Heraclides), 164; miracle-working, 166

alleged writings, accounts of, 155; 'Mystical Logos' attributed also to Hippasus, 320; credited with writings in the name of Orpheus, 150, 158; contrasted modern views of, 181

teaching and interests: doctrines of school attributed to the Master personally, 149; interest in mathematics, little early evidence for, 168; connected with music, 220ff.; with commerce, 222; theorem of, 53, 217, 265; his musical discovery, 220ff.; anecdotes on the subject, 223f.; religious teacher as well as philosopher, 148; combination in him of scientific and religious, 181; said to have first called the world kosmos, 208; his aim to discover kosmos in the world, for imitation in the soul, 288; taught transmigration of souls, 166; zeal for reforming society in accordance with his own moral ideas, 175

Pythagoreans and Pythagoreanism, 146ff.; relation to Oriental thought (India, China, Persia), 251ff.; difficulties in treating of, 146ff.; the a priori method, 171f.

sources: scantiness of contemporary sources, 153f.; sixth and fifth centuries, 157; summary of early information, 166f.; general account in Aristotle, 214f.; his lost book, 42; fourth-century sources exclusive of Aristotle, 161ff., 166ff.; most abundant from time of revival, 155; later sources and source-criticism, 170f.

external history, 175ff.; revolt against Pythagoreans, 178, 329; their emigration to Greek mainland, 179; effect of scattering of societies on continuity of tradition, 180

writings and sayings: no fragments from before time of Philolaus, 155; examples of Pythagorean Acusmata, 183f.; moral interpretations of these, 184; commentaries preserved and handed down by surviving exiles, 180f.; Pythagorean 'notebooks', ὑπομνήματα, 201 and n. 3, 266, 289

organization: a distinctive society, 167; two types of members, acusmatici and mathematici, 191ff.; secrecy, 147, 150ff., 167; silence, of novitiate and of school in general, 151

doctrine and aims, 181f.; pre-Platonic Pythagoreanism, 147; respect for tradition combined with progressive thought, ibid., 216f.; doctrines attributed to the founder, 149f.; not developed along identical lines, 314; religious and moral motives dominant, 181f.; a way of life sought, 148, 182; no real inconsistency between rational and religious sides, 250; these sides not to be treated in isolation, 306; scientific character of much of their thought, 289; experts in astronomy, harmonics and the science of number, 167

religious preoccupation: religious view of truth, 149; conformity with the divine, 199, 210; the kosmos, living and divine, 200f., 251; philosophy as basis for religion, 152, 199; mathematics a religious occupation, 153; resemblance to mystery-religions, 149, 150; tradition compared with Orphic writings, 150; religious teachings almost identical with Orphism, 182; kinship of all nature, 186f., 200, etc. (see under kinship); magical elements, 185; various bans and taboos, 163f., 167, 183; ban on flesh-eating, 187ff.; beauty and goodness in end not beginning, 251; on man and his place in nature, 182ff.

form, not matter, is permanent reality, 238, 317, 467

limit and unlimited: the ultimate notions, 207, 242; equated with good and evil, 207, 246; unlimited among sensible things, 241; itself a substance (Aristotle), 241; void (unlimited) a tenuous form of matter, 280; identifications with breath, void, time, 278, 280, 336, 340; limit imposed

Pythagoreans (*cont.*)
 both spatially (proportion) and temporally (regular motions of heavenly
  bodies), 337; mathematical aspect of the
  unlimited: extension without number or
  figure, 340; limit and unlimited the elements of numbers, 240; associated with
  odd and even respectively, 242 f.; explanation of motion, 241
 opposites: table of, 243, 245, 448 n. 3;
  harmonious blend of, 448; in what sense
  principles, 247 f.
 Pythagorean mathematics, 217 ff.; numbers
  and the cosmos, 212 ff.; its numerical explanation a generalization from Pythagoras's own discovery of musical ratios,
  221; types of relation, 229; numbers, in
  what sense *archai*, 273; independent
  existence of, 213, 225; difficulty of regarding as abstractions, 225; unit, both odd
  and even, 240; outside the number-series,
  244; treatment of Aristotle's account,
  246 f.; equated with good, 246; One not
  the sole principle, 248, 249; One
  reverenced as divine, 248; Pythagoreanism dualistic, as distinct from Ionian systems, 249; monistic theory Platonic, 249;
  the primal One a seed, 278; numbers
  represented as geometrical patterns, 242 f.,
  256; structure of things dependent on
  geometrical shapes and so on numbers,
  256 ff., 259, 266 ff.; numbers of point, line,
  etc., 259; fluxion theory, 263 f.; elements
  each assigned a regular solid, 266; numbers physically extended and independent,
  213, 280; numbers as boundaries, 274 f.;
  generation of things from numbers,
  229 ff.; leap from abstraction to physical
  bodies, 237, 239 ff., 266; *mimesis*, 229,
  230 f.; evidence and objections of
  Aristotle, 229, 233 ff., 236 f., 258, 273 f.;
  integers as things incompatible with incommensurable magnitudes, 265; numerical correlations: abstractions as numbers,
  213, 301 ff.; Aristotle's strictures on
  Pythagorean number symbolism, 302 f.;
  disagreement on which numbers, 303 f.;
  physical qualities explained by numerical
  ratio, 275; world a *harmonia*, 287; constructed according to a musical scale, 296;
  harmony of the spheres, 295 ff.
 soul: importance of, 195 f.; nature of, 306 ff.;
  immortal because akin to divine, 202 f.,
  306; divine because of numbers in harmony, 309, 315; happiness and the numbers of the soul, 164; soul as a harmony,
  307 ff.; soul *is* a harmony, of its own
  parts, 316; a state or arrangement of
  numbers (Arist. *Met.*), 316; yet death not
  final extinction, 312; more material views
  of medical members of school, 314 f.;
  deserts after death, 476; transmigration,
  186; impediment of body, 202 f., 312
 cosmogony, 266 ff.; *kosmos* produced from
  chaos, 250 f., 279; no single system to discover, 266; cosmogony of numbers criticized by Aristotle, 266; more physical
  account, 276; cosmos everlasting, 281;
  grows from seed, 278 f.; from centre outwards, 281; feeds on air, 281; the unit-
  seed has nature of fire, 281
 cosmology: wide scope of, 219 f.; passages
  descriptive of, 283 ff.; Philolaic scheme
  (planetary earth), 282 ff., probably work
  of Philolaus himself, 286 f.; central fire,
  282, 287 f., 290; relation of sun to it, 282 f.;
  shape and position of earth, 282, 283, 289,
  293 ff.; counter-earth, 282, 283; planetary
  orbits and distances, 285, 298, 301; geocentric scheme, 289 ff.; criticisms of
  Aristotle, 287 f., 340; time: drawn in from
  the Unlimited, 277, 336 ff.; identified with
  void and breath, 280; a time before time,
  338 f.; time as the enclosing sphere,
  339 f.
 subsequent influence: formative influence
  on Plato, 147; post-Platonic sources,
  169 ff.; revival in time of Cicero, 23;
  Neoplatonists, 155 f.; early Pythagoreanism obscured by late accounts, 23
 individual Pythagoreans, 319 ff.
Pyxus (town in S. Italy), 177 n. 1

qualitative differences, first reduced to quantitative by Anaximenes, 126 f.; ignored by
  Pythagoreans in favour of quantitative,
  238
quantitative, characteristic of modern physical
  treatment of things, 238; importance of,
  discovered by Pythagoreans, 238

rainbow, Anaximenes's account, 139, 393 n. 1;
  observed by moonlight (Anaximenes),
  139; in Xenophanes, 392 f.
ratios, of musical harmony, 223 and n.; distinguish different bodies, in Pythagoreans,
  275 and n. 2, in Empedocles, 258
Rathmann, W., 161 n. 1, 165 nn. 2 and 3

General index

Raven, J. E., **172**, 215 n. 2, **216**, **233** n. 2, **236** n. 1, 244 n. 3, 248 n. 2, **249**, 258 f., **262**, 263 n. 2, **264**, 269 n. 1, 275 n. 1, 276 n. 1, **280** n. 1, **302**, 330 n. 2, 408 n. 2

reality, in form and in matter, 467

recurrence, of seasonal changes, 453; *see also* repetition

Regenbogen, O., 407

regular solids, and elements, in Pythagoreanism, 267; date of their theoretical construction, 269 and n. 1

Reidemeister, K., 218 n.

Reinach, T., 297 n. 1

reincarnation (*see also* cycle of births, transmigration), 482, to solve Plato's problem of knowing, 167

Reinhardt, K., 131 n., 366 n. 1, **370**, 381, **387** n. 3, 408 n. 2, **415**, 444 n. 2, 454 n. 2, **455**, 466 n. 1, 473 n. 1, 483

relativity of judgments, and Protagoras's dictum, 401

religious background to Greek thought, sketch of, 196 ff.; religious explanations the most plausible in earlier stages of thought, 28

repetition, eternal and cyclic, of historical events, 281, 282, 321, 352, 389; a Pythagorean view, 458; in modern thought, 282 n. 1; of the whole cosmos, first attested in Empedocles, 389; relation to indestructibility of world, 282

respiration, as a god, 130; in Heraclitus, preserves life but not rationality in sleep, 430; sole means of contact with Logos during sleep, *ibid.*

res publica and πολιτεία, 23

Rhapsodic Theogony, attributed to Orpheus, 39

Rhegium, Pythagorean society persists at, 179

Rhoecus, 174

Richter, G., 174 n. 1

Ridgway, W., 226 n. 2

Rivaud, A., 335 n. 3

Robbins, F. E., 260 n. 1

Robertson, D. S., 475 n. 1

Rodier, G., 263

Rohde, E., 40 n. 1, 161 n. 1, **168**, **169**, 173 n. 2, 186 n. 1, **193**, 202 n.

Rome, philosophical influence of, 22

Ross, W. D., 62, 107 n., 153 n. 2, 239 n. 2, 243 nn., 259 n. 3, 303 n. 1, **342**, 343

Rostagni, A., 194 n. 1̊, **219**, **244** n. 1, **267** n. 2, **272**, **354** f.

Rostovtzeff, M., 15

Russell, Bertrand, 211 n. 2

Sabinus, 132 n. 2, 384

Sachs, E., 272

Saffrey, H. D., 245 n.

Sage. *See* Seven Sages

Sagra river, defeat of Crotoniates at, 174

salvation, ways of, 17, 199, 203

same, sense of, in Heraclitus, 443, 473

Samothrace, and Pythagoras, 254

Sandbach, F. H., xii, 158 n. 2, 297 n. 2, 305 n.

Santillana, G. de, 330 n. 2

šár, saros, astronomical period, 47

scales, diatonic, chromatic and enharmonic, investigations on by Archytas, 335

Sceptic School, 22; on Xenophanes, 395

Schiaparelli, G., 48 and n. 1

scholarship, later Greek cultivation of, 16

scholastics, influence of Plato, Aristotle, and Stoics on, 24

school, term as applied to Milesians, 43 f. and n. 2

science, Greek development of oriental, 34; Hellenistic application of to technology, 16

sea, drying up according to Anaximander, 92, 101, 388; encroached on land and *vice versa* (Xenophanes), 387 ff.; exhalations from (Heraclitus), 462 f.

seasons, cycle of, 80, 352, 452 f.

seed, in early philosophy, 278 n. 2; in Pythagorean cosmogony, 278, 292, 340; *spermata* of matter in Anaxagoras, 6

self-motion, suggests presence of life, 306

self-taught, *autodidaktos*, state not incompatible with divine inspiration, 415

Seltman, C. T., 174, 176, 177 n. 1

sensation, relation of to thought, in early Greek thought and Aristotle, 348; arises from interaction of *un*likes (Alcmaeon), *ibid.*; distrust of, 394, 397 f.; *see also* Heraclitus

separation, as cosmogonic process. See *apokrisis*, heaven

seven, significance of number, 303 f.

Seven Sages, 183; earliest list of in Plato, 50; Thales included in, 47, 49

sex, interest of primitive societies in, 62 n. 2; sexual analogy in cosmogonies, 28, 70, 91

Sextus Empiricus, account of Heraclitus's doctrine, 430

Shakespeare quoted, 297 n. 2, 435 n.

Sherrard, Philip, 212

534

General index

Sherrington, Sir Charles, on connexion of water and life, 71 f.
Sibyl, the, 414
Sicilian expedition, 8
Silloi, of Xenophanes, 365 f.
similarity and identity, difficulty of differentiating, 230; cf. 54 n.
Simmias, in Plato's *Phaedo*, 309, 313
Simplicius, character of his scholarship, 367
singers, status of at symposia, 364
Siris (town in S. Italy), 177 n. 1
Skemp, J. B., 324 n. 3, 342 n., 354 n. 1
σκιαγραφία, 274 n.
sleep, theory of Alcmaeon, 349; of Heraclitus, 430
Smith, G., 48 n. 2
Snell, B., 374 n. 3, 377 n. 2, 414 n. 2, **416** n. 3, **425** n. 5, **452** n., 477 n. 3, **482** n.
Socrates, 144, 232, 334, 403 n. 1, 418 and n. 2; marks new phase of philosophy, 7f.; defence of absolute values, 9; later influence, 9f., 22
solids, the regular, identified with elements by Plato, 267; by Pythagoreans, 266ff.; date of construction of regular solids, 268f.
Solon, 51, 166, 204, 388
solstices, 97, 135 n. 2
sophia, particular connexion with crafts, 31 n. 1
σοφιστής, applied to Pythagoras, 166; meaning 'poet', 166 n. 3
Sophists, 8
Sophocles, 400
sophos, σοφός, Sage, title given for practical wisdom, 47, 50
sophrosyne, in Plato, 317
Sotion, *Successions*, 320, 416
soul (*see also psyche*): associated with breath, 128ff., 184, 201, 307; with beans, 184, 187, 189; fate after death: belief in sixth and fifth centuries, 470f.; in Anaximenes, 131f.; in Alcmaeon, 356; in Heraclitus, 476ff. (*see also* cycle of births, immortality); of same substance as stars, 481; becomes a star at death, 350, 471, 480; atomic or material view, 18, 307 n. 1, 313f.; immortality of, 10, 201; Pythagorean notion of pre-existence not found in Persian religion, 255; Empedocles on its immortality, transmigration and apotheosis, 314; and its dual nature, 318; paramount importance of, to Pythagoreans' thinking, 195; their account of its nature, 203, 306ff.; equated with a

number by Pythagoreans, 302, 304; as self-moving number (Xenocrates), 263; 'numbers of the soul', 164, 168; taken as a *harmonia*, 307ff.; this view criticized by Aristotle, 308; *harmonia* theory used to refute immortality, 308ff.; 'an attunement of the four elements' (Dicaearchus), 315; later Pythagorean accounts, 321; connexion with motion, especially self-motion, 263, 350f.; with circular motion (Plato), 354; in Heraclitus, substantial identity with fire, 433; and exhaled from moist things, 434; treatment by Plato, 11, 214, 315, 318; by Aristotle, 14
sound, theories of, 226ff.
sources for Greek philosophy, xii, xiv, 25
space (*see also* void), in Pythagoreanism, belongs to realm of the unlimited, 257; empty, and Parmenides, 279; and body, not distinguished by early philosophers, 113, 279; treatment of by atomists, 113f., 279
Sparta, 8; Anaximander at, 75
Spenser, Edmund, quoted on opposites, 79
Speusippus, author of a monistic system, 249; and fragments of Philolaus, 202 n., 332; on *Pythagorean Numbers*, 260
sphere, constructed from pentagons and equated with dodecahedron, 268; celestial, constructed by Thales and Anaximander, 74; of different substance from the four bodies (Pythagorean), 272
sphericity, special perfection of in Aristotle, 2; compatible with lack of limit, 85; associated with divinity, 114; of Xenophanes's god, 377 and n. 2; of earth, when discovered, 293f.
Spintharus, father of Aristoxenus, 334 n. 1
spirit. *See* matter
spontaneous generation, 385f.
square, in Pythagoreanism, belongs to the limited, 243
stars, in Anaximander, 95, 113; in Anaximenes, 134, 135ff., 137f.; substance of, the 'fifth body' (Pythagorean), 270; the *aither*, 470; believed to be souls of dead men, 350, 471, 480; divinity of, 112, (Alcmaeon) 357; in Xenophanes, composed of ignited clouds, renewed daily, 392
Stebbing, L. S., 56
steering (κυβερνᾶν, οἰακίζειν), in Diogenes of Apollonia and Parmenides, 88; in Heraclitus, 438f.
Stella, L. A., 342

535

General index

Stobaeus (John of Stobi), *Physical Extracts*, as source, xiii

Stocks, J. L., 98 n. 1, 107 n., 165 n. 1, 204 n. 1

στοιχεῖον, Aristotelian term, 77; used for *arche*, 77, 460

Stoicism, 10, 17, 19, 132, 202 n. 1

Stoics, adopt and remould ideas of Heraclitus, 404

storks, foretell earthquakes, 73 n. 2

Strato, 16

Strife, and Love, in Empedocles, 6

stringed instruments, Greek: heptachord and octachord, 299 n. *See also* lyre

Styx, oath of gods by, 55

substance, and quality, approach to distinction of in Anaximenes, 116; substance in relation to geometrical elements, 239 f.

substratum (ὑποκείμενον), 55, 56, 77

successions (διαδοχαί), as sources, xiii

Suda, the (Suidas), 47 and n. 3, 73

suicide, condemned by Philolaus as contrary to religion, 167, 310

sun, common belief in its nourishment by moisture, 80; in Anaximenes, 134, 135; description of by Philolaus, 284 f.; by Empedocles, 286; by Xenophanes, 391 f.; in Heraclitus, 434, 483 ff., 486; myth of travel in golden boat, 138, 485; feeds on moisture, 434; in Anaximander, same size as earth, 96; eclipses of, *see* eclipses; larger than the earth (*Epinomis*), 296 n.; all-seeing, 474

Sybaris, 176, 177

Symbola, or *Acusmata*, Pythagorean, 183 ff.

symbols, use of by Heraclitus, 439

συμφυής, meaning of, 377 n. 1

Syracuse, fossils found at, 387

taboos, beliefs underlying, 186

Tannery, P., 46 n., 48, 323, 394 n. 1

Tate, J., 307 n. 3

Taylor, A. E., 94 n. 3, 124 n. 1, 210, **221**, 243 nn., 265 n. 2, **281**, **316**, 324, 338; quoted on Plato's *Timaeus*, 211

techniques, fundamental in oriental civilizations, 33; development of, as seen by Greeks, 400

Teichmüller, G., 138 n. 1

τεκμαίρεσθαι, 344 n. 2

teleology (*see also* design), characteristic of Aristotle's thought, 12

telos, ateles, teleion, 13, 207

Telys, demagogue at Sybaris, 176

temperament, influence of in individual philosophies, 117

ten. *See* decad

tension, in Heraclitus, 438 and n. 1

Terpander, 299 n.

Tertullian, hostility of to paganism, 24

Tethys, 55, 60, 410 n. 1

tetractys, 225 and n., 277, 288 n., 301, 316

Thales of Miletus, 1, 29, 40, 43, 45 ff.

date of, 46 ff.; ancestry, 50; length of life, 50; character in tradition, 50 f.; celestial sphere of, 74

mythological precursors, 58 ff., 68 ff.; as a forerunner of philosophy, 45

question of written works, 54 and n.

statesmanship, trading, engineering, interest in navigation and mensuration, 50; later exaggeration of his astronomical knowledge, 49; geometrical achievements assigned to, 52 f.

founder of 'physical' philosophy, according to Aristotle, 40, 45; water as *arche*, 54 ff.; evidence of Aristotle, 55 f.; earth floats on water, 59; reasons for choice of water, mythical, 58 ff., rational, 61 f.; water and life: hylozoism, 62 ff., 71 f.; *psyche* as the cause of motion, 65; animate not distinguished from inanimate, 66; all things full of gods, 65, 68

summary of his thought and achievement, 67 ff.

Theaetetus, 219, 268

Thebes, Pythagorean centre established at, 179

Themistius, on Anaximander, 72

Theo of Smyrna, quoted on the monad, 244

theocracies, oriental, 32 f.

Theodoret, xiii

Theodorus of Cyrene, 219, 265 n. 2

Theognis, 398 n. 1

theogonies, mythical, xi

theologi, Aristotle's use of term, 40

Theologumena Arithmeticae, on the decad, 260

Theophrastus, 16, 25, 122, 274; as source, xiii; on musical pitch, 228 f.

theoria, θεωρία, active contemplation, 212; linked by Pythagoreans with transmigration, 165 f.

Thesleff, H., 363 n. 2

Thomists, 24

Thompson, D'Arcy W., 104 n. 1

Thomson, G., **51** n. 1, **177** n. 2, **222** n. 1, **252**, 403 n.

Thomson, J. O., 393 n. 2

three, primacy of number, 2, 193

536

thunder and lightning, in Anaximander, 106 and n.; in Anaximenes, 139
thunderbolt, in Heraclitus, 428, 471 n.
Ti'amat, 59, 60
Timaeus, of Locri, 'On the World-Soul' forgery, 156, 332; *Timaeus*, of Plato, alleged to be taken from Philolaus, 330
Timaeus, of Tauromenium, historian, on Pythagoreans, 161, 170; on Xenophanes, 362
time, χρόνος, senses of, in English and Greek, 338 f.; distinguished from mere succession, 338; to Greeks unimaginable without ordered and recurrent motions, 280, 339; circularity of, 352, 452; relation to cosmological order, 338; Pythagorean conception of, 280; in Plato, to be identified with planetary motions, 339; time before time began, not absurd, 338; time and the unlimited, 336 ff.
Timon of Phlius, 366, 411
Titans, 141
toys, mechanical, invented by Archytas, 335
traditional conceptions behind philosophies, 118
transmigration of souls (*see also* cycle of births), 159, 165, 190, 354; a Greek doctrine, not Egyptian, 160; taught by Pythagoras himself, 186 f., 306; excluded in Aristotle, 14
τροπαί, whether of solstices or revolutions, 97
truth, speaking, in relation to Pythagoras and Persians, 254
turbans, 138

unit (monad), not itself a number (Pythagoreans), 240, 244; both odd and even, *ibid.*; primacy of; asserted by late writers on Pythagoreanism, 244; Cornford's theory on this, 244, 247, 250 f.; in Pythagorean cosmogony, appears as a *sperma*, 246; divinity of, (Xenophanes) 380 and n. 1, (Pythagoreans) 248
unity, primal, in Milesians, 4, 70; search for unity a universal phenomenon, 70; nondimensional, 261; no distinction between logical and material unity in Xenophanes, 380; importance in Pythagoreanism, *see* Pythagoreans
Untersteiner, M., 367 n. 2
Ure, P. N., 174 n. 1

values, Socrates's defence of absolute, 9; Pythagoreanism rooted in, unlike Ionian philosophies, 246

vegetarianism, *see* abstention
verbal similarity, significance assigned to, 425 n. 5
Verdam, H. D., 428 n. 2
Verdenius, W. J., 73 n. 2, 161 n. 1
verification, standard of, 345 and n. 1
virtue, relative view of, 9; in Epicureanism, 19; in Stoicism, 20
Vlastos, G., 77 n. 1, **81** n. 1, **89** n. 1, 126 n., 131 n., **166** nn. 2 and 3, **208** n. 1, 324, 345 n. 2, 408 n. 2, **416**, **429**, **433** n. 3, **439** nn. 1 and 3, 447 n. 4, **454** n. 2, **458** and n. 5, **463** n. 1, 465, 465 n. 1, **469** n., 489, 491, 492
Vohu Mana, universal Mind, Zoroastrian, 488
void, identified with air (Alcmaeon), 349, 358; 'drawn in' by the cosmos (Pythagorean), 277; identified with breath and the Unlimited, 278, 280, 340; separates numbers, 280; existence of denied by Parmenides and reasserted by atomists, 7. *See also* space
volcanoes, 292
vortex, universal, stars carried passively round by, 357
Voss, O., 323

Wachtler, J., **342** n., 343, 347 n. 3
Waerden, B. L. van der, 217 n., 218 n., 228, 265 nn., 282 n. 2, **287** n., 295 n. 2, 297 n. 1, **328**, **335** n. 1, 357 n.
Walzer, R., **454** nn., 472 n. 1
Wasserstein, A., 265 n. 2
water, importance of in Egyptian and Mesopotamian river-cultures, 58 f.; relation to life in ancient and modern thought, 71 f.; associated with foolishness, in Heraclitus, 433. *See also* Thales
way of life, religious, 4; the object of Pythagoreanism, 148; Plato quoted on, *ibid.*
Webster, T. B. L., 344 n. 2
Wedberg, A., 265 n. 1
Wehrli, F., 151 nn. 1 and 2, 170 n. 1, 173 n. 3, 199 n. 2
Weizsäcker, C. F. von, physicist, quoted, 70, 78, 225 f.
Wellmann, M., 202 n., 324, 342 n., **411** n.
wheel of birth, *see* cycle
White, M., 176 n. 1, 177 n. 1
Whitehead, A. N., 56 n. 1
Wightman, W. P. D., quoted, 33, 68, 70 f., 72, 102, 238
Wilamowitz, U. von, 131 n., 202 n., 204 n. 1, 267 n. 2, 309 n., 311 n. 3, 323, 332 n. 3, 475 n. 4

General index

Wilson, J. A., 102 n. 1

wind, explanation of by Anaximander, 105; by Anaximenes, 139; as cause of impregnation, 128 f.

Wind, E., xi

Woodbury, L., 81 n. 1, 428 n. 2

wool, taboo on burial in, 160, 167

words, magical conception of, 86; significance of word-play, 425 n. 5, 475 n. 2

world, as a *kosmos*, 207 f., 209; as a living creature, 200 n. 2, 278 f., 487 f.; in Anaximenes, 137; as god (Xenophanes), 380 ff.; according to all natural philosophers, had a beginning in time (Aristotle), 390; always existed (Xenophanes), *ibid.*

world-soul, in the *Timaeus*, 316

worlds, 'innumerable', 390; question of in Anaximander (ἄπειροι κόσμοι or οὐρανοί), 106 ff.; in the atomists, 113 f.; in Epicurus, 108, 109

Xanthus of Lydia, on fossils, 387 n. 2

Xenocrates, 222, 260, 264 f., 270 f., 291 n. 1; called soul a self-moving number, 263

Xenophanes, 4, 58 n. 2, 360 ff.; tradition, 366 ff.; date and life, 362 ff.

connexion with Elea and Eleatic school, 363 f., 368, 370; relationship with Parmenides, 369, 379

writings, 365 f.; poetical claims, 364; verse-forms, 365; epics, 365; reported work 'on nature', 366; imitated by Timon of Phlius, 366; disappearance of his works, 367

opinions upon: of Heraclitus, 368, 408; of Aristotle, 366, 369; of Theophrastus, 67; modern views, 361 f.

social and political outlook, 364 f.; disparagement of physical prowess, 364

destructive criticism, 370 ff.; condemns luxury, 365; opposition to poets, especially Homer and Hesiod, 370 f., 383 n., 386 f.; objections to their portrayal of the gods, and their anthropomorphism, 371, 373; expurgation of myths at symposia, 370; protests against impiety towards gods, 371 f.; satire on Pythagoras, 157; opposition also to Thales and Epimenides, 370; denial of validity of divinations or prophecy, 373; unity, interpreted in stricter sense than by Milesians, 368, 380, 383, 402

constructive theology, 373 ff.; question whether theologian, 361 f.; whether

monotheist or polytheist, 361, 375 f., no hierarchy of gods, 373; self-sufficiency of deity implied, 373; God not like man either in shape or in mind, 398; God has a body, 376; of spherical shape, 376 f., 378, 379; and finite, 378; said in Cicero's *N.D.* to be *infinitum*; God identical with the universe, 114, 377, 381 ff.; has no separate organs of perception, 375; is one, 375; single, whole, unmoving, 374; difficulties of immobile God, 381 f.; though essentially one, yet manifested in many forms, 376

cosmology: material and non-material, finite and infinite, not distinguished, 369 and n. 2; earth alleged to be taken as his *arche*, 384; the cosmos not infinite, 377 f.; ungenerated, 380, 382, 386; nature of the cosmos summarized, 382 f.

astronomy and meteorology, 390 ff.; how far dependent on Anaximander and Anaximenes, 391; no astronomy in extant verses, 390; heavenly bodies are clouds formed by evaporation from sea, 390, 392; sun, 391 f.; movement of, 394; numerous suns and moons, 393; effect on Heraclitus's conception of the sun, 485; moon, cloud 'felted', 392; earth flat-topped, 394; importance of the sea, 391; observation of fossils, 373, 387 and n. 2; alternation of wet and dry ages, 387 ff.; origin of life from the earth, 385 ff.

theory of knowledge, 395 ff.; emphasis on personal search, 399 f.; limitations of human knowledge, 395 f.; knowledge and opinion (seeming), 395 and n. 5, 399; no evidence of corresponding realms of existence, 397; contrast of opinion with divine certainty, 396 and n. 3, 397; distrust of senses, 394, 397 f.; relative character of judgment, 401; summing-up of his significance, 401 f.

Xuthus, Pythagorean, 319

ξυνιέναι, 347 n. 1

ξυνόν. *See* common

Yin–Yang, 252

Zalmoxis, 148 f.; and Pythagoras, 158 f.

Zancle (Messana), stay of Xenophanes at, 363

Zaratas (Zoroaster), 253

Zeller, E. (selected references), 107 n., 134 n. 1, 202 n., 251, 281, 298, 302, 366 n. 1, 410 n. 2, 453 n. 2

General index

Zen, as both Zeus and life (Heraclitus), 463

Zeno of Citium, Stoic, 19, 491

Zeno of Elea, 204, 262, 264, 265 and n. 1

Zephyr-eggs, 129

zero, unknown to Greeks, 240

Zeus, 27, 126, 129, 141, 196, 284, 287, 290, 374, 386, 429, 472 n. 2, 473; equated with Oromasdes, 249 n. 2

zodiac, discovery of obliquity of, 74, 97 n. 1

ζωή, distinguished from ψυχή, 202

Zoroaster (Zoroastres), 173 n. 3, 184 n., 250, 253

Zoroastrianism and Pythagoreanism, resemblances and differences, 254f.; and Heraclitus, 488